MARKETING RESEARCH

MARKETING RESEARCH

A PROBLEM-SOLVING APPROACH

SEYMOUR SUDMAN
University of Illinois, Urbana-Champaign

EDWARD BLAIR
University of Houston, Texas

Boston   Burr Ridge, IL   Dubuque, IA   Madison, WI   New York   San Francisco   St. Louis
Bangkok Bogotá Caracas Lisbon London Madrid
Mexico City   Milan   New Delhi   Seoul   Singapore   Sydney   Taipei   Toronto

Irwin/McGraw-Hill

A Division of The **McGraw·Hill** *Companies*

MARKETING RESEARCH: A Problem-solving Approach
International Editions 1998

Exclusive rights by McGraw-Hill Book Co – Singapore, for manufacture and export. This book cannot be re-exported from the country to which it is consigned by McGraw-Hill.

2 3 4 5 6 7 8 9 0 BJE PMP 20

ISBN 0-07-913670-2

Library of Congress Number 97-77262

Grateful acknowledgment is made for use of the following:

Photographs *Page 16* © Bonnie Kamin; *39* Courtesy of the Methodist Hospital; *54* Courtesy of Chrysler Corporation; *76* Courtesy of TBWA Chiat/Day & Infinity; *89* Reprinted by permission, Raymond R. Burke, E.W. Kelley Professor of Business Administration, Indiana University; *115* © James Martin/Courtesy of Pepsi-Cola & Minute Maid; *157* © R. Sidney/The Image Works; *186* © Spencer Grant/The Picture Cube; *679* Courtesy of Paragon; *680* Courtesy of Continental Airlines.

www.mhhe.com

When ordering this title, use ISBN 0-07-115862-6

Printed in Singapore

Preface

There are two schools of thought about learning. One school believes in the "no pain, no gain" theory, that only when you suffer do you benefit. The second school believes that only when the activity is enjoyable will there be an incentive to continue the behavior, and thus to benefit from it.

We are members of this second school, and have tried to write this book so as to maximize learning and minimize pain. We have kept our language simple, and have given lots of examples and lots of details to make the material more interesting. Some of the topics that arise in marketing research are more difficult than others, but we have done our best to present them in a way that will hold your interest and allow you to understand every single topic.

Why Did We Write This Book?

There are a large number of marketing research books available. Why did we write another one, and how do we see this book as different from the others?

Our goal was to write a book that would be *more practical* than other marketing research books: a book that, more than any other, would tell you *how to do marketing research* as well as *why to do it that way*. In using other marketing research books over the years, we have found that these books generally provide students with a good background in research issues, but it is left to a classroom instructor to show students how to do things. Our goal was to bring more of this practical material into the book, along with the background reasons. There are several benefits from doing so: (1) a book with more practical content is more useful outside a classroom context, or as a reference source after the class is over, (2) students gain a better understanding of theoretical issues if they can see the practical implications, and (3) instructors can run classes at a higher level, and have more fun in discussions, if students come to class with a better grasp of the material.

The practical orientation of this book is revealed in various ways:

- The book's organizational structure provides excellent support for anyone who is doing a marketing research project. Of course, the book can be used without a research project, but readers who are doing a project will find that the book leads them through the project from the initial formulation of research questions to the final presentation of a research report.

- The book contains many unique, practical features. For example, Chapter 5 allows readers to look up common marketing research questions and see which information sources are appropriate for each. Chapter 12 shows several marketing research questionnaires in their entirety, evaluates them, and shows how they can be improved. Chapter 14 provides automated sample size calculations. Chapter 20 provides a sample research report which readers can use as a template for their own reports. Chapter 23 discusses practical aspects of using marketing research in relationship marketing, database marketing, Total Quality

Management, and customer satisfaction research, as well as practical aspects of doing research on the Internet (Internet issues also are discussed in other places throughout the book).

- The book has a practical orientation built into the text. If you compare any chapter in this book with comparable chapters from other books, you will see that this book is more concrete about how to do things.

- The book has a variety of learning features that are intended to make the material come alive. These include many "case study" examples and author tips. These learning features, and the contents of the book, are described in greater detail below.

Earlier drafts of this book have been used in various classes, and we have received very positive feedback. Students have found the book interesting, readable, and, most important, useful. We hope that you will, too.

An Overview of the Book

As noted above, this book is organized to lead readers through a marketing research project, from the initial formulation of the research questions to the final presentation of the research report.

The book is divided into five sections. The first section, **An Overview of Marketing Research,** is designed to give you a broad background in marketing research and get you started on a research project if you are doing one. This section contains five chapters. Chapter 1 defines marketing research, provides an overview of the research process, describes the managerial questions that are typically addressed by marketing research, and offers general information regarding who uses marketing research, who does marketing research, and career paths in marketing research. Most people have some awareness of marketing research, but this chapter contains information that is likely to surprise you.

Chapter 2 describes the purpose, design, and contents of a marketing information system. Marketing information systems involve the gathering and dissemination of repetitive information such as market share data. Most large companies spend the majority of their marketing research expenditures on such systems, which are used to monitor markets and identify problems and opportunities as they emerge. We discuss information systems in this early chapter because they constitute the biggest part of marketing research for many companies, and because they often provide the context in which research projects are done. Systematic data collection is used to identify problems or opportunities in a company's marketing programs, and targeted research projects are used to study these problems or opportunities in greater detail.

Chapter 3 discusses issues in managing marketing research. Four broad topics are addressed: how to allocate responsibility for marketing research decisions, how to handle interactions between managers and researchers, how to organize and staff the research function, and how to choose and manage research suppliers. If you are doing a marking research project, this chapter will tell you how to define the project's objectives, how to set project parameters such as budgets and schedules, and how to work with managers in doing so.

Chapters 4 and 5 introduce the various information sources used in marketing research. Chapter 4 introduces the various sources of information and describes the ways in which each source is used in marketing research. Chapter 5 cross-references information sources with research applications. It allows you to start with common managerial questions (e.g., "what is our market share?"), and it describes the information sources that are used to answer each question.

At the end of the book's first section, you should have a broad overview of marketing research. You will have some skills related to marketing research projects, and know the types of questions that are commonly addressed in marketing research projects. You will know how to work with managers in defining the questions to be addressed in any given project, and how to set project parameters. You should know the various information sources that can be used in marketing research, and be able to choose the sources that are appropriate for your project.

The second section of the book, **Sources of Marketing Research Data,** provides additional detail about the most commonly used sources of marketing research information. The purpose of this section is to provide enough detail so that you are actually able to use the sources of information that you selected for a research project.

Chapter 6 starts by discussing sources of secondary information (i.e., information that has already been gathered). In the normal flow of a research project, it is useful to determine what is already known before rushing out to re-invent the wheel. This chapter lists the research questions that are commonly addressed with secondary information, and provides detailed information about how to access library and non-library sources for this information. The discussion includes coverage of computerized databases and the Internet, which is a rapidly growing source of information. The chapter concludes with a discussion and examples of syndicated data services that provide regular reports to subscribing companies.

Chapters 7, 8, and 9 discuss sources of primary information (i.e., original information). The three major sources of primary data are: (1) surveys, (2) focus groups and depth interviews, and (3) experiments. Chapter 7 tells you how to design and implement surveys, Chapter 8 tells you how to design and implement focus groups and depth interviews, and Chapter 9 tells you how to design and implement experiments. Also, an appendix to Chapter 9 discusses conjoint analysis, a popular research method that is a special type of experiment.

At the end of the book's second section, you should know not only which sources of information to use in a marketing research project, but also how to design and implement data collection efforts.

The third section of the book, **Tools for Primary Data Collection,** describes how to develop the measurement instruments and sampling plans that are needed in the process of implementing surveys, focus groups, depth interviews, and experiments. These topics are presented in the context of marketing surveys, because surveys are widely used and have the most formal requirements for instrument design and sampling. However, the general principles expressed in this section apply to focus groups, depth interviews, and experiments as well as to surveys.

The first three chapters in this section, Chapters 10–12, tell how to design effective questionnaires. Chapter 10 starts with individual questions, and discusses how to write questions that avoid common problems and provide the desired information. Chapter 11 then proceeds to the entire questionnaire, and discusses how to organize questions into an optimal sequence, how to lay out a questionnaire, and how to test a questionnaire to ensure that it works as intended. Then, to illustrate the principles given in Chapters 10 and 11, Chapter 12 shows several marketing research questionnaires, evaluates them, and shows how they can be improved. There is a knack to writing good questionnaires, and we hope that the many examples shown throughout these chapters, including the comprehensive examples shown in Chapter 12, will help you acquire that knack.

The other two chapters in this section, Chapters 13 and 14, discuss sampling issues. Chapter 13 presents a general overview of sampling: how to define a population of interest, how to work with lists of that population, how to choose a sampling procedure, how to draw a sample, how to maintain sample integrity during data collection, and how to report sampling information. Chapter 14 then discusses how to set sample size and how to maximize sampling efficiency.

At the end of the book's third section, you should be able to choose a research method, design the study, prepare the measurement instruments, design the sampling plan, and implement the research. In other words, you should be able to perform all aspects of research design and data collection.

The fourth section of the book, **Data Analysis,** turns from data collection to data analysis. This section contains five chapters. Chapter 15 discusses how to prepare data for analysis. Chapters 16–19 then discuss various analysis procedures. Chapter 16 discusses univariate procedures; i.e., procedures for analyzing the distribution of a single variable. Chapter 17 discusses bivariate procedures; i.e., procedures for analyzing the relationship between two variables. Chapter 18 discusses multivariate procedures in which one or more variables are considered to be dependent on the others (e.g., sales might be considered to be dependent on various marketing actions), and Chapter 19 considers multivariate procedures in which the goal is to measure relationships among three or more variables without treating any of these variables as dependent on the others.

The chapters in this section are not intended to replace a course in statistics, and consequently do not focus on statistics for statistics' sake. Rather, these chapters are intended to show how various analysis procedures are used to solve marketing problems. The emphasis in Chapters 16 and 17 is on relatively simple procedures. The procedures discussed in Chapters 18 and 19 are more complicated; even here, though, we focus on the meaning rather than the mathematics of the procedures.

At the end of the book's third section, you should be able to analyze marketing research data and interpret the results. You also should be aware of the ways in which various analysis procedures can yield misleading results.

The fifth and final section of the book, **Issues in Research Management,** covers a variety of topics. Chapter 20 completes our discussion of research projects by describing how to communicate research results in both written and oral form. We provide general template for research reports and provide a complete report as an example. We also discuss how to prepare effective charts and graphs, and we provide guidelines for effective oral presentations. Effective communication is crucial to the ultimate managerial effectiveness of a research project, and will be crucial to your own professional success.

Chapter 21 discusses some of the special issues that arise when marketing research is done in an international context. Chapter 22 discusses ethical issues in marketing research, including how researchers should treat research participants and how researchers and research clients should treat each other. Finally, Chapter 23 discusses topics that are likely to dominate marketing research in coming years.

These topics include the rapidly increasing use of the Internet for research purposes, as well as the use of research in relationship marketing, database marketing, Total Quality Management programs, and customer satisfaction programs.

Learning Features

As you go through this book, you will find a variety of learning features that we hope will increase your enjoyment of the book and understanding of the material. These learning features include the following:

- **Case Studies** illustrate the principles of marketing research. Some of these case studies have been drawn from business publications such as *Forbes, Fortune, Wall Street Journal*, and *Advertising Age*. Many others have been drawn from our own personal experience. These examples help to make the material more lively and interesting. Of course, they are supplemented by many examples within the text itself.

- **Author Tips** provide recommendations based on our experience. As with the case studies, the recommendations that are labeled as author tips are just the tip of the iceberg. Many, many other recommendations are contained within the text. These recommendations are a key part of the book's practical orientation.

- **Marketing Tools** are tables that summarize key points from the text. These tools provide useful reference lists to use in problem solving.

- **Critical Thinking Skills** are questions which invite you to stop and think about the material you have just read. Most of them ask you to think about how you would implement the recommendations that are given in the book. If you take the time to think about these questions, we think that you will gain a better understanding of the material. If you are an instructor, we think you will find most of these questions to be excellent vehicles for class discussion.

- **Discussion Questions** at the end of each chapter help to remind you of what you have read.

- **Marketing Research Challenges** at the end of each chapter function much like the "critical thinking skills" to encourage you to think about the material.

- **Internet Exercises** at the end of each chapter ask you to consider aspects of the chapter that relate to marketing research on the Internet. As with all areas of business today, the marketing research world is buzzing about the Internet, and Internet issues are covered throughout the book where appropriate.

- The introductory materials for each section of the book include a running description of a class project done for Apple Computer, along with examples of the work actually done by students who worked on this project. These materials help to illustrate the steps in a marketing research project, and how a project is done.

- The book is accompanied by a computer disk that enables you to implement material that is given in the text.

All of these learning features are directed toward the goal of producing a book that is interesting, readable, and useful.

About Us . . . and You

Since we (the authors) will be your guides to the field of marketing research, you may want to know a little about us. You will find biographical sketches elsewhere in the book. We both are professors of marketing at universities, and both have taught marketing research for many years. We have taught professional researchers as well as college students.

In addition to our teaching experience, we have, over a period of decades, published a great deal of research into better methods for doing marketing research, and have served as marketing and marketing research consultants to a wide variety of corporations, research companies, and government agencies. The methods that we describe in this book are ones that we have developed and used to solve real world problems, and we want to share our experience with you.

We recognize that people study marketing research for a variety of reasons. You may be considering marketing research as a career. If so, this book should give you a good foundation for your career, though it cannot replace practical experience. More likely, you plan to go into marketing management. If so, we hope that you find this book useful in teaching you what marketing research can do for you, and how to use it effectively. We hope that the book will be useful to you not only at the present time, but as a reference source in the future.

We would appreciate hearing from you if you have any reactions to the book, or thoughts about how we might make it more useful. We enjoyed writing it, and we hope you enjoy reading it. Please contact us through our Publisher's Web site— www.mhhe.com/business/marketing.

Acknowledgments

A large number of people made useful contributions to the development of this book. We first would like to thank our marketing research students at the University of Illinois at Urbana-Champaign and the University of Houston who used this book in earlier drafts and gave us valuable feedback. We also would like to thank Julie Lee, University of Hawaii, and Joan Phillips, University of Kentucky, who used earlier drafts of this book and prepared the end of chapter questions and the instructor's manual. We also owe a debt to Judy Harris, Florida International University, who made editorial suggestions, wrote the learning objective summaries, developed many of the Internet exercises, and developed many of the visual demonstrations used in the book.

Karen Westover and Dan Alpert, our editors at Irwin/McGraw-Hill, were endlessly patient with us as we went through our multiple revisions. Georgene Gallagher served as development editor and made significant contributions in making the book more user-friendly. A special word of thanks goes to our good friend Mike Houston of the University of Minnesota who reviewed our initial proposal and our many drafts of the book, and made many suggestions that improved the book.

We also would like to thank the following academics who offered numerous suggestions at various stages in the manuscript:

Greg Allenby, Ohio State University
David Andrus, Kansas State University
Andrew Brogowicz, Western Michigan University
John "Rusty" Brooks, Houston Baptist University
Mary Carsky, University of Hartford
Cornelia Droge, Michigan State University
Joel Dubow, St. Joseph University
Andrew Forman, Hostra University
Ralph Gallay, Rider University
Ronald Goldsmith, Florida State University
David Gourley, Arizona State University
Bonnie Guy, Appalachian State University
Curt Haugtvedt, Ohio State University
Douglas Hausknecht, University of Akron
Jamer Jeck, North Carolina State University
Peter Kaminski, Northern Illinois University
John Kuehn, University of Missouri-Columbia
Jim Leigh, Texas A&M
James Molinari, State University of New York-Oswego
Gordon Patzer, Northern Iowa University
David Schaitkin, South Hills Business School
Jagdip Sinha, Case Western Reserve University
Rajiv Sinha, Arizona State University
Ruth Smith, University of Virginia
David Snepenger, Montana State University
Bruce Stern, Portland State University
Jeff Tanner, Baylor University
Gail Tom, California State University-Sacramento
Jackie Twible, University of South Carolina
Mary Wolfinbarger, California State University Long Beach
Robert Wright, University of Illinois

Seymour Sudman
University of Illinois at Urbana-Champaign

Edward Blair
University of Houston

About the Authors

Seymour Sudman is Walter Stellner Professor of Business Administration at the University of Illinois, Urbana-Champaign which he joined in 1968. He teaches marketing research to undergraduates and survey methods to advanced students. Prior to that he was Director of Research for the Market Research Corporation of America and Director of Sampling and Senior Study Director at the National Opinion Research Center, University of Chicago.

He is the author, co-author or editor of twenty books and more than 200 publications in professional journals. His principal current areas of research involve sampling and cognitive aspects of survey research. His books *Applied Sampling* and *Asking Questions* with Norman Bradburn have been widely used. His recent publications include the following books: *Thinking About Answers: The Application of Cognitive Processes to Survey Methodology* with Norman Bradburn and Norbert Schwarz (1996): and *Answering Questions: Methods of Determining Processes Used to Answer Questions* edited with Norbert Schwarz.

Professor Sudman is on the editorial boards of seven professional journals and is currently chair of the American Statistical Association Advisory Committee to the Center for Disease Control Behavior Risk Factors Survey. He has consulted for many universities and federal agencies. He is a Fellow of the American Statistical Association and with Norman Bradburn the recipient of the American Association for Public Opinion Research Award for Exceptionally Distinguished Achievement.

Edward Blair is Professor and Chairman of Marketing and Entrepreneurship at the University of Houston which he joined in 1977. He has taught university courses on a variety of topics related to marketing research, including marketing, marketing research, sampling, survey methods, statistics, and multivariate analysis. He also is active in professional education, and has taught at the American Marketing Association's School of Marketing Research since its inception. Between his work for professional organizations and private companies. Prof. Blair has trained more than 1,000 marketing research professionals, including people from AT&T, Coca-Cola, IBM, and many other companies.

Professor Blair is widely published in journals such as the *Journal of Marketing, Journal of Marketing Research, Journal of Consumer Research*, and *Public Opinion Quartery*, and serves on the editorial boards of the *Journal of Marketing Research* and *Journal of Business Research*. He also has extensive experience as a marketing and marketing research consultant, advising organizations that range from small entrepreneurial ventures to large companies such as Shell, Chevron, Exxon, and Texaco.

Brief Contents

ontents

CHAPTER

5 Typical Ways of Answering Common
Research Questions

CHAPTER

7 Conducting Surveys 153

CHAPTER

8 Conducting Focus Groups and Depth Interviews   183

PART 3 Tools for Primary Data Collection   239

CHAPTER

11 Designing a Questionnaire   281

CHAPTER 12 Questionnaire Workshop: Evaluating Questionnaires   305

CHAPTER 13 Sampling   331

PART 4 Analyzing Data   409

CHAPTER 15 Preparing Data for Analysis   413

CHAPTER

18 Multivariate Analysis with Dependent Variables   501

CHAPTER

19 Multivariate Grouping Procedures   545

CHAPTER

22 Ethical Issues in Marketing Research   643

1 An Overview of Marketing Research

Imagine that you are an astronaut on the first spacecraft to Mars. Your first views of the planet, from far above, give you a global perspective. As you get nearer and nearer, more and more details become clear. You no longer see the whole planet, but you can put the details into a global perspective because of your earlier experience.

In a similar fashion, the first section in this book, **An Overview of Marketing Research,** is intended to give a global perspective of marketing research to help explain the detailed chapters that follow. Many of the topics that are briefly discussed in the Overview are covered in greater depth later in the book.

This overview of marketing research contains five chapters. Chapter 1 introduces the field of marketing research and describes the users and producers of research. Many people have an awareness of marketing research, but this chapter contains some surprising facts about the size of the field, the scope of the work, and the variety of its applications.

Chapter 2 describes the purpose, design, and contents of marketing information systems. Marketing information systems are used to identify marketing opportunities and problems. Many firms spend a large portion of their total market research dollars on such systems. It also becomes apparent in this chapter that the new computer technology has shaped the nature of collecting and storing data and the way in which marketing information systems are organized and staffed.

Chapter 3 discusses issues in managing marketing research. Four broad topics are discussed: how to allocate responsibility for research decisions, how to handle interactions between managers and researchers, how to organize and staff the research function, and how to choose and manage suppliers. This chapter is important because marketing research is not an end in itself but rather a tool of marketing management, and the management of the marketing research function has a significant impact on how effective it will be.

Chapters 4 and 5 provide an overview of marketing research data sources and the kinds of questions that are typically answered by each source of data. Chapter 4 describes various data sources, and Chapter 5 cross-references these sources with their applications to answering marketing research questions.

The broad overview of marketing research in these first five chapters reveals:

- What marketing research is and the common questions that are asked in marketing research
- The extent to which different types of organizations use marketing research, the different types of research suppliers, and the nature of career paths within marketing research
- What a marketing information system is and issues to consider in designing a marketing information system
- Some guidelines for managing the marketing research function within an organization and for managing a specific research project
- The various sources of marketing research data, the characteristics of each source, and the common research questions to which each source is applied

These chapters provide a context for the detailed information in later chapters.

One of the aims of this book is to help you actually conduct marketing research. Your first chance to do this may be in the research class for which this book is the text, or it may be in another class or on the job. We obviously cannot predict exactly what you will be faced with, but this book should be useful for a broad range of projects.

To illustrate the use of this book, the Introductions to each of the remaining sections discuss a real-world project that one of our marketing research classes worked on recently, what they did, and how they used the material in this book for reference. We think this example should be useful as you do your own research.

Sample Student Project

Marketing Research and the Real World: The Apple Computer Project

The campus representative for Apple Computers contacted one of us about the possibility of research to determine current student use of and attitudes toward Apple computers and their chief competition, IBM and IBM-compatibles. Apple has been traditionally strong on university campuses but has been facing ever-increasing pressure from the competition.

Apple had been marketing on campus primarily by offering student discounts for purchases made through the university's Micro Computer Order Center (MCOC). The Apple marketers were concerned about how students perceived the Micro Computer Order Center and where students were buying their computers, as well as their attitudes toward and use of various computers.

The project began with a visit by the Apple representative to the class. The Apple representative spelled out the problems as she saw them but admitted that there was much information that was not available to her. It was agreed that the first step for the class would be an extensive search of secondary sources so that Apple's current status, as well as recent trends in the computer industry, could be described. The class broke into teams and searched for sources of information, using the kinds of sources suggested in Chapter 6.

The following excerpt from one team's report shows general computer industry trends. It provides an overview of the marketplace.

Computer Industry Trends[1]

In 1993, more than 31 million U.S. households owned PCs; the installed base was over 38 million.

Increasingly, it is the use of computers in the home for business, entertainment, and hobby purposes that is driving demand for the product. Market growth was mostly driven by price cuts of 30 to 40 percent and the introduction of new low-cost PCs. A growing portion of sales will go to the replacement market; however, interest from first-time buyers will also increase.

Multimedia products have had a tremendous impact on the PC market. Potential uses include training, education, publishing, entertainment, voice and video mail, teleconferencing, public information, and document-imaging and archival systems. Proof of the effectiveness of multimedia is not yet conclusive, but early studies and many anecdotes suggest its great power as a learning aid.

Because computers can be used as efficient communication tools, managers as well as students are attracted to networks and are continually experimenting with the fastest way to access information. Networks can be used to provide data and information to users who read the information from data files; to send messages to other users; to participate in conferences, discussions, or even in conversations with others. In the past few years, there have been many improvements in the communication networks. Specialists are trying to decrease barriers of time and distance. According to *ComputerWorld* magazine, "Computer industry specialists predict the creation of a second-generation Internet, or Internet II. In this internetwork, a worldwide dial tone of sorts that will encompass telephone, videophone, videofax, and computers will let anyone communicate with anyone else anywhere in the world. This will most

[1]*U.S. Industrial Outlook 1994—Computer Equipment,* p. 26–17.

likely increase the use of computers for communication purposes."[2]

Computer usage is also seeing dramatic increases in education. Some schools are choosing a manufacturer as a total solution vendor for executing a networked approach to classroom technology (cabling classroom computers, providing teacher training in addition to administrative and courseware solutions).

A study done at the University of Minnesota[3] analyzes computer use for educational purposes. The report concludes that the United States needs to rethink the role of computers in schools. "It is important to improve upon what we have, for instance to upgrade existing technology, but it is even more critical to develop strategic plans for the future and to establish new institutions that insure adequate continuing [computer] education and training for all Americans."

Another trend in education is the premiere business schools' attempt to become totally networked. The John E. Anderson Graduate School of Management at UCLA, for example, has completely reengineered its computer infrastructure; the school set up labs with scores of PCs and Mac's, all linked to a minicomputer running a custom e-mail system for the 1200 students, 100 faculty members, and 180 staff personnel. About 80 percent of students will have their own computers next fall. Every Anderson student will be required to own a computer in the fall of 1996 in addition to a laptop, which is strongly recommended. Several graduate business schools are requiring their students to own computers, and the trend is likely to continue. In the future, every "good" graduate business school will require this.[4]

In addition, in the face of budgetary constraints, schools (especially secondary and high schools) are going about using distance teaching for subjects such as foreign languages.

Finally, we found an interesting comment on the supposedly different approaches of women and men in the use of computers. Computers may seem gender neutral, but men and women relate to them in very different ways. While women use computers, men love them. Men also spend more of their spare time playing on computers and trying to understand how they work. "The greatest predictor of success with computers is experience—mucking around," says Shelly Heller, a computer science professor at George Washington University in Washington, D.C.[5]

According to the *U.S. Industrial Outlook 1994*, the rest of the 1990s finally will witness the accomplishment of computers' evolution to become ubiquitous "information appliances." As the computer market matures, it will divide into more distinct segments. The success of miniaturized computers, as well as the development of a nationwide wireless communications infrastructure, will stimulate demand in the education sector. This sector has long been viewed as a potentially lucrative and underdeveloped market.

---

[2]Gordon Bell, "The View from Here," ComputerWorld, March 20, 1995, p. 91.
[3]Ronald Anderson, Vicki Lundmark, Shon Magnan, Tim Beebe, and Lis Palmer, *Computer Use in American Schools 1992: An Overview*, University of Minnesota, 1992.

[4]Tom R. Halfhill, "Starting from Scratch," *Byte*, March 1995, pp. 58–62.
[5]William M. Bulkeley, "A Tool for Women, A Toy for Men," *Wall Street Journal*, Mar. 16, 1994, pp. B1, B5.

1 An Introduction to Marketing Research

▨ OBJECTIVES

After reading this chapter, you should be able to answer the following questions:

1. What is marketing research?

2. What are the steps in a marketing research project?

3. What questions are commonly addressed by marketing research?

4. What is the value of marketing research?

5. Who uses marketing research?

6. Who produces marketing research?

7. What careers are available in marketing research?

8. What ethical issues are important in marketing research?

What Is Marketing Research?

This chapter is an introduction to marketing research. The opening section begins with a definition of marketing research. It then gives examples of situations in which marketing research was used, to illustrate the nature and variety of marketing research. These are followed by a discussion of the common denominator of those examples. Finally, there is an overview of the process of doing a marketing research project and how this book is organized. The rest of the chapter is devoted to general background on marketing research.

Definition and Examples

Marketing research is defined as *all activities that provide information to guide marketing decisions*. That is, marketing research is any information-gathering activity that is intended to guide strategic or operational marketing decisions about target markets, competitive strategies, product, price, place (distribution), or promotion.

Marketing research can take many forms. The common denominator in marketing research is not *how* it is done but *why* it is done. To illustrate this point, consider the following situations in which marketing research was used.

Minute Maid

The company that makes Minute Maid orange juice ran various promotions, such as coupons and price reductions, over a period of time. To measure the effects of these promotions on profitability, the company tracked Minute Maid sales before, during, and after the promotions. The company bought the data from a company that tracks sales on a market-by-market basis for a wide variety of grocery products.

The data showed that Minute Maid sales would increase during a promotion, then drop in subsequent periods because customers had stocked up. The net effect on sales volume was positive but often failed to compensate for the lower price. As a result, the company decided to run promotions less frequently.

Sears

A few years ago, Sears wanted to sell Goodyear tires through Sears stores. Until then, Sears had followed a policy of selling only its own brands, such as Roadhandler tires and Kenmore appliances, but the company was losing sales to other stores and had decided to change its policy.

Goodyear wasn't sure how to respond. Sears is the largest tire retailer in America, and it was estimated that Sears might sell as many as 2 million Goodyear tires annually. However, Goodyear feared that many of these sales would simply be drawn from other Goodyear outlets, possibly straining Goodyear's relationships with these other retailers without producing much new business for Goodyear.

To help Goodyear decide, Sears gathered records of the brands that were replaced when people bought tires at Sears. These records showed that Sears was selling more than 1 million tires a year to people who drove in with Goodyear tires on their vehicles. It seemed likely that many of these people would buy Goodyear tires if Sears had them—and, since they currently were buying Sears tires, their Goodyear purchases would represent new business for Goodyear. Given this information, Goodyear decided to sell tires through Sears.

A Stockbrokerage

A stockbrokerage used a three-part research project to help set its marketing strategy. In the first part of the project, the firm's key brokers were asked for their opinions regarding who the company's target customers should be and what the company should provide to them. This research showed that brokers favored a "carriage trade" positioning in which the firm would offer superior service to clients with a net worth of at least $500,000.

Next, library sources and real estate records were used to estimate the number of households with a net worth of at least $500,000 in the company's market area. These data showed that the number of households in this category was large enough for the company to meet its goals if it could attract 20 percent of them.

Finally, researchers conducted focus groups (group discussions) with targeted investors to learn how they handled their investments and what they thought of the company. In these discussions, it became obvious that the company would not attract 20 percent of these households and a broader target market was needed. The results were shared with the firm's key brokers to help obtain their support for a different strategy.

A Young Entrepreneur

A young entrepreneur named Rachel Ochoa was thinking about opening a bar in a business district of a large city, near some large office buildings. Her concept was to offer a wide variety of specialty beers, plus live progressive-rock bands on the weekends. Rachel thought this concept would appeal to young professionals in the area.

As part of researching her idea, Ochoa visited other bars and tried to talk with the owners and managers about her idea. Some of them were very helpful. They told Ochoa that her key to success, given her location, would be "after-work" business. They thought specialty beers would be a good concept for drawing young professionals after work, but they didn't think that bands would draw enough weekend business to cover the extra cost. Given this information, Ochoa dropped live music from her concept.

The Common Denominator

What is the common denominator of these examples? What makes all of them examples of marketing research? Quite simply, all of them describe situations in which information was gathered to guide marketing decisions.

As the examples suggest, marketing research can take a wide variety of forms. Marketing research can be formal or informal, onetime or continuing, "made" within the company or bought from outside, syndicated to many users or custom designed for a single user. It can use data from survey interviews, group discussions, casual conversations, sales records, library research, Internet searches, or other sources. Marketing research is defined not by its content but by its applications.

CASE STUDY 1.1

Market research does not have to be formal to be useful. Casual conversations with customers can also be a good source of information.

Lee Kun Hee, chairman of Samsung, the largest company in Korea, recently got an earful when he visited American retailers of Samsung's consumer electronics products. He heard "harsh complaints about shoddy products, unappealing designs, and poor after-sales service."

Mr. Lee immediately ordered senior executives from Samsung's electronics group to fly to America and visit retailers in the Los Angeles area. After they heard the same complaints, he warned them, "If we don't correct this, we won't be qualified to run street-corner shops."

Samsung subsequently made quality improvement a top priority, and the results are paying off. The company's products have received favorable evaluations in recent consumer publications, and sales are improving.

Source: Based on Louis Kraar, "Korea Goes for Quality," *Fortune,* April 18, 1994, pp. 153–159.

The methods used in marketing research are similar to those used in other business research and by social scientists such as economists, psychologists, and sociologists. If you've studied research in these settings, you will find this background useful in studying marketing research; similarly, what you learn about marketing research will be useful in other settings. The key to marketing research is not unique methods; rather, it is a focus on marketing decisions.

The Steps in a Marketing Research Project

Since the number of businesspeople who use marketing research to guide decisions is larger than the number of people who actually do the research, you are more likely to be a user than a doer of marketing research in your business career. However, anyone can become a more effective user by studying methods of research and the issues involved. Therefore, there is a great deal of "hands-on" content in this book. The book is organized according to the steps involved in doing marketing research and how to do them. After studying this book, you should know how to do a successful research project; or, if someone else does research for you, you should know what they are supposed to do.

The general steps involved in marketing research are as follows:

Step 1: Define Objectives and Set Parameters

At the start of any marketing research project, three things must be done: (1) defining the marketing issues to be addressed by the research, (2) specifying the information objectives that will address these issues, and (3) setting general parameters for the research in terms of budget, schedule, reporting procedures, and business arrangements. In other words, the general purpose of the research, its specific objectives, when it is due, and how much it will cost must all be specified.

This part of the research process is addressed in Chapters 1 to 3 of this book. The rest of Chapter 1 provides some general background on issues that are commonly addressed by marketing research, factors that influence the value of a particular project, and the types of companies that do research. Chapter 2 distinguishes between repetitive studies and onetime projects and discusses issues in gathering and reporting repetitive information. Chapter 3 describes how to define research objectives, set budgets and schedules, and make business arrangements. When you are finished studying these chapters, you should be able to set the objectives and parameters for a research project.

Step 2: Choose Data Sources

As already noted, information can come from many possible sources, including informal communications, library research, Internet searches, surveys, group discussions, and experiments. All of these data sources have strengths and weaknesses, and different sources are appropriate for different projects. You need to target the sources that are best for your research.

This part of the research process is addressed in Chapters 4 and 5. Chapter 4 describes various data sources and discusses the strengths and weaknesses of each. Chapter 5 then returns to the list of common marketing research questions given in Chapter 1 and describes the sources that are typically used in each situation. When you are finished studying these chapters, you should be able to choose the data sources that best fit a particular project.

Chapters 4 and 5 are grouped with Chapters 1 to 3 in Part 1 of this book because the setting of research objectives and parameters is not independent of the selection of data sources. Choosing a particular data source—for example, deciding to do a customer survey—has implications for both the cost of a research project and its likely schedule.

Step 3: Design and Implement Data Collection Procedures

The next step in the research process is designing and implementing the specific data collection procedures. For example, if you think a particular research question is best answered through a customer survey, you must design the survey procedures, write a questionnaire, and draw a sample of customers to be interviewed.

This part of the research process is addressed in Chapters 6 to 14, which are divided into two groups. The first group is Chapters 6 to 9, each of which provides detailed information about a particular way to gather research information. Chapter 6 describes how to get information from secondary (i.e., previously existing) sources, including library sources and the Internet; Chapter 7 describes the design and administration of surveys; Chapter 8 describes the design and administration of focus groups (i.e., group discussions) and depth interviews; and Chapter 9 tells how to design and administer experiments. Surveys, focus groups, depth interviews, and experiments are the most common methods of gathering "new" data in marketing research.

The next group of chapters, Chapters 10 to 14, continues by providing information about questionnaire design and sampling. Chapters 10 to 12 describe how to ask questions and design questionnaires, and Chapters 13 and 14 describe how to design and draw samples. These chapters are presented in a group by themselves because asking questions and sampling are basic tools in many forms of data collection, including surveys, focus groups, depth interviews, and some experiments. When you are finished studying these chapters, along with Chapters 6 to 9, you should be able to design and implement all aspects of data collection for most marketing research projects.

Step 4: Analyze the Data

Once data have been collected for a marketing research project, the next step is analyzing the data for the purpose of drawing conclusions. This purpose should be kept in mind throughout the marketing research process. Long before the data analysis stage, you should have planned your project according to the sequence we have outlined, that is, establishing the marketing issue you wish to explore; identifying the information you will need to address that issue; determining a way to collect that information; and deciding on how you will analyze the information you have collected. When you reach the analysis stage, you should be implementing your plan, not starting fresh and thinking "How can I analyze these data?"

The data analysis portion of the research process is addressed by Chapters 15 to 19. Chapter 15 tells how to prepare data for analysis, whereas Chapters 16 to 19 tell how to perform various data analysis procedures. When you are finished studying these chapters, you should be able to select the analysis procedures that best fit your needs, and you should be able to implement and interpret those analyses.

Step 5: Present the Results

Since the people who conduct marketing research often are not the people who use the results to make decisions, the research process has one final step beyond data analysis. This is presenting the results (and, if desired, action recommendations) to decision makers.

This part of the research process is addressed in Chapter 20, which describes how to write a research report and how to make a research presentation. When you are finished studying this chapter, you should know what to write in a research report, how to organize the report, what to show in a research presentation, and how to make a successful presentation.

This book has three final chapters that discuss "big-picture" research issues: Chapter 21 discusses marketing research in an international context, Chapter 22 discusses ethical issues in marketing research, and Chapter 23 discusses the use of the Internet and other current issues in marketing research.

Overview

Exhibit 1.1 summarizes the steps involved in the marketing research process, and the chapters that relate to each step. This book is intended to be a practical resource: those who are doing a marketing research project can use it to progress through that project in an organized way and will find a lot of practical information about how to do so; those who work with a researcher will have a better idea of what the researcher should be doing and whether he or she is doing a good job.

EXHIBIT 1.1

Steps in a
Marketing
Research
Project

Step	Related Chapters
Define the objectives and parameters of the research	Chapters 1-3
Choose data sources	Chapters 4, 5
Design and implement data collection procedures	Chapters 6-14
Analyze the data	Chapters 15-19
Present the results	Chapter 20

Some General Background on Marketing Research

The remainder of this chapter presents some general background about marketing research as it is seen in the business world, including:

- Issues most commonly addressed by marketing research
- Judging the value of a given research project
- A profile of those who use marketing research
- A profile of those who produce marketing research
- Career opportunities in marketing research
- Ethical issues in marketing research

Issues Most Commonly Addressed by Marketing Research

A basic form of analysis in marketing is the "4 Cs" analysis (Customers, Competitors, Company, and Climate). Marketing insights are drawn from answers to questions such as:

- Who are your customers? How much do they buy? Why do they buy? When do they buy? Where do they buy?
- Who are your competitors? How do you compare with your competitors in terms of sales volume, costs, customer satisfaction, and so on? What are your competitors' resources and plans?
- What are your own organization's resources? How effective are your marketing programs?

Critical Thinking Skills

lease return to the four examples at the beginning of this chapter. Decide how each study fits into the list of common marketing research questions presented in Marketing Research Tools 1.1. Do any of these studies ask questions not in our list?

■ What changes are occurring in the technological, social, regulatory, or economic climate in which you operate?

Since this is a basic form of marketing analysis, it should come as no surprise that many of the common questions addressed by marketing research relate to this framework. A list of common research questions is shown in Marketing Research Tools 1.1. This list is not intended to show all the specific questions that might arise in marketing research; it is simply intended to show some of the most common questions.

Another perspective on common marketing research activities is shown in Exhibit 1.2 (see page 14), which shows the percentage of companies engaged in various research activities according to a survey done by the American Marketing Association.

Judging the Value of a Given Research Project

Every company has a market share and every company sets prices, but, as Exhibit 1.2 shows, not every company does marketing research on these and other subjects. This leads to the question: "When should research be done?"

A simple question should precede any marketing research project: "Will this research more than pay for itself?" If the answer is "no," the project should not be done. Like any other business service, the ultimate purpose of marketing research is to increase an organization's bottom line.

The value of marketing research is defined as the ability to improve marketing decisions. Decision makers who use research should be right more often than if they just relied on their own judgment, even if they have long experience and good judgment. A higher percentage of correct decisions leads to increased profits as a result of correct decisions and a reduction of losses resulting from bad ones (Akerson, 1993; Townsend, 1992; Yokum, 1994; Zabriskie and Huellmantel, 1994). The fact that marketing research derives its value from improving the chance of making a right decision has three important implications.

1. *The dollar value of any given research project depends on the amount of money riding on related decisions.* It is impossible to justify a $20,000 research project when only $10,000 rides on the decision, but it is easy to justify a $20,000 project when millions of dollars are at stake. For this reason, large companies, which have large amounts of money riding on routine decisions, spend much more for marketing research than small ones do.

2. *If a decision has already been made and research will not affect it, research is not worthwhile.* Managers sometimes do "window-dressing" research to justify decisions they have already made. This is a poor use of marketing research. These projects may have political benefits for the manager but will not have economic benefits for the organization.

3. *The value of research depends on its ability to provide clear direction.* If a research project is begun without a clear idea of the decisions to be made and what the research is to be focused on, the chance of wasting money is high. It may be

(cont. on p. 15)

MARKETING RESEARCH TOOLS

1.1

COMMONLY ASKED QUESTIONS IN MARKETING RESEARCH

Customer Analysis	Competitive Analysis	Operational Analysis	Environmental Analysis
How big is the existing market?	What market share do you and various competitors hold?	How effective is your distribution?	How will technological developments affect this business?
How big is the potential market?	What future sales do you forecast for your organization and for the market as a whole?	How effective is your advertising?	How will changes in the media environment affect the market?
How fast is the market growing?		How effective are your sales promotions?	
What are buyers' background characteristics?	What percentage of potential buyers are aware of your brand and of competing brands?	How effective are your salespeople?	How will social changes affect the market?
How and why do buyers use the product or service?		How effective is your pricing?	How will regulatory changes affect the market?
Where do they buy the product?	How do potential buyers perceive your brand and competing brands?	How will customers respond to possible product changes?	How will changes in the general economic environment affect the market?
What process do they go through in buying the product?	What is the repurchase rate for your brand and competing brands?	How will buyers respond to a possible new product?	
How brand-loyal are the buyers?	How satisfied are your customers? How satisfied are competitors' customers?		
What market segments exist, and how large are the various segments?	What are your competitors' current marketing programs?		
	What are your competitors' marketing plans and strategies?		

EXHIBIT 1.2

Research
Activities
of 587
Companies

	% Doing
A. Business/Economic and Corporate Research	
1. Industry/market characteristics and trends	83%
2. Market share analyses	79
B. Pricing	
1. Cost analysis	60
2. Demand analysis:	
a) market potential	74
b) sales forecasts	67
3. Competitive pricing analyses	63
C. Product	
1. Concept development and testing	68
2. Brand name generation and testing	38
3. Packaging design studies	31
D. Distribution	
1. Plant/Warehouse location studies	23
2. Channel performance studies	29
E. Promotion	
1. Motivation research	37
2. Media research	57
3. Advertising effectiveness	65
4. Sales force compensation studies	30
5. Sales force territory structure	31
F. Buying Behavior	
1. Brand attitudes	53
2. Product satisfaction	68
3. Brand awareness	59
4. Segmentation studies	60

Source: Reprinted with permission from 1988 Survey of Marketing Research, published by the American Marketing Association, Thomas C. Kinnear and Ann R. Root, editors "Research Activities of 587 Companies," 1988, p. 43.

CASE STUDY 1.2

One of the new issues in marketing research is how to make effective use of the Internet. The Net has various possible applications to marketing research, including (1) tracking visitors to a Net site that contains information or advertising, (2) posting a questionnaire on the Net and gathering responses, (3) looking for statistical information on the Net, and (4) posting questions to a usenet to ask its members for advice.

The vice president for new product development for a valve manufacturer recently told us that this last use is a good one. He said:

So far, we haven't found the Net to be very useful for doing marketing research. For example, when we look for statistical information on markets we might enter, we usually can't find what we want on the Net, and, if we can, we usually can get the information more easily from a library or a trade association. And we haven't tried to do a questionnaire on the Net because we wouldn't have confidence in the representativeness of the respondents.

On the other hand, the Net has been very useful to us in learning <u>how</u> to do research. We've identified some user groups where we can post questions about how to do things, and we've gotten some great advice in this way. For example, we recently had a new product feasibility study done by a supplier who was recommended to us on the Net, and we were very happy with the results.

How to use the Internet for marketing research is discussed in appropriate places throughout this book.

interesting and fun to gather information for its own sake, but it is not good practice in commercial marketing research.

Who Uses Marketing Research?

You might expect any organization that does marketing to do marketing research. However, organizations vary greatly in their use of research.

There are several reasons for this variation across organizations. One reason is size differences—as noted previously, big organizations typically do more marketing research than small organizations do. Another reason is differences in philosophy—some companies are big believers in research, whereas others are not. A third reason is differences in industry characteristics. All these factors are discussed in the following sections.

Manufacturers of Nondurable Consumer Goods

The biggest spenders on marketing research are manufacturers of nondurable consumer goods, especially the big makers of grocery "packaged goods" such as Procter & Gamble, Colgate Palmolive, and Kraft–General Foods. These companies spend large sums of money on marketing research for various reasons:

- First, many grocery categories represent billions of dollars. For example, a market share shift of 0.1 percent in the cold cereal market represents more than $5 million in revenues. The stakes justify high research spending, and these companies are big enough to pay for it.

- Second, these companies have no direct contact with their ultimate customers. Since they sell to supermarket chains such as Kroger or Safeway, marketing research is the only way for them to learn about consumers.

- Third, the rapid purchase cycles for consumer nondurables leads companies to jockey for sales on a week-by-week basis. This means that companies want market information not just annually, not just quarterly, but weekly.

Also, marketing research is increasingly used by packaged goods manufacturers as a tool in the battle for advantageous shelf space in retail stores. The manufacturers provide retailers with marketing research to show how the manufacturers' products will provide profits for the retailers (Masterson, 1993; Riddell, 1992).

Manufacturers of Durable Consumer Goods

Manufacturers of durable consumer goods are the second largest spenders on marketing research. Companies such as General Motors, General Electric, Compaq, and Sony all have big research budgets. However, as a percentage of sales, they tend to spend less than the makers of nondurable goods do.

The reasons why makers of consumer durables spend heavily on research are similar to those that apply to nondurable products: the markets are large, the companies are large, and the companies do not have direct contact with their ultimate customers. The reason why makers of durables spend less than packaged goods companies as a percentage of sales is that durable goods don't have as much week-to-week fluctuation in pricing and promotional activity, so the manufacturers of durable goods don't need information as frequently.

Manufacturers of Business Products

A large subcategory of marketing research is called business-to-business research; this involves products whose buyers are organizations rather than individuals (Block, 1995; Gorelick, 1993; Hague, 1988; Kelly, 1984). As a percentage of sales, research spending by industrial goods manufacturers is similar to that by consumer goods manufacturers; for example, companies with annual revenues of at least $5 million in either group spend about 1 percent of sales on marketing research (Honomichl, 1995).

The major difference between consumer and business research is not in the spending level but in the type of research that is done. Consumer goods manufacturers spend much more money on studies that track retail sales of their products, whereas industrial goods manufacturers have little need for such data. Also, consumer goods makers tend to rely on methods such as telephone surveys, whereas industrial goods manufacturers are more likely to gather data through face-to-face contact with their customers.

Service Companies

As the service sector of the American economy has grown, its use of marketing research has grown accordingly. Service companies tend to spend less than manufacturers on marketing research because service companies tend to be smaller, but these companies have shown a faster rate of growth in their spending. Most noticeable in recent years has been the expansion of marketing research by financial institutions as competition has increased (Britt, 1993; Gridley and Brenner, 1991; Sullivan, 1992). There has also been rapid growth in marketing research activities by health care providers, including HMOs and hospitals (Elsesser, 1988).

It is often difficult to determine whether something is a product or a service, but this really doesn't matter as far as the market research activities that are conducted. Providers of consumer services tend to have research programs similar to those of consumer goods manufacturers, and industrial service providers tend to do research similar to that of industrial goods manufacturers. For example, all types of companies do research to measure customer satisfaction after a product is purchased or a service is provided (Triplett, 1994).

Nonprofit Organizations

Marketing research by nonprofit organizations constitutes a small segment of the total that probably will remain small. This is because most nonprofit organizations are relatively small and are similar to small businesses in that their research tends to be informal and inexpensive.

Retailers

Because retailers are such a visible part of marketing, it may surprise you to learn that they do little marketing research. There is an increasing trend for companies such as J. C. Penney, Shell, and McDonald's to do research on customer satisfaction (Collins, 1989; Justis, Olsen, and Chan, 1993). In general, though, retailers tend to rely on other companies or internal sales analysis for their research needs: they rely on real estate companies for location data, manufacturers for research on new products, and sales analysis to tell them whether or not to continue stocking older items.

Advertising Agencies

There has been a steady decline in the amount of market research done by advertising agencies during recent decades. Years ago, when many companies had no research expertise, ad agencies provided research services. This is still done for small clients that lack research capabilities. However, larger clients typically have research capabilities these days and prefer to use their own research staffs. As the vice president for marketing for a large company recently told us, "Whenever an agency does research on your marketing program, they always seem to conclude that you need to increase your advertising budget!"

Two research functions have remained mainly within advertising agencies: the evaluation of advertising effectiveness and the evaluation of potential advertising media. Effectiveness research is used to pick the best ads from various "executions" and then, after these ads have run, to see how well they did (Staffaroni, 1993). Media research is done to evaluate the suitability of various media as outlets for a client's advertising. Most advertisers, even large ones, get these data from advertising agencies because the agencies need this type of information for every client they serve and consequently employ people who are expert at this type of research.

Media Companies

Media companies (television and cable networks and stations, radio stations, magazines, newspapers, etc.) often conduct studies of their own audiences and of the general public. They use these studies in two distinct ways: (1) for internal marketing evaluation purposes and (2) as a selling tool, to show potential advertisers the type of audience they will get. Media companies spend most of their marketing research money for this latter purpose.

To the extent that information gathered by the media provide accurate information about audience characteristics, this information can help to increase advertising effectiveness. However, advertisers must realize that each medium will tend to provide data that are favorable to itself. Using data from independent services or comparing data from many different media helps to remove or reduce this bias.

Government Agencies

Government agencies don't usually use research for their own marketing purposes (except for tourism studies). However, government agencies can be a useful source of marketing research data, as discussed next.

Who Produces Marketing Research?

We've discussed the extent to which various industries use marketing research. But who produces it?

The major producers of marketing research are (1) syndicated research services, which track markets on an ongoing basis for multiple users; (2) job shops, which perform onetime research projects; (3) government agencies that publish data with marketing applications; (4) research users that do their own research; and (5) advertising agencies. These producers of marketing research are discussed in the following sections.

Syndicated Research Services

Syndicated research services are marketing research firms that track markets on an ongoing basis and sell the data to a number of clients. These data are used in clients' marketing information systems, which are described in Chapter 2.

The best-known example of a syndicated service is the A. C. Nielsen television ratings service. Nielsen, which is the largest research company in the world (and a subsidiary of Dun & Bradstreet), collects ongoing data concerning TV viewing in a national panel of households, and sells the resulting TV ratings to TV networks and advertising agencies that use the data to buy and sell advertising time.

Interestingly, while Nielsen is best known for its TV ratings, a much larger part of Nielsen's business is sales tracking for packaged grocery products. Nielsen measures product movement at a large number of participating stores, primarily through the use of checkout scanners, and sells the results to manufacturers who use them to estimate what their market shares are, how their sales respond to promotions, and other points of interest.

Other well-known syndicated services include:

- Information Resources, Inc. (IRI), which is a close competitor of Nielsen in tracking grocery products in the United States and is now entering other countries

- IMS, which tracks the market for pharmaceutical products and, like Nielsen, is a subsidiary of Dun & Bradstreet

- NPD, which tracks clothing, toys, restaurant dining, and petroleum products
- Simmons Market Research Bureau, which tracks magazine readership
- Arbitron, which tracks television viewing and radio listening in local markets
- Trendex, which tracks appliance purchasing
- F. W. Dodge, which tracks local building permits and automobile sales
- J. D. Power and Associates, which tracks owner satisfaction for automobiles and other products

As these examples suggest, syndicated services provide basic, industrywide data such as sales and market shares for competing products. This type of basic information is the "bread and butter" of market research, and syndicated services dominate the list of the largest market research suppliers. A list of the fifty largest market research firms in the United States is given in Exhibit 1.3 (see pp. 21–22); note the prominent positions of the syndicated services.

Job Shops

Job shops are market research suppliers that budget, design, and execute "custom" studies in response to client requests. Depending on their agreement with a client, they may be responsible for all parts of a study or only some parts. Even if a job shop is responsible for all parts, it is common for some of the work, especially data collection, to be subcontracted to other organizations.

The largest job shops in the marketing research industry include:

- Companies such as Gallup, Roper, and Louis Harris, which do marketing research and general public opinion polling. These organizations are best known for opinion polls that appear in newspapers, but they get most of their profits from marketing research.

- Companies such as Market Facts, National Family Opinion (NFO), and Home Testing Institute (HTI), which maintain large panels of prerecruited, preclassified people who can be sent questionnaires and products for testing. This is not quite a syndicated service because each project requires a different questionnaire and possibly a special subsample of the panel. Nonetheless, these companies develop standard procedures that are used repeatedly.

- Companies that measure the effectiveness of ads, such as Burke Marketing Research with its Day-After Recall service. These firms use the same or similar methods on each project—in Burke's case, a standard telephone survey done the night after a commercial airs on television—but each study is conducted as a distinct entity and sold to only one user.

Companies such as Gallup, Market Facts, and Burke are well known in the marketing field, but most job shops are small businesses with billings of less than $5 million per year. A job shop can be started without any employees because work can be subcontracted; all that is really needed is a client. This means that entry into the marketing research industry is easy. However, small firms have trouble surviving over the long haul unless they have special expertise or good client contacts.

Government Agencies

The U.S. government is the largest data collector and disseminator on the face of the earth. This information is not gathered for marketing research purposes, but much of it has marketing applications. For example, the federal government estimates the number of businesses of each type in each state and county, which is useful in setting sales territories for industrial goods.

State and local governments are also a good source of marketing research data. For example, state and local traffic departments measure vehicular traffic on major streets to decide where stoplights are needed; this information is useful to retailers in choosing store locations.

The use of government statistics is discussed in more detail in Chapter 6.

Critical Thinking Skills

Think of a specific product made by a specific company. Among the various producers of marketing research, which would be the best source of information in each of the following areas: market size, market share, customer satisfaction, ad awareness, price response, and regulatory trends?

In-House Operations

Most users of marketing research don't produce their own data because it is more efficient to use suppliers to do so. However, there are exceptions. For example, in-house work is commonly used for projects involving the analysis of internal accounting records. Companies may also do their own research for projects that involve library research or a small number of interviews with, say, industrial customers.

Regardless of who collects the data, data analysis and presentation of results to management are often done by an in-house research group.

Advertising Agencies

Many of the larger advertising agencies operate their own facilities for ad testing, either within their offices or at a shopping mall location. Some also have the facilities to host group discussions, which are useful in testing product concepts and getting a feel for how an ad campaign should approach customers. Also, virtually all agencies that are midsized or larger have a research department that evaluates media and helps agency executives prepare their media placement recommendations for clients.

Career Opportunities in Marketing Research

Marketing research plays a large role in the economy and provides a number of career opportunities.

Industry Size and Employment

Surveys of marketing research firms and of large companies estimate that about $3 billion are spent annually on market research in the United States, *not* counting in-house marketing research activities. In-house marketing research expenditures are estimated to be about one-half of expenditures on outside research, or $1.5 billion annually. The total estimated expenditures in the United States are thus $4 billion to $5 billion annually, and even more is spent in the rest of the world (Honomichl, 1995).

Based on data from the American Marketing Association and the U.S. Census Bureau, we estimate that about 50,000 people work full-time on marketing research activities, and thousands of interviewers work part-time (American Marketing Association, 1994).

In recent years, most of the growth in marketing research employment has come in supplier companies. The trend has been for companies that use marketing

(cont. on p. 23)

EXHIBIT

1.3

The Fifty
Largest
Marketing
Research
Suppliers

Rank	Organization	Headquarters	Worldwide Research Revenues* (millions)	Revenues from Outside U.S. (millions)
1	D&B Marketing Information Services	Wilton, CT	$2,388.1	$1,525.8
2	Information Resources Inc.	Chicago, IL	399.9	66.3
3	The Arbitron Co.	New York, NY	137.2	
4	Westat Inc.	Rockville, MD	124.0	
5	Maritz Marketing Research Inc.	St. Louis, MO	122.4	26.2
6	Walsh International/PMSI	Phoenix, AZ	111.6	25.1
7	The Kantar Group	London, UK	91.9	6.0
8	The NPD Group	Port Washington, NY	85.8	12.9
9	NFO Research Inc.	Greenwich, CT	73.1	2.0
10	Market Facts Inc.	Arlington Heights, IL	64.6	6.4
11	Audits & Surveys Worldwide Inc.	New York, NY	54.6	13.1
12	The M/A/R/C Group	Irving, TX	52.1	
13	Opinion Research Corp	Princeton, NJ	44.1	10.2
14	Abt Associates Inc.	Cambridge, MA	42.9	1.0
15	The BASES Group	Covington, KY	41.6	8.3
16	Intersearch Corp.	Horsham, PA	41.1	
17	MAI Information Group	Livingston, NJ	38.0	
18	Macro International Inc.	Calverton, MD	37.8	15.4
19	Walker Information	Indianapolis, IN	37.7	5.8
20	Elrick & Lavidge	Tucker, GA	34.6	.5
21	Roper Starch Worldwide Inc.	Mamaroneck, NY	31.5	1.8
22	J.D. Power and Associates	Agoura Hills, CA	30.3	
23	Burke Inc.	Cincinnati, OH	29.0	1.6
24	Creative & Response Research	Chicago, IL	27.1	
25	Lieberman Research Worldwide	Los Angeles, CA	23.4	2.8
26	Chilton Research Services	Radnor, PA	23.3	

*Total revenues that include nonresearch activities for some companies are significantly higher.

Continued

Rank	Organization	Headquarters	Worldwide Research Revenues* (millions)	Revenues from Outside U.S. (millions)
27	Yankelovich Partners Inc.	Norwalk, CT	23.2	1.4
28	M.O.R.-PACE Inc.	Farmington, MI	22.5	3.0
29	Wirthlin Worldwide	McLean, VA	22.3	.9
30	ASI Market Research Inc.	Stamford, CT	21.1	
31	Total Research Corp.	Princeton, NJ	20.9	5.5
32	Market Strategies Inc.	Southfield, MI	19.3	
33	Data Development Corp.	New York, NY	18.6	
34	Custom Research Inc.	Minneapolis, MN	18.5	
35	ICR Survey Research Group	Media, PA	17.9	
36	Response Analysis Corp.	Princeton, NJ	17.2	
37	IntelliQuest Inc.	Austin, TX	17.0	5.0
38	Market Decisions	Cincinnati, OH	15.1	
39	Research Data Analysis Inc.	Bloomfield Hills, MI	14.4	2.9
40	Matrixx Marketing Research	Cincinnati, OH	14.1	7.5
41	Conway/Milliken & Assocs.	Chicago, IL	12.4	
42	National Analysts Inc.	Philadelphia, PA	12.0	
43	Guideline Research Corp.	New York, NY	11.7	
44	Gordon S. Black Corp.	Rochester, NY	11.5	
45	Ross-Cooper-Lund Inc.	Teaneck, NJ	10.3	.1
46	BAI (Behavioral Analysis Inc.)	Tarrytown, NY	10.0	1.0
47	Newman-Stein Inc.	New York, NY	8.6	.4
48	TVG Inc.	Fort Washington, PA	8.6	
49	Marketing Research Services Inc.	Cincinnati, OH	8.5	
50	FRC Research Corp.	New York, NY	8.4	.3
Total, Top 50			$4,552.2	$1,760.1

Source: Reprinted with permission from *Marketing News*, published by the American Marketing Association, "The Honomichl 50," June 3, 1996, p. H4.

research to spend a larger share of their budgets purchasing outside research and to reduce their internal research staffs. Along with this, there has been a recent trend for large syndicated services to assign staff directly to their largest customers. These employees are physically located in the users' offices.

As marketing has become more international, so has marketing research. Many U.S. firms have marketing research activities in other countries. However, this globalization has not had significant effects on employment opportunities. Almost all researchers in any country are native to that country, regardless of where the headquarters of the parent company are located.

Career Paths in Marketing Research

How can someone break into marketing research? An education in marketing or marketing research is by far the most common way. Other entry routes include education in fields such as psychology, sociology, or statistics, where students receive training in research methods similar to those used in marketing research. The most typical marketing researcher currently has an M.B.A. with several courses in research methodology. Some older marketing researchers have only an undergraduate degree or no degree at all, but this is increasingly rare. The number of researchers with Ph.D.s is small but growing.

It is common for marketing researchers to start in general marketing and be transferred into the research function, after which they might stay in research or transfer back. Another career path is to start with a research company and rise through its ranks. As people progress, they often switch companies, and they sometimes start their own research companies after gaining experience and building contacts.

Marketing researchers usually benefit from some direct experience with marketing, either in selling or in management. Researchers can make better recommendations when they have been in the decision maker's shoes. An increasingly common practice is to have marketing managers work in marketing research as part of their career paths, to encourage the integration of research and decision making.

As in other areas of business, salaries in marketing research depend on an employee's educational level, experience, and competence, as well as the size and success of the employer. They also depend on the nature of the employer. Marketing researchers within a manufacturing or service firm usually earn less than people of comparable rank who work directly in marketing. Also, senior executives of marketing research suppliers usually earn more than equivalent research executives in client firms. In both cases, the differential is a function of decision-making responsibility: marketing researchers within manufacturing or service firms fulfill a staff function, whereas marketing managers and market research suppliers have direct responsibility for decisions that affect their companies' profitability. Decision makers usually earn more than people in staff positions.

Ethical Issues in Marketing Research

Ethical issues in marketing research include researchers' obligations to research participants, research suppliers' and clients' obligations to each other, and the special issues that arise when marketing research information is used in advertising or for selling purposes.

Illustrative questions include: Is it ever ethical to mislead or withhold information from research participants? If so, when can researchers do so, and what should they do to protect the rights of participants? When do research suppliers have an ethical responsibility to keep clients' data confidential, and when do they have an ethical responsibility to make their results public?

Ethical issues such as these are discussed in Chapter 22. This chapter is near the end not because the subject is unimportant or an afterthought but because ethical issues of marketing research can best be understood after a thorough grounding in the subject.

In this introductory chapter, we simply wish to acknowledge that ethical considerations are important, and we urge you to be aware of these issues. Many ethical violations in marketing research are made not deliberately but rather by people who simply are unaware of the ethical issues involved in research.

One question that is sometimes raised is whether the whole process of marketing research is ethical. The concern is that marketing researchers gather data from customers with the intent of manipulating them or persuading them to buy unneeded goods. However, we strongly believe that marketing research is ethical if practiced properly. The ethical marketer is interested in satisfying customers at the time of purchase and in the long run, not in deceiving them. To the extent that marketing research facilitates this process, we believe it is an ethical activity.

Summary

This chapter introduced the field of marketing research. The following points were covered:

1.   What is marketing research?

Marketing research consists of all activities that provide information to guide marketing decisions. The methods used in marketing research are similar to those used in other types of research. Marketing research is distinguished not by its methods but rather by its focus on marketing questions.

2.   What are the steps in a marketing research project?

There are five major steps in the research process: (1) defining objectives and setting parameters, (2) choosing data sources, (3) designing and implementing data collection procedures, (4) analyzing the data, and (5) presenting the results.

3.   What questions are commonly addressed by marketing research?

Common marketing research questions fall into four categories: (1) customer analysis, (2) competitive analysis, (3) operational analysis, and (4) environmental analysis. *Customer analysis* includes questions such as: How big is the market? What are the characteristics of buyers? What are their buying motives? What is their buying process? *Competitive analysis* includes questions such as: What is our market share? How do our marketing inputs, such as price and advertising, compare with our competitors? How do buyers perceive us relative to our competitors? *Operational analysis* includes questions such as: How does our sales volume vary across different salespeople or distributors? Are our incentives to salespeople or distributors commensurate with their sales? *Environmental analysis* includes questions such as: What regulations are being considered that will affect our market?

4. What is the value of marketing research?

Marketing research derives its value from helping managers make better decisions. It does not change the outcomes of those decisions; it simply helps managers know which course of action is best. Therefore, the value of marketing research in any given situation depends on the importance of the decision at issue, the level of uncertainty about the proper course of action, and the ability of the research to reduce that uncertainty.

5. Who uses marketing research?

All kinds of organizations use marketing research. However, the level of usage varies as follows:

- Large organizations typically spend more than small organizations on marketing research, because their decisions have greater financial implications.
- Manufacturers of products typically spend more than service companies, because they are more likely to be separated from their end users by layers of distribution.

Overall, the largest users of marketing research are the major manufacturers of nondurable consumer goods such as grocery products. Most of these companies spend millions of dollars on research each year.

6. Who produces marketing research?

Marketing research users sometimes produce their own research but more often use outside sources. *Syndicated services* are the largest outside source of marketing research; these services usually track information of general interest within an industry (such as sales volumes and market shares) and offer this information on a syndicated basis to all of the companies in the industry. *Custom job shops* are the next largest source; these companies, most of which are small, do special research projects for individual clients. Marketing research data also are produced by some *government agencies*, and *advertising agencies* often do ad testing and media efficiency research.

7. What careers are available in marketing research?

The most common route into the marketing research industry is through education. A student who has a strong interest in marketing research, along with an educational background in marketing, statistics, or social sciences, can take an entry-level position with a research organization and progress from there. Also, some researchers start in general marketing with a large company and transfer into the research function.

8. What ethical issues are important in marketing research?

Important ethical issues in marketing research include the obligations of a researcher to research participants, the obligations of research suppliers and clients to each other, and special issues that arise when marketing research information is used for advertising or selling. These issues are discussed in more detail in Chapter 22.

Suggested Additional Readings

Any student seriously interested in marketing or marketing research should join the American Marketing Association. In addition to its professional journals, it provides a directory of marketing and market research firms and has annually published, in

Marketing News, a report by Jack Honomichl about the leading firms in the market research industry.

The major U.S. trade publication reporting on marketing and marketing research is *Advertising Age*. The general business press, especially *The Wall Street Journal*, *The New York Times*, and *Business Week*, provide coverage of marketing and marketing research activities.

Discussion Questions

1. What are some reasons why a firm would want to conduct a market research study? What are some reasons why a firm would *not* want to conduct marketing research?

2. Compare and contrast how each of these marketers uses marketing research:
   a. Manufacturers of nondurable consumer goods
   b. Manufacturers of durable consumer goods
   c. Manufacturers of industrial products
   d. Service companies
   e. Nonprofit organizations
   f. Retailers
   g. Advertising agencies
   h. Media
   i. Governments

3. Below are four categories of questions that are commonly used in marketing research (taken from Exhibit 1.1). Match each of the six examples discussed in the beginning of the chapter with the question type each example most closely addresses.
   a. Describe the general market.
   b. Describe your organization's market position
   c. Measure the response to marketing actions.
   d. Monitor the general environment.

Marketing Research Challenges

1. Suppose you are looking for a job in marketing research. In what geographic locations are you most likely to find one? Use whatever sources are available to you to estimate the geographic locations of market research jobs.

2. Suppose you have had several years of experience and are considering the following three job opportunities:
   a. Market research manager in a large consumer goods firm
   b. Brand manager in the same or a similar firm
   c. Executive in a small market research supplier firm
   Discuss the comparative advantages and disadvantages of these three jobs from the perspectives of job satisfaction, salary, risk, and future opportunities. Which of these jobs is most appealing to you? Why?

Internet Exercise

The Marketing Research Job Board is an online bulletin board posted on the Marketing Research Resource Center. Access the site (at http://www.drgutah.com/guestbook/guestbook.html) and read through the available positions. What duties and responsibilities are typical for these jobs? What educational requirements seem necessary?

References

Akerson, Steven D. (1993). "Being a Little Off Can Make a Huge Difference." *Marketing News* 27 (August 16), p. A2.

American Marketing Association (1994). *Survey of Marketing Research*. (Chicago: American Marketing Association.)

Block, Martin P. (1995). *Business-to-Business Market Research: Identifying, Qualifying and Understanding Your Customers*. (Chicago: Probus.)

Britt, Phil (1993). "Basic Research Required." *Savings & Community Banker* 2, (Apr), p. 32.

Collins, A. (1989). "Store Location Planning: Its Role in Marketing Strategy." *Environment and Planning A* 21 (May), pp. 625–628.

Elsesser, Jan (1988). "Conducting Marketing Research in Health Care: The Changing Roles of Physician and Patient." *Journal of Advertising Research* 28 (October–November), pp. RC15–RC20.

Gorelick, Dick (1993). "Good Research Has Obvious—and Not So Obvious—Benefits." *Marketing News* 27 (Sept. 13), p. 16.

Gridley, Henry M., and Nancy L. Brenner (1991). "Trust Marketing—It Should Start with Consumer Research." *Bank Marketing* 23 (April), pp. 56–57.

Hague, Paul N. (1988). *The Industrial Market Research Handbook*. (New York: Franklin Watts.)

Honomichl, Jack (1995). "1995 Honomichl Business Report on the Market Research Industry." *Marketing News* 29 (June 5), pp. H1–H43.

Justis, Robert T., Janeen E. Olsen, and Peng Chan (1993). "Using Marketing Research to Enhance Franchisee/Franchisor Relationships." *Journal of Small Business Management* 31 (April), pp. 121–127.

Kelly, J. Steven (1984). "Research Lends Coherency to a Trade Show Marketing Plan." *Marketing News* 18 (March 2), pp. 4–5.

Masterson, Jim (1993). "Research Adds Value to Products." *Marketing News* 27 (Aug. 16), p. A6.

Riddell, Ken (1992). "The Art of Sales Promotion: A Good Promotional Program Starts with Good Research." *Marketing* 97 (Nov. 30), p. 1.

Staffaroni, James (1993). "Copy Testing—a True Team Effort." *Journal of Advertising Research* 33 (July–August), pp. RC2–RC3.

Sullivan, Michael P. (1992). "Selling to Seniors: Research Your Market." *Bankers Monthly* 109 (January), p. 36.

Townsend, Bickley (1992). "Market Research That Matters." *American Demographics* 14 (August), pp. 58–60.

Triplett, Tim (1994). "Abbott Labs Exec Tells Benefits of Satisfaction Measurement." *Marketing News* 28 (Apr. 11), p. 6.

Yokum, John (1994). "Invest for Success: It's Research That Makes Winning Programs." *Marketing News* 99 (June 6), p. 22.

Zabriskie, N. B., and A. B. Huellmantel (1994). "Marketing Research as a Strategic Tool." *Long-Range Planning* 27, pp. 107–118.

The Marketing Information System

 OBJECTIVES

LEARNING

After reading this chapter, you should be able to answer the following questions:

1 What is a marketing information system (MKIS)?

2 What information might a marketing information system contain?

3 What issues should be considered in designing a marketing information system?

4 How should the marketing information system be staffed?

5 How should the marketing information system be equipped?

6 What does a marketing information system look like?

This chapter discusses issues in designing a marketing information system (MKIS). As the name implies, a **marketing information system** is *a system for gathering and transmitting repetitive marketing research information.* The use of such systems has been growing rapidly. In 1985, a survey showed that two-thirds of *Fortune* 1000 firms that responded to a survey had an MKIS (McLeod and Rogers, 1985). Today, MKISs are universal among larger companies and have become common in smaller organizations.

Some people regard all marketing research activities as part of the MKIS. In our terminology, though, MKISs contain only information that is gathered and transmitted on a systematic, continuing basis. This emphasis on continuing data gives the MKIS a focus on problem identification research. **Problem identification research** is *research done to help managers identify problems and opportunities in marketing programs* (Bissell, 1995; Duclaux, 1995; Glazer, 1989; Morrall, 1994; Schwartz, 1989).

Problem identification research can be contrasted with problem-solving research. **Problem-solving research** is *research done to help managers decide between clearly defined courses of action.* For example, Borden's might face the question "Should we add caramel pecan fudge ice cream to our product line?" with the clearly defined alternatives of "yes" and "no." Research directed at choosing between these alternatives would be an example of problem-solving research. Problem-solving research is usually done on a special project basis because it serves a onetime, nonrecurring decision.

Problem identification research occurs at an earlier stage. Before developing a question as specific as "Should we add caramel pecan fudge ice cream to our product line?," Borden's might have been tracking sales and distribution for various types of ice cream. The company might have noticed several trends in the market: (1) grocers are giving more freezer space to ice cream, (2) this extra space is going to superpremium products and fancy flavors, and (3) sales of superpremiums and fancy flavors are rising at the expense of traditional products. These trends might have presented Borden's with both a problem (falling sales of traditional products) and an opportunity (to take more freezer space and increase sales with new products). The market monitoring that identified these trends would be an example of problem identification research. As the example suggests, problem identification research typically involves some type of ongoing monitoring and thus is well suited for systematic collection and reporting.

The purpose of an MKIS is to identify problems and opportunities at an early stage so that effective actions can be taken (Curry, 1993; Menon and Varadarajan, 1992; Moorman, 1995). It takes no genius to recognize that a problem exists if a product's market share has dropped so low that stores are refusing to stock it, but by that time it is probably too late to do anything except let the product die. Similarly, it takes no great skill to recognize that a profitable niche exists for a new product when a competitor has introduced a similar product with great success. An effective MKIS provides early information so that organizations can get a head start on the competition or, at the least, will not lag behind. This is increasingly important in the modern business world, where the rapid pace of change has made constant evolution essential to market success.

Problem identification and problem solving are not totally separate activities, and an MKIS may play an important role in providing the information needed to make decisions. In the ice cream example, the same market-tracking data might show both a problem (falling sales for traditional flavors) and its solution (caramel pecan fudge as the fastest-growing flavor not currently made by the company).

The Contents of a Marketing Information System

The abbreviation "MKIS" rather than "MIS" is used to denote a marketing information system because "MIS" usually refers to the more general concept of *management* information systems. A well-managed firm will have several information systems serving different purposes, and "MIS" is used to describe any or all of these systems. A *marketing* information system uses information specifically relevant to marketing decisions. It is primarily used by the marketing staff.

An MKIS may contain a broad range of data from both internal and external sources (Bakken, 1992; Riche, 1989) To illustrate this range of data, let's consider the information that might be useful in an MKIS for a hospital. Exhibit 2.1 (see page 32) shows some information a hospital might want to gather on an ongoing basis. You can probably think of other information that might be useful in a hospital MKIS, but the list in Exhibit 2.1 is enough to illustrate some basic ideas about MKISs:

- First, MKISs can be quite complex, and they can address a wide range of marketing issues.

- Second, MKISs, like all marketing research, can draw on a wide variety of data sources. For example, a hospital might use internal records, published data, patient surveys, trade association newsletters, and rumors about plans at other hospitals as part of its information system.

- Third, most organizations do not track every possible piece of information relevant to marketing programs. The contents of an MKIS are subject to cost-benefit considerations, and few hospitals would track all of the information we have listed.

As with all marketing research, smaller organizations will tend to spend less on an MKIS, because their smaller scale of operation provides less justification for information-gathering costs. A smaller organization can achieve lower expenditures in two ways: (1) it can gather less information, or (2) it can gather information less frequently, possibly using occasional projects to gather information that a bigger organization would collect regularly.

Author Tips

We usually recommend that small organizations accommodate their budgets by cutting back on the *amount* of information rather than the *frequency* of information. Infrequently gathered information cannot provide the "early-warning" capability provided by regular data collection. An analogy is that a captain who sends someone to see what happened when the ship hits a bump is more likely to see the ship sink than a captain who keeps a lookout posted. Also, some types of information are difficult to interpret unless they are gathered regularly. For example, regular tracking of customer satisfaction is needed to distinguish between random variation and meaningful trends.

Critical Thinking Skills

How could a hospital use each type of information shown in Exhibit 2.1 (see page 321)? For example, what should a hospital do if it sees that senior citizens in its service area are being replaced by young families? What should a hospital do if an increasing number of people in its area do not have regular doctors?

EXHIBIT 2.1

Possible
Information
for a Hospital
Marketing
Information
System

- The hospital might want to monitor patients' addresses, so it can map its service area.
- Within its service area, the hospital might want to monitor the size of the population, as well as health-related factors such as age, occupation, family size, and insurance coverage.
- The hospital might want to monitor the percentage of people in its service area who do not have a regular doctor and, among these people, the percentage who are aware of the hospital and consider it a good place to go for various medical services.
- The hospital might want to monitor the number of patients referred by each doctor on staff, as well as total revenues and profits generated by each doctor.
- The hospital might want to monitor variables such as service time in the emergency room, response time by ward nurses, food quality, and patient satisfaction with various aspects of hospital service.
- The hospital might want to monitor the activities of competing hospitals regarding facilities, incentives for doctors, prices, bids to insurance companies, and so on.
- The hospital might wish to monitor its market share of various services or among various market segments.
- The hospital might wish to monitor pending regulatory proposals such as changes in Medicare, Medicaid, and insurance regulations.

CASE STUDY 2.1

The ability to track certain information in an MKIS often depends on whether that information is available from commercial research companies or not.

For example, makers of packaged grocery products have built mutually lucrative relationships with research companies that use supermarket scanner data to track sales. Now marketers of household goods such as lint brushes, vacuum cleaners, and coffeepots hope to measure sales activity in their industries with the same type of data. A leading research company, IRI, has signed an agreement with the National Houseware Manufacturers Association to gather and report scanner data on nineteen categories of housewares.

"The benefits will be different for every member, but everybody will be able to analyze how the whole category is doing," said Thomas P. Conley, executive director and chief operating officer of the NHMA. "Manufacturers can use this information to prevent out-of-stocks, plan line extensions and make sales pitches to retailers."

The manufacturers' internal records show factory shipments for their own products, but they don't show market share or how products are moving at retail. The market-tracking data provided by IRI will fill in these gaps.

"What's really neat about the IRI data is they bring us closer to the package goods world, where we can understand the reality of where our business is [at the retail level], instead of where we think it is," said Carol Dores, director of consumer product development at Black & Decker.

Source: Based on Jeanne Whalen, "IRI Signs On to Track Household Goods Sales," *Advertising Age,* June 13, 1994, p. 37.

Designing a Marketing Information System

To this point, the purpose of an MKIS and the information that might go into one have been discussed. There are also other issues to consider in designing an MKIS. They include:

- What is the level of data aggregation?
- Who has access to the system?
- How recent are the data?
- What is the level of sophistication of the system?

What Is the Level of Data Aggregation?

Marketing information can be used at a completely disaggregated level, such as records of individual purchases by individual buyers. At the other extreme, information can be highly aggregated, such as a single number representing total company sales during some time period. Various other possibilities, such as total sales per customer, total sales per product, total sales per region, and so on lie in between.

One advantage of disaggregate data is that users have the flexibility to aggregate the data in any way they wish, whereas aggregate data usually can't be disaggregated (for example, you can add individual transactions to get total sales, but you can't break a total into individual transactions). Another advantage of disaggregate data is that they may be useful for "database marketing" as well as for market research. For example, catalog companies such as J. Crew and Victoria's Secret maintain transaction records that are used to identify (1) customers who have slow order cycles and should be sent fewer catalogs, (2) customers who have missed their usual order cycle and should be stimulated with a discount, and (3) customers who have missed several order cycles and should be dropped from further mailings.

Twenty years ago, the major complaint against disaggregate data was that they took too much computer storage capacity and were too costly (in machine time) to work with. With today's computers, which have larger memories and greater speed, this complaint is less relevant. Even with files containing millions of records, the capacity of modern computers is so large that sufficient data storage space is available. Nor are sorting and combining disaggregate data serious problems. Methods for doing this are now simple and relatively speedy.

Given that having data in disaggregate form has major benefits and fewer problems, it is clearly desirable for an MKIS to store data in the most disaggregate form possible. Most companies follow this principle, although the older tradition of storing partially aggregated data can be found in systems that were developed early and have not been changed.

Who Has Access to the System?

Three issues arise in connection with access to an MKIS: (1) Who should be allowed to manipulate the data and prepare reports? (2) Who should receive a particular report? and (3) What security measures are needed to protect the company's interests?

In the early days of MKISs, marketing managers rarely had the capability to manipulate MKIS data; rather, they would request information from computer programmers, who would write the needed programs and deliver the results in printed outputs. Since programming was costly, it was common for companies to develop standardized outputs that were run on a regular basis and distributed to all relevant managers. For example, a company such as Exxon might prepare a monthly sales report showing sales at each affiliated gas station and distribute this report to both regional sales managers and senior marketing executives.

This approach can create various problems. One problem is that a standard report may not provide every manager the specific information he or she needs. A second problem is that reports are designed to serve a wide group of managers, so any given manager is likely to receive some information he or she doesn't need. This leads to information overload, which can lead managers to ignore the reports. A third problem is that detailed information on company operations is floating around on printed documents that are only loosely controlled.

Fortunately, technology has come to the rescue. Many marketing managers now have personal computers that are linked to the system in which MKIS data are stored. These managers get occasional summary reports on market activity, but detailed information is not provided. Instead, managers directly access the database with a spreadsheet program such as Excel or a statistical package such as SAS to get the information they want. In a 1985 survey, McLeod and Rogers found that a majority of marketing managers used their terminals daily. Such systems can be controlled so that a given manager has access only to information needed for his or her function and cannot alter the main data file.

Of course, not all managers are comfortable with data handling, and some information is well suited to standard reports, so most companies still circulate standard reports. The trend, though, is for these reports to be less detailed.

How Recent Are the Data?

Recency refers to how frequently data in an MKIS are updated. Some forms of information may be updated daily; for example, Toys 'R' Us captures every transaction as it occurs and feeds the information, on a daily basis, into an automated system for re-ordering merchandise. Other data may be updated weekly, monthly, quarterly, or even annually.

All else equal, one would want the most recent data possible, but frequent updating increases the cost of the MKIS and is not always necessary. The benefits of having access to recent data should be balanced against the costs of obtaining it.

One factor that affects the need for recent data is the type of decision being supported by the data. Information that supports short-term decisions such as price adjustments should be as recent as possible, possibly even on line. However,

CASE STUDY 2.2

Texas Commerce Bank, a large, Texas-based subsidiary of Chase Manhattan Corp., recently saved a lot of money by cutting the frequency of management information reports.

A distribution clerk in the bank's Trust Operations division had the job of delivering a large, shrink-wrapped computer report that provided a number of senior managers with daily information about the division's activities. The clerk noticed that most of these reports went to waste. Only the last report of each month was taken out of its shrink wrap and used.

When the bank asked its employees to find ways to cut costs, the distribution clerk told his bosses about the wasted reports. Sure enough, the managers said they only needed a report at the end of the month. The daily reports were discontinued, saving the bank $60,000 per year.

This story shows how an organization can save money by questioning the way it does things. It also illustrates the point that most information is used at particular times, and reports should be timed accordingly. Marketing information systems that distribute information more often than needed or to a wider audience than needed simply waste money.

Source: Taken from Jim Barlow, "TCB Taking to Re-enginnering," *Houston Chronicle*, Dec. 22, 1996, p. E1.

information that supports long-term decisions such as target market selection may be needed only once a year.

The need for recent information also depends on the rate of change in the market. Consider the difference between Amana refrigerators and Compaq notebook computers. The computer market is far more volatile than the refrigerator market, with rapid changes in competitive conditions. Because of this volatility, Compaq needs weekly or monthly information on market conditions to adjust its marketing and production schedules; Amana, in contrast, can live with quarterly or even annual data.

What Is the Level of Sophistication of the System?

The level of sophistication of an MKIS relates to its data processing capabilities. In addition to containing raw data, all MKISs have data processing capabilities that vary across systems. At the lowest level, almost all information systems have the ability to sort and combine data into totals and to compute percentages and averages. These calculations are usually automated, so the MKIS reports the same summary calculations every time a report is issued.

At an intermediate level of sophistication, a system can be programmed to compute differences between current and previous results (such as this month versus last month). A system can also be programmed to print a report that highlights differences exceeding some trigger value. This means that managers are alerted to situations that require special attention.

If an MKIS is designed to produce such a report, there must be careful consideration of the level of change needed to trigger an alert. If that level is too high, important market changes may be missed. However, if it is too low, the situation is like an overly sensitive car alarm that goes off every time somebody passes, and meaningful changes tend to get lost among the noise. The amount of change needed to trigger an alert should be less than the normal variability that occurs even when no significant change is occurring in the market.

At higher levels of sophistication, some firms have complex forecasting procedures that are built into the MKIS. These systems use data from current and previous periods to make predictions about what will happen in the future if the marketing activities of the firm and its competitors remain unchanged or change in specified ways.

At the highest levels of sophistication, "expert systems" can be programmed to recommend actions in addition to providing analyses or forecasts. For example, American Airlines has an expert system that uses historical data and current bookings to forecast how many "full-fare" passengers will take a particular flight, then automatically sets the number of discount tickets that are available for that flight.

Marketing Research Tools 2.1 summarizes the issues and choices involved in designing an MKIS.

Critical Thinking Skills

How would you design an MKIS for a large bank with hundreds of locations? What information would you track? How would the system work in terms of data aggregation, access, recency, and sophistication? How, if at all, would you change the system if it were for a small bank with one location in a small town?

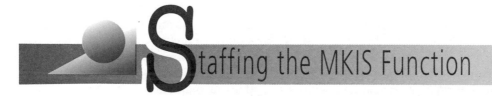

Staffing the MKIS Function

Running an effective MKIS requires computer expertise, knowledge of information sources, data analysis skills and knowledge of marketing. These skills currently tend to be found in different people.

Computer specialists are needed to design and install an MKIS and to modify it as new hardware, software, and data sources become available. Computer specialists also need to be able to communicate with the marketing users so that they can make the MKIS user friendly. There may also be special data needs that require new programming, but this should happen only rarely. Frequent need for special programming indicates a problem with the basic MKIS.

In addition to computer specialists, many large firms have information specialists on their MKIS teams. "Information specialist" is a designation for people who are basically librarians. These people should be knowledgeable about (1) the broad range of print sources with marketing research applications, (2) the growing number of on-line data services that provide marketing information, and (3) the data contained in the company's MKIS. In some industries, it is desirable to have information specialists with multilingual capabilities so that international sources within the MKIS can be scanned (Francese, 1995; Nijkamp, 1989).

MARKETING RESEARCH TOOLS

2.1

ISSUES TO CONSIDER IN DESIGNING A MARKETING INFORMATION SYSTEM

Level of data aggregation	Disaggregated			Aggregated
	Individual purchase records	Customer purchases in a period	Sales by region	Total sales in a period
Access	High			Low
	Interactive		Can request analyses	Standard reports
Recency	Very Recent			Not Very Recent
	Daily	Weekly	Monthly	Annual
Level of sophistication	High			Low
	Expert systems	Forecast models	Differences between periods	Sort and combine

This marketing research tool shows the range of choices available in designing an MKIS.

This is a good place to stress that many MKISs contain printed information as well as computerized data. Some have predicted that we will live in a paperless society in the twenty-first century, but many important information sources are currently found only in print. It is here that an information specialist who communicates well with the marketing staff can be invaluable.

In addition to computer specialists and information specialists, most companies staff their information systems with analysts who studied marketing and statistics in college or who have some marketing experience and who like to work with information. Also, companies increasingly follow a practice of rotating marketing people through the marketing research department. This practice helps to ensure that the research department understands the company's marketing activities.

A recent development that reflects the benefits of closer relationships between researchers and managers is for syndicated research services to place employees in the offices of their major clients. Some large clients have multimillion-dollar contracts with syndicated services; for example, in 1992 the Kraft–General Foods unit of Philip Morris spent an estimated $24 million on data from A. C. Nielsen (Stern and Gibson, 1993). As part of such a contract, Nielsen places one or more of its own staff in the client's office. These people serve only that client and develop a detailed understanding of the client's needs to go with their detailed understanding of the data being provided.

Exhibit 2.2 (see page 38) summarizes MKIS staffing needs.

EXHIBIT 2.2

Marketing Information System Staffing Needs

Computer Specialists

Staff with expertise to design and install an MKIS and to modify it as new hardware, software, and data sources become available. Computer specialists also need to be able to communicate with the marketing users so that they can make the MKIS user friendly. There may also be special data needs that require new programming.

Information Specialists

Librarians who are knowledgeable about (1) the broad range of print sources with marketing research applications, (2) the growing number of online data services that provide marketing information, and (3) the data contained in the company's MKIS.

Marketing Analysts

People who studied marketing and statistics (or social research methods) in college, or who have marketing experience, and who like to work with information.

Author Tips

We suggest that marketing managers have access to personal computers that can uplink with central data files, as well as software that can process information with only minimal instructions from the user.

Equipment Requirements for an MKIS

It is impossible to be specific about MKIS equipment because this depends on the special needs of individual firms as well as rapidly changing computer technology.

Remember that equipment is not the defining element of a successful MKIS. An organization that thinks of MKIS improvement in terms of bigger or faster computers is confusing information technology with information productivity. Good equipment helps, but the types of computer and software that are used are far less important than the types of information gathered, the way that information is organized and reported, and the way that information is used.

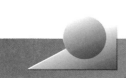

A Sample Marketing Information System

To illustrate the design and contents of a real-life marketing information system, we recently interviewed some people at The Methodist Hospital in Houston, Texas, about their MKIS. Here's a transcript of our conversation, with the authors labeled "Us" and The Methodist Hospital people labeled "MH."

Background Information and Trends

Us: To start, can you give us some background on The Methodist Hospital?

MH: Sure. The Methodist Hospital is a large, multiservice hospital located in the Texas Medical Center in Houston, Texas. Like most hospitals, we provide primary care services such as delivering babies and treating broken bones. We also are a "tertiary care center," which means that we treat people with complicated conditions who are referred to us by other health care providers. We are affiliated with the Baylor College of Medicine, a well-known medical school, and we have many top specialists on our staff. We are very proud of our doctors and of our patient outcomes data, which show that we provide superior-quality medical care.

Us: Can you tell us something about your market?

MH: Our ultimate customer is the patient who receives medical care in our hospital. Most of these patients come from the Houston area, but we also get quite a few foreign patients for services such as heart surgery. Other players in the market are the doctors who refer patients to our hospital and the insurance plans that pay for the care. If you define our market in terms of competitors, then you would say that we are in the Houston hospital market, specifically in the medical center, tertiary care market.

Us: Has your market changed in the past ten years?

MH: Definitely. Ten years ago, most people in Houston had "fee-for-service" health insurance. This meant their doctor could send them to any hospital and their insurance would reimburse reasonable costs. Today, most people have "managed care" insurance, which restricts them to certain hospitals or gives higher reimbursement at those hospitals. As a result, our key customer ten years ago was the doctor, but our key customer today is the insurance company. Also, ten years ago we could provide appropriate service and price it on a cost-plus basis, but today we have to offer a competitive price to the insurance company and then find a way to provide proper care at that price.

Critical Thinking Skills

Do you believe that other hospitals have experienced the same trends as The Methodist Hospital? What changes, if any, should these trends cause a hospital to make in the content or design of its MKIS?

Overview of the Marketing Information System

Us: Thanks for the background. Now, what kind of information do you track in your marketing information system?

MH: Our marketing information system tracks five general types of data:

- The first category is what we call "market utilization data." Basically, this is information that shows who are our patients, how much business are we doing, and what is our market share.

- The second category is competitive intelligence data related to our competitors' strategies and activities.
- The third category is patient satisfaction data, which measure how satisfied our patients were with the treatment we provided to them.
- The fourth category is public awareness and image data, which measure what the general public thinks of us.
- The fifth category is general demographic trends, which relate to future demand for hospital services in our primary service area.

Customer Tracking, Sales and Market Share Data

Us: Let's start with the market utilization data. What information do you track on your own patients?

MH: For inpatients who stayed in the hospital at least one night, we track the primary medical condition that was diagnosed, the medical procedures that were performed (such as heart surgery), the services that were provided (such as semiprivate room), the length of the stay, the care unit where the patient stayed, the type of insurance payer, the total charges, and the patient's age, zip code, and gender. For outpatients who did not stay overnight, we track the same information except for length of stay and care unit.

Us: Where do you get this information?

MH: From our billing system.

Us: Do you track each patient individually?

MH: No, we summarize the data. In other words, we track the total number of patients we treated in each diagnostic category, the total number of patients who received various services, and so on. This allows us to profile our customers in total.

Us: How about market share data? What information do you get, and where do you get it?

MH: We get market share data on every variable that we track, and we get it from the Texas Hospital Association. It's a cooperative system; you send your data to the THA, and you get back the same information for all other participating hospitals. In the Houston area, the participating hospitals account for about 85 percent of all hospital discharges, and all of our major competitors participate, so the data are excellent from our point of view.

Us: Do these data cover both inpatients and outpatients?

MH: We just use the data for inpatients. Most outpatient care is provided in doctors' offices or in other nonhospital settings, so the THA data don't have good enough market coverage to give us useful share estimates.

Us: How often do you update this information?

MH: We update and report to our management every six months.

Us: Which managers get the report?

MH: All middle and upper managers; basically, department managers and up.

Us: Is the information distributed in its own report?

MH: No. We used to distribute this information in a monthly marketing report, but other departments issued similar reports and our managers got buried in paper. Our senior management decided to go with one consolidated monthly operations report, and we were given one section of that report for marketing information. We use that space to provide market share data once every six months, and we use the space for other information in the other months.

Us: What specific market share information do you provide?

MH: Since we have limited reporting space, we provide highly summarized information. Usually, we use trend graphs that show market shares in selected diagnostic categories and selected geographic areas for our hospital and four key competitors.

Us: Is it the same information each time?

MH: No. We select the results that we think will have the highest general interest to our managers.

Us: Do managers have access to market share data that you don't show in the report?

MH: Yes, we've recently put the detailed information on a computer network with open access for managers.

Us: Are the managers allowed to manipulate the data to do their own analyses?

MH: Not at this time.

Competitor Tracking Data

Us: Okay, let's talk about your second category of information, competitor data. What information do you track?

MH: Well, the market share data that we just discussed tells us how much business our competitors are doing in various categories. We also try to track their strategies and their business plans.

Us: Where do you get that information?

MH: We use clipping services that cover various magazines and newspapers. These services are paid to send us copies of any articles that refer to our competitors. Our marketing staff also does its own monitoring of local news stories and trade publications. We also get a lot of information about our competitors' activities through informal conversations with people in the industry.

Us: How do you organize all of this information?

MH: We maintain computerized files on each of our major competitors. Whenever we get information, we type it up and enter it into the file.

Us: How often do you update this information?

MH: We enter information every time we hear something.

Us: How often do you organize it into a report?

MH: Once a month.

Critical Thinking Skills

re there differences in the levels of data aggregation that are appropriate for reports prepared for the board of directors and for middle managers? Why?

Us: Which managers get the report?

MH: This information goes into a market developments report that we present each month to our board of directors.

Us: Do middle managers get this report?

MH: No. Middle managers see market share information, as we've already discussed, but they don't get information about our competitors' plans and activities. That information goes to the board, because it is strategic in nature.

Us: What is the format of your report to the board?

MH: We make an oral presentation of any significant competitive actions.

Us: Do board members have direct access to the competitive intelligence files?

MH: No, they seem satisfied with the monthly report format.

Customer Satisfaction Data

Us: How about your third category of information, patient satisfaction data? What information do you track in this category?

MH: We do telephone surveys with 650 inpatients and 650 outpatients every quarter. The work is done by a research company from Nebraska. They call a sample of our recent patients and ask whether anyone in the family was recently treated in a hospital. If the people say "Yes," we ask which hospital—almost all of them identify our hospital—and then we ask how satisfied they were with various aspects of their experience.

Us: Do you use standardized questions, and do you probe why people were less than fully satisfied?

MH: Yes on both counts. The research company that does our surveys also works for hospitals in other cities. Since these hospitals don't compete with us, we've all agreed to use standard questions so we can compare our results with each other as well as with our own historical performance. Also, if people say they were less than very satisfied, we ask them why. We also ask if they ever got upset while they were in the hospital and, if so, why.

Us: How often do you update this information?

MH: Quarterly. That is, once every three months.

Us: How often do you report it to managers?

MH: Quarterly.

Us: Is the information reported in the monthly operations report that we previously discussed?

MH: No, the patient satisfaction results are presented in a separate report that runs about thirty pages and has a standard format. This report shows historical trends on key measures along with comparisons to other hospitals, and it highlights statistically significant trends.

Us: Which managers get this report?

MH: All middle and upper managers. Also, our senior vice president for quality improvement prepares a two-to-three-page summary that goes to our board.

Us: Do managers have direct access to the data?

MH: No. In fact, we don't even store the data in house. Our research supplier keeps the data and sends us reports.

Critical Thinking Skills

Would you change anything about The Methodist Hospital's procedures for measuring and reporting patient satisfaction? If so, what changes would you make? Why?

Awareness and Image Data

Us: Now let's talk about your fourth category of information, which is public awareness and image. What do you gather in this regard?

MH: We subscribe to a syndicated service called "HealthPoll." That service does three thousand telephone interviews per year in the Houston area. Among other things, it asks people which hospital comes to mind as a good place to receive treatment for medical conditions, such as back pain, heart disease, cancer, pregnancy, and so on. We like that measure because it shows our "share of mind" in various medical categories, and it reveals categories that are "open" because no hospital has a strong image. "HealthPoll" also measures general name awareness and whether people have a positive impression of the hospital.

Us: Is this like your patient satisfaction data in that you get reports but not raw data from the research supplier?

MH: Exactly.

Us: How often do you get the reports?

MH: Semiannually.

Us: And how often do you report this information to your managers?

MH: Even though we get the data semiannually, we break it up and report findings of interest once a quarter in the monthly operations report that we discussed earlier.

Us: So this information goes to all middle and upper managers?

MH: Right. We also make a short summary for our board.

Us: Do managers have direct access to the data?

MH: No, but they can get copies of additional tables that we don't show in the operations report.

Demographic Trend Data

Us: Your fifth category of information is general demographic trends related to future demand for hospital services. What information do you gather in this regard?

MH: We get two types of information. First, we have a supplier who sells us up-dated census information on the Houston area. We get the population size, population growth rate, age distribution, and income distribution for the whole Houston area and for every zip code. We get current figures and pro-jections for five years in the future. Second, the Texas Department of Insur-ance gives us reports that show the total number of households in Houston who belong to managed care health plans, and it shows enrollment for each plan.

Us: Do you gather any lifestyle or psychographic data?

MH: No, because we don't really market directly to the end user. We primarily market to doctors and health insurance plans, so all we need to know about our potential patients is how many of them will be available, where they will be located, and what kinds of insurance they will have.

Us: Earlier in our discussion, you said that you get quite a few foreign patients. Do you track those populations in any way?

MH: No, because the demand isn't dense enough. For example, we might get twenty patients a month from Mexico City, but it doesn't justify buying spe-cial information about that area.

Us: How often do you update your general demographic data?

MH: We buy updated census data about once every two years. We get the Texas Department of Insurance data once a year.

Us: How often do you report this information?

MH: We report both types of information about once a year. We don't necessarily report it when we get it; we just use it to fill in our section of the monthly op-erations report when we don't have other information to report.

Us: So it goes to all middle and upper managers?

MH: Right. And the reason we don't provide this information more regularly is that our managers don't have much they can do with it. Satisfaction data, market share data, and public image data are of immediate interest to our managers in showing how their sections are performing, but data on popula-tion trends and insurance membership are of less interest to them. Our main use for these data is at a central level, to help us decide where to increase ser-vice offerings and how to bid on managed care contracts.

Us: Do managers have access to the data?

MH: No.

Other Information

Us: Let's talk briefly about some types of information that you didn't mention. Do you track activity on a doctor-by-doctor basis?

MH: Yes and no. That information is available from our billing system, and our cost-accounting people use it. However, we don't pull it into our marketing information system and we don't disseminate it to managers, because our business somewhat depends on the goodwill of our doctors and we don't want to take a chance of embarrassing anyone.

Us: How about the regulatory environment? Do you track that?

MH: Like doctor activity, this is information that has marketing implications and is captured by our organization but is not considered part of the marketing information system. We have a government relations department that tracks regulatory activity and issues its own reports.

Us: How about cost data that might be relevant to pricing?

MH: We have cost data available in our accounting system, but we don't use it for marketing purposes. We've made a strategic decision to set prices according to competition, so instead of gathering cost data to help us decide what prices to charge, we simply set our prices according to competition, and it is up to our operations people to get their costs in line with those prices.

Us: How has your marketing information system changed, if at all, in the past five years?

MH: First of all, the content of the system has expanded. Five years ago, we weren't tracking competitors and we weren't tracking membership in insurance plans. Also, our market utilization data and our patient satisfaction data were in earlier generations and weren't as useful. For example, we measured satisfaction, but we didn't ask people why they were less than fully satisfied.

Also, five years ago, the only information that went to our board was some market utilization data. Now they also get patient satisfaction data, public image data, and reports on our competitors' activities. This is part of a general increase in our "marketing consciousness."

Also, five years ago, we, along with other departments, gave stand-alone monthly reports to middle and upper managers. Now, except for patient satisfaction data, everything is consolidated into the monthly operations report. The information is more highly summarized than before and has more interpretation added. It may seem odd, but we reduced the amount of information that we provide in order to increase the amount of information that managers pay attention to and use.

Us: Any changes in data access?

MH: We recently put our market utilization reports on a network where managers have open access to them. We'll probably have requests to do more in this regard as our managers become more comfortable with using computers.

Us: Thanks for all the information. We really appreciate your help.

Exhibit 2.3 (see page 46) summarizes The Methodist Hospital's marketing information system. It shows the various types of information tracked by The Methodist Hospital. For each type of information, it shows the source of data, the level of aggregation, the extent to which managers have access to the data, the recency with which data are reported, and the sophistication of data processing.

Earlier in the chapter, we listed various types of information that might be useful in a hospital's MKIS. If you compare that list with the information contained in The Methodist Hospital's MKIS, you will see that Methodist tracks most of the items listed, though it doesn't classify all of these items as part of the MKIS. The completeness of The Methodist Hospital's system reflects the fact that Methodist is a large, relatively sophisticated operation. Smaller hospitals are likely to have smaller information systems.

Note that The Methodist Hospital's MKIS has grown and changed over the past five years. The growth in Methodist's MKIS reflects an increasing marketing

EXHIBIT 2.3

Summary of The Methodist Hospital's Marketing Information System

Content (type of information)	Source of Information	Level of Aggregation	Access	Recency	Sophistication
Sales and market share	Internal billing records; industry cooperative data	The raw data are transaction based; in use, the data are aggregated on a per product and per market basis.	Midlevel managers and above get reports and can access the data.	Data are updated and reported every six months.	Transaction data are aggregated into totals; all subsequent processing is manual.
Competitive intelligence	Clipping services, media monitoring, street talk	Data are gathered on a per item basis and used on a per competitor basis.	Reports go to the board of directors.	Data are updated continually and reported monthly.	All processing and interpretation are manual.
Customer satisfaction	Proprietary survey data	Data are gathered on a per customer basis and aggregated.	Midlevel managers and above get reports; they can get more analyses but cannot access the data.	Detailed data are updated and reported quarterly; a summary index is reported monthly.	The system automatically makes trend comparisons and flags significant changes.
Awareness and image	Syndicated survey data	Data are gathered on a per household basis and aggregated.	Midlevel managers and above get reports; they can get more analyses but cannot access the data.	Data are updated semiannually and reported quarterly.	The system automatically makes trend comparisons.
General market size and trends	Secondary data from commercial vendor and insurance board	Data are aggregate in nature.	Midlevel managers and above get reports but cannot access the data.	Data are updated annually or biannually and reported sporadically.	All processing and interpretation are manual.

orientation in the hospital industry, as well as a trend in all industries toward increased use of marketing information. The changes in Methodist's system reflect the fact that most information systems change over time; in fact, if an MKIS never changes, the market may not be dynamic enough to justify monitoring it.

Summary

This chapter discussed marketing information systems (MKISs). The following points were covered:

1. What is a marketing information system (MKIS)?

An MKIS is a system for tracking markets on a regular basis. The purpose of an MKIS is to identify problems and opportunities at an early stage.

2. What information might a marketing information system contain?

An MKIS might contain a wide variety of information. Almost any of the common research questions related to customer analysis, competitive situation analysis, operational analysis, and environmental analysis might be addressed through an MKIS.

3. What issues should be considered in designing a marketing information system?

Apart from the types of information contained in the system, issues to consider in designing an MKIS include (1) the level of aggregation at which data should be stored, (2) how much direct access marketing managers should have to the data, (3) the frequency with which data should be entered into the system, and (4) the sophistication of the data processing functions performed by the system.

4. How should the marketing information system be staffed?

The MKIS staff should contain people with computer skills, people with knowledge of internally and externally available data, and people with a good understanding of the organization's marketing activities and information needs. Often, these skills are found in different people, so a large MKIS operation might have separate computer specialists, information specialists, and marketing specialists.

5. How should the marketing information system be equipped?

Specific equipment needs will vary greatly, depending on the requirements of the organization and the availability of new technology. In general, equipment issues are far less important than the selection of information to be gathered and the way that information is organized and used.

6. What does a marketing information system look like?

In the example given about the MKIS of The Methodist Hospital, Houston, Texas, the system contained five major categories of information: (1) market utilization data, (2) competitive intelligence data, (3) patient satisfaction data, (4) public awareness and image data, and (5) general demographic trends. For each category, there are different frequencies of reports and recipients of the data.

Suggested Additional Readings

It is dangerous to suggest books about MKIS because the technology is changing so rapidly. You may find the following books useful: David Curry, *The New Marketing*

Research Systems (New York: Wiley, 1993); and Rashi Glazer, *Marketing and the Changing Information Environment* (Cambridge, Mass.: Marketing Science Institute, 1989).

There are also several professional journals that present studies of information systems, such as *Information and Management* and *Journal of Management Information Systems.* These periodically have articles on MKIS. The use of such systems is also reported in the business press.

Discussion Questions

1. Why should companies consider creating an MKIS? Name some types of information that might be found in this MKIS and the sources of this information.

2. Discuss the difference between "problem identification research" and "problem-solving research."

3. Discuss the advantages and disadvantages of collecting disaggregated data. What about highly aggregated data?

4. Listed below are several product categories. Please indicate the degree of recency the product manger would require from the firm's MKIS. Would it be
   a. Monthly or less often?
   b. At least monthly?

   Categories
   Automobiles
   Women's clothing
   Bulldozers
   Spaghetti sauce
   Children's toys
   VCRs
   Microwave ovens
   Dishwashers
   Ski jackets
   In-line roller skates

Marketing Research Challenges

1. Using the business press, select a company and a new or modified product that has been recently introduced. Speculate about the kind of information in the company's MKIS that may have led it to develop this new or modified product.

2. Design an MKIS for (a) a major hospital in your community and (b) a clinic that employs four doctors. Specify the contents of each system, the summary reports that will be delivered to managers, which managers will get each report, and when the reports will be delivered.

Internet Exercise

The Methodist Hospital's marketing information system includes data from patient satisfaction surveys. This information is distributed quarterly in printed reports. In your opinion, what would be the advantages of posting current and historical data on a password-protected webpage, and allowing the hospital's managers to download information as desired? What would be the disadvantages, if any, of distributing satisfaction data in this way? If The Methodist Hospital created a webpage to distribute patient satisfaction data, should it continue to distribute printed reports?

References

Bakken, David G. (1992). "Combining Data-base Analysis, Survey Research Improves Marketing Success." *Marketing News* 26 (July 6), p. 19.

Bissell, John (1995). "More Packaged Goods Marketers Hearing the Call of the Data Base." *Brandweek* 36 (Aug. 7), p. 18.

Curry, David J. (1993). *The New Marketing Research Systems: How to Use Strategic Database Information for Better Marketing Decisions.* (New York: Wiley.)

Duclaux, Denise (1995). "Are You Getting the Most from Your MCIF (Marketing Customer Information File)." *ABA Banking Journal* 87 (July), p. 64.

Francese, Peter (1995). "Managing Market Information." *American Demographics* 17 (September), pp. 56–59.

Glazer, Rashi (1989). *Marketing and the Changing Information Environment.* (Cambridge, Mass.: Marketing Science Institute.)

McLeod, Raymond, and John Rogers (1985). "Marketing Information Systems: Their Current Status in *Fortune* 1000 Companies." *Journal of Management Information Systems* 1 (Spring), pp. 57–75.

Menon, Anil, and P. Rajan Varadarajan (1992). "A Model of Marketing Knowledge Use Within Firms." *Journal of Marketing* 56 (October), pp. 53–71.

Moorman, Christine (1995). "Organizational Market Information Processes: Cultural Antecedents and New Product Outcomes." *Journal of Marketing Research* 32, pp. 318–335.

Morrall, Katherine (1994). "Technology Updates Market Research Methods." *Bank Marketing* 26 (April), pp. 15–18.

Nijkamp, Peter (1989). "The Development of Retail Information Systems in the Netherlands." *Ekistics* 56 (September/October–November/December), pp. 259–261.

Riche, Martha Farnsworth (1989). "Getting It Together." *American Demographics* 11 (August), p. 8.

Schwartz, Joe (1989). "Databases Deliver the Goods." *American Demographics* 11 (September), pp. 22–25.

Stern, Gabriella, and Richard Gibson (1993). "Rivals Duel Bitterly for Job of Supplying Market Information." *Wall Street Journal* (Nov. 15), p. 1.

3 Managing Marketing Research

 OBJECTIVES

After reading this chapter, you should be able to answer the following questions:

❶ Who should be responsible for making decisions about marketing research?

❷ How should marketing researchers work with marketing managers?

❸ How should the marketing research function be organized and staffed?

❹ How should research suppliers be chosen and managed?

In this chapter, we expand our discussion of managerial issues in marketing research. Our discussion covers four broad topics: (1) how to allocate responsibility for marketing research decisions, (2) how marketing researchers should work with marketing managers, (3) how to organize and staff the marketing research function, and (4) how to choose and manage research suppliers.

Who Should Be Responsible for Making Research Decisions?

The most basic questions in marketing research management are (1) who should have the authority to decide *whether* to do marketing research and (2) who should have the authority to decide *how* to do it. For example, in a hospital, who should decide whether to measure patient satisfaction? If satisfaction is measured, who should decide which methods to use?

Who Decides Whether to Do Research?

The authority to approve marketing research on a particular topic can be given either (a) to operational managers who will use the information to guide their marketing decisions or (b) to a research manager who is responsible for providing managerially useful information. To illustrate these two approaches, consider the question of who would decide to measure patient satisfaction at a hospital.

Under the first approach, operational managers such as the hospital's chief executive officer, vice president for marketing, or director of nursing services would decide whether they want patient satisfaction data to guide their decisions; if so, the manager who wants this research would call the hospital's marketing research department or a marketing research vendor and arrange for the research to be done. The manager who commissioned the research would pay for it out of his or her general budget for operations and support.

Under the second approach, the hospital's marketing research manager would decide whether to measure patient satisfaction for the benefit of operational managers; if so, the research manager would arrange for the research and make the results available to appropriate managers. The cost of the research would be paid for out of a budget controlled by the research manager, or, if the research manager doesn't have a separate budget, the cost of the research would be charged to participating managers.

Which Approach Is Better?

The advantages of giving authority to operational managers should be obvious. Marketing research derives its value from improving marketing decisions, and operational managers are the people who make those decisions. It makes sense to let them decide what information they need and how much money that information is worth to them.

However, various problems can arise when managers have full control over research authorizations. One possible problem is that managers will fail to do useful research, either because they don't realize the value of research or because they fear that research will reveal deficiencies in their operations. For example, a hospital's director of nursing services might not measure patient satisfaction with nursing services, even though this information could be useful, because he or she fears that the results will expose the nursing department to criticism.

Another possible problem is a lack of continuity in MKIS research. Midlevel marketing managers tend to change jobs every two or three years, and the continuity that is so valuable in an MKIS may be lost if each new manager makes new research decisions. For example, if a hospital keeps changing its program for measuring patient satisfaction, it will be difficult to evaluate trends over time.

A third possible problem is a lack of coherence or efficiency across decision-making units in the organization. For example, it doesn't make sense to have the director of nursing services sponsor a survey in January to measure patient satisfaction with nursing services, the director of food services sponsor a survey in May to measure patient satisfaction with the food, and so on.

To minimize these problems, we recommend a structure in which (1) a marketing research manager has responsibility and budget authority for MKIS research and (2) operational managers have responsibility and budget authority for special research projects. This structure is used by most organizations that are large enough to have an MKIS. For example, it is used by The Methodist Hospital in Houston, Texas, whose MKIS was profiled in Chapter 2. This structure ensures coherence and continuity in the marketing information system, where they are most needed, and otherwise lets decision makers define their own information needs.

Critical Thinking Skills

In many cases, MKIS data can be used both to evaluate and improve operations. For example, the director of nursing at a hospital can use patient satisfaction data to help improve nursing services, whereas the CEO can use the same data to evaluate the whole nursing department. What problems, if any, does this imply for the relationship between researchers and managers?

Who Decides How to Do Research?

No matter who has the authority to decide *whether* to do marketing research, researchers should have the lead role in deciding *how* to do it. Researchers have more knowledge than managers about data sources and research methods.

In the common situation, where a manager initiates the decision to do a research project, the project should be designed through the following process. The first step should be a meeting between the manager and the researcher. The purpose of this meeting is to set research objectives and budget constraints. The manager should tell the researcher what she or he hopes to learn from the research, and how much she or he is willing to spend on the project.

Given this information, the researcher's next step is to recommend a general research plan and a budget. The research plan should specify the questions to be answered by the research, the methods to be used, and the contents of the final report.

CASE STUDY 3.1

The value of marketing research ultimately depends on its interpretation and use. This is seen in the story of the minivan.

Chrysler's minivans have been the most profitable product in the U.S. automobile market since being introduced in 1983. Other auto companies have introduced minivans but haven't been able to overcome Chrysler's early lead.

Amazingly, Chrysler was the *last* American automaker to research the minivan concept. Ford researched the concept and built a prototype in 1973, and General Motors tested a minivan virtually identical to Chrysler's in 1979.

What happened? Lee Iacocca was at Ford when the minivan was tested, and he says the research was favorable. He wanted to introduce the minivan, but company president Henry Ford II overruled him because the investment was large and Ford feared another Edsel. In fact, when Iacocca left Ford for Chrysler, the company allowed him to take its market research on the minivan because Ford considered it worthless.

At General Motors, executive Vince Barabba says, "We had the market research to support the viability of the minivan idea, but . . . we were considering a whole family of front-wheel-drive

vehicles, and . . . the van didn't make the cut."

Decision makers at Ford and GM did not have a special vision of the minivan—a special belief in the product—so they did not act despite favorable market research. The minivan was not introduced until Lee Iacocca, who *did* believe in the product, became president of Chrysler and could act on the combination of this innate belief and the supporting research.

Source: Based on Alex Taylor III, "Iacocca's Minivan," *Fortune,* May 30, 1994, pp. 56–66.

Critical Thinking Skills

From Case Study 3.1, what can you infer about who made the decision to do the minivan research at General Motors, Ford, and Chrysler? What does this case suggest about the relationship between who decides to do research and how the results will be used by line managers?

These recommendations can be given in the initial meeting, but it is often best to present them in a follow-up meeting, possibly accompanied by a written proposal. This keeps people from committing prematurely to a research plan that comes "off the top of the head." It also ensures that a realistic budget can be prepared to accompany the research plan.

If the manager approves the research plan and the budget, the researcher should proceed to design specific data collection procedures, such as the questionnaire and sampling procedures that will be used, if any. These specific procedures may or may not be presented for comments by the relevant managers. If they are presented to managers, comments should be solicited in a "What I like or don't like" form rather than a "How-to" form. This is similar to a restaurant; diners can tell the chef what they like or don't like, but most diners can't give the chef details about how to cook the meal.

How Should Researchers Work with Managers?

Researchers' ability to produce satisfactory research depends on more than just technical competence; it also depends on the manner in which they communicate with managers. Research can be brilliantly done yet not be satisfactory because it is not really what the managers wanted, because the managers expected even more, or because the managers don't know what to do with the results.

Some issues in researchers' interactions with managers are discussed in the next pages. First are problems that arise in defining managers' research needs; then how to manage managers' expectations about marketing research is discussed. Finally, the question of whether to include action recommendations with research reports is explored.

Defining Managers' Research Needs

Marketing researchers can encounter several problems in turning managers' information requests into research, projects; including:

- Managers may state research objectives that are not specific enough to guide the research design. In this situation, it is necessary to clarify the objectives.

- Managers may state a desire for broader objectives than they can financially afford. In this situation, the scope of the project must be narrowed.

- Managers may not initially express all their objectives for a project. This problem will surface at some point in the project approval process, but it is best to catch it early, because it is inefficient to have a series of meetings in which the researcher perceives the manager to be putting new issues onto the table and the manager perceives the researcher to be doing only part of the job.

- Managers may not realize all of their objectives in advance. It is frustrating to get halfway through the research and have someone say, "I wish we had also measured [some other issue]."

- Managers may misstate their objectives or have "hidden agendas" (unstated reasons why they want the work done), so that the research that responds to their expressed needs is not what they really want.

To illustrate some of these problems, assume a manager calls a researcher and says, as managers sometimes do, "We're thinking of introducing a new product, and we want to do some research to see whether it's a good idea."

This might strike you as a reasonable request. It certainly strikes managers that way. From the researcher's point of view, though, the request is not well enough defined. For example, does the manager want broad reactions to the product concept or specific reactions to product features and prices? Has the manager already identified target customers, or will this be part of the project? Does the manager want estimates of market size?

It is tempting to say, "yes" to all of the above, but this is usually not practical because these questions are best answered with different types of research, and the budget may not be large enough to do all of them. For example, to get responses to the product concept, the researcher might present the concept in a focus group discussion and just let people talk about it. To identify desirable market segments, the researcher might survey a broad cross section of potential buyers, with a few questions designed to measure response to the product and many questions designed to classify the respondents. To measure price sensitivity and feature preferences, the researcher might ask groups of customers to rank or score a series of product descriptions with varying features and/or prices. Most managers' budgets are not large enough to do all of these things.

Apart from the question of budget is the question of desire. The manager may already be committed to introducing the product and may not want research that questions the assumption that it will be introduced in some form. If so, the statement "We want to see whether the product is a good idea" has a limited meaning. At best, it means "Please compare alternate versions of the product to see which is best." At worst, it means "Please generate a sales forecast that shows that this product will be a success."

How can researchers solve these problems? How can they clarify research needs, narrow overly broad requests, identify unarticulated or unanticipated objectives, correct misstated objectives, and spot hidden agendas? The main answer is *"Ask questions."*

Researchers should begin every consultation by asking background questions about the business situation: who buys the product or service in question, how they buy it, where they buy it, who the competitors are, what the company's advantages and disadvantages are, and what the market trends are. The list of questions found in Marketing Research Tools 1.1 (in Chapter 1) can be used for this purpose. These background questions serve three purposes: (1) they provide a context that helps managers articulate their research needs, (2) they may reveal additional areas in which managers need research, and (3) they give the researcher a better understanding of the business, which always helps in designing research.

After acquiring background information, the researcher should ask questions that define the proposed research; that is, what the manager wants to learn, how the manager will use the information, who (or what) should be studied, what should be measured, how much the manager wants to spend, and when the manager wants to see results. If the available time, money, or manpower is not enough to satisfy all the manager's objectives, this should be noted as soon as possible so the manager can add resources or narrow the objectives.

It is also useful to ask whether the research is intended to resolve any problems or disputes within the organization and, more generally, whether the information will be used to influence anybody other than the manager. If so, the researcher should ask what is needed for the research to be credible to these other people.

These questions will help reveal hidden agendas, if any exist, and will give the researcher a broader understanding of what is desired.

Marketing Research Tools 3.1 summarizes the questions researchers can use, along with background questions about the market, to define specifications for a project. Follow-up questions may also be needed to clarify points of uncertainty. The goal should be to reach a point where what is needed is clear and it is not necessary to make assumptions. Every assumption a researcher makes about the business situation or about what the manager wants is a point where the project could go wrong.

More on Hidden Agendas

Throughout the process of specifying what is wanted in a research project, the researcher should be alert for resistance to certain possibilities. Such resistance may simply reflect managers' likes or dislikes for certain types of research but also may indicate hidden agendas.

For example, we were recently contacted by a consulting company that planned a series of educational programs for middle managers. The people who contacted us said they wanted to know whether potential customers would prefer the programs to be given on Fridays or Saturdays. When we asked about measuring other program preferences or the extent to which potential customers had *any* interest in the programs, the people from the company resisted.

Author Tips

If you do a research project for someone else, take notes and use "playback" to ensure that you have a proper understanding of the business situation and research parameters. During your information-gathering session, take notes. Then, at the end of the session, say to the person for whom you are doing the research, "Let me double check what you've told me." Read your notes back to him or her, and record any necessary changes.

MARKETING RESEARCH TOOLS

3.1

QUESTIONS USED TO SET PROJECT SPECIFICATIONS

If you find yourself in the position of doing a research project, start by asking background questions. Then, to set project specifications, ask the person who is commissioning the research:

- What information do you want?
- How will you use this information?
- Who (or what) should we study?
- What should we ask them (or what should we measure)?
- How much do you want to pay for the research?
- When do you need the results?
- Will the research be used to resolve any problems or disputes within your organization?
- Apart from problems, will the research be used to influence anyone other than yourself?
- (IF YES TO EITHER OF THE LAST TWO QUESTIONS) What is needed for the research to be credible to the people it is meant to influence?

This resistance didn't make sense to us, so we asked if there were a reason why. The people told us that their company's partners were split regarding the advisability of offering these educational programs. They said the original proposal had featured three all-day Friday sessions for each program and the partners who opposed the proposal had focused their arguments on this issue, claiming that managers would not want to lose three Fridays from work. They told us they did not want to open new areas for dispute with the partners who were against the proposal—they simply wanted to measure schedule preferences, choose the preferred schedule, and try to get the programs approved on this basis. Clearly, this "office politics" agenda was influencing their research preferences.

Revealing hidden agendas can raise ethical issues. In our situation, for example, should we simply do what we were asked, and test Fridays versus Saturdays, or should we insist on asking customers about their general interest in the programs? What if the results convinced us that the programs were a bad idea? Should we remain silent on this issue in our report, should we include a warning that our report did not address the viability of the programs, or should we openly criticize the programs' viability?

Some researchers prefer not to confront these issues. They would not have asked why the managers didn't want data other than schedule preferences; they would simply have done what the managers wanted. This ostrich approach has the merit of avoiding possible disputes with managers. On the other hand, it also makes it difficult for research to give maximum value.

We prefer to confront the issues. In the case of the educational programs, we said that it made no sense to measure schedule preferences among managers who weren't interested in the programs anyway. We suggested using an interest measure as a screen so that only people who indicated interest were asked for schedule preferences. We also said that we would report the percentage of people who expressed interest. The people who wanted the research agreed to this, which answered our concern that the research would be used to indicate schedule preferences without any context as to overall interest in the programs. This sort of happy ending is by no means guaranteed, but in our experience happy endings are common as long as researchers raise problems early in the process and in a tactful manner.

Managing Expectations About Research

Another concern in working with managers is managing their expectations about research. It is possible to do brilliant research that doesn't satisfy managers because they expected even more or expected something different.

The communication process we have described will help give managers realistic expectations about marketing research. It should ensure that managers know what questions the research will answer, how much the research will cost, and when it will be delivered. If the original information request was too broad, such as "I want to know whether this product is a good idea," this process should ensure that managers accept the need to narrow the scope of the project. If researchers feel ethically compelled to challenge managers' agendas, it should give fair warning.

It is also important to tell managers about the limitations of the research. For example, a manager who wants a sales forecast for a new product should be told that

CASE STUDY 3.2

Some years ago, downtown pedestrian malls were a hot concept in urban redevelopment. These malls were created by barring automobile traffic from certain downtown shopping streets. The goal was to create something like a shopping mall that would draw visitors downtown and revitalize retailing in the area.

In one midwestern city with a declining downtown area, members of the Downtown Merchants Association decided that a pedestrian mall would be a good idea for their city. To build support, they commissioned a survey in which downtown shoppers were asked to rate the area on various factors. Shoppers gave the downtown area good ratings for merchandise quality, selection, and prices; its worst ratings came in parking and getting around. These results were used to support the claim that a pedestrian mall would help revitalize downtown.

The mall was created, but it failed to stem the decline of the downtown area. This failure highlighted two limitations in the supporting research:

- First, asking customers what they like and don't like about your product will not necessarily tell you why noncustomers don't buy it. The two groups may have completely different perceptions. In this particular situation, a survey was done at a competing mall, and the mall shoppers did not mention parking and mobility as reasons for not going downtown. They said they didn't go downtown because it was old and dirty and did not have their favorite stores. The pedestrian mall did not address these problems and consequently did not attract new shoppers downtown.

- Second, the research was done to prove a point. The people who commissioned the research saw it as a way of supporting a decision that had already been made, not as a way to guide the decision, and the results were interpreted accordingly. In fact, the survey at the competing mall was done at the same time as the survey of downtown shoppers but was ignored because it didn't support the idea of a pedestrian mall.

This example is a reminder that the purpose of marketing research is to guide decisions. If a decision is already made and research is just window dressing, the research has no real value other than a political one.

marketing research can produce an excellent estimate of the number of potential customers who like the product and have the money to buy it but cannot produce an accurate sales forecast because sales also depend on factors such as marketing effectiveness and competitive response. Managers usually accept limitations if they are raised before the research, but they sometimes think researchers are making excuses for a bad job if limitations are mentioned only after the project is done.

Once managers have expectations regarding the research, it is important to deliver on those expectations. If any problems arise in delivering research as promised, managers should be told at the earliest possible date and given some revised basis for expectation. For example, a common "rookie" mistake by researchers is giving an optimistic date for project completion, then failing to deliver on time. It is far better to give a realistic date that can be met.

Should Research Reports Contain Recommendations?

Our final issue concerning researchers' interactions with managers is whether research reports should contain action recommendations. Research can be brilliant yet not satisfactory because managers don't know what to do with it. The purpose of action recommendations is to ensure that managers receive guidance for acting on the research.

Say, for example, that research shows that the percentage of patients who are "very satisfied" with the nursing care at a hospital has dropped from 86 percent to 78 percent during the past year. Is this a meaningful decline? What, if anything, should be done? Action recommendations will show managers whether the researcher considers the decline to be meaningful and how the researcher thinks the situation can be improved.

This example reveals some problems with the idea of action recommendations. Certainly, the researcher can tell managers that a decline in satisfaction rating is statistically significant (i.e., cannot be attributed to sampling fluctuations among the people interviewed). But is it really the researcher's job to tell managers what level of decline merits action? And what actions should the researcher recommend? The data don't provide a basis for saying anything other than "Do something about the nursing," which isn't a very helpful recommendation.

Some type of data interpretation is almost always desirable in reporting marketing research results. The specific form of interpretation, though, should depend on the nature of the research and on managers' preferences.

In *problem identification* research, such as the patient satisfaction example, interpretation should take the form of highlights such as a "Changes Worth Watching" report. This type of research usually does not provide a basis for specific recommendations. *Problem-solving* research, in contrast, does provide a basis for specific recommendations. For example, if Borden's does research to learn whether caramel pecan fudge ice cream should be added to its product line, this research should provide the basis for a "yes" or "no" recommendation.

Critical Thinking Skills

If patient satisfaction data at a hospital showed a drop in satisfaction with nursing care, what additional information, if any, would be needed to make specific action recommendations?

Even if research provides a basis for recommendations, managers may not want them. Some managers like to get recommendations to help them interpret research and give them someone to blame if decisions don't work out. Other managers, though, don't want recommendations because they feel that recommendations limit their freedom to interpret the research or that the researcher doesn't know all aspects of the decision environment (such as costs and internal politics). For these managers, it is best to summarize findings without explicitly recommending actions.

To avoid misunderstandings, managers should be asked during research planning whether they want recommendations and, if so, whether recommendations should be presented verbally, in writing, or both. Verbal presentation is a middle ground in which managers can hear the researcher's views without being committed to a written recommendation. Whether or not recommendations are given, reports should provide enough detail to allow managers to draw their own conclusions. Chapter 19 contains a more detailed discussion of how to present research results.

How Should the Research Function Be Organized and Staffed?

So far, we have dealt with the relationship between marketing researchers and line managers. We now turn to the internal management of marketing research activities. This involves questions such as:

- How should marketing research people fit into the organizational chart?
- Should marketing research be done inside the organization or by outside suppliers?
- How should marketing research activities be staffed?

The selection and management of outside suppliers will not be discussed at this time. Those topics are discussed in the final section of this chapter.

Marketing Research in the Organization Chart

The first question in placing marketing research within an organization is simple: Should the organization have at least one person devoted full-time to marketing research? This question is parallel to asking whether the organization should have a full-time accountant or a full-time lawyer. In all cases, the organization can save money by having a specialist on the payroll rather than buying from outside, but only if the organization has enough work to keep the specialist busy.

If an organization has enough work for several marketing research people, questions arise as to where to locate these people. Should they be grouped in a centralized marketing research department? Split across two or more research departments? Assigned, one or two at a time, to the staffs of operational marketing managers?

Arguments can be made for either centralized or decentralized marketing research. Spreading researchers around an organization has the benefit of keeping them close to the markets they study and the managers they serve. On the other hand, grouping researchers into a central department can bring cost benefits from economies of scale, improved capabilities as a result of specialization within the department, and less disruption when people leave the organization. Given these trade-offs, there is no perfect way of organizing

Critical Thinking Skills

As part of its marketing research program, a large hospital has made Jane Doe responsible for measuring patients' satisfaction with nursing services. In your opinion, should Jane Doe report to the director of nursing services or to someone else? Why?

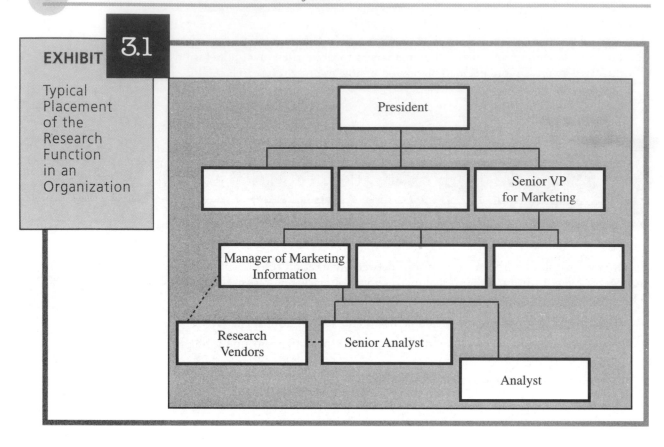

marketing research activities. Most large companies use a mixture of centralized and decentralized research. A recent trend in large consumer firms is to create a centralized "marketing information" group that handles MKIS activities and less centralized "marketing research" groups that handle special projects (Honomichl, 1994).

Once an organizational structure is chosen for research activities, reporting lines will follow this structure in a straightforward way. Exhibit 3.1 illustrates a typical example: a corporate marketing research department usually has a manager who reports to the company's vice president for marketing or chief executive officer. Divisional research units report to division heads or divisional marketing managers. Specialized research departments organized by technique rather than by product—such as a sensory testing department or an economic modeling department—usually report to the corporate research department. Researchers assigned to staff duty with line managers report to those managers.

 # The Make-or-Buy Decision

We have made several references to the possibility that companies buy marketing research from outside suppliers rather than "making" the research in house. The "make-or-buy" decision is present in all marketing research activities and obviously influences organizational and staffing decisions.

Make-or-buy decisions are not unique to marketing research. For example, should a firm prepare its own advertising or use an agency? Should a firm employ

CASE STUDY 3.3

Larry Moore is a Vice President of NPD Research, one of the nation's largest research companies. We asked Larry to comment on changes that he has seen in the research business in recent years. Here's what he said:

I work with NPD's services that track the markets for gasoline, motor oil, and car care products, so my principal clients are large oil companies. In dealing with these clients, one of the biggest changes that I have seen is corporate downsizing.

Ten years ago, most of these companies had ten to fifteen people in their market research departments. We provided these people with raw data from our tracking services and left it to them to interpret the data for managers in their companies.

Now most of our clients have only one or two people assigned to market research, and these people are completely occupied in managing research projects. They don't have time to interpret data, so the job has fallen to us. We have had to become much more active in interpreting our data in order to provide actionable results and good value to our clients.

janitors or use a cleaning service? Should a firm run its own manufacturing plants or contract for production? In all cases, the question is how to get the best job for the best price while protecting the organization's competitive position.

Doing research in house is cheaper than buying research if staff are fully utilized, but it is difficult to keep staff busy if all research is done in house. Research work, especially special projects, tends to come in spurts. Rather than building staff for peak situations and having them do make-work in off-peak periods, it is usually cheaper to have a small in-house staff and purchase services as needed. Outside research firms can make better use of people by flowing from one client's project to another's.

Another reason to use outside suppliers is that research suppliers often have special expertise (Bailey, 1990). An in-house researcher may keep busy by being a jack-of-all-trades—conducting a group discussion today, planning a survey tomorrow, analyzing data the day after—but, as the saying goes, a jack-of-all-trades is usually master of none. Using outside specialists can mean better-quality work.

Given the relative advantages of making and buying, here are some general rules regarding the "make-or-buy" decision in marketing research:

- Any project that requires special expertise or large-scale data gathering should be bought from outside suppliers.

- Smaller, simpler projects can be made or bought depending on the availability of company personnel.

- MKIS data that are available from syndicated services should be bought from those services if the quality is acceptable, because syndication splits the cost across a number of users.

- MKIS reports based on company accounting records, such as sales reports, should be made within the company.

■ Other MKIS data, such as customer satisfaction surveys, might be made internally if collected on a continuous basis, for example, if all patients leaving a hospital are asked how satisfied they were with various aspects of the service. If the data are not collected continuously—for example, if patient satisfaction is measured in annual surveys—they should be bought unless the organization has other activities that can be interscheduled with them.

Staffing Marketing Research Activities

The issues involved in whether to locate research within the organization and whether to make or buy research have implications for the people needed to staff the marketing research function.

Most small organizations don't do enough marketing research to keep a full-time person busy. They rely on ad agencies or outside suppliers, with operational managers purchasing research as needed. It is difficult for these companies to get full value for their research dollar, because there is no one inside the company who really understands research. In these companies, MKIS activities tend to be weak.

As organizations grow larger, they reach a point where they may have a full-time marketing research person. This initial person is usually titled "manager of marketing research" and reports to the vice president for marketing or the chief executive officer. The term "manager" reflects status rather than duties, because nobody other than a secretary actually reports to this person. In this situation, the research manager's success depends on his or her technical skills and ability to work well with operational managers.

As organizations continue to grow, they reach a point where they may have several marketing research people. Initially, these people are likely to be grouped together in a research department. The personnel in this department may include research technicians, research professionals, and intermediate managers, as well as an overall department manager. **Research technicians** are employees who perform structured, relatively noncreative tasks such as data collection and data analysis. They may report directly to the department manager if the department is small but are more likely to report to an intermediate manager with a title such as "programming supervisor." **Research professionals** are usually project managers who work with line managers in planning special projects. Research professionals may also include MIS specialists and, in larger departments, specialists such as experts in data analysis.

The manager of a multiperson research department is a manager in practice, not just in title. This manager may have experience as a staff researcher, but this person's technical skills are less important than his or her general management skills, skills in project scheduling, and ability to communicate with the operational managers who are served by the research department.

As companies become even larger, the research function is likely to split across a number of locations. However, unless the company is extremely large, the total number of marketing researchers employed by the company will be small. Because of this, opportunities within any given company are limited, and it is common for people to advance in marketing research by moving from one company to another.

How to Choose and Manage Research Suppliers

Much marketing research is bought from outside suppliers. This section discusses how to select and manage suppliers. There are four basic steps: (1) identifying potential suppliers for a research project, (2) communicating the project specifications, (3) evaluating suppliers' proposals and choosing a supplier, and (4) managing the supplier throughout the project (Stern and Dawson, 1989).

Identifying Potential Suppliers for a Research Project

The first thing to do when choosing a supplier for a marketing research project is identify potential suppliers. This can be done in various ways:

- Your company may keep a formal list of approved suppliers.
- You may know suppliers who have done good work in the past.
- You can call acquaintances for recommendations.
- You can call the marketing department at a nearby university and ask for recommendations.

Most companies do not keep lists of approved suppliers, but doing so has a couple of benefits. One is that the company is more open to consider new vendors and not get locked into working with old vendors that do mediocre work but are familiar quantities. Another is that incoming managers have some record of whom to call for research.

Communicating the Project Specifications

After identifying potential suppliers, it is essential to tell them what is wanted so they can present a proposal for the work. This can be done in various ways:

- Many firms issue a written request for proposal (RFP) that specifies (1) the topic to be studied, (2) the specific information needed, (3) the methods the firm considers appropriate for obtaining this information, (4) how the results are to be reported, (5) deadlines for the proposal and the final report, and (6) business matters such as payment terms, confidentiality, rights to the raw data, and rights to audit the supplier's records.
- Alternatively, a firm may issue an RFP that specifies a budget for the project rather than the preferred methods.
- A firm can verbally provide RFP-type information to potential suppliers.

Printed RFPs have an advantage over verbal communications because they provide all potential suppliers with uniform project specifications and make it easy to request proposals from any number of suppliers. Printed RFPs also help suppliers by forcing the client firm to answer many questions about the project. The disadvantage of RFPs is that they are time-consuming and require quite a bit of knowledge to prepare. Overall, RFPs make sense for big projects and big organizations, but usually not for small projects and small organizations.

Regardless of whether you use a printed RFP or verbal communications, you should solicit proposals only from suppliers who have some reasonable chance of getting the job. Don't waste the supplier's time or your own. Also, don't take a proposal from one potential supplier and ask another supplier to bid on doing the same thing. A reputable supplier will not bid under these circumstances, because passing one supplier's proposal to another for competitive bidding is considered unethical unless the first supplier was told this would happen and was paid for the time spent in developing the proposal. Research companies invest time and expertise in the proposals they give potential clients, and clients have an obligation to treat them fairly.

Evaluating Suppliers' Proposals and Choosing a Supplier

Once proposals are in, the next step is to evaluate the proposals and the companies that made them. This evaluation has three components:

- Evaluation of the research design
- Evaluation of the price
- Evaluation of the company that will do the work

In evaluating the research design, your concerns are (1) whether this research will answer all of the questions that were specified and (2) whether the design appears to be a valid, cost-effective way of answering those questions. If more than one supplier submits a proposal, the easiest way of evaluating research designs is by comparing proposals.

In evaluating the price, your concerns are (1) whether the price of the research fits your budget and (2) whether the price appears reasonable given the amount of work to be done. You are looking for a competitive price, but not necessarily the lowest one. An unusually low bid may be a sign that the supplier did not properly understand the job. It may also be a sign that the supplier is hungry for work, which is not a problem as long as the supplier can do the job properly.

Evaluating the company that will do the work is perhaps the most important part of the selection process. A record of good performance should weigh heavily in a supplier's favor. However, even if a supplier has done well in the past, a current evaluation is needed because the firm may have slipped. This is especially true for job shops, which are thinly financed and often have only two to three key people, who may leave the organization to join client companies or start their own businesses.

If you don't have past experience with a research supplier, Don Batson, the former director of marketing research for General Motors, suggests ten questions for evaluating potential suppliers. These questions are shown in Marketing Research Tools 3.2.

MARKETING RESEARCH TOOLS

3.2

TEN QUESTIONS FOR SCREENING A NEW SUPPLIER

1. Ask the supplier's recent clients: **Would you recommend this supplier?** The biggest mistake research buyers make is not checking references. Do not let the supplier give you just any three references; ask for references from the five most recent jobs, and check dates as well as evaluations.

2. Ask the supplier: **Do you have sufficient funds for this job?** Get a bank reference, and check it. Underfinanced suppliers are tempted to cut corners. If the supplier is well qualified but not well financed, make arrangements such as a fieldwork drawing fund to ensure that the supplier has enough cash to do all work properly.

3. Ask the supplier: **What parts of the project will be subcontracted, and how do you control subcontractors?** Many suppliers subcontract parts of the research, and you should know how they manage their subcontractors. A ready answer indicates that the supplier understands the issue and has procedures in place.

4. If the research involves survey interviews, ask the supplier: **May I see your interviewer's manual and data entry manual?** You don't have to read these manuals, but they should be readily available and should appear well used. The use of manuals suggests that formal management procedures are in place.

5. Also ask: **How do you train and supervise interviewers?** Supervision and training cost money and are not visible to clients, so some suppliers cut corners in these areas. The best suppliers do a good job of supervision and training as a matter of professional standards and welcome the chance to show off these standards.

6. Also ask: **What percentage of interviews are validated? How many invalid questionnaires are needed for you to do a 100 percent check on an interviewer's work?** If the answer is "What numbers do you want?," ask "What are your usual standards?" Interviewer cheating is most likely to occur in operations that do not have standards for finding and correcting it. You are looking for those standards, and you want them to be as high or higher than your own.

7. If the research involves survey interviews, ask the supplier: **May I see a typical questionnaire?** If the supplier shows you a questionnaire written for one of your competitors, leave immediately, because this is a violation of confidentiality and is unacceptable. Check to see whether the questionnaire will be easy for the respondent, the interviewer, and data entry people to use.

8. If the research involves any type of sampling, ask the supplier: **Who draws your samples?** Sampling is a technical aspect of research in which novices can easily make mistakes.

9. If the research involves any data being entered into the computer, ask the supplier: **What percentage of your data entry is verified?** Again, you are looking for standards, and the standard for data entry is 100 percent verification.

10. Ask your managers: **What do you think about this supplier?** Don't limit the value of research by using a supplier that your managers have doubts about. Also, the most useful research is research that produces new, even counterintuitive information, and managers often resist new information by raising the possibility that the supplier "did it wrong" or "didn't understand the issues." Make them raise any doubts at the start of the project, and save credibility questions for other problems.

Author Tips

Don't do business with suppliers that are willing to act unethically. If they act unethically toward others, they will act unethically toward you.

In addition to asking these questions, be alert for warning signs that indicate a lack of professionalism. These include:

- Disparaging competing researchers
- Offering to execute another researcher's proposal at a lower price
- Any other indications of willingness to violate professional ethics
- Extravagant promises about what the research will do
- Vague descriptions of research procedures
- Not listening

Managing the Supplier Throughout the Project

Once a supplier is chosen for a marketing research project, that supplier's performance must be managed throughout the project. This process actually starts before the project is awarded. The research client must establish, either verbally or in writing, the ground rules under which the research will be conducted, as well as the client's legal rights and obligations regarding the research.

Key ground rules include the following:

- The relationship between the client and the research supplier's project manager will be a professional relationship, with each respecting the other's position and responsibilities.
- The client will bypass the supplier's project manager and directly communicate with other people in the supplier's company *only* if there is a major problem with the project.
- The supplier's project manager will not bypass the client's project manager at all.
- The supplier will follow a "no-surprises" policy.

Several legal points must also be established:

- The supplier is an independent contractor, not an employee or agent of the client. As far as outsiders are concerned, it must be made clear that the supplier is a separate organization acting under contract.
- The client should have the right to audit all records related to the project, whether those records belong to the supplier or to a subcontractor the supplier uses (this means that the supplier must arrange subcontracts with "pass-through" audit rights).
- The research contract should specify the procedures to be used. If procedures are not specified, the contract should give the client approval rights over the procedures.
- The research supplier must guarantee the confidentiality of the research results and any materials used in the research. Information should not be disclosed to anyone unless the client gives express permission.
- The supplier should provide any raw data gathered in the study if you request them. In turn, the client should agree to respect the confidentiality of these data as indicated by a professional code of ethics (see Chapter 21).
- The supplier should agree to provide progress reports as the client requires.

- The client must agree to the payment schedule, and there should be some provision in the contract regarding who will pay for possible cost overruns.

Establishing all these points at the start of a research project greatly reduces the opportunities for misunderstandings and disputes and thus makes it easier to manage the project.

After the project begins, the client's project manager should remain involved with the project until completion. This involvement may take several forms, including review of questionnaires, sampling plans, and plans for data analysis. Some effort should be made to evaluate the quality of the data being gathered; for example, if the project involves interviewing people by telephone, the client's project manager should "listen in" on some interviews. Once the data are in, the client's project manager should check any data analyses to verify that they seem to be correct and that correct conclusions are being drawn.

At the end of the project, the last thing to be done is evaluation of the supplier for future reference. The client's project manager should make a written note of whether or not to hire this supplier for future use and post that note to an appropriate file. It is also helpful to make notes regarding the supplier's strengths and weaknesses and of any problems that may have arisen during the project (Moorman, Zaltman, and Deshpande, 1992).

One final point is important in project management: the research supplier should deliver results early enough so that the client has time to evaluate the data and ask for revisions if necessary. This ensures that managers within the client orga-

CASE STUDY 3.4

The marketing research business tends to be divided between suppliers that provide information and those that provide recommendations. Most syndicators fall into the first group, serving as neutral information providers to an entire industry. If they start to provide advice, their neutrality is brought into question, and clients may feel uncomfortable.

Nielsen Marketing Research recently entered an exclusive agreement to supply marketing research information to all of Kraft–General Foods (KGF) North American operations. "The partnership will produce new and unique ways to analyze sales data that give us a competitive advantage," said KGF spokesperson Michael Mudd.

Mudd's statement is controversial. "I can't see how you can agree to do that in the syndicated business," said Gian Fulgoni of IRI, Nielsen's leading competitor. He and his colleagues see the possibility of a conflict of interest if Nielsen truly develops services for KGF that are not provided to clients that are competitors of KGF.

Nielsen's John Costello does not view it that way. "We have been operating in a partnership direction for years," he said of the nature of client relationships. "Better relationships in a most challenging market for packaged-goods marketers are the best service we can provide."

Source: Reprinted with permission from *Marketing News,* published by the American Marketing Association, Howard Schlossberg, April 27, 1992, p. 13.

nization get a good impression of the research. First-draft results should not be shown to managers, even if they are anxious to receive them, because showing a first draft will rob the final report of its impact and leave the project manager vulnerable to being judged based on preliminary results and "top-of-mind" conclusions.

Summary

This chapter discussed the issues involved in managing the marketing research process. The following points were covered:

1. Who should be responsible for making decisions about marketing research?

Decisions about the contents of a marketing information system should be made by a research manager who has a dedicated budget for this purpose. Placing the MKIS under the direction of a research manager facilitates the continuity and coherence that are needed for it to be effective.

Decisions on whether to do special projects should be made by operational managers, who should pay for these projects out of their own budgets. Continuity is not so important in special projects, and giving authority to managers ensures that projects will be focused on their decision needs.

Regardless of who makes the decision of *whether* to do research on a particular topic, the responsibility for *how* to collect it should rest with researchers, who have better knowledge about research sources and techniques. In exercising this responsibility, researchers should work with operational managers to ensure that they can use the results.

2. How should marketing researchers work with marketing managers?

When planning a project, a researcher should ask lots of questions and make as few assumptions as possible. The researcher should begin by posing background questions about the business situation. After gathering background information, the researcher should ask what the manager wants to learn, how the information will be used, who (or what) should be studied, what should be measured, how much the manager wants to spend, and when the results are needed. The researcher should also ask whether the research will be used to influence people other than the person who is requesting the research. Then, before doing the research, the researcher should ensure that the manager understands what questions will actually be answered, how much the research will cost, when the research will be delivered, and any expected limitations of the research.

3. How should the marketing research function be organized and staffed?

Small companies usually start with a single researcher, who reports to a marketing manager or the president of the company. As the research function grows, it tends to be centralized in a research department. As companies become larger, the research function may split across several locations, with specialized functions such as economic modeling performed in a central location. Those who staff the research function may include managers, technicians, analytic specialists, and clerical staff.

One of the issues that influences staffing decisions is the decision of whether the organization should make or buy its marketing research. In general, any project that requires special expertise or large-scale data gathering should be bought from outside suppliers. Smaller projects can be made or bought depending on the availability of company personnel. MKIS data that are available from syndicated services should be bought, provided the quality is acceptable. MKIS data that are based on company records should be produced in house.

4. How should research suppliers be chosen and managed?

Potential research suppliers can be identified by: keeping a formal list of approved suppliers, using suppliers that have done good work before, calling acquaintances for recommendations, or calling the marketing department of a nearby university for recommendations.

When dealing with an outside supplier, it is important to establish ground rules for communication, clarify legal issues, remain involved with the project until it is completed, evaluate the supplier after the project is finished, and make sure the research supplier delivers the results early enough that they can be evaluated and any necessary revisions can be requested.

Suggested Additional Readings

Examples of the issues raised in this chapter are sometimes found in *Advertising Age*, *Marketing News*, the business press, and company annual reports.

Discussion Questions

1. What are the ethical implications of issuing a request for proposal (RFP) when you have already decided on a market research supplier?

2. Discuss the advantages and disadvantages of giving line managers full budgetary authority for marketing research.

3. Discuss when a firm should make rather than buy its marketing research.

4. As the marketing research buyer, how can you help the supplier maintain a "no-surprises" policy?

Marketing Research Challenge

Assume you are the market research manager in a medium-sized consumer goods company. The workload in your department has increased sharply in the past year. Discuss the pros and cons of hiring additional staff versus increasing your use of research suppliers. What recommendation would you make to the director of marketing?

Internet Exercise

Find homepages for various marketing research companies. Check out A. C. Nielsen (http://acnielsen.com), The Gallup Organization (http://www.gallup.com), NPD Group (http://www.npd.com) and J. D. Power and Associates (http://www.jdpower.com). Also, use a search engine to look for smaller research companies. Do these websites show what services the companies offer? Do they give you some impression about whether each company would be a good research provider? Based on these websites, how would you design a website to attract customers for a marketing research company?

References

Bailey, Robert (1990). "Key Trends in Package Goods Marketing Research That Are Reshaping the Research Industry." *Journal of Advertising Research* 30 (October–November), pp. RC3–RC6.

Honomichl, Jack J. (1994). "Point of View: Why Marketing Information Should Have Top Executive Status." *Journal of Advertising Research* 34 (November–December), pp. 61–66.

Moorman, Christine, Gerald Zaltman, and Rohit Deshpande (1992). "Relationships Between Providers and Users of Market Research: The Dynamics of Trust Within and Between Organizations." *Journal of Marketing Research* 29 (August), pp. 314–328.

Stern, Bruce, and Scott Dawson (1989). "How to Select a Market Research Firm." *American Demographics* 11 (March), p. 44.

4 An Overview of Data Sources

 OBJECTIVES

After reading this chapter, you should be able to answer the following questions:

❶ What are the different types of marketing research information?

❷ How can internal data sources be used to obtain marketing research information?

❸ How can secondary data sources be used to obtain marketing research information?

❹ How can primary data sources be used to obtain marketing research information?

Author Tips

Subsequent chapters in this book provide "how-to" detail about various external information sources. There are many chapters about how to gather primary data but only one chapter about secondary sources. This doesn't mean that secondary information is less important than primary information; there are simply more ways of creating new information than finding old information. A good researcher always checks what old information is available before gathering new information. After all, why reinvent the wheel?

In this chapter, we describe various sources of marketing research information and their strengths and weaknesses. In Chapter 5, these information sources are matched with common marketing research questions. Together, Chapters 4 and 5 are meant to show the range of information sources available and to help you make decisions about how to choose the best source of information for a particular need.

We begin by discussing internal information. Internal information comes from sources inside the organization, such as accounting records and salespeople's reports. Internal information is usually quick and inexpensive to get and should be used wherever it is useful. Its drawback is its narrow range of application; for example, to learn what buyers think about a product, it is necessary to go outside the manufacturer's organization and talk with them.

Next comes external sources of information. These are grouped into secondary and primary information sources. **Secondary information** is information that has already been collected for some other purpose; it comes from sources such as libraries, online services, or trade associations. **Primary information** is gathered fresh; it comes from sources such as survey interviews, group discussions, or market experiments. Like internal information, secondary information is relatively inexpensive and quick to obtain, but it may not be available or may not fit a particular situation. In contrast, primary information can be fit to almost any situation but may be expensive and time-consuming to get.

Sources of Internal Information

As already noted, internal information comes from sources inside the organization. Five types of internally available information are useful in marketing research: (1) sales and expense records, (2) salespeople's reports, (3) "street news," (4) executive judgments, and (5) extended internal information.

Sales and Expense Records

Every company has both sales and expense records. This information takes two forms, both of which are useful in marketing research. The first form is traditional accounting compilations, which are used to prepare income statements for an organization's operating units (i.e., sales and expenses for a product, a geographic division, or the entire company). The second is sales and expense information organized by customer or customer group, not by operating unit.

Traditional sales and expense data for operating units have several uses in marketing research. These include:

- Sales data for a product or a business unit can be analyzed to measure seasonal fluctuations and make short-term sales forecasts.
- Sales for a product can be correlated with prices to estimate the price elasticity of demand (i.e., the extent to which sales volume responds to price changes).
- Sales for a product can be correlated with advertising expenditures to estimate the advertising response function.
- Sales can be compared before, during, and after a promotion to measure the effects of the promotion.

Sales and expense data based on customers rather than operating units are less traditional but lie at the heart of database marketing, which is increasingly popular in marketing. **Database marketing** involves using purchase records and background data on individual customers to tailor what is offered to them or to develop target profiles for potential new customers. Examples of using internal information in this way include:

- A customer's purchase records can be analyzed to estimate that customer's buying cycle; then purchase reminders can be sent when the customer is "due" for a purchase (a dentist or doctor may do this), and promotional incentives can be sent to customers who seem overdue (catalog merchandising firms do this).
- The profitability of an individual customer or a group of customers can be calculated to determine whether price concessions or marketing expenditures are justified.
- Heavy purchasers can be compared with light purchasers to develop a profile of key target customers (Fletcher, Wheeler, and Wright, 1994; Johnson, 1995; Nowak and Phelps, 1995; Roman, 1993; Steinborn, 1994; Stevenson, 1989; Swigor, 1995).

Case Study 4.1 (see page 76) gives another example of database marketing: a situation in which purchase records were used to optimize the length of leases for Infiniti automobiles.

The likelihood of having good internal records on individual customers varies across companies. Companies that sell directly to end users, such as many service providers and makers of heavy equipment, usually have good records. Companies that sell through intermediate distributors, such as most consumer goods companies, generally do not. In these companies, internal records show only sales for the first step in the distribution channel and do not go as far as the end user.

Selling through distributors not only limits the availability of information about end users but also creates problems in matching sales and expense data at an aggregate level. For example, manufacturers of grocery products face the problem that retailers stock up *before* major promotions and it may be months before reorder volume shows whether a promotion was effective. This timing problem is a major reason why manufacturers supplement sales and cost records with the types of outside syndicated data discussed later in this chapter.

Perhaps the major problem with using sales and expense records is the difference between what has happened and what is yet to come. Sales and expense records provide information on what has happened in the past, but future conditions may be different. The past is usually our best predictor of the future—but not always.

Database marketers identify potential customers from their prior purchasing behavior.

Source: Guess Who Didn't Take a Nap? 1993. Rick Kirkman and Jerry Scott. Reprinted with special permission of King Feature Syndicate.

CASE STUDY 4.1

What is the optimal length of an automobile lease? Infiniti and other automakers have found that the answer lies in an analysis of internal records.

The length of a lease period requires a balancing act for an automaker. Shorter leases enhance brand loyalty and repurchase rates because they bring customers back to the showroom sooner. However, shorter leases also require higher monthly payments because they are concentrated in the time period when a car depreciates fastest. Longer leases allow lower payments, which can attract more buyers.

By analyzing internal records concerning sales levels and repurchase rates under different lease conditions, Infiniti has decided that thirty-six months achieves an optimal balance for its cars. Meanwhile, Ford and General Motors have chosen twenty-four months for their less expensive cars, and some European luxury cars have chosen forty-eight months to make payments affordable.

Source: Arlena Sawyers, "Short Leases: They'll Be Back," Reprinted with permission from the June 13, 1998 Issue of *Advertising Age.* Copyright Crain Communications, Inc. 1994.

Salespeople's Reports

A second type of internal information is salespeople's reports. Four types of reports can be useful: (1) request and complaint reports, (2) lost sales reports, (3) call reports, and (4) activity reports.

Request and complaint reports show customer requests that cannot be fulfilled and customer complaints. For example, a customer might request a product the company doesn't make, an option that is not available, or purchase terms that are not offered. A customer might complain about slow delivery, poor product performance, and so on. Documenting these occurrences helps the company recognize problems and opportunities.

Lost sales reports provide information on lost sales opportunities. Salespeople often know why business has been lost and to which competitor. Reports that provide this information can alert management to trends and patterns. Of course, the validity of these reports depends on customers being honest with salespeople and salespeople being honest with the company, so the reports must be treated cautiously.

Call reports show the time and dates of sales call, the company and person visited, the issues discussed, and the outcome of the visit. These reports are oriented toward managerial control of selling activities. They also help salespeople keep track of their accounts and help managers determine whether a salesperson is seeing the right people at the right times and doing the right things.

Activity reports summarize a salesperson's activities over some time period: how many calls were made, to whom, on what dates. These are also oriented toward managerial control of selling activities. They allow managers to spot problems, such as steady customers who are not being visited enough, and to compare the activities of successful and less successful salespeople, which can be useful for training purposes.

The biggest limitation on using salespeople's reports is the workload they put on the sales force. Salespeople are hired to sell, not to complete reports. Also, imposing reports on salespeople can cause resentment if they see the reports as nonproductive paperwork. Often, it is necessary to "sell" reports to the sales force, so that both salespeople and their managers see the reports as worthwhile.

Critical Thinking Skills

Among the four types of sales force reports discussed here—request and complaint reports, lost sales reports, call reports, and activity reports—which would you give highest priority if your company sold multimillion-dollar construction projects? How about if your company were a shoe retailer? Why?

"Street News"

Another type of internal information is **"street news"** about customers' or competitors' activities. For example, one of your salespersons might visit a customer who asks, "Are you planning to introduce an updated version of your production-scheduling software? Someone from Exotek was here last week, and he said they're going to release an update in April." One of your software designers might hear this news at a technical conference. Or your advertising agency might hear that Exotek is working on an ad campaign for a new release. Any of these chance conversations might give you valuable information that a competitor plans to introduce a new product.

In most companies, "street news" ends where it begins. The salesperson doesn't mention the conversation with the customer: then, when the sales manager tells the sales force that Exotek has a new release, the salesperson says "Oh, yeah; someone at Monarch Chemical told me about that." The software designer tells another designer about his conversation, but nobody tells the marketing department. As a result, most companies don't get maximum value from this information.

"Street news" should be made a regular part of the company's marketing information system. This can be accomplished by:

- Establishing guidelines regarding the types of information desired (such as any information regarding competitors' plans for new products or new facilities).

- Communicating these guidelines to people in your organization and establishing a reporting system; the reporting system can be "Heard on the Street" forms for people to fill out, a "Market Hotline" for people to call, or occasional group meetings to ask what people have heard.

- Regularly analyzing and reporting this information.

Formal systems for handling "street news" are particularly important in situations in which people who hear this information don't have much contact with the people who must act on it. This tends to occur in large companies and in situations in which the information needs to cross organizational units, such as from engineering to marketing.

Critical Thinking Skills

Return to Chapter 2 and look at the discussion of The Methodist Hospital's marketing information system. Does this system capture "street news"? If so, how?

Executive Judgments

A fourth source of information from inside the company is **executive judgments,** or key executives' opinions and insights. Marketing research uses for executive judgments include the following:

- Panels of executives can screen new product ideas to decide which ideas should be introduced without research, which ideas should be studied, and which ideas should be killed.

- Panels of executives can be asked to make judgment-based sales forecasts.

- In developing mathematical models of relationships between marketing inputs and sales, executives can give opinions about which variables to include and how their relationships might look.

Data for executive judgment exercises can be gathered in various ways. One approach is to gather individual judgments and aggregate these results without giving the judges a chance to consult one another. Another approach is to have the executives meet as a group and develop a consensus opinion. In a third approach called the **Delphi method,** each executive makes an independent judgment; then he or she is given information about other people's judgments and is allowed to change his or her mind. A variation on the Delphi method is to gather individual judgments, then have a group meeting at which these judgments are discussed and consensus is reached.

This latter approach has the advantages of both individual and group judgments. Individual judgments ensure that everyone expresses an independent opinion and everyone is heard. Group judgments allow the group to converge on the best judgment, which is not necessarily the average of the individual judgments.

Extended Internal Information

The fifth type of internal information is **extended internal information.** This is information that comes from companies that supply goods or services to a company. This information can be thought of as internal information because it is not available *except* to important clients.

Extended internal information most often comes from advertising agencies or media. These businesses often maintain data files that show area populations, social and economic profiles, media habits, and so on. Such data are useful to any business in planning advertising campaigns and may be useful for other purposes as well.

Caution is needed when using extended internal information. The supplier of this information may have a vested interest in your decision and may slant the information that is released. Also, the quality of the information may be suspect.

Author Tips

Historical sales data and executive judgments can both be used for sales-forecasting purposes. Projections based on historical data give good results when forecasts are done for relatively short periods (such as a year) and conditions are stable. Executive judgments are good for long-range forecasts and for situations in which the company or its environment is changing.

General Comments

Marketing Research Tools 4.1 summarizes the various sources of internal information. Internal data sources tend to have specific applications and will not apply to all research projects. However, if internal data do apply to the problem at hand, their low cost and ready availability make them a good source of information.

MARKETING RESEARCH TOOLS

4.1

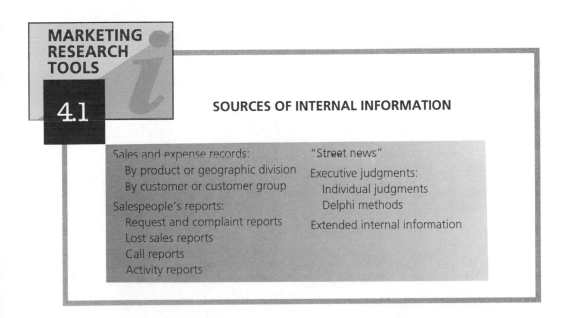

SOURCES OF INTERNAL INFORMATION

Sales and expense records:
   By product or geographic division
   By customer or customer group
Salespeople's reports:
   Request and complaint reports
   Lost sales reports
   Call reports
   Activity reports

"Street news"
Executive judgments:
   Individual judgments
   Delphi methods
Extended internal information

CASE STUDY 4.2

Internal or syndicated data can be used to track a company's market performance, and special projects using surveys or other techniques can be used to determine the reasons for changes in that performance.

For example, internal sales records at Kentucky Fried Chicken–Japan showed a 10 percent drop in customers during 1993. The company served chicken to 120 million Japanese customers in 1993, down from 135 million in 1992 despite having the same number of restaurants.

To learn *why* this decrease occurred, the company turned to a survey. Toshiki Nakata, deputy general manager in the planning and administration department of KFC-Japan, says that the results were clear: recession-plagued Japanese customers said, "Your food is very good, but you're a bit expensive."

KFC-Japan responded with a value strategy aimed at its biggest customer group, eighteen-to-twenty-six-year-olds who eat at KFC restaurants located in or near train stations (these restaurants produce more than half of KFC's Japanese sales, with the remainder coming from suburban locations where women buy dinner for their families). KFC cut the price on its biggest-selling meal, two pieces of chicken with a side dish, to 500 yen, the denomination of one Japanese coin. "We call it our 'one-coin price,' " says Mr. Nakata.

The price cut produced an immediate increase in customer counts. However, the ultimate wisdom of KFC's strategy will not be known for some time, because it triggered a price war in the Japanese fast-food market. In the end, the company might be worse off.

In addition to illustrating the combined use of tracking data and special projects, this example shows that market research findings should not be considered by themselves in determining management action; other business factors and competitors' likely reactions should also be taken into account.

Source: Based on Jack Russell, "U.S. Fast Food Giants in Japan Slice Prices," *Advertising Age,* June 13, 1994, p. 64.

Sources of Secondary Information

If information needs can't be satisfied by internal sources, the next place to turn is external sources of secondary information. The reason for turning to secondary information before primary information is that secondary information costs less to acquire. However, as with other used things, secondary information must be carefully evaluated before it is used.

This section briefly discusses library and nonlibrary sources of secondary information. Secondary sources are discussed in more detail in Chapter 6.

Library Sources

Libraries contain four types of material that might be used in marketing research projects: (1) books, (2) government documents, (3) periodicals, and (4) computerized databases.

Books are useful for "how-to" information about marketing and marketing research. For example, the book you are now reading describes how to do marketing research; books that tell you how to do database marketing, how to select ad media, and so on are also available. However, books are usually *not* useful as sources of statistical information and market forecasts. The problem is timeliness: if an important event happens today, it will be in the newspaper tomorrow, a magazine next week, and a book in nine months' time or longer. The length of time needed to print books makes it impossible to get timely statistics from them.

Government documents are useful for general statistics such as population data and market size estimates. For example, if you plan to open a jewelry store and want to know population and jewelry expenditures for an area, you will find government documents useful. However, if you want to know information such as market shares for different jewelry stores or specific jewelry preferences among the area population, you won't have much luck with government documents. The government doesn't collect this type of information.

Periodicals, which are also called serials, are magazines, newspapers, academic journals, and other publications issued periodically. They contain a wide variety of information that is useful in marketing research. Trade journals are particularly useful; these magazines cover specific industries and are the best source for market share estimates as well as general news about an industry. Other useful magazines include general marketing publications such as *Advertising Age* and *Sales and Marketing Management*, which provide information on current marketing trends, and academic journals such as *Journal of Marketing* and *Journal of Marketing Research*, which describe the latest research methods.

Computerized databases also contain a wide variety of useful information. Much of the information available from government documents and periodicals is also available on computerized databases that can be found in research libraries. Also, there is explosive growth in the databases available on the Internet, use of which doesn't require a visit to the library.

Nonlibrary Sources

Secondary information can also come from places other than a library. This includes information from (1) trade associations, (2) government agencies, (3) media companies, (4) local private sources, (5) syndicated data services, (6) personal networking, and (7) the Internet.

Most industries have *trade associations* to which companies in the industry belong. These associations are good sources of informal information about industry trends. Also, many associations publish key operating ratios for their industry, such as expense rates and profit rates. The primary limitation on this information is its availability; some trade associations have it, some don't.

Author Tips

Local information should be carefully evaluated before it is used. This information varies widely in quality. Also, chambers of commerce, power companies, and media companies maintain information with a goal of encouraging business development, so the information they provide may be biased on the optimistic side.

Other kinds of information may be available from *government agencies*, *media companies*, and *local private sources* such as *chambers of commerce* and *power companies*. For example, a retailer who wants information on a potential store site might be able to get local business activity and population data from the local chamber of commerce. Population data might also be available from local utilities, based on electrical, gas, or water connections. Short-term population growth can be estimated by examining construction permits at the city planning office. Vehicular traffic data for nearby streets will be available through the city, county, or state traffic department. Data on people's shopping patterns may be available from local media based on surveys they have done.

Syndicated data services can be viewed as another nonlibrary source of secondary information. As discussed in previous chapters, syndicated data services gather data for sale to many clients. They specialize in information such as sales volume and market shares for all of the companies in an industry. Some companies, such as J. D. Power and Associates, also syndicate customer satisfaction data.

Another source of secondary information is *personal networking*. Neighbors, friends, and past work acquaintances may sometimes provide useful information. Keeping a file of business cards from these sources and from people met at trade shows and association meetings is a good way to get started in the search for information. The first network contact may not yield results, but using referrals from the people contacted often does.

Finally, the *Internet* is growing by leaps and bounds as a source of information. In the near future, many traditional library sources of information, as well as much trade association data, will be available on the Internet.

Marketing Research Tools 4.2 summarizes potential secondary data sources.

MARKETING RESEARCH TOOLS

4.2

SOURCES OF EXTERNAL SECONDARY INFORMATION

Library sources:
- Books
- Government documents
- Periodicals
- Computerized databases

Nonlibrary sources:
- Trade associations
- Government agencies
- Media
- Local sources such as chambers of commerce and utilities
- Syndicated data services
- Personal networking
- Internet

Sources of Primary Information

If internal and secondary information sources can't provide the information needed, it's time to turn to primary data. Almost any type of information can be obtained through a custom-designed research project. However, primary data are used as a last resort because they tend to be much more expensive than internal or secondary data.

Most of the primary information collected in marketing research is gathered through two basic methods. The first is observation of events or occurrences; information gathered through this method is called **observational data.** The second is asking people questions; information gathered through this method is called **self-report data** (though our discussion includes examples in which respondents report about someone or something other than themselves).

This section discusses six methods of gathering primary information. First is observation. Then surveys and depth interviews, which use self-report data, are discussed. Focus groups are included in the discussion of depth interviews. Next are discussed panels and experiments, which can use either observational or self-report measures. Finally, test markets are discussed.

Observation

Observation is just what the name implies: observing people, objects, or events. Observations can be made by human observers or mechanical devices. Examples include the following:

- The A. C. Nielsen Company connects "audimeters" to the televisions in participating households to measure TV show ratings.

- Participants in "scanner tracking" panels use something like a credit card when they buy groceries, and the purchases are automatically entered into their households' data files.

- Toy manufacturers invite children to play in a room containing various toys, and observers record which toys are used.

- Advertising researchers show ads to people and mechanically record physiological responses such as eye pupil dilation or galvanic skin response, which supposedly indicate interest.

- Interviewers sometimes do "pantry audits" to observe what products people have in their pantries.

- Service shoppers visit stores or restaurants and record information about the service they receive.

- Advertisers often count coupon redemptions as a measure of the effectiveness of alternative promotions.
- Retailers watch security videotapes or draw "traffic flowcharts" to learn how shoppers move through stores.

In some of these situations, similar information could be gathered by self-report methods, but observation has certain advantages. Observation doesn't suffer from respondents forgetting what happened or distorting their answers to make a good impression.

Two terms that are relevant to the idea of distortion are obtrusive (versus unobtrusive) and reactive (versus nonreactive) measurement. **Obtrusive** means that the object being measured is aware of the measurement; **reactive** means that the object reacts by changing in some way. Research participants are aware of self-report measures, and they may react by changing their answers to make a good impression. For example, people who self-report television viewing might overreport *Masterpiece Theater* viewing and underreport *Gilligan's Island* viewing because they want to seem more cultured. Observational data may be less obtrusive, less reactive, and therefore more accurate.

Of course, observational measures can be reactive if people know they are being observed. For example, people who know that their TV viewing is being monitored may watch different shows than usual, at least until they get used to being monitored. This raises the issue of whether it is ethical to observe people without telling them. In general, it is ethically appropriate to observe public behaviors such as movement through a store without telling people, but for nonpublic behaviors, such as TV viewing, participants have a right to give their informed consent before being observed.

The major problem with observation relative to self-report measures is limited applicability. For observational data to be feasible, the phenomenon of interest must be observable; mental states such as attitudes are thus ruled out. Also, it must occur often enough or predictably enough so that you don't spend all your time waiting for it to occur. Not too many phenomena satisfy these criteria.

Surveys

Surveys are used widely in marketing research, especially consumer research. They gather self-report data by means of structured interviews. The identifying characteristic of surveys is the use of a standardized questionnaire, which gives surveys certain advantages and disadvantages compared with less structured interviewing methods.

The advantages of surveys are as follows: (1) the use of a structured questionnaire means that all respondents are asked the same questions in the same order, which facilitates data analysis; (2) the use of a structured questionnaire allows the researcher to control the interview without being present; (3) the use of a structured questionnaire allows survey interviews to be done by mail or telephone, which means they can be done more cheaply than interviews that require personal interaction; and (4) the use of mail or telephone, plus the lower cost per interview, makes it possible to do a large number of interviews with a broader cross section of the market.

The disadvantages of surveys, compared with less structured interviewing, are (1) the structured interview reduces flexibility; (2) deep feelings and hidden motivations cannot be probed very well; and (3) questions are best limited to items that have short, direct answers.

Given these strengths and weaknesses, surveys are good for measuring "facts" such as how many people are aware of a brand, how many people have bought an item, how many people were satisfied with a purchase, and so on. Surveys are not as good for in-depth profiles of individual respondents or for measuring "stream-of-consciousness" thinking.

How to do surveys is discussed in Chapter 7, how to write questionnaires in Chapters 10 to 12, and how to select a sample of respondents in Chapters 13 to 14.

CASE STUDY 4.3

The president of a marketing research and consulting company says:

We do a lot of customer satisfaction research for clients. A few years ago, we did this research as follows. First, we would identify the important dimensions of product or service quality by talking with managers from a client company and conducting focus groups with their customers. Then, after we knew the dimensions, we would conduct a customer survey. We would ask customers to rate the client's performance on each important dimension. We also would ask customers to tell us how an "excellent" company would rate on that dimension, and we would use those ratings as a benchmark to identify dimensions on which the client needed to improve.

We found that this research was limited because it identified problem areas but didn't tell our clients how to fix them. We tried asking customers to suggest ways in which performance could be improved, but this usually was not successful.

These days, we do the same general type of research, but instead of asking customers to rate a generic "excellent" company on each dimension, we ask them to tell us the name of a specific company with excellent performance and to rate that company's performance on the dimension. Now, we can tell our client not only the areas in which improvement is needed but also the names of "benchmark" companies to emulate. Our client then studies the products or services of those companies to learn how they achieve excellent performance and reengineers its operations as necessary to match that excellence.

This example shows some of the variety possible in market research. Within a single project, this company might use executive interviews, focus groups, customer surveys, and competitor analysis.

Depth Interviews and Focus Groups

Like surveys, **depth interviews** rely on self-reports to obtain information. However, depth interviews are less structured than surveys. The interviewer usually has a list of topics to be covered and may use fixed questions to get respondents started on these topics, but the overall goal is to let respondents express their thoughts freely. These interviews are done in person (mail and telephone don't work), and a skilled interviewer is needed to manage the unstructured interaction. The sessions usually take thirty to ninety minutes, which is much longer than the typical survey interview.

Depth interviews can be conducted with either individuals or groups. In marketing research, group interviews, called **focus groups,** are far more common than individual depth interviews.

The major advantage of focus groups and depth interviews is that they can gather complex information that doesn't come across well in a survey. The disadvantages are that each interview is very costly and it is difficult to obtain participation for such long interviews, so focus groups and depth interviews tend to have small sample sizes and limited population coverage. Given their strengths and weaknesses, focus groups and depth interviews are best suited for concept testing, motivational research, and interviewing corporate buyers whose companies may spend large sums on a particular product or service.

Chapter 8 discusses how to do focus groups and depth interviews. Also, while these methods usually do not use formal questionnaires or sampling procedures, the discussions of questionnaire design and sampling contained in Chapters 10 to 14 have general relevance.

Panels

Another source of primary data is panels. **Panels** are groups of research participants that provide information over time. This information can be collected through observation (as in the Nielsen TV panel) or self-reports. Panels are sometimes compared with surveys; it is said that a survey provides a snapshot of the population, whereas a panel provides a moving picture.

The major reason for using panels is to track individual purchasing units over time, so that brand switching and other changes in behavior can be measured. For example, if Kraft–General Foods distributes a "50¢ off" coupon for Maxwell House coffee, the company can use grocery panel data to determine how many of the people who used the coupon bought Maxwell House on their previous coffee purchase, how many switched from Folger's, and so on. The same type of information can be obtained in a survey by asking people whether they used the coupon and what brand they usually buy, but panel data will be more accurate.

Panels can also be used to provide ready access to specific types of consumers. For example, research companies such as NFO, HTI, and Market Facts operate panels of people who agree to respond to any mail questionnaires the company might send them. Certain types of people, such as people who change their own motor oil, can thus be efficiently located and interviewed by mail. These surveys are usually onetime affairs with no longitudinal tracking (i.e., no tracking over time).

The greatest weakness of panel research is the fact that many people are not willing to accept the commitment required by a panel, while many others drop out after a short time. As a result, it is difficult to keep panels representative of the population. Also, panels tend to be more expensive than surveys because panel members must be given some reward for their ongoing effort. Most surveys do not reward respondents.

Experiments

An **experiment** is a study in which a researcher actively manipulates one or more experimental variables (such as product features, price levels, advertising levels, or advertising appeals), then measures the effects of these manipulations on one or more dependent variables of interest (such as sales or product preference). The dependent variable(s) can be measured by either observation or self-report.

Experiments are motivated by a desire to remove uncertainty about the effects of the manipulated variable(s). For example, consider a supermarket chain that has higher produce sales in stores in which the produce department is painted green than those in which it is painted yellow. However, the departments painted green also happen to be located in the newest, biggest stores. In this example, there is uncertainty about the effect of color; the higher sales in green-painted departments may be caused by newness or store size, not by color. Before committing to a major redecorating program, the company may want to experiment with paint color.

To do the experiment, stores might be randomly assigned to one of two groups. Produce departments will be painted yellow in one group and green in the other. Then comparative sales will decide which wall color is better. The validity of this comparison depends on how well factors other than wall color are equalized between the groups, but the company is bound to feel the comparison is more valid after having attempted to control the process.

Since the whole purpose of experimentation is to isolate the effects of the manipulated variable(s), experiments are useful only to the extent that the effects of other variables can be controlled or eliminated. However, this is very difficult to do in real marketplace situations, where competitors' actions are uncontrolled. Also, it may not be feasible to perform certain manipulations in a real environment; for example, it isn't practical to test the effects of a product's features by changing the product from market to market or from week to week.

In order to improve control or make the manipulations feasible, experiments are often done as **laboratory studies** rather than **field studies.** A laboratory is any controlled environment. For example, if customers are invited to a research facility where they express their preferences among products with manipulated features, this would be a laboratory study.

The price paid for the improved control of a laboratory setting is a loss in realism. Experiments can be valuable sources of marketing information, but the line

Critical Thinking Skills

If you were the brand manager responsible for marketing a frozen orange juice with $40 million in annual sales, would you be willing to spend $100,000 per year for syndicated data that show weekly sales and market share? Would you be willing to spend an additional $100,000 for panel data with purchase records for individual households? Why or why not?

between control (called **internal validity**) and realism (called **external validity**) is a difficult one to tread.

How to do experiments is discussed in Chapter 9. Also, the discussions of questionnaire design and sampling contained in Chapters 10 to 14 have general relevance to experimental procedures.

Test Markets

Test markets are the final source of primary information. New or revamped products are introduced into selected markets so their actual market performance can be tested. A test market can be thought of as a form of simple experiment.

The value of test marketing should be obvious. Asking people whether they will buy a product provides useful information, but test marketing provides an acid test of whether a product will sell. It also provides an opportunity to work out product design and/or distribution problems before risking a full market introduction.

Test marketing has some major weaknesses that make it appropriate only for the most promising and riskiest products. First, test markets are expensive, often costing hundreds of thousands of dollars. Second, the researcher does not have full control over the test marketplace, and competitors may disrupt the market to "jam" the results. For example, when the makers of Scope mouthwash attempted to test market an antiseptic-flavored version of their product in Kansas City, the makers of Listerine responded with heavy local couponing and the introduction of a new, low-priced product that disrupted the test. Third, because only a few markets are used, choosing nonrepresentative markets can result in a misleading test. For example, New York City is generally viewed as a unique place that should not be used as a test market. Fourth, test marketing takes considerable time to conduct and gives competitors time to catch up or imitate. Several large companies have adopted a "no-test-marketing" policy for this reason.

Also, test marketing is inappropriate for a product that will have large start-up costs before any can be produced. If there are heavy start-up costs, the manufacturer is likely to enter the full market—if it enters the market at all—so that as much as possible of the start-up costs can be recovered. Heavy design and tooling costs are the reason why automobiles, for example, are not test-marketed.

To get the benefits of test marketing without the costs and problems, companies have begun to look at alternatives, such as testing in "virtual markets." For example, at Indiana University, a subject sitting at a computer monitor travels through a "virtual store" and does his or her normal shopping (see accompanying pictures). The "shopper" picks a package from the shelf by touching its image on the monitor; the package then flies to the center of the screen, where the shopper can examine it by using a trackball to rotate the package. The shopper can then put the package into his or her "cart" or return it to the shelf. This system is used like a test market to evaluate responses to new products, as well as to test how customers might respond to changes in packaging, shelf space, and/or shelf location for existing products.

Marketing Research Tools 4.3 (see page 90) summarizes potential sources of primary information. A summary of the strengths and weaknesses of and typical uses for various information sources is given in Marketing Tools 4.4 (see pages 90–91).

In Indiana University's Customer Interface Lab, a consumer travels through a virtual store and views shelf fixtures stocked with virtually any kind of product.

Source: Raymond Burke, "Virtual Shopping," *OR/MS Today,* August 1995, p. 28.

MARKETING RESEARCH TOOLS

4.3

SOURCES OF PRIMARY INFORMATION

Observational data:	Depth interviews:	Experiments:
Human observers	Individuals	Field
Electrical/mechanical devices	Focus groups	Laboratory
Coupon redemption	Panels	Test markets
Pantry audits		
Surveys		

MARKETING RESEARCH TOOLS

4.4

SUMMARY OF INFORMATION SOURCES

Source	Strengths	Weaknesses	Typical Uses
Internal sources:			
Sales and expense records	Low cost, ready availability	Limited scope	Forecasting sales, measuring sales response to marketing inputs, database marketing
Salespeople's reports	Low cost, can measure lost opportunities	May be biased, burdens sales force	Evaluating salespeople, identifying opportunities
Market intelligence ("street news")	Provides early warning about market changes	Difficult to collect and analyze	Predicting competitors' actions
Executives' judgments	Low cost, exploits executives' wisdom	May have low precision	Forecasting long-range trends, setting structure for market models
Extended internal information	Low cost	May be biased	Evaluating advertising media

SUMMARY OF INFORMATION SOURCES—CONTINUED

Source	Strengths	Weaknesses	Typical Uses
Secondary sources:			
Library sources	Low cost, wide scope	Usually doesn't fit exact needs	Measuring market size and growth
Trade associations	Low cost	Often not available	Obtaining data on industry trends and performance standards
Local sources	Low cost	May be biased	Measuring local market size and business patterns
Syndicated services	Lower cost than primary sources	Often not available	Measuring sales, market share, response to promotions
Personal networking	Low cost	Unorganized	Advice on methods or suppliers
Internet	Low cost	Limited content, can be hard to access	Market statistics, advice on methods
Primary sources:			
Observation	Not subject to reporting bias	Can't measure mental states	Measuring sales activity, traffic flows
Surveys	Low cost per interview, broad population coverage	Limited to structured questions, can't go into depth	Measuring user characteristics and usage patterns
Focus groups and depth interviews	Can go into depth	Expensive, poor population coverage	Concept testing, probing buying motivations, interviewing executives
Panels	Shows changes over time	Expensive; limited participation	Measuring brand loyalty, response to promotions
Experiments	Strong test of causation	Difficult to do outside lab setting	Taste testing, preliminary ad testing
Test markets	Realistic	Tremendously expensive, tips off competitors	Testing new products

Summary

This chapter described various sources of marketing research information. The following points were covered:

1. What are the different types of marketing research information?

We classified information sources along two dimensions: *internal* versus *external* and *primary* versus *secondary*.

Internal information comes from sources inside the organization. It is usually quick and easy to get but has a narrow range of applications. External information is collected from sources outside the organization.

External information can be either secondary or primary. Secondary information has already been collected for some other purpose. It may be readily available but may not be exactly what you want. Primary information is collected fresh by the researcher. It can be customized to be whatever you want but is expensive and time-consuming compared to secondary data.

2. How can internal data sources be used to obtain marketing research information?

Sales and expense records can be used to make short-term sales forecasts, to measure response to price and promotions, and, if kept on a customer-by-customer basis, to model the buying patterns and profitability of individual customers and develop a profile of key customers. *Salespeople's reports* can be used to obtain information about customers or sales call activities. *"Street news"* can provide informal information about competitors or industry trends. *Executive judgments* can be used for new-product development and sales forecasting.

3. How can secondary data sources be used to obtain marketing research information?

Within the library, *books* can provide "how-to" information, *U.S. government documents* can provide general statistics such as population data, *periodicals* can provide a wide variety of specific information, and *computerized databases* can provide much of the data from government sources and periodicals in edited form.

Outside the library, *trade associations* may provide informal information about industry trends, *local governments* and *chambers of commerce* may provide data about local business activity, *syndicated data services* may have industry data, *personal sources* may have useful knowledge, and the *Internet* may provide access to a wide variety of information sources.

4. How can primary methods of data collection be used to obtain marketing information?

Primary research studies use two major forms of data collection: observation and self-reports. *Observation* can be used to gather objective information about buyer behavior but cannot capture states of mind; it shows what people do but not what they think. In contrast, *self-report methods* can provide data about states of mind but are subject to biased reporting in their measures of behavior.

Among self-report methods, *surveys* use a standardized questionnaire, whereas *depth interviews* and *focus groups* use interactive discussion to probe narrow topics. Surveys are better for obtaining broad population coverage and counting objects, whereas depth interviews and focus groups are better for probing buyers' opinions and motivations.

Panel research is used to gather information over time from the same participants, either through observation or self-reports. Panels are the best method for measuring changes at the level of individual customers. *Experiments* actively manipulate one or more variables to see how the manipulation affects a dependent variable of interest; this is the best way of confirming the existence of causal relationships. Finally, *test markets* can be used to work out potential problems before risking full market introduction.

Suggested Additional Readings

This chapter is an overview of techniques that are discussed in greater detail in later chapters. For additional readings related to any specific technique, see the suggested readings at the end of the chapter discussing it.

Discussion Questions

1. What is the difference between primary and secondary information? Discuss the advantages and disadvantages of each.

2. Suppose you are the brand manager for a line of mountain bikes. Your sales have been growing at the rate of 6 percent per year for the past three years. What role might secondary data play in evaluating the market position of your brand of mountain bike?

3. What are some of the advantages and pitfalls of relying solely on internal information?

4. What is meant by "extended" internal information, and why is it appropriate to use caution when relying on this type of information?

5. Why are secondary data often preferred to primary data?

6. Your R&D department just developed a new technological innovation to make industrial fans more efficient. You have been asked to assess the market feasibility of this new technology. What secondary sources would you use? What primary methods?

7. Following is a list of how primary sources might be used. What primary data collection method should be used for each research objective?
   a. Concept testing
   b. Measuring usage patterns
   c. Testing line extensions for consumer products
   d. Measuring product movement
   e. Testing advertisements
   f. Executive interviewing
   g. Measuring brand loyalty
   h. Product formulation tests (e.g., taste tests)
   i. Measuring user characteristics
   j. Measuring traffic flows
   k. Measuring response to promotions

Marketing Research Challenge

Imagine that you are working for a firm that operates a chain of retail clothing stores for children on the East Coast. You are considering expansion into other regions of the United States, starting with the Midwest. Discuss the sources you would use to identify likely new locations. Remember that the cost of obtaining the data is a factor, but not the only one. Would you recommend any primary data collection?

Internet Exercise

Among the sources of information listed in this chapter, which apply to the Internet? What types of research questions can be answered via the Internet?

References

Fletcher, K., C. Wheeler, and J. Wright (1994). "Strategic Implementation of Data Base Marketing—Problems and Pitfalls." *Long-Range Planning* 27, pp. 133–141.

Johnson, Bradley (1995). "Behind All the Hype Lies a Crucial Hidden Asset." *Advertising Age* 66 (Oct. 2), p. 30.

Nowak, Glen J., and Joseph Phelps (1995). "Direct Marketing and the Use of Individual Level Consumer Information." *Journal of Direct Marketing* 9 (Summer), pp. 46–60.

Roman, Ernan (1993). "Zeroing In on the Customer Base: AT&T Is Among Companies Employing Integrated Direct Marketing." *Business Marketing* 78 (November), p. 40.

Steinborn, Deborah (1994). "Know Your Customers Better Through an MCIF: PC-based Marketing Customer Information Files Offer Community Banks a Way to Target Households for Cross-selling." *ABA Banking Journal* 86 (June), p. 29.

Stevenson, John (1989). "The State of the Art." *Direct Marketing* 52 (August), pp. 68–70.

Swigor, J. Timothy (1995). "Marketing Databases: An Art Beyond Science." *Direct Marketing* 58 (July), pp. 23–25.

CHAPTER

5 Typical Ways of Answering Common Research Questions

OBJECTIVES

LEARNING

After reading this chapter, you should be able to answer the following questions:

❶ What data sources are typically used to answer questions related to customer analysis?

❷ What data sources are typically used to answer questions related to competitive analysis?

❸ What data sources are typically used to answer questions related to operational analysis?

❹ What data sources are typically used to answer questions related to environmental analysis?

In Chapter 4, we introduced various sources of marketing research information. In this chapter, the list of common research questions from Chapter 1 is repeated and the sources that are typically used to answer each question are described. This chapter has two goals. First, matching the information sources with applications should give you a stronger feeling for the usefulness of various sources. Second, the chapter provides a "directory" of marketing research that is organized by questions rather than sources. The rest of this book is organized according to sources, not questions, because there is less repetition in discussing marketing research this way; however, if you need to do a marketing research project, you will start by posing questions. We hope you can bring these questions to this chapter, get some ideas about good information sources, then refer to the appropriate source chapters for guidance in how to do the project.

Customer Analysis

The following questions are common in customer analysis:

- How big is the existing market?
- How big is the potential market?
- How fast is the market growing?
- What are buyers' background characteristics?
- How and why do buyers use the product or service?
- How and where is the product bought?
- How brand-loyal are buyers?
- What market segments exist, and how large are the various segments?

These questions are typically answered as follows.

How Big Is the Existing Market?

Market size is generally defined as the total dollar sales for a product category. Estimates of market size are usually drawn from secondary sources of information.

In some industries, syndicated services provide estimates of market size at both the national and local levels. For example, a company such as Pillsbury can obtain estimates of supermarket sales in its product categories, both nationally and locally, from A. C. Nielsen.

If syndicated data are unavailable, estimates of total national market size can usually be found in library sources. The ***American Statistics Index (ASI)*** provides market size estimates published by the U.S. government, the ***Statistical Reference Index (SRI)*** provides estimates published by private sources, and a librarian can suggest other indexes or sources. These sources are discussed further in Chapter 6. Estimates prepared by the government are usually accurate but are presented according to Standard Industrial Classification (SIC) group without sensitivity to product subcategories. For example, soft drinks are not separated into regular and diet drinks. Estimates prepared by trade associations or by analysts who follow the industry for investment purposes may have useful breakdowns of product subcategories.

Estimates of market size for regions or localities are more difficult to find unless the product is subject to special tax or registration requirements, such as alcoholic beverages or automobiles. If it is, data should be available from appropriate government authorities or from commercial firms that tabulate and sell the information. For example, the Texas secretary of state's office will sell, for about $50, a printout showing alcohol tax receipts for a one-month period for every establishment in Texas that has a liquor license. If a product is not regulated, subnational market size estimates might be available from library or trade association sources; these are not always available, however. The *Encyclopedia of Associations* is a useful source of the names of trade associations.

Market size estimates for product subcategories in subnational territories are usually not directly available and must be estimated as portions of broader figures.

Be aware that any definition of an industry is arbitrary, so that different sources are likely to define the industry differently and thus make different estimates of its size. It is important to know how the industry was defined in any estimates that you use and to think about the industry definition that is most appropriate for your needs.

Critical Thinking Skills

A company that plans to introduce a new valve gets different estimates of the size of the valve market from different sources. Why does this matter, and what should the company do?

How Big Is the Potential Market?

A product's **potential market** is the total dollar sales for that product if all potential customers purchase all they need. The first step in estimating potential market size is calculating the total number of potential buyers, that is, the number of people, households, or businesses that potentially could use the product. This estimate will almost always come from secondary sources. U.S. government documents, especially census data, are a good source of basic data on population, households, and business establishments in cities, counties, and states. If you need data for submetropolitan areas or for population subgroups not broken out by the government, they may be available from commercial data sources or sources such as chambers of commerce and utility companies.

The second step in estimating potential market size is estimating the likely **adoption rate,** that is, the percentage of potential buyers who will buy the product. For example, not every household with a television set will buy cable TV, and not every cable TV household will buy a paid movie channel. To estimate the number of potential buyers who will adopt the product, it is necessary to consider factors such as their interest in the product and purchasing power.

The eventual adoption rate might be estimated from actual sales data; these could include the adoption rate for this product in a test market, adoption rates for similar products, or early sales results for this product in this market. For example,

Author Tips

Sometimes you can find ready-made estimates of potential market size in secondary sources such as trade journals. For example, you might find an estimate that retail activity on the Internet will grow to $60 billion by the year 2010. Be wary of such estimates. In our experience, they are usually too high, reflecting the optimism of people within a growing industry.

the Bass New Product Growth Model uses as little as three months of sales history to project ultimate adoption rates for durable goods (Bass, 1969). Another common way of estimating the adoption rate is by using a survey that measures potential buyers' interest in the product and/or potential benefit from it. For example, Urban and Hauser (1980) describe a procedure in which people are asked whether they "definitely would buy, probably would buy, might buy, or would not buy" a new product. They suggest using 90 percent of the "definites," 40 percent of the "probables," and 10 percent of the "mights" to get a reasonable estimate of adoption.

The quality of any such estimate depends heavily on the extent to which the product is similar to previous products, so that customers understand it and precedents exist. It is very difficult to estimate eventual adoption rates for really innovative products. A famous example is the projection, made in the 1940s, that the ultimate worldwide demand for high-speed computers would not exceed ten machines. No one could foresee the transition from mainframe to personal computers and the manifold expansion of their uses.

The third and final step in estimating potential market size is estimating how much the average buyer will spend once in the market. This figure is typically estimated from sales results in the existing market, if available. Another possibility is estimating sales per buyer based on survey results regarding likely usage frequency.

How Fast Is the Market Growing?

Measures of historical market growth are typically obtained from the same secondary sources that are used for estimates of existing market size. Forecasts of future growth are also obtained from secondary sources. ***Predicasts Basebook*** and ***Predicasts Forecasts*** are well-known sources, available in most big libraries, that provide estimates of historical and forecasted market growth.

What Are Buyers' Background Characteristics?

In consumer markets, you may be interested in buyers' **demographic characteristics,** such as age, income, gender, marital status, family size, and education. You may also want to know their media consumption habits (what TV shows they watch, what magazines they read, etc.).

Demographic information may be available from syndicated services. If syndicated data are not available, demographic data can be obtained through consumer surveys done specifically for the manufacturer or retailer who commissions the research. Information on buyers' media habits is often available from the various media, which provide audience information to potential advertisers and/or their ad agencies. These data are likely to overstate the buying influence of audience members, but they may be useful anyway, and in any case they are free.

Another important kind of information comes from **psychographic characteristics,** the attitudes, tastes, and preferences that influence purchase behavior. These are also called **lifestyle characteristics.** Surveys are the most common sources of psychographic data on consumer markets.

In industrial markets, data such as the size of companies that are potential customers and their industries are important. Descriptions of customers in industrial markets will typically come from salespeople's reports. Descriptions of buyers for the entire industry, if available, will typically come from research reports published by a trade association.

How and Why Do Buyers Use the Product or Service?

Questions about how and why buyers use a product are important because the answers tell the company how to present products in its advertising, how to improve products, and which product attributes to focus on. For example, knowing that cream of mushroom soup is mostly used in casseroles tells Campbell's that the best way to encourage use of this soup is to publish casserole recipes. Casserole recipes would not help as much for chicken noodle soup, which is used differently.

Information on usage patterns and motivations may be available through secondary sources, but the most common source of usage information is user surveys in which people respond to questionnaires regarding how often they use the product, in what settings, for what purposes, and so on. Focus groups can also be used to learn about people's consumption. This format gives users more freedom to discuss what the product means to them, how they use it, and problems they have encountered with it. Focus groups are particularly valuable for products with high symbolic value, such as luxury automobiles, and for industrial goods that have complex usage environments. You will never understand the luxury-car market if you simply ask people to tell you how often they drive their cars, to what places, and so on. A focus group will tell you what the car means to them and how they feel when they drive it.

How and Where Is the Product Bought?

It is also important to determine where buyers get the product, how they pay for it, the length of the interval between purchases, how much time buyers spend shopping for the product, how they obtain information about it, whether they buy in anticipation of needing the product or on a "need-it-now" basis, whether they stock up or buy as needed, and so on. All of this type of information can be obtained from buyer surveys, possibly augmented by panel data.

How Brand-Loyal Are Buyers?

A special question about purchase patterns concerns brand loyalty in the market. **Brand loyalty** is broadly defined as the extent to which a consumer repurchases the same brand instead of other brands of the same product. This concept is important because it influences promotional strategies and new-product opportunities. In markets with high levels of brand loyalty, special deals or promotions will not attract customers from other brands, and new products will be adopted slowly. Markets with low brand loyalty, in contrast, offer the possibility of rapid change.

Brand loyalty in industrial markets can be determined from salespeople's reports concerning customers won and lost. Strictly speaking, this provides loyalty data only on one's own customers, but salespeople and industry contacts can be used to extend the analysis to the entire market.

Loyalty measures for consumer markets are usually obtained from syndicated panel data, if available. Since panels track participants over time, they can measure brand-switching behavior. If syndicated panel data are not available for the industry, loyalty will typically be measured through surveys that ask about purchase histories.

It is important to distinguish between *constrained* loyalty and *felt* loyalty. Some markets show high levels of brand loyalty simply because there are not many products available, so consumers don't have much choice. These markets will respond to new products differently than will markets in which buyers feel committed to their brands. *Felt* loyalty, if measured, may be obtained through surveys or focus group discussions.

What Market Segments Exist, and How Large Are the Various Segments?

Market segmentation is the practice of grouping buyers by certain characteristics or behaviors so that different marketing strategies can be used on the different segments. Segmentation is usually done on the basis of demographic characteristics, psychographic characteristics, media usage, product usage patterns, product-buying patterns, and/or brand loyalty. Consequently, the basic information for market segmentation comes from the same sources used to determine these other characteristics. Segmentation is simply a matter of analyzing these data.

Marketing Research Tools 5.1 summarizes the data sources used for various aspects of customer analysis.

Competitive Analysis

In addition to analyzing customers, market research may be used to describe your organization's competitive position in the market. Relevant questions include:

- What market share do you and various competitors hold?
- What future sales do you forecast?
- What are the awareness levels for various brands?
- How do buyers perceive various brands?
- What are the repurchase rates for various brands?

MARKETING RESEARCH TOOLS

5.1

SOURCES USED FOR CUSTOMER ANALYSIS

Research Question	Typical Sources
Market size	Syndicated data, library sources, trade associations
Market potential:	
Number of potential buyers	Library sources
Likely adoption rate	Historical data, surveys
Amount spent per buyer	Surveys, internal sales data
Market growth rate	Library sources
Buyer characteristics:	
Consumer demographics	Syndicated data, surveys
Media use	Media surveys
Consumer psychographics	Syndicated data, surveys
Business buyer characteristics	Salespeople's reports, trade associations
Usage patterns	Surveys, focus groups
Buying patterns	Surveys, consumer panels
Brand loyalty:	
Business buyers	Salesperson reports
Consumers	Consumer panels, surveys, focus groups
Market segments	Same sources as for buyer characteristics

- How satisfied are customers with various brands?
- What are your competitors' resources and strategies?

These questions typically are answered as follows.

What Market Share Do You and Various Competitors Hold?

An organization's overall market share can be calculated by dividing its sales (obtained from internal accounting records) by an estimate of the total market size.

Estimates of competitors' market shares may come from various sources. One possibility is a syndicated research service that covers the industry. This is how grocery products such as Tide detergent obtain market share data. If there is no syndicated service, share estimates may be available from trade association sources or from investment analysts who track the industry. For example, as noted in Chapter 2, The

Methodist Hospital in Houston, Texas, gets market share data from the Texas Hospital Association.

Another possibility is to estimate market shares from survey data. Respondents are asked whether they buy the item in question, how much they buy, and which brand(s) they buy, and the results are used to estimate the percentage of the market belonging to each brand. Share estimates obtained in this manner are subject to substantial errors because of memory lapses, other sources of response error, and sampling fluctuation. However, they are better than nothing and may be the only estimates available if the industry is too small for outsiders to track.

In addition to measuring overall market share, companies often want to know their market shares within specific market segments. These estimates may be available from syndicated data but more likely will come from survey data.

What Future Sales Do You Forecast?

Short-range sales forecasts for existing organizations are usually based on trends in historical sales data. For example, a forecast of weekly sales for the coming year would be based on trends in weekly sales data over the past several years. These trends would be calculated with methods such as multiple regression analysis, which is discussed in Chapter 18, or exponential smoothing, which is discussed in many statistics textbooks. For example, M&M/Mars uses regression procedures to forecast weekly sales of Snickers candy bars, and Southwestern Bell Telephone uses exponential smoothing to forecast short-range demand for telephone services.

Short-range sales forecasts for the entire market can also be estimated from historical trends. They might also be found in secondary sources such as *Predicasts Forecasts.*

Long-range sales forecasts for individual companies usually involve forecasting sales for the entire industry, then applying some market share assumption. The industry sales estimate follows our previous discussion of potential market size; that is, it relies on estimates of the number of potential buyers, the likely adoption rate, and the amount spent per buyer. The market share estimate is typically drawn from executives' judgments.

In some cases, you might want to forecast sales for a product or a business that does not yet exist—for example, if you plan to start your own business. The methods used for this type of forecasting are different for small entrepreneurial ventures and big companies.

For entrepreneurial ventures, which are heavily constrained by resource limitations, sales forecasts are usually based on the amount of resources available for marketing activities. Library sources and/or trade associations are used to obtain key productivity ratios, such as sales per square foot for retail businesses, sales per sales call, or whatever. These ratios are multiplied by the planned number of square feet, planned number of sales calls, or whatever. For example, if you plan to open a science fiction book store with 1,200 square feet and specialty book stores average $200 in sales per square foot per year, this yields a sales forecast of $240,000 per year (1,200 × $200). This figure can be checked against an estimate of total market size to determine whether the implied market share seems reasonable.

In larger companies, which have fewer resource constraints, new-product sales forecasts are made by estimating market share for the new product. For example, in introducing a product such as Rice Krispies Treats, Kellogg's has the ability to put the product onto every supermarket shelf in America and to spend millions of dollars in advertising, so the real question is the percentage of potential buyers that will prefer the new product to the alternatives. Specialized techniques such as conjoint analysis, which is discussed in Chapter 9, are used to generate share estimates. These estimates are then multiplied by estimates of total market size to produce sales projections.

What Are the Awareness Levels for Various Brands?

Buyer awareness is a measure of how well a product or service is known. Obviously, before you can sell a product or service, buyers must be aware that it exists. Buyer awareness is usually measured through surveys. For example, users of hair shampoo might be asked:

- "When you think of hair shampoo, what is the first brand that comes to mind?" This is a "top-of-mind" recall measure.

- "What are all the brands of hair shampoo you can think of? Any others?" This is a "complete category" recall measure.

- "I'm going to read some names to you. Please tell me which names you recognize as brands of hair shampoo." This is a "recognition measure."

Whatever measure is used, it is likely to be applied in the context of a survey.

How Do Buyers Perceive Various Brands?

Brand perceptions are usually measured through surveys. For example, potential buyers might be asked to rate various brands along various dimensions or simply to tell which brand offers the best performance along each dimension; other questions can also be asked. The answers provide some indication of where your brand stands relative to competitors.

What Are the Repurchase Rates for Various Brands?

The repurchase rate—the percentage of buyers who return to a brand on consecutive purchases—gives an indication of brand loyalty and is a "bottom-line" measure of customer satisfaction. For industrial products, the repurchase rate can be measured through salespeople's reports. For consumer products covered by consumer panels, the repurchase rate can be measured from syndicated panel data. Otherwise, the repurchase rate can be measured through surveys.

Repurchase rates are particularly crucial in test markets for new products, because they tell whether a product will be able to hold customers who try it.

Critical Thinking Skills

Victor Smith is planning a business that will sell customer satisfaction surveys to restaurants. How would you forecast this company's sales? Rachel Ochoa is planning a bar in a business district that will offer a wide variety of specialty beers. How would you forecast this company's sales?

How Satisfied Are Customers with Various Brands?

Historically, customer satisfaction has been measured through company-sponsored surveys. This is still the most common way of obtaining satisfaction data; however, in more and more industries, overall customer satisfaction is viewed as basic industry data, like market share, and is collected and sold on a syndicated basis. The J. D. Power and Associates owner satisfaction ratings for new cars are an example. These ratings are purchased by Toyota, Nissan, Ford and every other automaker.

Another measure of customer satisfaction is the number of complaints received about a product. Although this is not a good measure of total satisfaction, since only a small percentage of dissatisfied customers will take the trouble to complain, trends in complaint rates can be used as indicators of increased or decreased satisfaction.

What Are Your Competitors' Resources and Strategies?

It is useful to have information on competitors' financial positions, key personnel changes, changes in plant capacity or other resources, new products under consideration, target markets, and marketing strategies.

Financial data for publicly traded companies is available from annual reports. In addition, many companies obtain credit reports on their competitors. Other information might come from industry gossip and other "street news."

Personnel changes, plant expansions, and new products also tend to be discussed within an industry, especially in the trade press and at trade shows. Gathering this information for marketing research purposes simply requires some system of capturing "street news."

Target markets and selling strategies can usually be inferred from competitors' marketing activities, such as advertising content, ad placement, places where their salespeople seem active, and so on. Again, this is simply a matter of recording and analyzing information that is all around you.

Some forms of competitive intelligence are illegal or unethical. These include sneaking into competitors' plants, bribing competitors' employees, other forms of "industrial espionage," and using planning documents that people bring with them if they leave a competitor to join your organization.

Marketing Research Tools 5.2 summarizes the data sources used for various aspects of competitive analysis.

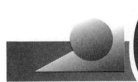

Operational Analysis

Questions that arise under the heading of operational analysis include:

- How effective is your distribution?
- How effective is your advertising?

MARKETING RESEARCH TOOLS

5.2

SOURCES USED FOR COMPETITIVE ANALYSIS

Research Question	Typical Sources
Market share	Internal sales records, secondary sources, syndicated data, trade associations, surveys
Sales forecasts	Historical sales data, secondary sources, executive judgments
Brand awareness	Surveys
Brand images	Surveys
Repurchase rates:	
Business buyers	Salesperson reports
Consumers	Consumer panels, surveys
Customer satisfaction	Surveys, syndicated data, complaints
Competitors' resources and strategies	Financial reports, "street news"

- How effective are your sales promotions?
- How effective are your salespeople?
- How effective are your pricing strategies?
- How might customers respond to product changes?
- How might buyers respond to a new product?

The answers to these questions allow companies to evaluate marketing programs and target areas for improvement. Following are the typical sources used to answer these questions.

How Effective Is Your Distribution?

The two most common questions in assessing distribution effectiveness are "What percentage of potential outlets carry our product?" and "What sales do we generate per outlet?"

The first of these measures, known as outlet penetration, is most relevant for manufacturers of consumer goods that are bought on convenience or impulse, because sales of these types of products depend heavily on their availability. Outlet penetration is less relevant for consumer shopping goods, such as furniture, or for industrial goods that are sold by distributors with active sales forces. For example, a maker of industrial wire cable such as Hitachi Cable America doesn't want *every* cable distributor to carry its product; it wants the *best* distributors, with the best sales forces.

Manufacturers in some industries, such as packaged grocery products, can obtain outlet penetration data from syndicated distribution audits. These audits tell which outlets carry the item and which outlets had the item in stock when checked. In industries where syndicated data are not available, outlet penetration can be measured by assembling a list of potential outlets (obtained from secondary sources) and comparing this list with the list of outlets serviced by your organization (obtained from accounting records).

The second measure of distribution effectiveness, sales per outlet, is obtained from accounting records. Sales are simply divided by the number of outlets serviced. For example, if a company services 1,000 stores and has annual sales of $500,000 for a product, then sales per outlet are $500,000/1,000 = $500.

It is useful to calculate sales per outlet separately for different types of outlets (grocery stores, drugstores, etc.) and/or to split outlets into "top producers," "medium producers," and so on. These analyses help you decide which outlets should receive priority in your marketing efforts and can be used to project the sales increase that might result from increased distribution in any particular type of outlet.

It is also helpful to know your competitors' sales per outlet. Knowing this information helps you shape incentive programs for distributors who carry competing products. For example, if the average drugstore sells $500 per year of a competitor's product, with a gross margin of 30 percent, you know you have to produce more than $150 in margin to get drugstores to favor you.

Sales per outlet for other brands are sometimes available through syndicated distribution audits. More often, this type of information must be assembled through a survey of distributors.

How Effective Is Your Advertising?

Advertising effectiveness can be measured at various levels: (1) the extent to which people are aware of an ad, (2) the extent to which advertising changes the number of people who are aware of the brand, (3) the extent to which advertising changes people's impressions of the brand, and (4) the extent to which advertising results in sales.

Ad awareness is measured through surveys. These surveys are usually conducted by companies that specialize in ad testing. For example, Burke Marketing Research tests "day-after recall" for television commercials, and Daniel Starch, Inc., tests recall of magazine ads.

Brand awareness can also be measured through surveys, as discussed earlier in this chapter. The effectiveness of an ad campaign could be tested by measuring brand awareness before and after the campaign and calculating the change.

The extent to which advertising changes people's impressions of a brand can be tested in similar fashion. Surveys may be used to take the appropriate measures before and after a campaign, and the changes can then be calculated. In addition, reactions to specific ads are sometimes measured in advertising agencies' testing labs, where potential buyers are shown ads and asked for their reactions.

The extent to which advertising results in sales can be tested in two ways. The simplest way is by comparing sales levels before and after a specific campaign, as described in Case Study 5.1. The other, more general way, is by using multiple regression analysis on historical sales and advertising records to calculate the apparent effect of advertising on sales. Multiple regression analysis is discussed in Chapter 18.

CASE STUDY 5.1

Taster's Choice coffee uses market share to demonstrate the success of its long-running series of commercials featuring the "Taster's Choice couple." For several years, consumers have been intrigued by the couple's romance, from their first meeting as new neighbors to the surprise visit of a young man calling the woman "Mom." A year after the first commercial ran in November 1990, Taster's Choice surpassed Folger's and Maxwell House to become the number one instant coffee. Between 1989 and 1993, the brand's market share rose from 20.7 percent to 24.0 percent—a gain of more than three share points in a market worth hundreds of millions of dollars each year. This type of sales result is the acid test of advertising effectiveness.

Source: Leah Rickard, "Taster's Choice Rolls Love Potion Number 9," p. 70. Reprinted with permission from the March 28, 1994 issue of *Advertising Age.* Copyright Crain Communications, Inc. 1994.

How Effective Are Your Sales Promotions?

The biggest users of sales promotions, whether aimed at consumers (coupons, rebates, cents-off packages, sweepstakes, etc.) or "the trade" (discounts to distributors), are the large manufacturers of packaged grocery products.

Many years ago these manufacturers judged the effectiveness of promotional efforts by simple participation. Coupons would be evaluated by the number of coupon redemptions, trade promotions would be judged by the volume of orders, and so on. The basic data came from accounting records. Case Study 5.2 (see page 108) provides an example of this type of analysis in the unconventional context of a promotion for TV programs.

Today, promotions for packaged grocery products are more likely to be evaluated through complex analyses of consumer panel data. Manufacturers study the data to see whether people who redeem a coupon are being drawn from competitors or whether the company is simply giving discounts to its own customers. Also, sales are analyzed to see whether they are "extra" sales or simply drawn from future periods (that is, buyers are stocking up at favorable prices).

How Effective Are Your Salespeople?

A variety of measures go into evaluating sales force performance. How many calls do salespeople make? How are calls allocated between prospects and customers? What is the ratio of calls to purchases (the call-to-close ratio)? What is the average transaction size? Are sales made at profitable prices? Does the mix of products sold indicate that salespeople are pushing the more profitable items? These questions can be answered by analyzing salespeople's call records along with records of sales transactions.

In most organizations, sales force evaluation is *not* done by marketing researchers. It is considered to be the job of sales managers. The marketing research group is responsible, however, for providing the data used by sales managers in setting quotas for how much each salesperson should sell. These quotas are typically based on estimates of the sales potential for each salesperson's territory.

CASE STUDY 5.2

The purpose of most sales promotions is to produce a short-term boost in sales, so market researchers usually measure the success of promotions according to short-term sales results. However, other measures can also be used.

For example, the ABC television network conducted a promotional contest to stimulate interest in its daytime soap operas. Here's how the promotion worked:

- The network ran magazine ads inviting potential viewers to enter the contest by mailing in their phone numbers and watching ABC soaps during an eleven-day promotional period.
- On those eleven days, the network aired one-minute "mini soaps" featuring scenes from upcoming episodes of ABC shows. Each evening, ABC soap stars called twenty-five randomly selected entrants and asked them to predict how the "mini soap" would be resolved in the upcoming episode. Those who answered correctly won prizes.

The success of this promotion could have been measured by audience ratings. However, since ratings can be affected by many factors, ABC decided to measure the success of this promotion according to the number of entries. More than 100,000 people mailed in their phone numbers, the highest number ever for an ABC promotion.

Source: William A. Robinson, *Best Sales Promotions,* Lincolnwood, Ill.: NTC Business Books, 1987.

How Effective Are Your Pricing Strategies?

Effective pricing requires two types of knowledge. First, it is necessary to have some idea of the demand curve for a product so that sales at various price levels can be estimated. Second, it is necessary to know what competitors are charging.

Price elasticity, which defines the slope of the demand curve for a product or service, can be estimated from historical accounting data: periods in which the price changed can be identified, and sales records can be consulted to determine customers' response.

Unfortunately, this type of analysis usually provides an incomplete picture of price sensitivity. A real-life demand curve is irregular, with sudden shifts in demand as a product crosses a breakthrough price at the lower end or a price ceiling at the higher end. For example, when videotaped movies routinely sold for $70, film critic Roger Ebert predicted that sales would take off if their price fell below $20; he turned out to be right. For another example, if the price of store-brand green beans (such as Kroger) goes above that of national-brand green beans (such as Green Giant), sales of the store brand will drop to nothing. To measure such sudden shifts, a company must use a wide variety of prices. Most organizations vary their prices only within a fairly narrow range.

Also, for most companies, price reductions are done on a promotional basis, and it is difficult to separate the "price" effect from the "promotion" effect. For example, if sales of Tropicana orange juice triple when it goes on sale for 50¢ off, this doesn't mean that the brand would sustain a trebled sales volume if there were a 50¢ reduction in the "everyday" price.

If historical data cover too narrow a price range, the broader demand curve is usually estimated with conjoint analysis. **Conjoint analysis** is a "what-if" experiment in which buyers are presented with different possibilities and asked what they would buy. We discuss conjoint analysis in more detail in Chapter 9.

The second type of price information, competitive price data, may be easy or difficult to obtain. If products are sold at publicly posted prices, it is easy to know these prices. For example, retailers can send employees to check prices at competing stores. However, if prices are individually negotiated with customers, then accurate price data may be difficult to get. In this situation, most organizations rely on informal communications with customers to keep in touch with competitors' pricing.

How Might Customers Respond to Product Changes?

The likely response to possible product or service changes may be estimated from some type of self-report data. Survey-based measures are probably the most common device. For example, if a retailer wants to estimate the number of customers it would lose by dropping its credit card, it might do a survey with questions concerning (1) the most important reason why people choose this retailer over others, (2) ratings of the importance of various factors, including availability of the credit card, (3) expected shopping behavior if the credit card were not available, and (4) customers' ownership levels of alternative credit cards.

Focus groups can also be used to measure responses to possible product changes, and conjoint analysis has become increasingly popular for this purpose.

All these methods presume that buyers can understand the changes just by hearing about them. Some changes, such as new flavors or new scents, must be experienced. Almost all food companies operate test kitchens where employee volunteers and sometimes plant visitors participate in taste tests. Similarly, manufacturers of toiletries and cleaning products ask employees to participate in scent tests. If new-product formulations do well in employee tests, research companies are hired to recruit consumers and run similar tests among them. The results are by no means guaranteed: "new Coke" was introduced after it won taste tests with more than 100,000 cola drinkers, but it failed in the marketplace because of other factors.

How Might Buyers Respond to a New Product?

Typically, the first step in testing the feasibility of a new product is measuring the size and nature of the market. How many buyers or potential buyers are there? What perceptions do they have of existing products relative to their "ideal" products? How many buyers express dissatisfaction with their choices? Are trends in buyers' values and/or preferences creating new opportunities? The answers to these questions tell whether the market is worth pursuing.

CASE STUDY 5.3

Sometimes marketing problems cannot be completely addressed by market research.

In an effort to revive its flagging Almay cosmetics brand, Revlon has released advertising that directly compares Almay to Clinique cosmetics on value. The headline for a mascara ad bluntly says that "Clinique mascara can cost twice as much as Almay mascara."

Some experts criticize Revlon's aggressive strategy, saying that it will not help Almay's image in an image-driven business. They wonder whether Revlon has forgotten the credo of its founder, Charles Revson: "What we're selling is hope in a jar."

Revlon claims to have market research supporting its position. Rosie Albright, Almay's executive vice president for marketing, says, "We tested the campaign with consumers [in focus groups] and it tested well . . . we made sure the testing showed that we did [the comparison] in a very tasteful way."

However, the image question is not easily resolved by focus group testing. Focus groups can give an immediate response to an ad message but not a long-term response. The concern among Revlon's critics is that aggressive, price-oriented advertising will produce good short-term results but diminish the perceived quality and value of Almay cosmetics in the long run.

This is a situation in which market research is of limited value because managers must "bet their instincts" long before long-term results are available.

Source: Based on Suein L. Hwang, "Makeup Ads Downplay Glamour for Value," *Wall Street Journal,* June 20, 1994, p. B6.

As discussed earlier in this chapter, market size estimates are obtained from secondary sources, and product perceptions are measured through self-report procedures. Trends are measured through demographic forecasting services and other research companies that specialize in trend reporting. Usually, a review of the trade press will uncover reports of key trends affecting the industry.

Once a new-product idea is developed, the next step is usually "concept testing" with focus groups: the product idea is described to a group of potential buyers, who give their reactions.

If the new product survives concept testing, it goes into development. For consumer products, the development phase may involve taste testing, scent testing, color testing, and so on to discover the ideal product formulation. Also, surveys may be used to fine-tune customers' preference data.

Once the product has been developed, it goes into use testing to uncover any problems. In consumer markets, this involves recruiting people to use the product. After a trial period, these people discuss any problems they had with the product and indicate whether they would buy it if available. The posttrial "willingness to purchase" level is compared with the pretrial level and should be higher if the product is to be successful. In industrial markets, a few customers are recruited to serve as **beta test sites** to use a new product and give feedback about it. These sites operate just like household testers.

MARKETING RESEARCH TOOLS

5.3

SOURCES USED FOR OPERATIONAL ANALYSIS

Research Question	Typical Sources
Distribution:	
Outlet penetration	Syndicated data, internal and secondary sources
Sales per outlet	Internal sales records
Competitors' sales per outlet	Syndicated data, distributor surveys
Advertising effectiveness	Surveys, sales records
Sales promotion effectiveness	Sales records, consumer panel data
Pricing effectiveness	Sales records, consumer panel data, competitive price surveys
Responses to product changes	Surveys, focus groups, conjoint analysis
Responses to new products	Market size data, focus groups, surveys, conjoint analysis, use testing, test markets

In industrial markets, beta test sites are generally the end of the road for new-product research; the next step is product launch. In consumer markets, a test market may follow the in-home testing.

Marketing Research Tools 5.3 summarizes the data sources used for various aspects of operational analysis.

Environmental Analysis

Relevant questions about the general environment include:

- How will technological developments affect this business?
- How will media changes affect the market?
- How will social changes affect the market?
- How will legal and regulatory changes affect the market?
- How will economic changes affect the market?

The typical data sources used to answer these questions are as follows.

How Will Technological Developments Affect This Business?

Technological developments can affect markets in many different ways. For example:

- Almost all markets are affected by ongoing changes in computer and telecommunications technologies that are changing the ways people work, shop, and communicate. Voice mail, the multiplication of long-distance phone companies, and the Internet are prime examples.

- The economics of product design and manufacturing can be affected by developments related to component materials; for example, the automobile market is affected by changes in metals, plastics, and ceramics technologies.

- The economics of manufacturing and distribution can be affected by developments in management technologies such as just-in-time inventory management systems that eliminate the need for large storage facilities but increase the need for precise production and shipment schedules.

In general, the effects of relevant technological developments will be felt by every company in an industry. Therefore, the industry as a whole will track these developments, and information will be available in articles in trade magazines, reports issued by trade associations, and seminars held at trade shows.

In addition to monitoring these sources of information, companies sometimes appoint internal task forces to make special studies of important technological issues. These task forces may supplement available data by interviewing technology "gurus" such as university professors and consultants.

How Will Media Changes Affect the Market?

In general, companies rely on their advertising agencies to track changes in the media environment and to recommend appropriate changes in promotional programs.

How Will Social Changes Affect the Market?

Social changes that are relevant to marketers take two primary forms:

- Demographic changes that affect the number of people within a particular buying group; for example, the increasing number of older people in the United States has increased the demand for nursing homes.

- Attitudinal and/or lifestyle changes that affect demand for a product; for example, a trend toward casual lifestyles has reduced the demand for men's suits.

Some companies track demographic changes through internal reports, relying on secondary sources such as U.S. Census data. Other companies buy market-tracking reports from consulting companies or learn about relevant changes through sessions at industry conferences.

CASE STUDY 5.4

General population data can help companies identify promising markets. For example, the age trend in the U.S. population is leading fashion designers into the home furnishings business.

The median age of Americans is thirty-four today and should be thirty-seven by the year 2000. This aging promises growth in the home furnishings market because "as people get older they spend more time at home, and more money on it," according to Carl Steidtmann, a retailing economist. Accordingly, designers such as Ralph Lauren and Adrienne Vittadini have introduced lines of home furnishings products.

Fashion designers are not the only ones planning for an older population. Marriott has shifted resources from the hotel business to nursing homes, and car manufacturers are working on safer information panels and control systems for drivers with declining vision and reflexes.

All the demographic information that supports these business decisions is readily available from secondary sources. Market researchers need only go to the library and look it up.

Source: Based on Amy Feldman and Joshua Levine, "Sprucing Up the Cocoon," *Forbes,* Jan. 4, 1993, pp. 64–65.

Changes in attitudes and lifestyles are usually tracked through syndicated reports produced by specialized research companies. For example, the Yankelovich company produces a social monitoring report that is bought by many producers of consumer goods.

How Will Legal and Regulatory Changes Affect the Market?

Most trade associations and trade magazines monitor legal and regulatory actions that are relevant to their industries. Companies within the industry are notified of developments by means of (1) regular "Washington roundup" reports that are issued by the trade association or published in the trade magazine, (2) special reports that appear in the same sources, and/or (3) seminars that are given at trade shows or conferences.

Most large companies supplement this information with informal reports obtained from lobbyists who represent the company in places of government.

How Will Economic Changes Affect the Market?

Most large and medium-sized companies prepare their own economic forecasts for their industries. They rely on secondary sources such as government reports for their basic data.

SOURCES USED FOR ENVIRONMENTAL ANALYSIS

Research Question	Typical Sources
Technological changes	Trade associations, trade press, trade shows
Media changes	Advertising agencies
Social changes	Library sources, syndicated reports
Legal and regulatory changes	Trade associations, trade press, trade shows
Economic changes	Trade associations, trade press, trade shows, other secondary sources

Smaller companies are more likely to monitor economic conditions by means of "economic outlook" reports that appear in trade magazines, trade association reports, and/or sessions at industry conferences.

Marketing Research Tools 5.4 summarizes the data sources used for various aspects of environmental analysis.

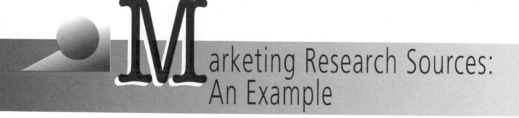

Marketing Research Sources: An Example

To illustrate some of the preceding discussion, we follow the research process behind 5 Alive!, a frozen juice product developed by Minute Maid, Inc. (formerly Coca-Cola Foods, Inc.).

Minute Maid is a leading maker of fruit beverages, with a product line that includes Minute Maid juices and Hi-C drinks. As a result, the company tracks beverage markets closely. One of the things it tracks is how various beverages are used and perceived. Regular survey data, for example, tell the company that orange juice is used almost exclusively as a breakfast beverage, despite years of effort by the Florida Citrus Commission to convince people that orange juice is "not just for breakfast anymore."

Around 1980, image studies of the beverage market showed Minute Maid that many people define beverages within a three-dimensional space defined by refreshment, nutrition, and deliciousness. Milk, for example, is seen as high in nutrition, low in refreshment, and either high or low in deliciousness depending on whether the person likes milk or not. Coca-Cola is seen as low in nutrition, high in refreshment, and high in deliciousness. Lemonade is seen as low in nutrition, high in refreshment, and medium in deliciousness. Orange juice is seen as high in nutrition, low in refreshment, and high in deliciousness.

Simultaneously, social trend research bought by the company showed a strong movement toward "natural" products and an increasing concern with nutrition.

Putting the usage, image, and social trend studies together, managers at Minute Maid thought they saw an opportunity. The movement toward natural foods suggested that consumers would like to drink nutritious juices in refreshment contexts. However, there were no juices that scored well on both nutrition *and* refreshment. Somebody suggested that such a product might be created by blending juices.

Thus the company decided to blend five citrus juices: orange, tangerine, grapefruit, lemon, and lime. Orange and tangerine would make the drink delicious; orange and grapefruit would make it nutritious; and lemon and lime would make it refreshing.

Of course, consumers might also perceive that orange and lemon would combine to make the beverage taste bad, tangerine and lime would combine to make it unhealthy, and the five juices together would generally make an awful mess. To test this possibility, Minute Maid commissioned a series of focus groups for concept-testing purposes. These focus groups showed favorable reactions to the idea.

Next, product developers concocted various blends of the five juices. These blends were evaluated in a series of taste tests by employees who took time off from work to participate. Five blends made the finals; then, in taste tests among these five, one blend took 80 percent of the vote.

The winning formula was blended in larger batches for an in-home product test. Several hundred grocery shoppers were recruited to take the product into their homes for two weeks and use it. At the time of recruitment, 60 percent of the shoppers said they thought they would buy the product, as described to them, if it were available in stores. After they used the product for two weeks, this figure rose to 80 percent.

These figures were excellent compared with those of previous products tested, so the company decided to take the product to a full-scale test market. Before doing so, however, it commissioned some additional work. Early in the process, even before concept testing, researchers had checked market size information for the overall juice market and had determined that the new product could meet the company's sales volume requirements if it achieved even a small share of this market. Now that additional data on consumer reactions were available, the researchers developed more refined estimates of the product's sales potential.

Also, researchers began testing names for the new product. The product was conceived as a frozen juice product. Management decided, without research, not to create a new brand name and to place the product under the company's Snow Crop brand rather than the Minute Maid brand. This decision was based on a fear that a product failure would damage the valuable Minute Maid name, plus a feeling that the Snow Crop brand needed more market presence to be effective.

However, the product needed more than the Snow Crop name alone. A testing company specializing in names was engaged to generate and test a list of possible names for the product.

Testing involved checks to make sure the company could legally use each name, as well as consumer focus groups to measure perceptions of each name. Among the names tested, 5 Alive! was selected as conveying the concept of a refreshing blend of five citrus juices. (Subsequently, the Snow Crop name was dropped and the name became just 5 Alive!.)

5 Alive! entered test markets in two locations. Like most test markets, these markets were chosen because their populations were representative of the nation and they were distinct media markets for advertising purposes (as opposed to a place like Princeton, New Jersey, where television ads for a test product would have to be placed on both New York and Philadelphia stations at tremendous expense and with premature exposure of the product to millions of people). Another factor in test market selection is the presence of a large consumer panel, so that panel data are available. This allows the manufacturer to track trial and repurchase of the product among participating households.

Minute Maid bought distribution audit data for these test markets to track distribution of the new product. The company also commissioned surveys to measure awareness, trial, and repeat buying of the new product. A bad result on any of these would have helped diagnose the reasons if the test market results were discouraging.

Fortunately for the company, the results from the test markets were encouraging, and the product proceeded to a national launch. It has remained in the juice market ever since.

Marketing Research Tools 5.5 summarizes the research questions that were considered in the development and launch of 5 Alive! and the sources used to answer these questions.

MARKETING RESEARCH TOOLS

5.5

RESEARCH USED TO DEVELOP AND LAUNCH 5 ALIVE! JUICE

Research Question	Information Source
Usage and perceptions of existing beverages	Custom surveys (special projects)
Social trends	Syndicated surveys
Potential market size	Syndicated sales data
Product concept testing	Focus groups
Product formulation	Taste experiments with employees
Consumer acceptance of the formulated product	In-home product trials
Ability to sell the product successfully	Test marketing

Summary

This chapter discussed the information sources typically used to answer common marketing questions. The following points were covered:

1. What data sources are typically used to answer questions related to customer analysis?

Information about the size of the market or the market growth rate might be obtained from a syndicated data service, government publications, trade association publications, or other secondary sources. Information about the characteristics of buyers and their habits might be obtained from salespeople's reports (for an industrial product) or from buyer surveys, syndicated services, or focus groups.

2. What data sources are typically used to answer questions related to competitive analysis?

Information about market share can be obtained from syndicated sources, trade associations, investment analysts, or buyer surveys. Information for sales forecasts can be obtained from historical sales data (for short-run forecasts); from secondary or syndicated data (for long-run forecasts); or from government publications, trade associations, and other secondary sources (for a new business). Buyer awareness and perceptions can be measured with survey data. Repurchase rates can be measured with data from salespeople's reports (for an industrial product) or from syndicated panel data or buyer surveys. Customer satisfaction can be measured with surveys or syndicated data. Information on competitors' strengths and weaknesses can be obtained from published sources, vendors, and the trade press.

3. What data sources are typically used to answer questions related to operational analysis?

You can determine the effectiveness of a company's distribution by using data from a syndicated distribution audit or secondary and accounting information. You can determine the effectiveness of advertising by using surveys to track brand awareness, by conducting tests, or by analyzing sales and advertising expense records. You can determine the effectiveness of sales promotions and pricing by analyzing sales records or using the information available from consumer panels. You can determine how customers would respond to possible product changes by means of surveys, focus groups, or experiments. You can test prototype products by similar means.

4. What data sources are typically used to answer questions related to environmental analysis?

You can track changes in the technological, social, economic, and regulatory environment of a market by using information from trade associations, articles in the trade press, or syndicated reports.

Suggested Additional Readings

As with the previous chapter, this chapter is an overview of specific methods that are covered in the coming chapters. Additional readings for any technique will be found at the end of the chapter covering it.

Discussion Questions

1. How would you go about testing a new product?

2. Pepperidge Farm, Inc. has an idea to add a new diamond-shaped chocolate cookie with hazelnuts to its product line to maintain its market share. What research should be done first?

3. What is a "Beta test"?

4. What are the three steps used to estimate potential market size? Specify the type of data you would use in each step?

5. What is the advantage of using panel data to measure consumers' reactions to product-related changes?

6. You are the new assistant brand manager for a car wax product that is sold to consumers through retail establishments. Your boss asks you to assess the distribution effectiveness of this product. How might you do this?

7. How would you assess the rate of market growth for coffee?

8. What are typical questions that market research is used to answer?

Marketing Research Challenge

Using sources available to you, select a product or service and answer as many of the following questions as you can. Document the sources of your answers.

1. What is the size of the total market in dollars and number of customers?

2. Who are the customers? What are their characteristics, media habits, and so on?

3. Where is the product or service purchased or obtained?

4. How is the product or service used?

5. Are there any distinct market segments?

6. Discuss any additional sources of information that you are aware of that you could not obtain because the data are syndicated or proprietary.

Internet Exercise

"Starch scores" are used to test the effectiveness of magazine advertisements in attracting readers. Visit the Roper Starch site (http://www.roper.com/survey/index.htm) to learn about this research procedure. Take the five question quiz and see if you can guess the Starch readership scores of various ads. Roper will send you the answers via e-mail in a few days.

References

Bass, F. M. (1969). "A New Product Growth Model for Consumer Durables." *Management Science* 15 (January), pp. 215–217.

Urban, Glen L., and John R. Hauser (1980). *Design and Marketing of New Products*. (Englewood Cliffs, N.J.: Prentice Hall.)

PART

Sources of Market Research Data

Chapters 4 and 5 gave an introduction to marketing research sources and how they are used. The next four chapters describe these sources in enough detail so that you will actually be able to use them, or to evaluate someone else's use of them.

Chapter 6 starts with available secondary sources, because in the normal flow of research activities it is useful to determine what is already known before rushing out to reinvent the wheel. The chapter discusses, in detail, how to access library and nonlibrary sources of secondary information, including computerized databases, and then describes how to evaluate the quality of secondary sources. The chapter ends with a discussion and examples of syndicated services.

Sources of primary data are described in Chapters 7, 8, and 9. The three major sources of primary data are (1) surveys, (2) depth interviews and focus groups, and (3) experiments. Chapter 7 begins with a discussion of surveys: the advantages and disadvantages of different survey methods, appropriate uses for each method, guidelines for effective interviewing, and how to manage a survey.

Chapter 8 discusses focus groups and depth interviews, which provide richer information than surveys but with smaller, less representative samples. Methods for conducting them are described, as are the strengths, weaknesses, and appropriate uses of these procedures.

Chapter 9 examines the use of experiments in market research. After a series of examples to demonstrate the many forms that experiments can take, the logic of experimentation and the use of control groups to ensure valid results are illustrated. The advantages of field versus laboratory experiments are given, and various issues in experimental design are introduced. An appendix to Chapter 9 discusses conjoint analysis, a widely used market research method that is a special type of experiment.

Sample Student Project

Since Apple was primarily interested in university student use of computers, the students in the class searched for information about how students at other universities used computers and how they evaluated Apple computers and IBM-compatibles. In addition to the published sources, students were able to locate mentions of surveys that had been done at other campuses, and in several cases they obtained copies or summaries of these studies. An excerpt of one of the team's reports is given.

Student Ownership of Computers

A comprehensive study done on computer use in education was performed by the University of Southern California.[1] The study covered three years: 1990, 1991, and 1992, encompassed all types of colleges, and contained data on student ownership of computers. The colleges surveyed were grouped in five categories: public universities, private universities, four-year public colleges, four-year private colleges, and community colleges. The following graph, labeled "Student Ownership of Computers," presents some of the results of this study. As we can see, the percentage of students who "have or own" computers on American campuses has increased steadily over the periods surveyed, from 15.8 percent in 1990 to 20.5 percent in 1992. Another notable observation is that computer

ownership among college students increased for all five types of postsecondary educational institutions.

Student Ownership Trends

The next figure, labeled "Computer Use Trends by Students," shows the trends in computer usage by graduate and undergraduate students. The graph shows computer use in the home for both schoolwork and nonschoolwork uses. 1984 data were given only in the aggregate usage and were scaled by the proportions to represent graduates and undergraduates—the proportion of usage by graduates and undergraduates is a relatively constant percentage of the total usage. The 1999 figure is purely a graphical extrapolation of the trends in computer usage presented here. From the graph we can infer that present ownership percentage is around 50 percent. With the limitations of the data considered, there appears to be considerable potential for market penetration.

[1]*Campus Computing 1992—the EDUCOM–USC Survey of Desktop Computing in Higher Education*, Los Angeles: The James Irvine Foundation Center for Scholarly Technology.

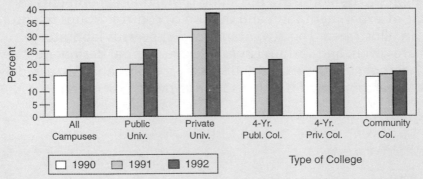

Student Ownership of Computers

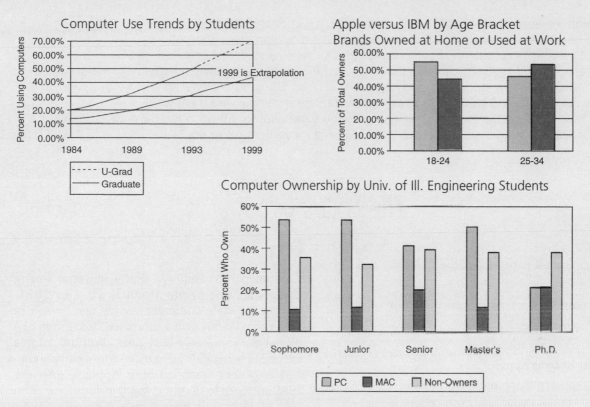

Computer Use Trends by Students

Apple versus IBM by Age Bracket
Brands Owned at Home or Used at Work

Computer Ownership by Univ. of Ill. Engineering Students

Ownership by Brand

The figure above, "Apple versus IBM by Age Bracket, Brands Owned at Home or Used at Work," displays data from Simmons Market Research that illustrates the brand penetration of Apple in the relevant age categories for graduate and undergraduate students. Although this graph is for the general U.S. population, it indicates that in these age categories, Apple brand commands over 40 percent "usage or ownership."

The University of Illinois Engineering Student survey shows a substantially different ownership pattern. Apple brand computers command a far smaller percentage of the student engineering population. An estimate of overall Apple ownership within the engineering student population at the University of Illinois is that approximately 15 percent of all engineering students own Apple brand computers. See graph labeled "Computer Ownership by Univ. of Ill. Engineering Students."

As the graph shows, 64 percent of sophomores, 66 percent of juniors, and 60 percent of seniors own computers. An interesting result of this study is the lower percentage of computer owners among graduate engineering students. This may be due to increased access of graduate students to university computers, which precludes the need to purchase a computer for studies.

Summary

A key point about computer use by students is that student computer use does not mirror that of the general population. Students are a distinct group of users whose ownership patterns, usage patterns, and frequency of use are substantially different from the general population within the same age groups. Based on the available data, we estimate that approximately 50 percent of all students own a computer. Between 15 and 40 percent of student computer owners own Apple computers.

Uses of computers differ by the students' year in school, yet usage for word processing is uniformly high by all groups. Students use computers far more frequently than the general public, and we would expect them to be a far more demanding market segment than the overall population.

Although the analysis of secondary data was useful, it was clear that a new survey would need to be done at the university to answer the most important questions raised by Apple. In considering how to design their survey, the students consulted Chapter 7. Several of the groups decided to conduct focus groups to obtain a better understanding of how students thought about computers. Using the material in Chapter 8, they invited students to a focus group facility on campus, fed them with pizza, tape-recorded the focus groups, and prepared summaries for others in the class and for Apple management. A summary of one of the focus groups is given.

The Focus Group

The focus group was targeted toward eliciting responses from a panel about the following areas of interest:

- Computer ownership and satisfaction
- Purchase decision variables
- Buyer motivation
- IBM versus Apple
- Computer shopping:
  - Micro Computer Order Center
  - Shopping habits

This report details the results of the focus group conducted October 6, 1995, at 12:00 P.M. at the Survey Research Laboratory of the University of Illinois.

Focus Group Composition

Eleven participants attended the focus group session, in response to posters placed around the University of Illinois campus that advertised free pizza and $6.00 for anyone who would participate in a focus group on computer use. The following table indicates the composition of the focus group:

Number	Major
2	Master's of Business Administration
1	Graduate Advertising major
1	Undergraduate History major
2	Undergraduate Sociology majors
1	Doctoral student in French
1	Finance/Accounting major
1	Undergraduate Liberal Arts major
2	Undergraduate Engineering majors

Computer Ownership

Computer ownership was almost universal among the group and predominantly IBM or IBM-compatible-style computers—only one person in the group did not own a computer. The group displayed the commonly held contention that people are intensely brand-loyal to their style of computer—Apple owners defended their Apple against the IBM-compatible users during the discussion. The identified brands were Apple, Gateway, Zeos, Leading Edge, Compaq, and a "home built" model.

Uses for Computers

The group had limited uses for computers, but they used them intensely for those applications. The uses described by the participants are listed:

Use	Number of Users
Word processing	All participants
E-mail	All participants
Internet	All participants
Excel spreadsheets	1/2 participants
Computer-aided design	Engineers

Buyer Motivation to Purchase a Computer

Buyer motivations for purchasing computers seemed centered on convenience—typical response was "The computer labs are not open all night, I live off campus, and need access all night long." Other responses included that they wanted Internet or e-mail access at home, they needed it for work, or "It was a great price—I just couldn't resist." In all, the respondents seemed to feel that having a computer at home was rather essential for schoolwork.

Purchase Decision Variables

Information on the Purchase

The first source for information on where to buy a computer was friends and associates. This source was mentioned by all participants. In particular, some of the participants had sought out people responsible for assembling or maintaining university computer systems for advice on their personal purchase. Examples given were professors and computer lab personnel. Computer magazines, such as PC magazine, were also mentioned, as well as the influence of knowledgeable salespeople. Computer advertisements "didn't tell you anything" and were viewed to be misleading.

Product Purchase Factors

Factors considered in the purchase decision were primarily service oriented—it was a very important variable to the whole group, and the general consensus was that they were willing to pay more for good, reliable service. Close behind this was the reliability and accuracy of technical support. The participants indicated that brand name was important, as long as it had a reputation for good service, and had a good warranty. Price was not so much a factor for these participants—"we'll pay extra for good service." Other variables mentioned were the financing plan available and the style, size, and weight of the machine.

Of the hardware features, the most important seemed to be the expandability of the machine—did it have extra slots and the capability to be upgraded to keep the machine current with technology. Other important features, in order of importance, were:

- Does it have an internal modem
- Size and speed of the memory
- Size of the hard drives
- Speed of the processor
- The available software "bundle"

The software bundle sparked some controversy, for many felt that they should be able to "customize" their software bundle and not be forced to accept that which the manufacturer offered preloaded on the machine.

Where They Shop

The bulk of the group like the major discount retailers the best. Two of the participants (one Apple owner and one other owner) had shopped at the Micro Computer Order Center. The other Apple owner in the group had purchased his Apple from mail order.

Likes and Dislikes—Apple Versus IBM Compatible

The following table details the likes and dislikes of the IBM-compatible owners versus the likes and dislikes of the Apple owners.

IBM-Compatible Owners

Likes	Dislikes
Ease of use	Memory
Price	Microsoft

Apple Owners

Likes	Dislikes
Ease of use	Software availability
Software bundle	Lack of interoperability with IBM
	Lack of choice in hardware

The selection decision seemed to be based on the perception that an IBM clone is cheaper for the same features (megabytes, megahertz) than the Apple—Apple is viewed as the "pricey" machine. Also, some users are precluded from using an Apple machine because the engineering software they need is not available for Apple. Finally, the perception was that IBM architecture is the "industry standard," although most agreed that the Apple brand is easier to use.

The Micro Computer Order Center (MCOC)

Sixty percent of the focus group had used MCOC, although there were some negative comments about the experience. In particular, the Apple buyer was just handed some forms; in contrast, the IBM buyer received "very good service." None of the users of the center liked the three-day wait, or the fact that they had to pick up their goods at central stores. In general, the observation was that "[the] prices are good, but you can find better."

Issue Areas—The "Hot Buttons"

The two areas of discussion that raised voices in the group were the issues of promotions and Microsoft. Promotions were viewed almost universally as a way to "cheat the customer," or to sell them substandard goods by hiding the defect (such as too little memory). In the end, if you buy on promotion, the group felt it would cost you more to upgrade the machine. This was appreciated as a means to get into computer ownership without having to pay the full price for what you would eventually need.

Microsoft corporation was despised by most members of the group. They articulated the Microsoft strategy as "design low-quality products, and then charge you for the upgrades to fix the bugs." Microsoft marketing was viewed as trying to dominate the computer industry, was described as "heavy handed," and in general the group felt that Microsoft preyed on the consumer.

6

Secondary and Syndicated Data

◨ OBJECTIVES

After reading this chapter, you should be able to answer the following questions:

❶ How is secondary information located in a library?

❷ How is secondary information located outside a library?

❸ How is secondary information located on the Internet?

❹ How is secondary information evaluated?

❺ How are secondary and syndicated information used within a marketing information system?

Secondary information was discussed in Chapter 4, and some of its applications were discussed in Chapter 5. This chapter provides more detail about how to locate and evaluate secondary data. It discusses three general sources of secondary information: (1) library sources, (2) nonlibrary sources, and (3) the Internet. After these sources are reviewed, there is a discussion of how to evaluate secondary information.

Most of the chapter is written as if secondary information is to be used in the context of "special project" research. However, secondary data also play an important role in marketing information systems. Therefore, following the discussion of how to locate and evaluate secondary information, issues in using secondary data within the MKIS are discussed. This final portion of the chapter includes some discussion of syndicated data as a special category of secondary information and an example of a syndicated report.

Syndicated data are usually bought new from commercial services: however, syndicated data are similar to secondary data in that a user cannot control the research procedures (because an independent research firm creates the data for many users) and the motive for using these data is cost savings. Syndicated data are an important component of the marketing information systems of most large companies.

Locating Secondary Information in Libraries

The key to successful library research is recognizing how to locate the information needed. Different types of information, from different sources, are accessed in different ways.

In Chapter 4, library sources were separated into four categories: books, periodicals, U.S. government documents, and computerized databases. These information sources are accessed in different ways. Books are accessed through the library's catalog. **Periodicals**—journals, magazines, newspapers, newsletters, and other serial publications—are accessed through various indexes and abstracting services. Government documents are accessed through other specialized indexes. Computerized databases and other sources of information such as company annual reports are often not listed with other library holdings. This information may be found by consulting special business libraries, asking librarians for advice, and browsing the Internet (Crispell, 1989; Daniells, 1985).

To illustrate the principal access routes for library sources, let's consider seven types of secondary information that can be found in libraries and are relevant to market research:

- Industry statistics
- Nonstatistical background on an industry

- Information on specific companies
- Estimates of sales potentials of various geographic territories
- Media cost and coverage information
- Information on marketing research methods
- Academic marketing research on some topic

Industry Statistics

Industry statistics such as market size, market growth rates, and key expense ratios might be found in government documents or materials from private sources.

Government Documents

U.S. government statistics are found through the ***American Statistics Index (ASI)***, which provides a guide to federal statistical sources. The *ASI* is published in two volumes—an index volume and an abstracts volume. You can use it as follows:

1. Start with the index volume. This volume is organized by subject. Look up subject headings that might be appropriate for your purposes. If you are interested in statistics on restaurants, for example, you might try headings such as restaurants, eating establishments, food, and so on. It is important to try a variety of headings unless you immediately hit exactly what you want.

2. Look under the various subject headings for items with promising titles. Each item ends with an abstract number. Copy this number for promising items.

3. Go to the abstracts volume. Find the abstract numbers that you copied, and read the abstracts. If an abstract looks good, look in the title section of the abstract for a number with a small empty circle in front of it. This is the Superintendent of Documents (SuDoc) number, by which U.S. government publications are organized and stored, just as books are stored by Dewey decimal number or Library of Congress number.

4. Use the SuDoc number to find the shelf location of the publication containing the statistical data you need. Some documents may be in microfiche form and stored in a different location from the printed documents. Some data may be on CD-ROM or diskettes. There is a strong trend for federal agencies to make their data available for use on computers.

The library may not have the publication needed. Most libraries at large universities and in large cities carry a wide variety of government statistical publications; however, if the publication needed is not there, a librarian can help locate it elsewhere.

Private Sources

Statistics from private sources are accessed through the ***Statistical Reference Index (SRI)***. The *SRI* works exactly the same way as the *American Statistics Index*. Look under possible subject headings in the index volume to find promising titles, copy the abstract number, then look in the abstracts volume for the description and location of the data.

Author Tips

If your library doesn't take a publication, your librarian may be able to get it for you through interlibrary loan. If not, you can check a periodicals directory for the name, address, and telephone number of the publisher, call the publisher to inquire whether the item you want is available as a back issue, and order it if so. This may seem time consuming and costly, but it beats creating data from scratch.

The big difference, of course, is that the *SRI* is not used for government documents. Instead, it refers to articles in sources such as trade magazines or industry yearbooks published by trade associations. A librarian can provide the list of periodicals that a library receives. It will indicate whether the library takes a specific publication and, if so, where it is stored.

Marketing Research Tools 6.1 summarizes how to use the *ASI* and *SRI* indexes to locate statistical information on an industry.

Other Sources

In addition to the *ASI* and *SRI* indexes, there are some sources that can routinely be checked for industry statistics:

- **U.S. Industrial Outlook,** published by the U.S. Department of Commerce, provides statistical data for the current year plus economic projections for the next five years for about 350 industries. Analyses are given for the current situation, the short-term outlook, and long-term prospects.

- **Standard & Poor's Industry Surveys** contain verbal discussions of business prospects for various industries and statistical data on leading competitors.

- **Predicasts Basebook** contains historical statistics on industries, such as historical sales data. **Predicasts Forecasts** contains future projections of industry statistics.

Managers and researchers often find financial and operating ratios useful. **Financial ratios** are used to evaluate the financial health and performance of a business; they include figures such as net profit margin (the ratio of net profit to total sales), return on assets (the ratio of net profit to assets), and financial leverage (the ratio of liabilities to net worth). **Operating ratios** are used to evaluate a business's operating performance; they include figures such as inventory turnover (the ratio of sales to inventory) or expense ratios (the ratio of some expense category to sales). Financial and operating ratios give managers information about performance standards for their industry and whether or not their firm is competitive. This type of information is available from **Robert Morris Associates' Annual Statement Studies, Dun & Bradstreet's Industry Norms and Key Business Ratios, Leo Troy's Almanac of Business and Industrial Financial Ratios,** and **Financial Studies of the Small Business.**

Nonstatistical Background on an Industry

Nonstatistical background is often useful when researching an industry. This includes material such as general trends in the industry, current activities of leading competitors, key success factors, personnel moves, and so on.

Some of this information, such as guidelines on how to start a business in the industry and key success factors, may be available in books. However, most of this information will be found in trade journals devoted to the industry. A principal source for locating this material is the **Predicasts F & S Index.**

HOW TO FIND STATISTICAL INFORMATION ON AN INDUSTRY

To Find	Do This
Government statistics	1. Use the *American Statistics Index (ASI)*.
	2. In the index volume, check appropriate subject headings to find promising items.
	3. Check the abstracts volume for descriptions and SuDoc numbers on these items.
	4. Use SuDoc numbers to find items in the library.
Private statistics	1. Use the *Statistical Reference Index (SRI)*.
	2. In the index volume, check appropriate subject headings to find promising items.
	3. Check the abstracts volume for descriptions and locations on these items.

The *F & S Index* is a key source for marketing research because it has excellent coverage of trade magazines. *The Wall Street Journal Index* may also be of use. Other well-known periodicals indexes, such as the *Reader's Guide to Periodical Literature* and the *Business Periodicals Index*, cover magazines written for a broader audience and usually do not add to the information found through the *F & S Index*.

There are two sections in the *F & S Index*. One section indexes articles by company name. If you are doing research on IBM, for example, you can look up "IBM" and get references to articles that relate to the company. The other section of the *F & S Index*, which is of more use in industry analysis, indexes articles according to Standard Industrial Classification (SIC) number. SIC numbers identify categories of manufacturers and distributors.

To find information on an industry with the *F & S Index*:

1. Check the SIC directory in the front of the *F & S Index* to learn the SIC number for the industry or product of interest to you. If this directory leaves you uncertain about the appropriate number, ask your librarian for the *SIC Manual,* which gives specific examples of the products covered by each number.

2. Look under the appropriate number in the SIC section of the *F & S Index* to identify potentially interesting articles.

Critical Thinking Skills

Where are the *American Statistics Index* and the *Statistical Reference Index* kept in your library? Use these indexes, or any other source listed here, to estimate the current market size for (a) automobiles, (b) bottled water, (c) diesel fuel, and (d) industrial ball valves. Do you observe differences across products in the availability of statistical information?

3. The magazines in which those articles appear will be listed in abbreviated form. Check the front of the *F & S Index* for the list of publications indicated by each abbreviation, then start looking for the magazines you need.

Critical Thinking Skills

Use the *F & S Index* or other sources to locate nonstatistical information on (a) automobiles, (b) bottled water, (c) diesel fuel, and (d) industrial ball valves. Is it easier to get information about some industries than about others?

Marketing Research Tools 6.2 summarizes how to use the *F & S Index* to find nonstatistical information on an industry. A search of the *F & S Index* may not identify every possible article that might be useful, and it might be helpful to do some extra browsing through trade journals for information. The *F & S Index* is useful even for this purpose, because the best magazines to browse are those that have good articles listed in the index.

Also, since business is increasingly international in scope, foreign periodicals may also be useful (though most libraries will probably not subscribe to international trade publications). There is an *F & S International Index,* which is helpful in this regard. Also, *Ulrich's International Periodical Directory* or the *Standard Periodical Directory* will help identify relevant publications.

Marketing Research Tools 6.3 summarizes the various library sources that can be used to find information on an industry.

Information on Specific Companies

We've already mentioned that the *F & S Index* has a section organized by company name that indicates articles about a company that have appeared in the business press. It is also wise to check the *F & S Index* section organized by SIC number, because useful information about a company may appear in an article that is focused more on the industry than on the company. *The Wall Street Journal Index* also has a section organized by company names that may be useful to you.

You might want financial data on a company, possibly to assess its potential strength as a competitor. If the company is based in the United States and publicly held, the best source of financial information is the company's annual report. Many university business libraries maintain extensive collections of annual reports, either in printed form or on microfiche. Also, annual report data are summarized on widely available computerized databases, such as the *Compact Disclosure* system.

Annual reports are the best source of financial data because they are predictable: they come out every year, and they follow standard accounting formats for reporting sales and income. However, they may gloss over a company's problems or overestimate its opportunities. *Corporate and Industry Research Reports* presents a less biased picture. This source consists of reports on industries and companies prepared by stockbrokerage companies to guide investment decisions. Most university business libraries carry these reports on microfiche, with a printed index to the reports. Stockbrokers can also be contacted to learn whether their companies have research reports on a particular company.

If information about a company is not readily available, it may be for any of various reasons. First, the company may be a subsidiary of a larger company and not listed on its own. Second, the company may be privately owned. Third, the company may be foreign.

To learn whether the company is a subsidiary of another company, check the *Directory of Corporate Affiliations or Who Owns*

Critical Thinking Skills

Do you think it would be easier to find information on General Motors or Toyota? General Motors or Ozarka Water? Why?

MARKETING RESEARCH TOOLS

6.2

HOW TO FIND NONSTATISTICAL INFORMATION ON AN INDUSTRY

To use the *Predicasts F & S Index:*

• Identify the SIC number of interest to you.

• Look under this number in the SIC section of the *F & S Index* to identify the titles of interesting articles.

• Start looking for the magazines you need.

MARKETING RESEARCH TOOLS

6.3

LIBRARY SOURCES OF INDUSTRY INFORMATION

American Statistics Index (ASI)
Dun and Bradstreet Industry Norms
Financial Studies of the Small Business
Leo Troy's Almanac of Business and Industrial Financial Ratios
Predicasts Basebook
Predicasts Forecasts
Predicasts F & S Indexes
Robert Morris Associates' Annual Statement Studies
Standard Periodical Directory
Standard and Poor's Industry Surveys
Statistical Reference Index (SRI)
Ulrich's International Periodical Directory
U.S. Industrial Outlook
The Wall Street Journal Index

Whom. Then, if the company is a subsidiary, use the parent company's name in addition to the subsidiary's name.

To learn whether the company is private, check *Major U.S. Private Companies* or some other business directory such as *Dun and Bradstreet's Million Dollar Directory* or the *Thomas Register of American Manufacturers.* If the company is private, it will be difficult to get library information about it. Instead, talking with people in the industry may provide better information.

Marketing Research Tools 6.4 (see page 132) summarizes the library sources that can be used to find information about specific companies.

Estimates of Sales Potentials of Various Geographic Territories

There are three principal reasons to gather territorial estimates of sales potential. First, an organization might only sell within some limited area, and data on industry sales and sales potential may be needed for that area. Second, territorial data can help define sales force territories with equal potential. Third, there may be a need for location analysis for a potential retail business.

General Estimates of Sales and Sales Potential

Research on territorial sales is, to some extent, a subset of general industry analysis. Sales data for regions, states, counties, or cities might be found in the course of a general industry analysis using the *Statistical Reference Index*, *American Statistics Index*, or *F & S Index*.

Other sources are more specifically directed toward local areas. The **County and City Data Book** provides population and general business activity data for U.S. counties and cities. Its companion volume is the **State and Metropolitan Area Data Book**. **County Business Patterns,** another government publication, provides more specific business data at the county level by SIC code. **Survey of Buying Power,** which is *not* a government publication, contains population, income, and expenditure data for counties and cities. **Dun & Bradstreet's Market Profile Analysis** contains population data at the level of census tracts, which are sections of large cities. All these sources should be available in a library's reference section.

MARKETING RESEARCH TOOLS

6.4

LIBRARY SOURCES OF COMPANY INFORMATION

Company annual reports
Compact Disclosure (database)
Corporate and Industry Research Reports
Directory of Corporate Affiliations or Who Owns Whom
Dun and Bradstreet's Million Dollar Directory
Major U.S. Private Companies
Predicasts F & S Index
Thomas Register of American Manufacturers
The Wall Street Journal Index

To illustrate the kind of information that is available and how it might be used, Exhibit 6.1 (see page 134) shows a page from the *County and City Data Book*. This page contains data for counties in the State of Alabama. Column 161 shows per capita sales in eating and drinking places. This information could be used, along with population data, to estimate the size of the restaurant and bar market in each county. The table also shows that Houston, Madison, and Montgomery Counties have the highest per capita sales in the state, which might make them of special interest to a bar or restaurant chain looking for locations.

Additional information can be found in the various U.S. censuses. The *Census of Population and Housing* is published once every ten years. The *Census of Manufactures, Census of Construction Industries, Census of Wholesale Trade, Census of Retail Trade, Census of Service Industries, Census of Agriculture,* and *Census of Governments* are published every five years. We encourage you to look at these publications in your library to see the volume of information they provide. Census data become outdated in rapidly growing areas and rapidly changing industries, but they remain useful elsewhere. Heavy users of census data can receive it directly from the government on CD-ROM disks (Burka, 1992; Riche, 1990). See Figure 6.1.

(cont. on p. 136)

Author Tips

If the industry you are studying is taxed at the state level, you may be able to obtain state, county, and city sales data from the state's taxing authorities. This applies to retail businesses in states with sales taxes and to sales of gasoline, cigarettes, and alcohol.

Figure 6.1 Homepage for the U.S. Census Bureau (http://www.census.gov)

EXHIBIT 6.1

Excerpt from County and City Data Book

Retail trade establishments with payroll, 1982

County	Number	Total (Mil. dol.)	Per capita[1] (Dollars)				Paid employees[2]	Annual payroll (Mil. dol.)
			General merchandise group stores	Food stores	Apparel and accessory stores	Eating and drinking places		
	156	157	158	159	160	161	162	163
UNITED STATES	1 330 316	1 039 028.7	517	1 037	245	438	14 467 813	123 618.7
ALABAMA	20 581	13 927.5	419	910	212	274	192 402	1 563.6
Autauga	133	89.4	245	756	123	212	1 128	8.6
Baldwin	552	312.0	315	1 128	147	333	4 371	33.6
Barbour	143	59.6	182	829	149	236	940	7.1
Bibb	64	27.9	152	659	89	75	371	3.1
Blount	132	65.4	181	526	79	100	761	6.2
Bullock	56	21.0	D	605	166	77	272	2.0
Butler	137	66.5	248	871	159	255	982	7.0
Calhoun	566	411.7	436	799	226	258	5 603	45.8
Chambers	165	98.3	108	809	55	149	1 213	9.7
Cherokee	100	35.0	88	462	109	110	479	3.4
Chilton	162	80.0	238	810	102	124	1 006	8.2
Choctaw	99	30.1	77	748	56	239	541	3.3
Clarke	198	96.5	323	1 118	141	203	1 304	10.1
Clay	70	28.7	142	748	53	90	382	2.8
Cleburne	48	14.6	112	297	15	82	210	1.4
Coffee	258	143.1	369	801	195	204	1 949	14.7
Colbert	330	202.9	365	839	153	330	2 945	21.6
Conecuh	71	33.4	D	596	65	122	372	2.9
Coosa	20	3.9	–	114	–	9	53	.4
Covington	253	123.2	298	1 020	174	165	1 648	13.1
Crenshaw	67	23.8	83	661	31	51	313	2.4
Cullman	312	198.4	278	899	185	192	2 418	19.2
Dale	214	109.7	214	624	63	192	1 664	11.6
Dallas	298	168.3	409	806	167	213	2 667	20.3
De Kalb	263	123.8	181	639	117	159	1 579	13.2
Elmore	177	89.0	D	783	63	84	1 075	8.6
Escambia	257	130.9	336	811	239	212	1 802	14.2
Elowah	566	380.9	506	1 076	232	321	5 349	42.8
Fayette	90	47.7	228	849	130	119	598	4.9

County								
Franklin	163	90.3	306	759	103	146	1 052	8.2
Geneva	110	47.0	193	836	75	28	589	4.3
Greene	54	26.2	163	877	47	116	311	2.1
Hale	60	26.4	67	732	47	40	308	2.6
Henry	75	36.7	D	872	D	94	473	3.9
Houston	608	431.7	318	1 146	331	424	5 984	48.7
Jackson	222	133.0	264	700	106	132	1 717	13.6
Jefferson	3 546	3 033.9	512	1 059	393	382	42 104	354.6
Lamar	82	35.0	73	787	205	59	417	3.4
Lauderdale	458	307.3	704	851	278	267	4 597	35.6
Lawrence	85	45.0	154	466	61	91	507	3.7
Lee	386	292.6	548	938	133	354	4 580	32.7
Limestone	207	121.9	233	779	157	215	1 658	13.8
Lowndes	45	18.5	D	477	D	28	185	1.5
Macon	87	40.8	D	540	90	73	541	3.8
Madison	1 051	872.9	617	893	269	428	12 661	105.4
Marengo	135	74.6	305	929	135	141	1 016	8.5
Marion	148	67.3	310	778	179	103	899	6.4
Marshall	407	265.1	522	967	264	249	3 368	25.8
Mobile	1 949	1 599.5	582	1 079	173	357	21 438	184.5
Monroe	106	58.6	257	885	93	149	772	6.4
Montgomery	1 103	949.0	496	933	287	406	13 220	113.7
Morgan	550	359.7		950	243	277	5 055	41.8
Perry	61	19.7	82	431	84	41	366	2.3
Pickens	105	34.6	71	571	32	39	464	3.7
Pike	173	86.6	292	787	193	320	1 363	9.9
Randolph	99	42.2	171	814	129	77	574	4.3
Russell	211	104.7	269	890	73	187	1 548	11.1
St. Clair	147	81.7	122	583	43	94	749	6.3
Shelby	266	150.7	134	858	64	157	2 065	16.3
Sumter	93	33.4	288	790	D	139	542	3.6
Talladega	398	219.3	325	971	187	191	3 070	24.0
Tallapoosa	202	100.3	226	749	199	167	1 502	11.6
Tuscaloosa	768	565.0	559	1 098	259	349	8 543	68.9
Walker	364	232.2	275	857	245	201	2 890	24.6
Washington	53	26.0	D	358	22	28	240	1.9
Wilcox	77	26.1	120	681	D	64	313	2.4
Winston	124	56.3	354	929	81	152	726	5.7

[1] Based on resident population estimated as of July 1, 1982.
[2] For pay period including March 12, 1982.

Critical Thinking Skills

chain of fast-food restaurants is thinking about expanding to your town. It wants to know the total number of locations the town might support, as well as the neighborhood population and vehicular traffic at specific potential sites. What information sources would you use to get this information?

Analysis for Purposes of Sales Territory Definition

Geographic analysis for purposes of sales territory definition might use any of the sources listed in the preceding paragraphs. Also, if an organization sells to businesses, a business directory can be used to locate and count potential customers. Local analysis can be done from the Yellow Pages, and regional or national analysis can be done from specialized directories that cover various industries and/or regions. If a library does not have an appropriate directory, contact the relevant trade association (how to locate trade associations is discussed later in this chapter).

Retail Location Analysis

Retail location analysis presents special problems in measuring territory potentials because it requires extremely detailed geographic data. If a choice is to be made between possible locations in a large city, countywide or even citywide population data are of little value. What is needed is data for very small geographic areas, such as census tracts (usually covering about 4,000 people) or even city blocks.

These data can be found in the *Census of Population and Housing* or local updates of the census. Also, the local chamber of commerce and/or the marketing research office at the local power company may be able to help find reliable local updates of census data.

In a retail location analysis, it is also important to know how much traffic flows past the site. If the primary concern is pedestrian traffic, as with locations within shopping malls or on crowded downtown streets, a count will probably have to be made. If the primary concern is vehicular traffic, though, information on traffic flow can be found in the city's traffic department. In unincorporated areas, the state's traffic department fulfills the same function.

Various commercial firms "package" population data or other sales potential data to make it easier to use. If a company's research budget is sizable, it may be easier to contact one of these firms than to search for population information in the library.

Marketing Research Tools 6.5 summarizes the library sources that can be used to find information about state or local markets.

Media Cost and Coverage Information

The best source of media cost and coverage information is the various *Standard Rate and Data Service* publications: *SRDS Radio*, *SRDS Spot Television*, *SRDS Magazines*, and so on. These publications provide "rate cards" for various media outlets (what they charge for various sizes and locations of ads), plus some indication of the size and demographic characteristics of their audiences.

It is also possible to get audience analysis data from syndicated services such as Simmons reports (on magazines) or Arbitron or Nielsen reports (on radio and television stations). Of course, if an advertising agency is used, it will provide the desired media information as a client service.

MARKETING RESEARCH TOOLS

6.5

LIBRARY SOURCES OF LOCAL INFORMATION

County and City Data Book
County Business Patterns
Dun and Bradstreet's Market Profile Analysis
State and Metropolitan Area Data Book
Survey of Buying Power
*U.S. Censuses (Agriculture, Construction Industries, Governments,
     Manufactures, Population and Housing, Retail Trade, Service
     Industries, Wholesale Trade)*

Information on Marketing Research Methods

Books are a good source of "how-to" information on marketing research methods. Sources of information on doing a retail location analysis, doing a marketing survey, and running a focus group discussion can all be found in the subject index in a library's book catalog.

Books are a good source of information on techniques because they allow more thorough explanation of the subject than a magazine article can provide. Also, the length of time it takes to get a book into print is usually not a problem, because "how-to" advice does not change very quickly.

Locating Academic Research

Academic marketing research tackles broad questions about marketing, such as "If people laugh at a commercial, will this translate into positive feelings toward the product?" and "What factors seem to influence companies' choices of distribution arrangements in foreign markets?" Academic research is generally not focused on a particular company or industry and generally does not provide statistical information such as market size, market share, and so on.

The best way to locate academic research that is relevant to marketing research is through *Psychological Abstracts,* which indexes articles from journals that cover psychological issues. This index covers *Journal of Marketing, Journal of Marketing Research, Journal of Consumer Research, Journal of Advertising,* and many others.

To use *Psychological Abstracts,* look in the subject index under various headings that might cover the topic you are studying. The index will give you an abstract number for each article related to a given heading. Find these numbers in the main body of the abstracts to get citations and descriptions for articles of interest.

Other academic indexes that might be useful are *Economic Abstracts* and *Sociological Abstracts.*

The All-Purpose Source

One library source not mentioned so far is **Statistical Abstract of the United States.** This volume, published annually by the U.S. Census Bureau, contains a wide variety of current statistics and trend information drawn from government sources and from the most reliable commercial and academic sources. Here are some of its sections:

- *Vital Statistics, Health, and Nutrition.* These sections provide information on births, deaths, marriages and divorces, health expenditures, availability and utilization of medical professionals and facilities, and consumption of foods and beverages. These sections have marketing applications from cradle to grave, from baby food to casket manufacturers.

- *Education.* This section has statistics on the number of schools and students in various places, as well as expenditures for elementary, secondary, and postsecondary education. These data are used by textbook publishers and other suppliers of school equipment.

- *Climate.* This section has data on temperature, precipitation, and relative humidity. These data have application to sales of soft drinks and air conditioners, locations for ski resorts, and so on.

- *Recreation and Travel.* This section reports levels of book reading, sales of records, tapes, and CDs, sales of household camera and video equipment, and attendance at various sporting events.

Statistical Abstract is so inexpensive and useful that any marketing researcher will want to have a copy. It is seldom the last word on a subject, but it is often a fast, easy way to start finding information on a business opportunity.

Computerized Databases

The past decade has seen an explosion in the availability of computerized databases. At the time this book is being written, there are about 4,500 online databases available, of which several hundred have marketing research applications. In addition, many databases are available on CD-ROM disk.

Many of these computerized information sources are duplicates of databases available in print form—for example, the *F & S Index* is now available in both print and computerized form. The guidelines given for finding library information remain valid because the information sources remain the same, even though the access medium changes from printed volumes to computer terminals. Computerized information searches can be expensive because of access and time charges, but they are very cost effective if the service being used has helpful information.

Author Tips

In our experience, the most useful sources for learning about information available through computerized search are two directories published by Cuadra/Elsevier: *Directory of Online Databases* and *Directory of Portable Databases* (for CD-ROM files). These directories contain enough information about the contents of various information services to allow you to decide whether to try a service.

A Word of Advice

We have pretty well covered the main access routes for library information, but we have one last word of advice: ask the librarian for help! A good research librarian can help save time on most searches.

Locating Secondary Information Outside Libraries

Nonlibrary sources of secondary information include trade associations, government sources, the media, and local sources such as utilities and chambers of commerce. Here is how to find information from these sources.

Trade Associations

Trade associations may be helpful in two ways. First, many trade associations gather and publish statistical information on their industries, especially data on the costs of doing business. If this information cannot be found through library sources, it may be available directly from the association. Second, trade association officials know a great deal about industry trends and participants. They may be able to provide informal information on the industry and/or names of people who know about the industry.

To identify relevant trade associations:

1. Ask your librarian for the *Encyclopedia of Associations,* which lists all kinds of associations. Specifically, you will need the index volume and the volume devoted to business organizations.

2. Look in the index volume under relevant subject headings. For example, if you are looking for information on vacuum cleaner manufacturers, you might try subject headings such as "Vacuum Cleaners," "Household Appliances," "Electrical Appliances," "Appliances—Electrical," and so on. The index will supply the names of relevant associations and a listing number for each association.

3. Use the listing numbers to find association listings in the main directory. Each listing will give the name of the association, its address, its telephone number, and some idea of what it does.

Critical Thinking Skills

What trade associations might be able to help you with information on the following markets: (a) automobiles, (b) bottled water, (c) diesel fuel, and (d) industrial ball valves? Use the *Encyclopedia of Associations* to find out.

4. Call the associations that seem promising, and ask to speak to someone who might be able to help you.

Trade association people are usually cooperative with research requests. However, don't be too surprised if they tell you that certain information is not available to nonmembers. Unlike libraries, trade associations do not exist to serve the public—they exist to serve their members.

Government Sources

Government sources can provide various types of information that are useful in marketing research projects. For example, state tax collectors can provide sales data (or at least tax data) for taxed industries, and state or local traffic authorities can provide vehicular traffic flows along various streets.

People who work for government agencies often have substantial knowledge about related industries, over and above what is published in statistical reports. Your telephone book should have listings for various local, state, and federal agencies. Decide which agencies might have the information you need and call them. Your initial call may be unsuccessful, but you will be referred, and you will usually find the person you need within three or four calls. Case Study 6.1 describes an example of this process.

Media Companies

Media companies can provide data on the characteristics of their audiences. This information is used to choose media for ad campaigns.

Advertising agencies generally provide this information for their clients. If you don't have an agency but still need media data, do the following:

1. Describe the characteristics of your target customers.

2. Identify the media that might be most appropriate for reaching them.

3. Call the appropriate media companies, ask for the research manager, and ask that person for the necessary information.

As with trade associations, you may be turned down if you are not a potential client.

Local Sources

Various private sources may be able to provide local information for a research project. For example, a local power company may be able to provide current population data for small geographic areas. The local chamber of commerce may also be able to provide population data and may have directories or other statistics on local manufacturers. Information about real estate developments might be obtained from the real estate reporter at a local newspaper.

CASE STUDY 6.1

We were recently asked by a Taiwanese trading company to help it find an American company that could supply them with stainless steel pot bearings, a highly specialized product that is used in the construction of large highway bridges.

Without leaving the office, we looked under "Steel" in the Yellow Pages to identify companies that made or distributed steel products. We called some of them to see if they carried the product or knew who did. However, the product is so specialized that the regular steel companies did not know anything about it.

Next, we tried the state highway department. We called the agency's general number and asked the receptionist to refer us to someone who might be able to tell us the name of a company that makes a product used in bridge-building projects. She referred us to a general manager. He suggested that we try the department's engineering office, because it was responsible for designing highway bridges and might be knowledgeable about the products used in them. He gave us the phone number for the engineering office.

We called that number and repeated our request. We were referred to "Mr. Highway Bridge," the engineer who knew everything there is to know about designing highway bridges. After asking us if we realized that stainless steel pot bearings would be used only in a bridge with unusually long spans, he told us that the product might be made by a company from Ohio, and he gave us the phone number for their regional agent. The regional agent referred us to the home office, which confirmed that the company made the product and could supply it to the Taiwanese buyer.

In total, it took us about twenty minutes to start with blind phone calls and, through referral, find one of the very few companies in the world that make this product.

Locating Secondary Information on the Internet

The **Internet** is growing by leaps and bounds as a source of secondary information in marketing research. It provides access to information about companies and industries, access to a wide variety of statistical data, and access to newsgroups where researchers can post queries and get answers.

For Internet information on a specific company, the first place to look is the company's homepage, if it has one. Internet addresses for these sites are easy to guess; for example, Nike's homepage is at http://www.nike.com, and Microsoft is at http://www.microsoft.com. Homepages usually contain background information on the company and information about the company's products. They are a good source of competitive intelligence, and a good marketing information system should monitor competitors' homepages for announcements about new products or new marketing programs.

For financial data on companies and industries, the best Internet sources are sites that provide information for investors. Three such sites are Wall Street Research Net (http://www.wsrn.com), CompanyLink (http://www.companylink.com), and Deloitte & Touche PeerScape (http://www.peerscape.com). These sites provide industry performance profiles, stock prices and financial data for individual companies, and general information such as news clippings and press releases.

For other types of information, there are many Internet sites of potential interest. For example, the U.S. Census Bureau homepage (http://www.census.gov) provides access to a wide variety of industry and demographic statistics, including the *County and City Data Book* and *Statistical Abstract of the United States.* The American Marketing Association homepage (http://www.ama.org) provides links to various AMA publications.

Of course, it is also possible to find information on the Internet without knowing about specific sites. Just access an Internet search engine, such as Infoseek or Alta Vista, enter keywords for the search, and follow the links that come up. For example, if you want market size information for vacuum cleaners, try linking keywords such as "vacuum cleaners" and "sales statistics" and follow the resulting trail.

At the present time, the biggest problem with using the Internet for general searches is that search engines aren't efficient enough to cope with the huge amount of available information. This leads to two problems. The first problem is too great a volume of material. It is as if you sent someone to a huge library to get information on vacuum cleaner sales, and that person brought back every single document that had the words "clean" or "sales" anywhere in them. Figure 6.2 exemplifies what can happen when too broad a search is requested, in this instance using the keywords "new product development."

The second problem with using the Internet for general searches is not enough prioritization. A search for vacuum cleaner sales may elicit a document that provides exactly what you want, but this document may be buried amid thousands of useless documents. This inefficiency can make general Internet searches frustrating.

By the time you read this chapter, the efficiency of Internet research may have been substantially enhanced by new generations of search engines. But even if problems remain, using the available search engines for the Internet is a *must* for any thorough secondary research project. One of the basic goals in a secondary research project is to obtain all available information, and there is an excellent chance that the Internet will contain information not found in your library. The Internet is especially useful in identifying commercial and international data sources that are not available in most libraries.

Also, if you are searching for general information on the Internet, such as advice on how to use some research procedure or where to find some data, you can post your question to a newsgroup or listserve and hope for a reply from someone who knows the answer. **Newsgroups** are electronic bulletin boards where messages can be read by anyone who accesses the site. **Listservs** are electronic mailing lists where messages are automatically sent to all list subscribers.

Critical Thinking Skills

Earlier in this chapter, we suggested that you use library sources to find information on (a) automobiles, (b) bottled water, (c) diesel fuel, and (d) industrial ball valves. Try to find the same information on the Internet. Compare how long it takes and what information you find.

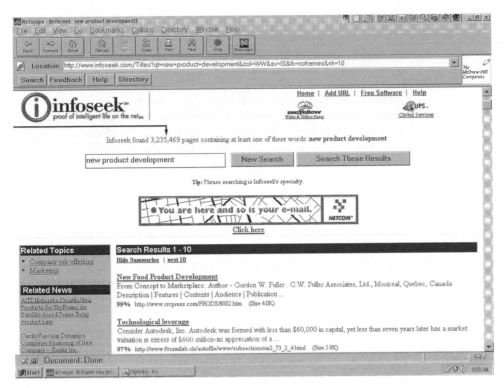

Figure 6.2   General queries with Internet search engines often provide too much information to be useful. For example, a search for information on "new product development" using the Infoseek engine generated 3,235,469 sites! Imagine trying to find the item you want in that list.

The Internet contains thousands of newsgroups and listservs, so whatever your question, there is likely to be an appropriate place for you to ask it. You can locate and access newsgroups by using an Internet browser, such as Netscape Navigator, and a newsgroup searching service, such as Deja News (http://www.dejanews.com). You can find a list of marketing related listservs at Mousetracks (http://nsns.com/MouseTracks).

Evaluating Secondary Information

It is important to evaluate secondary information before it is used. One way to evaluate secondary information is by using a checklist of who, what, why, when, where, and how.

- *Who sponsored the research?* Research doesn't just happen: somebody commissions it and pays for it. Some research sponsors are not knowledgeable about data quality and pay enough to get only low-quality information. Also, some research sponsors are hoping for certain results and encourage the researcher to take an approach that ensures these results.

Consider population statistics as an example of how a research sponsor might influence the evaluation of secondary data. Population estimates prepared by the U.S. government can usually be treated as unbiased. They may, however, contain errors—for example, it is usually assumed that census figures underestimate the numbers of young black and Hispanic men in large cities—but the Census Bureau does not have any ax to grind in generating population figures and tries to get its estimates correct. On the other hand, population estimates prepared by chambers of commerce may be high. These groups have a booster mentality and usually want their city to look as large as possible.

- *Who conducted the research?* Research can often be judged by the qualifications and reputation of the researcher. Secondary information can be trusted more when the research firm that did the study has a reputation for integrity and good work.

    U.S. government data score high on researcher quality because the government employs many outstanding research professionals and has well-developed statistical standards. Trade association data, on the other hand, show much greater variation in quality.

- *Who provided the information?* The people or companies that provided the data should be representative of your market. Engineers' opinions may not predict managers' behavior, census tracts may not coincide with your trading area, and individual attitudes may not explain household buying decisions.

- *Who reported the information?* People sometimes publicize findings that are favorable to them and suppress other information. For example, have you ever wondered how every brand of headache tablet on the market can have a major hospital study that shows it to be most effective against pain?

    Biased reporting is more likely to occur when data are reported by a research sponsor rather than the actual researcher. Most, though not all, researchers worry that biased reporting will damage their reputations. Also, researchers are more aware of the professional ethics regarding biased reporting. Ethical issues are discussed in Chapter 22.

    Be especially careful about using secondhand reports of secondary information. *Information may be quoted erroneously or out of context, so it is necessary to check original sources to avoid repeating errors.* One general rule is always to use original sources of secondary information or to label clearly the information as thirdhand.

- *What information was gathered?* How relevant is the information to our specific problem?

- *Why was the information gathered?* Information that was gathered to make a point may be biased. We may question media companies' studies of their audiences' buying power even without knowing the details of the research, simply because we know the research was done for purposes of selling advertising in the medium that sponsored the research.

- *When was the information gathered?* Market conditions may have changed since the information was gathered. A three-year-old study of brand-choice motives for buying personal computers will probably no longer apply. Also, the information must be evaluated with respect to seasonality. A study of tennis participation conducted during the summer months might overstate the potential for year-round sales of tennis items.

- *Where was the information gathered?* Regional or national differences between the research site and the specific market being researched may limit the value of the information.

- *How was the information gathered?* Was the research design appropriate? Was sampling of respondents done properly? What measurement procedures were used? Were key variables measured in the same way the user would measure them?

A summary of questions to ask about secondary information is given in Marketing Research Tools 6.6. Most sources of secondary information do not provide enough documentation to allow a thorough evaluation of the information. A good general policy on missing documentation is that "no news is bad news." However, if all secondary information with incomplete documentation is tossed aside, there will be nothing left. It is necessary to fill in the blanks and make reasonable guesses about details of the research.

Author Tips

The best protection against bad secondary information is using more than one information source. For example, when looking for market size estimates, don't stop at the first one you find; keep looking for more. Multiple sources allow you to compare sources for consistency and to use disagreements among sources to reach a better understanding of the characteristics and usefulness of each source.

MARKETING RESEARCH TOOLS

6.6

QUESTIONS TO ASK ABOUT SECONDARY INFORMATION

Question	Issue
Who sponsored the research?	Are they unbiased?
Who conducted the research?	Are they competent?
Who provided the information?	Are they representative of the target market?
Who reported the information?	Are they unbiased?
What information was gathered?	Is it relevant?
Why was the information gathered?	Is it objective?
When was the information gathered?	Is it still timely?
Where was the information gathered?	Is it similar to your market?
How was the information gathered?	Was it done correctly?

CASE STUDY 6.2

One problem in international research using secondary data is interpreting economic statistics across nations. For example, the Czech Republic's gross domestic product fell by more than 20 percent between 1990 and 1993—yet the economy actually improved. Says Prime Minister Václav Klaus: "[In 1991,] my two sons, at the time twenty-one and sixteen, had never in their lives entered a private grocery shop, butcher shop, hairdresser. Today, within a mile of where we live, there probably is not one state-owned shop, café, or service. To measure [the difference in service and variety] in quantitative terms has absolutely no meaning."

Similarly, comparisons of consumer incomes across countries must consider differences in prices, differences in state subsidies for basic costs such as transportation, and differences in family structure, which influence costs such as child care. Middle-class consumers in developing nations often have disposable incomes that are much higher than their total incomes might suggest.

Source: Based on Richard C. Morais, "Hong Kong of Europe," *Forbes,* June 20, 1994, pp. 69–70, and Rahul Jacob, "The Big Rise: Middle Classes Explode Around the Globe, Bringing New Markets and New Prosperity," *Fortune,* May 30, 1994, pp. 74–90.

Secondary and Syndicated Information in the Marketing Information System

The entire discussion regarding the location of secondary information applies whether the information is being gathered for a special project or as part of an MKIS. However, there are some additional considerations in using secondary data within the context of an MKIS.

Published Information

As discussed in Chapter 2, MKISs serve a monitoring function that helps organizations identify marketing problems and opportunities. This means that an MKIS will receive a steady flow of secondary materials and must evaluate them for useful information.

The direct cost of trade magazines and other printed sources is relatively small; in fact, many trade magazines are entirely supported by advertising and are sent free to companies in the industry. This may be an encouragement to subscribe to a large number of publications. However, somebody must scan these publications, and this is the limiting factor on using them.

Trade publications and other sources of secondary data may be divided into two groups: (1) key publications that *often* have useful information, and (2) other publications that *occasionally* have useful information. Both types of publications should be used in the MKIS, but the less useful should be reviewed periodically for possible deletion. A publication that provides no *unique* information over some reasonable period of time (perhaps a year) should be dropped from the system.

For the publications that are retained, we suggest a two-tier scanning procedure. First, the table of contents for each issue of key publications should be photocopied and distributed to marketing managers (of course, many managers will receive personal copies of the most important publications). Managers should be encouraged to request copies of articles that look useful. These requests can be made via telephone calls to the company library or by some form of printed request sheet. This system allows managers to exercise their own judgment about what is and is not useful.

Second, an information specialist should scan all publications received by the MKIS. The information specialist should prepare monthly reports that give key industry statistics, trends in these statistics, and any other trends the information specialist has noticed; they should also summarize key articles in the trade press. This system makes sure that less important publications receive proper attention and provides some order to the information-monitoring process.

Syndicated Data

Syndicated data are data prepared by a commercial firm for multiple users. These data can be viewed as a form of secondary information, because any given user must take them "as is." Since syndication allows data collection costs to be spread over several users, it makes good sense for any company to purchase syndicated data for its MKIS if such data exist and are of reasonable quality (Edmonston, 1994; Haran, 1995; Russell and Kamakura, 1994).

Syndicated data can be very costly in absolute terms. For example, most large manufacturers of consumer packaged goods spend several million dollars a year on syndicated market-tracking data. Although costly in absolute terms, these data are cheap relative to what it would cost each company to collect the information by itself.

Syndicated data are generally provided to clients in different ways to fit different companies' MKIS requirements. Smaller companies with limited research expertise usually receive only printed reports, along with oral presentations from the research company's representatives. If these companies want special analyses, the research company does the analysis and provides the results in both printed and oral form. Larger firms receive not only the printed reports and oral presentations but also computer files that allow them to create their own analyses and reports. In addition, the major syndicated services are now placing their own employees in the offices of large clients to help them use the data.

Chapter 1 listed some of the well-known syndicated services. To give a better idea about the data provided by some of these services, Exhibit 6.2 (see page 148) shows a sample page from a syndicated report on the clothing industry, issued by NPD Research. The table shows total brassiere sales by product type for various

Author Tips

For most companies, the marketing information system should scan not only the U.S. trade press but also the international trade press. Business is increasingly international, and new developments in any part of the world may have significant consequences for your company. Scanning the international trade press may require employing information specialists or other employees who are multilingual.

EXHIBIT 6.2

Sample Page
from a
Syndicated
Report

ANNUAL BRA REPORT
VERTICAL DOLLAR SHARE

	Total	Department	Top 50 Dept.	Major	Other	Specialty
Total	100.0	100.0	100.0	100.0	100.0	100.0
Product type						
Regular	83.3	87.8	87.2	91.6	87.7	80.6
Longline	1.6	1.2	1.3	.2	2.0	3.9
Maternity	.9	.1	.1	.2		1.4
Nursing	1.9	.9	.9	1.6		2.8
Training	.8	.5	.6		.4	.1
Sport	8.0	5.3	5.3	4.8	5.8	4.4
Strapless	1.6	2.3	2.6	1.4	.5	2.6
Bra & panty set	1.9	1.9	2.0	.2	3.6	4.2
Padding	100.0	100.0	100.0	100.0	100.0	100.0
Slight	19.1	21.1	21.5	19.3	19.7	13.1
Regular/full	3.3	5.7	6.2	5.8	1.1	3.6
None	77.6	73.3	72.3	75.0	79.2	83.4
Nonwire	47.5	34.1	31.4	41.5	47.8	38.9
Chest size	100.0	100.0	100.0	100.0	100.0	100.0
32 or smaller	4.6	4.7	4.9	5.3	2.0	3.7
34	24.6	27.9	27.2	34.6	23.2	26.7
36	31.0	34.4	36.3	25.2	31.1	25.4
38	20.2	20.0	18.8	25.3	22.9	18.7
40	9.2	7.8	7.7	5.2	12.1	6.6
42+	10.2	4.9	4.6	4.4	8.3	19.0
42	5.4	3.8	3.6	4.4	4.6	5.3
44	2.9	.8	.8		2.5	5.5
46	1.1	.3	.2		1.2	4.9
48+	.8	.1	.1			3.3
Other	.2	.4	.4		.3	

Source: "Annual Bra Report-Vertical Dollar Share." Reprinted with permission of NPD Research Inc.

retail outlets. For example, in 1993, 8 percent of all bras sold were sports bras, but in department stores sports bras accounted for only 5.3 percent of sales. This might simply reflect a difference between these stores' customer base and the market at large—for example, the average department store customer might be older and less inclined to exercise—or it might reflect an opportunity for department stores to build their sales of sports bras.

Summary

This chapter provided details about how to locate and evaluate secondary data. The following points were covered:

1. How is secondary information located in a library?

Industry statistics might be found in government documents (accessed through the *American Statistics Index*) or in private sources (accessed through the *Statistical Reference Index*). Nonstatistical background on an industry or a company can be found with the *Predicasts F & S Index*. These three indexes are the major tools for library-based marketing research.

In addition, financial data on companies can be obtained from their annual reports or from Standard & Poor's publications. Information on research methods is found in books, which are accessed through library book catalogs. Academic research results are found in academic journals, which are accessed through indexes such as *Psychological Abstracts*. Information on computerized databases may be found in *Directory of Online Databases*. Additional information can be found with help from a librarian.

2. How is secondary information located outside a library?

Trade associations may be able to provide statistical information on their industries; they are located by using *Encyclopedia of Associations*. Government employees often have knowledge about the industries they work with; they may be located by calling the relevant agency and asking for referrals. Media companies can provide data on the characteristics of their audiences. Chambers of commerce, utility companies, and other private sources may be able to provide local information such as population statistics.

3. How is secondary information located on the Internet?

Secondary information on the Internet is located through keyword searches. Call up your preferred search engine, enter your keywords, and follow the resulting links.

4. How is secondary information evaluated?

To evaluate secondary information, the following questions should be asked: Who sponsored the research (is the researcher unbiased)? Who conducted the research (is the researcher competent)? Who provided the information (is the researcher representative of the target market)? Who reported the information (is the researcher unbiased)? What information was gathered (is it relevant)? Why was the information gathered (is it objective)? When was the information gathered (is it still timely)? Where was the information gathered (is it similar to your market)? How was the information gathered (was it done correctly)?

5. How are secondary and syndicated information used within a marketing information system?

Published data should be scanned by an information specialist who prepares regular reports, and tables of contents for key publications should be distributed to managers.

Syndicated data can be provided to companies in a form that is convenient for them. Most smaller companies settle for printed reports and oral presentations. Most larger companies also receive computerized data files and may have an employee of the research company assigned to their site.

Suggested Additional Readings

We strongly urge you to go to your local library and examine as many of the sources discussed in this chapter as are available to you. At a minimum, you should look at

Statistical Abstract of the United States, City and County Data Book, and other available census and government data to see what they contain. If your library has any online services or CD-ROM readers, it would be useful to gain experience in using them.

Discussion Questions

1. What is secondary information and what are the benefits and limitations of using secondary information in marketing research?
2. Name some of the major secondary sources commonly used to locate industry statistics such as market size and growth.
3. How would you evaluate the quality of data from secondary sources?
4. What are the advantages of computerized databases as a secondary information source?
5. Your boss asks you to find out the size of the U.S. soft drink market. What secondary information would you use?
6. What is syndicated data, and why would syndicated data be part of a marketing information system?

Marketing Research Challenge

Select a firm you might like to work for. In preparation for a job interview with that firm, use the sources listed in this chapter to find out as much as you can about that firm, its competition, and the industry it is in. (If it is a diversified firm, limit yourself to discussing only one of the major industries of which it is a part.) You should certainly discuss the firm's products and marketing activities, but other data such as organization, finances, history, and so on are also useful.

Internet Exercise

What are the top five U.S. cities in the number of Hispanic residents? What are the top five cities in the percentage of Hispanic residents? What about the number and percentage of residents over 65 years of age? Find the answers to these secondary research questions on the webpage for the *County and City Data Book,* located at http://www.census.gov/stat_abstract/ccdb.html.

References

Burka, Karen (1992). "Publishers Beef Up Lists With Census Data." *Folio* 21 (June), p. 30.

Crispell, Diane (1989). "How to Hunt for the Best Source." *American Demographics* 11 (September), p. 46.

Daniells, Lorna M. (1985). *Note on Sources of External Marketing Data* (Boston: Harvard Business School).

Edmonston, Jack (1994). "Syndicated Research Is Wonderful, Right?" *Business Marketing* 79 (August), p. 12.

Feldman, Amy, and Joshua Levine (1993). "Sprucing Up the Cocoon." *Forbes* 151 (Jan. 4), pp. 64–65.

Haran, Leah (1995). "Data Pump Up Promotions." *Advertising Age* 66 (Oct. 9), p. 20.

Riche, Martha Farnsworth (1990). "Look Before Leaping."*American Demographics* 12 (February), p. 18.

Russell, Gary J., and Wagner A. Kamakura (1994). "Understanding Brand Competition Using Micro and Macro Scanner Data." *Journal of Marketing Research* 31 (May), pp. 289–303.

Wall Street Journal (1994). "Sales of Cigarettes Decline as Competition Heats Up." *Wall Street Journal* (Feb. 24), p. B6.

Conducting Surveys

◨ OBJECTIVES

After reading this chapter, you should be able to answer the following questions:

❶ What are the strengths and weaknesses of surveys compared to other self-report methods of data collection?

❷ What are the advantages and disadvantages of personal surveys, intercept surveys, telephone surveys, and mail surveys?

❸ How can participation rates in surveys be increased?

❹ How is a survey interview conducted?

❺ How should interviewers be chosen, trained, and supervised?

❻ How can surveys be managed and their costs controlled?

Survey interviews are commonly used in market research. Their identifying characteristic is a fixed questionnaire with prespecified questions. Using a fixed questionnaire allows a researcher to control the interview without being present and reduces the demands placed on interviewers. Surveys generally use interviewers who, although trained, are part-time workers paid at a modest rate.

The major strength of surveys compared with other self-report procedures is broad coverage of the respondent population. Broad coverage is possible because the relatively low cost of surveys allows the researcher to contact many respondents, and the relatively low demands placed on respondents encourage a high percentage to cooperate. The major weakness of surveys compared with other self-report procedures is that only limited information can be obtained from each respondent. Deep feelings and hidden motivations can't be probed very well. Because of these strengths and weaknesses, surveys provide good data about the population at large but limited data about individual respondents.

This chapter discusses various issues that arise in conducting surveys. Perhaps the most critical issue is the method of administration. Market research surveys typically take one of four forms:

- Personal surveys, in which face-to-face interviews are conducted at respondents' homes or offices

- Intercept surveys, in which face-to-face interviews are conducted with people intercepted at some public location such as a shopping mall

- Telephone surveys, in which people are interviewed over the telephone

- Mail surveys, in which people complete self-administered questionnaires that are mailed to them

In the following sections of this chapter, we discuss these methods of administration. For each method, the general procedures used are described and the method is evaluated along various dimensions, which are shown in Marketing Research Tools 7.1. After a discussion of each method, we give an overview of their characteristics and describe appropriate uses for each.

The remaining sections of the chapter discuss how to gain access to respondents and encourage participation in surveys; how to conduct survey interviews; how to hire, train, and supervise interviewers; and how to control survey costs and quality.

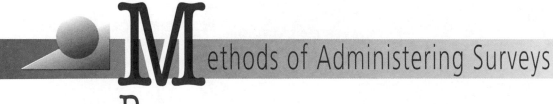

Methods of Administering Surveys

Personal Surveys

The oldest form of survey research is **personal interviews** conducted at a respondent's home or workplace. This method allows excellent control over who actually

MARKETING RESEARCH TOOLS

7.1

CONSIDERATIONS IN CHOOSING A SURVEY METHOD

Questionnaire design	What constraints does this method impose on the questionnaire? Does it allow us to do what we want?
Sampling	What constraints does this method impose on getting a sample of respondents? Will it allow us to get a sample of adequate quality?
Response quality	Will any characteristics of this method discourage accurate answers?
Time and cost	How long will the study take to complete? How much will it cost?

answers the questions and maximum flexibility in the questionnaire design. However, the fact that interviewers must travel to respondents' homes or offices makes personal interviewing costly relative to other methods.

Because of its high cost, personal interviewing is rarely used in American consumer research. It is mostly used (1) for consumer research in countries where telephone surveys are not culturally accepted and (2) for surveys of business executives. Business surveys are often done with respondents who control large budgets and often use many open questions, which require probing and elaboration. The individual value of these respondents and the complexity of the interviews justify the expense of personal interviewing.

General Procedures for Personal Surveys

Personal household surveys are usually conducted without an advance appointment. Most contacts are made in the evenings and on weekends, since these are the times that people are most likely to be home. Even then, callbacks are frequently necessary. Typically, three callbacks are made after an initial call but attempts then cease if the respondent cannot be located.

In many cartoons, the interviewer and respondents are shown standing at the door. In practice, both the respondent and interviewer will be much more comfortable if the interviewing is done in the house, with both sitting down.

In-office interviews for surveys of business executives are usually done by advance appointment. A sample of organizations is drawn for the survey, appropriate people are called and asked for appointments, and the interviewers then go to respondents' offices and conduct the interviews at the appointed times. Several calls may be needed to locate the proper respondent within an organization (Meyers, 1993).

Questionnaire Design Issues

The flexibility of personal surveys in terms of questionnaire design is unrivaled among the possible methods of data collection. This is because:

- The interviewer can strictly control the order of the questions.
- The interviewer can probe unclear answers. This allows for the use of complex questions.
- The interviewer can implement branching instructions. **Branching** involves asking or not asking certain questions depending on the answers to previous questions.
- The interviewer can show the respondent lists of response categories to help with questions that have many categories.
- The face-to-face nature of the interview allows the interviewer to show the respondent products, packages, or advertisements.
- The face-to-face, personal connection allows the interviewer to explore unstructured, "conversational" topics.
- The face-to-face connection allows a lengthy interview; in fact, interviews lasting an hour or more are not uncommon.

All this flexibility makes personal surveys a preferred method when their cost is not prohibitive.

Sample Quality of Personal Surveys

Sample quality in personal surveys is excellent. You can draw careful samples, and you know exactly who the respondent is. Although there may sometimes be problems with locked entrance doors to apartment buildings, the face-to-face interaction helps increase cooperation once a respondent is reached.

Response Quality of Personal Surveys

Research shows that the quality of data provided by respondents is quite similar across methods of administration. The only real advantage of personal surveys is that their flexibility allows a wider range of questions.

Costs of Personal Surveys

Cost is the big disadvantage of personal surveys. Personal interviews for business-to-business surveys almost always cost more than $200 an interview, plus travel expenses, and can run as much as $1,000. Gifts to respondents add to this total; it is not uncommon to give incentives worth $50 or more per respondent.

Intercept Surveys

Because of the high cost of personal surveys, most American consumer surveys that use face-to-face interviewing are done by intercepting visitors to some public place such as a shopping mall or a city street. **Intercept surveys** allow face-to-face interviewing at a much lower cost than in-home surveys because travel costs are eliminated.

General Procedures for Intercept Surveys

The most popular location for intercept surveys is shopping malls, because they provide access to a general population that is appropriate for most consumer research. In fact, intercept surveys are so commonly done in shopping malls that they are often called "mall surveys." The organization conducting interviews in a mall pays rent to the mall for space to conduct the interviews.

In most intercept surveys, interviewers are sent into the mall to recruit anyone who looks as if she or he might qualify for the survey. People are approached and asked to participate in interviews on the spot. If they agree, the interview is administered and the respondent is thanked, paid (in some cases), and returns to other mall activities. If they refuse, the interviewer continues on to the next person.

The interview is usually administered by an interviewer using a paper-and-pencil form. Sometimes, respondents are given a self-administered questionnaire or are seated at a computer terminal for a computer-administered questionnaire.

Questionnaire Design Issues

Since intercept surveys are done face to face, they offer the same basic flexibility as a personal survey. The major difference is that intercept surveys are conducted under greater time pressure. In most cases, the interview should not take more than a few minutes unless respondents are compensated, because people won't accept a prolonged interruption of their activities.

Sample Quality of Intercept Surveys

Sample quality is a weak point of intercept surveys. This method is not used for surveys of business executives, except for occasional studies done at trade shows, because business executives are not often found on a street corner or in a shopping mall. Even for consumer studies, it can be difficult to find good intercept sites. Most marketing research intercepts are done in shopping malls, but many malls refuse access even when offered rental payments. This limits the extent to which the respondents will represent a general population.

Even with access to a mall, low cooperation rates impair the quality of the sample. Most mall researchers report cooperation rates of 50 percent or less. This is not surprising since many shoppers have limited time, and nobody came to the mall to be

CASE STUDY 7.1

An alternative to calling people who were selected in an intercept survey is to have them call you. This is how the Gallup Organization has been measuring opinions about new movies. Gallup 800 Interactive replaces the live interviews used by most exit polls with a toll-free number that moviegoers are asked to call within two hours after the movie. Moviegoers who call are asked what they thought of the movie, whether they would recommend it to friends, and whether they might buy the movie sound track or video. The data obtained in this fashion have been very useful to movie studios.

A similar method has been tried in the restaurant industry, with mixed results. Some midpriced, table service restaurant chains such as Olive Garden have had good luck with a system in which patrons are given a $5 coupon that is activated by calling a toll-free number and responding to a computerized customer satisfaction interview. However, Kentucky Fried Chicken tried a similar system and was disappointed in the results. It appears that fast-food customers won't take the time to call a toll-free number, presumably because they don't have a high enough involvement in the transaction and they are very time-sensitive.

Source: Marcy Magiera, "Gallup Returns to Movie Research," *Advertising Age,* Apr. 11, 1994, p. 30.

interviewed. An alternative that can be used to reduce this problem is to ask for the shopper's phone number and then to conduct the interview later by telephone.

In some cases, intercept surveys are not used to capture a general population but simply to profile visitors to the intercept site; for example, to profile shoppers at a mall or visitors to a zoo. Such studies are highly appropriate and can produce excellent information if well designed. Sampling procedures for these kinds of studies are discussed in Chapter 13.

Response Quality of Intercept Surveys

All available evidence suggests that people who respond to intercept surveys give answers that are comparable in quality to answers obtained from other survey methods. The limited time available in mall surveys does not appear to hurt the quality of the answers from respondents.

Costs of Intercept Surveys

The reason for using intercept surveys rather than personal surveys is that intercept surveys are cheaper. There are no travel costs (because respondents come to the interview place), no time is spent on people who aren't available, and no time is spent on follow-ups of people who weren't contacted on the first try. The interviews are usually short, and production rates of five or more interviews per hour from each interviewer are not uncommon. As a result, mall interviews usually cost in the range of $10 to $20 per interview, plus fixed costs.

Fixed costs cover the rental of mall space and the hiring, training, and supervision of interviewers. These costs usually amount to at least $1,000 per location and are allocated over all the interviews done in that mall. The larger the sample chosen in each mall, the smaller the fixed cost per interview. For this reason, mall sample sizes are usually in the range of 50 to 200 interviews per mall.

Telephone Surveys

Telephone surveys are widely used in market research, especially consumer research. They offer better population coverage than intercept surveys but are limited by the fact that interviewers cannot show things to respondents.

General Procedures for Telephone Surveys

Telephone surveys begin with the selection of a sample of telephone numbers. In surveys of organizations, companies are selected and phone numbers are obtained for those companies. In consumer surveys, the phone numbers are drawn directly from a directory or with a technique called **random digit dialing** (this technique is discussed in Chapter 13). When random digit dialing is used, the interviewer doesn't know who he or she is calling, only what number is being called.

Once the sample is drawn, interviewers telephone the selected people (or selected numbers) and request cooperation with the survey. If the desired respondent isn't in, the interviewer asks for a good time to call back and tries later. Callbacks should continue until (1) the interview is completed, (2) the interview is refused, (3) the potential respondent is found to be ineligible, or (4) some previously established limit on the number of callbacks is reached.

Telephone interviewers generally work from central offices, and most big research companies use computer-assisted telephone interviewing (CATI) systems. In a CATI system, the interviewer sits in front of a computer monitor on which the questions appear and enters the answers directly into the computer. Use of computers makes possible:

- Automatic use of branching instructions.
- Editing data as they are being collected rather than in a separate and costly step. For example, if the possible codes for a question are "1" if an item was purchased and "2" if it was not, an interviewer who inadvertently punches "3" will be told that this is not an acceptable code and can immediately correct the error.
- Improved supervision of interviewers. We discuss this point later in this chapter.
- Same-day availability of the data for analysis.

Questionnaire Design Issues

Since telephone surveys are administered by interviewers, they offer good control of the question sequence, good ability to implement branching instructions, and the opportunity to probe unclear answers.

Of course, since telephone interviews are not conducted face to face, it is not possible to show products, packages, or advertisements to the respondent unless they

Critical Thinking Skills

If you wanted to use an intercept survey to gather opinions from a representative cross section of students at your university, what intercept location(s) would you use? Why? What percentage of students would you expect to cooperate if the questionnaire took two minutes? If it took twenty minutes? How, if at all, would you expect the resulting sample to be different from the student population at large?

have been mailed in advance. Also, it is not possible to provide respondents with printed lists of responses for questions with many alternatives. Because of this point, and because respondents must be able to keep the question and the response alternatives in their heads, questions should be kept simple and the number of response alternatives should be limited.

Interview length is generally not a problem in telephone surveys, contrary to the expectations of many novice researchers. Interviews up to twenty minutes long are common and do not cause problems. However, it is possible that a survey call will come at a time that is inconvenient for the respondent. Since the interviewer cannot see this, it is polite to ask if the respondent is free to talk. If not, an appointment should be made for a more convenient time.

Sample Quality of Telephone Surveys

The sample quality of telephone surveys depends on three issues: (1) whether the potential respondents have telephones, (2) whether those phones are identified in lists such as the telephone directory, and (3) whether the potential respondents are willing to participate.

For consumer surveys, telephone availability is generally not an issue. Industrialized countries such as the United States have almost universal phone ownership, and consumer research in less developed countries is generally directed at a middle-class population that owns phones. The use of random digit dialing methods solves the problem of unlisted numbers.

The major sampling problems of consumer telephone surveys are nonavailability and noncooperation. Currently, telephone calls to specific individuals will, on average, find fewer than 25 percent of them at home on the first call. The people who are contacted on the first call are likely to be housewives, retired people, and other stay-at-homes. This creates a bias toward less active people unless the survey organization calls back until the designated respondents are reached. A good organization will make at least five calls, spread across weekdays, weeknights, and weekends, before giving up on a respondent.

Noncooperation is a more difficult problem to solve. About one-third of all respondents who initially refuse an interview will later give one to a different interviewer, and most survey organizations have interviewers who specialize in converting refusals to interviews. Even so, refusal rates remain over 20 percent in many telephone surveys.

One way to reduce both refusals and noncontacts is to broaden the definition of who is eligible to respond. Surveys that accept information from any member of a household usually get cooperation rates 10 to 20 percent higher than surveys directed at specific individuals. The reason is simple: the request is referred to the person in the household who is most likely to cooperate. Of course, this approach works only if the person who cooperates knows the answers to the questions. An intermediate approach is to ask for a specific individual and then, if this person refuses or is unavailable, to ask whether any other member of the household is knowledgeable about the survey topic and then interview that person instead.

The major concern of all telephone survey organizations is not current refusal rates among consumer populations but rather that legal or technological barriers will significantly reduce cooperation rates in the future. There is significant consumer dissatisfaction with telemarketing, and this unhappiness has grown as the practice has become more pervasive. To date, legislation intended to control telemarketing has recognized the difference between sales efforts and marketing research, but this distinction may not hold in the future. Also, the ever-growing use of answering machines as well as other technical innovations makes it possible for respondents to screen incoming calls and to refuse to be interviewed simply by not answering.

Telephone surveys of business populations present somewhat different issues from those posed by consumer surveys. Virtually all businesses have listed telephone numbers, and any call placed during business hours should get through. The problem in industrial surveys, apart from obtaining cooperation, is locating the proper person within the organization to interview. Usually, this is done by starting with a job title and then getting referred from one person to another until the right person is reached. The telephone is ideal for this purpose. In fact, industrial mail surveys generally require advance telephone calls to identify names, titles, and exact addresses of people to whom questionnaires should be sent.

Once the proper respondents are identified, reaching them may still be a problem. A secretary or other "gatekeeper" may limit access to them. Methods of gaining access and cooperation are discussed later in this chapter.

Response Quality of Telephone Surveys

Much research has been done to compare the quality of responses in telephone and personal interviews. Overwhelmingly, this research shows no significant differences in the response quality of data obtained from respondents for market research purposes.

Whereas response quality is similar between telephone and personal interviews, the quality of the data recorded by interviewers may differ. Interviewer errors in computerized telephone interviews that provide automatic editing are less common than in personal interviews that use paper-and-pencil data collection. The advantage vanishes if the telephone interview does not use computers or the personal interview does.

You might think that data quality in telephone interviews would benefit from the close supervision possible in a central facility, but this has not been demonstrated.

Costs of Telephone Surveys

The cost per interview for telephone surveys is comparable to that of intercept surveys. The cost of a telephone interview usually falls in the range of $10 to $25, with the exact figure depending on the length of the interview, the amount of screening needed to locate eligible respondents, and the level of long-distance charges.

Mail Surveys

Inexperienced researchers almost always think of self-administered mail surveys when considering a survey. Mail is perceived to be inexpensive, and mail surveys don't require an interviewing staff.

Critical Thinking Skills

If you were to do a telephone survey of students at your university, what calling times would give you the best chance of finding people at home? What percentage of students would you expect to reach on the first call? How, if at all, would this group differ from the student population at large? What percentage would you expect to reach within five calls? How, if at all, would this group differ from the student population at large?

Unfortunately, mail surveys also suffer from some major limitations, which are noted in the following subsections. These limitations make mail surveys inappropriate for many projects. However, when they are appropriate, or when they are used in combination with other methods, mail surveys can be efficient data collection procedures.

General Procedures for Mail Surveys

In a mail survey, a sample of addresses (and usually names) is drawn from a list, mailing labels are prepared, and the questionnaire is sent out with a cover letter. Some studies begin with an advance postcard to explain the survey and alert respondents that it is coming.

Two weeks after the initial mailing, a follow-up questionnaire and letter are sent to nonrespondents. Two weeks later, a second follow-up questionnaire and letter are sent. If total response is not satisfactory after this second follow-up, it is possible to use telephone interviews to survey a sample of the nonrespondents and measure whether they are different in some way from respondents.

Questionnaire Design Issues

A major limitation of mail surveys is that they can be used only for short surveys with mainly closed questions. For surveys of the general public, experience has shown that response rates drop sharply if the questionnaire is longer than four pages (Erdos and Morgan, 1970). Longer questionnaires of up to twelve pages are sometimes possible with professionals who are highly motivated, such as lawyers who are participating in a survey conducted by their state bar association, but this is usually not the case for consumer surveys.

The questions on a mail questionnaire should offer response categories or at least not require substantial amounts of writing. For example, respondents to mail surveys will write the brand name of a product or the name of the store where it was purchased, but most will not write even a short answer on why they made a purchase decision. This reluctance to answer open questions stems not only from the time and effort required but also from the fact that many respondents are uncertain of their spelling and grammar and do not want to be embarrassed. Open questions in mail surveys usually reduce the cooperation rate substantially while yielding little useful information.

Another limitation to mail surveys is that they permit very little branching. Even very simple branching instructions are likely to confuse some respondents. It is possible, however, to ask a question about the ownership or purchase of a product and then to follow with questions about the product such as brand name and the respondent's reasons for choosing that brand. Respondents will understand that the later questions do not apply if they do not own the product.

Still another complication in mail surveys is that question order cannot be controlled as it is in personal interviews. You have to assume that respondents will read all the questions before answering any of them. This makes it possible for questions at the end of the questionnaire to influence questions at the beginning, which may sometimes be undesirable. Also, questions intended to measure respondents' levels of knowledge about a product, service, or issue don't work well because respondents are free to look up the answers or ask someone else.

Sample Quality of Mail Surveys

Response rates are a major sampling issue in mail surveys. Mail surveys often have response rates lower than 50 percent, with rates as low as 10 percent for badly done studies. These low response rates create a risk of high *nonresponse bias* (i.e., a risk of large differences between data for the overall population of interest and data for those who responded).

There are two major sources of nonresponse bias in mail surveys with low cooperation rates. First, since mail surveys of the general population require respondents to have reasonable reading skills, cooperation rates are generally higher for people with higher levels of education. A second, and more serious, fact is that cooperation on mail surveys is influenced by respondents' interest in the topic. In attitude surveys, those who feel strongly about something are more likely to respond than are those who don't care. For new products or services, those who are interested are more likely to respond, producing overestimates of market interest.

These biases become smaller as sample cooperation increases, but they never vanish entirely from mail surveys. Unlike telephone and face-to-face surveys, in which people refuse before they really know anything about the topic, you must assume that nonrespondents to a mail survey looked at the questionnaire and decided they weren't interested.

Another sampling problem in mail surveys is that you can't be certain who the respondent is. Most industrial mail surveys can be assumed to come from a subordinate of the person you wanted to interview, and we've seen estimates that one-third of consumer mail surveys are filled out by someone other than the designated respondent.

Nonresponse rates and wrong-respondent identity problems in industrial studies are especially severe when researchers fail to make phone calls to identify the right person for mailing purposes. The simpleminded notion of addressing the questionnaire to a job title (e.g., "Purchasing Director"), or to the highest level in an organization with instructions that the questionnaire be forwarded to the right person, usually winds up with the questionnaire being thrown into a wastebasket. You must telephone the organization and identify the proper respondent by name, title, and address.

In consumer research, some research companies offer mail panels for survey purposes. These panels are households that have agreed, often for incentives, to answer mail surveys from the research company. These panels are usually balanced by education and other demographic variables to reduce sample bias. They offer a good way to get relatively quick, relatively high response rates at mail costs. However, they cannot be viewed as truly random samples.

Response Quality of Mail Surveys

Within the limits previously mentioned, the response quality of mail surveys should be about as good as that obtained by other methods of administrations. Indeed, when respondents in either business or household surveys must look up information from records, the data from mail surveys may be more accurate and complete.

Costs of Mail Surveys

Mail surveys are less expensive than telephone or in-home surveys, but they are not as cheap as an inexperienced researcher might expect. This is because careful mail survey procedures require follow-ups to nonrespondents and some form of respondent compensation, as discussed later in this chapter. The highest rates of cooperation are obtained when the initial questionnaire mailing is preceded by an advance postcard and followed by two additional mailings to nonrespondents. Each of these mailings increases the cost of the study. Total data collection costs for well-done mail surveys usually run from $5 to $10 per completed interview.

CASE STUDY 7.2

The Gelb Consulting Group is a company that has done many marketing research projects, including many feasibility studies for new, high-tech products in the oil and gas industry. The company's clients for these studies include Shell Oil, Schlumberger, Halliburton, and the Gas Research Institute.

John Elmer of the Gelb Consulting Group says:

Mail surveys have many limitations, but we get excellent results from using mail surveys to test response to new technologies in business-to-business markets.

Our general procedure is as follows. First, we develop a list of potential respondents. In some studies, we can buy an acceptable list, but we usually have to do at least some list building. We identify companies that might use the product or service that is being tested, and we telephone those companies to identify the people who will be key decision makers in adopting the technology.

Concurrently with developing the list of potential respondents, we develop the questionnaire. This has three parts. First, we write the questions that we want to ask. Second, we design any graphics that are needed to explain the technology or to make the questionnaire more interesting. Third, we convert this material into a computerized questionnaire that will run on any computer.

We then copy this questionnaire onto diskettes and send the diskettes to potential respondents, along with a printed cover letter that introduces the diskette and tells respondents how to use it. We send this material by FedEx to get respondents' attention.

Respondents read the diskette, enter their answers right on it, and send it back, using prepaid delivery. We usually get a response rate of at least 40 percent. If necessary, we call people to encourage them to respond.

The response to this method has been excellent. The potential respondents in these studies are technically oriented buyers, usually engineers by training, who feel very comfortable with computer-based materials. They seem to like answering in this format, as opposed to answering on paper. More important, the computerized presentation allows us to do some neat things with graphics and really explain the technology. This feature is popular with the respondents, because it is their job to keep up with new technologies. The computerized presentation helps us by serving as a questionnaire, but it helps the respondents by providing them with technical education.

Perhaps a more serious cost in mail surveys is time. Mail surveys generally take longer in the field than do interviewer-conducted surveys. With the time required for mail to be sent and returned and for follow-up, mail surveys usually take at least two months. If speed is of the essence, you shouldn't use a mail survey.

Methods of Administration: An Overview

Marketing Research Tools 7.2 gives an overview of alternative methods of administration.

MARKETING RESEARCH TOOLS

7.2

METHODS OF ADMINISTRATION COMPARED

	Mail	Telephone	Intercept	Personal
Questionnaire issues:				
Length	Keep to 4 pages	20 minutes or more	Keep to 5 minutes	An hour or more
Open questions	Big problem	Some problem	Some problem	No problem
Probing	Not possible	Possible	Possible	Best
Complex questions	Big problem	Some problem	Some problem	No problem
Number of response categories	No limit	Keep to 4	No limit if cards shown	No limit if cards shown
Branching	Big problem	No problem	No problem	No problem
Question order	No control	Controlled	Controlled	Controlled
Sampling issues:				
Population coverage	No problem if list good	Usually no problem	May be problem	Usually no problem
Response rate	10–60%	50–70%	<50%	50–90%
Identity of respondent	Not known	Known	Known	Known
Cost:				
Cost per interview	$5–$10	$10–$25	$10–$20	>$200

The strengths and weaknesses of the various methods lead to the following general recommendations:

- All surveys work best when they include only simple questions about concrete phenomena, such as what people bought, when they bought it, where they bought it, when they used it, how they used it, where they used it, and how satisfied they were with it. Depth interviews or focus groups are better for asking *why* people used a product, unless a relatively shallow level of information is acceptable.

- Personal surveys are appropriate for surveys of executives, especially if the questionnaire contains many open questions. However, personal surveys are too expensive for most consumer research.

Critical Thinking Skills

A university wants to do a survey of college freshmen, to learn how they decided which school to attend. The university hopes to use this information to enhance its effectiveness in recruiting students. Which method of administration would you recommend for this survey? Why?

- Telephone surveys are the general fallback method. They should be used when the limitations of mail and intercept surveys present problems and a personal survey is too expensive.

- If it is necessary to show products, packages, or advertisements to respondents but cost is an issue, mall intercept surveys are generally the appropriate method.

- Mail surveys are least expensive whenever their limitations do not prevent their use. As a general rule, they are good for highly educated respondent groups such as doctors, lawyers, accountants, and executives if the topic, the sponsor, or other factors can be used to motivate response.

Across the various methods, increases in questionnaire flexibility, sample quality, and/or response quality are generally accompanied by increases in cost. A general rule applies: choose the cheapest method that provides acceptable data for the purposes of your research.

CASE STUDY 7.3

The latest place to do surveys is the Internet. Many companies ask people who visit their websites to respond to questionnaires. Exhibit 7.1 presents an example.

Internet surveys can be viewed as a form of intercept survey, in that interviews are conducted with visitors to some site. However, Internet surveys have some limitations over and above those usually encountered in intercept surveys. These limitations are:

- If the questionnaire is posted on the company's own website, the sample is limited to people who have an active interest in the company. The closest comparison would be to an intercept survey conducted by a retail store among people who visit the store. This sample might be ideal for some purposes, but it certainly doesn't represent the market at large.

- The response rate is *very* low, further reducing the representativeness of the sample. In essence, respondents to an Internet survey should be viewed as people who volunteered for the research.

- The questionnaire is limited in much the same way as mail questionnaires. The questionnaire must be brief, with simple questions. (On the other hand, automated branching is possible.)

Despite these limitations, Internet surveys have an obvious attraction: they are free, except for the cost of creating the questionnaire and processing the data. There are no interviewer compensation, no mall rent, no long-distance charges, and no postage. If the limitations are bearable given the purpose of the research, Internet surveys can be an attractive way to go.

EXHIBIT

7.1

Internet
Customer
Survey

The Domino's Pizza Consumer Survey   http://www.cominos.com/survey/index.htm

Info   Info   Survey   Jobs   Home

We'd like to hear your thoughts and suggestions. Please complete this short survey and you'll automatically be entered into our drawing to win a Domino's Pizza Party. *Take a look at this month's winner!

Name

Email

Street Address

City

State

Zip Code

Country

Age

Sex
○ Male
○ Female

The Domino's Pizza Consumer Survey   http://www.dominos.com/survey/index.htm

1. When was the last time you ordered a pizza from Domino's?
(Check only one response)
○ Within the past 30 days
○ Within the past 90 days
○ Within the past year
○ More than a year ago
○ Never

2. In a typical month, how many times do you order pizza for carryout or delivery from any establishment?
(Check only one response)
○ Never
○ Once a month
○ Two to three times a month
○ Four or more times a month

3. In a typical month, how many times do you order pizza for carryout or delivery from DOMINO'S?
(Check only one response)
○ Never
○ Once a month
○ Two to three times a month
○ Four or more times a month

4. What is your favorite type of pizza?
(Check only one response)
○ Regular, hand-tossed crust
○ Deep Dish/Pan Pizza
○ Thin Crust
○ Other

5. How many hours a week do you surf the Net?
○ 0-10
○ 11-20
○ More than 20

6. Have you tried our Garlic Crunch crust yet?
If so, what did you think?

7. Other comments, suggestions or questions:

Submit   Reset

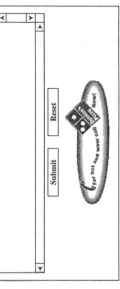

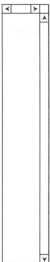

Obtaining Cooperation from Respondents

Once a method of administration is selected, researchers face the issues of how to reach respondents and how to get them to participate.

Gaining Access to Respondents

The first task involves getting through to respondents. This is generally a straightforward matter: get the best possible list, contact potential respondents, and screen if necessary to identify eligible respondents.

For personal and telephone surveys of business buyers, the biggest access problems occur in appointment setting. Many executives have secretaries who zealously guard their bosses from interruption. These gatekeepers may require you to leave a message, and there is little motivation for the potential respondent to return that message.

It is often possible to get around gatekeepers by calling before or after business hours, because most executives arrive earlier and/or leave later than their secretaries. If eight to five is a normal business day in your part of the country, a 7:30 A.M. or 5:30 P.M. call may show results. It pays to try both before and after business hours because some people are more receptive in the morning, when they haven't become bogged down in work yet, whereas others are more receptive in the evening because they're ready for a break. Of course, calling outside business hours requires a direct line into the executive's office. If it is necessary to go through a closed switchboard or an unattended desk, early or late calls are impossible.

Another technique for getting access to executives is for an interviewer to start with a higher level executive in the organization and ask to be referred to the potential respondent. Then, when the interviewer calls the potential respondent's office, he or she can tell the secretary that he or she has been referred and name the higher level executive. Most secretaries will connect such calls if the respondent is in. If the respondent is not in, call back instead of leaving a message; the respondent has little incentive to return your call.

In consumer telephone surveys, gaining access to individual respondents is simply a matter of persistence. As mentioned earlier, initial efforts to find people at home tend to miss most of the potential respondents. Just keep calling. Sooner or later, you'll find most people at home.

In mail surveys of businesses, advance telephone calls to identify the proper respondents are a must. Very few mailing lists will be good enough to be used immediately without phoning in advance.

In consumer mail surveys, access is mostly a matter of list quality. An outdated list might produce an excessive number of bad addresses, which lead to undeliverable questionnaires. If this happens, a mail-order list company may be able to help—for a fee, of course—or you might put a clerk to work checking old and new telephone books or other sources that might show where people have moved.

Researchers sometimes turn to intermediaries such as professional associations for help in gaining access to respondents or encouraging participation. This help might come in the form of high-quality sampling lists not generally available or endorsements of a study that will help persuade potential respondents to participate. Intermediaries can sometimes be helpful, but often they are only a handicap and should be ignored. Even if they eventually decide to cooperate, they take a long time to make up their minds and in the process delay the research. A general rule is to avoid getting intermediaries involved with your study unless there are clear benefits that outweigh the added costs of both time and money.

Critical Thinking Skills

One way of gaining access to respondents in businesses is to start at a higher level in the organization and be referred down to the potential respondent. Do you see any ethical issues in this procedure?

Encouraging Participation

Some people will agree with almost any request to participate in a marketing research survey. Others will *never* agree to participate. Other people—a substantial part of the population—are in the middle. They may or may not participate, depending on the persistence of the survey organization, the effectiveness of the request, and the topic of the survey.

In face-to-face and telephone interviews, it is the skill of the interviewer that ultimately determines whether a wavering respondent will cooperate. In mail surveys, cooperation is determined by the cover letter that accompanies the questionnaire, the questionnaire itself, and any monetary incentive. We discuss these here.

Encouraging Cooperation in Face-to-Face and Telephone Interviews

In every survey organization, there are striking differences in the levels of cooperation that different interviewers obtain. Some interviewers almost never get refusals; others find it difficult to obtain high cooperation levels.

As a general rule, new interviewers have much lower cooperation rates than do long-term interviewers. The implication for selecting a field organization to conduct your survey is that, all else being equal, an organization with more long-term experienced interviewers will produce higher cooperation rates.

Some survey organizations use the interviewers who have the highest cooperation rates as specialists in converting refusals to interviews. The less productive interviewers get as many interviews as they can, and the people they can't get are turned over to the converters. Of course, this kind of follow-up costs money.

People sometimes ask whether paying respondents for face-to-face or telephone interviews increases cooperation rates. For personal and telephone surveys of consumers, the general answer is "no." However, paying respondents does increase cooperation in the following situations:

- When respondents are required to go to a central location for an interview
- When respondents are required to perform certain clerical activities, such as keeping diaries
- When respondents participate in repeated interviews, as is true for members of a panel
- When respondents are professionals who expect to be paid for the time they spend in an interview

Encouraging Cooperation in Mail Surveys

The single most important factor in increasing the cooperation rate in mail surveys is the use of effective advance and follow-up procedures. Advance notification should come three to five days before the initial questionnaire mailing, and follow-ups should occur at two-week intervals after the initial mailing. Two-week intervals allow sufficient time for the mail to be received and returned. A few additional questionnaires are always returned later, but waiting longer stretches out the data collection period and ultimately increases costs.

Advance notification is usually done by postcard. The purpose is simply to let respondents know that a questionnaire is coming, so that they won't discard it as junk mail, and to give them some brief idea why they should respond to the questionnaire.

Follow-up mailings are done to encourage response. Some people intend to respond but don't get around to it; follow-ups may prompt them to action. Other people will realize that the questionnaire is important to you when they see a follow-up, and this will motivate them to respond.

We recommend that a new copy of the questionnaire be sent with each follow-up mailing. Reminder postcards are cheaper but are ineffective if the respondent has misplaced or discarded the questionnaire. Follow-up material is sent only, of course, to those who have not yet returned the questionnaire. This means that it is necessary to have an identification number on each questionnaire so that it can be logged in when returned. It is useful to explain in the cover letter that the identification number is there so that respondents who have returned the questionnaire will not be sent follow-up letters.

Apart from advance notification and follow-ups, the next most effective method of increasing mail response is to enclose a monetary incentive with the questionnaire. Monetary incentives increase cooperation by 5 to 10 percentage points in general population samples. Currently, for general population samples, the preferred incentive is a crisp new dollar bill. The cover letter should make it clear that this money is intended as a small token of appreciation. The cover letter should not imply that the money is provided to compensate respondents for their time, because it doesn't. Enclosing money with the questionnaire encourages response because many people are reluctant to take the money and ignore the request. Promising to send money later doesn't work nearly as well, even if the amount is larger, because this tactic does not create a sense of obligation.

It is standard procedure to enclose a stamped, self-addressed envelope for the respondent to return the completed mail questionnaire. Stamps are more effective at encouraging cooperation than return envelopes without postage because some respondents are reluctant to waste the postage. Experiments have not shown that special kinds of stamps or colored envelopes have any important effect on cooperation rates.

In addition, cooperation can be increased slightly with a persuasive cover letter that stresses how survey participation will ultimately benefit respondents by improving the goods or services they use. This cover letter should be kept short because many respondents will not read a long letter. Marketing Research Tools 7.3

MARKETING RESEARCH TOOLS

7.3

EXAMPLE OF A COVER LETTER

Official letterhead	WASHINGTON STATE UNIVERSITY Pullman, Washington 99163 DEPARTMENT OF RURAL SOCIOLOGY Room 23, Wilson Hall
Date mailed	April 19, 1971
Inside address in matching type	Oliver Jones 2190 Fontana Road Spokane, Washington 99467
What study is about; its social usefulness	Bills have been introduced in Congress and our State Legislature to encourage the growth of rural and small town areas and slow down that of large cities. These bills could greatly affect the quality of life provided in both rural and urban places. However, no one really knows in what kinds of communities people like yourself want to live or what is thought about these proposed programs.
Why recipient is important (and, if needed, who should complete the questionnaire)	Your household is one of a small number in which people are being asked to give their opinion on these matters. It was drawn in a random sample of the entire state. In order that the results will truly represent the thinking of the people of Washington, it is important that each questionnaire be completed and returned. It is also important that we have about the same number of men and women participating in this study. Thus, we would like the questionnaire for your household to be completed by an <u>adult female.</u> If none is present, then it should be completed by an adult male.
Promise of confidentiality; explanation of identification number	You may be assured of complete confidentiality. The questionnaire has an identification number for mailing purposes only. This is so that we may check your name off the mailing list when your questionnaire is returned. Your name will never be placed on the questionnaire.
Usefulness of study; "token" reward for participation	The results of this research will be made available to officials and representatives in our state's government, members of Congress, and all interested citizens. You may receive a summary of results by writing "copy of results requested" on the back of the return envelope, and printing your name and address below it. Please <u>do not</u> put this information on the questionnaire itself.
What to do if questions arise	I would be most happy to answer any questions you might have. Please write or call. The telephone number is (509) 335-8623.
Appreciation	Thank you for your assistance.
	Sincerely,
Pressed blue ball point signature	*Don A. Dillman*
Title	Don A. Dillman Project Director

shows an example of a good cover letter. Although not shown in the example, a typical cover letter includes a toll-free telephone number or an offer to accept collect calls on a regular number if respondents have any questions they want to ask.

Finally, the actual design of the questionnaire is also of great importance in mail surveys. Questionnaires that look easy and professionally designed will get better responses.

Optimum Levels of Effort

As the previous discussion indicates, it generally costs money to increase survey participation rates. Efforts to increase the participation rate involve the vigorous pursuit of respondents who are harder to locate or recruit. This effort may reduce sample bias, but it definitely increases cost.

Decisions on the extent to which such efforts are justified in any given study ultimately depend on the judgment of the researcher. Although we can give no general rules, here are some common practices:

- The percentage of respondents not reached in telephone surveys is a direct function of the number of follow-ups. Good-quality efforts will use five or more callbacks in telephone surveys, and top-quality efforts will use ten or more.

  This level of effort is common in industrial marketing research, but not in consumer research. Three to six callbacks is a more common level in consumer research, and many consumer research projects use no callbacks at all, relying instead on quotas (for age, sex, and/or employment status) to control sample composition. If no callbacks are made, the sample will be biased toward less active respondents who spend more of their time at home than at work or in other activities away from home.

- Top-quality practice in mail surveys is to send an advance notification before the initial mailing and two follow-ups after. If the cooperation rate is sufficiently high after two follow-ups—say, 50 percent or higher—nothing else is necessary. If the cooperation rate is still too low, follow-up telephone calls can be made to a sample of nonrespondents to obtain information on this group.

  Most market research organizations use lower standards than this. Few use advance notifications, and many do not send follow-ups to nonrespondents.

- The decision on whether to try to convert initial refusers depends on the purpose of the study and the resources available. Often, research managers will set an acceptable level of cooperation and the survey organization will budget to meet this level. For many market research surveys, this cooperation level is set around 60 percent. Refusers are contacted only if their responses are needed to achieve the desired cooperation rate.

Survey Interviewing

Once respondents are contacted and agree to cooperate, the interview begins. In this and the next sections of this chapter, we discuss how to choose, train, and supervise interviewers and how to conduct survey interviews. This information will be helpful both in doing research interviewing and in evaluating survey organizations.

Choosing, Training, and Supervising Interviewers

Choosing, training, and supervising a group of survey interviewers requires skill and experience and is not a job for an inexperienced researcher to tackle unaided. A good job in these areas pays off: an experienced, well-trained, and carefully supervised staff of interviewers can substantially improve the quality of data obtained.

Choosing Interviewers

The hiring of interviewers is normally handled by field supervisors in survey organizations. Most good field supervisors were themselves successful interviewers.

Studies show that background characteristics generally don't predict interviewers' performance very well. However, the following characteristics are common to successful interviewers:

- *Education:* Interviewing requires intelligence and communication skills, and these are most common among people with higher levels of education.

- *Energy:* Interviewing requires substantial energy, persistence, and optimism, even if the interviewer is in a centralized telephone facility and no travel is necessary.

- *Availability:* Even the best interviewer is of little value if not available when needed.

- *Previous experience:* This is a positive factor because it indicates some familiarity with the job and some willingness to do it. Some companies are reluctant to hire experienced interviewers because they fear that the interviewers will have picked up bad habits at other places, but most people will adjust their work habits to fit an organization's policies.

Training Interviewers

Once selected, interviewers must be trained. Training occurs at two levels. All interviewers, even experienced ones, should receive initial training on how to conduct interviews following the organization's standard policies. Then they should receive specific training related to each new study.

The general training covers issues such as how to obtain cooperation from reluctant respondents, how to probe if answers are incomplete, and how to avoid influencing respondents' answers. There is also instruction on clerical activities, such as filling out time sheets.

Normally, the general training consists of home study from an interviewer's manual (such as the *SRC Interviewer's Manual* published by the Survey Research Center at the University of Michigan), in-office lectures from field supervisors, and, most important, the conducting of mock and actual interviews. Mock interviews are conducted with other interviewers or supervisors role-playing the role of respondents, while actual interviews are conducted either with acquaintances or strangers as a supervisor watches or listens. This general training might last from one day to several days, depending on the organization and the previous experience of the interviewer.

Specific training on a particular survey again includes home study of an interviewer's manual prepared for that study, in-office discussion of the study and the questionnaire by a field supervisor and the project director, and some mock interviewing. Such training might take only a few hours for a simple survey but several days for a complicated project.

Some organizations give virtually no training on specific studies but observe interviewers carefully during the initial interviews. We agree that close supervision during the early phases of a study makes sense, but we do not think that it can take the place of at least some initial training.

Author Tips

If you are hiring a company to do survey research, check its training methods. Answers such as "We'll be happy to train the interviewers any way you want" are not acceptable. The organization should have specific practices in place—which can be modified on request—and an interviewer's manual. An absence of training materials is a sign of a low-quality operation.

Supervising Interviewers

The task of an interviewing supervisor is to make sure that data collection is done properly. Supervisors should be available during interviewing periods so they can answer any questions that interviewers may have. They also should monitor each interviewer's work and retrain the interviewer if needed. In some cases, if an interviewer's work is very poor, supervisors may have to recommend termination.

Supervision is easiest in centralized locations, such as malls or telephone facilities. Most centralized telephone sites are wired so that supervisors can listen in on interviews without the interviewer or respondent knowing that the interview is being monitored. In computer-assisted telephone interviewing (CATI) systems, the supervisor can also watch a computer screen identical to the one seen by the interviewer. Thus, the supervisor knows instantly if the interviewer has made an error, either in what she or he says or what she or he enters on the keyboard. The supervisor should not interrupt an interview in progress, but at the end of the interview she or he can discuss the case with the interviewer and correct any problems.

In mall intercept studies, supervisors can observe interviews but do not know what the interviewer has written until the interview is over. They can then check the questionnaire for possible clerical errors. It is good survey practice for a supervisor to be present most of the time while mall intercept interviewing is being conducted.

The presence of a supervisor also acts as a quality control measure to prevent interviewers from fabricating interview results. Such fabrication is called **curbstoning.** This term dates from the early days of market research, when in-home interviews were common; some interviewers would sit on the curb and fill in the questionnaires themselves instead of knocking on doors.

Regardless of whether or not a survey is done in a centralized facility, interviewer cheating is controlled by validation procedures in which a random sample of respondents are recontacted and asked a few questions from the initial interview. Knowing that the interviews will be checked is a strong deterrent to cheating.

Conducting Interviews

A good survey interviewer is a task-oriented "people person" who likes to meet people and has rapport with them. Rapport is important in convincing respondents that their answers are important and in convincing them to give these answers to a stranger. However, the interviewer should not become the respondents' friend. Chumminess makes it more important to respondents to present themselves favorably to the interviewer and can result in less accurate answers. Respondents should feel that the interviewer cares *whether* they answer the questions but not what answers they give.

Thus, the interviewer should be warm yet professional. He or she should be task-oriented; he or she wants to do the interview well but does not desire a social relationship beyond the interviewing task. He or she should avoid extraneous conversation with respondents and show neither approval nor disapproval of their answers.

Some respondents will be hesitant about participating in a survey. A good interviewer will use his or her warmth with these people, explain the objectives of the survey and the scientific nature of the sampling if necessary, and generally cajole them into participating and finishing.

Some respondents may be uneasy about some of the questions, such as questions about their income, and hesitate to answer. This is not the place for warmth. A good interviewer will proceed with such questions as if they were the most normal thing in the world and she or he does not care what answers are given.

Author Tips

Ask potential interviewing suppliers about their validation standards. If they ask "What do you want?" ask for *their* usual standard. The company should have standards in place that can be modified if desired. As with training procedures, an absence of standards is a sign of low quality.

Commenting on the respondent's answer makes for good cartoons but bad research practice.

Source: Adjectives Will Cost You Extra, 1979. DOONESBURY © G. B. Trudeau. Reprinted with permission of Universal Press Syndicate. All rights reserved.

Some respondents will ramble. As soon as she or he realizes that the respondent is talking, not answering, a good interviewer will use the first pause to return to the interview with a probe or with the next question, whichever is appropriate. This does not mean the interviewer should have a "hurry-up" orientation. A good interviewer will avoid nontask conversation but will take as much time as necessary to do the task properly. The interviewer should hear out a respondent who gives a long answer to the question and should record that answer, even if the question has precoded response categories.

A good interviewer will read the entire question and all of the response categories, even if the respondent answers before the reading is finished. Respondents may change their answers when they hear the entire question.

If the respondent gives an unclear or inappropriate answer to a question, a good interviewer will probe for an acceptable answer. She or he will not speed up the interview by deciding what answer the respondent meant to give or by leading the respondent to a particular answer. Proper probing involves rereading the question and the response categories. If the answer clearly lies between acceptable categories, the probe involves asking which category the answer is closer to (for example, "Would that be closer to two times a week or three times a week?"). The probe should never involve explaining the question, because the risk of biasing the answer with explanations or examples is greater than the risk of obtaining a biased answer due to misunderstanding.

The temptation to abridge questions or response lists, to rephrase questions, or to use leading probes becomes almost unbearable with "spacy" respondents. A good interviewer resists this temptation.

When the respondent gives an acceptable answer to a question, a good interviewer simply records the answer and moves to the next question. He or she does not express surprise or disbelief at the answer, nor does he or she express approval or disapproval.

In addition to proper interviewing techniques, a good interviewer must have professional deportment and, for face-to-face interviewers, a professional appearance. The interviewer's appearance or deportment should not draw respondents' attention away from the interview. A simple hairstyle, subdued cosmetics, and neat, conservative clothing are appropriate, as are good grammar and a professional manner. Male interviewers in industrial surveys should wear a coat and tie.

Marketing Research Tools 7.4 is a summary of interviewing guidelines.

Critical Thinking Skills

Test yourself as an interviewer. Make up a brief questionnaire, or use an existing questionnaire, and interview a friend or family member. See how well you can follow our interviewing guidelines. Tape-record the interview and listen to it.

Controlling Survey Costs and Quality

While a survey is in progress, the people responsible for conducting or buying the study may want information relevant to the project schedule and sample quality, such as the number of interviews that have been completed and the numbers of

MARKETING RESEARCH TOOLS

7.4

GUIDELINES FOR SURVEY INTERVIEWING

1. Maintain a task orientation.
2. Be warm with respondents who are hesitant about participating in the survey.
3. Be cool with respondents who are uneasy about a question, and act as if asking this question is the most normal thing in the world.
4. If a respondent rambles, use the first pause to return to the interview with a probe or with the next question.
5. Take as much time as necessary to do the task properly. Hear out and record long answers.
6. Read the entire question and all of the response categories.
7. If the respondent gives an unclear or inappropriate answer, probe for an acceptable answer.
8. Do not lead the respondent to a particular answer. Reread the question and the response categories; don't suggest a category, and don't explain the question.
9. When the respondent gives an acceptable answer, record that answer, and move on. Do not express surprise, disbelief, approval, or disapproval.

noncontacts, initial refusals, and final refusals. Cost-control information relating actual expenditures to budgeted ones can also be useful, especially if the budget is tight and there are indications of a budget overrun.

Controlling the Interviewing Schedule and Sample Quality

The basic document used to monitor scheduling and sample quality for telephone and in-home surveys is the **interviewer report form (IRF).** An IRF is maintained for each potential respondent in a survey sample; it records the timing and outcomes of efforts to contact and interview the respondent. Marketing Research Tools 7.5 (see page 178) shows an example of an IRF.

Whenever desired, IRFs can be tabulated to show the number of interviews completed, the number of people who have refused interviews, the number who have been called with no contact, the number of calls that have been made, and, if recorded, the average length of an interview. Most survey organizations have computerized control systems into which IRF data are logged daily; this is easiest in CATI systems, in which the IRF is shown on the computer screen and the interviewer enters control information on line.

For mail surveys, interviews are logged into the computer as they are returned. This not only provides control information but also is used to remove respondents from the list of those who are to receive follow-up mailings.

MARKETING RESEARCH TOOLS

7.5

EXAMPLE OF AN INTERVIEWER REPORT FORM

UNIVERSITY OF ILLINOIS
Survey Research Laboratory
Interviewer Report Form

Quest. # _____
Study # _____
_____
_____

Contact Attempt	Date	Time	Disposition	Final		Appointments/Notes/Other	Interviewer ID#
				Yes	No		
01	_____	_____	_____	1	2	_____	_____
02	_____	_____	_____	1	2	_____	_____
03	_____	_____	_____	1	2	_____	_____
04	_____	_____	_____	1	2	_____	_____
05	_____	_____	_____	1	2	_____	_____
06	_____	_____	_____	1	2	_____	_____
07	_____	_____	_____	1	2	_____	_____
08	_____	_____	_____	1	2	_____	_____
09	_____	_____	_____	1	2	_____	_____
10	_____	_____	_____	1	2	_____	_____
11	_____	_____	_____	1	2	_____	_____
12	_____	_____	_____	1	2	_____	_____
13	_____	_____	_____	1	2	_____	_____
14	_____	_____	_____	1	2	_____	_____
15	_____	_____	_____	1	2	_____	_____

Interviewer Notes: _____

_____

_____

_____

_____

Intercept surveys are usually completed within a few days, and there is no need to follow up on noncontacts. Because of this, some intercept surveys use no control records at all. We think this is a mistake. The number of refusals and the number of potential respondents who were ineligible should be recorded for purposes of evaluating the interviewing effort, evaluating the sample, and planning future studies.

Cost Control

Keeping track of costs in an ongoing survey is closely related to keeping track of response rates and interview lengths. Response rates are the key factor, especially when a survey is screening for some small group within the broader population. For example, a survey that seeks 400 buyers of some product and assumes that these buyers make up 5 percent of the population will plan to conduct 8,000 screening interviews to get 400 buyers (8,000 × .05 = 400). If the target group turns out to make up only 4 percent of the population, 8,000 screening calls will yield only 320 buyers, and the researcher will need to decide whether to reduce the target sample size or absorb the cost of another 2,000 screening interviews to get 80 more buyers.

To recognize and control such situations, preliminary estimates about response rates should be checked against actual experience during the survey. This is done either by monitoring results continuously or by stopping when one-third or one-half of the interviews have been done so that a cost analysis can be made. If this analysis indicates cost overruns because of unexpected sample difficulties, the survey organization can advise the client and request a budget increase or a sample size reduction. Reasonable clients recognize the need to make changes in the face of unexpected events, but they expect to be notified early enough to consider alternative courses of action. If a

CASE STUDY 7.4

One issue in planning a survey is deciding when to do it. The results of a survey—or any research project—can depend on the time when it is done. For example:

- The University of Houston did two surveys of its undergraduate students. Both surveys included a question asking students to cite areas of the university that should be changed. In the first survey, done in the third week of a fall semester, 10 percent of the students cited registration as an area to be changed. In the second survey, done in the eleventh week, only 5 percent of the students cited registration. Apparently, the pain of registration fades with time.

- Similarly, a research manager at a large hospital told us, "If we measure patient satisfaction right after a patient leaves the hospital, it tends to be lower than if we wait awhile. Minor irritations about the food, the nurses, and the bill fade as time goes by, and people mostly remember the hospital as the place where they got well."

If results are likely to be time-sensitive, a researcher must think about the best time to gather data, or must balance the data collection across different time periods.

survey organization does not inform the client of cost overruns until the study is completed and nothing can be done to contain costs, the client is likely to balk at additional payments or at the very least to mistrust future bids from this organization. Remember, researchers should always follow a rule of "no surprises for the client."

Whereas interviewer wage costs can be monitored continuously, other costs can be tabulated less frequently. Telephone charges for long-distance calls, for example, need to be estimated on the basis of IRF data because the actual bills will not arrive until long after the interviewing for a project is complete. Other staff costs, derived from time sheets, are usually tabulated weekly.

In preparing cost-control information, data should be entered in their most disaggregate form. This is critical to detailed analysis of why budget overruns, if any, are occurring, and for the careful budgeting of future studies.

Summary

This chapter discussed survey research methods. The following points were covered:

1. What are the strengths and weaknesses of surveys compared to other self-report methods of data collection?

The major strength of surveys is broad coverage of the population due to the relatively low cost of administration and relatively high cooperation rate. The major weakness of surveys is that only limited information can be obtained from each respondent.

2. What are the advantages and disadvantages of personal surveys, intercept surveys, telephone surveys, and mail surveys?

Personal surveys offer maximum questionnaire flexibility and sample quality but are expensive. In general, they are used only for surveys of business buyers and for consumer research in countries where telephone surveys are not appropriate.

Intercept surveys, usually conducted in shopping malls, allow objects to be shown to respondents at a lower cost than in personal interviews. However, sample quality is not as high as in personal or telephone surveys, and the questionnaire cannot take more than a few minutes to complete.

Telephone surveys offer sample quality similar to that of personal surveys at a much lower cost. However, it is not possible to show products, packages, or ads, and response alternatives must be limited.

The major advantage of mail surveys is low cost. The disadvantages include a number of limitations on both the questionnaire and sample quality.

3. How can participation rates in surveys be increased?

In face-to-face and telephone interviews, participation rates depend mainly on: (1) the number of callbacks used to reach unavailable respondents and (2) the quality and experience of the interviewer in gaining cooperation. In mail surveys, response can be increased by using prenotification postcards, follow-up mailings, monetary incentives, self-addressed stamped envelopes with real stamps, a persuasive cover letter, and a professional questionnaire.

4. How is a survey interview conducted?

A good interviewer is warm yet professional. She or he establishes a rapport with respondents to make them feel at ease but avoids extraneous conversation and shows neither approval nor disapproval of their answers. A good interviewer must have a professional appearance (for face-to-face interviewers) and professional deportment.

5. How should interviewers be chosen, trained, and supervised?

Good interviewers are educated, energetic, available, and experienced. They should receive general training on interviewing techniques, as well as specific training related to each new study. Supervisors should listen to a sample of each interviewer's work and retrain as necessary.

6. How can surveys be managed and their costs controlled?

A key issue in managing surveys is keeping track of response rates. If response rates are not as high as planned, the researcher must decide whether to absorb the costs of contacting additional respondents. Interviewer report forms (IRFs) can be used to monitor response rates and work in progress.

Suggested Additional Readings

In addition to the market research literature, there is a more general literature on surveys that you may find useful. Norman M. Bradburn and Seymour Sudman, *Polls and Surveys: Understanding What They Tell Us* (San Francisco: Jossey-Bass, 1988) is an introduction to survey methods intended primarily for users and the general public. Two short, simple, but sound books are Ronald Czaja and Johnny Blair, *Designing Surveys* (Newbury Park, Calif.: Sage, 1996), and Floyd J. Fowler, *Survey Research Methods* (Newbury Park, Calif.: Sage, 1984). Two more advanced versions intended for professionals are Peter H. Rossi, James B. Wright, and Arnold B. Anderson, eds., *The Handbook of Survey Research* (Orlando, Fla.: Academic, 1983), and Eleanor Singer and Stanley Presser, eds., *Survey Research Methods: A Reader* (Chicago: University of Chicago Press, 1989). A similarly advanced-level book is Robert M. Groves, *Survey Errors and Survey Costs* (New York: Wiley, 1989). Groves and Robert L. Kahn are the authors of a good book on telephone methods, *Surveys by Telephone* (Orlando, Fla.: Academic, 1979). A more recent review of the telephone survey literature is Robert M. Groves, Paul P. Biemer, Lars E. Lyberg, James T. Massey, William L. Nicholls II, and Joseph Waksberg, *Telephone Survey Methodology* (New York: Wiley, 1988). The best and most widely used book on mail surveys is Donald Dillman, *Mail and Telephone Surveys: The Total Design Method*, (New York: Wiley, 1978). Finally, there is an excellent annotated bibliography by Graham R. Walden, *Public Opinion Polls and Survey Research: A Selected Annotated Bibliography of U.S. Guides and Studies from the 1980s* (New York: Garland, 1990).

Discussion Questions

1. What is a survey and how does it differ from other data collection methods?
2. What are the major strengths and weaknesses of surveys compared to other self-report procedures?
3. What are three methods of survey administration? Discuss the advantages and disadvantages of each method.
4. What kind of research method would you use to measure how customers perceive the quality of services provided by service establishments such as hotels, restaurants, and airlines?

5. What factors should a researcher consider before conducting a survey?

6. What are some of the ways that computers and interactive technology are revolutionizing the way marketing research surveys are being conducted?

Marketing Research Challenge

Suppose you have developed a new salad dressing and wish to estimate its market potential so you can decide whether or not to proceed with market introduction. Describe the survey procedure you would use to test consumer reactions toward the new product. Note that in addition to the methods discussed in this chapter, you may consider combining procedures.

Internet Exercise

Case Study 7.3 discusses using the Internet as a place to conduct surveys. Summarize the pros and cons of using the Internet in this way. In what circumstances would an Internet survey be more appropriate than a mail or telephone survey? In what circumstances would it be less appropriate?

References

Erdos, P. L. and A. J. Morgan (1970). *Professional Mail Surveys* (New York: McGraw-Hill).

Meyers, Gerald (1993). "Interviewing Trade Execs Is Not like Interviewing Consumers." *Marketing News* 27 (June 7), pp. H20–H21.

8 Conducting Focus Groups and Depth Interviews

 OBJECTIVES

LEARNING

After reading this chapter, you should be able to answer the following questions:

① What are the strengths and weaknesses of focus groups as a research method?

② What are good uses of focus group research?

③ How is a focus group organized and conducted?

④ What are the strengths and weaknesses of individual depth interviews?

⑤ What are good uses of depth interviews?

⑥ How is a depth interview organized and conducted?

Like surveys, focus groups and depth interviews use self-reports to obtain information. Unlike surveys, these methods do not use fixed questionnaires. The focus group moderator or depth interviewer starts only with a list of topics to be covered and doesn't ask questions so much as moderate the respondents' flow of thought about these topics. The sessions last a long time—90 to 120 minutes for focus groups, 30 to 90 minutes for depth interviews—and cover a narrow range of topics. The long duration and narrow focus of focus groups and depth interviews are what give them their names.

The general method of depth interviewing, whether in groups or individually, comes from the field of psychoanalysis. This is why focus groups and depth interviews don't use fixed questionnaires. The philosophy of psychoanalytic interviewing is that unstructured discussion allows respondents to reveal their feelings and beliefs in their own natural language with their own natural structure. Psychoanalytic methods also assume that important feelings or beliefs may be buried beneath the surface and will emerge only if respondents discuss a topic at length.

The strengths of focus groups and depth interviews are their ability to get a great deal of information from each respondent, their ability to get complex information about attitudes or motivations, and their ability to capture how respondents structure the topic of interest. These methods are well suited to concept testing, motivational research, and interviews of executives (where the usual research goal is to get large amounts of information from a small number of respondents).

The major weakness of focus groups and depth interviews is their inability to get broad population coverage because of small samples and low response rates. The length and personnel requirements of these methods make them very expensive and limit the number that can be done. Also, the length of these interviews, and the fact that most of them are done at researchers' facilities, reduces the number of people who will cooperate. Because of these limitations, focus groups and depth interviews are not as well suited as surveys for most routine studies of buying and consumption behavior.

Currently, focus groups are much more common than depth interviews in consumer research, primarily because they are less expensive. Individual depth interviews are more likely to be used in business-to-business research, in which executives are interviewed. Even in business markets, though, focus groups are common.

Because focus groups are more common than individual depth interviews, this chapter begins with a discussion of general procedures for focus groups, the strengths and weaknesses of focus groups, and appropriate uses for focus groups in marketing research, followed by a more detailed discussion of how to conduct focus groups. The chapter concludes with a discussion of individual depth interviews.

Focus Groups

The use of focus groups in market research has grown rapidly over the past twenty-five years. Twenty-five years ago, few companies used focus group interviews in their market research programs. Today, virtually all marketing research suppliers in the United States are capable of conducting focus groups, and many small research companies specialize in this method. The rise in focus groups has resulted from the increasingly prohibitive costs of personal surveys, combined with a continuing need for marketers to hear spontaneous comments from their customers.

Actually, the term "focused group interview" was originally applied to a type of survey. Large groups of people, usually radio-show audiences, would be asked structured questions and would record their answers to these questions. This type of "focused group" disappeared at least thirty years ago; today, a **focus group** is a small group discussion without a fixed questionnaire. It is unstructured so that spontaneous thoughts and ideas can surface.

General Procedures for Focus Groups

A focus group usually consists of six to fifteen people drawn from a population relevant to a company's marketing activities. These people have been contacted by a research company and asked to come to a group discussion on the indicated topic. They have been offered a financial incentive to come, usually $25 to $50. The focus group is usually held in a room that has circular seating, a microphone for tape recording, and a one-way mirror through which the discussion can be viewed and/or videotaped (Edmondston, 1994; Feig, 1989; Goldman and McDonald, 1987; Greenbaum, 1993a,b; Higginbotham and Cox, 1979; Hoeffel, 1994; Krueger, 1988; Morgan, 1988; Templeton, 1994).

A photograph of a focus group in session is shown on the next page.

Participants are greeted by a receptionist as they arrive for the session. Their attendance is registered, and they may be given a brief background questionnaire to complete. They are subsequently ushered into the focus group room. The focus group room usually has plenty of drinks for everyone and may have cookies, doughnuts, or sandwiches.

A **focus group moderator** is a person trained to conduct an unstructured discussion on a prespecified list of topics. The moderator begins the session by welcoming the participants and thanking them for coming. She or he then describes the plan for the session; she or he might simply tell the participants the general topic for the discussion, or she or he might tell them several specific topics that she or he would like to cover. These topics are broadly stated; for example, how people feel about banking in general, how they feel about their banks, and what they would like to see changed about their banks.

To start the discussion, the moderator might go around the room and ask each participant to answer a couple of easy questions such as "Where do you bank?" and

A focus group in session.

Author Tips

An important task for the moderator is to help everyone's opinions emerge, even if they disagree with comments that other participants have made. The moderator might sense that a particular person disagrees with something that has just been said and say to that person, "You look as though you might have a different opinion about that. What is your opinion?" The moderator's goal is to encourage each participant to reveal his or her feelings and, without seeming to criticize anyone, to show the participants that they need not agree with the others. It is not constructive, for example, to have a debate about the "true" or "proper" feelings anyone should have toward banking.

"About how long have you banked there?" The moderator then presents the first topic in the form of a general question for the table at large: "What are your feelings about banking?"

Once the discussion begins, the moderator doesn't talk much, preferring to let group members stimulate one another. The moderator will prefer not to change the subject, but simply to follow up interesting comments or keep the conversation going by asking people "Why do you feel that way?" The points she or he follows up on will be those that relate to any specific reasons why the focus group is being held. For example, if a bank is thinking about redecorating its interior, the moderator will tend to follow up on any comments related to the bank's decor.

The moderator will also try to bring shy participants into the discussion by directly asking them, "What is your opinion, Joe?" Sometimes an initial stimulus is all that is needed to get someone into the discussion. If a participant remains shy—and most focus groups will have one or two people who remain quiet—the moderator occasionally will check this person's opinions, but mostly will leave the person alone. Repeatedly asking someone to participate may stress that person and disrupt the flow of discussion.

The moderator will work from a list of topics to be covered in the session. For example, Exhibit 8.1 shows the topic list from a focus group on health care. When a topic seems exhausted or the session has reached a predesignated time for moving to another topic, the moderator changes the subject to the next topic. The session proceeds in this manner until the discussion is exhausted or time has run out. The moderator will close the session, thank the participants for coming, and remind them to see the receptionist for their payment.

An audiotape of the session—and a videotape as well, if the session has been videotaped—will immediately be labeled and given to the project director. Subsequently, the tape may be transcribed to a typed record, and the project director will use this transcript to select quotations to be used in the report to the client.

EXHIBIT 8.1

Discussion Guide for a Focus Group on Health Care

1. Welcome and introductions

2. Current health status and medical problems

3. When do you go see a doctor?

4. Relationship with health care providers:
   Kinds of contact/time spent
   Difficulty in seeing doctor/making appointments
   Cost
   Ease in getting to provider

5. Physical examinations:
   Does doctor explain what is happening?
   Can you influence what tests are performed?
   How are results communicated?
   How is the decision made to get a physical exam?

Strengths and Weaknesses of Focus Groups

Compared with surveys, focus groups offer greater depth and flexibility. For example, Case Study 8.1 describes a situation in which the informality of a focus group allowed the rapid discovery of an important point that would have been hard to get in a survey (because the researcher would not have thought to include a relevant question). On the downside, focus groups cost much more than surveys on a per person basis and are limited to people who are willing to go to a research facility.

Compared with individual depth interviews, focus groups have the advantages of (1) lower cost per person, (2) a possible stimulating effect from group interaction, and (3) higher vividness to managers. This higher vividness does not come from any implicit difference in the methods but rather from the fact that most focus groups are observed and/or videotaped, whereas most individual depth interviews are not. The disadvantages of focus groups, compared with individual interviews, are that focus groups (1) obtain less information from each respondent, (2) are somewhat less flexible regarding the use of physical stimuli such as pictures, and (3) may be less complete at the individual level because many participants may not comment on a given issue discussed by the group.

Overall, individual interviews are more flexible than focus groups from a purely methodological point of view. The greater popularity of focus groups stems from their lower cost and the fact that managers find them more vivid.

Good Uses of Focus Groups

The widespread growth of focus groups has led to both good and bad uses of the method. Good uses include the following:

CASE STUDY 8.1

Here is a story that shows how the unstructured information provided by focus groups can be useful. Dean's Formal Wear is a retail chain that rents and sells tuxedos. About three years ago, the company diagnosed a marketing problem. It held more than 50 percent of the tuxedo *rental* business in its market but less than 10 percent of the tuxedo *sales* business.

The company decided to target tuxedo sales as a growth opportunity. It ran advertising that featured "tuxedos for sale" at very attractive prices. However, these efforts produced only a slight increase in tuxedo sales.

The company asked a marketing consultant for help. He says:

We started with a theory that Dean's had such a strong rental image that people didn't think of Dean's as a place to buy tuxedos, despite the advertising. To check this theory, we ran a small survey in which we asked people to name stores where they could buy a tuxedo. The results surprised us: most people named Dean's. People knew that Dean's sold tuxedos but just weren't buying from Dean's.

We tried a focus group to see if we could learn the reasons why. We brought in ten men who had bought tuxedos during the previous six months: four from Dean's and six from other stores.

I started the discussion by going around the room and asking each man whether he had bought a tuxedo and where he had bought it. Then I asked one of the men who had not bought from Dean's whether he knew that Dean's sold tuxedos. "Yes," he said. I asked why he hadn't bought his tuxedo at Dean's. He said, "I didn't want a used tuxedo." I saw several other men nodding in agreement, so I asked the group members to raise their hands if they thought that a tuxedo bought at Dean's would be used. Eight of the ten raised their hands, including two men who bought their tuxedos at Dean's. I said to one of them, "You thought Dean's sold you a used tuxedo?" "Sure," he said. "That's why their prices are lower. Myself, I didn't really care if the tuxedo was used, and it seemed to be in good condition, so I decided to save the money."

The group kept talking for another hour, but I already had the information I needed. People weren't buying from Dean's because they thought that Dean's would sell them a used tuxedo. On our advice, Dean's began to advertise <u>brand-new</u> tuxedos for sale; sales doubled within six months and continue to grow to the present day.

- Focus groups are great for concept testing (**concept tests** are tests of whether buyers like a new-product concept, done before a lot of money is spent on product development). If a new-product concept is run past a focus group, participants' reactions will fall into one of three categories: they love it, hate it, or are in between. If they love the concept, it is a winner and can be developed further. If they're in between, more detailed research may be needed. If they hate it, the idea should be dropped.

CASE STUDY 8.2

Focus groups that are used to test responses to new-product concepts should reflect the environment in which those products will be marketed. A large bank learned this lesson the hard way.

The bank developed a new type of checking account that offered more services for a higher fee than a regular checking account. Focus groups were used to test the concept. These focus groups showed favorable consumer response, so the bank introduced the new type of account. Unfortunately, it flopped. Contrary to what the focus groups had suggested, customers did not sign up for these accounts.

In an effort to learn why the product had failed, the bank reviewed transcripts of the focus groups for warning signs. This review showed that participants in the groups had initially been negative to the account concept but had warmed up as they learned more about it and were highly enthusiastic by the end of the discussion. Unfortunately, the bank did not have the luxury of talking with customers for forty-five minutes when it marketed these accounts. The marketing relied on advertising that never got past the negative first impression.

Researchers must be sensitive to this issue in testing new-product concepts. If a product will be sold through lengthy, face-to-face sales calls, it makes sense to provide research participants with a great deal of product information before measuring their responses. However, if the product will be sold in a mass-marketing context, it may be more appropriate to measure first impressions.

- Focus groups are also good for learning how people use a product and what it means to them. For example, Norma Larkin, director of consumer research for Nabisco, says that focus groups helped the company design a successful advertising campaign for Oreo cookies. Focus groups revealed that many adults view Oreos as a cherished memory of childhood and perceive the product to be almost magical in its ability to make people feel good. This led Nabisco to a successful ad campaign, "Unlocking the Magic of Oreo," which was designed to bring out all the good things about being a kid.

- Focus groups are good for exploring problems or complaints that people have had in connection with a product, as well as ways of addressing these problems or complaints. In this regard, focus groups can be a good source of ideas about product improvements.

- Focus groups are good for exploring why people hold certain views about a brand or why they evaluate a package or an advertisement the way they do.

- Focus groups can be used to show researchers which issues to cover in a survey questionnaire.

The principal *bad* use of focus groups is as a substitute for surveys. Most marketing research surveys cost more than $10,000 if a reputable research company does the work. Focus groups are more expensive on a per participant basis, but a focus group can be conducted for less than $5,000. This leads some research clients on

Focus group results shouldn't be used for quantitative estimates.

Source: Fugitive from the Cubicle Police, 1996. DILBERT. Scott Adams. Reprinted by permission of United Features Syndicate, Inc.

MARKETING RESEARCH TOOLS

8.1

GOOD AND BAD USES OF FOCUS GROUPS

Good uses:
    Concept testing for new products
    Understanding how people use a product or what it means to them
    Probing attitudes and their underlying bases
    Exploring customers' problems or complaints with a product
    Identifying issues to be covered in a structured questionnaire

Bad use:
    As a substitute for surveys

tight budgets to use one or two focus groups as an alternative to a survey. Researchers will run these groups almost as if they are a group survey, going around the room to get each participant's response to structured questions and analyzing the data in a quantitative fashion typical of survey analysis ("40 percent of the participants felt that . . .").

The problem, of course, is that a focus group isn't a survey. If a survey is the best method for a particular problem but the research budget is only $5,000, it is necessary to find a way to do a $5,000 survey rather than switch to focus groups. Using focus groups instead of surveys for financial reasons ignores the basic strengths and weaknesses of the two methods.

Marketing Research Tools 8.1 summarizes the good and bad uses of focus groups.

How to Organize and Conduct Focus Groups

Specific issues in doing focus group research fall into four broad categories: choosing the location, recruiting participants, moderating the discussion, and reporting the results.

Choosing the Location

There are two factors to consider in choosing a location for a focus group:

- The location should be convenient and comfortable for respondents. Many people will not show up to a focus group if it requires them to drive a long distance, go to a bad neighborhood, or even go to an unfamiliar place.

- The facility should be well designed for group discussion. Desirable features include (1) a reception area where participants can be greeted, (2) seating in the discussion room that allows all group members to see one another, (3) a discussion room that is large enough to avoid crowding, with comfortable seats and pleasant decor, (4) ideally, the ability to observe the discussion from another room, (5) an observation room that is soundproofed and wired so the observers can hear the group but the group can't hear the observers, (6) videotaping facilities, and (7) a setup such that the video camera and the observers can see the faces of as many participants as possible.

A focus group can be held in a private home, at the client company's offices, at a hotel, or at a special facility operated by a research company.

A home offers an informal, relaxing environment that may be conducive to discussion; on the other hand, a home may be difficult to find, and some participants may feel uncomfortable going to a stranger's home. Private homes also lack facilities for observing or videotaping discussions. In general, private homes are not used except in special circumstances, such as a focus group of hospital volunteers that is held in the home of a member of the volunteer association's board of directors.

Holding the focus group at company offices makes it easy for managers to attend but creates a variety of other problems. Even if a comfortable, informal room can be provided for the group, the general surroundings of a business and an office building make the setting somewhat formal. Observation facilities are usually not available, and the location may not be convenient for participants, especially if the offices are in a business district and the participants are consumers.

Hotels offer convenient locations that should be familiar to participants. However, they typically lack observation facilities, and they may not be comfortable. Hotels have comfortable chairs in their guest rooms but usually not in their meeting rooms, where focus groups will be held. The atmosphere may also be somewhat formal. In general, hotels are better locations for focus groups involving businesspeople than for those involving consumers.

Most focus groups are held at specialized facilities operated by research companies. These facilities are located in malls or other places where people feel comfortable, and they have all the desired reception and observation facilities. The research company that provides the facility can also provide other services, including recruiting participants, greeting and registering participants, arranging catering, paying participants after the focus group, and providing a session moderator.

Prices for a full-service focus group—for which a research supplier takes full responsibility for arranging a facility, recruiting participants, moderating the session, and so on—run from about $2,000 to $5,000 depending on where in the country the group is held. This includes payments to participants. If the client provides a moderator and produces the report, the price will normally be about $1,000 lower.

The choice among focus group facilities often depends more on location than on the facility's features. For example, Sharpstown Mall in Houston, Texas, is a popular location for consumer focus groups. The focus group facility at Sharpstown Mall is not especially nice, but it is adequate, and the location is terrific. This mall has nearby populations of upper-middle-class people, lower-middle-class people, middle-middle-class people, homeowners, apartment dwellers, Anglos, Hispanics, African Americans, and Asians, so almost any desired type of consumer can be recruited to the mall. This convenience makes the focus group facility at Sharpstown Mall more attractive for many studies than other, nicer facilities are.

Critical Thinking Skills

What location in your community would be ideal for a consumer focus group facility?

Recruiting Participants and Forming Groups

The desired population for a focus group is set according to the general research objectives. Whatever population is desired, decisions must be made regarding (1) how to recruit members of this population, (2) what incentives to offer for participation, (3) how many people to recruit, and (4) how to form these people into groups.

How to Recruit

Every research organization that offers focus group services maintains a file with the name, address, and telephone number of everyone who has participated in the organization's focus groups during the past few years. These files also contain background information such as the age, sex, race, and occupation of each participant.

An organization's first instinct when asked to recruit a group is to use the files of previous participants. Using the files allows it to match any demographic requirements for the group without screening new people. It also allows it to be confident that most of the people contacted for the group will cooperate. This makes its job quicker and easier.

Unfortunately, using previous participants means that a focus group will be filled with experienced respondents, some of whom may be **"professional respondents"** who have participated in many previous groups. Most research clients prefer to avoid these people, out of fear that they will not be as spontaneous as less experienced participants or that they will dominate the discussion. A standard policy in good research organizations that is designed to avoid "professional respondents" is not to use participants within six months of a prior focus group. Even so, it is best to specify that the research company is *not* to use its files in recruiting participants for your focus groups.

If the research company is not allowed to use its files, it will recruit participants by random telephone calls or mall intercepts. The advantage of random calls is that they should produce a broader sample than a sample drawn from mall visitors. The advantage of mall recruitment, if the discussion facility is located at the mall, is that recruits are known to visit the mall and are more likely to show up for the session.

However potential recruits are located, they are screened to verify that they fit the group requirements. If eligible, they are also asked whether they have participated in a group discussion at a research facility during the past six months (or, if you prefer, during the past year). If not, they are told that the research company is looking for people to participate in a discussion group. They are told the day, time, and place of the discussion and the payment for participating, and they are asked whether they would be willing to participate in this discussion. If so, they are asked for a mailing address so the recruiter can send them a formal confirmation, and a confirmation letter and a map are mailed to them.

The confirmation letter mentions the date, starting time, ending time, and place of the discussion as well as the compensation rate. This letter helps participants remember and find the session and also reassures them that the project is legitimate.

What Incentives to Offer

Incentives are necessary to get people to attend a focus group discussion. The only questions are what kind of incentive to use and how big it should be.

For consumer focus groups, cash incentives are used almost exclusively. Payments can be as low as $15, but $25 to $50 is the norm in most cities. Clients who want to encourage participation are usually advised to give $50. Larger amounts do not significantly increase cooperation, and the research company may complain that a higher payment will "break the scale."

For groups of businesspeople or professionals, gifts or charitable contributions are sometimes used, but cash incentives are still the norm. For these groups, $35 is a low amount, $50 is typical, and $100 or more is not uncommon (Fedder, 1990). If a gift or charitable contribution is given, the value should be in the same range as a cash incentive. Cash is really the best incentive. Clients are sometimes concerned that a cash payment will seem to place an inappropriately low value on the participant's time, but this can be avoided by positioning the payment as "a small honorarium of $50."

How Many People to Recruit

The typical size of a focus group is six to ten participants, though larger groups are sometimes used. Smaller groups can have more intimate discussions, whereas larger groups allow for a greater range of opinions. If a group becomes too large, it is difficult to bring everyone into the conversation.

Every organization has its own standards regarding the number of people who should be recruited to fill a group. Unless the compensation is unusually high, most focus group recruiters assume that only about half the recruits who agree to participate will actually show up.

Critical Thinking Skills

What kinds of people would you seek for a focus group to be used for concept testing on a new, inexpensive sports car? What differences, if any, would you expect if these people were recruited from visitors to a mall in your locality versus being recruited by random phone calls?

How to Compose the Group

In general, it is desirable to fill focus groups with people who are similar in some regard. Professional groups, of course, are similar in that they are all doctors, businesspeople, or whatever. Consumer groups might be made similar in terms of socioeconomic background, gender, race, type of work, stage in the family life cycle, or other factors.

Participants certainly don't have to be identical to one another, and the group might be boring if they were. However, when people don't share some common bond, it can be difficult for them to loosen up and share their feelings, or the group may split into cliques—working women against housewives, Anglos against African Americans, childless adults against parents, and so on. This damages the quality of the discussion. Discussion is particularly restricted by large differences in social status: lower-class or lower-education respondents often feel intimidated and do not talk. If the discussion concerns personal topics, men and women may not feel comfortable being in the same group.

The problem with breaking a population into subgroups is that a larger number of focus groups are needed to cover the population. Most focus group projects are budgeted for only one to four groups. This limits the extent to which people can be broken into subgroups and guarantees some diversity within groups.

Critical Thinking Skills

If you were planning two focus groups to be used for concept testing on a new, inexpensive sports car, would you separate male and female participants into separate groups? Would you separate any other types of respondents? What would you offer as an incentive for participation?

Moderating the Discussion

Like a good survey interviewer, a focus group moderator should be a task-oriented "people person" who relates easily to participants but focuses on getting the job done. The focus group moderator also needs skills in conversation management and detailed knowledge about the purposes of the focus group, so he or she can bring everybody into the discussion, steer the discussion away from unproductive topics, and recognize and encourage useful avenues for discussion.

Earlier in this chapter, some techniques for moderating focus groups were mentioned. The focus group moderator should be a moderator, not a leader—or, perhaps more accurately, lead the discussion unobtrusively. A good moderator never interjects his or her opinions into the discussion. If the group participants are doing well on their own, a good moderator says nothing. He or she talks only when he or she wants to involve people ("How do you feel about that, Jane?"), when he or she wants to encourage further discussion on some point ("How do the rest of you feel about that?" or "Why do you feel that way?"), or when he or she absolutely must change the topic of discussion. This isn't to say that the moderator is passive; he or she must actively but *unobtrusively* guide the discussion.

If an active, outgoing participant is recognized during the general chitchat that often occurs before the discussion starts, this person may be asked to sit in the chair next to the moderator. A shy person should be placed in a chair across from the moderator. This allows the moderator easily and naturally to look at the shy person and solicit his or her comments. Having the aggressive person at the moderator's side allows the moderator to control this person by looking away from him or her (which has a subtle "body language" effect) or even by gently pressing the aggressive person's arm to stop him or her from talking.

Changes in topic are accomplished as much as possible by following up on comments made within the group, rather than by saying "Another topic we want to discuss is . . . " In general, the moderator should not worry about the sequence of topics: he or she wants to cover all the topics on the discussion guide, but maintaining a natural flow of discussion is more important than maintaining a topic order.

Sometimes companies use focus groups as a cheap alternative to a survey, and they want to get participants' feelings about a series of structured issues. In this situation, the focus group moderator must be more intrusive and must structure the discussion to satisfy client needs. This is a poor use of focus groups that ignores the strengths of the method.

Reporting Focus Group Results

Most researchers feel that focus groups should be viewed as a "nonquantitative" technique. That is, if your emphasis in focus group analysis is to count the number of times some issue is mentioned or to count the number of people who agree with some opinion, you are using the wrong method. Your emphasis in interpreting focus groups should be on ideas, themes, and relationships.

Focus group analysis should generally be done from a typed transcript of the session(s). The analyst reads the transcript, draws important themes or ideas from it, and writes a narrative that reports these ideas and their implications. The emphasis isn't on the number of people who said something but rather on what they said. A focus group report should read like a story rather than a series of tables.

Verbatim comments from the transcript are used in the report to illustrate themes and ideas. For example, the verbatim comments in Exhibit 8.2 were used in

EXHIBIT 8.2

Verbatim Comments from a Focus Group Concerning Direct Deposit of Social Security Checks

"The government doesn't have to tell me how to handle my money. I'll do it myself."

"If the check didn't come to me, I'd never get out of the house."

"Going downtown is a treat. Going to the bank gives me an excuse to go downtown."

"I pay my bills with cash. I don't know how to handle a checking account."

"I have other checks to deposit, so I do it all at one time."

"The mails are safer than direct deposit. I don't trust computers."

"I like to meet my friends at the bank and visit with them."

"A retirement magazine story was unfavorable towards direct deposit."

"I want to feel the money in my hand."

"I can take care of my own finances."

reporting the results of several focus groups in which retired people talked about banking services. The specific issue that stimulated these comments was the desirability of "direct deposit" service for Social Security checks.

The analyst used these verbatim comments to support a conclusion that many participants were resistant to direct deposit services. On a broader level, the analyst also used them to show that banking activities represent more than a series of routine financial transactions for retired people; they involve feelings of independence, competence, and social participation. These points couldn't have been made as powerfully without the verbatim comments.

Incidentally, this example illustrates the special nature and value of unstructured interviewing techniques. Had the bank's research staff written survey questions about direct deposit services prior to seeing the results of the focus groups, they would have asked about convenience and security but not about independence, competence, or social participation. The focus group allowed customers' feelings about these issues to surface and stimulated bank managers to think about how these feelings might relate to other aspects of bank service, such as training tellers to greet customers by name and placing chairs and coffee in the lobby.

Transcript preparation usually takes a couple of days and costs $100 to $200. These costs aren't significant compared with the overall time and cost involved in a focus group study, but they sometimes motivate researchers to proceed without the transcripts. Instead, the researcher will listen to the audiotape or view the videotape of the focus group, jot down comments that strike his or her interest, and write the report based on the resulting impressions. We think it is a mistake to proceed with a report to the client without having the benefit of a written transcript to draw on for better evaluation of the focus group.

Of course, the managers who observe a focus group will draw their own conclusions about the discussions, even before they see a report. This is both a strength and weakness of focus groups. The strength is immediacy: managers who observe focus groups feel really close to the data. The weakness is that managers will sometimes latch onto one particular comment and ignore the broader content of the group discussion. This can lead to misinterpretation of the results.

Author Tips

It is a mistake not to prepare a transcript of a focus group discussion. Reading the transcript allows much better evaluation of the *entire* discussion, including comments that seem meaningful only when you look back on them. The transcript also simplifies the use of verbatim comments because all you need to do is "cut and paste" (which is simple on the computer). Finally, the transcript is a useful appendix for the final report, because it allows readers to draw their own conclusions. This is useful because a focus group analysis can be somewhat subjective.

Individual Depth Interviews

An individual **depth interview** is an unstructured conversation on a given topic between a respondent and interviewer. The general purpose of individual depth interviews is the same as that of focus groups, that is, to obtain attitudes and feelings about a product or service that would not surface in a structured interview. Individual interviews are more likely to be used under two circumstances:

(1) when the researcher wants all participants to express opinions on the same topics, as is common in executive interviewing, and (2) when the researcher wants participants to respond to physical stimuli such as projective measures.

A **projective measure** is a stimulus that encourages respondents to project their thoughts and feelings. Some common techniques are as follows:

- Respondents might be asked to draw pictures. For example, people might be asked to draw pictures of a good accountant and a bad accountant, to identify the physical cues that lead to inferences about service quality.

- Respondents might be asked to describe a situation. For example, respondents might be asked to describe a situation in which people would eat Doritos chips.

- Respondents might be asked to describe the type of person who would use some product. For example, the Pillsbury company recently discovered that women tended to describe the user of Pillsbury cake mix as a grandmother, whereas the user of Duncan Hines cake mix was described as a younger working woman.

- Respondents might be asked to look at an ambiguous picture and describe it.

- Respondents might be asked to look at a scene with something missing and complete it. For example, people might be asked to look at a partial grocery list and say what else this person would buy.

It is possible to use projective measures in face-to-face surveys or in focus groups, but this method is most commonly associated with individual depth interviews.

CASE STUDY 8.3

Researchers at the McCann-Erickson ad agency were baffled after interviewing some low-income southern women about insecticides. The women strongly believed that a new brand of roach killer sold in little plastic trays was more effective and less messy than traditional bug sprays. Yet they had never bought it, sticking stubbornly with their old sprays.

To try to understand this contradiction, the researchers asked the women to draw pictures of roaches and write stories about their sketches. What McCann-Erickson hoped to do was probe the women's subconscious feelings about roaches. The results are shown in the accompanying illustrations.

According to Paula Drillman, the agency's director of strategic planning, the roaches in the pictures were all male, symbolizing men who the women said had abandoned them and left them feeling poor and powerless. "Killing the roaches with a bug spray and watching them squirm and die allowed the women to express their hostility . . . and have greater control over the roaches," she says.

The roach pictures are just one of many projective methods McCann-Erickson has tried. "We've tried using a whole battery of psychological techniques—some new and some old—to understand the emotional bonds between consumers and brands," says Drillman. "You have to sell on emotion more than ever because it's a world of parity products out there."

continued

In addition to using drawings, McCann-Erickson is also asking consumers to write newspaper obituaries for brands. The agency's researchers say they learn a lot about a product's image depending on whether people describe the brand as young and virile and the victim of a tragic accident or as a worn-out product succumbing to old age.

"I TIPTOED quietly into the kitchen perhaps he wasn't around. I stretched my arm up to the light. I hoped I'd be alone when the light went on. Perhaps he is sitting on the table I thought. You think that's impossible? Nothing is impossible with that guy. He might not even be alone. He'll run when the light goes on I thought. But what's worse is for him to slip out of sight. No, it would be better to confront him before he takes control and invites a companion'."

"ONE NIGHT I just couldn't take the horror of these bugs sneaking around in the dark. They are always crawling when you can't see them. I had to do something. I thought wouldn't it be wonderful if when I switched on the light the roaches would shrink up and die like vampires to sunlight. So I did, but they just all scattered. But I was ready with my spray so it wasn't a total loss. I got quite a few...continued tomorrow night when night time falls."

"A MAN LIKES a free meal you cook for him, as long as there is food he will stay."

CASE STUDY 8.4

Projective measures underlie a recent advertising campaign for Tostitos chips. "It's very interesting. We'd hand people paper and say, 'Draw your occasion for eating Tostitos,'" says Mike Munro, product manager for Frito-Lay. "And they would draw parties, many people at a gathering."

The brand's $20 million "You got Tostitos, you got a party" campaign from BBDO Worldwide, New York, capitalizes on that association. TV commercials show comedian Chris Elliott partying with supermodels, partying aboard a yacht, and partying at his local Internal Revenue Service office. This campaign, along with the overall growth in demand for Mexican foods, is credited with boosting Tostitos sales from approximately $500 million in 1994 to $650 million in 1995.

Source: Adapted from Jeanne Whalen, "Tostitos Tastes New Life." Reprinted with permission from the December 11, 1995, issue of *Advertising Age.* Copyright, Crain Communications Inc. 1995.

General Procedures for Depth Interviews

Depth Interviews with Consumers

Depth interviews with consumers are usually done at the researcher's office. People from the target population are recruited by telephone to come to the site and are given a monetary incentive for participating, just as in focus groups.

When respondents arrive at the interviewing site, they are usually given a self-administered questionnaire to fill out before the depth interview. This questionnaire may simply gather background data such as age, marital status, and so on, but it may also gather product preference or usage data. The depth interview begins as soon as possible after a respondent returns the completed questionnaire. The interviewing room is usually furnished in a simple, businesslike manner and contains means of audiotaping the interview and possibly for observing.

The session begins with simple questions designed to start the respondent talking. These questions might relate to the background questionnaire; the interviewer might say things such as "I see that you have two children—is that correct? How old are they?" Once the ice is broken, the interviewer gives the respondent a brief, general introduction to the interview, for example, "Today, I'd like to show you some pictures of shopping situations and get your reactions to them." The interviewer then asks a question to start the interview. This question is usually general in nature: for example, the interviewer might show the respondent a vague sketch of a woman taking a package of Maxwell House coffee from a grocery shelf and ask the respondent, "Here's our first picture. What thoughts do you have as you look at this picture?"

If the respondent starts slowly in discussing this stimulus—for example, "I don't know. . . . It's a picture of someone buying coffee. . . . [long pause]"—the interviewer might simply wait patiently or might spur the respondent with nondirective probes such as "What more can you tell me?" If the respondent stops talking entirely, or if the interviewing plan calls for it, the interviewer might focus the respondent on a specific aspect of the stimulus, for example, "Tell me about the person in that picture. What kind of person is she?"

Of course, projective stimuli aren't necessary in a depth interview. The interviewer might start the discussion without any stimulus other than a question such as "In your mind, what kind of person drinks Maxwell House coffee?" or "How is coffee used in your household?" Almost any question will do as long as it starts the respondent talking about the desired topic.

There are two schools of thought about what the interviewer should do once the respondent begins talking. One school says that the interviewer should never change the subject—she or he should simply draw respondents out with nondirective probes such as "Why do you say that?" or "Can you tell me more about that?" (Silence also works: if the interviewer maintains an expectant silence, most respondents will start to talk to fill the conversational vacuum.) Under this approach, the interviewer uses selective follow-ups on respondent comments to keep the interview focused on areas of interest. However, even with skillful follow-ups, each interview is likely to have a different topic sequence, and some interviews will never reach certain topics.

Another school of thought says that the interviewer's first responsibility is to cover a prespecified topic list for the interview; she or he shouldn't change the subject if she or he can introduce all topics by following up respondent comments, but she or he must change the subject if some topics are not being covered. Even under this approach, changes in topic should come fairly late in the discussion. The choice between these two approaches basically depends on how much importance is placed on having a set of interviews in which all respondents comment on all topics.

An individual depth interview for a consumer research project usually lasts thirty to ninety minutes. When time is up or the discussion runs dry, the interviewer closes the interview, thanks the respondent, and takes the respondent to a receptionist to receive an incentive.

Depth Interviews with Executives

A depth interview with a businessperson is usually done at the respondent's office, and monetary incentives are usually not provided. Instead, the executive may be offered a copy of the study's report as an incentive for participating (Woodside and Wilson, 1995).

When the interviewer arrives at the respondent's office (at an appointed time), the interview usually begins immediately, with no self-administered questionnaire and no warm-up discussion. The interview is usually more structured than consumer depth interviews—the interviewer introduces each desired topic with a prepared question. The interview usually lasts thirty to sixty minutes.

Critical Thinking Skills

 hy don't depth interviews with executives use the same procedures as depth interviews with consumers? Why don't depth interviews with consumers use the same procedures as depth interviews with executives?

Strengths and Weaknesses of Depth Interviews

The key strengths of depth interviews relative to surveys are (1) depth and (2) point of view. It sounds redundant, but depth interviews go more deeply into a subject. Also, whereas surveys ask respondents to comment on the world as the researcher has organized it, depth interviews force the interviewer to enter the respondent's world. Opinions are expressed in respondents' own words and organized the way they themselves see fit.

The key weaknesses of depth interviews relative to surveys are (1) cost and (2) data generalizability. The high cost of depth interviews results in small sample sizes—few depth interviewing projects use more than thirty participants—and sample representativeness may be suspect. People who are willing to participate in depth interviews may not reflect the population of all consumers. Also, surveys obtain standard data that fits well with objective, quantitative analysis. Every respondent in a survey answers the same questions, in the same language, in the same order, with more or less the same level of depth. In contrast, respondents to depth interviews discuss different issues, in different language, in different orders, with different levels of depth. This makes the analysis of depth interviews subjective. Researchers must interpret ideas and themes rather than counting things, and the things that respondents *don't* mention in depth interviews may be as important as what they do mention.

The strengths of individual depth interviews relative to focus groups are (1) greater depth of data from individual respondents and (2) more flexibility in using projective materials. The weaknesses of individual interviews relative to focus groups are (1) a higher cost per person, (2) no possible gains from group interaction, and (3) less vivid and interesting data for managers.

As noted earlier in this chapter, the difference in vividness is not implicit in the methods but is simply a function of the fact that individual depth interviews usually aren't observed or videotaped, whereas focus groups almost always are observed and/or videotaped. Managers experience data from individual interviews via research reports, but they experience data from focus groups firsthand. This is what makes focus groups more vivid.

Good Uses of Individual Depth Interviews

Given the strengths and weaknesses of individual depth interviews, they are good for the same things as are focus groups. Specifically:

- Depth interviews are good for understanding why people use a product or why they use it in a particular way. For example, a coffee drinker might brew one cup of double-strength coffee each morning and drink this coffee, even though he doesn't like the taste, as part of "psyching up" for the day. Depth interviews can measure this kind of phenomenon—the meaning of consumption behavior—better than any other method. If depth interviews of several consumers show consistent patterns in usage or meaning, this information can be helpful in generating insights for ad design or product improvements.

- Sometimes depth interviews are helpful just because they give marketers a better feeling for customers' lives (or businesses). When Joe Plummer was head of research for the Young & Rubicam advertising agency, he told a story in this regard. He said that quantitative research methods had showed two market segments for Lincoln automobiles: "old rich" buyers, who bought the car for its traditional comfort, and "new rich" buyers, who bought the car because of what it said about them. Despite these clear-cut descriptions, the creative people in the ad agency had trouble visualizing the customers and making effective ads. To make the customers "come alive," the research department conducted depth interviews with several customers from each segment. These interviews were done at the customers' homes. The interviewers took many pictures and talked extensively about the customers' lives but didn't particularly talk about automobiles. When these interviews were given to the creative advertising people, the creative people felt for the first time that they really understood the customers, and subsequently they designed some very effective advertising that related Lincoln automobiles to how people lived.

- Depth interviews are good for measuring the underlying bases for brand images. In surveys, you can ask respondents how they evaluate your product. In depth interviews, you can ask them why they feel that way, and you can pursue the matter in depth.

- Depth interviews, like focus groups, can be used as a first step in developing a structured questionnaire. For example, knowing (from depth interviews) how people use a product, why they use it, and how they talk about it can be useful in developing an overall approach to the questionnaire, deciding which questions to ask, and phrasing questions.

Summary

This chapter discussed focus groups and depth interviews. The following points were covered:

1. What are the strengths and weaknesses of focus groups as a research method?

Focus groups offer more depth and spontaneity than surveys, but they don't offer broad population coverage. They also cost much more per person. Compared with individual depth interviews, focus groups cost less, but they also gather less information from each participant.

2. What are good uses of focus group research?

Good uses of focus groups include concept testing for new products, learning how consumers use a product and what it means to them, exploring people's problems and complaints with a product, exploring why people hold certain views about a brand, and helping marketers develop questions for a survey. A bad use for focus groups is as a substitute for a survey.

3. How is a focus group organized and conducted?

Focus groups can be held in a variety of locations. Specialized facilities operated by research companies are usually the best sites. Participants may be recruited through random telephone calls or mall intercepts and are usually paid between $15 and $50. The typical size of a focus group is six to ten participants, and it is usually desirable to fill the group with people who are similar in some way. A good focus group moderator unobtrusively leads the discussion and draws out opinions.

4. What are the strengths and weaknesses of individual depth interviews?

Individual depth interviews offer more depth and spontaneity than surveys, but they cost more and don't provide broad population coverage. Compared with focus groups, depth interviews gather more data from individual respondents and allow more flexibility in using projective materials, but they also cost more and do not allow gains from group interaction.

5. What are good uses of depth interviews?

Good uses of depth interviews are measuring and understanding consumers' habits in using a product, measuring the underlying bases for brand images, and helping marketers develop questions for a survey.

6. How is a depth interview organized and conducted?

In depth interviews done with consumers, people from the target population are recruited by telephone to come to the site, and they receive a monetary incentive to participate. The interviewer starts with simple questions to break the ice, then gives the respondent a general introduction to the topic and lets him or her talk. The typical interview lasts thirty to ninety minutes. In business research, the interview is usually conducted at the respondent's office. There is usually no structured questionnaire and no warm-up discussion. The interview usually lasts thirty to sixty minutes.

Suggested Additional Readings

There are several books that expand on the discussion in this chapter, especially the discussion of focus groups. These include:

Alfred Goldman and Susan S. McDonald, *The Group Depth Interview: Principles and Practices* (Englewood Cliffs, N.J.: Prentice-Hall, 1987).

Thomas L. Greenbaum, *The Practical Handbook and Guide to Focus Group Research* (New York: Lexington, 1993).

James Higginbotham and Keith Cox, eds., *Focus Group Interviews: A Reader* (Chicago: American Marketing Association, 1979).

Richard Krueger, *Focus Groups: A Practical Guide for Applied Research* (Newburg Park, Calif.: Sage, 1988).

David Morgan, *Focus Groups as Qualitative Research* (Newbury Park, Calif.: Sage, 1988).

Jane Farley Templeton, *The Focus Group: A Strategic Guide to Organizing, Conducting, and Analyzing the Focus Group Interview* (Chicago: Probus, 1994).

Discussion Questions

1. What are the strengths and weaknesses of qualitative research (i.e., focus groups and depth interviews)?

2. Compare the strengths and weaknesses of focus groups relative to surveys. Compare the strengths and weaknesses of focus groups relative to depth interviews.

3. What are some good uses for focus groups?

4. Why is it generally desirable to fill focus groups with people who are similar in some regard?

5. What skills are needed by an effective focus group moderator?

6. Under what circumstances would you want to use individual depth interviews?

7. What are the strengths and weaknesses of individual depth interviews relative to surveys? What are the strengths and weaknesses to individual depth interviews relative to focus groups?

Marketing Research Challenge

The best way to get a feel for focus groups and what they can do is to participate in one. Suppose you are interested in learning how college students use and feel about their personal computers. Prepare a discussion guide that consists of a half-dozen or so issues that you wish to explore. Recruit a group of four or five friends, and conduct a focus group lasting about an hour and a half with you acting as moderator. Tape the discussion. Prepare a report that summarizes the discussion.

Internet Exercise

Look for Internet newsgroups that relate to automobiles. On one of these newsgroups, post a question to see what people think about some car (or, if you can think of a new-product concept related to automobiles, post a question to see what people think about that concept). Based on this experience, how would you evaluate newsgroups as a possible substitute for focus groups; i.e., as a vehicle for people to engage in unstructured discussions about products or experiences? (Tip: access the DejaNews site at http://www.dejanews.com if you need help finding a newsgroup or posting a message.)

References

Edmondston, Jack (1994). "Handle Focus Group Research with Care." *Business Marketing* 79 (June), p. 38.

Fedder, Curtis J. (1990). "Biz-to-Biz Focus Groups Require a Special Touch." *Marketing News* 24 (Jan. 8), p. 46.

Feig, Barry (1989). "How to Run a Focus Group." *American Demographics* 11 (December), pp. 36–37.

Goldman, Alfred, and Susan S. McDonald (1987). *The Group Depth Interview: Principles and Practices* (Englewood Cliffs, N.J.: Prentice-Hall).

Greenbaum, Thomas L. (1993a). *The Practical Handbook and Guide to Focus Group Research* (New York: Lexington Books).

Greenbaum, Thomas L. (1993b). "Who's Leading Your Focus Group?" *Bank Marketing* 25 (March), p. 31.

Higginbotham, James, and Keith Cox (eds.) (1979). *Focus Group Interviews: A Reader* (Chicago: American Marketing Association).

Hoeffel, John (1994). "The Secret Life of Focus Groups." *American Demographics* 16 (December), pp. 17–19.

Krueger, Richard (1988). *Focus Groups: A Practical Guide for Applied Research* (Newbury Park, Calif.: Sage).

Morgan, David (1988). *Focus Groups as Qualitative Research* (Newbury Park, Calif.: Sage).

Templeton, Jane Farley (1994). *The Focus Group: A Strategic Guide to Organizing, Conducting, and Analyzing the Focus Group Interview* (Chicago: Probus).

Woodside, Arch G., and Elizabeth J. Wilson (1995). "Applying the Long Interview in Direct Marketing Research." *Journal of Direct Marketing Research* 9 (Winter), pp. 37–55.

9 Conducting Experiments

 OBJECTIVES

LEARNING

After reading this chapter, you should be able to answer the following questions:

❶ What is an experiment?

❷ What is experimental validity?

❸ What is the difference between a laboratory experiment and a field experiment, and when is each appropriate?

❹ How are threats to internal validity controlled?

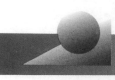

Introduction to Experiments

What Is an Experiment?

An **experiment** is a study in which the researcher actively manipulates one or more causal variables, then measures the effects of this manipulation on one or more dependent variables of interest. For example:

- A magazine company printed various cover designs and asked people in its office to indicate the design they liked best. This experiment measured the effects of cover design on preference.

- The same company printed magazines with the two most popular cover designs, shipped these magazines to newsstands in different cities, and measured sales for each design. This experiment also measured the effects of cover design on sales.

- A maker of grape jelly created several jelly formulations by varying the levels of sweetness, thickness, and grape flavor intensity. For each formulation, the company recruited mothers to use the jelly in their homes for two weeks. Afterward, the company asked the mothers to rate the jelly along dimensions such as appearance, spreadability, and children's reactions to the product. The company also gave the mothers a choice between a $35 cash payment for participating in the study or $32 plus two 12-ounce jars of the jelly they tested. This experiment measured the effects of sweetness, thickness, and flavor intensity on product ratings and "purchase" frequencies.

- A radio manufacturer created sixty-four descriptions of AM-FM clock radios to represent different combinations of: four different price levels ($9.95, $14.95, $19.95, and $24.95), two different types of alarm (music only and music/buzzer), two different types of power source (cord only and cord plus battery), and four different brand names (Sony, Panasonic, Emerson, and Goldstar). The manufacturer then asked consumers to rank these sixty-four descriptions from most preferred to least preferred. This experiment measured the effects of price, alarm type, power source, and brand name on preference.

These four studies differ in many ways, but all have one common feature—in all four studies, researchers actively manipulated certain experimental variables and measured the effects of those manipulations on some dependent variable(s) of interest. **Experimental variables,** also called **experimental factors,** are causal variables that are manipulated in an experiment to see if they have an impact on sales, preferences, or some other outcome of interest. **Dependent variables** are the outcomes of interest that may be influenced by manipulating experimental variables. The active manipulation of causal variables is what makes all of these studies experiments.

As the four examples show, experiments can take many forms. They can be done in an office, where people look at magazine covers; in the actual marketplace, where people buy magazines; in people's homes, where they use jelly; or anywhere else. Any number of variables can be manipulated, using either physical manipulations ("Look at these cover designs"; "Taste this jelly") or hypothetical manipulations ("Imagine these radios"). They can measure any number of dependent variables through observation (how many people choose $32 plus two jars of jelly) or self-report ("Please rate the jelly on the following dimensions"). Measures can be taken on individuals, household, companies, markets, or any other unit. Experimental research is not defined by the source of data or the method of measurement; rather, it is defined by active manipulation of causal variables.

Controlled Versus Uncontrolled Experiments

Critical Thinking Skills

Review the experiments described in the introduction to this chapter and say for each experiment which variables are experimental and which variables are dependent.

According to our definition, experiments occur whenever people take actions and observe the results. This definition is very broad, and it includes simple experiments such as lowering prices to see whether sales go up, painting the walls of a store to see whether sales are affected, and so on. The simplest experiments typically apply a manipulation to a single participant or group of participants, then use a "before-and-after" comparison to measure the effects of that manipulation. These studies are said to use a "single-group, pretest-versus-posttest" design.

Simple experiments often present problems in interpreting results. For example, if a supermarket tests the price response for eggs by dropping prices $.10 per dozen, and sales in the week after the price cut are 20 percent *lower* than the week before, does this mean that the supermarket should raise its egg prices? What if the experiment were done in the week after Easter? What if the American Medical Association issued a report that egg consumption raises the risk of heart disease? What if a competing store reduced the price of its eggs by $.20 per dozen?

This example illustrates a common problem of simple experiments: they fail to control the effects of events other than the manipulation. Changes in some dependent variable can be measured, but it is not possible to determine whether those changes are the result of the manipulation or of other, unmanipulated events. Under these circumstances, there is not much point in doing an experiment. For an experiment to have value, it is necessary to "control" the effects of other events that are likely to influence the dependent variable, so that changes in this variable reflect the results of manipulations.

One way of controlling the effects of nonmanipulated variables in experiments is to do the research in a laboratory environment. In a laboratory, competitors' prices can be controlled, the information given to research participants can be controlled, and so on. Unfortunately, laboratory environments aren't always realistic for marketing purposes (the pros and cons of laboratory versus field settings are discussed later in this chapter), and extraneous events can occur even within a laboratory.

Another way of controlling the effects of nonmanipulated variables is by using comparison groups in the experiment. For example, a supermarket chain could measure response to egg prices by lowering prices in one group of markets while holding prices constant in another group. The group of markets where prices are lowered is the **experimental group,** and the group of markets where prices are held constant is the **control group.** If the two groups are chosen so that they are initially equivalent, the effect of the manipulation can be measured by comparing the groups. Any extraneous events (other than the price cut) should have the same impact on both groups and thus cancel out.

A **controlled experiment** is one that uses some control procedure to minimize the chance that spurious external factors distort the relationship between causal and dependent variables. The two most common forms of control are (1) the use of a laboratory environment in which the occurrence of extraneous events can be minimized and (2) the use of a comparison group in which the effects of extraneous variables can be equalized.

Why Conduct Experiments?

The basic motivation for conducting experiments is control. Experiments are done because they allow researchers to control the effects of extraneous variables and, in so doing, to isolate the effects of manipulated variables and verify that these variables really do affect the dependent variable.

Consider the example used in Chapter 4 to introduce the concept of experiments. A company operates a chain of grocery stores. The produce departments are painted green in some of the company's stores and yellow in others. Sales of produce are higher in the stores where the produce department is painted green. These are also the newest, biggest stores. Should the company paint all its produce departments green?

In this example, an experiment is not needed to generate a comparison between green- and yellow-painted produce departments. This comparison exists naturally. However, the natural comparison suffers from causal uncertainty. Stores with green produce departments *may* have higher sales because green is a better color for selling produce. However, they may also have higher sales because they are newer, because they are bigger, or for some other reason. In fact, the observed relationship may be misleading—green may actually be a *worse* color than yellow, and the newer, bigger stores might do even better if they weren't painted green. Before painting all the produce departments green, the company will want to reduce this causal uncertainty and isolate the effects of wall color.

A wall color experiment can accomplish this goal. By randomly assigning stores to experimental color groups—one group to get green walls in the produce department and one group to get yellow walls—the company can form groups that are as equal as possible regarding store age, store size, and any other variable that might affect produce sales. The company can check this equality by testing whether average produce sales in the two groups are similar before the experiment. Then the company can proceed to paint the produce departments in experimental stores.

The company can assume that any subsequent differences in produce sales between the experimental groups must be caused by the color manipulation, because other variables have been equalized in the process of randomly assigning stores to color groups. Alternately, if the company doesn't completely trust the equalization, it can measure the *change* in produce sales before and after painting the walls of each participating store and compare the experimental groups on this measure of change. The logic of this analysis is that even if the groups are not perfectly equal before the experiment, the color of the wall is the only factor that can account for different amounts of change in the two groups.

If the company's wall color experiment is well designed and well executed, it will successfully control the effects of all nonmanipulated variables and provide a conclusive answer regarding the better color. This control is the central purpose of experimentation.

Alternatives to Experimentation

Experimentation is not the only way of isolating the effects of causal variables; they can also be isolated by computational procedures. In our wall color example, the company could take the green- and yellow-painted produce departments as they are—complete with differences in store age, store size, and other factors—and adjust for these other variables as follows:

- The company can calculate sales per square foot in the produce department and use the sales-per-square-foot measure to compare green- and yellow-painted departments. If green-painted departments have a higher average sales per square foot, green will be considered the better color. This computation will remove the effects of store size from the color comparison—or, to put it another way, this computation will show the effects of wall color over and above the effects of size.

- The company can calculate produce sales as a percentage of total store sales and use this percentage-of-sales measure to compare green- and yellow-painted departments. If green-painted departments account for a higher percentage of store sales on average, green will be considered the better color. This procedure will remove the effects of store age, store size, and any other variables as long as the effects of these variables on produce sales are proportional to their effects on total sales.

- The company can use multiple regression analysis (discussed in Chapter 18) to measure the effects of store age, store size, and any other desired variables on produce sales. Then, for each store, the company can calculate expected produce sales based on the regression analysis and compute the difference between actual produce sales and expected sales. Green- and yellow-painted departments can be compared on this difference measure. If green-painted departments have the higher average (of actual sales minus predicted sales), green will be considered the better color.

When to Experiment

Computational adjustments to isolate effects are common in marketing research—probably more common than experiments, in fact, because computational adjustments have certain advantages over experiments. It is usually faster and cheaper to use naturally occurring data and isolate effects by means of computational procedures than to plan and conduct an experiment. Also, the application of computational adjustments to naturally occurring data allows researchers to study the phenomena of interest under realistic market conditions, which is not always possible in experiments. For example, in the radio experiment given as the fourth example at the beginning of this chapter, it would not be feasible for a manufacturer to create sixty-four different types of radios, including radios with other companies' brand names, and market all of these radios.

However, computational procedures also have two important disadvantages compared with experiments. First, not every factor can be adjusted for. The green-painted produce departments in our grocery study may differ from the yellow-painted departments in many ways other than store size and store age. When computational adjustments are used to eliminate variables one at a time, it is possible to miss an important variable. A well-designed experiment eliminates *all* causal variables other than those of interest.

Second, computational procedures are limited to naturally occurring levels of the causal variable. For example, if our grocery company wants to evaluate a sunny orange color for produce departments, in addition to green and yellow, this cannot be done by analyzing the existing departments, because orange walls are not found in the "natural" data. Experiments are not limited in this way. In an experiment, the company can simply add a group of stores to be painted sunny orange.

The advantages and disadvantages of computational procedures compared to experiments lead to two conditions under which experiments are appropriate in marketing research. These are:

1. An experiment is necessary whenever you want to evaluate responses to marketing actions that do not exist in the present market.

2. Even if you are studying phenomena that exist in the present market, an experiment makes sense when the isolation of a particular causal variable is an important research objective and the costs, inconvenience, and possibly limited realism of experimentation do not prohibit its use.

In our produce department example, an experiment will be necessary if the company wants to test wall colors other than green and yellow. If the company cares only about green and yellow, which occur "naturally" in the company's stores, then experimentation will probably not be used because the costs and inconvenience of redecorating stores on an experimental basis are substantial. Instead, the company will probably rely on computational procedures and hope that it can adjust for all relevant variables. Realism will not be a factor in choosing whether or not to experiment in this project, because the contemplated experiment would use realistic conditions.

In the magazine cover, jelly, and radio examples given at the start of this chapter, experimentation would be used because all these studies are designed to test stimuli that do not occur in the present market.

Critical Thinking Skills

The makers of Tropicana orange juice would like to know the extent to which advertising expenditures affect sales. What are the pros and cons of answering this question through experimentation as opposed to analyzing existing data? Which approach would you recommend in this situation?

Experimental Validity

Internal Validity

Internal validity is the extent to which an experiment controls the effects of all non-manipulated variables so that differences among experimental groups on the dependent variable can be regarded as valid effects of the manipulations. Of course, this removal of causal uncertainty is the basic purpose of an experiment.

Threats to internal validity in experiments include:

1. **Selection bias.** The subjects* assigned to some experimental groups may be different from the subjects assigned to other groups, and subsequent differences among the groups may be caused by these differences between subjects rather than the experimental manipulations. For example, in our wall color example, stores assigned to the green color condition might be smaller or older than stores assigned to the yellow condition, with the result that green-painted departments would get worse results than they deserve.

2. **Treatment effects.** The very act of conducting an experiment may affect the dependent variable in a way that alters or masks the effects of the manipulations.

   One type of treatment effect is called a **Hawthorne effect,** in which all experimental groups react to being in the experimental spotlight. In our wall color experiment, customers and employees might simply react to the fact that the produce departments are being painted. The experiment might fail to show legitimate differences between green and yellow wall colors because the "redecoration effect" overwhelms this difference.

   Another type of treatment effect is **demand effect** (Shimp, Hyatt, and Snyder, 1991). People who participate in experiments tend to act the way they think they should act—that is, they try to comply with the demands (or "demand characteristics") of the situation. This can affect their responses to the experimental stimuli. Consider, for example, the magazine cover experiment, in which a magazine company showed various cover designs to its employees and asked which design they preferred. In this experiment, the possibility that some designs are better than others for grabbing people's attention on magazine racks will not be captured very well, because subjects will pay attention to *all* the covers. They will do this because they assume that careful attention is desired.

   Subjects may also try to guess the purpose of an experiment and "help" the researcher get good results. In the magazine cover experiment, one of the covers might be the current design whereas others are new designs under consideration. Some of the employees may choose a new design not because they prefer it but rather because they think this is the desired answer.

   A third type of treatment effect relates to **evaluation apprehension.** Subjects may view the experiment as a test or as an opportunity to make a favorable impression on the researcher. In our grocery store experiment, the produce managers in experimental stores may feel that the experiment is testing them as well as the wall color, and these managers may exert special efforts during the period of the experiment. The effects of evaluation apprehension are closely related to Hawthorne effects and demand effects.

3. **Testing effects.** The process of measuring a dependent variable may influence the way in which subjects respond to experimental manipulations and/or to later measures of the dependent variable.

   Say, for example, that an advertising agency compares two different television commercials for a restaurant using the following procedure: subjects are given a pretest questionnaire to measure their attitudes toward the restaurant,

---

*"Subjects" are the participants in an experiment. They can be people, households, stores, businesses, or market areas. In our supermarket wall color experiment, for example, the subjects are produce departments.

If people know what result you want, you might get biased data.

Source: Fugitive from the Cubicle Police, 1996, DILBERT. Scott Adams. Reprinted by permission of United Feature Syndicate, Inc.

then are shown one of the experimental commercials, then are given a posttest to measure their subsequent attitudes. This study is likely to have a testing effect. As soon as subjects see a commercial for the restaurant, they will remember the pretest measure and view the commercial in the context of that measure. This may affect their responses to the commercial.

Note that the testing effect in this example is actually a "testing-by-treatment interaction" in which the pretest heightens the possible demand effects. Testing-by-treatment interactions are more common than simple testing effects.

4. *History effects.* History effects arise when some outside event that affects the dependent variable happens during the experiment. For example, in the wall color experiment, if a competing grocery chain offers very low produce prices during the experiment, this might create an impression that painting the walls actually causes sales to decline. History effects are particularly troublesome when they affect treatment groups disproportionately. For example, if the competitor that offers low prices during the wall color experiment has stores that compete with nine of the green stores but only five of the yellow stores, this might create an appearance that yellow is a better color because the yellow stores have higher sales.

5. *Maturation effects.* Maturation effects occur when some change that is unrelated to the manipulations but affects the dependent variable occurs *within subjects* during an experiment. For example, in our wall color experiment, one of the stores might lose a good produce manager during the experiment and subsequently suffer from lower sales. This would lower the average produce sales in that store's treatment group.

6. *Mortality effects.* Some subjects may fail to complete the experiment. For example, in our grocery experiment, one of the stores may have a fire and be dropped from the study. If the subjects that leave the study are different in some way from those that stay, this mortality will influence the observed effects. As with all threats to internal validity, mortality is a particular problem when it affects different treatment groups disproportionately.

Exhibit 9.1 provides a pictorial illustration of history, maturation, and mortality effects.

EXHIBIT 9.1

Illustration of Some Threats to Internal Validity

Beginning of the Study   End of the Study

 History

History effects occur when the environment changes during the experiment. It is not possible to determine if the results are due to the manipulation or to the environmental change.

Beginning of the Study   End of the Study

 Maturation

Maturation effects occur when the subjects change during the experiment. It is not possible to determine if the results are due to the manipulation or to the change in the subjects.

Beginning of the Study   End of the Study

 Mortality

Mortality effects occur when subjects fail to complete the experiment. It is not possible to determine if the dropouts would have responded to the manipulation in the same way as those who remain.

MARKETING RESEARCH TOOLS

9.1

THREATS TO INTERNAL VALIDITY

Threats	Causes
Selection bias	Innate differences in subjects
Treatment effects:	
Hawthorne effects	Reaction to being in the spotlight
Demand effects	Participants' desire to please researcher
Evaluation apprehension	Participants' desire to look good
Testing effects	Sensitization to measurement procedures
History effects	External events during the experiment
Maturation effects	Internal changes in subjects
Mortality effects	Dropouts from the experiment

Marketing Research Tools 9.1 summarizes the threats to internal experimental validity and the causes of each.

External Validity

As already noted, an experiment is internally valid to the extent that the observed differences among treatment groups are valid effects of the manipulations. An experiment is externally valid to the extent that effects that occur in the experiment approximate those in an actual market situation. **External validity** is also sometimes called **generalizability,** because it refers to the extent to which experimental effects will generalize to the marketplace (Smead, Wilcox, and Wilkes, 1981).

Our wall color experiment would be high in external validity because it is done in the marketplace. Similarly, the magazine cover experiment in which different covers were sent to different newsstands would score high in external validity. Test markets in which a new or revised product is promoted and sold are very high in external validity (Waldrop, 1992, 1993). On the other hand, the experiment in which magazine company employees look at different covers in the office would score *low* in external validity, because the covers are not shown under realistic market conditions and the subjects may not be representative of the magazine's buyers.

Designing Experiments

There are no standard rules for designing experiments, because experiments can take so many different forms. There are, however, some general decisions to be made in designing any experiment. These decisions include:

- Should the experiment be done in a laboratory or the field?
- How many manipulated factors should be tested?
- What design should be used to test multiple factors?
- What should the levels and duration of the manipulations be?
- What should the measurement procedure for the dependent variable(s) be?

Laboratory Versus Field Experiments

A **laboratory experiment** is any experiment that studies the phenomena of interest outside their natural setting. The term "laboratory" does not refer to a particular location for the research; it simply refers to any context other than a natural one. For example, the radio experiment described at the beginning of this chapter, in which subjects expressed preferences for different radio descriptions, is a laboratory experiment because the subjects ranked paper-and-pencil descriptions of radios rather than buying real radios from real stores. The magazine cover experiment in which company employees chose a preferred design was also a laboratory experiment.

A **field experiment,** in contrast, studies the phenomena of interest in a natural setting. The grocery wall color experiment is a field experiment, as was the magazine cover experiment in which different covers were sent to different newsstands.

The distinction between laboratory and field experiments is not always clear cut. Consider the experiment in which a jelly manufacturer gave various formulations to mothers for in home use. The mothers subsequently rated the jelly along various dimensions and chose between $35 compensation and $32 plus two jars of jelly. This *was not* a field experiment regarding purchasing behavior, because the subjects did not buy the jelly under natural circumstances. However, it *was* a field experiment regarding product evaluation, because people evaluated the jelly after using it in a natural manner. Also, although the experiment did not measure actual store purchases, it did measure whether subjects would "spend" $3 for two jars of jelly. Compared with a taste test in which company employees eat different types of jelly in a testing kitchen and indicate which they would buy, the "mothers" study is much closer to a field experiment of purchasing behavior.

The advantage of field experiments over laboratory experiments is that field experiments offer more realistic conditions and hence tend to have higher external validity. The advantages of laboratory experiments are that (1) they are usually much cheaper than field experiments, (2) they allow manipulations that may not be possible in the field, such as changing competitors' prices, (3) they don't disrupt field marketing programs, and (4) they offer better control over nonmanipulated events and hence may have higher internal validity. In most marketing research projects, these advantages outweigh the higher realism of a field experiment, especially if a laboratory study can be designed with natural elements. As a result, laboratory experiments are more common than field experiments in marketing research.

A field experiment is preferable to a lab experiment only when all five of the following conditions exist:

1. The experiment involves one or two factors that can be studied with a small number of treatment groups (field experiments become much more difficult to implement as the number of treatment groups increases).

2. The factors you want to study can be manipulated in the field.

3. The disruption that a field experiment will bring to your existing marketing program is not important.

4. Either the cost of a field experiment is not significantly higher than the cost of a lab experiment, or the financial implications of the decision are high enough that the extra cost of a field study seems small in comparison.

5. External validity is more important than internal validity.

This last condition might seem silly, because external validity has no value without internal validity. There is no value in generalizing spurious effects. However, a situation might exist in which previous research has shown that a relationship exists between the experimental and dependent variables, and the purpose of the current research is to measure the scale of this relationship under field conditions (laboratory experiments often produce magnified effects because the variables are, in a sense, being studied under a microscope). If this is the situation, realism is more important than control.

A possible evolution from laboratory to field experiments is illustrated by the magazine cover experiment described at the beginning of this chapter. The magazine company used laboratory testing to evaluate several possible new covers; then, after one design "won" the lab tests, the company used a field experiment to test this winner against the old design under newsstand conditions before making a full commitment to the new cover.

In our wall color experiment, a field test would be appropriate from the start. Only one factor is of interest, and it has only two levels. This factor is manipulable in the field, and the experiment is unlikely to disrupt the company's business. Also, to acquire useful data, the company must display produce within large areas of color—a green paint chip is not the same as a green produce department. Large-scale color testing might be accomplished in various ways, but a field experiment is about as cheap and easy as anything else.

Critical Thinking Skills

esign a *laboratory* experiment for the makers of Tropicana orange juice to measure the effects of advertising on sales. Design a *field* experiment to measure the effects of advertising on sales. How much do you think it would cost to run each of these experiments? Which would have higher internal validity? Why? Which would have higher external validity?

How Many Factors Should Be Used?

The simplest experimental designs vary one factor and keep everything else constant, allowing for measurement of the effect of that one factor. For example, Case Study

9.1, which describes an extremely simple experiment, shows that such experiments can be useful.

In many situations, though, marketers are interested in studying the effects of several factors. For example, a jelly manufacturer might be interested in several aspects of its product: thickness, sweetness, and fruit flavor intensity. In this type of situation, it is possible to do a series of experiments to measure the effects of these factors individually, but the optimum procedure is to test all of the factors simultaneously in a single, multifactor experiment.

There are two reasons why a multifactor experiment is preferable. First, the cost of one multifactor experiment is less than the total costs of several single-factor studies. Second, and more important, multifactor experiments allow measurement of not only the main effects of each factor but also the interactions among factors. For example, a jelly manufacturer might discover an interaction between thickness and flavor intensity, such that a more intense flavor is preferred for a thick formulation but a less intense flavor is preferred for a thin formulation. Such effects can be seen only if the factors are studied in combination.

Although the ability to study factors in combination is attractive, few marketing experiments use more than four factors. One reason is that complex interactions are difficult to interpret, so increasingly complex experiments offer no additional benefit. The other reason is that it can be difficult to manage a lot of different experimental groups, and the number of groups increases geometrically as the number of factors increases. For example, a jelly experiment with three levels of thickness and three levels of sweetness requires 9 groups (3×3) if all combinations of thickness and sweetness are used. An experiment with three levels each of thickness, sweetness, flavor intensity, and price requires *81* groups ($3 \times 3 \times 3 \times 3$) if all combinations are used. In fact, the number of experimental groups in a large multifactor study with all combinations could quickly outstrip the number of available participants!

CASE STUDY 9.1

The Oldsmobile Aurora is considered a crucial product in General Motors' effort to attract "baby-boom" car buyers back to GM cars. One small but interesting feature of the Aurora is its logo. Other Oldsmobile vehicles carry the division's famous "rocket" logo. The Aurora carries its own logo, a stylized *A*.

According to a recent article in *Business Week,* this logo decision was based on a simple two-group experiment. GM researchers recruited target customers for the Aurora and split them into two groups. One group saw the Aurora with a stylized *A* logo, and the other saw it with a traditional rocket logo. People in each group were asked to rate the car on a variety of dimensions. The result: ratings were significantly lower when the rocket logo was used.

Of course, the result of this experiment has implications that go well beyond the Aurora. It suggests that the Oldsmobile brand name is currently not attractive to baby boomers.

Source: Kathleen Kerwin, "GM's Aurora," *Business Week,* Mar. 21, 1994, p. 88–95.

Author Tips

In using a fractional design, it is essential to anticipate which of the experimental variables will have interaction effects and to use a design that allows you to separate these effects from the main effects of other variables. This requires quite a bit of expertise, so get help from an expert on experimental design.

Types of Multifactor Designs

Once a multifactor experiment has been decided upon, the next question is whether the design of that experiment will be "full factorial" or "fractional." A **full factorial design** is a multifactor design in which all possible combinations of manipulation levels in the experiment are used; a **fractional design** omits some combinations (Kuhfeld, Randall, and Garratt, 1994).

The advantage of fractional designs is that they use fewer treatment groups. For example, Exhibit 9.2 shows a fractional design for the radio experiment described at the start of this chapter, in which a manufacturer wanted to study the effects of four price levels, two types of alarm, two types of power source, and four brand names on consumer preferences. A full factorial design for this study would use 64 combinations ($4 \times 2 \times 2 \times 4$), but the fractional design shown in Exhibit 9.2 uses only 16 treatment groups.

The disadvantage of fractional designs is that the reduced number of treatment combinations has the effect of confounding the main effects of some variables with the interaction effects of other variables, which can lead to misleading results. This point is demonstrated in Appendix 9.1 at the end of this chapter.

Because a fractional design can lead to misleading results, full factorial designs should be used if the number of treatment groups is manageable. If the number of treatment groups is not manageable—for example, if it seems unreasonable to expect people to take the time to rank sixty-four radio combinations—a fractional design should be used to reduce the number of combinations to a manageable level.

Choosing the Levels and Duration of Manipulations

Another decision to be made in planning an experiment is setting appropriate conditions for the manipulations. Are green and yellow the best colors to test in our wall color experiment? How about green, yellow, and sunny orange? How about a light beige? If green and yellow are used, which shades of green and yellow are best? Should the green or yellow colors be used by themselves or as background colors with some surface design? Should sales be measured immediately after painting the walls, or should the company allow some time for the novelty to wear off? If so, how much time? Two weeks? Two months?

As these decisions are made, it should become obvious that the ability to design a good experiment depends very heavily on how much is already known about the topic. Experiments are not very good for "exploratory" research, in which the main goal is to uncover interesting facts about the market. Experiments are better for "confirmatory" research in which relationships that you already know something about are isolated and validated.

EXHIBIT 9.2

Example of a Fractional Design

A radio manufacturer wants to study the following experimental variables:

- Four price levels ($9.95, $14.95, $19.95, and $24.95)

- Two types of alarm (music only and music/buzzer choice)

- Two types of power source (cord only and cord plus battery)

- Four brand names (Sony, Panasonic, Emerson, and Goldstar)

A full factorial design will use 64 combinations ($4 \times 2 \times 2 \times 4$).
Here is a fractional design that uses 16 combinations:

Sony Music only Cord only $9.95	Panasonic Music only Cord/battery $9.95	Emerson Music/buzzer Cord only $9.95	Goldstar Music/buzzer Cord/battery $9.95
Sony Music/buzzer Cord/battery $11.95	Panasonic Music only Cord only $11.95	Emerson Music only Cord/battery $11.95	Goldstar Music/buzzer Cord only $11.95
Sony Music/buzzer Cord only $19.95	Panasonic Music/buzzer Cord/battery $19.95	Emerson Music only Cord only $19.95	Goldstar Music only Cord/battery $19.95
Sony Music only Cord/battery $24.95	Panasonic Music/buzzer Cord only $24.95	Emerson Music/buzzer Cord/battery $24.95	Goldstar Music only Cord only $24.95

Note that this design does not include all possible combinations. For example, it does not include:

- Sony, music only, cord/battery, $9.95
- Sony, music/buzzer, cord only, $9.95
- Sony, music/buzzer, cord/battery, $9.95

However, it does use every level of every factor at least once, and it makes some attempt to use each level of each factor with different combinations of the other factors.

This is only one of many possible fractional designs for this study. We could prepare other 16-group designs that use different combinations, or we could prepare designs with a different number of groups.

Critical Thinking Skills

The makers of Tropicana orange juice want to use a field experiment to determine how changes in advertising expenditure levels might affect sales. In designing this experiment, what levels of ad expenditure would you use? How long would the experiment run? When would you measure the effects?

Experimental manipulations should be determined according to some theory or some previous findings. For example, in the wall color experiment, the motive for the experiment is an observation that produce sales are different for two paint colors already in use. Therefore, since previous findings have shown that these colors are of interest, these will be the colors used in the experiment. The decision regarding how long to wait before measuring the effects of painting should be based on management's prior experience with redecoration programs or on expert advice about the duration of redecoration effects.

Experimental manipulations are also affected by the intrinsic constraints on experiments. Consider, for example, an experiment in which different advertisements are tested by showing them to subjects at an advertising agency's research facility. This type of experiment usually shows a test ad only once and measures response within thirty minutes of exposure. The reason for this "single exposure, immediate response" procedure is simple— the agency can't keep subjects at the research facility forever. The agency would really like to know how people respond to the ad when it is shown repeatedly over a period of weeks, but this is not possible given the experimental setting.

Choosing the Dependent Measure(s)

The issues that arise in choosing dependent measures for an experiment include: Will observation or self-report data provide a better result? If self-report data are desirable, how should the questions be phrased and organized? When should the measures be taken? If observational data are better, how should the observations be obtained and over what period of time?

In making these decisions, one should seek:

- Measures that correspond as closely as possible to the market phenomena of interest: sales, attitude toward the brand, awareness of the brand, and so forth
- Measures that make the research as easy and interesting as possible for participants
- Measures that satisfy situational constraints

Consider, for example, the experiment in which mothers tested jelly formulations at home, rated the jelly on various criteria, and subsequently had the choice of receiving $35 for their participation or $32 plus two jars of the jelly they tested. The percentage of subjects who took $32 plus two jars of jelly might be considered a better dependent variable than the various product ratings, because this measure is closer to the market phenomenon of interest: purchase behavior. On the other hand, actual purchase behavior was not used in the experiment because it could not be measured within the lab constraints.

Controlling Threats to Internal Validity

Controlling Selection Bias

Experimental procedures should be designed to minimize threats to internal validity. The most pervasive of these threats is **selection bias,** which occurs when the subjects assigned to some treatment groups are somehow different from the subjects assigned to other treatment groups.

Six methods can be used to minimize the existence or effects of selection bias. These methods, and guidelines for using them, are as follows:

1. *Randomization.* Random assignment of subjects to treatment groups is the primary method for reducing selection bias in experiments. In fact, randomization is so important that Cook and Campbell (1979) call experiments without randomization "quasi experiments." Exhibit 9.3 (see page 222) shows how randomization works. This method should be used whenever possible.

2. *Blocking.* It is possible to have bad luck in a random assignment process so that experimental groups are not equalized on some important variable. Blocking provides a safeguard against this possibility. It designs one or more nonmanipulated variables into an experiment to ensure that the treatment groups are equalized on those variables.

   Say, for example, that a company uses twenty-four stores in a wall color experiment for produce departments and wants to be sure that the experimental groups are equalized on store size. It can sort the twenty-four stores into three size groups—the eight smallest, the eight in the middle, and the eight largest—then randomly assign four stores from each size group to each of the two wall color conditions. This will ensure that the green and yellow wall color groups each contain a fair mixture of store sizes. If a store does not participate for some reason, it will be replaced with another store from the same size group. In this example, size is a "blocking variable," and the store groups are "blocked on size."

   If the statistical significance of experimental effects is important, blocking offers a benefit beyond equalizing groups. When the dependent variable varies across levels of the blocking variable—for example, sales would vary across levels of store size—the variance in the dependent variable that is "explained" by the blocking variable is removed from the "residual" or "error" variance, and it becomes easier to find statistically significant effects for the manipulated variable(s).

   We suggest the following rules for when to block:

   - You *may* want to block for purposes of equalization if your experiment will have fewer than twenty subjects per experimental group. Blocking is usually not needed to equalize larger groups because the probability of bad luck in group assignments becomes lower as group size increases. Even with small sample sizes, computational adjustments may offer a more flexible way of achieving the same goals as blocking.

Assume that twenty subjects are assigned to two experimental groups. Ten subjects are old, and ten subjects are young.

Old Subjects

Young Subjects

Selection bias would occur if all (or most) of the young subjects were in one group and all (or most) of the old subjects were assigned to the other, because after the experiment, it could not be determined if the results were due to the manipulation or to the age of the subjects.

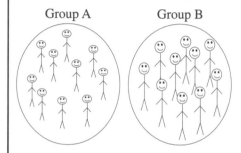

Selection Bias

With randomization, each subject is randomly assigned to a group by, for example, flipping a coin.

B B A B A B A B A B

A B A B A A B A A B

Randomization can control selection bias. Note, however, that it does not ensure that equal numbers of old and young subjects will be assigned to the two groups.

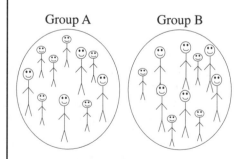

Random Assignment

- You definitely *should* block if you want to test whether the effects of your manipulated variables "interact" with the blocking variable. Blocking will allow you to test for interaction effects within the context of your experiment.

- You also *should* block for purposes of increasing the statistical significance of effects if significance is important and you can identify a blocking variable that relates to the dependent variable.

Note, by the way, that blocking is done in conjunction with randomization and is not a replacement for it.

3. *Matching.* "Matching" is another way of ensuring that experimental groups are equalized on some variable. If a company has twenty-four stores, it can sort them into twelve sets so that each set contains two stores matched as closely as possible on size. Then the company can randomly assign one member from each set to the green walls condition and one to the yellow walls condition. Like blocking, this matching procedure should ensure that the color groups are balanced on size.

    To many inexperienced researchers, matching looks even better than blocking because it controls the group assignments at a finer level. However, subjects that are matched on one variable are often different in other ways. A novice should not use matching unless an expert advises this method.

4. *Computational adjustments.* It is possible to adjust for differences among subjects with various computational procedures. For example, in the wall color experiment, simple regression analysis (discussed in Chapter 17) can be used to predict produce sales from store size, then the difference between predicted and observed produce sales can be used as the dependent measure. Alternately, simple sales per square foot can be used as the dependent measure. Either method should remove differences in produce sales that are attributable to store size.

    Like blocking, computational adjustments can be used in conjunction with randomization. It is always a good idea to check experimental groups for equality on nonmanipulated variables that might affect the results and adjust for any nonmanipulated variables that show significant differences among groups.

5. *Pretest-versus-posttest comparison.* In the wall color experiment, we can measure produce sales before and after painting the walls in each participating store, then use the before-versus-after difference as the dependent variable. This method—pretest-versus-posttest comparison—will adjust for prior sales differences among the stores regardless of whether those difference are caused by store size, store age, or some other factor.

    The problem with pretest-versus-posttest comparisons for experiments involving human subjects is that pretests can cause testing effects by alerting subjects to the nature of the experiment. We discuss ways to minimize these undesired effects in the following section of this chapter.

6. *Repeated measures.* Pretest-versus-posttest comparisons control for differences among subjects by measuring the effects of the experiment with reference to each subject's own baseline. A similar adjustment exists in **repeated measures designs,** in which manipulation effects are measured by taking subjects' responses to different treatment conditions at different points in time. In the wall color experiment, for example, the same stores would be painted each of the colors in turn.

The possibility of testing effects is very high with repeated measures designs. Consider our wall color experiment as an example. Shoppers won't be affected by measuring each store's sales prior to the experiment, but shoppers might well be affected if we give each store green paint for six weeks followed by yellow paint for six weeks.

Because of the high likelihood of testing effects, we recommend that you not use repeated measures as a method for controlling selection bias. Instead, repeated measures designs should be viewed as a way to do experiments when the number of subjects is very limited.*

Marketing Research Tools 9.2 summarizes the guidelines for using the various methods for minimizing selection bias in experiments. Random assignment of subjects to groups is the simplest and best of these procedures and should be used whenever possible.

---

*Repeated measures designs are also called "within subjects" designs because the experimental effects are measured within subjects. Designs in which the effects are measured by comparing different groups of subjects are called "between subjects" designs. An experiment also can use a "mixed between and within subjects" design.

MARKETING RESEARCH TOOLS

9.2

WAYS OF CONTROLLING SELECTION BIAS

Method	When to Use
Randomization	Randomize whenever possible.
Blocking	*Consider* blocking when you are particularly worried about the effects of some nonmanipulated variable and treatment group sizes are smaller than 20 or sample cooperation is related to the variable. *Do* block when you want to test for an interaction between nonmanipulated and manipulated variables.
Matching	Do not match unless advised to do so by an expert.
Computational adjustments	Always test to see whether treatment groups are equal on nonmanipulated variables that are likely to have large effects on the dependent variable(s). If treatment groups differ significantly on some variable, adjust for that variable.
Pretest-versus-posttest comparisons	In general, do not use this method with human subjects unless you feel confident that testing effects will not be a problem. *Do* use this method when working with nonhuman subjects.
Repeated measures	Do not use this method to control selection bias. Instead, use it to get the most out of a limited number of subjects.

Controlling Treatment and Testing Effects

Treatment effects and testing effects—for example, Hawthorne effects, demand effects, evaluation apprehension, and testing reactions—are a particular concern in experiments done with human subjects. People know that they are in an experiment, and they usually try to do well and please the experimenter.

The primary way to minimize treatment effects in lab experiments is to conceal the manipulations. Say, for example, that you wish to test alternate executions of a magazine ad for Hunt's catsup. If you show subjects this ad by itself, they will pay close attention to it, and they will assume that you hope to hear favorable comments. You will get a more natural response if you make a portfolio with several dozen advertisements, place the Hunt's ad in the middle, and ask subjects to look through the portfolio before you ask some questions. The subjects will pay close attention to the first few ads in the portfolio, but their attention will quickly fade and they will not pay any special attention to the test ad.

Another way of minimizing treatment effects in lab studies is to misdirect subjects about the true purpose of the experiment. For example, in "theater tests" of television commercials, audience members are usually told that they will be evaluating a pilot show for television and commercials will be shown only for the sake of realism. This cover story leads subjects to pay more attention to the show and less attention to the commercials, as they would do if viewing at home. Note that when subjects are misdirected about the purpose of the experiment, ethical standards require that they be "debriefed" and told the true purpose at the end of the session. We discuss ethical standards in Chapter 22.

In field experiments, it is sometimes difficult to conceal the experimental manipulations or the purpose of the experiment. Consequently, the principal way of minimizing treatment effects in field experiments is simply waiting until they pass. For example, in our wall color experiment, customers may show an initial response simply because the walls have been painted, regardless of color, and employees may work with special enthusiasm because they know they are being studied. However, these effects will fade within a few weeks, and the company will then be able to measure the effects of the manipulation.

Some variables such as price and advertising change often in the marketplace, so consumers are unlikely to realize that they are in an experiment when they see changes in these variables. Such variables do not require long waiting periods to eliminate treatment effects.

Testing effects are controlled through the same mechanisms used to control treatment effects. In our earlier discussion of testing effects, we noted that these effects occur primarily in the form of testing-by-treatment interactions, in which testing heightens demand effects. As a result, procedures that minimize treatment effects will also minimize most testing effects.

Critical Thinking Skills

How would you control selection bias in a lab experiment to measure the relationship between advertising levels and sales for Tropicana orange juice? How would you control selection bias in a field experiment to measure this relationship?

Summary

This chapter discussed experiments. The following points were covered:

1.   What is an experiment?

An experiment is a study in which the researcher actively manipulates one or more experimental variables and measures the effects of this manipulation on one or more dependent variables of interest. The purpose of experimentation is to reduce causal uncertainty.

2.   What is experimental validity?

The validity of an experiment has two components: internal validity and external validity. Internal validity is the extent to which nonmanipulated variables are completely controlled, so that differences among experimental and control groups can be regarded as valid effects of the manipulations. External validity, or generalizability, is the extent to which the effects that occur in the experiment will occur in the actual market.

Internal validity is crucial to an experiment, because the fundamental purpose of experimentation is to control extraneous effects. The sources of threat to internal validity are selection bias, treatment effects, testing effects, history effects, maturation effects, and mortality effects.

3.   What is the difference between a laboratory experiment and a field experiment, and when is each appropriate?

A lab experiment is any experiment that studies the phenomena of interest outside their natural environment. A field experiment is done in the natural environment. In general, lab experiments are cheaper and more flexible and have higher internal validity. In general, field experiments have higher external validity.

A field experiment should be conducted when (1) the experiment has one or two factors that can be studied with a small number of treatment groups, (2) these factors can be manipulated in the field, (3) the disruption that a field experiment will bring to your existing marketing program is not important, (4) the cost of the field experiment is justified, and (5) external validity is more important than internal validity.

4.   How are threats to internal validity controlled?

The primary way of controlling for selection bias (i.e., differences between subjects) is by randomly assigning subjects to treatment groups. Other ways of controlling for differences between subjects are blocking, matching, making computational adjustments, making pretest-versus-posttest comparisons, and using repeated measures.

In laboratory experiments, the primary way of minimizing testing and treatment effects is by concealing the manipulations or by misdirecting subjects about the true purposes of the experiment. In field experiments, the principal way of minimizing these effects is by waiting until they pass.

Suggested Additional Readings

There are many excellent books on experimental design. Some of the best include:

David R. Boniface, *Experimental Design and Statistical Methods for Behavioural and Social Research* (London: Chapman and Hall, 1995).

William G. Cochran and Gertrude M. Cox, *Experimental Designs* (New York: Wiley, 1982).

D. R. Cox, *Planning of Experiments* (New York: Wiley, 1991).

Allen Louis Edwards, *Experimental Design in Psychological Research* (New York: Harper and Row, 1985).

David M. Gardner and Russell W. Belk, *A Basic Bibliography on Experimental Design in Marketing* (Chicago: American Marketing Association, 1980).

John J. Kennedy, *An Introduction to the Design and Analysis of Experiments in Behavioral Research* (Washington, D.C.: University Press of America, 1985).

Roger E. Kirk, *Experimental Design: Procedures for Behavioral Sciences* (Monterey, Calif.: Brodes-Cole, 1995).

Leslie Kish, *Statistical Designs for Research* (New York: Wiley, 1987).

John Neter, William Wasserman, and Michael H. Kutner, *Applied Linear Statistical Models: Regression, Analysis of Variance, and Experimental Designs* (Homewood, Ill.: Irwin, 1990).

Paul R. Rosenbaum, *Observational Studies* (New York: Springer, 1995).

B. J. Winer, *Statistical Principles in Experimental Design* (New York: McGraw-Hill, 1991).

Examples of experimental designs can also be found in almost every issue of *Journal of Consumer Research* and *Journal of Marketing Research*.

Discussion Questions

1. What is an experiment and why are they used in marketing research?

2. What is meant by controlled experiments? How can a researcher "control" for the effects of nonmanipulated variables?

3. What is meant by internal and external validity?

4. Why is external validity sometimes called "generalizability"?

5. What are some common threats to internal validity in experiments?

6. How do lab experiments and field experiments differ? What are the advantages of lab experiments over field experiment? What are the advantages of field experiments over lab experiments?

7. When is a field experiment preferable to a lab experiment?

8. Are experiments better used for "exploratory" research or "confirmatory" research? Why?

Marketing Research Challenge

A well-known advertising program of a few years back reported the results of taste tests in which consumers tasted both Coke and Pepsi. Imagine that you are conducting such a taste test in your community. How would you design such a taste test to be as realistic as possible and not to favor one brand over the other? Specifically, you should consider but not limit yourself to the following issues:

a. Where would you do the taste test?

b. Would you attempt to control the order in which people tasted the two drinks? If yes, how?

c. Would you attempt to control the temperature at which the drinks were served? If yes, how?

d. Would you serve the drinks in marked or unmarked containers, cans, glasses, or paper cups?

e. How much would you let each person drink of each brand?

Internet Exercise

Many online catalogs (such as Lands' End at http://www.landsend.com and Eddie Bauer at http://www.ebauer.com) allow customers to view merchandise after going through a series of steps to specify what they want to see (e.g., at Lands' End, click on "the store," then "women's," then "tailored clothing," then "silk wing collar blouse"). Explore these sites to see how they do it. Now, design an experiment to test whether presenting merchandise in this way is better than presenting it in another way, such as automatically displaying "specials" that customers have not asked to see. How would you design the experiment? What dependent variable(s) would you use? What threats to internal validity would you encounter, and how would you control them?

References

1. Cook, Thomas, and Donald Campbell (1979). *Quasi-experimentation: Design and Analysis Issues for Field Settings* (Chicago: Rand-McNally).

2. Kuhfeld, Warren F., Randall D. Tobias, and Mark Garratt (1994). "Efficient Experimental Design with Marketing Research Applications." *Journal of Marketing Research* 31, pp. 545–557.

3. Shimp, Terence A., Eva M. Hyatt, and David J. Snyder (1991). "A Critical Appraisal of Demand Artifacts in Consumer Research." *Journal of Consumer Research* 18 (December), pp. 273–283.

4. Smead, Raymond J., James B. Wilcox, and Robert E. Wilkes (1981). "How Valid Are Product Descriptions and Protocols in Choice Experiments?" *Journal of Consumer Research* 8(1), pp. 37–42.

5. Waldrop, Judith (1992). "All-American Markets." *American Demographics* 14 (January), pp. 24–27.

6. Waldrop, Judith (1993). "When Tulsa Burps, McDonald's Apologizes." *American Demographics* 15 (July), pp. 44–45.

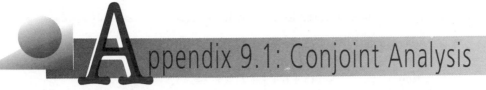

Introduction

Despite its name, conjoint analysis is not a data analysis procedure like factor analysis, cluster analysis, or regression analysis (these techniques are discussed in later chapters). Rather, it is a type of "thought experiment" designed to show how various elements of products or services (elements such as price, brand name, and features) predict customer preferences for those products or services. Conjoint results can be used for various purposes including market segmentation and predicting market shares for new or improved products. This last application is where conjoint analysis is most useful.

The basic method of conjoint analysis is as follows. People are asked to imagine products or services that vary along some dimensions of interest and to score these products or services in some way. The scoring usually is done by ranking the descriptions in order of preference. For example, we asked a friend of ours to express his preferences among movies that varied on three dimensions, each with two levels:

- Star of the movie: Eddie Murphy or Clint Eastwood
- Type of movie: action or comedy
- Price of admission: $6 or $7

We constructed a movie description using all eight possible combinations of these features ($2 \times 2 \times 2 = 8$), then wrote each combination on a separate card. One card looked as follows:

> Action movie
> Starring Eddie Murphy
> Admission price $6

Another card looked as follows:

> Comedy
> Starring Eddie Murphy
> Admission price $7

We arranged the eight cards in random order, gave them to our friend, and asked him to rearrange the cards from most preferred (first choice) to least preferred (eighth choice). His rankings are summarized as follows:

	Eddie Murphy		**Clint Eastwood**	
	Action	*Comedy*	*Action*	*Comedy*
$6	5th	3rd	1st	7th
$7	6th	4th	2nd	8th

Average scores for the levels of each variable are as follows:

$$
\begin{aligned}
\text{Eddie Murphy} &= (5+6+3+4)/4 &= 4.5 \\
\text{Clint Eastwood} &= (1+2+7+8)/4 &= 4.5 \\
\text{Action} &= (5+6+1+2)/4 &= 3.5 \\
\text{Comedy} &= (3+4+7+8)/4 &= 5.5 \\
\$6 &= (5+3+1+7)/4 &= 4.0 \\
\$7 &= (6+4+2+8)/4 &= 5.0
\end{aligned}
$$

Taken at face value, these average scores suggest that our friend is indifferent between Eddie Murphy and Clint Eastwood as stars (both got the same average score), prefers action movies to comedies (action movies scored closer to first, on average), and prefers to pay $6 rather than $7. A closer look at the data shows an interaction between star of movie and type of movie—our friend prefers Clint Eastwood over Eddie Murphy in an action movie and Eddie Murphy over Clint Eastwood in a comedy. This interaction makes the finding of no difference between stars somewhat misleading.

This, in a nutshell, is conjoint analysis. Now let's consider some of the things that can be accomplished with this procedure.

Measuring Attribute Importance with Conjoint Analysis

One of the things you can do with conjoint analysis is measure the relative importance of product attributes. Consider our friend's ratings of the Eddie Murphy movies:

	Action	*Comedy*
$6	3rd	1st
$7	4th	2nd

Our friend's first choice shows that he prefers comedies to action films—at least when Eddie Murphy is the star—and that he would rather pay $6 than $7 admission price. (In general, any subject's first choice when all combinations are shown will reveal his/her most preferred level for all dimensions. However, the "best of everything" choice may not be available if only some subset of combinations is shown.)

Subsequent choices show the second most preferred level on each dimension, the third most preferred level, etc. They also show the relative importance of the dimensions by revealing which elements are sacrificed and which are retained. In making his second choice from the Eddie Murphy movies, our friend no longer could have his preferred movie type *and* his preferred price. He had to sacrifice one or the other. He sacrificed his preferred price: he paid a $7 price and kept the comedy. This decision indicates that within the context of this design—Eddie Murphy movies, comedy or action, $6 or $7 admission price—price is less important than movie type to our friend.

The extent to which product elements are sacrificed or retained shows up in the differences among average scores for the various factor levels. For example, our friend's ratings for Eddie Murphy movies produced the following:

$$
\left.
\begin{array}{lclcr}
\text{Action} & = & (3+4)/2 & = & 3.5 \\
\text{Comedy} & = & (1+2)/2 & = & 1.5
\end{array}
\right\} \ 2.0
$$

$$
\left.
\begin{array}{lclcr}
\$6 & = & (1+3)/2 & = & 2.0 \\
\$7 & = & (2+4)/2 & = & 3.0
\end{array}
\right\} \ 1.0
$$

The larger difference across levels of movie type (2.0 versus 1.0 across levels of price) indicates that movie type was more important to our friend. The higher importance of movie type led to a score pattern in which the better movie type got extremely high ratings and the worse movie type got extremely low ratings, which produced a lot of spread in average scores across the levels of this attribute. The lower importance of price led to a back-and-forth score pattern and less spread in average scores across the levels of this attribute.

A special feature of conjoint analysis is its ability to reveal complicated patterns of preference across levels of product or service attributes. Consider the following ratings of televisions by price and brands given by a potential television buyer:

Price	Sony	Zenith	Goldstar
$250	1st	3rd	9th
$300	2nd	5th	10th
$350	4th	6th	11th
$400	7th	8th	12th

Close inspection of these ratings suggests several conclusions. First, this person prefers a Sony television at the lowest possible price. Second, within the $250–$350 price range, she will pay an extra $50 to get a Sony TV rather than a Zenith, but she won't pay an extra $100. Third, once we hit $350, she won't pay the extra $50 for the Sony anymore; perhaps she is hitting a budget limit at this point. Fourth, this person avoids Goldstar, suggesting that this brand is unacceptable to her for some reason. Average scores for the various attribute levels are as follow:

$$
\begin{array}{lclcr}
\$250 \text{ price} & = & (9+3+1)/3 & = & 4.33 \\
\$300 \text{ price} & = & (10+5+2)/3 & = & 5.67 \\
\$350 \text{ price} & = & (11+6+4)/3 & = & 7.00 \\
\$400 \text{ price} & = & (12+8+7)/3 & = & 9.00 \\
\\
\text{Sony} & = & (1+2+4+7)/4 & = & 3.50 \\
\text{Zenith} & = & (3+5+6+8)/4 & = & 5.50 \\
\text{Goldstar} & = & (9+10+11+12)/4 & = & 10.50
\end{array}
$$

These scores show that this person prefers a $250 price to a $300 price to a $350 price to a $400 price, and Sony to Zenith to Goldstar. No surprises there. Overall, brand is more important than price, as indicated by a range of 7.00 (10.50 − 3.50) across brand levels versus 4.67 (9.00 − 4.33) across price levels. However, this range of 7.00 is mostly caused by the Goldstar televisions. The difference in average scores is 5.00 between Goldstar and Zenith, compared with only 2.00 between Zenith and Sony. These numbers reveal what we've already seen through inspection—that a switch from Sony to Zenith is less serious to this subject than a switch from Zenith to Goldstar. Similarly, a rise in price from $350 to $400 is more important than a rise from $250 to $300 or $300 to $350, and more important than a switch from Sony to Zenith even though brand overall is more important than price.

This television example shows the special value of conjoint analysis. Simple, direct questions in a survey or a depth interview would be able to measure this person's preferred levels of brand and price, as well as the overall importance of these variables to her. However, the importance functions for both brand and price are nonlinear (a brand change, or a price increase of $50, has different impact at different points on the scale). It would be difficult to get at this nonlinearity in a direct questionnaire, and it would be very difficult to quantify these functions. Conjoint analysis does the job, though.

Estimating Sales for New or Improved Products

A popular use for conjoint analyses is estimating sales for new or improved products. A related use is identifying product improvements that will yield maximum sales for minimum costs.

Consider our television example. Say that current market prices for Sony, Zenith, and Goldstar televisions are as follow:

Sony	Zenith	Goldstar
$350	$300	$250

At these prices, our subject should buy the Sony television unless something happens to change or thwart her preferences. (The Sony television at $350 was preferred to the Zenith at $300 and the Goldstar at $250.) However, what if the prices changed? Using the conjoint results, Sony management can see that a $50 price rise in its brand (to $400) will cause this subject to switch to Zenith, even if Zenith also raises its price $50 (to $350). Zenith management can see that a $50 price cut in its brand (to $250) also will cause the subject to switch to Zenith unless Sony responds with a price cut of its own. Goldstar is out of luck: this subject doesn't seem willing to consider Goldstar under any circumstances.

So far, we've only analyzed one subject. However, a large conjoint analysis project might gather data from hundreds of subjects. Other people might remain loyal to Sony despite a $50 price rise, or prefer Zenith from the start. To estimate the overall effects of a $50 price rise for Sony, we would do the following:

- For each subject, identify the television with the highest ranking among those available on the market. This would be done twice—first with Sony at its initial price and then with Sony at the increased price.

- Assume that each subject will buy the television with the highest ranking unless other factors such as availability interfere with this choice.

- Count the subjects for whom Sony is the most preferred television at its initial price. If desired, weight these subjects by the probability that they will buy a television during some time period. (For nondurable products, subjects would be weighted by their expenditure levels in the product category.) Calculate these subjects as a (weighted) percentage of all subjects. This percentage represents the share of market that prefers the Sony television at its initial price over other televisions on the market.

- Count the subjects for whom Sony is the most preferred television at the increased price. Calculate these subjects as a (weighted) percentage of all subjects. This percentage represents the share of market that prefers the Sony television at an increased price over other televisions on the market.

The difference between the two share estimates can be used directly as an estimate of potential share change associated with a $50 price rise. This difference also can be scaled in some way—for example, the comparison between Sony's initial "preference share" and Sony's actual market share might be used to estimate how the "preference share" loss will translate in actual share loss. We also can identify specific competitors who will gain or lose customers, and we can use other questionnaire data to identify the characteristics of customers who will shift brands.

In a similar fashion, we can estimate the effects of changes in any attribute covered by the conjoint analysis—price, warranty terms, product features, or whatever the company has chosen to study in the conjoint procedure. We can use this "what if" modeling, in conjunction with a profit model that includes cost data, to identify changes that will optimize the profitability of a product.

We also can use this type of "what if" modeling to study the effects of a new market entrant: Given the new entrant's characteristics, how much share will it gain? From which competitors will this share be drawn? What will be the characteristics of the new entrant's buyers? We can use this information to develop optimal responses to a competitive entry; or, if the new entry represents our own line extension, we can optimize the new product so it minimizes cannibalization of our existing products and/or maximizes total profit for the entire product line.

Other Uses for Conjoint Analysis

Other uses for conjoint analysis include market segmentation, measuring price elasticity, and measuring the value of advertising.

Segmentation

Cluster analysis, which is discussed in Chapter 19, can be used to group the conjoint respondents according to similarities and dissimilarities in the values they attach to various attribute levels. This analysis will group the respondents into clusters that care about different product attributes: e.g., people to whom brand name is important, people to whom price is important, people to whom product features are important, etc. In other words, the analysis will segment the market according to product feature preferences, which is related to segmenting on desired benefits.

Benefit segmentation is cheaper to accomplish with survey questionnaires in which respondents directly indicate the relative importance of various product attributes. Therefore, conjoint analysis should not be used for the primary purpose of market segmentation. However, if a conjoint analysis is done for other purposes, such as forecasting market reaction to product improvements, a segmentation analysis is a nice bonus.

Elasticity

If price is included in the conjoint task, one of the outputs you get from the analysis is a value function for price, which provides a form of elasticity information.

As with segmentation information, elasticity can be obtained more cheaply from survey data than from conjoint analysis. For example, to get elasticity information for a television set, simply describe the set to people and ask whether they would be willing to pay $X for it. Split the respondents into five groups, and give each group a different value for X; then develop a rough demand curve by plotting the percentage who say they will buy at each price. Alternately, ask people the maximum they would pay, and develop a demand curve by plotting the percentage who will pay at least $10, $20, $30, $40, . . . $210, $220, etc. Either of these procedures will provide elasticity information less expensively than a conjoint analysis. Therefore, a conjoint analysis should not be used for the sole purpose of estimating elasticity, but the elasticity estimates you get from a conjoint analysis are a nice bonus.

Value of Advertising

Conjoint analysis also can be used to measure the value of advertising, as follows. Measure whether subjects are aware of your brand and whether they hold certain beliefs about it. Then compare conjoint results between aware and unaware subjects, or between subjects who do and don't hold some belief. For example, our television subject, who didn't want a Goldstar television even when it was $150 cheaper than a Sony or a Zenith, might be unfamiliar with the brand. An analysis across all of the subjects who are unfamiliar with Goldstar might show that, on average, Goldstar needs to be $120 cheaper than Zenith for these subjects to choose Goldstar. In contrast, analysis of the subjects who know about Goldstar might show that the average subject in this group will choose Goldstar if it is $50 cheaper than Zenith. If results like these are obtained, the $70 difference between familiar and unfamiliar subjects would provide a basis for calculating the benefits of advertising to build knowledge about Goldstar televisions.

Issues in Using Conjoint Analysis

Several issues must be considered in designing a conjoint analysis study or deciding whether to do one.

The big issue regarding whether to do a conjoint analysis is cost. In general, conjoint analysis requires face-to-face data collection: the procedure is too difficult to administer over the telephone or in mailed questionnaires. Face-to-face data collection means a high cost per interview. This means high study costs, small sample sizes, or both.

Because of cost considerations, conjoint analysis usually should be reserved for studies of possible product improvements or new product development. The ability of conjoint analysis to model market response is especially valuable in these applications. Conjoint analysis usually should *not* be done for the primary purposes of measuring the importance of product attributes or market segmentation; cheaper methods provide adequate data for these purposes.

Another key issue in whether to do a conjoint analysis is task realism. The procedure is a hypothetical exercise, and subjects must be able to visualize the descriptions and reliably choose among them. Conjoint analysis usually is not appropriate for designing radically new products because subjects can't reliably judge the product descriptions.

If conjoint analysis is appropriate for a particular research project, the following implementation issues exist:

1. Are all appropriate factors included in the design? You'll want to choose the factors of most relevance to your marketing program. Also, when you measure a difference between Sony and Zenith televisions, you usually want subjects to

rank the Sony and Zenith as if they were identical on everything except the factors used in your conjoint procedure. Subjects tend not to do this very well, and it helps them if you explicitly include other factors in the design.

2. Have you used appropriate levels of the chosen factors?

3. How should the study be designed? You might want to do a conjoint analysis with 6 different brands, 5 different prices, 2 levels of guarantee, and 10 other levels of product features. If all combinations are used, you'll have $6 \times 5 \times 2 \times 10 = 600$ product descriptions. Obviously, it isn't practical to expect a respondent to sort out 600 descriptions—a general rule of thumb is to limit yourself to no more than 30 descriptions. This means that you will have to (1) drop factors from your research, (2) keep all the factors but study them two or three at a time, or (3) use some subset of the possible combinations.

An arrangement that uses all possible combinations of features is called a "full factorial design," or just a "factorial design." An arrangement that uses only some of the combinations is called a "fractional factorial design," or simply a "fractional design." Most commercial applications of conjoint analysis use fractional designs.

The possible problem with fractional designs can be seen by revisiting our friend's movie rankings. We reduced the descriptions to represent a $2 \times 2 \times 2$ "Latin Square" arrangement of stars, movie types, and prices. A Latin Square is a fractional design that has the following layout (where A, B, etc. indicate factors and A1, A2, etc. indicate levels of the factors):

$2 \times 2 \times 2$ Latin Square				$3 \times 3 \times 3$ Latin Square			
	A1	A2			A1	A2	A3
B1	C1	C2		B1	C1	C2	C3
B2	C2	C1		B2	C3	C1	C2
				B3	C2	C3	C1

For our movie descriptions, a $2 \times 2 \times 2$ Latin Square gave our friend four combinations to rank. These combinations, and his rankings, were:

			Ranking
A1-B1-C1	=	Eddie Murphy, Action movie, $6	3rd
A1-B2-C2	=	Eddie Murphy, Comedy, $7	2nd
A2-B1-C2	=	Clint Eastwood, Action movie, $7	1st
A2-B2-C1	=	Clint Eastwood, Comedy, $6	4th

Average scores for the various factor levels were as follows:

$$Eddie\ Murphy = (3 + 2) / 2 = 2.5$$
$$Clint\ Eastwood = (1 + 4) / 2 = 2.5$$

$$Action = (1 + 3) / 2 = 2.0$$
$$Comedy = (2 + 4) / 2 = 3.0$$

$$\$6 = (3 + 4) / 2 = 3.5$$
$$\$7 = (1 + 2) / 2 = 1.5$$

As before, these averages show that my friend is indifferent between Eddie Murphy and Clint Eastwood and prefers action movies to comedies. However, the scores also show that my friend would rather pay $7 than $6, which we know to be wrong.

The reason for this misleading finding is that the comparison of $6 versus $7 prices coincided with a comparison of a Clint Eastwood comedy and Eddie Murphy action film versus a Clint Eastwood action film and Eddie Murphy comedy. My friend doesn't prefer a $7 price—it just looks that way because he prefers Clint Eastwood action films and Eddie Murphy comedies. The main effect of price is confounded with the interaction between star of movie and type of movie, and the interaction between star and type overpowers the price effect.

This example illustrates the advantage and disadvantage of fractional designs. The advantage of fractional designs is that they require participants to rank fewer product descriptions. The disadvantage of fractional designs is that they confound the main effects of some variables with the interaction effects of other variables, and therefore can yield misleading results.

In general, fractional designs are necessary to capture all the product features of interest—but if you use a fractional design, get help from an expert.

4. Are your respondents properly motivated? A big concern in conjoint analysis studies is that respondents may not take the task seriously. It's important not to overtax the respondents' motivation by giving them too big a task. This is the reason we generally prefer not to ask respondents to rank more than 30 product descriptions.

Alternatives to Conjoint Analysis

There are various alternatives to conjoint analysis as we have described it. These include survey procedures, conjoint analysis with different methods for gathering or analyzing the data, and choice modeling.

Survey procedures can be used for purposes similar to conjoint analysis. For example, if you want to identify product improvements that will get buyers to switch to your product, you can simply recruit a sample of buyers who buy from your competitors and ask them whether they will switch to your product if certain changes are made. If you want to measure the relative importance of various product attributes, you can directly ask for importance ratings. We've already noted that conjoint analysis provides certain quantitative information that can be difficult to get from surveys, but survey procedures are cheaper than conjoint analysis and always should be used if possible. In general, conjoint analysis should be viewed as a close-up look at buyer preferences that is used only after other methods have given a general picture of these preferences and only if a close-up is needed.

If conjoint analysis is used in a research project, it can be implemented using procedures other than those we have described. We've described a procedure in which respondents sort cards to produce a ranking. It's also possible to use computerized procedures in which respondents see a pair of product descriptions on a screen and choose the one they prefer, then see another pair and choose the one they prefer, and so on until the full set of rankings can be reconstructed using the logic that if A > B and B > C then A > C. The underlying program shows the descriptions and records the data as people respond. We've had good luck using this procedure with technical populations; we FedEx potential respondents a diskette containing the program that runs the conjoint task, they complete the task, and they FedEx the diskette back to us. It's also possible to use a dependent variable other than preference ranks, for example, we've given subjects a fixed budget to spend across the various alternatives. The resulting data are analyzed just as we analyzed the rankings, by calculating average scores for each attribute level.

Conjoint data also can be analyzed by more sophisticated methods than the simple averaging we used. This averaging assumes that the data have "interval" scaling (equal distances among scale points, so that the distance from 1 to 2 equals the distance from 2 to 3, etc.). Ranking data do not really satisfy this assumption. The problem can be solved by using an analysis procedure that does not assume interval data—for example, the LINMAP procedure or the monotone regression used in packages such as CONJOINT. These procedures go beyond our scope; however, they almost always produce the same conclusions as simple averaging.

Finally, choice modeling is a technique that serves the same general purposes as conjoint analysis and has grown in popularity in recent years. In choice modeling, subjects are given a series of product description sets—usually with no more than four descriptions in a set—and are asked to choose which product they would buy from each set (the set may include "no purchase" as an alternative). For example, subjects might be given a set with a Zenith television at $300 and a Goldstar television at $250 and asked which they would choose. Then the subjects might be given a set with Zenith at $300, Goldstar at $250, and Sony at $350, and again asked to choose. The patterns of choice switching—how many people took Zenith in the first set but Sony in the second, how many people took Goldstar in the first set but Sony in the second—can be analyzed to reveal the similarity of various alternatives to each other, and the relative importance of various attributes in motivating choice.

Choice modeling has an advantage over conjoint analysis in that it works directly with choice measures, which have more application than preference measures to actual market behavior. However, choice modeling generally requires more skill than conjoint analysis to design and analyze, and we consider choice modeling beyond the scope of this book.

3 Tools for Primary Data Collection

In the previous section, surveys, depth interviews, focus groups, and experiments were discussed. To use any of these tools in marketing research, a measurement instrument and a procedure for selecting research participants are needed. Measurement instruments and sampling plans are the basic tools of primary data collection.

Therefore, this section describes how to develop measurement instruments and sampling plans. These topics are presented in the context of surveys, because surveys are widely used and have the most formal requirements for instrument design and sampling. However, the general principles in this section apply to depth interviews, focus groups, and experiments as well as to surveys.

Chapters 10 to 12 focus on the design of effective questionnaires. Chapters 13 and 14 discuss procedures for sample selection.

Question writing turns out to be more difficult than might be expected, because language and communication are very complex processes and what appears to be a simple question can be difficult to ask, answer, or interpret. Chapter 10 discusses how to write questions that give the needed answers and how to avoid questions that give misleading answers.

Also, questions do not appear in isolation. They are parts of a questionnaire, and the overall design of the questionnaire can have a major impact on the answers to individual questions. Chapter 11 tells how to assemble individual questions into an effective questionnaire. Then, to illustrate question writing and questionnaire design principles, Chapter 12 presents several real-world questionnaires and gives detailed comments about each of them.

Sampling methods have been carefully developed by statisticians during the past fifty years, and Chapters 13 and 14 introduce methods for selecting samples that provide accurate information. Chapter 13 presents a general overview of sampling: how to define a population of interest, how to work with lists of that population, how to choose a sampling procedure, how to draw a sample, how to maintain sample integrity in data collection, and how to report sampling information. Chapter 14 then elaborates on issues related to determining how big the sample should be and how to maximize sampling efficiency.

Sample Student Project

The Questionnaire

After detailed discussions with the Apple representative and conducting focus groups with students, the class was ready to develop a questionnaire to measure student purchase, use, and attitudes toward computers. They used Chapters 10 to 12 of this book to help them design a four-page self-administered questionnaire. A copy of the final questionnaire is given on the following pages.

The topics to be included in the questionnaire were discussed and jointly agreed upon by the students and the Apple representative. The first eight questions of the questionnaire asked about current uses and purchasing of computers by students. Questions 9 to 12 asked about features of a computer that were important to students and how they rated these features on IBM-type computers and Apple computers. Questions 13 and 14 referred specifically to the Micro Computer Order Center, and the final classification questions asked about year in school, major, and where students lived.

Survey of Computer Usage
University of Illinois
Fall, 1995

Class _____

CIRCLE THE NUMBERS THAT APPLY.

1. Do you ever use computers?

Yes 1
No . . . . 2→(SKIP TO Q.15)

2. Do you use computers regularly for the following applications?

	Yes	No
Word processing/desktop publishing	1	2
Data analysis (SPSS, etc.)	1	2
Graphics	1	2
E-mail/The Internet (WWW, Gopher, Mosaic, etc.)	1	2
Computer design (CAD, CAM)/programming languages	1	2
Games	1	2
Databases (i.e., dBase IV)	1	2
Other (SPECIFY)	1	2

3a. About how often did you go to a Campus Computing Site Organization (CCSO) in the past seven days.

_____ times

Never . . . . .0→(SKIP TO Q.4)

3b. When you went to a CCSO site, which computers did you use? (CIRCLE ALL THAT APPLY.)

IBM compatible 1

Apple/Macintosh 2

NeXT 3

Workstations 4

4. Do you own a personal computer?

Yes 1

No . . . . 2→(SKIP TO Q.9a)

5. What brand of computer is it?　　_____

6. Is your computer a laptop?

Yes 1

No 2

7. In what year did you get this computer? . . . . 19 _____

8a. Did you buy this computer or was it a gift?

Bought 1

Gift . . . . 2→(SKIP TO Q.9a)

8b. Where did you buy this computer?

University of Illinois Micro Computer Order Center (Central Stores) 1

Mail order 2

Discount stores (Circuit City, Best Buy, Walmart, etc.) 3

Computer stores 4

Personal sale (used or person-to-person sale) 5

Other (SPECIFY) 6

8c. What sources of information did you use in making your purchase decision? (PLEASE CIRCLE ALL THAT APPLY.)

Friends or acquaintances 1

Other family members or relatives 2

Magazines (Computer World, PC World, etc.) 3

Newspaper advertisements 4

Salespeople 5

Brochures, literature from computer companies 6

Continued

9a. How important would each of these features be to you in choosing what computer to buy when you decide to buy a computer?

	Not at all important						Very important
Speed	1	2	3	4	5	6	7
Ease of use	1	2	3	4	5	6	7
Memory size	1	2	3	4	5	6	7
Modem	1	2	3	4	5	6	7
Reliability	1	2	3	4	5	6	7
CD-ROM	1	2	3	4	5	6	7
Expansion capabilities	1	2	3	4	5	6	7
Software installed at purchase	1	2	3	4	5	6	7
Availability of other software	1	2	3	4	5	6	7
Price	1	2	3	4	5	6	7
Service	1	2	3	4	5	6	7

9b. What brands of computers would you consider buying? _____

_____

10a. How likely are you to be using a computer at work when you leave the university? Would you say you are very likely, somewhat likely, not very likely, or not at all likely to be using a computer at work?

Not at all likely .... 1→(SKIP TO Q.11)

Not very likely 2

Somewhat likely 3

Very likely 4

10b. Would you be more likely to be using an IBM-compatible computer or an Apple/Macintosh computer at work, or don't you know what kind you might be using?

IBM/IBM compatible 1

Apple 2

Either one 3

Don't know 4

11. Whether or not you currently own or use them, how would you rate IBM or IBM-compatible computers on the following categories?

	No Opinion	Poor					Excellent
Ease of use	0	1	2	3	4	5	6	7
Service	0	1	2	3	4	5	6	7
Reliability	0	1	2	3	4	5	6	7
Speed	0	1	2	3	4	5	6	7
Graphics	0	1	2	3	4	5	6	7
Software available to do what I want to do	0	1	2	3	4	5	6	7
Price	0	1	2	3	4	5	6	7

12. Whether or not you currently own or use them, how would you rate Apple/Macintosh computers on the following categories?

	No Opinion	Poor						Excellent
Ease of use	0	1	2	3	4	5	6	7
Service	0	1	2	3	4	5	6	7
Reliability	0	1	2	3	4	5	6	7
Speed	0	1	2	3	4	5	6	7
Graphics	0	1	2	3	4	5	6	7
Software available to do what I want to do	0	1	2	3	4	5	6	7
Price	0	1	2	3	4	5	6	7

13. Have you ever heard of the Micro Computer Order Center?

Yes 1

No .... 2→(SKIP TO Q.15)

14a. Have you ever visited the Micro Computer Order Center:

Yes 1

No .... 2→(SKIP TO Q.15)

14b. How would you rate the Micro Computer Order Center on the following dimensions?

	No Opinion	Poor						Excellent
Price	0	1	2	3	4	5	6	7
Before sales service	0	1	2	3	4	5	6	7
Knowledge of staff	0	1	2	3	4	5	6	7
After sales service	0	1	2	3	4	5	6	7
Convenience	0	1	2	3	4	5	6	7
Selection choices	0	1	2	3	4	5	6	7

15. What year in school are you?

Freshman 1

Sophomore 2

Junior 3

Senior 4

Graduate student 5

16. What is your major field of study? _____

Continued

17. Where do you live?

Dormitory 1

Fraternity/sorority 2

Apartment building 3

Other 4

18. Aside from personally owned computers, are there any computers available for residents' use where you live?

Yes 1

No 2

19. Do you have any other comments about computers that you would like to tell us?

_____

_____

_____

_____

_____

_____

Thank you very much!

Sampling

Sampling issues required a good deal of discussion. The students wanted a large sample so that analyses could be done separately for students in different academic programs. This large sample size led to the decision to use a self-administered form. Mailing or putting the questionnaires in student mailboxes was considered but rejected because of concerns that the response rate would be too low unless multiple mailings or follow-ups were used. The need to complete the project within a semester made these follow-up activities impractical.

After considering, and rejecting, passing out the questionnaires at various computer sites and other locations on campus, the decision was made to pass the questionnaires out in classes, with the permission of the instructor. Using a published list of all the classes being taught that semester, a simple random sample of forty classrooms was selected based on the procedures described in Chapters 13 and 14. Members of the research class passed out questionnaires to all members of the selected classes. As happens in the real world, some classes had to be replaced because they were no longer meeting. Attached to the questionnaires were self-addressed, postage paid envelopes for students to return their completed questionnaires. (Postage and printing costs were paid by the client, Apple.) Because the questionnaire was short and the topic was considered important, cooperation by instructors and students was high. To increase cooperation, students who gave their names were entered in a lottery that offered six cash prizes of $50 each paid for by Apple. A copy of the letter attached to the questionnaires is given here.

Dear Fellow Student:

As you know, the use of computers on this campus has grown so rapidly that there is no good information available on what student needs are. As part of an advanced research class, we are conducting a survey for the university and its computer suppliers to determine what is happening and what these needs are so that you may be better served.

We are sampling a group of selected classes so that we can find out the different needs of all parts of the campus. Your response is very important. Would you take a few minutes at your convenience in the next day or two to fill this questionnaire out and return it in the enclosed envelope by campus mail to the Survey Research Laboratory?

To encourage you to participate, we will have a lottery among all the questionnaires that are received and will offer six awards of $50 each to the winners. To participate in the lottery, your questionnaire must be received by _____. Please give us your name, address, and phone number in the space below so that we can notify you if you are a winner. Note that your name will never be associated with the questionnaire so that your answers are completely confidential.

Thanks very much for your help.

First names of students

Your name _____

Address _____

Phone number _____

10 Asking Questions

 OBJECTIVES

LEARNING

After reading this chapter, you should be able to answer the following questions:

❶ How can the right questions for a research project be determined?

❷ How can the chance that respondents will properly interpret a question be maximized?

❸ How can the chance that respondents will know the answer be maximized?

❹ How can the chance that respondents will give an answer without distorting it be maximized?

❺ What are the relative advantages of open and closed questions?

❻ What are the principles of response category design?

❼ How many questions should be used to measure a phenomenon?

❽ What are standard ways of asking some common classification questions?

The most common way of obtaining marketing research information is by asking questions. Because questioning is such a common activity, many people think that asking and answering questions is easy. In fact, this is far from true. There is an old saying, "A fool can ask questions that a wise man cannot answer."

To get good results from questions, you must meet four requirements:

- You must ask the right questions (given the research objectives and the business situation).

- Respondents must properly understand your questions.

- Respondents must know the answers.

- Respondents must be willing and able to tell you those answers without distorting them.

Marketing Research Tools 10.1 summarizes these requirements and lists the issues that are associated with each requirement. In this chapter, these issues are discussed, and ways of minimizing problems in each area are suggested. Other issues in question writing are then discussed, and standard ways of asking some common questions are provided.

A few points about this chapter are in order:

- The principles discussed in this chapter apply to any type of research: surveys, depth interviews, and so on. The primary examples are surveys, but the requirements for effective questions are the same for all types of research.

MARKETING RESEARCH TOOLS

10.1

THE REQUIREMENTS FOR GETTING GOOD RESULTS FROM QUESTIONS

Requirement	Related issues
You must ask the right question.	Does the question fit the research objectives? Does the question fit the way the market works?
Respondents must understand the question.	Do they understand the words in the question? Do all of them interpret the question in the same way? Do they interpret the question in the way you intended?
Respondents must know the answer.	Were they there? Can they remember? If the question asks for an opinion, do they have one? If the question asks for intentions, are they meaningful?
Respondents must be willing and able to respond accurately.	Do they think that some answers are socially desirable?

- This chapter only covers individual questions; Chapter 11 covers how to design questionnaires.

- Questioning is an art as well as a science, and everyone has his or her own style. There are many "right" ways of asking a question. This chapter will not so much describe how to ask good questions as suggest how to avoid bad ones.

Asking the Right Questions

In marketing research, questions are asked because the answers will help improve marketing decisions. This connection between questions and decisions means that a question can be technically perfect—clearly stated, easy to understand, easy to answer—yet still be a bad question because it does not properly serve the marketing purpose at hand.

Say, for example, that you want to measure awareness of a clothing store within its market area. There are many ways of doing so, as shown in Exhibit 10.1. All of these questions are clearly stated and easy to understand. However, they may not be equally suitable for every marketing research purpose.

To choose the best question form, you have to know why you are asking the question. Most marketing researchers measure awareness because they think that awareness has something to do with sales. The next question is exactly *how* awareness relates to sales. The answer will suggest the best way of measuring awareness.

For example, it may be believed that higher awareness of a clothing store leads to higher sales because awareness *determines a shopping sequence*. The first store that people think of as a good place to buy clothes may be the first store they visit when they shop. They may go to a second store only if the first store can't satisfy them, go to a third store only if the second store can't satisfy them, and so on. If this is the situation, there is little value in being the tenth store that people think of or in being recognized but not recalled by shoppers. This suggests that the best awareness question for a clothing store might be a limited recall measure, such as the first store that comes to mind.

On the other hand, when measuring awareness for brands of blank videotape, you may believe that awareness simply *sanctions alternatives*. Many people buy videotapes by going to a store that sells tapes and buying any reputable brand that is on sale. Awareness simply sanctions an alternative by qualifying it as a reputable brand. In this situation, the best awareness question might be a recognition measure. It doesn't matter if a brand is the first, third, or tenth brand that people think of—only that it is recognized as a reputable brand.

To help ask the right question in a marketing research project two rules should be followed:

1. Ask whether the question is consistent with how the market works. If this is not known, ask someone who knows. For example, before writing a question to measure awareness, ask someone to tell you how awareness relates to sales in this particular market.

EXHIBIT **10.1**

Ways of Measuring Awareness of a Store

Recognition measures

In recognition measures, respondents demonstrate awareness of a store by saying that they recognize the store's name when it is shown or read to them. Examples include:

- I have a list of clothing stores. As I read each one, please tell me whether or not you have heard of that store. How about . . .

- I have a list of store names. As I read each one, please tell me whether it is a clothing store. If you're not sure about a store, just tell me that you're not sure. How about . . .

- Duna is a clothing store with locations downtown and in the Baybridge, Northtown, and Seven Oaks shopping centers. Have you heard of this store?

Recall measures

In recall measures, respondents demonstrate awareness of a store by naming it from memory. Recall measures pose a more difficult task than recognition measures for the respondent, and the number of people who can recall a store (product, advertisement, etc.) will always be smaller than the number who say they recognize it. Examples of recall measures include:

- What are all the names of women's clothing stores that you can think of? (PROBE: Any others?)

- What are all the stores that sell women's clothing in the Baybridge Mall that you can think of? (PROBE: Any others?)

- When you think of places to buy women's clothing, what are the first three stores that come to mind?

- When you think of places to buy women's clothing, what is the first store that comes to mind?

- Which women's clothing store uses the slogan "You've got style"?

The first two recall measures given can be analyzed for whether respondents name the store, regardless of order, or can be analyzed for the order in which stores are mentioned. The third and fourth recall measures implicitly concern themselves with order. The "first-to-mind" question is commonly called a "top-of-mind" awareness measure.

2. Specify how you will use the results to draw conclusions about the market, and ask yourself whether those conclusions address the research objectives.

If a question is consistent with the way in which the market works and it addresses the research objectives, then the question being asked is probably the right one. Marketing Research Tools 10.2 summarizes these points.

MARKETING RESEARCH TOOLS

10.2

WAYS OF HELPING YOURSELF ASK THE RIGHT QUESTION

1. Ask whether the question fits the way the market works.
2. Ask whether the question addresses the research objectives.

CASE STUDY 10.1

A marketing director for a hospital chain told us this story:

We operate a physician referral service under the telephone number 444-CARE. We view this service as an important part of our support services for doctors, and we advertise it heavily.

At one point, we decided to test whether our advertising had created awareness of 444-CARE. We did a telephone survey and used unaided recall to measure awareness of physician referral services. That is, we simply asked people to tell us the telephone numbers for any physician referral services they could recall.

The results showed that less than 1 percent of the population could name 444-CARE. We were incredibly depressed and felt that our advertising had been a big failure, until somebody pointed out that calls to 444-CARE are heavily correlated with advertising levels. We get hundreds of calls per week when we advertise heavily; when we stop advertising, the phone stops ringing. Obviously, the advertising is working.

So why doesn't our advertising produce awareness, at least as measured by unaided recall? We formed two theories to explain this situation. First, people might look in the Yellow Pages for physician referral services and call 444-CARE because they recognize it, even though they can't spontaneously recall it. Second, people who need a doctor might notice the advertising, call the number, then promptly forget the number. I favor this second theory because of the close correlation between the timing of the advertising and the timing of the calls.

Whichever theory is correct, the recall measure was inappropriate for our situation. If the first theory is correct, a recognition measure would be more appropriate. If the second theory is correct, it just doesn't make sense for us to measure awareness, because enduring awareness is not part of the buying process for our service.

This story shows that to ask the right question, it is necessary to have a theory of how the market works.

Understanding the Question

There are three issues related to respondents' understanding or interpretation of a question:

- Do respondents understand the words in the question?
- Do all respondents interpret the question in the *same* way?
- Do respondents interpret the question in the way *you intended*?

Do Respondents Understand the Words in the Question?

The simplest reason for problems in understanding a question is that people don't understand some of the words. Consider this example, taken from an actual marketing research questionnaire targeted at consumers:

Q: Does your home have power conditioning equipment to protect your critical equipment against power fluctuations?

This may be a reasonable question for a questionnaire aimed at electrical engineers, but it is a poor question for the general public. Many people will answer this question without asking for help because they don't want to appear ignorant, but they won't understand the term "power conditioning equipment," and they can't give meaningful answers if they don't understand the term. A less technical version might be "Do you have anything in your home to protect your electrical devices against power surges?"

Even if people understand all of the words in a question, they may have trouble with the question as a whole. Consider this example:

Q: Part of our research is to learn what people mean when they use certain words. If people asked you what you thought of a certain TV program, you might tell them you thought it was excellent, terrible, or so-so. If you wanted to, you could use these words to give a TV program a score. For example, you might give it a 50 every time someone said it was so-so. If someone used a word that was ten times more favorable than so-so, you would give it a 500 because $50 \times 10 = 500$. If someone used a word that was only half as favorable as so-so, you would give it a 25 because half of 50 is 25.

I am going to read you a short list of words that could be used to describe TV programs, movies, products, or almost anything else. If "so-so" is worth 50 points, please tell me what number you would assign to each of these other words. You can give each word any number above zero, no matter how large it is. Let's start with "bad." If "so-so" is worth 50 points, what number would you assign to "bad"?

This question was used in a telephone survey of the general population, and many respondents had trouble understanding it. The individual words in the question are understandable, but the question as a whole is too long and complex.

Do All Respondents Understand the Question in the Same Way?

A more subtle issue in question writing is whether all respondents understand the question in the same way. Consider this example:

Q: What is your income?

This question seems easy to understand. The problem is that different people will interpret the question in different ways. Some people will answer with their monthly income, while others will give their annual income. Some will give their personal income, while others will give their family income. Some will give their pre-tax income, while others will give their take-home income. Some will give their income only from their job, while others will give their income from all sources. As a group, the answers will be uninterpretable.

The problem in this example is that the word "income" has several interpretations. The more general a word is, the more likely this is to occur. Exhibit 10.2 lists some simple words that sometimes cause problems in questionnaires because they have different meanings in different contexts. Additional definition may be needed to keep these words unambiguous in a question. For example, instead of simply saying "you," the phrase "you yourself" can be used if information is wanted about the respondent and "you and your household" can be used if information is wanted about the entire household. The general rule is to define fully the question for the respondent.

EXHIBIT 10.2

A Rogue's Gallery of Problem Words

Stanley Payne, in his classic book *The Art of Asking Questions* (Princeton, N.J.: Princeton University Press, 1980) gave a "rogue's gallery" of words that seem simple but cause problems in questions because they are interpreted in different ways by different people. These words include:

any, anybody, anyone, anything: May mean "every," "some," or "only one."

fair: Meanings include "average," "pretty good," "not bad," "favorable," "just," "honest," "according to the rules," "plain," or "open."

just: May mean "precisely," "closely," or "barely."

most: A problem if it precedes another adjective, since it is not clear whether it modifies the adjective or the noun as in "most useful work."

saw, see, seen: May mean "observe," or may mean "visit."

you: May be interpreted to refer to the individual or a group such as a household.

Try to think of ways a question might could be misinterpreted.

Do Respondents Understand the Question the Way You Intended?

Even if respondents understand the question and they all interpret it in the same way, they may not understand the question in the way you intended. Consider this example:

Q: What are all the reasons why you bought your groceries at ValuLand rather than some other store? (PROBE: Any others?)

This question seems straightforward, but we know of a supermarket company that lost a lot of money because it misinterpreted the answers. The company used this question in several surveys and found that low prices, merchandise selection, and good service were leading factors in choosing where to buy groceries. Store location seemed less important. Based on these results, the company opened some large stores on the outskirts of medium-sized cities. The stores had good prices and excellent merchandise selection but poor locations. They did poorly.

The problem was one of interpretation. Most people restrict their grocery shopping, as well as their thinking about grocery shopping, to stores within a reasonable distance of their homes. When you ask, "Why do you shop at ValuLand?," they answer the question as if it said "Why do you shop at ValuLand rather than another store close to you?" They may not mention location as a reason for store choice because they think only of stores with acceptable locations; however, they will not shop at a store with an inconvenient location. In using the results, the company failed to realize that respondents were answering the question in this way.

Similar problems arise whenever questions are used to judge the importance of marketing variables that act as "screens" in buying decisions. People won't say they bought a product because of advertising—but if they hadn't seen the product advertised, they wouldn't have known about it and wouldn't have bought it. People won't say they bought a medium- or high-priced product because of its price—but if the price was out of their range, they wouldn't have bought the product. In using the answers to these and other questions, it is important to consider what respondents had in mind when they answered.

Minimizing Problems of Understanding or Interpretation

Use the following rules to avoid problems of understanding or interpretation:

1. *Be specific.* Interpretation problems often arise because a question is too broad. For example:

   Q: In the past six months, has your household purchased any major appliances new from the store?

   This question presents a problem because different respondents will have different definitions of "major appliances." You'll get better results if you ask:

   Q: I have a list of household appliances. As I read each one, please tell me whether or not your household has purchased this type of appliance new from the store during the past six months. How about . . .

	Yes	No
A refrigerator?	1	2
A kitchen range or oven?	1	2
A microwave oven?	1	2
Etc.		

2. *Specify who, what, when, where, and how.* For example, here is a revision of our income question that attempts to specify whose income, from what sources, over what time:

   Q: In 1997, about what was your total family income before taxes? Please count income from all members of your household, and from all sources including sources such as interest and dividends.

3. *Specify how the answer should be given.* Consider this example:

   Q: Overall, how satisfied were you with the care you received at that hospital?

   If this question is asked, you'll get all kinds of answers: "Excellent," "Very satisfied," "I didn't have any problems," "The food wasn't very good," and so on. These answers will be difficult to interpret as a group. You'll do better if you put respondents on the same scale, such as:

   Q: Overall, how satisfied were you with the care you received at that hospital? Were you very satisfied, moderately satisfied, slightly satisfied, or not at all satisfied?

   Even if you don't give response categories, you can tell respondents how many answers to give. For example:

   Q: What are the *two most important reasons* why you bought your groceries at ValuLand rather than some other store?

4. *Use simple language.* A good rule is to limit questions to words that a child would understand and to avoid technical language (of course, technical language is acceptable in questions aimed at technicians).

5. *Try to use words with only one meaning.*

6. *Use numbers rather than indefinite adjectives to measure magnitudes.* For example, rather than ask people whether they use a product "regularly," use specific numbers to measure usage frequency. This avoids confusion over the interpretation of "regular."

    In some situations, an indefinite measure may be better. For example, a person who says he "often" has trouble with his car may be a better potential customer for a new car than someone who says he "sometimes" has trouble, even if the second person actually has trouble more frequently.

7. *Ask questions one at a time.* For example, the following question might confuse people, and can be tricky to answer:

    Q: In the past six months, have you bought a television or a VCR?

    You'll do better if you ask:

    Q: In the past six months, have you bought a television?

    then

    Q: In the past six months, have you bought a VCR?

Critical Thinking Skills

What comprehension problems, if any, would you encounter with the question "Are you a full-time student?" Can you think of a better way of asking this question?

8. *Before proceeding with a research project, pretest the questionnaire.* This will show whether respondents have trouble understanding any of the questions. Chapter 11 discusses pretesting methods in more detail.

9. *Pretest the questionnaire to learn what respondents have in mind when they answer key questions.*

    The pretesting process can be speeded and questionnaire development costs reduced by the use of questions that have been tested and used in earlier studies, by either you or someone else. It is important, however, to be certain that these questions worked well. Otherwise, mistakes may simply be copied.

    Marketing Research Tools 10.3 summarizes how to minimize problems associated with incorrect or inconsistent understanding of a question.

Knowing the Answer

If respondents understand a question properly and consistently, the next issue is whether they know the answer. This is a big issue. Ultimately, data quality is limited by respondents' knowledge, which in turn is limited by the following factors.

MARKETING RESEARCH TOOLS

10.3

WAYS OF MINIMIZING PROBLEMS RELATED TO UNDERSTANDING THE QUESTION

1. Be specific.
2. Specify who, what, when, where, and how.
3. Specify how the answer should be given.
4. Use simple language.
5. Try to use words with only one meaning.
6. Use numbers (rather than indefinite adjectives) to measure magnitudes.
7. Ask questions one at a time.
8. Pretest the questionnaire to see whether respondents have trouble understanding some of the questions.
9. Pretest the questionnaire to learn what respondents have in mind when they answer key questions.

Were They There?

Sometimes respondents can't answer questions because they weren't there. Say, for example, that an interview is being conducted with "the person who knows the most about health events in this household." In most families, this is the wife. During the interview, you ask whether anyone in the family has been hospitalized during the past six months, and you learn that the husband was hospitalized for kidney stones. In such a situation, if you ask the wife questions about the nursing care in the hospital, she may not know because she wasn't there.

Proxy respondents (respondents who provide information about others in their households and organizations) are not necessarily bad. For example, if the wife handled the bills for her husband's hospitalization, she will be in a better position to answer questions about the performance of the hospital's business office. The hospitalization was his experience, but the paperwork was *her* experience. Also, she will know as well as her husband does that the hospitalization occurred, and she may have a better memory for details such as when it occurred. The key question is not so much "Was she there?" as "Does she know?" If proxy respondents know the information you want, they will give acceptable data, though proxy reports on average are slightly less accurate than self-reports.

Author Tips

The problem of respondents not knowing the answers because they weren't there is particularly serious in business research. Organizational buying, for example, often involves many people, and no one person has the whole story. Business research also presents a problem because people change jobs; you may find yourself asking questions about a purchase to a person who wasn't on the job when the purchase was made.

Can They Remember?

Even if questions are asked about something that happened to respondents personally, they might not know the answers because they didn't notice or can't remember. For example, the last time you bought hair shampoo, did you check the price? If you did check the price, do you remember it?

When we say that people forgot something, we don't necessarily mean that there is no trace of the event left in memory. Consider this example:

Q: In the past two months, about how many times have you dined at restaurants, including fast food restaurants?

Given enough time and effort, people may be able to recall every single time they went to restaurants during the past two months. However, respondents will not make unlimited efforts to search their memories. If the number of restaurant meals is more than four or five, respondents will rely on stereotypical knowledge such as "I eat lunch out every day" or on some other method of quickly generating an estimate. Whatever method they use to answer the question, their answers will be approximate rather than exact (Sudman, Bradburn, and Schwarz, 1996).

Common problems associated with memory errors in marketing research include the following:

- People tend to *overestimate* purchase and consumption frequencies for short time periods. This occurs because people are uncertain about the dates of their activities, and, when uncertain, they include rather than exclude events in an effort to be helpful (Schwarz and Sudman, 1994; Sudman and Bradburn, 1974).

- People tend to *underestimate* purchase and consumption frequencies for long time periods. This occurs because people lose track of events over a long period of time.

- If people are asked to report what brand they purchased, they tend to overreport brands that are heavily advertised, because advertised brands are more likely to come to mind.

The severity of memory-based errors depends on various factors, including (1) the respondent's motivation to think carefully, (2) the importance to the respondent of whatever is being measured, (3) the uniqueness of whatever is being measured, and (4) the recency of whatever is being measured. For example, a home purchase may have occurred years ago, but because of its importance and its uniqueness, most respondents will remember a home purchase better than grocery purchases made a few weeks ago.

Do They Have Opinions?

Attitude and opinion questions present special problems associated with people not knowing the answer. These problems arise because respondents often don't have definite attitudes about the subjects covered in the questionnaire. Consider this example:

Q: I have a list of hospitals in our area. As I read each one, please tell me how you would rate that hospital as a place to receive care: excellent, good, fair, or poor. How about . . .

	Excellent	Good	Fair	Poor
Eastside Hospital?	4	3	2	1
Lakeview Hospital?	4	3	2	1
Presbyterian Hospital?	4	3	2	1
St. Peter's Hospital?	4	3	2	1

Most respondents to a question like this will *not* have definite attitudes about all of the hospitals. However, they will create opinions on the spot, based on what little knowledge they have.

If respondents create opinions on the spot, their answers will depend on the specific context and wording of the question. This instability makes attitude data difficult to compare across studies. Nonetheless, many researchers find such data useful. They argue that people make buying decisions based on their opinions, however poorly founded those opinions may be, so it is useful to measure opinions even among people who haven't thought much about a topic.

Are Intentions Meaningful?

Intention measures are closely related to attitude measures in the strain they place on respondents' knowledge. Consider this example:

Q: If there were a local magazine like *Consumer Reports* that evaluated restaurants, auto repair shops, plumbers, stores, and other local businesses, what is the likelihood that your family would subscribe to this magazine? Would you say your family definitely would subscribe, probably would subscribe, might or might not subscribe, probably would not subscribe, or definitely would not subscribe?

Marketing researchers often complain that questions such as this are poor predictors of behavior. For example, Urban and Hauser (1993) suggest that you can expect purchases from only 90 percent of the "definitely would" respondents, 50 percent of the "probably would" respondents, and 10 percent of the "might or might not" respondents. Even these figures vary widely from one situation to the next.

Intention data have three problems. The first, very simply, is that people may not know what they will do until the actual situation arises. This is particularly a problem for innovative products. If you ask people, "Would you buy Tide detergent if it came with a lemon scent?," most respondents can accurately predict their behavior because they can accurately envision the product. However, they may not be able to envision accurately a more innovative product. Anything you can do to increase respondents' knowledge about the product—such as letting them see it and/or giving them its price—will help you to get better intention data.

A second problem is that the lead time between intentions and behavior may be very short. For example, imagine asking people, "How many AA batteries do you intend to buy during the next six months?" People don't *intend* to buy AA batteries six months in advance—they just buy batteries when they need them. A better estimate of battery purchases can be made by asking how many batteries respondents have bought during the past six months.

A third problem with intention measures is that respondents may overreport their buying intentions because they want to be nice to you. After all, it does not cost anything to say they will buy your product. To minimize this problem, try to avoid a direct intention measure. For example, instead of asking people whether they would subscribe to a magazine like *Consumer Reports*, you might give them a list of magazines (including the proposed magazine) and ask which ones they would choose. For industrial products, you might simply "qualify" potential buyers according to their usage patterns, available funds, and general interest in the product. This will allow you to report a solid estimate of the number of qualified buyers available for sales efforts rather than a shaky estimate of how many companies intend to buy.

Minimizing Problems Arising from Respondents Not Knowing the Answers

Data problems resulting from respondents' limited knowledge are to some extent beyond a researcher's control. However, here are some ways of minimizing these problems.

1. *Qualify respondents for knowledge.* Ask whether he or she is the person who made the purchase, whether he or she has formed an opinion on the subject, etc.

2. *Use the right time frame, which depends on the frequency and importance of the event being measured.* Rare and important events, such as automobile accidents, can be remembered after several years. Automobile purchases might be measured over the previous twelve months. Purchases of furniture or appliances might be measured over one to three months. Mundane events such as grocery purchases might be measured over one or two weeks. When even this period is too long, as with behaviors such as television watching, consider other methods such as diaries to replace recall entirely.

    Some researchers avoid the issue of time frames by asking about "typical" behavior, for example, "How much do you spend in a typical week?" or "What brand do you usually buy?" This approach can create problems with consistent definitions across respondents, so it is generally not recommended.

3. *Consider providing cues to aid memory.* A **cue** is any type of spoken or printed reminder given the respondent to improve memory. Cues can be provided by giving examples of the behavior, such as:

    Q: People drink beer in many places—at home, at restaurants, at bars, at sporting events, at friends' homes, etc. During the past month, did you drink any beer?

    The problem with cueing through examples is that respondents tend to think only in terms of the examples. Don't use examples if you want respondents to consider something more general.

    Cues can also be provided by separating a question into specifics; for example, rather than ask, "During the past month, what magazines did you read?," you might ask:

Critical Thinking Skills

What knowledge problems, if any, would you encounter if you tried to measure people's long-distance telephone usage over the past year? How would you minimize these problems?

Q: During the past month, which of the following magazines did you read? How about . . .

	Yes	No
TV Guide?	1	2
People?	1	2
Etc.		

4. *Consider using bounded recall to prevent respondents from misplacing events in time.* **Bounded recall** is a procedure in which you interview people at the start of a time period to set a baseline, then interview them at the end of the period to identify changes. For example, to measure refrigerator purchases over a six-month period, you would ask respondents about their refrigerators at the start and end of that period.

   The problem with bounded recall is that it requires two interviews and therefore is time consuming and expensive. An alternative is to "quasi-bound" the time frame in a single interview, for example:

   Q1: Have you bought a refrigerator during the past twelve months?
   Q2: Was that purchase made during the past *six* months?

   This procedure allows respondents to "help you out" by reporting a purchase in the longer time frame, then encourages them to think more carefully about the shorter time frame.

5. *Consider asking respondents to check records such as receipts or invoices before answering the question.* This method is useful in some business research but is too much bother in most consumer studies.

6. *Give people specific information — product prototypes, prices, and so on—before measuring purchase intentions for new products.*

7. *Compare subjective measures across time, objects, or people.* For example, it may be helpful for a bank to know that 58 percent of its customers say they are "completely satisfied" with the speed of service at the drive-in facility, but it is even more helpful to know that "Last year, 64 percent were completely satisfied" or "The average bank scores 63 percent completely satisfied" or "72 percent of commercial customers were completely satisfied versus 47 percent of retail customers."

8. *Try to cope with the natural imprecision of respondents' answers by using multiple measures for important concepts.* Say, for example, that you want to estimate the amount of sales a store will lose if it discontinues its store credit card. The problem with asking people, "How much less will you spend if the store drops its credit card?" is that they really don't know the answer. In this situation, you might use various measures to measure how much people spend, how they use their credit cards, whether they have other credit cards, and the role of credit cards in store choice. These measures will give you multiple perspectives on the issue and allow you to draw better conclusions.

9. *Remember that respondents' knowledge constrains the quality of self-report data.* These data should be interpreted and presented as if they were approximate, not exact, and patterns in the data rather than specific facts should be focused on.

Marketing Research Tools 10.4 (see page 263) summarizes the various ways of minimizing problems associated with not knowing the answer to a question.

Willingness to Respond

The Problem of Social Desirability

Assuming that people understand a question and know the answer, they must still decide whether or not to answer and whether or not to give an accurate answer. The key problem here is accuracy. Most people who agree to be interviewed will answer all of the questions (except perhaps for income, which gets refusal rates of 5 to 25 percent). However, respondents want to present themselves in a favorable light and to "be nice" to the interviewer. If they feel there are social norms about which answers are "right," they may edit their answers to be more socially desirable.

Consider these questions:

Q: During the past month, since *(DATE)*, did you drink beer even once?

    Yes . . . . 1 (ASK A)
    No . . . . 2 (GO TO X)

(IF YES)

Q: About how often did you drink beer during the past month?

    Once 1
    2–3 times 2
    About once a week 3
    2–3 times a week 4
    4–6 times a week 5
    About once a day 6
    More than once a day 7

Some people will incorrectly answer the first question "No" because they don't want to admit to drinking. Other people will underreport their consumption frequency because they don't want to come across as heavy drinkers. Overall, beer consumption will thus be underreported (Bradburn, Sudman, and Associates, 1979).

Next consider this question:

Q: During the past month, have you read any books other than for work or school?

Usually, book reading is overreported, because people consider reading to be a socially desirable activity.

Now consider this question:

Q: If there were a local magazine like *Consumer Reports* that evaluated restaurants, auto repair shops, plumbers, stores, and other local businesses, what is the likelihood that your family would subscribe to this magazine? Would you say your family definitely would subscribe,

MARKETING
RESEARCH
TOOLS

10.4

WAYS OF MINIMIZING PROBLEMS RELATED TO KNOWING THE ANSWER

1. Qualify respondents for knowledge.
2. Use the right time frame.
3. Consider providing cues to aid memory.
4. Consider using bounded recall.
5. Consider asking respondents to check records.
6. Give people specific information—product prototypes, prices, and so on—before measuring purchase intentions for new products.
7. Compare subjective measures across time, objects, or people.
8. Use multiple measures for important concepts.
9. Interpret and present self report data as if they are approximate, not exact, and focus on patterns rather than specific facts.

probably would subscribe, might or might not subscribe, probably would not subscribe, or definitely would not subscribe?

We have already discussed this question. Respondents are likely to assume that the researcher wants a favorable response, so they will be positive just to be nice. In general, if respondents think you care which answer they give, some will give the answer they think you want.

Minimizing the Problem

More than thirty years ago, Allen Barton, a Columbia University survey researcher, gave a tongue-in-cheek description of the methods used to overcome problems with social desirability in survey questions. These methods, which still work, are shown in Exhibit 10.3 (see page 264).

Other things can also be done to reduce concerns about social desirability. These include the following:

1. *Train interviewers to maintain a professional attitude when asking questions.* The interviewer should maintain a task-focused attitude and convey to respondents that she or he cares *whether* they answer a question but not *how* they answer it.

2. *Use comparative choice or preference measures when measuring response to a new product.* If you simply ask, "Would you buy this new product?," some respondents will answer "yes" to be nice to you.

The pollster's greatest ingenuity has been devoted to finding ways to ask embarrassing questions in nonembarrassing ways. We give here examples of a number of these techniques, as applied to the question "Did you kill your wife?"

The Casual Approach:
"Do you happen to have murdered your wife?"

The Numbered Card:
"Would you please read off the number on this card which corresponds to what became of your wife?" (*Hand card to respondent.*)
1. Natural death
2. I killed her
3. Other (What?)
(*Get the card back from respondent before proceeding!*)

The Everybody Approach:
"As you know, many people have been killing their wives these days. Do you happened to have killed yours?"

The "Other People" Approach:
(a) "Do you know any people who have murdered their wives?"
(b) "How about yourself?"

The Sealed Ballot Technique:
In this version you explain that the survey respects people's right to anonymity in respect to their marital relations, and that they themselves are to fill out the answer to the question, seal it in an envelope, and drop it in a box conspicuously labeled "Sealed Ballot Box" carried by the interviewer.

The Kinsey Technique:
Stare firmly into respondent's eyes and ask in simple, clear-cut language such as that to which the respondent is accustomed, and with an air of assuming that everyone has done everything, "Did you ever kill your wife?"

Putting the Question at the End of the Interview.

Source: Alan J. Barton, "Asking the Embarrassing Question," *Public Opinion Quarterly,* 1958, pp. 67–68.

3. *Check questions for social loading.* (A **loaded question** is one that encourages a certain response.) Marketing Research Tools 10.5 gives suggestions for how to avoid loaded questions.

4. *Do not reveal the identity of the sponsoring company if you are asking for evaluations of the company's products.* Respondents will tend to say nice things about the sponsor, and you would rather have brutal honesty.

5. *Use* **open questions** *(questions without response categories) to measure the frequency of socially sensitive behaviors.* If the question is **closed** (i.e., has categories), respondents may be reluctant to choose the highest category.

RULES FOR AVOIDING LOADED QUESTIONS

1. *Avoid "angel" or "devil" words that respondents will embrace or avoid.* For example, "Do you support union czars in their efforts to force every American worker to join a union?" doesn't leave much doubt about the desired response. "Union czar" and "force" are loaded terms.

2. *Avoid extreme words such as "always" and "never."* For example, "Do you think the oil industry is doing everything possible to protect our environment, or do you think it could improve in this area?" Who is doing *everything* possible? Who could not improve?

3. *Avoid appeals to the norm.* For example, "Do you feel, as most people do, that air pollution is a serious threat to our future?" (Sometimes you may want to include an appeal to the norm to encourage people to admit socially undesirable behavior they might otherwise conceal.)

4. *Don't ask subjective questions with "Yes-No" answers.* For example, ask, "Would you rate the quality of care at Eastside Hospital as excellent, good, fair, or poor?" rather than "Do you think Eastside Hospital offers good care?" "Yes-No" opinion questions tend to elicit *yea saying*, because respondents want to be polite.

5. *When contrasting alternatives are given, try to balance them.* For example, "Do you think Pepsi is better or worse than Coke?" is loaded toward "better" because respondents treat "worse" as a stronger word than "better." Try "Would you say that Pepsi is better than, about the same as, or not as good as Coke?"

6. *When sets of alternatives are given, try to balance them across types of alternatives.* Consider, for example, "If you were on a desert isle with only one pain reliever, which brand would you want: Tylenol, Bayer, Anacin, or Excedrin?" Tylenol will win this comparison easily. Not only is it the first brand given, but it gets the acetaminophen vote to itself while the others have to split the aspirin vote.

---

6. *Use longer questions to reduce the social stigma attached to certain answers.* For example:

Q: Many people say that they just don't have time for reading anymore. In the past month, have you read any books other than for work or school?

This example uses an "everybody does it" approach to legitimize certain responses. Respondents are given an opportunity to tell the interviewer "No—I love to read, but I just haven't had time lately." Longer questions slow the interview, so we recommend that you use this approach only for key items.

7. *Try to maximize respondents' motivation to report carefully and accurately.* Various methods have been used for this purpose. For example, Charles Cannell at the Survey Research Center, University

Author Tips

In business-to-business research, it is often necessary to identify the sponsor. People are reluctant to answer questions about their business operations if they don't know who is doing the research and why.

Critical Thinking Skills

Give an example of a question for which the answers might be affected by social desirability. How would you minimize these effects?

of Michigan, has had good results from asking survey respondents for signed promises that they will do their best to give accurate answers.

The best motivator for most respondents is a feeling that the interview is a professional undertaking. This feeling is fostered by details such as professional printing of the questionnaire, a professional introduction to the interview, formal language in the questionnaire, business clothing for interviewers if respondents will see them, and proper training so that interviewers appear professional.

Marketing Research Tools 10.6 summarizes the various ways of minimizing problems associated with respondents not being willing and/or able to report accurately.

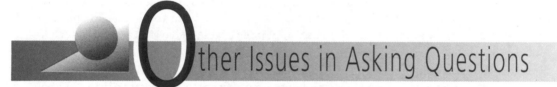

Other Issues in Asking Questions

Apart from asking the right question and having respondents understand it, know the answer, and be willing to give the answer, there are some other issues that arise in writing questions. These issues, which are discussed in this section of the chapter, include the following:

- Should questions be open or closed?
- If questions are closed, what are the general principles of response category design?

MARKETING RESEARCH TOOLS

10.6

WAYS OF MINIMIZING PROBLEMS ASSOCIATED WITH WILLINGNESS AND ABILITY TO ANSWER ACCURATELY

1. Train interviewers to maintain a professional attitude.
2. Use comparative choice or preference measures when measuring response to a new product.
3. Check questions for social loading.
4. In consumer studies, do not reveal the identity of the sponsoring company if you are asking for evaluations of the company's products.
5. Use open questions to measure the frequency of socially sensitive behaviors.
6. Use longer questions to reduce the social stigma attached to certain answers.
7. Try to maximize respondents' motivation to report carefully and accurately.

- How many response categories should be used?
- For opinion questions, should "No opinion" or "Neutral" categories be provided?
- How many questions should be used to measure a subjective variable?
- How should knowledge be measured?

Should Questions Be Open or Closed?

As already mentioned, closed questions provide response categories and open questions do not. Which is better?

Closed questions have some advantages over open questions:

- They encourage response by making it easy. Respondents don't need to articulate a response; they just need to pick a category.
- They reduce the cost of coding answers into categories, because the answers are obtained in categories.
- They reduce the amount of probing needed to get codable answers, which makes for a quicker, more standardized interview.
- They encourage people to give answers they otherwise might not think of.

On the other hand, closed questions have some disadvantages:

- They can lead respondents by suggesting which answers are "normal."
- They make it easy for respondents to answer without thinking or caring.
- They require more pretesting because you need to know the possible answers in advance to provide appropriate categories.
- They limit the richness of the data and can be boring for respondents. Case Study 10.2 illustrates this point.

Overall, open questions generally work better than closed questions in situations where there is a preference for rich, unstructured information and personal

CASE STUDY 10.2

When Helen Kaufman was in charge of marketing research for Clairol, she said that she listened in on a telephone interview that included the question "I have a list of reasons why women color their hair. As I read each one, please tell me whether this was a reason why you colored *your* hair."

After the interviewer read several reasons that did not apply to the respondent, the respondent got irritated and said, "Look, do you want to know why I colored my hair?" "No," said the interviewer, "just answer the questions."

This story not only illustrates bad interviewing technique—the interviewer should have recorded whatever the respondent wanted to say—but also shows how closed questions can straitjacket responses and alienate respondents.

interviewing is used. These situations include focus groups, depth interviews, and executive interviewing. Open questions are also advisable when you don't know what answers to expect.

Closed questions work better than open questions in situations where there is a preference for inexpensive, structured information. This fits most consumer surveys. Closed questions also work well when data are gathered by telephone, and they are a *must* for self-administered questionnaires, because most respondents simply will not write answers to open questions.

Principles of Response Category Design

If you use closed questions, the response categories should conform to some general principles. These principles are as follows:

1. *The categories must be exhaustive.* Every respondent with an answer should have a way of giving that answer. This means that:

   - Lists of amounts or frequencies should have "Or less" (or "Zero") at the bottom and "Or more" at the top.
   - Lists of reasons for buying, stores to shop at, and so on should have "Other" as the last response category.

2. *The categories should be mutually exclusive if respondents are to choose only one.* For example, what answer should a respondent give if she shopped at a mall five times and the categories are "1 to 5," "5 to 10," and so on?

3. *In general, don't list "Don't know" or "No answer" as response categories on questionnaires.* Train interviewers to record these answers if they are given, but use the absence of listed categories to discourage these answers. The exceptions to this rule are: (a) a "Prefer not to answer" category should be provided for questions on income or other questions to which a substantial number of respondents will refuse and (b) a "Don't know" or "No opinion" category should be provided when this is a legitimate response, for example, when you ask an attitude question without screening for knowledge.

4. *Ordered response categories should relate to one underlying dimension.* For example, the categories "Excellent-Good-Average-Fair-Poor" are undesirable because they contain four *absolute* evaluations (excellent, good, fair, poor) and one *relative* evaluation (average). In this example, the "Average" category should be dropped. A simple way of ensuring undimensionality is by using a base word with adjectives: "Very satisfied–Somewhat satisfied–Not satisfied," for example, or "Above average–Average–Below average."

   Sometimes multidimensional response categories reflect separate questions. Consider this example:

   Q: How would you rate the taste of Eagle Brand Honey Roast Peanuts? Would you say they are very sweet, sweet, bland, salty, or very salty?

There are at least two questions here: "How *sweet* are Eagle Brand Honey Roast Peanuts?," "How *salty* are Eagle Brand Honey Roast Peanuts?," and possibly "How *flavorful* are Eagle Brand Honey Roast Peanuts?"

5. *Response categories should be presented in order, low to high or high to low.* If you think the order of presentation will influence the answers, consider using each sequence for half the respondents.

6. *In general, quantities should be measured with specific numbers ("1 to 3," "4 to 6," etc.) rather than indefinite terms ("very often," "pretty often," etc.).* However, as noted earlier in this chapter, in some situations the subjective evaluation may be more useful.

Marketing Research Tools 10.7 summarizes these principles.

How Many Categories Should Be Used?

In discussing the appropriate number of response categories for a question, it is helpful to distinguish questions about three types of phenomena: **qualitative phenomena** (for which the possible responses represent different categories, not different quantities), **subjective quantitative phenomena** (for which the possible responses represent different subjective quantities), and **objective quantitative phenomena** (for which the possible responses represent different objective quantities).

Qualitative Phenomena

Let's start with qualitative phenomena, such as "Why did you buy your furniture at Smith's rather than some other store?" or "Which stores did you visit when you shopped for furniture?" These questions have natural response categories—the

MARKETING RESEARCH TOOLS

10.7

PRINCIPLES OF RESPONSE CATEGORY DESIGN

1. The categories must be exhaustive (cover all possible answers).
2. The categories should be mutually exclusive if respondents are to choose only one.
3. In general, do not list "Don't know" or "No answer" as response categories on questionnaires.
4. Ordered response categories should relate to one underlying dimension.
5. Ordered categories should be presented in order, low to high or high to low.
6. In general, quantities should be measured with specific numbers rather than indefinite adjectives.

different possible answers—and you need to have enough categories to accommodate these answers. However, you may choose to combine some of the answers into broader categories. For example, consider this question:

Q: What were your reasons for buying your furniture at Smith's rather than another store? (READ CATEGORIES AND CIRCLE THE NUMBERS OF ALL THAT APPLY)

Smith's everyday prices? 1
Smith's sale prices? 2
How close the store is to your home? 3
How close the store is to other stores that you shop at? 4
How knowledgeable the salespeople were? 5
How friendly the salespeople were? 6
Etc. . . . .

If you wanted to reduce the number of categories, you could make the categories broader. For example:

Q: What were your reasons for buying your furniture at Smith's rather than another store? (READ CATEGORIES AND CIRCLE THE NUMBERS OF ALL THAT APPLY)

Smith's prices? 1
Smith's location? 2
Smith's employees? 3
Etc. . . . .

Subjective Quantitative Phenomena

Now let's consider subjective quantitative phenomena, such as "How satisfied were you with the speed of service?" These items are different from qualitative phenomena in that there are no natural response categories. For example, you could measure satisfaction on a scale of 1 to 7, 0 to 100, "Very satisfied–Somewhat satisfied–Not satisfied," "Completely satisfied–Mostly satisfied–Somewhat satisfied–Dissatisfied," and so on. For this type of question, the number of categories depends on the amount of discrimination you want and whether you want to use **labeled scales** (for which the categories have verbal labels, such as "Very satisfied–Somewhat satisfied–Not satisfied").

Most labeled scales use only three to five categories, because problems can arise when the number of categories is larger. One problem is that respondents who hear a large number of verbal categories may need to have them repeated (this is a problem in telephone interviews). Also, it can be difficult to generate a large set of verbal categories that are unidimensional and clearly distinct. (Test yourself: try to generate nine distinct categories of satisfaction.)

Most unlabeled scales use seven to nine points. In principle, they could use more, but respondents can't usually discriminate among more than seven to nine levels. For example, if customer satisfaction is measured on a scale of 0 to 100, answers will cluster at 10, 20, 30, and so on.

Objective Quantitative Phenomena

Now let's consider objective quantitative phenomena, such as "What is your income?" or "In the past three months, about how many times have you visited

Eastlake Mall?" These items differ from subjective phenomena in that they use simple numerical scales with no need for verbal descriptors. As a result, the only question is how much discrimination you want.

The best discrimination is obtained from open questions that obtain an exact number, for example, an exact income or an exact number of visits. However, you might use categories to make a question less threatening; for example, income questions usually use broad categories so as not to seem too personal. You might also use categories to make a question easier; for example, it is easier for respondents to say whether they have visited a mall "0," "1 to 5," "6 to 10," or "More than 10" times rather than give an exact number.

In general, therefore, the rule of thumb in measuring objective quantities is to use full discrimination, unless it is not needed and the question can be made easier or less threatening without it. If these conditions apply, the number of categories depends entirely on the needed level of discrimination. For example, if all that is needed is to separate respondents into high, medium, and low groups, only three categories are necessary.

In defining categories for quantitative measures, the following guidelines apply:

- There may be theoretical reasons to split the scale at certain points. For example, age measures normally have a split at 18, the age at which people become legal adults in most states, and 65, the most common retirement age.

- If you wish to compare your results with other research, you should use the same categories. For example, most media research uses age categories of 18 to 24, 25 to 34, 35 to 49, 50 to 64, 65 and older.

- If there are no theoretical or comparative reasons to use specific categories, try to split respondents into relatively equal groups. For example, in setting four categories, try to set boundaries so that 25 percent of respondents fall into each group. This arrangement will be useful in data analysis.

  Of course, designing response categories according to the underlying population distribution requires information about this distribution. If you don't have results from a previous study to guide you, you can do a pretest with an open question to get a feeling for the distribution.

Should Subjective Measures Have a "Neutral" Category?

Over the years, there has been some dispute about whether subjective measures should include categories such as "no opinion," "undecided," or "neutral."

For opinion measures, the argument in favor of these categories is to remove people who don't really have an opinion. The argument against them is that people make buying decisions based on their opinions even if those opinions are not well founded, so everyone should be forced to declare an opinion.

For **bipolar measures** (measures with positive and negative responses), there is debate about whether to use a "neutral" category. A bipolar measure with a neutral category might look like this: "strongly agree, somewhat agree, *neither agree nor disagree*, somewhat disagree, strongly disagree." Researchers who oppose "no opinion" categories also tend to oppose "neutral" categories, because they want people to declare a position. The problem is that answers given by undecided or neutral respondents who are forced to express an opinion will be unreliable.

We recommend including a "no opinion" option with opinion questions. We also recommend including a "neutral" category with bipolar measures.

How Many Questions Should Be Used to Measure a Phenomenon?

The next issue to be considered is: How many questions should be used to measure a phenomenon?

To illustrate the argument for multi-item measures, let us consider how to measure verbal skills. Verbal skills can be measured by having people answer a single question, such as "Inch is to foot as ounce is to _____?" However, this measure would provide little discrimination among respondents, and it would not be a reliable measure because someone with poor verbal skills might get lucky on this item, whereas someone with good verbal skills might mess up. Better discrimination and better reliability would be produced if respondents were asked a series of questions and a total score were computed for each person. This is the logic behind tests such as the Scholastic Aptitude Test.

Now let us say that we want to determine whether people should be classified as "deal-prone" for marketing purposes. The situation parallels our measurement of verbal skills. Deal-proneness can be measured with a single item, such as:

Q: How often are your buying decisions influenced by the availability of coupons, rebates, or sales? Would you say very often, pretty often, not too often, or never?

However, more discrimination among respondents and more reliable results will be produced if a multi-item measure is used, such as:

Q: I have a series of statements that might apply to your shopping habits. As I read each statement, please tell me whether you strongly agree, agree, disagree, or strongly disagree with that statement. Here we go . . .

	SA	A	D	SD
I usually check the newspaper for coupons	4	3	2	1
I will buy a product I don't usually buy if I have a coupon for it	4	3	2	1
I'm much more likely to go into a store if it is having a sale	4	3	2	1
Etc.				

The improved discrimination and reliability of multi-item measures come with an obvious disadvantage; multi-item measures use more questions for a single phenomenon, so the research is more expensive and/or fewer measures can be taken. Because of this added cost, it is important to use the smallest number of items needed to get satisfactory results. This number will depend on four factors:

- *If different items are largely redundant, fewer of them are needed.* For example, little benefit is gained from adding a second, third, or fourth question to measure age. If each item is somewhat unique—as might be the case in the deal-proneness measure—more items are needed, and the number of items needed rises as the inconsistency rises.

- *If the focus is on groups of respondents, rather than individuals, fewer items are needed.* This point goes back to the earlier comment that discrimination can be achieved across respondents. Psychologists sometimes use more than 100 items in personality measures or academic achievement tests, but they are trying to develop detailed measures for individuals. Marketing researchers are usually more interested in total markets or in market segments.

- *If a phenomenon is less important to the overall research project, fewer items are justified.* For example, if deal-proneness is a minor aspect of our research, it is not necessary to take the time needed for a twenty-item measure of deal proneness.

- *If a questionnaire is long, then fewer items may be justified.* For example, a ten-item scale might be used to measure consumers' attitudes toward a single brand of computer, but the questionnaire would get too long if a ten-item scale were used for each of ten different brands.

Because of the emphasis on group data in marketing research, market researchers usually use no more than ten items to measure even the most difficult phenomena, and single-item measures are the norm.

How Should Knowledge Be Measured?

Respondents may be asked whether they have heard about a brand, know some feature of a product, or have some other form of knowledge. The problem with such questions is that respondents may overclaim knowledge for reasons of social desirability (Nadeau and Niemi, 1995).

One method of identifying or reducing overclaiming of knowledge is simply to ask for additional information. Thus, people who say they have heard of KLM can be asked "What business is it in?" To make such questions less threatening, it is best to add a phrase

Critical Thinking Skills

If you were conducting a survey to measure Sears' store image and wanted to compare Sears' image with the image of one other store, how many questions would you use to measure store image? How many questions would you use if you wanted to compare Sears with three other stores? What questions would you ask?

to indicate that knowledge isn't really that important. The question might be phrased as "Do you happen to know . . . " or "Can you recall, offhand, what business it is in?"

Another way of measuring the extent to which knowledge is overclaimed in brand-awareness studies is by using a **sleeper** (fictitious brand). Usually, 10 to 20 percent of respondents to brand-awareness studies will report having heard of a sleeper. For new and little-known brands, sleeper questions can be used to indicate the level that should be deducted from the brand's results to get a "true" awareness level. A brand with 15 percent of respondents who claim to have heard of it may really be known by hardly anyone.

Sleepers have less application to well-known brands. For example, if 12 percent of respondents think they have heard of Speed King restaurants, this does not mean that only 88 percent of the 100 percent who say they have heard of McDonald's are answering correctly. Also, sleepers are problematic because the number of people who think they are familiar with a sleeper will depend on how plausible it looks and sounds. It doesn't make sense to say that the level of "true" awareness for Rally restaurants should depend on which sleeper the Rally result is compared with.

In some situations, you might want to measure respondents' knowledge of important quantities. For example, a maker of energy-saving lightbulbs might want to ask, "Do you happen to know the total annual cost of using regular sixty-watt lightbulbs in a typical table lamp?" Questions like these should be open, as response categories will provide cues to respondents, who will tend to select a middle category without really having any knowledge.

Standard Ways of Asking Classification Questions

Almost all questionnaires have questions that are used to classify respondents into groups. We urge that you not invent your own classification questions but use those that are widely used by others, especially federal statistical agencies such as the Bureau of the Census. Using standard questions will help you avoid mistakes and allow you to compare your sample composition with census data or other results.

Following are standard ways to ask common classification questions. Of course, different research organizations may use different wordings.

 Household Size and Composition

For many product categories, household size is a key variable related to consumption levels. The most straightforward question is simply:

Q: Including yourself, how many people are currently living in your household?

If you need information about household composition, the household size measure can be followed with appropriate questions such as:

Q: How many of these people are children less than six years old?

Gender

If you wish to determine the respondent's gender, you can ask "Are you male or female?" If an interviewer is administering the questionnaire, it is more diplomatic to code gender without asking unless there is some reason for uncertainty.

Age

The best way of asking about age is:

Q: In what year were you born?

This question has two advantages over "What is your age?" First, your age changes every year but your year of birth stays the same, so people are more accurate concerning their year of birth (this is particularly true for older people). Second, some people like to shave a few years off their age (especially around deciles such as thirty, forty, fifty, etc.). They are less likely to do this if you ask for the year of birth.

Income

Income is highly related to purchase behavior. It is also a highly sensitive subject. In general, open questions are appropriate for sensitive subjects, but a closed question works better for income. A good income question is:

Q: What was the approximate annual income from employment and all other sources for all members of your household, before taxes, last year in 19XX? Was it . . .

Less than $10,000?	1
$10,000 to $24,999?	2
$25,000 to $49,999?	3
$50,000 to $74,999?	4
$75,000 to $99,999?	5
$100,000 or more?	6
(PREFER NOT TO ANSWER)	9

The use of a categorical format shows respondents that an exact income is not required and reduces the sensitivity of the income question.

Income is a very sensitive topic in surveys.

Education

For some products, education may be more important than income. The standard question is:

Q: What is the highest grade of school you finished and got credit for in regular school or college?

Own or Rent

Homeownership is important for ownership and purchasing of many appliances. The standard question is:

Q: Do you or your family own the place where you live, are you buying it, do you pay rent, or what?

Race

Racial groups are important market segments for some products. For face-to-face interviews, respondents' race may be observed. Where this is not possible, or where there is some uncertainty, ask the following question:

Q: What race do you consider yourself? Are you white, African American, Hispanic, Asian, or something else?

Some respondents are sensitive about how they are described and will tell you so. In general, though, asking race does not bother most respondents.

Organization Size

It is often possible, especially for larger organizations, to get a size measure from public sources. Three types of size measures may be found:

- Total number of employees
- Total annual revenues
- Total value of assets

If outside data are not available, you should ask the size question that fits best with the product or service you are selling. Thus, an insurance company doing research on the need for a new benefits program will be interested in the number of employees, whereas an insurance company doing research on the need for asset coverage will be more interested in asset value.

Sometimes organizational respondents prefer not to reveal revenue or profit figures, but they usually don't mind telling you the number of employees they have. All of these size measures are highly correlated, so it may be a good idea to ask about the number of employees if there is resistance to other size measures.

Since many firms and organizations have more than one location, a researcher must make clear whether information about the entire organization or only a specific site is wanted. Also, if the number of employees is requested, it is necessary to specify whether the figure wanted is the number of full-time employees, the total number of employees including part-timers, the number of "full-time equivalent" employees, or what. Here is a sample question:

Q: Counting both full-time and part-time employees of all types, about how many people work at this company office?

Final Comments

The goal in writing questions is not to get perfect information; this is impractical. Rather, the goal is to get information that is as good as it can be, given the complexities of language and the limitations on respondents' knowledge.

As with other aspects of research, it is important that you not reinvent the wheel. It is almost always better to use existing questions than to write new ones. Using existing questions makes a research job easier, reduces the need for pretesting, and makes it possible to compare results across studies to measure trends.

Obviously, the first source for previous questions should be a company's files. All organizations should keep copies of previous questionnaires, indexed so that specific questions can be located. Other sources of questionnaires include media research provided to a company and syndicated services that a company buys.

Also, any questionnaire used by the federal statistical agencies and by nonprofit survey research organizations may be used. These can be located using archives of survey data. The largest of these archives are at the Roper Center (University of Connecticut), the Inter-University Consortium for Political and Social Research (University of Michigan), the Institute for Research in Social Science (University of North Carolina), and the National Opinion Research Center (University of Chicago).

Summary

This chapter discussed how to ask questions. The following points were covered:

1. How can the right questions for a research project be determined?
To make sure that the right questions are being asked, determine whether they are consistent with how the market works and whether they are consistent with the research objectives.

2. How can the chance that respondents will properly interpret a question be maximized?
To maximize the chance of proper interpretation: (1) be specific, (2) specify who, what, when, where, and how, (3) specify how the answer should be given, (4) use simple language, (5) try to use words with only one meaning, (6) use numbers rather than indefinite adjectives to measure magnitudes, (7) ask questions one at a time, and (8) pretest the questionnaire.

3. How can the chance that respondents will know the answer be maximized?
To maximize the chance that respondents will know the answer: (1) qualify respondents for knowledge, (2) use a proper time frame, (3) consider providing memory cues, (4) consider using bounded recall to prevent respondents from misplacing events in time, (5) consider asking respondents to check their records, (6) give people specific information before measuring purchase intentions for new products, (7) anchor subjective measures with comparisons across time, objects, or people, (8) use multiple measures for important concepts, and (9) treat self-report data as approximate rather than exact.

4. How can the chance that respondents will give an answer without distorting it be maximized?
To maximize the chance that respondents will answer without distortion: (1) train interviewers to maintain a professional attitude, (2) use comparative choice or preference measures when estimating response to new products, (3) avoid "loaded" questions, (4) don't reveal the sponsoring company unless necessary, (5) use open questions to measure the frequency of socially sensitive behaviors, (6) use longer questions to reduce the social stigma attached to certain answers, and (7) try to maximize respondents' motivation to report accurately.

5. What are the relative advantages of open and closed questions?
The advantages of closed questions are that they make it easy to respond, reduce the coding task, require less probing, and may encourage people to give good answers they might otherwise overlook. The disadvantages are that they may lead respondents by suggesting which answers are "normal," they make it easy for respondents to answer without thinking or caring, they require more pretesting, and they limit the richness of the answers. Overall, open questions are better for focus groups, depth interviews, and executive interviews; closed questions are better for most consumer surveys.

6. What are the principles of response category design?
The principles of response category design are as follows: (1) the categories must be exhaustive, (2) the categories should be mutually exclusive if respondents are to choose only one, (3) in general, "Don't know" or "No answer" should not be listed as response categories on questionnaires, (4) ordered response categories should relate

to one underlying dimension, (5) ordered categories should be presented in order, low to high or high to low, and (6) in general, objective quantities should be measured with specific numbers rather than indefinite adjectives.

7. How many questions should be used to measure a phenomenon?
The number of items that should be used depends on (1) the extent to which different items are needed to capture fully the phenomenon of interest, (2) the extent to which the research is focused on groups versus individuals, (3) the importance of the phenomenon, and (4) the length of the questionnaire. Marketing research usually focuses on groups, so single-item measures are the norm, and multi-item measures rarely have more than ten items.

8. What are standard ways of asking some common classification questions?
Standard formats for measures of household size and composition, gender, age, income, education, home ownership, race, and organization size were given.

Suggested Additional Readings

The material in this and the next two chapters is amplified upon in Seymour Sudman and Norman M. Bradburn, *Asking Questions* (San Francisco: Jossey-Bass, 1982). An earlier book by Stanley L. Payne, *The Art of Asking Questions* (Princeton, N.J.: Princeton University Press, 1951), if available, is still an enjoyable book to read and contains much useful advice. Another general book on question wording is A. N. Oppenheim, *Questionnaire Design, Interviewing and Attitude Measurement* (New York: St. Martin's, 1992).

If you are interested in research on questionnaire design, you may want to consult Howard Schuman and Stanley Presser, *Questions and Answers in Attitude Surveys* (Orlando, Fla.: Academic, 1981), and three books edited by Norbert Schwarz and Seymour Sudman: *Context Effects in Social and Psychological Research* (New York: Springer, 1992); *Autobiographical Memory and the Validity of Retrospective Reports* (New York: Springer, 1994); and *Answering Questions* (San Francisco: Jossey-Bass, 1996). Seymour Sudman, Norman M. Bradburn, and Norbert Schwarz, *Thinking About Answers* (San Francisco: Jossey-Bass, 1996), reviews the recent research on how people answer questions and how to improve these answers.

Two bibliographies on questionnaire design are Wayne W. Daniel, *Questionnaire Design: A Selected Bibliography for the Survey Researcher* (Monticello, Ill.: Vance Bibliographies, 1979), and Anthony G. White, *Survey and Questionnaire Design: A Bibliography* (Monticello, Ill.: Vance Bibliographies, 1986). Many examples of questionnaire design studies are presented in *Public Opinion Quarterly*.

Discussion Questions

1. What are the four requirements that must be satisfied to ensure good results from self-report data?

2. How can you help minimize respondents' misunderstanding of a question?

3. Marketing researchers are often asked to measure the purchase intentions of customers. That is, managers often want to know how likely consumers are to buy their product. What are some of the problems associated with trying to measure consumer intentions?

4. What can an interviewer do to encourage a participant's willingness to respond?

5. Discuss the advantages and disadvantages of using open versus closed questions.

6. Marketing researchers have used both verbal and numerical scales. When is it better to use a verbal scale? When is it better to use a numerical scale?

7. What are some reasons marketing researchers include a middle category such as "No opinion" or "Don't know" or "Undecided"? Why do some researchers choose not to include a middle category? What do you recommend?

Marketing Research Challenge

Suppose you are interested in getting measures of the exercise activity of students at your school. Write a question (or series of questions) that attempts to obtain this information. Ask these questions separately of each of a small group of friends. Then ask the respondents what they thought you meant by exercise and the time period they thought was being covered. Do they all agree on what the question meant? Does their understanding of the question agree with what you had in mind? If yes, congratulations! You have written a good question. If no, try to revise the question to remove any remaining ambiguities.

Internet Exercise

Search the Internet for marketing research questionnaires (try keywords such as "customer survey" or "questionnaire"). Pick one that looks interesting. In your opinion, what are the information objectives for the questionnaire? Do you think the right questions have been asked? Do the questions meet our requirements that respondents must understand the question, know the answer, and be willing to answer accurately? How, if at all, would you change the questions to meet these requirements better ?

References

Bearden, William O., Richard G. Netemeyer, and Mary F. Mobley (1993). *Handbook of Marketing Scales: Multi-item Measures for Marketing and Consumer Behavior Research* (Newbury Park, Calif.: Sage).

Bradburn, Norman M., Seymour Sudman, and Associates (1979). *Improving Interview Method and Questionnaire Design* (San Francisco: Jossey-Bass).

Nadeau, Richard, and Richard G. Niemi (1995). "Educated Guesses: The Process of Answering Factual Knowledge Questions in Surveys." *Public Opinion Quarterly* 59, p. 323.

Schwarz, Norbert, and Seymour Sudman (eds.) (1994). *Autobiographical Memory and the Validity of Retrospective Reports* (New York: Springer).

Sudman, Seymour, and Norman M. Bradburn (1974). *Response Effects in Surveys* (Chicago: Aldine Publishing).

Sudman, Seymour, Norman M. Bradburn, and Norbert Schwarz (1996). *Thinking About Answers* (San Francisco: Jossey-Bass).

Urban, Glen L. and John R. Hauser (1993). *Design and Marketing of New Products* (Englewood Cliffs, N.J.: Prentice Hall).

Designing a Questionnaire

⊠ *OBJECTIVES*

After reading this chapter, you should be able to answer the following questions:

1. What questions should be included in a questionnaire?

2. How should questions be ordered?

3. How does the method of administration affect the questions asked?

4. What principles should guide the physical format of a questionnaire?

5. How can a questionnaire be tested?

A questionnaire is not just a collection of questions. An interview should be a structured, task-oriented conversation between the interviewer and the respondent. Social formalities such as introductions should be observed, and the conversation should be properly organized. Ideally, there should be a logical flow to the conversation, and the respondent should be told when the topic is changed. Also, the questionnaire should be easy for the interviewer to administer.

This chapter discusses how to develop, organize, and test questionnaires. It is organized into five sections:

- Planning questionnaire content
- Ordering the questions
- Administering the questionnaire
- Formatting the questionnaire
- Testing the questionnaire

The sections on planning, ordering, and testing apply to all questionnaires and all types of research. The other sections, on methods of administration and physical format, specifically address survey questionnaires. These topics do not really apply to depth interviews and focus groups.

Planning Questionnaire Content

Setting Information Goals

The first step in designing a questionnaire is to make a list of the research objectives. The project's research objectives should then be translated into information goals that are specific enough to guide question formulation. In doing so, it can be very helpful to think ahead to the types of tables and graphs that can be used to illustrate the final report.

To see how research objectives are turned into a list of information goals, consider the following example drawn from our own experiences. Managers at Smith's, a retail chain, faced a decision on whether to close their credit card operation. The cost of processing transactions on the chain's credit card was higher than the cost of processing transactions by cash, check, or outside credit cards. However, the managers felt that credit customers might shop less with the chain if the credit card were dropped. To help determine the best course of action, they asked us to estimate the amount of sales they would lose if they dropped the credit card. This was the overall research objective.

The first thing we did was to analyze internal data on credit sales in various merchandise departments. We found that some departments with expensive merchandise did as much as 40 percent of their business on credit, whereas other departments had virtually no credit business. This gave us an idea about which departments would face the greatest loss from dropping the credit card. We also searched company records to see how sales had reacted to previous changes in credit policies, and we searched secondary sources to learn about other companies' experiences after dropping their own credit cards.

After doing this internal and secondary research, we designed a survey of credit card holders to estimate their reactions to having the card withdrawn. We had only one research objective in this survey: to estimate sales loss. In principle, therefore, we could have asked just one question: "If Smith's Stores drop their credit cards, how will your spending at Smith's be affected?" However, people often give poor predictions of their behavior, and we thought that other questions might improve our estimates of sales loss. We ultimately developed a list that included the following information goals:

- We wanted to know whether the store credit card holders also had Visa, Master-Card, and/or American Express cards. This would tell us whether they would have a way of charging purchases if the Smith's card was withdrawn.

- We wanted to know whether credit card holders also sometimes paid for purchases at Smith's by other means. This would tell us whether a loss of credit business would be likely to carry additional business with it.

- If cardholders sometimes used other means to buy things at Smith's, we wanted to know how much they charged to their Smith's account and how much they spent using other payment forms. This would tell us the *amount* of potential loss.

- We wanted to know whether people thought they would spend less, more, or about the same at Smith's if the Smith credit card were withdrawn. This would give us some idea of the number of customers who might be affected and, when analyzed along with background questions such as income, would give us some idea of the types of customers affected. Knowing the types of customers would allow us to estimate the effects on Smith's stores serving different markets.

- We wanted to know how much less, or how much more, people thought they would spend at Smith's if the Smith credit card were withdrawn. This would tell us the potential dollar impact on sales.

- We thought that people might say that withdrawing the cards would cause them to shop less at Smith's even if store credit wasn't important to their shopping decisions. Therefore, we wanted people to rate the importance of store credit in choosing where to shop for Smith's kind of merchandise. Knowing how many people felt that credit was "very important" would give us some additional basis for estimating the number of people who would be affected by withdrawing the Smith's credit cards.

- We also wanted importance ratings for other factors. This would allow us to put the ratings for store credit into context. If store credit were rated "very important" by 40 percent of respondents but this was by far the lowest score among factors such as price, selection, and location, this would tell us that store credit was actually a minor selection factor.

Critical Thinking Skills

A university wants to do a telephone survey of college freshmen to learn how they decided which school to attend. The university hopes to use this information to enhance its effectiveness in recruiting students. What specific information goals would you set for this project?

- We wanted to know the store where Smith's cardholders had made their most recent purchase of the kind of merchandise sold at Smith's, and we wanted to know their most important reason for choosing that store. We wanted to see how many people spontaneously mentioned their Smith's credit cards as the most important reason for store choice, to get a different measure of the importance of credit.

This list of information goals isn't quite finished. For example, we wanted other information such as background data on the cardholders. The list is enough, though, to show that it takes thought and creativity to translate research issues into information goals. It also shows that a list of information goals should lead directly into question development.

Translating the Information Goals into Questions

Once you have a list of information goals, the next step is to translate those goals into questions. Our previous chapter discussed principles for how to ask questions, so we won't repeat that discussion.

When the list of questions is finished, it should cover all information goals and all research objectives. At this point, it is also good to have an idea of how you will analyze and present the results.

Does the List of Questions Need to Be Trimmed?

The last step before organizing the questions into a questionnaire is to check whether the list needs to be trimmed.

The appropriate length of a questionnaire depends on the interviewing method. Interviews of up to ninety minutes are feasible for focus groups and depth interviews. Face-to-face survey interviews can take up to thirty to sixty minutes, depending on respondents' interest in the topic. Telephone interviews can generally take up to twenty minutes, though interviews lasting more than an hour have been used for topics that respondents find especially interesting. Mail surveys present the most severe constraints, because many respondents decide whether to participate based on the length of the questionnaire. Repeated experience has shown that mail questionnaires should not exceed four pages for most marketing research surveys.

Researchers faced with a four-page limit sometimes try to accommodate extra questions by cramming them together or using small type fonts, but this is a mistake. Respondents look not only at the questionnaire's length but also at how difficult it seems. Cramming questions together makes the questionnaire look difficult and cancels any benefits of the reduced length.

In situations where the list of questions is too long for the available time or space, it is necessary to prioritize goals and trim the list or to change the method to one that allows for a longer interview.

Author Tips

If the list of questions that covers your information goals is short, you may be tempted to add extra questions. Resist this temptation. Unless you have a specific use for these questions, they will add to the cost of the interview and burden respondents to no good purpose.

Ordering the Questions

Once a list of questions that corresponds to your information goals has been drawn up, these questions must be organized into a questionnaire. In doing so, order effects must be considered, a logical flow for the questionnaire must be developed, and rapport with respondents must be established.

Minimizing Order Effects

As a general rule, questions should be arranged in a sequence that minimizes order effects. An **order effect** occurs when the answer to a particular question is influenced by the context of previous questions. For example, if we ask people, "What are all the reasons you shop at Smith's Stores?" *after* asking them "Do you have a Smith's credit card?," more people will mention the credit card than if we ask the "reasons" question first, because the credit card question will cue them to think about credit cards.

One well-known order effect is the relationship between general attitudes toward a product and attitudes toward specific attributes. It has been found that starting with a general question usually doesn't affect answers to specific attribute questions, but starting with specific questions *may* affect responses to the general question. Because of this, it is best to follow a **funnel sequence** in which questions are ordered from general to specific. For example:

Q: *Overall,* how would you rate Smith's Stores as a place to shop for furniture?

Q: How would you rate Smith's prices?

Q: How would you rate Smith's merchandise selection?

This sequence presumes that respondents will be able to give meaningful answers to the general attitude question. If this is not true, we recommend an **inverted funnel,** which orders questions from specific to general. In an inverted funnel, respondents' answers to the specific questions will provide them with a context for the general question. When using inverted funnels, it is necessary to ask about all relevant attributes, because many respondents will answer the general question as if it referred only to the listed attributes.

Another possible order effect relates to **branching questions,** which are asked only if a qualifying answer has been given to a previous question. Say, for example, that you ask whether a respondent bought any shoes during the past six months; if the answer is "yes," you ask where she bought the shoes, why she chose that store, and how she paid for the purchase. If the answer is "no," the questions about where, why, and price are skipped.

Then you ask whether the respondent bought any hosiery during the past six months. If so, you ask where, why, and how she paid. Then you ask about cosmetics. By this point, the respondent will recognize that a "yes" answer to the purchase question triggers several more questions, and she may be tempted to reduce the length of the interview by not reporting purchases.

The way around this is to ask all of the purchase questions first, before the respondents know there will be follow-up questions, and then to return and ask the follow-up questions for the purchases respondents made.

Developing a Logical Flow

Most respondents to a questionnaire feel more comfortable and give better answers if they can see the logic of the questionnaire. We recommend five rules for organizing questionnaires in a logical way:

1. If topics or questions have some natural sequence (e.g., "What did you buy?," "How did you use it?," "What did you think of it?"), follow this sequence.

2. If the questionnaire deals with several topics, complete the questions on one topic before moving on to a new topic.

3. If some of the questionnaire topics are related and some are not, ask questions on related topics before moving to unrelated topics.

4. When asking questions about a series of behaviors, such as a respondents' last three mall visits, follow chronological order backward in time, that is, the most recent visit, the visit before that, and so on. This is the easiest way for most respondents to remember historical events, because it is easiest to remember the most recent event, and thinking about this event helps respondents remember earlier ones.

5. When changing topics, use a transitional phrase to make it easier for respondents to switch their train of thought. Phrases such as "Now I'd like to ask you some questions about . . ." alert the respondents to changes in topic and help them follow the questionnaire.

Some researchers feel that switching back and forth across topics reduces possible order effects or keeps respondents from going onto "autopilot" and not really thinking about the questions. These are legitimate concerns, but the major concern should be making the questionnaire easy for the respondent and interviewer to follow. Also, if the questionnaire switches back and forth without some clear logic, or if other constructions designed to "trap" careless respondents (such as reversing numbers on opinion questions so that 7 means "good" on one item and "bad" on the next) are used, the researcher runs the risk of alienating respondents. They don't like being trapped or tested.

Establishing Rapport

At the start of an interview, some respondents may worry that they will be made to look foolish or ignorant. Others may not be worried but are not really "into" the interview. Better cooperation and better data can be had by building a rapport with the respondent.

Try to start the questionnaire with easy, nonthreatening questions that might be interesting to respondents. These questions should relate to the stated topic of the interview. Some researchers like to open with a "throwaway" question, such as "What is your favorite TV program?," but it is better to build the logic of the questionnaire from the very first question. The "throwaway" question may be easy and interesting, but we don't want respondents to wonder, "If this is a questionnaire about shopping habits, why are they asking about my favorite TV show?"

Knowledge or awareness questions—for example, "What are all the brands of hair shampoo you can think of?"—may threaten some respondents and should not be asked at the start of a questionnaire. The initial questions should be items for which there is no wrong answer, such as attitude questions or nonthreatening questions about product use—for example, "In the past six months, have you bought anything at a Smith's store?"

In face-to-face or telephone interviews, open questions—for example, "What things do you like best about your current car?"—work well because they get the respondent talking and create personal involvement. Open questions should never begin a mail questionnaire, though. Respondents are not likely to participate if they have to write an essay.

Some questionnaire writers start with demographic questions such as age or education because these questions are easy to answer. However, these questions don't obviously relate to the questionnaire topic and may be threatening to some respondents. Demographic questions work better at the end of the interview, where they can be introduced with an explanatory transition statement such as "Now we have some questions to help us classify your answers." The exception is when demographic questions are needed to determine whether respondents fit the target group. If your telephone questionnaire is intended only for married women between eighteen and thirty-four years of age, for example, you will probably start with an age and a marital status question to qualify the respondent, and pick up other background information at the end of the interview.

Once rapport has been established and respondents are at ease, you can ask difficult and/or threatening questions. Respondents may, of course, refuse to answer some questions. We have found that telling them at the start of the interview, "If you prefer not to answer any question, just let me know and we will go on to the next question," actually increases trust and reduces the number of people who refuse to answer.

An Example of Ordering Questions

To illustrate our comments about question order, we continue with the Smith's Stores example. In developing a questionnaire for this project, we put the information goals listed earlier in this chapter into the following order:

1. First, we asked for the name of the store where respondents had made their most recent purchase of the kind of merchandise sold at Smith's, and their most important reason for choosing that store.

2. Next, we asked respondents to rate the importance of various factors in choosing where to shop for this type of merchandise. Within this sequence we included a rating for store credit cards.

3. Next we asked respondents to estimate:

    - How much they had spent at Smith's Stores during the past twelve months.

    - (IF ANY) How much of this spending had been charged to a Smith's credit card.

Critical Thinking Skills

A university is planning a telephone survey of college freshmen and wishes to ask questions on the following topics: (1) what two schools had been the respondent's top college choices, (2) what information the respondent had received on those schools, (3) from what sources the respondent had gotten that information, (4) among six specific colleges, which schools the respondent had considered applying to, (5) to which of these schools the respondent had applied, (6) to which other schools the respondent had applied, (7) by which schools the respondent had been accepted, (8) at which school the respondent had enrolled, (9) why the respondent had chosen that school. If you were designing this questionnaire, how would you order these questions? Why?

- (IF ANY) Whether they thought they would have spent more, about the same, or less at Smith's if they didn't have a Smith's credit card.
- (IF MORE OR LESS) How much more (or less) they would have spent.

4. Finally, we asked respondents various background questions. This background sequence included questions on whether they had Visa, MasterCard, and/or American Express cards.

The logic of this sequence is as follows:

- We started with the "reasons for shopping" questions because of possible order effects. We wanted to measure reasons for shopping before we introduced the subject of credit, so that respondents would give their reasons without being cued to think about credit. Similarly, we wanted to get the open-ended reason for store choice before we cued respondents by listing possible reasons in the rating measure.

- We asked respondents about *total Smith's spending*, then about *credit spending* (which can be compared with total spending to reveal noncredit spending), then about *likely changes in spending*, because we thought these questions formed a natural sequence that would give us the information we wanted.

- We placed the questions on credit card ownership into the background section because we thought they fit better with the background questions than with the shopping questions. Also, asking these questions outside the background section would make it seem that credit cards were a focal topic rather than a background issue, and we wanted to downplay this point.

The question sequence that we chose for this project thus reflects considerations of order effects and natural question sequences. It also reflects considerations about rapport. The sequence begins with easy behavioral measures about respondents' shopping experience and places the potentially sensitive questions about credit card ownership at the end.

Administering the Questionnaire

Questionnaires can be either self-administered or administered by an interviewer. If done by an interviewer, they can be administered by telephone or face to face (in a personal or intercept interview). Methods of administration were discussed in Chapter 7.

The method of administration has various implications for questionnaire design, as discussed in the following sections.

Types of Information

Certain types of information may or may not fit a particular method of administration.

For example, mail surveys may be appropriate when respondents are asked to check records or consult with others, as in some studies of organizational buying behavior. However, if you don't want respondents to talk with others, mail surveys can cause problems, because this factor is uncontrolled. Respondents may even give mail questionnaires to someone else for completion; there are estimates that about one-third of mail questionnaires for consumers are completed by someone else in the household, and the figure may be higher for questionnaires directed to executives.

If you want respondents to react to physical stimuli, face-to-face interviews are best. Telephone surveys are very limited in this regard, though it may be possible to send materials to respondents in advance of a phone interview.

Open and Closed Questions

Open questions (questions without response categories) can provide rich information. They work well in personal interviews, reasonably well in telephone interviews, and not at all well in mail surveys.

Respondents to mail surveys are reluctant to write essay answers, not only because these answers take time and effort, but also because some respondents don't want to embarrass themselves by making errors in spelling or grammar. As a result, many respondents leave open questions blank, and others simply throw away the questionnaire. The presence of open questions in a mail survey significantly reduces cooperation without providing much helpful information.

It is possible to obtain *short* open answers in mail surveys. Questions for which the answer is a number (e.g., "In what year were you born?" or "How many television sets are in your home?") do not cause problems, and questions with short verbal answers (e.g., "What brands of cars do you and other members of your household own?") are generally usable.

Also, although open questions are not generally recommended for mail questionnaires, a good way of ending a mail survey is with the following question:

Q: **Is there anything else that you would like to tell us? Please use the space below.** *(followed by an open space)*

This question is provided in case the questionnaire missed anything and to give respondents an opportunity to express themselves. As a practical matter, though, the question rarely provides useful information, and most respondents leave it blank.

Question Difficulty and Probing

In mail surveys, no interviewer is present to probe unclear answers or to set respondents straight if they misinterpret questions. As a result, all questions must be simple and straightforward. If respondents don't understand a question or don't know how to reply, they will give unusable answers or throw the questionnaire away.

Telephone interviews are better than mail surveys in this regard, but they are still not as good as face-to-face interviews. Telephone interviewers cannot see looks of puzzlement on respondents' faces and must rely on long pauses or other verbal cues to suggest that respondents are having difficulties with the question.

Number of Response Categories

The maximum number of response categories that can be used for closed questions depends on the method of administration. Telephone questionnaires present the greatest limitation in this regard. In telephone interviews, respondents can't see the response alternatives and must be able to remember them. Also, lists of response alternatives can seem to go on forever when they are being read over the telephone. Because of this, no more than four response categories should be used for telephone questions.

There are some exceptions to this rule. Some attitude questions might say something like "On a scale of 1 to 7, where 1 is not at all satisfied and 7 is completely satisfied, how satisfied were you with the speed of checkout the last time you bought anything at Smith's?" This type of purely numerical scale is no problem in a telephone interview.

Also, you might have a set of response categories that really constitute a series of "yes-no" questions. For example, "Which of the following were reasons why you bought your furniture at Smith's rather than some other store?," followed by a list of reasons. Respondents will respond to these categories one at a time and will not need to keep the entire list in mind, so length is not a problem.

Self-administered and face-to-face interviews generally do not present problems regarding the number of response categories. In face-to-face interviews, response categories with more than four choices can be printed on cards and given to respondents (for example, "What was the most important reason you bought your furniture at Smith's rather than some other store? Was it one of the reasons listed on this card or something else?"). With self-administered questionnaires, respondents have plenty of time to read the categories and choose an answer, so large sets of categories are not a problem.

Branching

Branching, or **skipping,** is a procedure in which certain questions are not asked if they don't apply to a respondent (based on the answers to previous questions). Exhibit 11.1 shows an example of branching.

The use of branching is common in surveys because it allows the questionnaire to fit the specific circumstances of the respondent. There are, however, significant differences across methods of administration in how branching may be used.

Branching is most easily done in computer-assisted telephone interviews (CATIs). In CATI systems, the interviewer sits at a computer terminal and questions appear on the screen. Answers are entered into the computer, which can be programmed to skip to the next appropriate question depending on the answer given.

EXHIBIT 11.1

Question
Sequence with
Branching

3. In total, about how much money did you spend at Smith's Stores during the past twelve months?

$ _____ (IF ZERO, GO TO Q4)

(IF MORE THAN ZERO)
   3A.   About how much of that was charged to a Smith's credit card?

$ _____

   3B.   In total, do you think you would have spent more money at
         Smith's, less at Smith's, or about the same amount at Smith's if
         you didn't have a Smith's credit card?

More 3
About the same . . . 2 (GO TO Q4)
Less 1

(IF MORE OR LESS)
   3B1.   About how much (more/less) do you think you would
          have spent?

$ _____

4.   Now we have some questions to help us classify the answers. In what year
        were you born?

(YEAR) _____

Branching conditions can be very complicated—for example, if a respondent indicated in previous answers that she has an eight-year-old son named Kyle who was hospitalized during the past six months, the computer can present a question that reads "When your son Kyle was in the hospital . . ." and can skip this question for people who have not had a pediatric hospitalization in the household. Branching occurs automatically, so interviewer errors resulting from missed branching instructions are eliminated.

In paper-and-pencil interviews, whether done by telephone or face to face, the interviewer must record each answer and follow instructions to find the next appropriate question. Usually, this means that branching instructions must depend only on the most recent questions asked. Even well-trained interviewers may make mistakes in branching, with the number of mistakes depending on the complexity of the branching instruction and the number of questions to be skipped. When a "skip pattern" crosses more than one page of the questionnaire, interviewers sometimes have trouble finding the next question to be asked.

The use of complex branching is impossible for self-administered surveys unless they are done by computer. If even well-trained interviewers make errors, it should not be surprising that respondents have trouble following the branching instructions. Any questionnaire requiring more than the simplest skips (where respondents skip one or two questions based on a single answer) should be done using telephone or face-to-face administration.

Order Effects

An important difference between self-administered questionnaires and telephone or face-to-face interviews is that many respondents read through self-administered questionnaires before starting to answer and therefore know all the questions before answering any of them. For this reason, mail surveys are not appropriate if order effects are important.

Response Differences by Method of Administration

Critical Thinking Skills

Look back at the information goals for our Smith's Stores example. In your opinion, could this project be done effectively as a mail survey? As a telephone survey? As a face-to-face interview? How, if at all, would the questionnaire differ between methods of administration?

A general question that arises is whether the same question will get the same responses across different methods of administration. There has been quite a bit of research on this subject, and the answer in the overwhelming majority of situations in marketing research is "yes." There may be more overclaiming of socially desirable behavior in face-to-face or telephone interviews as compared to self-administered interviews, but most questions obtain similar responses across different methods. This means that you can choose a method of administration strictly according to cost and data limitations and that you can generally combine methods if you want.

Marketing Research Tools 11.1 summarizes the various implications of method of administration for questionnaire design. As this table shows, self-administered questionnaires generally have more limitations than telephone questionnaires, which in turn have more limitations than face-to-face questionnaires.

Formatting the Questionnaire

Once the information goals have been listed, the questions written, the questions put into order, and a method of administration selected, it is time to prepare the actual physical questionnaire. The goal in doing so is to make the questionnaire as easy as possible for respondents, interviewers, and data processing people to use.

Questionnaire format is discussed in this section, and several rules for formatting questionnaires are given. The discussion is directed toward printed (paper-and-pencil) questionnaires, but many of the same rules apply to computer questionnaires.

MARKETING RESEARCH TOOLS

11.1

HOW METHOD OF ADMINISTRATION AFFECTS QUESTIONNAIRES

Issue	Mail	Telephone	Face to Face
Questionnaire length	Keep to 4 pages	Depends on respondent interest	Depends on interest (intercepts must be brief)
Identity of respondent	Not known	Known	Known
Open questions	Big problem	No problem	No problem
Probing	Not possible	Better	Best
Complex questions	Big problem	No problem	No problem
Number of response categories	All that fit onto page	Keep to 4 or use numbers	All that fit onto card
Branching	Big problem	No problem with CATI	Some problem
Question order	No control	Controlled	Controlled
Sensitive topics	May be best	Handle with care	Handle with care

Also, although every researcher and research organization has its own format preferences, most professionals follow principles similar to those given here.

Rule 1: Use a Booklet Format

There are four reasons why a booklet format is desirable: (1) it prevents pages from being lost or misplaced, (2) it makes it easier for the interviewer or respondent to turn pages, (3) it makes it possible to use a double-page format if needed, and (4) for a mail questionnaire, a booklet looks more professional and is easier to follow.

The questionnaire should be printed on both sides of the page to conserve paper and, for mail surveys, to reduce mailing costs and make the questionnaire look shorter. Leave plenty of "white space" so that the questionnaire does not appear cramped.

Rule 2: Identify the Questionnaire

Questionnaires need a date, the title of the study (and study number, if appropriate), and the name of the organization conducting the survey. This information allows a marketing research organization to keep questionnaires from several studies organized.

Identifying material is normally placed at the beginning of the questionnaire, where it is easy to see yet does not interfere with the questionnaire's flow.

Rule 3: Do Not Crowd the Questions

We have already said that self-administered questionnaires should not be crowded, because crowding makes the questionnaire look more difficult. The same rule applies to questionnaires that interviewers will use. Also, be sure to leave enough space for open-ended answers, because interviewers will shorten answers to fit the available space.

Rule 4: Use Large, Clear Type

Some researchers try to save paper by using small type. This is always a mistake in telephone and face-to-face interviews because it is difficult to read and greatly increases the chance that interviewers will misread questions or make other mistakes. In mail surveys, smaller print may allow the questionnaire to fit within a four-page limit, but it also makes the questionnaire look more difficult, especially to older respondents, who don't see fine print well.

Rule 5: Number All Questions and Use an Outline Form for Branching

Each question should be numbered, and branching instructions should be supported with an "outline" format in which questions are indented if some respondents will skip them. Exhibit 11.1 (see page 291), which shows an example of branching questions, also illustrates outline format. Note how the outline form gives the interviewer visual support for the branching instructions.

Rule 6: Do Not Split Questions Across Pages

Interviewers and respondents find it confusing if a question is split over two pages and are more likely to make mistakes. This problem is especially serious when response categories for a closed question are split across pages, because interviewers and respondents tend to overlook the categories on the second page. If the entire question cannot be fitted onto a page, including response categories, the question should be started at the top of the next page.

This rule also applies to branching sequences, where possible. Splitting the branching sequence across pages disrupts the visual cues provided by indentation and makes it more difficult for the interviewer to find the end of the sequence. This makes mistakes more likely.

Unfortunately, long branching sequences may not fit onto one page. When this happens, it is best to make a page break at the end of the sequence, so the interviewer can find the next question (for respondents who skip the sequence) at the top of a page.

Rule 7: Put Special Instructions on the Questionnaire

Some questions require special instructions for the interviewers or respondents. For example, interviewers are normally trained to read response categories to respondents. If response categories are to be used for coding purposes, but the interviewers are not to read them, the interviewers should be instructed "DO NOT READ CATEGORIES." Also, interviewers should be instructed that each question has only one answer unless otherwise specified. If respondents are allowed to give several answers to a question—for example, if respondents are to tell *all* the reasons they bought their furniture at Smith's Stores—interviewers should be instructed to "CIRCLE ALL THAT APPLY" or "RECORD ALL ANSWERS."

In soliciting a list of reasons, interviewers may be directed to "PROBE: Any other reasons?" In a face-to-face interview, interviewers may be directed to "GIVE CARD A," which contains a list of response categories or some other exhibit. In recording the number of hours per day that respondents watch television, interviewers may be directed to "RECORD TO NEAREST HALF HOUR." When branching is needed, interviewers may be directed to "GO TO QUESTION 4" or to ask a question only if the previous answer was "IF MORE THAN ZERO." In a face-to-face interview, interviewers may be directed to "RECORD—DO NOT ASK—RESPONDENT'S SEX." Exhibit 11.1 (see page 291), which illustrates branching questions, also contains examples of some of these instructions.

Special instructions should appear on the questionnaire, rather than in a separate set of interviewer instructions, so they can guide the interviewer as she or he moves through the interview. They should be identified with a different typeface than the questions, such as **boldface,** CAPITALS, or *italics,* so that it is easy to distinguish between instructions for the interviewer and material to be read to respondents.

Instructions should be placed in the most useful possible location. Branching instructions should be placed immediately after answers that trigger skips, because this is where they are most useful to the interviewer (see questions 3 and 3B in Exhibit 11.1 for examples). Instructions that warn the interviewer not to ask some question should be placed immediately *above* that question (see questions 3A and 3B1 in Exhibit 11.1). Instructions to probe, to circle all answers, and so on should be placed at the end of the question to which they apply. For example:

Q: What are all the reasons you bought your furniture at Smith's rather than some other store? (CIRCLE ALL THAT APPLY)

Instructions to record the answer in some form should be placed on the line where the answer will be recorded (see questions 3, 3A, 3B1, and 4 in Exhibit 11.1, where a dollar sign or the word "YEAR" is used to indicate the desired response form).

Self-administered questionnaires generally need more instructions than telephone or face-to-face questionnaires because there are no trained interviewers. Respondents must be told *exactly* how to fill out the questionnaire.

Rule 8: Use Vertical Answer Formats for Closed Questions

Putting only one answer onto each line makes it easier for respondents, interviewers, and data processors to know which answer has been chosen. Compare the following two formats:

Q: What is your favorite brand of cereal?

Brand A ___ Brand B ___ Brand C ___ Other ___

Q: What is your favorite brand of cereal?

Brand A 1
Brand B 2
Brand C 3
Other 4

Don't worry that a vertical format takes too much space. This is a virtue, not a problem. The empty space makes the questionnaire look easier and provides room for comments, if any. A vertical format also makes it easy for interviewers to find the next question and for data entry staff to locate the answers.

Checklist questions are the exception to the rule about vertical answer formats. Exhibit 11.2 shows an example of a **checklist question,** which is a question that asks

EXHIBIT 11.2

Example of a Checklist Question

2. I have some specific factors that might influence where you would shop for furniture. As I read each one, please tell me whether you consider that factor to be very important, somewhat important, or not important in choosing a store for furniture. How about . . .

	Very important	Somewhat important	Not important
The convenience of the store location?	3	2	1
The store's everyday prices?	3	2	1
Sale prices?	3	2	1
Whether the store takes credit cards such as Visa, MasterCard, and American Express?	3	2	1
Whether you have a credit card from the store?	3	2	1
The quality of the store's merchandise?	3	2	1
The selection of merchandise?	3	2	1
How often the store is out of stock of merchandise you want?	3	2	1
The helpfulness of the salespeople?	3	2	1
The speed of service?	3	2	1

about a series of items with a common response format. In checklist questions, the vertical dimension is used for the various items, and the response categories are arranged horizontally.

Rule 9: Precode All Closed Questions

In Exhibits 11.1 (see page 291) and 11.2 (see page 296), note that all the response categories have been precoded with numbers to facilitate data entry and processing. Closed questions should always be precoded like this. Precoding allows the interviewer or respondent simply to circle the right answer, and it forces the questionnaire writer to think ahead to how the data will be coded and analyzed.

It may also be desirable to "precolumn" the questionnaire, depending on how data will be entered into computer files. In precolumning, the right-hand margin of the questionnaire is reserved "for office use only," and that margin is used to show the column in the data file where each response will be entered. Exhibits 11.1 and 11.2 are *not* precolumned. If you use modern statistical software, the columning information will be built into the data entry screen, so precolumning is not needed.

Rule 10: Record the Times When the Interview Begins and Ends

For planning and budgeting purposes, it may be useful to know how long an interview lasts. This information is easily obtained by leaving a space at the beginning of the interview for the interviewer to record the time the interview started and a space at the end to record the time the interview ended.

Rule 11: Provide a Beginning and an End to the Interview

At the start of a telephone or personal interview, it is necessary to (1) locate the proper respondent, (2) obtain a time to call back if the respondent is not available, (3) introduce the interviewer, the research company, and the questionnaire to the respondent, and (4) tell respondents that they need not answer any question they prefer not to answer. Many researchers don't include this last point, but we think it is ethically appropriate and often makes for better cooperation from respondents.

Exhibit 11.3 (see page 298) shows two introductions for a questionnaire on health care services. The first introduction contains all of the desired elements and was used in a telephone survey with a good cooperation rate. The introduction may seem cumbersome, but it has the advantage of "preprogramming" much of the interviewer's job.

Author Tips

In Exhibits 11.1 and 11.2 (see pp. 291, 296), the numerical codes for quantitative items have been assigned so that a higher number always means a higher quantity (higher importance, higher expenditure, etc.), regardless of the order in which categories are presented to the respondent. The first time we precoded a questionnaire, we assigned the codes in order of presentation. Then, when we analyzed the data, we kept getting confused because higher numbers meant "more" on some of the questions and "less" on other questions. We ended up writing a lot of recoding instructions so that higher always meant "more." Ever since then, we have built this principle into our precoding, and we suggest you do the same.

The second introduction was used by a different research company for the same questionnaire and is more typical of introductions used in marketing research. It gets the respondent into the interview as quickly as possible, but it doesn't provide much information. This type of introduction needs to be supplemented with training and/or a separate instruction sheet that tells interviewers what to do if various problems arise (such as the desired respondent not being available).

There will need to be some interviewer training and instructions even if you use the long introduction shown in Exhibit 11.3, because interviewers will need to be prepared for questions and comments such as:

"How was I selected?"

"How did you get my phone number?"

"How long will this take?"

"Give me your name and phone number. I want to verify that this is a legitimate call."

"You don't want to talk with me. My family doesn't have any health problems."

EXHIBIT 11.3

Examples of Questionnaire Introductions

Introduction #1

Hello. My name is *(YOUR NAME)*, and I am calling from Harmon Research, a marketing research company. We are conducting an opinion survey about health care in this area. I need to speak with the person who is most responsible for health care decisions in your household. Would that be you?

- **(IF THIS IS PROPER RESPONDENT)**

  If you prefer not to answer any question, please let me know and we will go on to the next question. If you do help us by answering a question, please be as truthful and as accurate as you can.

- **(IF PROPER RESPONDENT IS NOT AVAILABLE)**

  When might I reach that person?   (RECORD TIME ON REPORT
                                        FORM)
  Whom should I ask for?   (RECORD NAME ON REPORT
                                        FORM)

Introduction #2

Hello, my name is *(YOUR NAME)*, and I'm calling from Harmon Research, a marketing research company. I need to speak with the person who is *most responsible* for health care decisions in your household? Is that you?

Yes . . . . . [ ]   (CONTINUE)
No . . . . . [ ]   (ASK TO SPEAK TO THE PERSON MOST
                        RESPONSIBLE)

Note that, even in our long introduction, we did not tell respondents how long the interview would last. This is because the actual interviewing time often varies depending on the answers the respondent gives. If asked, however, interviewers should give an honest answer, such as "It takes most people between ten and twenty minutes."

At the end of the interview, interviewers should be reminded to say "Thank you" for the help they have received from respondents. Interviewers may, for example, tell respondents, "Those are all the questions we have. Thanks very much for your help." They can continue to ask, if desired, "May I have your first name in case my supervisor wants to call and verify that I talked with you?" Then, "Thanks again."

Introductions and endings for self-administered questionnaires are a little bit different from those for telephone and face-to-face interviews. The ending should be the same: thanking the respondent for participation. The beginning, though, will simply indicate who should complete the questionnaire. An explanation of the questionnaire and appeal for cooperation will be given in a separate cover letter. Cover letters were discussed in Chapter 7.

Marketing Research Tools 11.2 summarizes the rules for designing a physical questionnaire.

Critical Thinking Skills

Look for a copy of a questionnaire, for example, a restaurant's service questionnaire. Does this questionnaire follow our rules for questionnaire design? If not, do the rule violations cause problems?

MARKETING RESEARCH TOOLS

11.2

RULES FOR DESIGNING THE PHYSICAL QUESTIONNAIRE

1. Use a booklet format.
2. Identify the questionnaire.
3. Do not crowd the questions.
4. Use large, clear type.
5. Number all questions and use an outline form for branching.
6. Do not split questions across pages.
7. Put special instructions on the questionnaire.
8. Use vertical answer formats for closed questions.
9. Precode all closed questions.
10. Record the times when the interview begins and ends.
11. Provide a beginning and an end to the interview.

Testing the Questionnaire

Anytime a questionnaire is written, there is a chance that some of the questions will cause problems. Questionnaire testing is needed to identify and eliminate these problems. This section discusses ways of testing questionnaires and some of the issues encountered in testing.

Basic Tests for Questionnaires

The most basic test for questionnaires is to have as many people as possible look at the drafts of the questionnaire. Other researchers may be asked to review the questionnaire and warn of any problems they see. These researchers could be people in your own office, other professional colleagues, or a consultant you use as a sounding board. The worst questionnaire problems will be uncovered by these reviews.

Another basic test is to administer questionnaire drafts to people in your office—secretaries, professional researchers, whomever. Questions that seem unambiguous to you may cause problems for people with different points of view. In administering the questionnaire to people in your office, you obviously don't care about their answers. The important thing is to note where they have questions or problems and then to revise those sections of the questionnaire.

A somewhat more costly and time-consuming way of detecting problems with the draft questionnaire is through cognitive interviews. In a **cognitive interview,** people from the target group for the research are recruited (and paid) to come to a central location and go through the interview, and are asked to "think out loud" while they do so to show how respondents interpret the questions and construct their answers. Cognitive interviews can be done by the questionnaire writer, but it is usually better to have an interviewer (or an interviewing supervisor) administer the questions. The interview is tape-recorded so that it is easy to go back over sections that caused problems.

Some respondents in cognitive interviews may not be talkative and may not provide enough information about their thought processes. If this happens, the interviewer is instructed to probe with questions such as "What did you think we meant when we asked . . . ?" and "How did you go about answering that question?" It takes only a few cognitive interviews to spot and eliminate major problems in the questionnaire.

Pretests (Pilot Tests)

Pretests (or **pilot tests**) involve administering the questionnaire under field conditions to a sample of ten to fifty respondents. This testing usually comes after the questionnaire has gone through basic testing and been revised. Pretests may use standard respondents (as targeted in the research) or may be specially aimed at respondents who are expected to have the most difficulty with the questionnaire.

The major purpose of the pretest is to uncover any remaining problems in the questionnaire. The pretest is also used to time the interview. Timing information can be used for budgeting purposes, or it may suggest that the questionnaire needs to be shortened to fit the interviewing budget. Finally, the pretest is used to identify questions that are not useful, even though they don't cause problems, because almost everyone answers the question in the same way and the question therefore does not distinguish among respondents. These are sometimes called "Do you love your mother?" questions.

Unlike respondents in cognitive interviews, pretest respondents are not asked to think aloud. Questions about difficulties with the questionnaire are asked at the end of the interview and may provide useful information, although by then respondents may have forgotten some small difficulties.

The results of the pretest should, of course, be used to revise the questionnaire. If significant revisions are done, additional testing may be needed. A common mistake is to schedule a pretest but then to schedule the main study so shortly afterward that it is impossible to incorporate any pretest changes into the main study. It doesn't make sense to do a pretest to discover problems and then ignore these problems in conducting the study.

Interviewer Testing

In preparing for pretests and pilot tests, it is necessary to train interviewers and prepare written instructions. During this phase, it may turn out that the interviewers do not understand what is wanted. Such difficulties must certainly be addressed in training and may mean that the questionnaire needs to be revised.

Of Time and Testing

Testing questionnaires costs only modest amounts of money. The bigger issue is that testing takes time, and there are usually strong pressures to obtain information quickly. Imperfect but timely information is better than perfect information a year later.

There is no rule about how much questionnaire testing is necessary; there is always a trade-off between time and quality that will drive this decision. Large tracking studies that cost millions of dollars and will be implemented over a period of years obviously deserve the most complete testing possible. Small studies that managers need "yesterday" will have to get by with rough, quick testing. No single process applies. However, the following principles are useful:

1. With new questionnaires, it is a mistake to rely on the expertise of the questionnaire writer and not do testing. Even the most experienced researcher is unlikely to write a perfect questionnaire.

2. The marginal benefit from each additional test drops rapidly unless earlier versions are totally rewritten.

3. Every questionnaire has some key measures. If the key measures are working well, it may be possible to ignore small problems with less critical items.

4. In some studies, time is not a critical factor. For these studies, it makes sense to spend a little extra time to get better data.

In general, a questionnaire should not be tested any longer than necessary. It is crucial, though, that enough testing be done to avoid flaws that will ruin the entire study. If this happens, the study will need to be done again, and then time really becomes a problem. To paraphrase an old motto, "Question in haste, repent at leisure."

Marketing Research Tools 11.3 summarizes the steps in designing and implementing a questionnaire, from the initial development of information goals through testing to implementation.

MARKETING RESEARCH TOOLS

11.3

STEPS IN DESIGNING AND IMPLEMENTING A QUESTIONNAIRE

1. Prepare a list of information needs.
2. Determine the method of administration.
3. Conduct a search for existing questions.
4. Draft new questions or revise existing questions.
5. Sequence the questionnaire to minimize order effects, develop a logical flow, and establish rapport.
6. Determine skip instructions for branching.
7. Format the questionnaire to minimize confusion.
8. Precode all closed questions.
9. Get peer evaluations of draft questionnaire in group sessions and/or individually.
10. Revise the draft and test the revised questionnaire on yourself, coworkers, friends, and relatives. Revise again if necessary.
11. Possibly conduct cognitive interviews with a small sample. Revise the questionnaire as necessary.
12. Prepare interviewer instructions for a pretest and train interviewers. Revise the questionnaire if new problems are uncovered.
13. Pretest the questionnaire on a small sample. Obtain comments of respondents and interviewers. Revise as necessary.
14. Prepare final interviewer instructions and train interviewers.
15. Proceed with interviewing.
16. After all interviewing is completed, analyze interviewer reports and debrief interviewers and coders to determine whether there were any questionnaire problems that would affect analysis.

Summary

This chapter discussed how to plan, construct, and test a questionnaire. The following points were covered:

1. What questions should be included in a questionnaire?

Make a list of your information needs before you write any questions. Trim the questionnaire if it is too long, and don't ask extra questions just because you have room.

2. How should questions be ordered?

To minimize order effects, arrange questions from the general to the specific. To give the questionnaire a logical flow, group related topics together. Ask questions about behavior in backward chronological order, and use transitional phrases when switching topics. To put the respondent at ease, start the questionnaire with easy, nonthreatening questions and save demographic questions until the end.

3. How does the method of administration affect the questions asked?

Questions in a self-administered survey must be simple and straightforward, with little or no branching and little or no use of open questions. In a telephone survey, closed questions should usually have no more than four response categories. In face-to-face interviews, there is more flexibility.

4. What principles should guide the physical format of a questionnaire?

Use a booklet format. Identify the questionnaire with the date, the title of the study, and the name of the organization conducting the study. Don't crowd the questions, and use large, clear type. Number all questions, use an outline form to guide branching, don't split questions across pages, and try not to split branching sequences across pages.

Put interviewer instructions on the questionnaire as needed, use vertical answer formats for closed questions, and precode all closed questions. Record the times when the interview begins and ends. Provide a beginning and an end to the interview by including introduction and conclusion phrases in the questionnaire.

5. How can a questionnaire be tested?

The most basic test for a questionnaire is to have as many people as possible look at drafts of it. Administer it to people in your office to see where they have questions or problems. Also consider using cognitive interviews in which people think out loud as they complete the questionnaire, and pretest the questionnaire under field conditions. You should also test the instructions and interviewer training materials to ensure that interviewers know how to administer the questionnaire.

Suggested Additional Readings

See the suggestions at the end of Chapter 10, especially Seymour Sudman and Norman M. Bradburn, *Asking Questions: A Practical Guide to Questionnaire Design* (San Francisco: Jossey-Bass, 1982). Three additional references on questionnaire design are Patricia J. Labaw, *Advanced Questionnaire Design* (Cambridge, Mass.: Abt Books, 1981); Paul R. Lees-Haley, *The Questionnaire Design Handbook* (Huntsville, Ala.: Rubicon, 1980); and Judith Lessler, Roger Tourangeau, and William Salkes, *Questionnaire Design in the Cognitive Research Laboratory* (Hyattsville, Md.: U.S. Department of Health and Human Services, 1989).

Discussion Questions

1. Why is questionnaire length more important for mail surveys?

2. How does the method of administration affect questionnaires on each of the following issues?

   Questionnaire length
   Identity of respondent
   Open questions
   Probing
   Complex questions
   Number of response categories
   Branching
   Question order
   Sensitive topics

3. What are "order effects"?

4. You are developing a questionnaire to administer to participants after they test-drive a new "electric" car. You will be asking the participants to rate the new car on its speed, handling, and comfort, in addition to an overall rating. How should you order the following questions?

   How would you rate the electric car on its handling?
   How would you rate the electric car on its comfort?
   Overall, how would you rate the electric car as a vehicle to own?
   How would you rate the electric car on its speed?

5. What is branching and why is it used?

6. What is the purpose of pretesting a questionnaire?

7. How does a questionnaire differ from "just a collection of questions"?

8. Why should you test a questionnaire? Why might you not want to? What are the trade-offs of testing versus not testing?

Marketing Research Challenge

Design a questionnaire to measure potential interest in a new product. (Make one up, or get an idea from the business press.) Ask a fellow classmate to critique your questionnaire in exchange for critiquing his or hers. Revise your questionnaire on the basis of the critique. Pretest the questionnaire on fellow students, friends, parents, and relatives.

Internet Exercise

Refer back to the questionnaire that you evaluated in the Internet Exercise for Chapter 10. How, if at all, would you change this questionnaire if it were to be administered by telephone? How, if at all, would you change the questionnaire if it were to be administered face to face?

12

Questionnaire Workshop: Evaluating Questionnaires

◪ OBJECTIVES

After reading this chapter, you should be able to answer the following questions:

❶ How can a questionnaire be evaluated?

❷ How should a questionnaire be revised?

Chapters 10 and 11 provided a great deal of information about how to write questions and organize questionnaires. The purpose of this chapter is to make that material more concrete by applying it to specific questionnaires.

Four questionnaires are used as examples in this chapter. Our general format for discussing each of these questionnaires is as follows:

- First, some background on a research project is given and the research objectives are stated.

- Next, a questionnaire that is intended to satisfy those objectives is presented.

- Next, the questionnaire is evaluated.

- Finally, for two of the examples, a revised questionnaire that resolves the problems identified in our evaluation is presented.

As you read through the chapter, you will find that you don't always agree with our evaluations and revisions of the questionnaires. This is typical of questionnaire design. If a questionnaire writing assignment is given to ten experts in questionnaire design, they will produce ten different questionnaires. All these questionnaires will have points of similarity, but each will reflect a unique approach to satisfying the research objectives and a unique writing style. Each will be "correct" in its own way. There isn't any one "right" way to write a questionnaire; the rules in Chapters 10 and 11 don't so much describe how to write good questionnaires as how to avoid writing bad ones.

Example 1

The Research Problem

This example relates to a chain of inexpensive, sit-down restaurants—a Denny's type of operation. For the chain to be promoted effectively, food and service quality must be consistent across the restaurants. Therefore, the company has designed a program to monitor quality at each of its restaurants on an ongoing basis.

The program will work as follows. Copies of the proposed questionnaire will be placed in a rack on each table in the company's restaurants. The questionnaire will ask customers to comment on the food, service, and prices. Completed questionnaires will be picked up by waiters and waitresses and taken to the manager on duty, who will place them in a box. Once a month, results from the questionnaires will be tabulated and reported for each restaurant.

The Questionnaire

The proposed questionnaire is shown in Exhibit 12.1.

EXHIBIT 12.1

Questionnaire #1

Your Opinions Count!
We'd like to hear your comments about our restaurant.

1. How was the food?

   Excellent _____   Good _____   Fair _____

2. How was the service?

   Excellent _____   Good _____   Fair _____

3. How were the prices?

   Reasonable _____   High _____   Low _____

4. Other comments

   _____

   _____

Questionnaire Evaluation

Some good features of this research effort (including the questionnaire) are that:

1. The proposed research program uses a fixed questionnaire and fixed data collection methods on a "tracking" basis. The results for any given restaurant may not be meaningful in isolation, but comparisons across locations and across time will allow the company to identify operations that are below average and/or declining.

2. The length of the questionnaire is well suited to the data collection environment. The questionnaire can be faulted for gathering only limited data. However, a self-administered questionnaire for restaurant patrons *must be* brief. People will not take the time to complete a long, detailed questionnaire.

3. Given the brevity of the questionnaire, the topics seem well chosen. If only two questions could be asked about a restaurant dining experience, they would be about the food and the service, and "value" seems to be a good topic for a third question.

4. Closed questions are appropriate for the data collection environment.

   Those are the good points. Some of the weaknesses of the questionnaire are that:

1. The results are likely to give a misleading picture of overall customer satisfaction because very few patrons will complete the questionnaire, and those who do cannot be regarded as typical of the average patron after the average meal. This **sample bias,** the difference between all customers and those who fill out the questionnaire, may not be a problem if results are used on a consistent basis across locations and time, but it is still undesirable.

2. There is a problem with the data collection method. Servers will be motivated to destroy questionnaires that criticize the service. Similarly, site managers will be motivated to destroy questionnaires that criticize the restaurant, and to "manage" their results by stuffing the ballot box with positive questionnaires.

3. As already noted, the questionnaire is very limited. This may be necessary given the data collection environment, but it means that the results will have limited diagnostic value.

4. Respondents are not given a response alternative that allows them to comment negatively on the food or service. In addition to knowing how many patrons liked the food and service, we'd like to know how many thought they were poor.

5. This questionnaire breaks the rule for vertical layout of response categories. However, the horizontal layout helps create an impression that the questionnaire will "just take a second" and seems unlikely to cause any problems.

6. Respondents are not told what to do with the questionnaire after completing it. Instructions should be given at the bottom of the form.

Overall, the crucial issues in this research program relate to sample bias and data security. A questionnaire revision will not address these issues. Rather than revise the existing questionnaire and, in doing so, implicitly accept the general research design, we would recommend that the company consider different methods that would reduce the sample bias and data security problems.

One such method would be to use intercept surveys rather than table cards. In **intercept surveys,** patrons on their way out will be approached by interviewers and asked to answer a few questions about the restaurant. This method will reduce data collection problems and provide a less biased cross section of patrons. It will also allow a somewhat longer questionnaire. The disadvantages of intercept surveys, compared with table cards, are that they cost more and can be done only periodically.

Another method of evaluating service quality would be to use **service shoppers,** that is, people who are paid to visit a restaurant or store, make a purchase, and evaluate the service on a prepared rating sheet. The advantages of service shoppers, compared with table cards, are improved data security and much more detailed evaluations. The disadvantage of service shoppers is that monthly evaluations for any given restaurant will be based on only a small number of service encounters.

If the restaurant chain adopts an intercept survey program, a questionnaire will be needed for this program, but it will not simply be a revision of the current questionnaire. If the chain adopts a service shopper program, a rating form will be needed, but this form again will not be a revision of the current questionnaire.

Overall, this first example illustrates the following points about questionnaires:

- A questionnaire cannot be evaluated separately from the context and motives of the research.

- Questionnaire design rules need not be followed slavishly.

- A questionnaire design that breaks the rules may be desirable in some situations.

- A well-written questionnaire will not save poorly conceived research.

- Sometimes the best thing to do is not to revise a questionnaire but rather to go back to the drawing board and redesign the entire research project.

Critical Thinking Skills

Given this restaurant company's objectives, design a questionnaire that might be used for an intercept survey of patrons.

Example 2

The Research Problem

This example relates to the Houston Astros baseball team. As a major-league baseball team, the Astros play eighty-one home games in a regular season. These games are attended by a mixture of season ticket holders and single game attenders. Of course, people who buy single game tickets may come to more than one game in the course of a season. The Astros promote attendance in various ways, including:

- Direct mail solicitations for season ticket sales
- Game promotions such as "Bat Day" and "Jacket Day"
- Billboard advertising that promotes the team but not any particular game
- Television commercials with voice-overs that promote specific games
- Radio commercials that promote specific games
- Newspaper ads that promote specific games
- A mobile ticket van that visits various shopping centers

The Astros wish to do a survey of fans to learn more about the people who attend Astros games. Astros executives don't have a specific decision objective for this project, but they feel that a fan survey will provide useful guidance in placing advertising and planning promotions.

The team considered two options for this project: (1) a telephone survey of the general population and (2) an intercept survey done at one or more Astros games. The intercept survey would cost less per interview and focus attention on people who actually attend games. The telephone survey would allow the team to learn about people who do not attend games but might be motivated to do so. On balance, Astros management decided that an intercept survey would be preferable.

An intercept survey could be done in various ways. Fans could be intercepted as they entered the stadium, at their seating areas, or as they left. The questionnaire could be self-administered or administered by an interviewer. In considering various options, Astros management decided to intercept people as they entered. The team felt this was best because people would dislike any effort to intercept them while the game was in progress, and they would be in a hurry to leave after the game. The team decided to use self-administered questionnaires because employees with no training as interviewers could distribute large numbers of questionnaires to incoming fans, and the distribution process would not cause congestion near the entrance gates. To entice fans to return these self-administered questionnaires, the team planned to use the questionnaires as entries in a prize drawing to be held at the end of the third inning. The team also planned to place prominently labeled collection boxes throughout the stadium, to distribute pencils along with the questionnaires, and to print the questionnaires on a card stock that could be used without backing.

Astros management requested that the survey provide the following information about fans:

- Where do they live?
- Are they season ticket holders?
- How many people came with them?
- How many children?
- How many games do they attend?
- Why did they come to this game?
- What radio stations do they listen to?

The Questionnaire

The proposed questionnaire is shown in Exhibit 12.2.

Questionnaire Evaluation

This questionnaire has some good features. It generally uses closed questions, which are appropriate to a self-administered questionnaire. The questions are direct, and questions 4 and 5 nicely specify to whom the question refers. The questionnaire has an introduction and an end, and it tells respondents what they should do with the completed forms.

Now let's talk about possible improvements:

1. Questions 1 and 1A are well written but unnecessary. The zip code information obtained at the bottom of the questionnaire provides better data.

2. Question 2 is well written but should specify whether the respondent should count himself or herself.

3. The categories used in questions 2 to 5 may or may not be reasonable, depending on the exact purposes of the question and the expected distribution of answers. For example, if the team's purpose is to learn how many people come by themselves, how many come in small groups, and how many come in large groups, question 2 may need only three categories. Also, although the format is attractive for a self-administered study, the most flexible way of gathering these data would be to provide spaces in which respondents write the appropriate numbers.

4. Question 3 needs to define "children." Are sixteen year olds children?

5. Question 4, which asks about season ticket ownership for everyone in the group, asks respondents for information they may not have. It might be better simply to ask whether the respondent himself or herself is attending on a season ticket or a single game ticket.

6. Question 5 is pretty good, but it needs to specify whether tonight's game should be counted.

7. Question 6 is overambitious. The obvious goal of this question is to get a fairly complete list of the respondent's radio stations. However, the question ignores a basic rule of surveys: no one person needs to carry the load. The purpose of this

EXHIBIT 12.2

Questionnnaire #2

We are conducting a survey to learn more about you, our fan. We want to make your attendance at Astros games as enjoyable as possible.

To fill out the survey, check the boxes that most nearly describe you. Drop the completed form in any of the orange and blue boxes located near concession stands. After the third inning, we will draw names to win a NEW VCR, ASTROS TICKETS, and OTHER PRIZES.

1. In what city do you live? _____

(IF HOUSTON)

A. In what part of Houston do you live?

☐ Inside the Loop   ☐ South
☐ North   ☐ Southwest
☐ Northeast   ☐ West
☐ East   ☐ Northwest
☐ Southeast

2. How many people are in your group at tonight's game?

☐ 1   ☐ 2–3   ☐ 4–5   ☐ 6 or more

3. How many of them are children?

☐ 1   ☐ 2–3   ☐ 4–5   ☐ 6 or more

4. How many people in your group, including yourself, are Astros season ticket holders?

☐ 1   ☐ 2–3   ☐ 4–5   ☐ 6 or more

5. How many games have you yourself attended this season?

☐ 1   ☐ 2–3   ☐ 4–5   ☐ 6 or more

6. What four radio stations do you listen to most often?

_____   _____

_____   _____

7. Why did you come to tonight's Astros game?

_____

_____

_____

We need your name and address for our prize drawing.

NAME: _____

ADDRESS: _____

CITY, STATE, ZIP: _____

Thanks for your help. Please drop this form in any orange and blue box to enter our drawing.

survey isn't to learn what each respondent does—the purpose is to learn what Astros fans *in general* do. If the respondent's favorite radio station is requested and data are gathered from several hundred respondents, a nice distribution of radio stations will be provided.

8. Question 7 will not work in a self-administered survey. Fans will not write essays about their reasons for attending—especially when they are sitting in the stadium and writing with a golf pencil on an unbacked form. The question must be closed.

9. To close question 7, it is necessary to think about the motivation for the question. Why docs Astros management want to know why people come to a particular game? Does it hope to learn whether people come for the baseball versus some other social purpose? Does it hope to learn what types of promotions are effective in drawing people? Does it hope to learn how many people make a last-minute decision and thus might be influenced by advertising on game day and preceding days? Whatever the purpose, it is likely that a more specific question will provide more useful information.

10. If the rule that background questions should come after topic questions is to be followed, question 1 belongs at the end of the questionnaire, and question 6 should probably follow question 7. This is not terribly important in this questionnaire because the questionnaire's express purpose is to learn something about the fans' backgrounds, and also because respondents can see the questionnaire from start to finish before they answer the questions.

Questionnaire Revision

Exhibit 12.3 shows a revised questionnaire that reflects the preceding comments.

Example 3

The Research Problem

This example relates to an electric utility. The company wished to evaluate the potential residential market for equipment that protects against power fluctuations and outages.

As you may know, electrical service is subject to variability. The voltage flowing into a home or business occasionally surges or drops and sometimes goes out completely. Power fluctuation can damage electrical devices or cause them to perform improperly, and power outages cause electrical devices to stop working altogether.

EXHIBIT 12.3

Questionnnaire
#2 Revised

?

We are conducting a survey to learn more about you, our fan. We want to make your attendance at Astros games as enjoyable as possible.

To fill out the survey, check the boxes that most nearly describe you. Drop the completed form in any of the orange and blue boxes located near concession stands. After the third inning, we will draw names to win a NEW VCR, ASTROS TICKETS, and OTHER PRIZES.

1. Are you attending tonight's game on a season ticket or a single game ticket?

    ☐ Season ticket   ☐ Single game ticket

2. Counting tonight's game, how many Astros games have you attended this season?

    ☐ 1   ☐ 2–3   ☐ 4–5   ☐ 6 or more

3. Counting yourself, how many people are in your group at tonight's game?

    ☐ 1   ☐ 2–3   ☐ 4–5   ☐ 6 or more

4. How many of the people in your group are less than 13 years of age?

    ☐ 1   ☐ 2–3   ☐ 4–5   ☐ 6 or more

5. When did you decide to attend tonight's game? Was it today, before today but during the past week, or earlier than the past week?

    ☐ Today   ☐ Past week   ☐ Earlier

6. What promotions, if any, might influence you to attend an Astros game? (CHECK ALL THAT APPLY)

    ☐ $2 off tickets   ☐ Prize drawings

    ☐ Family discounts   ☐ Country music concert

    ☐ Free parking   ☐ Rock music concert

    ☐ Free Astros mug   ☐ Tailgate parties

    ☐ Free child's cap   ☐ Home run derby

7. What is your favorite radio station?

(FILL IN) _____

We need your name and address for our prize drawing.

NAME: _____

ADDRESS: _____

CITY, STATE, ZIP: _____

Thanks for your help. Please drop this form into any orange and blue box to enter our drawing.

Users of electricity can protect themselves from the effects of power outages by buying devices with built-in battery backups or by buying generators to be used when the power goes out. They can protect themselves from the effects of line fluctuations by connecting electrical devices to surge suppressors.

The power company wanted to estimate how many of its residential customers might be interested in buying generators or surge suppressors from the company and how much they might be willing to pay. To accomplish this goal, the company planned a survey of residential customers to measure the following general objectives:

- Customers' awareness of power supply problems
- Customers' willingness to purchase or lease corrective equipment
- Customers' willingness to purchase or lease corrective equipment from the power company
- The amount that customers are willing to pay

The Questionnaire

The proposed questionnaire is shown in Exhibit 12.4.

Questionnaire Evaluation

This is a terrible questionnaire. Let's note some of the problems.

1. The introduction uses technical jargon and, in effect, tells the respondent, "I'm about to ask you some questions you won't understand."

2. Question 1 asks about "equipment systems" that are "critical" to the "everyday functions" of the home. Some definition of these terms might be necessary.

3. The format of question 1 is messy. There isn't any need for the numbers in front of the equipment types.

4. Question 2 asks for information the respondent may not have. Also, the purpose of the question is not clear. The power company should already know how often power outages occur. If the purpose of the question is to identify people who perceive power outages as a problem, it would probably be better to ask for this perception directly.

5. Question 3 seems somewhat ambiguous. What is meant by being "familiar" with this equipment?

6. In question 3, the "Not very familiar" response category should be dropped. It isn't distinct from the "Somewhat familiar" category.

7. Question 4 uses jargon terms ("Uninterruptible power supply equipment" and "Power conditioning equipment"). If you were a respondent, would you know that "uninterruptible power supply equipment" refers to generators and "power conditioning equipment" refers to surge suppressors?

8. Question 4 is also two questions in one. Separating these questions will make the questionnaire easier to use.

(Cont. on p. 318)

EXHIBIT 12.4

Questionnnaire #3

Hello, I'm _____ of _____, a public opinion research firm. We have been retained by Western Shores Power to survey some of their residential customers about power interruptions to electrical service in your area.

Western Shores Power is evaluating the need for uninterruptible power equipment and power conditioning equipment to protect residential customers from power interruptions. I would like to ask you a few questions to help us determine the scope of this problem and find solutions geared to residential customers' needs.

Please be assured that all information will remain completely confidential and will be used for statistical purposes only.

1. I'm going to read you a list of equipment systems that may or may not be critical to the everyday functions of your home. For each system I read, please tell me if this equipment is critical to the everyday functions of your home, even during a power outage. (READ LIST—ROTATE)

What about	Yes	No
1. Computers?	1	2
2. Medical diagnostic equipment?	1	2
3. Security systems?	1	2

   4. (READ) Is there any other system that is critical to the everyday functions of your home, even during a power outage? (SPECIFY)_____

   (IF NONE OF THE ABOVE APPLY, THANK AND TERMINATE)

2. During the past year, how many times has there been an electrical power outage at your home? (READ CATEGORIES)

None	1
1–6	2
7 or more	3

3. How familiar are you with equipment that can be used to protect against power fluctuations and outages? (READ CATEGORIES)

Very familiar	1
Somewhat familiar	2
Not very familiar	3
Not familiar at all	4
Unsure (DO NOT READ)	5

Continued

EXHIBIT 12.4

Questionnnaire
#3—Continued

As you may know . . .

Uninterruptible Power Supply (UPS) is designed to protect critical equipment against ALL power fluctuations, including a total power outage. The backup power capability for power outages will vary with the customer's needs.

Power Conditioning Equipment is designed to protect against power fluctuations only.

4. Considering everyday home uses for your critical equipment, is there a need for either (1) uninterruptible power supply equipment or (2) power conditioning equipment to protect critical equipment from power fluctuations?

Uninterruptible power supply equipment	1
Power conditioning equipment	2
Both (DO NOT READ)	3
Neither (DO NOT READ)	4
Don't know/No answer	5

5. Does your home currently have uninterruptible power supply equipment or power conditioning equipment to protect your critical equipment against power fluctuations or outages?

Yes/Uninterruptible power supply equipment	1
(GO TO Q7 & Q9)	
Yes/Power conditioning equipment	2
(GO TO Q8 & Q9)	
Yes/Both (GO TO Q7–9)	3
No (GO TO Q6)	4
Don't know/No answer	5

(IF NO IN QUESTION 5, ASK:)

6. What are the reasons you do not currently use uninterruptible power supply or power conditioning equipment in your home? (DO NOT READ)

1.	Do not experience power-related failures of critical equipment (GO TO Q10)	1
2.	Initial cost of equipment (GO TO Q7–9)	2
3.	Cost of maintaining equipment . . . . (GO TO Q7–9)	3
4.	Not familiar with the equipment . . . . (GO TO Q7–9)	4
5.	Other (SPECIFY) (GO TO Q7–9)	5
6.	Don't know/No answer	6

7. Considering the importance of your critical equipment, if **uninterruptible power supply** equipment that would protect all critical systems from power failure were available at a cost of $_____ **per month,** would you be interested in looking at this system? (READ CATEGORIES—TOP TO BOTTOM, BOTTOM TO TOP—STOP WHEN ANSWERED) What if the cost were:

$50 or more?	1
Between $25 and $50?	2
Between $15 and $25?	3
Less than $15?	4
No level (DO NOT READ)	5
Don't know/No answer	6

8. Considering the importance of your critical equipment, if a **conditioned power system** that would protect all critical equipment from power fluctuations were available at a cost of $_____ **per month,** would you be interested in looking at this system? (READ CATEGORIES—TOP TO BOTTOM, BOTTOM TO TOP—STOP WHEN ANSWERED) What if the cost were:

$50 or more?	1
Between $25 and $50?	2
Between $15 and $25?	3
Less than $15?	4
No level (DO NOT READ)	5
Don't know/No answer	6

9. A number of companies provide uninterruptible power supply equipment and power conditioning equipment. Assuming that this equipment is available at a reasonable price, which of the following arrangements would you prefer? (READ CATEGORIES)

Deal directly with vendor	1
Deal directly with Western Shores Power	2
Other (DO NOT READ) (SPECIFY)	
_____	3
No interest (DO NOT READ)	4
Don't know/No answer	5

10. For classification purposes only, do you live in a house or an apartment?

House	1
Apartment	2

Those are all of our questions. Thanks for your help.

9. Question 5 is two questions in one and uses jargon. The branching instructions are complicated by the failure to separate the questions.

10. Question 6 is open, and interviewers are expected to code respondents' answers in the appropriate categories. However, the categories given in this question do not seem very complete. In fact, the most common answers received during field interviews were "Don't know" and "Other." The high rate of "Don't know" answers suggests that respondents had trouble with the question.

11. Question 6 appears to allow multiple answers: respondents are asked for *reasons* (plural). However, interviewers are not told to circle all answers that apply, and it is not clear how the branching instructions would be affected by multiple answers.

12. The branching instructions in question 6 are awkward. It would be better if questions 7 to 9 were indented to show the branching pattern and if interviewers were simply told to CONTINUE rather than told to GO TO questions 7–9.

13. There isn't any need for the numbers in front of each response category in question 6.

14. Interviewers are asked to specify the exact nature of "other" responses in question 6 but are not given space to write these answers.

15. Interviewers will need to be trained to interpret the vague instructions given in questions 7 and 8.

16. The DO NOT READ instruction that follows the "No level" category in question 7 and question 8 is misplaced. It comes too late to alert the interviewer.

17. The "Don't know/No answer" category in questions 7 and 8 should also have a DO NOT READ instruction.

18. Question 9 could be written more directly, and the term "vendor" may not be familiar to respondents. Here is an alternative wording: "If you bought a generator, would you prefer to buy it from Western Shores Power or from some other company?"

19. Question 9 also repeats some of the problems we have noted in earlier questions: it is two questions in one, the DO NOT READ instructions are poorly placed, and the "Don't know" category needs a DO NOT READ instruction.

20. Questions 1 and 2 seem redundant with question 4, at least in purpose, and might be eliminated. Presumably, the purpose of questions 1 and 2 is to determine whether the respondent might benefit from a generator and/or surge suppressor. This is the same purpose as question 4, which addresses the issue more directly.

Overall, this questionnaire has severe technical deficiencies. These are not all of its deficiencies, though, or even its worst deficiencies. The questionnaire could be revised to eliminate the jargon, the double-barreled questions, and the format problems, and it would still be a bad questionnaire. The reason is that this questionnaire asks the wrong questions.

Consider questions 3 to 9, which are the heart of the questionnaire. Respondents are asked whether they know about equipment that reduces problems from power variation (question 3), whether they would benefit from such equipment (question 4), and whether they own such equipment (question 5). If they don't own such equipment, they are asked why not (question 6). They are also asked how much they would pay for the equipment (questions 7 and 8) and whether they would buy from the power company (question 9). Taken together, questions 3 to 9 represent a coherent, though poorly executed, sequence that presumes a deliberative purchase model. In other words, these questions presume that people who buy generators or surge suppressors deliberate the purchase in advance and that key marketing questions include (1) "How many people know about the products but need to be convinced of their benefits?," (2) "How many people see the benefit of the products but need to be activated as buyers?," and (3) How many activated buyers need to be convinced that the power company is the best vendor for these products?"

However, most people who own a surge suppressor bought it as an add-on purchase with some other item such as a computer. Awareness of surge suppressors was irrelevant before the person developed a need by buying the other item, and the development of this need was essentially simultaneous with purchase. In this context, it is of little use to measure how many people have a general awareness of surge suppressors. Similarly, there is little benefit in asking whether respondents own equipment that would benefit from a surge suppressor or whether they like the power company as a stand-alone supplier of surge suppressors, since surge suppressors are bought on an unplanned, add-on basis at the same point of sale as the equipment with which they are used.

Generators do not fit a deliberative purchase model any better than surge suppressors do. The power company that sponsored this research is located in a coastal area where almost all consumer purchases of generators are made immediately before or after a major storm. People might be willing to buy their generators from the power company, but purchases would be on an immediate, "as needed" basis and would not really depend on awareness or careful shopping. (The commercial market for surge suppressors is much less crisis-driven.)

This questionnaire should not be revised until researchers meet with managers at the power company to reconsider the nature of the residential market for generators and surge suppressors and reevaluate the research objectives.

Critical Thinking Skills

Given the way in which surge suppressors and generators are purchased by consumers, how would you design a study to evaluate whether the power company can be a viable vendor of these products?

Example 4

The Research Problem

The final example concerns a chain of sporting goods stores that offers its own credit card. The chain currently has about $10 million in annual sales on this card, and it costs about $800,000 to run the credit operation (to evaluate applicants, issue cards, process transactions, prepare bills, mail bills, and collect payment). In other words, the expense rate for processing charges on the chain's own card is about 8 percent of credit sales. In contrast, the chain is charged about 1.5 percent to process Visa and Mastercard transactions and 3.5 percent for American Express (the chain takes all these cards).

If the chain dropped its credit card and switched the $10 million in sales to "third-party" credit cards (Visa, etc.), it would save at least $450,000 in annual costs. However, dropping the chain's credit card might also cause lower sales because customers would no longer have an incentive to shop at this particular chain. It isn't clear whether the net result would be profitable.

The chain has undertaken a three-step research project to help it decide what to do about the credit operation. In the first step, the chain gathered national statistics on the costs of retail credit departments. These statistics showed that the chain's costs are in line with national averages; therefore, significant gains from streamlining the credit department are not likely. In the second step, the chain analyzed sales from each merchandise department to identify areas that might be hard hit by a decline in credit sales. As expected, this analysis showed that the bigger-ticket items are more vulnerable. Now, in the third step, the chain plans a telephone survey of its credit customers. The purpose of this survey is to estimate the extent to which these customers will spend less at the chain's stores if the credit card is withdrawn.

Given that the chain plans to do a survey to evaluate the credit operation, it also wishes to learn how its customers rate it on various dimensions. In particular, the chain's last major study, done five years ago, showed that customers rated the chain low on having merchandise in stock. The chain wishes to know whether it has improved on this dimension.

The Questionnaire

This research problem was introduced in Chapter 10. There it was noted that respondents might not give accurate answers when asked whether they would shop less if the chain's credit card were withdrawn. The value of attacking this issue with multiple measures such as (1) open-ended measures of credit card importance in determining store choice, (2) closed-end measures of credit card importance, (3) measures of the extent to which customers have third-party credit cards available, and (4) direct measures of how people think their shopping would change was discussed. An appropriate ordering for these topics was also discussed.

A proposed questionnaire is shown in Exhibit 12.5.

Questionnaire Evaluation

This questionnaire generally reads and flows well. It also seems well suited to the research objectives. The instructions and precoding are solid. We would recommend only minor changes in it, as follows.

1. Spacing should be added throughout the questionnaire and the double-columning of questions and answers eliminated. The current format saves paper but will be difficult for interviewers to use.

2. Branching sequences should not be split across pages if possible.

3. It is not a good idea to ask about five different merchandise categories at the start of the questionnaire. One motive for doing so is to show how credit cards vary in importance across merchandise categories, but this has already been shown by the company's analysis of credit purchases. Another motive is to

(Cont. on p. 326)

EXHIBIT 12.5

Questionnaire #4

Hello, I'm _____ of _____, a marketing and opinion research firm. We are conducting a study with people who have purchased from sporting goods stores during the past year.

A. Have you purchased from any sporting goods stores during the past year?

B. IF NO: Has anyone else in your household purchased from sporting goods stores during the past year?

IF NO, TERMINATE.

CONTINUE INTERVIEW WITH A PERSON WHO HAS SHOPPED SPORTING GOODS STORES.

1. To begin, I have some questions about products you may have purchased, either for yourself or for someone else. In the past twelve months, have you purchased any type of athletic shoes?

Yes	1	(ASK Q1A–Q1D)
No	2	(GO TO Q2)

(IF YES)

1A. Where did you make your most recent purchase of athletic shoes?
(STORE) _____

1B. What was the most important reason you bought those shoes at (*STORE IN Q1A*) rather than at another store? (DO NOT READ CATEGORIES)

Price	1
Sale	2
Location/convenience	3
Merchandise quality	4
Merchandise selection	5
Salespeople	6
Availability of credit	7
←Other (SPECIFY)	0

(_____)

1C. How much did you spend on that purchase? (TO NEAREST DOLLAR) $_____

1D. Did you pay cash, use a store charge account, or use another credit card such as a Visa, MasterCard, or American Express?

Paid cash (check)	1
Store charge	2
Other credit card	3

2. In the past twelve months, have you purchased any active sportswear such as tennis clothes, leotards, swimsuits, etc.?

Yes	1	(ASK Q2A–D)
No	2	(GO TO Q3)

(IF YES)

2A. Where did you make your most recent purchase of active sportswear?
(STORE)_____

Continued

2B. What was the most important reason you made that purchase at *(STORE IN Q2A)* rather than at another store? (DO NOT READ CATEGORIES)

Price 1
Sale 2
Location/convenience 3
Merchandise quality 4
Merchandise selection 5
Salespeople 6
Availability of credit 7
←Other (SPECIFY) 0

(_____)

2C. How much did you spend on that purchase? (TO NEAREST DOLLAR)

$ _____

2D. Did you pay cash, use a store charge account, or use another credit card such as a Visa, MasterCard, or American Express?

Paid cash (check) 1
Store charge 2
Other credit card 3

3. In the past twelve months, have you purchased any exercise equipment such as weights, exercycles, rowing machines, etc.?

Yes . . . . 1 (ASK Q3A–D)
No . . . . 2 (GO TO Q4)

(IF YES)

3A. Where did you make your most recent purchase of exercise equipment?

(STORE)_____

3B. What was the most important reason you made that purchase at *(STORE IN Q3A)* rather than at another store? (DO NOT READ CATEGORIES)

Price 1
Sale 2
Location/convenience 3
Merchandise quality 4
Merchandise selection 5
Salespeople 6
Availability of credit 7
←Other (SPECIFY) 0

(_____)

3C. How much did you spend on that purchase? (TO NEAREST DOLLAR)

$ _____

3D. Did you pay cash, use a store charge account, or use another credit card such as a Visa, MasterCard, or American Express?

Paid cash (check) 1
Store charge 2
Other credit card 3

4. In the past twelve months, have you purchased any hunting, fishing, or camping equipment, either for yourself or for someone else?

Yes . . . . 1 (ASK Q4A–D)
No . . . . 2 (GO TO Q5)

(IF YES)

4A. Where did you make your most recent purchase of hunting, fishing, or camping equipment?

(STORE) _____

4B. What was the most important reason you made that purchase at *(STORE IN Q4A)* rather than at another store? (DO NOT READ CATEGORIES) (_____)	Price . . . . Sale . . . . Location/convenience . . . . Merchandise quality . . . . Merchandise selection . . . . Salespeople . . . . Availability of credit . . . . ←Other (SPECIFY)	1 2 3 4 5 6 7 0

4C. How much did you spend on that purchase?
(TO NEAREST DOLLAR) $ _____

4D. Did you pay cash, use a store charge account, or use another credit card such as a Visa, MasterCard, or American Express?	Paid cash (check) . . . . Store charge . . . . Other credit card	1 2 3

5. In the past twelve months, have you purchased any other type of sporting equipment including balls, bats, rackets, gloves, helmets, or anything we've not mentioned so far?	Yes . . . . 1 (ASK Q5A–D) No . . . . 2 (GO TO Q6)	

(IF YES)

5A. What sort of sporting equipment did you purchase most recently?
(DESCRIPTION) _____

5B. Where did you purchase that equipment?

(STORE) _____

5C. What was the most important reason you made that purchase at *(STORE IN Q5A)* rather than at another store? (DO NOT READ CATEGORIES) (_____)	Price . . . . Sale . . . . Location/convenience . . . . Merchandise quality . . . . Merchandise selection . . . . Salespeople . . . . Availability of credit . . . . ←Other (SPECIFY)	1 2 3 4 5 6 7 0

5D. How much did you spend on that purchase?
(TO NEAREST DOLLAR) $ _____

Continued

EXHIBIT 12.5

Questionnnaire
#4—Continued

5E. Did you pay cash, use a store charge account, or use another credit card such as a Visa, MasterCard, or American Express?

Paid cash (check) 1
Store charge 2
Other credit card 3

6. I have some specific factors that might influence where you would shop for athletic shoes, sportswear, and sporting equipment. As I read each one, please tell me whether you generally consider that factor to be very important, somewhat important, or not important in choosing a store for this type of merchandise. How about . . .

	Very important	Somewhat important	Not important
The convenience of store locations?	1	2	3
The store's prices?	1	2	3
Special sales?	1	2	3
Whether the store takes credit cards such as Visa, MasterCard, and American Express?	1	2	3
Whether the store has its own charge accounts?	1	2	3
The quality of merchandise carried by the store?	1	2	3
The selection of merchandise?	1	2	3
The availability of your desired brand names?	1	2	3
How often the store is out of stock on the merchandise you want? . . .	1	2	3
The helpfulness of the salespeople?	1	2	3
The speed of service?	1	2	3

7. In total, about how much have you spent in the past twelve months on sporting goods including athletic shoes and sportswear?

(TO NEAREST DOLLAR) $ _____

(IF RESPONDENT SPENT MORE THAN $0)
7A. About how much of that did you spend at Smith's Stores?

(TO NEAREST DOLLAR) $ _____

8. Do you have a Smith's charge account?   Yes . . . . . 1 (ASK Q8A,B)
                                                No . . . . . 2 (GO TO Q9)

(IF YES)
8A. During the past twelve months,   More . . . . 1 (ASK Q8A1)
would you have spent more,   Same 2
about the same, or less at   Less . . . . 3 (ASK Q8A1)
Smith's Stores if you did
not have a charge account?

(IF MORE OR LESS)
8A1. How much do you think you would have spent at Smith's
Stores?
(TO NEAREST DOLLAR) $ _____

8B. A minute ago, you estimated that you spent *(SEE Q7A)* at Smith's
Stores in the past twelve months. About how much of that was
charged to your Smith's account?
(TO NEAREST DOLLAR) $ _____

Now, for classification purposes only . . .

9. What is your age category? Is it   Under 18? 1
                                              18–24? 2
                                              25–34? 3
                                              35–49? 4
                                              50–64? 5
                                              65 and over? 6
                       (DO NOT READ)   Refused 7

10. Which of the following categories best describes your family income
before taxes for 1996? Would it be . . .

                                              Under $10,000? 1
                                              $10,000–$14,999? 2
                                              $15,000–$24,999? 3
                                              $25,000–$49,999? 4
                                              Over $50,000? 5
                       (DO NOT READ)   Refused 6

11. What is your Zip Code?   (NUMBER) _____

12. (DON'T ASK) Sex   Male 1
                                              Female 2

Those are all of our questions. Thanks for your help.

Critical Thinking Skills

For each of the revised questions in Exhibit 12.6, explain why the question was revised, whether or not you find our revision an improvement, and what alternative version you suggest.

ensure that every respondent answers with respect to at least one category or to show the chain how its competitors vary across merchandise categories. These are worthwhile motives, but they can be achieved by simply asking about the respondent's most recent purchase and identifying the type of merchandise bought at that time.

4. Note that the questionnaire screens respondents for purchases at sporting goods stores. The screening criterion should be changed to sporting goods purchases, because this would allow the pickup of purchases from all competing stores, not just sporting goods stores. Then the type of merchandise bought on the most recent purchase should be asked, followed by the questions currently listed as questions 1A to 1D in connection with that purchase. These questions would no longer be part of a branching sequence, because the overall questionnaire screen would ensure that all respondents would answer these questions.

5. Some minor definitional points could be added in a couple of places.

6. A question on respondents' ownership of third-party credit cards that are accepted by the chain should be added.

Questionnaire Revision

Exhibit 12.6 shows a revised questionnaire that reflects these comments.

EXHIBIT 12.6

Questionnaire #4 Revised

Hello, I'm _____ of _____, a marketing and opinion research firm. We are conducting a study with people who have purchased sporting goods, including athletic shoes or sportswear, during the past year.

A. Have you purchased any sporting goods, including athletic shoes or sportswear, during the past year?

B. IF NO: Has anyone else in your household purchased any sporting goods, including athletic shoes or sportswear, during the past year?
IF NO, TERMINATE.

CONTINUE INTERVIEW WITH A PERSON WHO HAS BOUGHT SPORTING GOODS

1. On your most recent purchase of sporting goods, including athletic shoes or sportswear, what merchandise did you buy?
(MERCHANDISE) _____

2. At what store did you make this purchase?
(STORE) _____

3. What was the most important reason you bought that merchandise at *(STORE IN Q1A)* rather than at some other store? (DO NOT READ CATEGORIES)

Price	1
Sale	2
Location/convenience	3
Merchandise quality	4
Merchandise selection	5
Salespeople	6
Availability of credit	7
(_____) ←Other (SPECIFY)	0

4. How much did you spend on that purchase? (TO NEAREST DOLLAR)

$ _____

5. Did you pay cash, use a store charge account, or use another credit card such as a Visa, MasterCard, or American Express?

Paid cash (check)	1
Store charge	2
Other credit card	3

6. I have some specific factors that might influence where you would shop for sporting goods, including athletic shoes or sportswear. As I read each one, please tell me whether you generally consider that factor to be very important, somewhat important, or not important in choosing a store for this type of merchandise. How about . . .

	Very important	Somewhat important	Not important
The convenience of store locations?	1	2	3
The store's prices?	1	2	3
Special sales?	1	2	3
Whether the store takes credit cards such as Visa, MasterCard and American Express?	1	2	3
Whether the store has its own charge accounts?	1	2	3
The quality of merchandise carried by the store?	1	2	3
The selection of merchandise?	1	2	3
The availability of your desired brand names?	1	2	3
How often the store is out of stock on the merchandise you want? . . .	1	2	3
The helpfulness of the salespeople? .	1	2	3
The speed of service?	1	2	3

Continued

EXHIBIT 12.6

Questionnnaire #4 Revised—Continued

7. In total, about how much have you spent in the past twelve months on sporting goods including athletic shoes and sportswear?

(TO NEAREST DOLLAR) $ _____

(IF RESPONDENT SPENT MORE THAN $0)
7A. About how much of that did you spend at Smith's Stores?

(TO NEAREST DOLLAR) $ _____

8. Do you have a Smith's charge account?

Yes . . . . 1 (ASK Q8A,B)
No . . . . 2 (GO TO Q9)

(IF YES)

8A. During the past twelve months, would you have spent more, about the same, or less at Smith's Stores if you did not have a Smith's charge account?

More . . . . 1 (ASK Q8A1)
Same 2
Less . . . . 3 (ASK Q8A1)

(IF MORE OR LESS)
8A1. How much do you think you would have spent at Smith's Stores?

(TO NEAREST DOLLAR) $ _____

8B. A minute ago, you estimated that you spent *(SEE Q7A)* at Smith's Stores in the past twelve months. About how much of that was charged to your Smith's account?

(TO NEAREST DOLLAR) $ _____

9. Which of these other credit cards do you have? (CIRCLE ALL THAT APPLY)

Visa? 1
MasterCard? 2
American Express? 3

Now for classification purposes only . . .

10. What is your age category? Is it . . .

Under 18? 1
18–24? 2
25–34? 3
35–49? 4
50–64? 5
65 and over? 6
(DO NOT READ) Refused 7

11. Which of the following categories best describes your family income before taxes for 1996? Would it be . . .

Under $10,000?	1
$10,000–$14,999?	2
$15,000–$24,999?	3
$25,000–$49,999?	4
Over $50,000?	5
(DO NOT READ) Refused	6

12. What is your home Zip Code?   (NUMBER) _____

13. (DON'T ASK) Sex

Male	1
Female	2

Those are all of our questions. Thanks for your help.

Summary

This chapter illustrated questionnaire design by evaluating four questionnaires. The following points were covered:

1. How can a questionnaire be evaluated?

The first step in evaluating a questionnaire is to consider the research objectives and how the market works. Is the questionnaire consistent with the market context? (Remember, as noted in Chapter 3, the first step in planning a project is to establish this background information.) Is the questionnaire consistent with the research objectives? Will the answers to the questions provide clear guidance for the marketing decisions at issue?

Next, consider the individual questions. Are they clear and easy to understand? Will respondents interpret the questions in the way intended? Will respondents be willing and able to answer the questions?

Now think about the overall questionnaire. Does the questionnaire have a beginning and an end? Does it start with an easy, nonthreatening question? Is the question sequence appropriate? Is the physical format easy to use?

Finally, consider how the questionnaire will be administered. Is the length of the questionnaire appropriate for the method of administration? Are question formats consistent with the method of administration? Are potential problems with data security controlled? Are the instructions for administering the questionnaire and coding the responses clear?

2. How should a questionnaire be revised?

In revising a questionnaire, start with the research objectives and the business situation. If the current questionnaire and research design reflect a proper understanding of the business and fit the research objectives, you simply need to fine-tune the questionnaire to eliminate any technical defects. However, if the questionnaire or the research design reflects flawed assumptions about the business or is poorly suited to the objectives, fundamental revisions are needed and you may have to scrap the existing questionnaire.

In "fine-tuning" the questionnaire (or developing a new questionnaire), follow the principles described in Chapters 10 and 11. If your revised questionnaire satisfies these principles, meets the research objectives, and reflects a proper understanding of the business, you should be successful. Of course, the specific wording of the questions and the specific arrangement of the questionnaire will reflect your own style and will not be exactly the same as what someone else would do.

Remember to keep your focus on the research objectives. If a revised question is better written than the original but isn't as well suited to the research objectives, it isn't a better question. An important issue in this regard is *data continuity*. If the existing question has been used in previous research and there is value to be gained from comparing the new results to the old results, the question should generally be left as is.

 # Discussion Questions

This chapter includes examples of questionnaires. The discussion questions from Chapter 11 apply here.

 # Internet Exercise

This chapter showed a questionnaire used by the Houston Astros baseball team for an "in stadium" fan survey. How, if at all, would you change this questionnaire if it were to be administered via the Internet?

13 Sampling

 OBJECTIVES

LEARNING

After reading this chapter, you should be able to answer the following questions:

1. What are sampling error, nonsampling error, and sample bias?

2. How should a population be defined for sampling purposes?

3. What is a sample frame, and how can frame problems be fixed?

4. What is the difference between probability and nonprobability sampling, and when is each appropriate?

5. How is a probability sample drawn?

6. How should research be executed to maintain sample integrity?

7. What information should be provided in a sampling report?

Think of a supermarket chain in your town. If this company hired you to measure how consumers evaluate its stores relative to the competition, would you try to interview every single person in town? The answer, obviously, is "no." It would cost too much money and take too much time to gather data from everyone in town. Instead, you would rely on a sample of the population.

This situation is typical in market research. In rare situations, usually in business-to-business research, the population of interest is very small and it is feasible to gather data from every member of the population. In most projects, though, the population is large enough that data may be gathered from a sample rather than the population.

Sampling and Nonsampling Errors

It is obviously desirable for the data from a sample to reflect the population of interest accurately. For example, if a survey is done for a grocery chain and the data show that 36 percent of the respondents rate the chain's checkout service as the best in town, this 36 percent figure should be an accurate reflection of feelings among the population at large. There are three reasons why it might not:

- Nonsampling error
- Sampling error, also known as sampling variance
- Sample bias

Nonsampling error consists of all error sources unrelated to the sampling of respondents. These include (1) errors that occur because people give incorrect answers, (2) errors that occur because of failures or fluctuations in physical measurement instruments, and (3) errors that occur in coding or data entry. These sources of nonsampling error are controlled, to the extent possible, by using good measurement principles and by exercising good control over coding, data entry, and data analysis.

Sampling error refers to the fact that samples do not always reflect a population's true characteristics, even if the samples are drawn using fair procedures. For example, if a coin is flipped ten times, then ten more times, then ten more times, and so on, it will not always come up "heads" five times out of ten. The percentage of "heads" in any given sample will be affected by chance variation. In the same way, if 100 people are asked which grocery chain has the best service in town, the percentage who name any particular chain will be affected by chance variation in the composition of the sample.

The level of sampling error is controlled by sample size. As a sample gets larger and larger, the distribution of possible sample outcomes becomes tighter and tighter around that of the true population figure. To put it another way, a larger sample has less chance of producing results that are uncharacteristic of the population as a whole.

Sample bias refers to the possibility that members of a sample differ from the larger population in some systematic fashion. For example, if opinions about a supermarket chain are measured by questioning shoppers at that chain's stores, the results may not reflect opinions among people at large. A sample of the store's customers is likely to produce a biased sample of people at large, at least as far as opinions about the store are concerned.

Unlike sampling error, sample bias is *not* controlled by sample size. Increasing the sample size does nothing to remove systematic biases; for example, whether 50 or 500 store customers are questioned, they still will not be a representative sample of people at large. Rather, sample bias is controlled by defining the population of interest before drawing the sample, selecting a sample that represents the entire population fairly, and obtaining data from as much of the selected sample as possible.

People who are unsophisticated about sampling usually think that sample size is the most important consideration. In presenting research results, you'll be asked about sample size more often than you'll be asked about sampling procedures. This focus on sample size probably occurs because size is the most visible aspect of the sample. Whatever the reason, the focus on sample size is misplaced. Sample *bias* is a far more serious issue than sample *size*. If the right information is not gathered from the right people, it does not really matter how much information has been gathered or how many people it has been gathered from.

This chapter discusses how to create unbiased samples. The sampling process is broken into a series of steps, which are shown in Marketing Research Tools 13.1, and a description of what to do at each step is given.

Critical Thinking Skills

Consider a grocery store chain in your town that uses a mail survey to measure consumers' evaluations of various stores. What sample bias might arise in this survey?

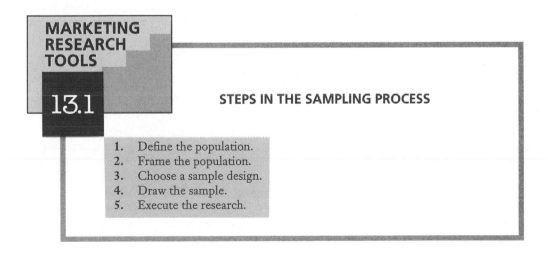

MARKETING RESEARCH TOOLS

13.1

STEPS IN THE SAMPLING PROCESS

1. Define the population.
2. Frame the population.
3. Choose a sample design.
4. Draw the sample.
5. Execute the research.

Defining the Population

The first step in the sampling process is defining the population. A **sample** is, by definition, a subset of a larger population. The **population,** or **universe,** is the entire set of elements being studied. For example, in our grocery store example, the desired population would probably consist of people who live in areas where the chain has stores and who shop for groceries.

Before selecting the sample, it is necessary to have a clear idea of the population to be studied. Failure to think carefully about the needed population often leads to the use of samples that are convenient but do not match what is needed. Case Study 13.1 illustrates this point.

Two questions must be answered in defining a population for sampling purposes:

- What are the population units?
- What are the population boundaries?

Defining Population Units

The first step in defining a population is defining the population units. Is the population made up of individuals, households, companies, factories, transactions, sales

CASE STUDY 13.1

One of the most common sampling errors in marketing research is using information from existing customers to determine how sales to other people might be increased. Customers are used because they are easy to locate. However, people who *do* buy the product cannot really give you the viewpoint of people who *don't* buy the product.

We recently saw a clear example of this problem. A chain of nursing homes measured its public image by interviewing every person who was responsible for registering a patient at one of the chain's nursing homes. These people were questioned regarding how they had heard of the home and what they thought about it. The results were tabulated every month and distributed in an "Image Tracking Report." This report showed the chain's image to be stable during a six-month period during which there was heavy media coverage about poor care in the homes and admissions to the homes dropped sharply.

The problem, of course, is that the relevant population for public image research is all *potential* customers, but the population being studied was all *actual* customers. Since people who heard the bad news stayed away from these nursing homes, the research could not determine the company's image problems.

Information drawn from the wrong population is not much help.

Source: DOONESBURY © G. B. Trudeau. Reprinted with permission of Universal Press Syndicate. All rights reserved.

dollars, or what? Exhibit 13.1 (see page 336) presents one example: Is the appropriate population unit defined by number of customers or sales dollars?

The definition of population units for any given research project depends on what product or service is being studied, what market segments are of interest, and what phenomena are of interest. For example, someone doing a project on consumers' long-distance telephone usage would probably study households, because long-distance service is a household-level purchase. For clothing or cosmetics, individuals rather than households would probably be studied, because these products are bought at the individual level.

Many products have complex purchase patterns that complicate population definition. Some cereals and bath soaps, for example, may be used by every member of a household, and others are used by only one. In industrial research, some companies use centralized buying, and others allow individual departments or even individual employees to make purchase decisions. The only general advice that can be given in such situations is that the definition of the population should match the purchase process as much as possible.

It is also important to recognize that the data source need not be the same as the population member. Individuals may speak on behalf of households, companies, and/or sales dollars. This use of proxy reporters does not change the definition of the population. Case Study 13.2 (see page 337) and Exhibit 13.1 illustrate this point.

Setting Population Boundaries

Once the population units have been defined, the next step is setting the boundaries of the population. **Population boundaries** are the conditions that separate those who are of interest to a research project from those who are not. For example,

EXHIBIT 13.1

What Is the
Population
Unit?

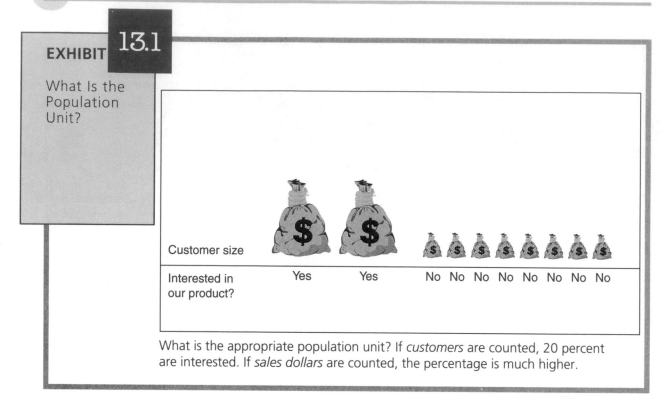

Customer size										
Interested in our product?	Yes	Yes		No	No	No	No	No	No	No	No

What is the appropriate population unit? If *customers* are counted, 20 percent are interested. If *sales dollars* are counted, the percentage is much higher.

Critical Thinking Skills

Define the population units and population boundaries for a *consumer* survey on long-distance telephone usage. Then define the population units and population boundaries for a *business* survey on long-distance telephone usage. In each project, from whom will you actually get information?

common boundary conditions in marketing research include (1) whether a person has bought the product in question within some qualifying time frame, (2) whether that person intends to buy within some time frame, (3) whether that person is in the geographic market, and (4) whether that person is an adult.

Four broad criteria should guide the setting of population boundaries. The first criterion is that a boundary should clearly separate subjects who are of interest from those who are not. This often requires making difficult judgments. For example, if a population is intended to consist of firms in some particular line of business, a decision must be made as to whether firms with only a small fraction of their business in the specified line should or should not be included.

The second criterion is that population boundaries must be stated in operational terms so that data collectors can tell who should be measured and who should not. "Adults in the Chicago area" is not an operational definition, because it doesn't tell interviewers whether they should gather data from eighteen-year-old women in Gary, Indiana. "Beer drinkers" is not an operational definition, because it doesn't tell interviewers whether they should interview someone who drank one beer, once in his life, seven years ago. Operational definitions of population boundaries should take forms such as "people who are at least eighteen years

CASE STUDY 13.2

When a company drills an oil or gas well, it is common practice to identify the companies that operate other wells near the planned drilling site. A drilling engineer contacts the operators of those wells and requests information on the geological structures and problems encountered during the earlier drillings. It is industry practice to provide this information on request.

An entrepreneur saw an opportunity to make this process more efficient by establishing a computerized library of drilling records. This way, when a company needed drilling information for wells near some site, the drilling engineer could make one call and get all the needed information—for a fee, of course.

To test industry response to the idea, the entrepreneur conducted a mail survey of all companies that had drilling operations within the planned market area. This population contained about seventy-five companies. The entrepreneur sent a questionnaire to the manager of drilling operations at each company and to one drilling engineer at each company. The overall response rate to the survey was 62 percent, which is good for this kind of mail survey. Of the people who responded, 46 percent said that their companies would be interested in subscribing to the planned service.

The overall sampling procedure in this research seems fine. It is difficult to quarrel with a sample that uses every possible customer for a new service. However, it is not really possible to interpret the finding that "of the people who responded, 46 percent said that their companies would be interested in subscribing to the planned service." This is partly because of measurement issues—the fact that 46 percent of respondents expressed interest doesn't mean that 46 percent will buy—but also because of issues related to the definition of population units.

If the desired population consisted of individual respondents, the 46 percent figure would be meaningful. However, the customers for this service will be *companies*, not individuals, and the data from this survey must be interpreted in some way to express interest at the company level. For example, a company might be counted as being interested only if the drilling engineer and drilling manager both express interest, on the theory that a purchase will require interest from both.

There are other issues as well. The companies in this industry vary enormously in their levels of drilling activity, with 7 out of the 75 companies accounting for more than 60 percent of the wells and hence more than 60 percent of the potential revenues. The 46 percent figure is thus rather misleading: if the interested companies include the 7 key customers, the service looks promising, regardless of the other companies' opinions. If the interested companies do not include those 7 customers, the service is probably doomed. The data must be weighted to reflect each company's revenue potential.

This example shows a common sampling problem in market research. The desired unit of study is sales dollars, or potential sales dollars. However, dollars (and companies) cannot speak. Only people speak, so the data are gathered from people. It is important to remember, though, that these people speak on behalf of the true units of interest, and the results must be interpreted accordingly.

old and have their principal place of residence within the 312 area code" or "people who have drunk beer at least once during the past three months."

In addition to being operational, it is helpful if population boundaries are easy to implement. Household income is an example of a variable that might be useful as a population boundary in consumer research but is difficult to implement. Income measures do not receive good response, especially at the beginning of a questionnaire, which is where they are needed if a population is being screened on income. Despite the possible usefulness of income as a boundary variable, it is better to use other variables if at all possible.

Finally, population boundaries may be set with an eye toward the cost-effectiveness of the research. For example, a telephone survey to measure opinions about a supermarket might be limited to certain telephone exchanges that are expected to account for the large majority of customers, although it is recognized that some customers who come from outside the area will be missed by this definition.

Framing the Population

Author Tips

The cost effectiveness criterion in population definition should be applied with caution. We have seen researchers define the population too narrowly in an effort to make their research more efficient and consequently miss an opportunity to discover interesting new markets. When in doubt, it is better to draw population boundaries too broadly than too narrowly.

After defining the population, a frame of the population must be obtained before sampling can begin. A **frame** is a list or system that identifies every member of the population so that a sample can be drawn without the necessity of physically contacting every member of the population.

Lists are generally the preferred type of frame. With a printed directory or a computerized file that identifies all of the population's members, it is simple to draw the sample right from the list. However, lists are not always available. In such a situation, some sort of counting system must be used to keep track of population members and identify the selections; for example, every fourth shopper, the third house on every other block, and so on.

The following discussion of sampling frames begins with a discussion of the use of lists and then continues with a discussion of other types of frames.

Obtaining a List

The first and most difficult step in using a list for sampling purposes is obtaining it. Existing lists should be used whenever possible because they are cheaper than custom-made lists. For example, if you are asked to survey the local population to measure opinions about a local supermarket chain, one way of getting a list of the population would be to send someone from door to door to record the address of every occupied housing unit. A second way would be to use a published city directory. Obviously, it is much easier and cheaper to use the directory.

The following types of lists may be obtained from the following sources:

- *A national list of the general population.* Although marketers as well as market researchers would love to have one, there is no list of the entire population or all the households in the United States. There is, however, a national list of listed telephone numbers. Companies such as Survey Sampling, Inc., sell samples drawn from this list for a reasonable fee.

- *National lists of population subgroups.* There are no national lists of men, women, young people, old people, African Americans, whites, high-income people, low-income people, and so on. There are mailing lists that provide this sort of information, but although mailing lists are useful to direct marketing organizations, they are usually worthless in drawing a good sample. Mailing lists are derived primarily from membership and subscription lists and thus do not provide good samples of broader groups.

- *Local lists of the general population.* Lists of names (arranged alphabetically) and addresses (arranged alphabetically by street and by numbers within streets) are available in city directories published by R. L. Polk for most cities in the range of 50,000 to 800,000 people. These directories are usually available for free use at the local public library or chamber of commerce. Since the directories are revised every two or three years, the street address directory is reasonably accurate, missing only some new construction. The alphabetical list, however, is subject to many more errors over time since many families move. For this reason, it is seldom used for sampling.

  Local telephone directories also provide lists of households. These directories must be used with caution: the nonlisted rate in most large American cities exceeds 35 percent, though it is much lower in smaller towns.

- *Lists of organization members.* Lists of an organization's members are usually available from the organization itself. The question is whether the organization's listed members constitute a good representation of the desired population. For example, a list of church members will not include everyone who attends services at the church and certainly will not include *potential* members. A list of American Marketing Association members will not include every person who works in marketing.

- *Local lists of businesses.* The telephone directory (White Pages) provides a list of local businesses among its other listings. If a list of specific types of businesses is desired, a good place to look is the Yellow Pages, although some businesses are not listed. If the local chamber of commerce has a good research operation, it may be able to provide better lists of businesses in certain categories.

- *National or regional lists of businesses.* Lists of business establishments with addresses and telephone numbers, grouped by SIC code, are available from Dun & Bradstreet. These lists are reasonably current with new establishments but are slower to drop establishments that have gone out of business.

Although all lists are subject to error, the quality of existing lists is usually as good as or better than lists that could be obtained by starting from scratch. Also, of course, the use of existing lists is cheaper.

Problems with Lists

Once a list is obtained, there are problems that must be dealt with. Ideally, a list will contain every member of the population once and only once; that is, there will be a one-to-one correspondence between the list and the population. Few lists meet this standard, and sampling procedures must compensate for the list's deficiencies.

There are four ways in which list and population elements can deviate from one-to-one correspondence. First, there may be population members that are not listed. This is called **omission,** because the elements have been omitted from the list. Second, there can be listings that aren't in the population. This is called **ineligibility,** because the listed elements are not members of the population and therefore are ineligible for inclusion in the sample. Third, there can be two or more listings corresponding to a given population member. This is called **duplication,** because the population member is duplicated in the list. Fourth, there can be two or more population members corresponding to a given listing. This is called **clustering,** because the list member corresponds to a cluster of population elements.

These four list problems and their effects can be illustrated by thinking about the telephone directory as a list of adults, as follows.

- First, the telephone book *omits* people who have moved to town recently, have unlisted telephone numbers, or do not have a telephone. As a result, these people will be omitted from any sample drawn from the telephone book. This will produce a sample that underrepresents groups such as new residents, unmarried women, schoolteachers, wealthy people with unlisted phones, and poor people with no phones.

- Second, many telephone directory listings are for businesses, and some are for children. These listings are *ineligible* for a sample of adults. If adjustments are not made for these ineligibles, a sample from the telephone book will produce fewer eligible selections than desired.

- Third, some people such as doctors and lawyers may have two listings, without any clear indication that one is an office listing and therefore ineligible. If something is not done about these *duplications*, the sample will contain a disproportionately large number of professionals. To see why this is true, consider the fact that selections are drawn from the list, not directly from the population. If professionals make up 5 percent of the population but 10 percent of the list, a random sample from the list will be made up of 10 percent professionals.

- Fourth, most households have only one telephone listing, regardless of how many adults live in the household. Adults who live in two-adult households will thus have only half the chance of being selected that single adults will have. This is because the clustered population members (such as married couples) split one listing and therefore have only one chance of selection, whereas the single adult is always selected. To put this another way, if single adults make up 5 percent of the population but 10 percent of the telephone listings, 10 percent of the sample will be made up of single adults. If something is not done about clustering, a sample from the telephone book will overrepresent single adults, many of whom are relatively young or relatively old. Many marketing variables will be affected by this bias.

Fortunately, even though list problems are unavoidable in most studies, there are methods for dealing with them. Marketing Research Tools 13.2 summarizes these methods, which are subsequently discussed.

MARKETING RESEARCH TOOLS

13.2

POTENTIAL PROBLEMS WITH SAMPLING FRAMES

Problem	Possible Solutions
Omissions (population elements omitted from the list)	Ignore omissions. Augment the list. Create a new list.
Ineligibles (list elements that are not in the population)	Drop ineligibles and adjust the sample size.
Duplications (multiple listings for population elements)	Cross-check the list. Subsample duplicates. Weight the data.
Clustering (multiple population elements per listing)	Take the whole cluster. Subsample within clusters. Weight the data.

Coping with Omissions

Omission is simultaneously the easiest and most difficult list problem to deal with. It is easiest because the major way of coping with omissions is to ignore them and hope that the resulting bias is not serious. This is an easy, if unsatisfactory, way of coping. Omission is the most difficult list problem because if you do decide to tackle the problem, you may have to locate omitted elements and list them. This is likely to be costly and time consuming.

When to Worry About Omissions

As a general rule, a list may be used if it contains more than 90 percent of the population and does not omit important subgroups. If the list contains 50 to 90 percent of the population and/or omits important subgroups it may be used but should be supplemented. If the list contains less than 50 percent of the population, it should generally not be used, because it will be cheaper and more accurate to develop a new list than to fix the available list.

Of course, an evaluation of list coverage requires a reliable outside estimate of the size of the population. Estimates of this type are often made on the basis of U.S. Census reports. For example, a current list of retail drugstores contains about 50,000 listings. The 1992 *Census of Businesses* also reports that there are about 50,000 drugstores. Thus, this list seems to be a good one to use for sampling drugstores.

Critical Thinking Skills

Estimate the number of household listings in your local telephone book and compare this with an estimate of the town's population. After making any necessary adjustments, what is your best estimate of the percentage of households that is listed?

In situations where a list needs to be augmented, there are two procedures that may provide satisfactory results. These are (1) random digit dialing (RDD) for telephone surveys and (2) screening of selected areas to generate complete lists.

Random Digit Dialing

Few consumer telephone surveys these days use telephone directories because of the large percentage of unlisted numbers, which accounts for more than half of all residential numbers in cities such as New York, Chicago, and Washington D.C. Instead, researchers use **random digit dialing (RDD)** to reach unlisted as well as listed numbers. Random digit dialing is the dialing of random numbers in working telephone exchanges so that unlisted numbers can be included.

Researchers who use RDD for the first time often ask "Won't people with unlisted numbers be upset about the call and refuse to participate?" Actually, cooperation rates for people with unlisted numbers are almost as high as those for people with listed numbers. Most people do not get unlisted numbers to avoid research interviews, and most do not mind if they are called for this purpose. Some respondents with unlisted telephone numbers will ask the interviewer how she or he got the number, so interviewers should be given a description of the sampling procedure to read to those who ask, but this is good practice in any survey.

The problem with random digit dialing is that, although it reaches unlisted numbers, it can be costly because it also reaches a large number of business and nonworking numbers. For example, in an early study, Gerald Glasser and Gale Metzger (1972) estimated that if one starts with a working telephone exchange and selects the last four numbers purely at random, only about one in five of the selected numbers will yield a working household number.

Several methods are used to reduce the fraction of unusable numbers obtained in random digit dialing. The method most widely used in marketing research is to purchase lists of household numbers from organizations such as Survey Sampling, Inc. These companies use a computer tape of all listed telephone numbers in the United States, which are sorted into numeric sequence, making it obvious where large batches of numbers are not in use. Thus, in a particular telephone exchange, only numbers ranging from 0000 to 2700 may be in use, with other numbers reserved for future expansion. Eliminating these higher numbers from the sample eliminates most nonworking numbers. Survey Sampling has also compiled a list of business telephone numbers from the Yellow Pages and can eliminate known business numbers from the list of household telephone numbers by matching the two lists. Given these screening procedures, about two-thirds of all random numbers reached are working household numbers.

It also is possible to avoid nonworking numbers with a procedure developed by Joesph Waksberg and Warren Mitofsky (Waksberg, 1978). The procedure starts with a screening call to a number selected at random from a working telephone exchange (a computer file of current working exchanges is available from AT&T). If this first number is a working number, additional calls are made within the bank of 100 numbers until a prespecified number of households is reached. For example, suppose the number dialed is (217) 555-1234 and is a working household number. Additional calls would be made at random to the bank of numbers between (217) 555-1200 and 1299. If the initial number is not a working number, no additional numbers would be used from that series. The major saving resulting from this procedure is that series with *no* working numbers are quickly eliminated. Waksberg-Mitofsky sampling yields about 50 percent working household numbers.

Somewhat looser RDD methods combine the use of directories with random digit dialing. Two such methods are (1) selecting a sample of numbers from the printed telephone directory and adding one to the last digit of each selected number, so that 555-1234 becomes 555-1235; and (2) selecting a sample of numbers from the directory and replacing the last two digits of each selected number with a two-digit random number. These methods, like Waksberg-Mitofsky sampling, yield about 50 percent working household numbers. In theory, the "adding one" and "replacing two" sampling methods are biased because they miss new batches of numbers added since the directory was printed and favor banks of numbers that have a higher percentage of numbers listed in the directory. In practice, though, the biases are not serious in most market research studies.

Screening Selected Areas

If a list is inadequate and the use of telephone methods is not feasible, it is always possible to send someone to selected areas to search for the units of the desired population. For example, if the population of interest is establishments that sell soft drinks, there is probably no complete list. It would, however, be possible to send a lister into a geographically defined area to search for such establishments. Since such a search is expensive, it should be done only in selected areas, which are called "clusters" for sampling purposes. (Cluster sampling is discussed in Chapter 14.)

Coping with Ineligibles

The second problem with lists is ineligibles. Coping with ineligibles is straightforward: they should not be selected. Since they are not in the population, they should not be in the sample.

There are two ways of keeping ineligibles out of a sample. First, the entire list can be screened for eligibility before sampling, with all ineligible listings being deleted. This is often not practical because the eligibility factor is not visible in the list; for example, a telephone book will not show whether people fall into some targeted age group. The other approach is to screen selected elements for eligibility *after* sampling and drop ineligibles at that time. This is the usual method employed.

Dropping ineligibles means just that—dropping them, not replacing them. Inexperienced researchers sometimes think that an ineligible should be replaced by taking the next name on the list, but this procedure gives an extra chance of selection to population members who are listed after ineligibles and may cause sample bias. The proper method is simply to adjust the sample size for shrinkage due to ineligibility and drop ineligible listings when encountered.

Adjusting the sample size is done as follows: if *e* percent of the list is eligible, the adjusted sample size is n/e, where n is the desired sample size. For example, if a sample of 300 freshmen at a given university is desired and only 20 percent of those listed in the college directory are freshmen, the adjusted sample size to be chosen from the directory is $300 \div .20 = 1,500$. A sample of 1,500 names from this directory should yield 300 freshmen.

Estimates of eligibility rates can be obtained either from prior experience or by studying a small pilot sample. Since these estimates may not be exactly accurate, it is a good idea to estimate eligibility on the low side so you are sure to get a large enough sample. Say, for example, that you think that freshmen will account for 20 percent of the listings drawn from a college directory, but that the eligibility rate for any given sample could be anywhere from 15 to 25 percent. The 15 percent figure should be used. In other words, if you want 300 eligibles, an initial sample of $300 \div .15 = 2,000$ should be drawn. Then, if this sample yields 400 eligibles (an eligibility rate of 20 percent), you can randomly choose 300 for retention or 100 for deletion. The result will still be a random sample: a random sample plus a random sample equals a random sample, and a random sample minus a random sample equals a random sample.

When eligibility is to be determined through screening interviews, both the low and high eligibility estimates should be used in planning sample size. In our example, the lowest eligibility estimate, 15 percent, means that a sample size as large as 2,000 may be needed to produce 300 eligibles. The highest estimate, 25 percent, means that a sample size as small as 1,200 may be needed ($300 \div .25 = 1,200$). To protect yourself in this situation, draw a sample of 2,000 but don't release the entire sample for screening. Instead, draw a random subsample of 1,200 from the 2,000; release this subsample and hold the other 800 selections for use if needed. If the first 1,200 selections yield 240 interviews (an eligibility rate of 20 percent), draw 300 ($60 \div .20 = 300$) of the holdout selections. This procedure gives you as many selections as you need without producing expensive and unnecessary data.

A common error is to draw the larger sample (2,000 in our example), release the entire sample for data collection, and simply stop the research when the desired number of eligibles is obtained. This procedure is incorrect, because the first observations obtained will be the observations that are easiest to get; for example, in a survey, these observations will tend to be of housewives and retired people. Any sample released for data collection should be worked completely to avoid bias in favor of the easy observations.

Incidentally, when adjusting the sample size to allow for ineligibles, it is appropriate to adjust for the expected cooperation rate. The adjusted sample size is *n/ec*, where *n* is the desired sample size, *e* is the eligibility rate, and *c* is the expected cooperation rate. If 300 usable observations are desired and 20 percent of the selections are expected to be eligible and 60 percent to cooperate, an initial sample size of $300 \div [.20 \times .60] = 2,500$ is needed.

Critical Thinking Skills

Colgate-Palmolive is doing a study of consumer potential for a lemon-scented antibacterial dishwashing liquid detergent. From previous research, it knows that about 70 percent of all households currently use a dishwashing detergent and would be eligible for the study. It expects a cooperation rate of about 60 percent. What sample size should it start with if it hopes to get a completed sample of 1,000 interviews?

Coping with Duplications

The third problem with lists is duplications. If a sample is selected from a list that contains duplications of some elements, but none of the duplicated elements is selected more than once, has the duplication caused any problems? The answer is "yes."

The basic problem with duplication is that it gives *groups* of population members disproportionate chances for selection into the sample. Even if individual duplicated elements are not chosen more than once, their *group* is chosen at a higher rate. The group of population members who appear twice on the list is overrepresented by a factor of two compared with the group of members who appear once; the group of population members who appear three times on the list is overrepresented by a factor of three; and so on. This overrepresentation will cause sample bias if the duplicated elements are different from the nonduplicated elements on some variable of interest to the research.

An example will help to illustrate the problem with duplicated elements. Suppose a study of potential customers for a new catalog is being done. There is no single list of potential users, but it is decided that a combination of customer lists from five other catalogs would make an acceptable frame. A problem arises because the same person may be on more than one list, and interest in the new catalog is likely to differ between people who are on all five customer lists and people who are on only one.

There are three ways of correcting for duplicate listings. The "brute strength" method is to cross check the list, identify duplicates, and remove them. This can easily be done if the list is computerized. For example, if the five lists of catalog buyers are contained in computer files, one consolidated list that excludes duplicates can be constructed.

A second method is to draw the sample and check only the selected elements to determine how many times they are duplicated in the total population list. Then, to restore equal probabilities of selection, sample members that are listed k times would be retained at the rate of $1/k$; that is, members that appear twice in the list would be retained at the rate of one-half; members that appear three times at the rate of one-third; and so on. This method is appropriate for noncomputerized lists. It will cause some shrinkage in the sample size, which can be handled in the same way as shrinkage for eligibility.

The third method, which is usable in surveys, is to ask selected population members how many times they appear in the list. Under this method, all of the data gathered are retained, because it would be wasteful to discard completed interviews, but observations are weighted by the inverse of their number of times in the list. That is, sample members who say they are listed k times are weighted by $1/k$.

This last method obviously requires that sample members know how many times they are listed. It should be used only when there is good reason to believe that this assumption is true and when checking the list is difficult or impossible.

Author Tips

In cross-checking a list, the same household might be represented by people with different first names, and the same person might be represented with variations in the name or address. If you look at the "junk mail" that comes to your home, you'll probably see these types of variations. Because of these variations, computerized cross-checking usually doesn't remove all of the duplications in a list, but it should reduce them to a level at which they cause negligible sample bias.

Coping with Clustering

The final problem with lists is clustering. Clustering is similar to duplication in that it involves unfair representation of some group of population members rather than complete exclusion or inclusion. The difference is that clustered elements are underrepresented in the sample, and duplicated elements are overrepresented.

Here is an example of clustering. A town has 100,000 adults, 50,000 married and 50,000 single. The 50,000 married adults form 25,000 households, each with one telephone number. The 50,000 single adults form 50,000 households, each with one telephone number. A sample of 300 numbers for a telephone survey will produce 100 "married" numbers and 200 "single" numbers (because the single people account for two-thirds of the telephone numbers). If one adult at each number is interviewed, the sample will include 100 married adults and 200 single adults. This is a fair sample of households but not of individuals. Married people account for one-half of the adults in town, but, because they are clustered on the list, they account for only one-third of the adults in the sample.

There are three basic ways of coping with clustering:

- First, data can be gathered from all population elements in the selected clusters. For example, in our married/single example, data could be gathered from both adults at each "married" number, which would produce data from 200 married people and 200 single people. Some adjustment to the initial sample size would be needed if the data collection budget allows only 300 observations.

    This method provides a fair chance of selection for every member of the population. Unfortunately, as the married/single example shows, it also produces a sample that contains related cluster members. Of 400 population members in that sample, 200 are related to each other. Because of this problem, taking entire clusters is a good idea only when clusters are relatively small and relatively few in number.

- Second, population members within clusters can be sampled at some fixed rate. The usual rate for sampling individuals within households is one-half. In the married/single example, only half of the "single" households would be retained (the others would be dropped), and data would be gathered from one randomly chosen person in each of the "married" households. This would produce a sample size of 100 people from the 100 "married" households and 100 people from the 200 "single" households. A sample size adjustment would be needed to get 300 interviews. This approach works well when clusters are common but small, as in households.

- Third, it is possible to compensate for clustering by randomly selecting one population member from each cluster and weighting that observation by the size of the cluster. This is the best approach when clusters vary widely in size, as in business populations.

Author Tips

Sampling within households is the most common way of coping with clustering in telephone surveys where individual consumers are of interest. A handy way of selecting someone within a household is by asking for the person whose birthday occured most recently. This procedure will create a sample of individuals that is random for all practical purposes.

Framing a Population Without a List

In some marketing research projects, sampling must be done without a list of the population. For example, if an intercept survey is being done to profile the visitors to a shopping mall, there will not be a list of visitors. Sampling without lists is done from "counting frames," as follows:

1. The size of the population is estimated.
2. A sample of numbers between 1 and n, where n is the population size, is selected.

3. The population is counted, and data are gathered from the appropriately numbered members.

For example, in a sample of visitors to a shopping mall, if 10,000 shoppers are expected to enter the mall during the interviewing period and 500 are to be selected, 500 numbers between 1 and 10,000 can be randomly selected. Alternately, every twentieth number after some random start (10,000 ÷ 500 = 20) can be taken. Shoppers will then be counted as they enter the center, and the shoppers with appropriate numbers can be approached.

Counting frames are subject to the same problems as lists: omission, ineligibility, duplication, and clustering. Omission results from underestimating the population size (or the sizes of population subgroups). For example, if the number of visitors to a shopping mall is estimated at 10,000 and this estimate is too small, all shoppers beyond the ten thousandth have no chance of selection because they don't appear in the sampling frame.

Ineligibility results from some of the counted elements not meeting population criteria. For example, counting the visitors to a mall is easiest if every visitor is counted, but some of the visitors might not fit the requirements that have been set for the population (regarding age, gender, product usage, or other factors). Ineligibility also results from overestimating the size of the population (or of population subgroups). A sample may be smaller than expected because only 9,412 shoppers visited the mall during the interviewing period, even though 10,000 were expected. In effect, the numbers 9,413 through 10,000 were ineligible elements in your sampling frame.

Duplication and clustering usually result from a mismatch between the counting units and population units. Say, for example, that a sample of *people* who shop at some mall is desired but the implicit counting unit is visits to the mall. Some people will visit the mall more than others, and the extra visits will constitute duplications in the counting frame (Nowell and Stanley, 1991; Sudman, 1980).

In general, the available solutions for problems in counting frames are more limited than the solutions for problems in lists. Omission is solved by simply estimating population size on the high side. Ineligibility is solved by screening for ineligibles. Duplication and clustering are usually solved by weighting data after they are gathered, because the absence of list documentation makes it impossible to clean or check the sampling frame prior to data collection.

Designing the Sampling Procedure

Once the population of interest to a research project has been defined and the population has been framed in some fashion, the next decision is what type of sampling design to use.

There are two general types of sampling designs: probability samples and nonprobability samples. **Probability samples,** also called **random samples,** use some random process to select population elements for the sample and give every population element a known, nonzero chance of selection. **Nonprobability samples** do not use a random process; instead, elements are selected by judgment or convenience.

The two types of samples rely on different mechanisms to derive samples that are representative of the population. Probability samples rely on chance. The idea is that if selections are made purely by chance, a large sample will naturally contain a representative cross section of the population. Nonprobability samples, in contrast, rely on judgment or on nothing. The idea is that samples can be judgmentally controlled to produce a representative cross section of the population—or that a representative cross section is not actually needed for the research purposes at hand.

Types of Probability Sampling

There are three broad types of probability samples. In **simple random sampling (SRS)** (including **systematic sampling**), population members are selected directly from the sampling frame. This type of sample gives an equal probability of selection to all population members that appear in the frame. Simple *r*andom *s*amples will be referred to as "srs," and samples that give *e*qual *p*robabilities of *s*election for *e*very (population) *m*ember will be referred to as "epsem" samples.

In **stratified sampling,** the population is separated into subgroups, called strata, and separate "srs" are drawn for each subgroup. For example, in drawing a sample of students from a university, graduate and undergraduate students might be separated and each group sampled separately. A stratified sample can be "epsem" if desired, but the usual reason for stratified sampling is to sample different groups at different rates.

In **cluster sampling,** the population is separated into subgroups called "clusters," and a sample of clusters is drawn. It is also common to subsample within selected clusters. For example, in drawing a sample of students from a university, we could randomly select classes, then students within classes. Cluster samples are usually designed as "epsem" samples; the purpose of cluster sampling is not to sample the subgroups at different rates but simply to draw the sample in clusters for reasons of convenience or cost.

Simple random sampling is the basic version of probability sampling. Stratified sampling and cluster sampling are special types of sampling that can improve the cost-effectiveness of research under certain conditions. This issue is discussed in Chapter 14.

Types of Nonprobability Sampling

Nonprobability sampling can assume many forms. One form is **judgment sampling,** in which researchers control sampling down to the element level and actively use judgment regarding the representativeness of elements. An example of judgment sampling is test market selection, in which individual cities are chosen to be representative of many others. The logic of judgment sampling is that expert judgment and past experience can ensure a representative sample.

Another form of nonprobability sampling is **convenience sampling,** in which a researcher studies whichever population members are easily available. You have probably been part of a convenience sample when you participated in a research project for class credit. This type of sampling includes **volunteer samples** and catch-as-catch-can samples obtained at places such as shopping malls. The usual logic behind convenience samples is that they produce a sample that is "good enough" for research purposes. For example, a researcher might argue that scent preferences are pretty similar among people. Therefore, a convenience sample of mall shoppers is just as good as any other sample for testing the scents of different furniture polishes.

Quota sampling is another form of nonprobability sampling. In quota sampling, data gatherers are given quotas for the number of observations to be gathered in various population groups (e.g., men 18 to 34 years of age, men 35 to 64, men 65 plus, women 18 to 34, women 35 to 64, women 65 plus) and are left on their own to fill these quotas. The general selection mechanism may be specified—for example, an interviewer might be told to call people who are listed on certain pages of the telephone book—but the ultimate composition of the sample is governed by quotas rather than probabilities.

When Should Probability and Nonprobability Samples Be Used?

In general, probability samples are preferable to nonprobability samples. Probability samples allow you to use probability-based statistical procedures, such as confidence intervals and hypothesis tests, in drawing inferences about the population from which the sample was drawn (these procedures are discussed in Chapters 16 to 19). Also, nonprobability samples are subject to possible biases that don't affect probability samples. These possible biases include the following:

- The respondents who are easy to get or who volunteer for research may not be typical of the broader population.

- People may use a judgment sample to promote their own agendas. For example, we recently encountered a situation in which a software company was planning research to determine why sales in certain markets were down. The marketing executive who was in charge of the research "knew" that the problem was poor performance by the technical service department, rather than poor marketing, and he wanted certain customers selected to "prove" that service was a problem.

- Nonprobability samples tend to be biased toward well-known members of the population. For example, if you were asked to choose ten representative colleges as locations for research on students' reactions to a new product, which ten would you choose? If you are like most people, your selections will overrepresent familiar names, such as major state schools.

- Nonprobability samples also tend to be biased against unusual population members. For example, in choosing representative colleges, most people will exclude religious seminaries, because these colleges are perceived as "unrepresentative." The effect of these exclusions is to underestimate the true variability in a population.

Despite these possible biases, there are situations in which nonprobability samples are adequate or even preferable to probability samples. These situations are as follows:

- *When the sample is very small.* The statistical law of large numbers suggests that sample sizes of twenty or more should allow reasonable confidence that

Critical Thinking Skills

A university wants to learn about the problems its freshmen experience in making the transition to college, so it can design and prioritize programs to keep students in school. The university plans to gather this information from freshmen who sign up for interviews in exchange for extra credit in an Introduction to Psychology class. Is this sample acceptable for the research purposes? If not, what problems do you see?

probability samples are representative of the population. However, smaller samples are on shaky ground. For example, consider the situation in which two representative cities are to be selected for test-marketing a new product. Probability sampling cannot be relied upon for a representative sample of size two. In this situation, the cities should be selected judgmentally.

- *When the population is homogeneous on the variable being studied.* For example, there is not likely to be much variance across groups of people in preference for cake mixes. A convenience sample of mall shoppers will provide adequate comparisons between products at a much lower cost than a probability sampling for in-home testing.

- *When informal, exploratory research is being done.* For example, most product concept testing is done with small convenience samples, as is most pretesting for questionnaires. Much insight can be gained at low cost from these nonrepresentative samples.

- *When it is desired to screen out "loser" products.* For example, suppose a manufacturer of frozen baked goods develops a new strawberry cheesecake in its test kitchens. It might test this product by giving samples to employees or visitors to the factory. If these people like the product, the firm can continue with more careful tests. However, if the new cheesecake gets a poor reception from employees and visitors, it almost certainly should be dropped.

Drawing the Sample

Given a sampling design, the next step in the sampling process is physically drawing the sample. If you are using some nonprobability design such as judgment sampling or volunteer sampling, you will simply choose your judgment sample, or post notices and wait for your volunteers to sign up. If you are using a probability sample, there are various methods for drawing probability samples, and you will want to use the method that is easiest and best for your particular sampling situation. The basic methods are (1) simple random sampling, (2) systematic sampling, and (3) physical sampling. In this section of this chapter, the application of these methods to various samples is illustrated and the conditions under which each method is appropriate are discussed.

Simple Random Sampling

Simple random sampling uses some chance mechanism to draw population members directly from the sampling frame. This can be accomplished with physical selection procedures or through the use of random numbers.

An example of physical selection procedures would be listing each population member on a slip of paper, mixing the slips of paper in a bowl, and drawing slips of paper to get the sample. Another physical procedure would be numbering the population members and selecting numbers by rolling dice, spinning a roulette wheel, or drawing bingo balls. These types of procedures are appealing because they are concrete, and everyone is familiar with games of chance that use these mechanisms. However, physical procedures can be cumbersome; for example, imagine how long it would take to make a slip of paper for every adult in your town, then draw 500 slips from a drum. Physical procedures also present difficulties in achieving randomness; it is not easy to mix slips of paper to the point of randomness.

A preferable method for drawing simple random samples is to number the members of the population and draw random numbers to determine which members are selected. Random numbers can be obtained from either of two sources: a computer or calculator can generate as many random numbers as needed, or a random number table such as Appendix A at the back of this book can be used. Appendix A, like most random number tables, is drawn from *A Million Random Digits* by the Rand Corporation.

Appendix A is printed in blocks of five digits, but these groupings in the table are only for ease in reading. This is a table of random *digits*. The numbers in Appendix A can be read as one-digit numbers, two-digit numbers, three-digit numbers, or whatever is desired. If a population with fewer than ten members is being sampled, the numbers in Appendix A should be read as one-digit numbers, because that's all that is necessary. If a population with 33,207 members is being sampled, the numbers in Appendix A should be read as five-digit numbers, to cover the possibility of drawing all numbers from 00001 through 33207.

To draw numbers from Appendix A (or any other random number table), start anywhere and move in any direction. An easy procedure is to start at the beginning and read down. The only errors to avoid are (1) starting at a given place because you like the distribution of numbers at that place, or (2) rejecting a sample because it doesn't look right. Obviously, these destroy the probability character of the sample and make it a judgment sample.

Some of the random numbers chosen might be larger than the size of the population. These numbers will be discarded, as will any duplicate numbers. For example, if the population has 33,207 members, random numbers in the range of 33208 to 99999 (as well as 00000) should be ignored. If you hit a number that is already in the sample, it should be ignored.

Marketing Research Tools 13.3 (see page 352) illustrates simple random sampling in action. It describes how Appendix A was used to select an "srs" of 25 from a population with 33,207 members.

Two points about Marketing Research Tools 13.3 are noteworthy. First, the sample does not *seem* perfectly random. No population members above 30,000 are selected, whereas five between 1 and 1,000 are selected. This, of course, is sampling variation in action. The sample is random, but most random samples do not represent their population perfectly. Smaller samples are particularly likely to exhibit serious peculiarities.

Author Tips

In using simple random sampling to draw elements from a population of 33,207, about two-thirds of the five-digit numbers you hit will fall outside the population range. You can increase the yield of usable numbers by using some system such as reading the numbers from 50001 to 83207 as if they were 00001 to 33207, but it is difficult to keep everything straight when you do so. It is easier to use a large random number table and only take numbers that directly correspond to population members.

SIMPLE RANDOM SAMPLING ILLUSTRATED

Goal: Select an "srs" of 25 from a population with 33,207 members.

Method: Begin at the start of Appendix A, and read five-digit numbers going down the left-hand side of the page. Any numbers between 00001 and 33207 are used to indicate selected population members; other numbers are ignored.

Moving down the column, the first five numbers are:

51007
50993
56399
93213
45930

Ignore all of these numbers which do not correspond to population members. Continuing down the page, the following usable numbers are found:

26625
11496
04016
00260
26375
03447
08571
15694
00363
24894
08475
10995
08319
19616
09886
22505
00985

The bottom of the page has been reached, with only 17 selections. Return to the top of the page, move two places to the right, and begin to read five-digit numbers down the page. (One can also move one place to the right or to any other place in the table—the whole table is random.)

Moving down the page the following usable numbers are derived:

00780
21313
22427
00008
28361
01625
26006
29146

At this point, the desired 25 selections have been derived.

The second thing of interest is that simple random sampling can be cumbersome. Counting up to the 33,207th population member wouldn't be as bad as making 33,207 slips of paper, but it wouldn't be pleasant. Similarly, finding 500 usable numbers in a random number table is a chore. For these reasons, we recommend simple random sampling only when a computerized list is being drawn from or when the population and sample are small enough to work with easily.

Systematic Sampling

Systematic sampling is a procedure that samples every ith member of a population after a random start between 1 and i. For example, to draw a sample of 25 from a population of 33,207, you would do the following:

- First, divide the population size by the desired sample size to get the sampling interval i (which is rounded *down* to the nearest whole number). In our example, $33,207 \div 25 = 1,328$, which means we will take every 1,328th population member after some random start.

- Next, draw a random start s between 1 and i. The use of a random start ensures that every population member has an equal chance of selection.

- Proceed to take population members numbered s, $(s + i)$, $(s + 2i)$, $(s + 3i)$, and so on.

This procedure is illustrated in Marketing Research Tools 13.4. To get a random start between 1 and 1,328, we looked in Appendix A and went across the top row looking for an eligible number. The second number from the left— 1007 —was usable. Therefore, our systematic sample consists of population members: $s = 1,007$, $(s + i) = (1,007 + 1,328) = 2,335$, and so on. Marketing Research Tools 13.4 shows the result.

When sampling from computerized lists, systematic sampling does not save much time compared with simple random sampling. After all, the computer is doing the work. In manual sampling, though, systematic sampling can save a great deal of time. It is necessary to draw only one random number, and it is much quicker to count every ith element than to number all of the population members.

As far as sample quality is concerned, systematic samples are generally the same as simple random samples, but differences can occur. Systematic sampling has a potential advantage in that it spreads selections through the sampling frame and will not bunch selections as simple random sampling can. Systematic sampling also has a potential disadvantage. If the list exhibits **periodicity**—a recurring sequence of population members—and the sampling interval coincides with that sequence, systematic sampling can produce an unrepresentative sample. For example, we once saw a list that went man-woman-man-woman, which wasn't realized until a systematic sample with an even sampling interval was chosen, and all of the selections were women.

Author Tips

It is rare to encounter periodicities that cause problems with systematic samples. Even so, sampling frames should always be checked for periodicity before drawing systematic samples. Also, if the sampling frame can be reorganized without too much effort, it is a good idea to put the frame into some type of order (women before men, large companies before small, etc.) to ensure that the systematic procedure will spread selections across different types of population members. This allows you to reap the benefits of systematic sampling without risking potential problems.

(cont. on page 356)

MARKETING RESEARCH TOOLS

13.4

SYSTEMATIC SAMPLING ILLUSTRATED

Goal: Select a systematic sample of 25 from a population with 33,207 members.

Method: Divide the population size by the desired sample size to get a sampling interval ($33,207 \div 25 = 1,328$). Take a random starting number between 1 and i, the sampling interval. Using four-digit numbers across the top row of Appendix A, located at the end of this book, a random start of 1,007 is derived. Therefore, the sample is as follows:

Selection	Calculation	Population Member Number
1	s	1,007
2	$(s + i)$	2,335
3	$(s + 2i)$	3,663
4	$(s + 3i)$	4,991
5	$(s + 4i)$	6,319
6	$(s + 5i)$	7,617
7	$(s + 6i)$	8,975
8	$(s + 7i)$	10,303
9	$(s + 8i)$	11,631
10	$(s + 9i)$	12,959
11	$(s + 10i)$	14,287
12	$(s + 11i)$	15,615
13	$(s + 12i)$	16,943
14	$(s + 13i)$	18,271
15	$(s + 14i)$	19,599
16	$(s + 15i)$	20,927
17	$(s + 16i)$	22,255
18	$(s + 17i)$	23,583
19	$(s + 18i)$	24,911
20	$(s + 19i)$	26,239
21	$(s + 20i)$	27,567
22	$(s + 21i)$	28,895
23	$(s + 22i)$	30,223
24	$(s + 23i)$	31,551
25	$(s + 24i)$	32,879

EXHIBIT 13.2

Simple
Random and
Systematic
Sampling

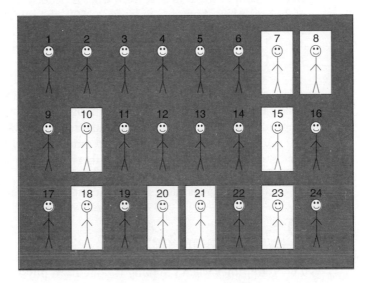

Simple Random Sampling: To sample 8 members out of a population of 24, randomly draw numbers between 1 and 24. Here, members 7, 8, 10, 15, 18, 20, 21, and 23 were randomly drawn.

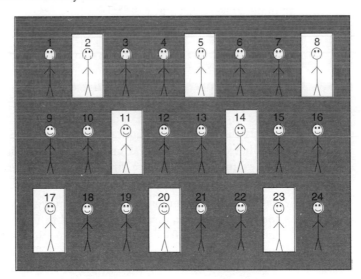

Systematic Sampling: To sample 8 members out of a population of 24, calculate a sampling interval $i = 24/8 = 3$. Take every third member after a random start between 1 and i. Here, member 2 was randomly chosen as the start.

You may encounter situations in which initial application of systematic sampling yields a sample size different from what is needed. For example, if you need a sample of 200 members from a population of 500, the calculated sampling interval is 500 ÷ 200 = 2.5. If this interval is rounded down to 2, an initial sample of 500 ÷ 2 = 250 is derived. This sample is too large. If the interval is rounded up to 3, a sample of 500 ÷ 3 = 167 is derived. This sample is too small.

The solution is to round in the direction of the larger sample and randomly delete the extra selections. Oversampling and deleting are almost always easier than undersampling and adding. The deletions can be done systematically; for example, if every fifth selection is skipped, an initial sample of 250 will be reduced to a sample of 200. One should not, of course, stop sampling in the middle of a list when the desired sample size is reached, because this results in a sample biased toward the earlier part of the list.

Exhibit 13.2 illustrates single random sampling and systematic sampling.

Physical Sampling

There are times when sampling is done from physical sources such as printed directories or file drawers that contain customer records. In such situations, the fastest way to draw a sample is with systematic sampling based on physical measures.

Sampling from Directories

Systematic sampling from printed directories is done as follows:

1. First, divide the needed sample size by the number of pages in the directory to calculate the number of selections per page. For example, if a population with 33,207 members is listed in a directory with 176 pages and you want a sample size of 500, then 500 ÷ 176 = 2.84 selections per page (round up to 3 to produce oversampling rather than undersampling).

   If the number of pages is larger than the needed sample size, divide the number of pages by the sample size to determine a sampling interval for pages. For example, if you have a directory of 176 pages and a needed sample size of 25, then 176 ÷ 25 = 7.04 pages per selection (round down to 7 for oversampling).

2. Second, draw a random sample of as many locations as you need per page. Say, for example, that a directory is printed in four columns per page, with each column containing 104 lines, and you want three selections per page. In this situation, select one random number between 1 and 104 to indicate a selected line in each column and one random number between 1 and 4 to indicate a column to be skipped on each page. This will give three selections per page, as desired.

3. Third, make a template to facilitate sampling. Take a piece of light cardboard that is at least as long as the directory pages (manila envelopes or file folders make excellent templates). Align the top of the template with the top of the printed column in the directory, and mark the selected lines on the template.

4. Fourth, draw the sample by placing the template against the appropriate columns of the directory and selecting the population members indicated by the marks on the template. Align the template with the first printed line rather than

the top of the page, because print location can vary from page to page. Repeat this procedure from the first through the last pages of the directory. Do not stop when the desired sample size is hit—work the whole directory and randomly delete excess selections.

This procedure is described in terms of lines, rather than directory listings, because lines are the basic printed unit and are more flexible than listings.

In some directories, different listings may have different numbers of lines. When this occurs, the selection procedure should be geared to the most common listing length. For example, if most listings take two lines, some take three, and a few take four, the third and fourth lines should be treated as ineligibles. If a selected line corresponds to the first two lines of a listed population member, the member is taken for the sample; if the selected line corresponds to the third or fourth line of a listing, the listing is ignored. This will prevent the listings with extra lines from having extra chances of selection. Also, any blank lines should be treated as ineligibles. These factors should be considered when calculating the eligibility rate and the needed sample size.

Physical sampling procedures go much faster than simple random sampling or systematic sampling as long as a directory has regular print and the listings occupy similar numbers of lines. If the printing is irregular or the listings vary greatly in length, plain systematic sampling may work best.

Sampling from File Drawers

Physical sampling from file drawers follows procedures similar to physical sampling from directories. Say, for example, that customer records are kept in 25 file cabinets, each with four drawers. To draw a sample of 100 customer files, you would do the following.

1. Measure the depth of the drawers: for example, 30 inches each.
2. Calculate the total length of the files: 25 cabinets × 4 drawers per cabinet × 30 inches per drawer = 3,000 inches of records.
3. Divide the total file length by the needed sample size to get a physical sampling interval: 3,000 inches ÷ 100 selections = 30 inches per selection.
4. Draw a random starting point expressed in fractions of an inch or millimeters.
5. Pull the files in the first drawer together tightly. Lay a tape measure (or ruler or yardstick) over these files, and locate the random starting point. Take the file that corresponds to that point, plus the files that come at appropriate intervals after the starting point.

In order to work with convenient sampling intervals, it may be helpful to round the interval down to the nearest inch. This will produce oversampling, just as rounding the interval down produces oversampling in sampling from directories. Also, the files may be different widths reflecting how much interaction the customer has had with the institution. If an "epsem" sample of files is desired, it will be necessary to use some standard width and regard widths over that amount as ineligible. This is parallel to the fact that listings may occupy different numbers of lines in a directory.

Critical Thinking Skills

Take your local telephone directory, and design a procedure to draw a sample of 500 households from that directory.

CASE STUDY 13.3

An electric utility in the Midwest decided to offer an "energy consulting" service in which a representative of the company would analyze ways in which a home could be made more energy-efficient. The utility did a survey to estimate how popular this service would be among homeowners, to help the company plan staffing and support levels.

The company mailed questionnaires to all of its residential customers—about 200,000 homes—with their March power bills. About 10,000 homeowners responded. The returned questionnaires indicated a very high level of interest in the service, so the power company geared up for heavy demand. However, actual demand proved far less than anticipated.

There are at least three reasons why this survey produced misleading results:

- First, the survey was done right after people had paid a series of winter power bills, so interest was inflated above its baseline level.
- Second, it is easier for people to *say* they're interested in a service than to *use* the service. This relates to the discussion in Chapter 10 on the measurement of intention.
- Third, and of most interest in this chapter, the obtained sample is biased because of poor research execution.

Note that we say the *obtained* sample is biased. There is nothing wrong with the original sample—in fact, it's a census! The problem is one of execution and follow-through. The 10,000 homeowners who responded were only 5 percent of the people who received questionnaires and should be viewed as a sample of *volunteers* rather than as a random sample of the *population*. In fact, probably the best way of interpreting this research would have been to assume that the 95 percent of the population that didn't respond to the questionnaire wasn't interested in the service.

The utility company would have been far better off if it had used its research funds for a much smaller telephone survey of its customers and had worked this sample to get a 70 percent or better response rate. Even with a mail survey, the company would have done better with a smaller, multiwave study using the procedures described in Chapter 7.

This example shows that a good initial sample is of no use if the researcher fails to protect its integrity in execution. The example also shows that a large sample—in this case, a sample of 10,000 people—is not necessarily a good sample.

Executing the Research

With the sample drawn, all that remains is to execute the research. This step, executing the research, is referred to as part of the sampling process because good execution is necessary to preserve the quality of the original sample. Case Study 13.3 illustrates this point by describing a situation in which poor execution ruined a good sample.

There are two components of good research execution. First, a method that encourages participation from the highest possible percentage of selected population members should be chosen. The methods that have the highest participation rates for self-report data are in-home (or in-office) surveys and telephone surveys. Selection of any other method—intercept survey, mail survey, depth interviews or focus groups at a central site, and panel research—should be accompanied by an awareness that you are losing sample quality in exchange for lower price or richer data.

Second, use callbacks or follow-up procedures that ensure that virtually all selected population members will be contacted for the research and encouraged to respond. In mail surveys, we recommend prenotification plus two follow-ups. In telephone surveys, we suggest at least five callbacks to people who don't answer when called. These callbacks should be spread across weekdays, weekday evenings, and weekends.

Some marketing researchers use telephone survey procedures without callbacks. If nobody answers a phone, the interviewer discards the number and proceeds to another. Used without controls, this procedure produces very high numbers of retired people and housewives, because they are the people who are most likely to be home when called. To control this obvious bias, researchers set quotas for age, sex, and employment groups (Lavrakas, 1993).

Quota sampling procedures aren't terrible; for example, Seymour Sudman (1976) has shown that age and employment quotas applied to random samples without callbacks can produce samples similar to those obtained with callbacks. However, if different numbers are called until someone is found at home, the sampling procedure will find the least active and most accessible members of the population. This can be a biasing factor in research. For example, if the research concerns food preparation habits and callbacks are not used in a telephone survey, it should be assumed that the results will overstate the frequency of at-home food preparation.

Reporting the Sample

After the research project is completed, a sampling report should be included with the final report of findings. A good sample report contains the following components:

- A detailed definition of the target population
- A description of the list or framing procedures used
- A description of the sampling design, including sample size
- Details related to sample execution, such as the number and timing of callbacks
- Response rates
- A definition of the population actually represented by the research and acknowledgment of the sample's limitations

We suggest that two response rates be reported. The first is the *completion rate* (or total response rate), which measures how effective you were at obtaining data from all sample members. This figure is calculated as

$$\text{Completion rate} = \frac{\text{Number of observations}}{\text{Initial sample size} - \text{Ineligibles}}$$

The second measure of response is the *cooperation rate*, which measures how well you did at getting data from selected population members you were able to reach. This figure is calculated as

$$\text{Cooperation rate} = \frac{\text{Number of observations}}{\text{Initial sample} - \text{Ineligibles} - \text{Noncontacts}}$$

For example, if you do a survey with an initial sample size of 1,000 from which you obtain 606 interviews, 198 refusals, 6 breakoffs (interviews that are started but not completed), 136 noncontacts, and 54 confirmed ineligibles, the completion rate is 64 percent (606/946) and the cooperation rate is 75 percent (606/810).

Note that noncontacts and refusals must be differentiated in order to calculate the cooperation rate. This is not possible in mail surveys, so the only response rate possible from a mail survey is the completion rate.

Summary

This chapter discussed sampling. The following points were covered:

1. What are sampling error, nonsampling error, and sample bias?
Factors that can result in a sample not being representative are: *nonsampling error*, which includes all error sources unrelated to sampling, *sampling error*, which refers to chance variation in the sample, and *sample bias*, which occurs when the sample differs from the population in some systematic way.

2. How should a population be defined for sampling purposes?
A sampling population is the set of elements about which you would like to draw conclusions. To define a population, it is necessary to specify (1) the population units and (2) the population boundaries. The boundaries must be stated in operational terms.

3. What is a sample frame, and how can frame problems be fixed?
A frame is a list or system that identifies every member of the population symboli-

cally. Ideally, the frame should have a one-to-one correspondence with the members of the population. This may not occur because of omissions, ineligibles, duplications, or clustering.

The response to omissions is to ignore them if the problem is small, augment the list if the problem is moderate, and replace the list if the problem is severe. Random digit dialing is used to handle unlisted numbers in telephone surveys.

The response to ineligibles is to drop them when encountered. If ineligible elements cannot be recognized in the frame, it may be necessary to screen for them in the field. Either way, the initial sample size should allow for losses due to ineligibility.

A possible response to duplicate listings is (1) deleting them from the frame prior to sampling, (2) retaining selected elements at a rate that is inverse to the number of times each selected unit is listed, or (3) asking each selected participant how many times she or he is listed and weighting the observations by the inverse of the number of listings.

A possible response to clustering is (1) including each member of a selected cluster, (2) sampling within clusters, or (3) randomly selecting one element in each cluster and weighting for cluster size.

4. What is the difference between probability and nonprobability sampling, and when is each appropriate?

Probability samples draw elements from the population by random selection. They rely on chance to produce a representative sample of the population. Nonprobability samples do not use random selection. They rely on judgment (or nothing) to produce a representative sample of the population.

Probability samples are generally preferable to nonprobability samples. However, nonprobability samples are appropriate when (1) the sample size is smaller than 20, (2) the population is homogeneous on the variable being studied, (3) the research is exploratory, or (4) the purpose of the research is to screen out "loser" products.

5. How is a probability sample drawn?

With *simple random sampling (SRS)*, population members are numbered and random numbers are drawn to determine which members are selected. With *systematic sampling*, a random start is followed by every *i*th population member. With *physical sampling*, a systematic sample is taken according to locations on a page or some other physical arrangement.

6. How should research be executed to maintain sample integrity?

To maintain sample integrity, choose a method that encourages participation from the highest possible percentage of selected population members, and use callbacks or follow-up procedures to ensure that virtually all selected population members will be contacted for the research.

7. What information should be provided in a sampling report?

A sampling report should include a detailed definition of the target population, a description of the list or framing procedures used, a description of the sampling design, the sample size, details related to sample execution, response rates, a definition of the population actually represented, and acknowledgment of sample limitations.

Suggested Additional Readings

Much of the material in this chapter and the next is taken from Seymour Sudman, *Applied Sampling* (Orlando, Fla: Academic, 1976), which you may want to consult for additional details. The other classic sampling books are Leslie Kish, *Survey Sampling* (New York: Wiley, 1965), Morris H. Hansen, William N. Hurwitz, and William G. Madow, *Sample Survey Methods and Theory (2 vols.)* (New York: Wiley, 1953), and Frank Yates, *Sampling Methods for Censuses and Surveys* (London: Griffin, 1981). Other useful books on sampling are W. Edwards Deming, *Sampling in Business Research* (New York: Wiley, 1990), Graham Kalton, *Introduction to Survey Sampling* (Newburg Park, Calif: Sage, 1983), Paul S. Levy and Stanley Lemeshow, *Sampling of Populations*, (New York: Wiley, 1991), and, on a more theoretical level, William Cochran, *Sampling Techniques* (New York: Wiley, 1963).

Discussion Questions

1. What is the difference between sampling error and sampling bias? How can the researcher control for each of these? Which is more serious? Why?

2. What is nonsampling error? Give examples. How can you control for nonsampling error?

3. What is a sampling frame? What frame(s) would you use if you wanted to conduct a survey of the faculty of your college or university?

4. What are some of the ways you might cope with each of the following problems when using a list as your sampling frame?
    a. omissions
    b. ineligibles
    c. duplications
    d. clustering

5. What are the types of sample designs? How do they differ? When should each be used? Which method is best?

6. You want to assess the effectiveness of a recent media campaign advertising "summer weekend specials" to an amusement park. Since no list of customers exists, how might you frame the population?

7. Specify whether each of the following sampling procedures results in a probability or a nonprobability sample:

    Judgment sampling
    Simple random sampling
    Systematic sampling
    Volunteer sampling
    Cluster sampling
    Convenience sampling
    Quota sampling
    Stratified sampling

8. When should you avoid using systematic sampling?
9. What are two components of good sample execution?

Marketing Research Challenge

Select a simple random sample of 300 students from a disk or listing of students at your school. You may use either computer or counting methods, and either systematic or regular random samples. Describe what you did, paying special attention to how you handled ineligibles, duplications, and omissions.

Internet Exercise

In Chapter 12, we showed a questionnaire used by the Houston Astros baseball team for an "in-stadium" fan survey. If this survey were conducted via the Internet, rather than in the stadium, what incentives would you offer to encourage participation, and how would you let potential respondents know about the survey? How, if at all, would the Internet sample be different from the in-stadium sample? Which sample would be better?

References

Glasser, Gerald L., and Gale D. Metzger (1972). "Random Digit Dialing as a Method of Telephone Sampling." *Journal of Marketing Research* 9, pp. 59–64.

Lavrakas, Paul J. (1993). *Telephone Survey Methods: Sampling, Selection, and Supervision* (Newbury Park, Calif: Sage).

Nowell, Clifford, and Linda R. Stanley (1991). "Length-biased Sampling in Mall Intercept Surveys." *Journal of Marketing Research* 28 (November), pp. 475–479.

Sudman, Seymour (1976). *Applied Sampling* (Orlando, Fla: Academic Press).

Sudman, Seymour (1980). "Improving the Quality of Shopping Center Sampling." *Journal of Marketing Research* 17, pp. 423–431.

Waksberg, Joseph (1978). "Sampling Methods for Random Digit Dialing." *Journal of the American Statistical Association* 73, pp. 40–46.

14

Determining Sample Size and Increasing Sample Efficiency

◪ *OBJECTIVES*

After reading this chapter, you should be able to answer the following questions:

❶ What is sampling error?

❷ How can the sample size needed to produce a desired confidence interval be determined?

❸ How can an optimum sample size be determined by using the value and cost of information?

❹ How can the sample size be set by using other guidelines?

❺ How is stratified sampling used to reduce sampling errors?

❻ How is cluster sampling used to increase the cost-effectiveness of research?

This chapter enlarges on the discussion of sampling, including procedures for determining sample size, an aspect of sample design that was not discussed in Chapter 13. Whereas Chapter 13 focused on the issue of *sample bias,* this chapter focuses on the issue of *sampling error.* As noted in Chapter 13, sampling error is the chance variation that will cause most samples to differ from the population to some extent, even if the sampling procedure is unbiased.

Subsequent sections of this chapter discuss sampling error in more concrete terms and show that the level of sampling error is determined by sample size. The relationship between sampling error and sample size means that sample sizes can be calculated to produce acceptable levels of sampling error. Formulas that can be used to calculate sample sizes that produce desired levels of sample error are introduced, and issues to consider when applying these formulas are discussed.

This initial discussion of sample size might be said to follow a "confidence interval" approach. There is also another statistical approach to setting sample size: the "value of information" approach. The value of information approach is less familiar to people than the confidence interval approach, but it fits well with some marketing research applications. Therefore, after discussing the confidence interval approach to setting sample size, we discuss the value of information approach. We also discuss various nonstatistical procedures for setting sample size and the usefulness of these procedures.

Once a sample size or budget is determined, there are ways of making the sample more efficient by use of stratification and clustering. The final sections of this chapter discuss these topics.

Sampling Error Illustrated

The concept of sampling error is best illustrated by showing the samples available from a small population. Exhibit 14.1 shows a *very* small population—five people named Ann, Bob, Carl, Dave, and Edna. Ann is a twenty-four-year-old female, Bob is a thirty-year-old male, Carl is a thirty-six-year-old male, Dave is a forty-two-year-old male, and Edna is a forty-eight-year-old female. The average age of this population is thirty-six, and the population is 60 percent male.

Exhibit 14.2 (see page 368) shows all of the samples of size 1, 2, 3, 4, and 5 that can be drawn from this population, assuming that no population member is repeated in a sample. A sample of size 5, of course, is a complete census of the population. Exhibit 14.2 also shows (1) the mean age of each sample, (2) the percentage of each sample that is male, and (3) averages across all samples of a given size. Again, these are *all* of the samples that can be drawn from our five-person population.

Three important facts can be seen in Exhibit 14.2:

■   First, when an average across all of the sample means (or percentages) for samples of a given size is calculated, the samples have the same average as the popu-

Exhibit>EXHIBIT **14.1**

A Small
Population

Population Member	Age	Gender
Ann	24	Female
Bob	30	Male
Carl	36	Male
Dave	42	Male
Edna	48	Female

lation as a whole. This is what statisticians mean when they say that the "expected value" of a sample mean equals the population mean.

- Second, the mean (or percentage) for any single sample need not be the same as the population mean. In fact, *most* of the sample means will differ from the population mean. In a commonsense use of the word "expect," one doesn't expect a sample mean to equal the population mean exactly.

- Third, the distribution of sample means (or percentages) becomes more tightly concentrated around the overall population mean as the sample size increases. In statistical terms, the variance of the sample means across samples of a particular size gets smaller as the sample size gets larger.

The term **sampling error** refers to the standard deviation of the distribution of sample means (standard deviations are discussed in Chapter 16). In statistical notation, this term is written as $s_{\bar{x}}$. The equation that relates the sampling error to the sample size is

$$s_{\bar{x}} = \sqrt{\frac{s^2}{n}\left(\frac{N-n}{N}\right)\left(\frac{N}{N-1}\right)},$$

Equation 14.1

where $s_{\bar{x}}$ is the estimated sampling error for the variable being measured, s is the estimated standard deviation for this variable in the population at large, n is the sample size, and N is the population size.

The last two terms in this equation, $(N-n)/N$ and $N/(N-1)$, are called the "finite population correction" (FPC) and the "correction for sampling without replacement," respectively. Multiplied together, they reduce to $(N-n)/(N-1)$. This combined term is trivial unless the sample constitutes a fairly large proportion of the population—say, more than 10 percent—which occurs fairly often in industrial marketing research but rarely in consumer research. When trivial, the term is usually discarded from the equation, leaving

$$s_{\bar{x}} = \frac{s}{\sqrt{n}}.$$

Equation 14.2

Critical Thinking Skills

If the standard deviation of an expenditure measure is $4,000 and the relevant population consists of 500 businesses, use Equations 14.1 and 14.2 to calculate the sampling error for samples of size 200 from this population.

EXHIBIT 14.2

All Possible Samples from Our Small Population

	Mean Age	Percent Male
All samples of *n* = 1:		
Ann	24	0
Bob	30	100
Carl	36	100
Dave	42	100
Edna	48	0
Average	**36**	**60**
All samples of *n* = 2:		
Ann, Bob	27	50
Ann, Carl	30	50
Ann, Dave	33	50
Bob, Carl	33	100
Ann, Edna	36	0
Bob, Dave	36	100
Bob, Edna	39	50
Carl, Dave	39	100
Carl, Edna	42	50
Dave, Edna	45	50
Average	**36**	**60**
All samples of *n* = 3:		
Ann, Bob, Carl	30	67
Ann, Bob, Dave	32	67
Ann, Bob, Edna	34	33
Ann, Carl, Dave	34	67
Ann, Carl, Edna	36	33
Bob, Carl, Dave	36	100
Bob, Carl, Edna	38	67
Ann, Dave, Edna	38	33
Bob, Dave, Edna	40	67
Carl, Dave, Edna	42	67
Average	**36**	**60**
All samples of *n* = 4:		
Ann, Bob, Carl, Dave	33	75
Ann, Bob, Carl, Edna	34½	50
Ann, Bob, Dave, Edna	36	50
Ann, Carl, Dave, Edna	37½	50
Bob, Carl, Dave, Edna	39	75
Average	**36**	**60**
All samples of *n* = 5:		
Ann, Bob, Carl, Dave, Edna	**36**	**60**

The Confidence Interval Approach to Sample Size

In the previous section of this chapter, we showed that a sample mean will generally *not* equal the population mean, though sample means will average around the population under repeated sampling. This principle holds true for any statistics we might calculate from a sample—means, proportions, correlations, regression coefficients, or any other statistic.

This creates a problem. Most research projects result in only one sample result. This sample will not, in general, reflect population statistics perfectly because of random variation in sample composition. However, it is not possible to tell how much any specific sample differs from the full population unless data are available for the population—and it wouldn't be necessary to do research if they were.

The sampling error *can*, however, be used to express probabilities that your sample results fall within a given range of the population figures. The sample mean, for example, follows a "normal" distribution, and the sampling error is the standard deviation of that distribution. Since 95 percent of the values in a normal distribution fall within ±1.96 standard deviations from the mean of that distribution, this means that 95 percent of the sample means should fall within $\pm 1.96 s_{\bar{x}}$ of the average sample mean, that is, within $\pm 1.96 s_{\bar{x}}$ of the population mean. For example, if the estimated sampling error for annual expenditure on ice cream in a given population is $30, there is a 95 percent chance that a sample mean will fall within +$58.80 ($1.96 \times \$30 =$ $58.80) of the population mean. In statistical terms, we would say that we have a "confidence interval" of ±$58.80 with a 95 percent "confidence level," or simply that the "95 percent confidence interval" is ±$58.80.

To use the confidence interval approach to sample size, take this calculation and work it backward, as follows:

1. Start with a desired confidence interval, and calculate the sampling error needed to produce this interval. For example, if a 95 percent confidence interval ($I_{95\%}$) of ±58.80 is desired, the required sampling error is

$$I_{95\%} = 1.96 \times s_{\bar{x}}$$
$$58.80 = 1.96 \times s_{\bar{x}}$$
$$s_{\bar{x}} = 58.80 \div 1.96 = 30.00.$$

2. Plug this sampling error into Equation 14.1 (see page 367), or, if the population is large, use the simplified Equation 14.2. For example, if a desired sampling error of 30.00 is plugged into Equation 14.2, the result is

$$s_{\bar{x}} = s/\sqrt{n}$$
$$30.00 = s/\sqrt{n}.$$

3. Now, if s, the standard deviation of the variable being studied, is estimated, n, the sample size needed to produce the desired sampling error and hence the desired confidence interval, can be solved for.

Author Tips

The confidence interval approach to sample size assumes that you have a good reason for specifying the desired width of the confidence interval. If this is not true, it may be more appropriate to (1) set the sample size in some nonstatistical way, as discussed later in this chapter, (2) use Appendix 14.1 or SAMPLER to calculate the associated confidence intervals, and (3) think about whether those confidence intervals are satisfactory given the purposes of your research. If they are not, try other sample sizes until you are satisfied.

Critical Thinking Skills

If the hospital marketing director in Case Study 14.1 wanted to have a confidence interval of ±1 percent (instead of 4 percent) for the same estimates, what sample size would she need? If she wanted to have a confidence interval of ±1 percent for differences between satisfaction measures, what sample size would she need? (See Appendix 14.1 for help.)

To streamline the calculations, Steps 1 and 2 can be combined into one step that omits the intermediate calculation of a sampling error; for example, if Equation 14.2 is used to calculate sampling error, the "one-step" calculation is

$$I_{95\%} = 1.96 \times (s/\sqrt{n}).$$

Rearranged, this becomes:

$$\sqrt{n} = (1.96 \times s)/I_{95\%}.$$

So:

$$n = [(1.96 \times s)/I_{95\%}]^2$$

Appendix 14.1, at the end of this chapter, automates this process. It provides tables and help sheets that can be used to determine the sample size needed to produce a desired confidence interval. It also provides tables that can be used to determine the confidence interval associated with a given sample size. The following comments about this appendix are in order:

- Appendix 14.1 applies to confidence intervals for two common types of estimates: *proportions* and *means*. Means are averages; when you answer the question "What is the average value of some variable?," you are estimating a mean. Proportions are percentages; when you answer the question "What percentage of the population has some characteristic?," you are estimating a proportion.

- The tables and formulas shown in Appendix 14.1 are for 95% confidence intervals. If you prefer to work with 90% confidence intervals, use 1.645 instead of 1.96 in the formulas.

- The tables and formulas in Appendix 14.1 are based on Equation 14.2 and do not take the finite population correction into account. If the sample will be a substantial proportion of the population, the formulas shown in Tables 14.1–4 should be augmented to include the FPC. To do this, find s^2 or $p(1 - p)$ in the formulas and multiply this term by $(N - n)/(N - 1)$. Then solve the augmented formula.

Case Study 14.1 shows how Appendix 14.1 can be used to determine sample size. As the case study notes, each such calculation results in the sample size needed to satisfy one particular confidence interval goal. If a marketing research project has multiple goals, including estimates of population subgroups, each desired confidence interval will carry its own required sample size. Most research projects have some goals that require small samples and others that require large samples, and the sample size that is ultimately chosen often represents a compromise between these objectives.

To automate your sample size calculations further, the computer disk accompanying this book has a file called SAMPLER.EXE, which is an executable file that you should be able

CASE STUDY 14.1

A hospital marketing director is planning a patient satisfaction survey. She plans to report the percentage of patients who say they were "completely satisfied" with various aspects of the hospital's performance. She would like to be 95 percent confident that her estimates fall within ±4 percent (that is, within ±.04) of the population figure for each measure. How big a sample does she need?

Use Appendix 14.1 to answer this question. According to the table of contents for that appendix, instructions on how to calculate sample sizes can be found in Help Sheet 14.1. This help sheet asks whether one is estimating an *average* (i.e., a mean) or a *proportion* (i.e., a percentage). The marketing director wants to know the percentage of patients who respond "Completely satisfied" on each of a series of measures, so she will be estimating a series of proportions. The help sheet refers you to Table 14.1 for sample sizes associated with estimates of proportions. Therefore, go to Table 14.1.

In Table 14.1, the ±4 percent confidence interval desired by the marketing director falls between two columns—those for 3 percent and 5 percent. You also need to pick a row that indicates the percentage of patients you expect to be "completely satisfied." Help Sheet 14.3 suggests methods of making this choice. Since the hospital will be estimating percentages for a series of satisfaction measures, let's assume that at least one of them will fall near 50 percent (.50), which is the figure that requires the largest sample size. This puts you onto the bottom row of the table, where you will see that a 3 percent confidence interval requires a sample size of 1,068 and a 5 percent interval requires a sample of 385.

It is a mistake to think that the sample size needed for a 4 percent confidence interval will be halfway between the sample sizes needed for 3 percent and 5 percent. If you solve the formula given in Table 14.1 for sample sizes not shown in the table, you will find that a 4 percent confidence interval requires a sample size of 600.

Before using this sample size, you must consider whether to adjust it for the finite population correction. If the hospital is large and the patient satisfaction survey is being planned on an annual basis, the answer is probably "no." A large hospital will have several thousand patients per year, and the anticipated sample is likely to be less than 10 percent of the population. At this level, the FPC will not materially alter the sample size.

Please note that our calculations apply only to estimates of the proportion of patients who are completely satisfied with the hospital's services. If the hospital's marketing director has other research objectives, each piece of information will carry its own required sample size. Also, if subgroup analyses (e.g., separate satisfaction estimates for patients who were in different hospital wards) are desired, each subgroup will have a needed sample size, which will depend on whatever confidence interval goals the marketing director sets for the subgroup estimates.

Most marketing research projects have many research objectives, some of which require small samples and some of which require enormous samples. Resource constraints usually require some compromise on the most difficult objectives.

to open on any computer. SAMPLER automates the process given in Appendix 14.1 and goes one step further by automatically including the finite population correction so that no further adjustment is needed for small populations. You might want to study Appendix 14.1 to see this process in hard-copy form, then use SAMPLER for your sample size and confidence interval calculations.

The "Value of Information" Approach to Sample Size

The confidence interval approach is the traditional statistical approach to sample size calculation. However, this method has significant weaknesses when applied in marketing research. It doesn't separate research on which companies are betting their futures from research where small amounts of money are at stake, research on new products from research on old products, or projects with a $200 cost per observation from projects with a $5 cost per observation. The only factors that drive this approach are the confidence interval goal and the innate variability of the population; factors such as the cost of research and the value of the decision do not enter the calculations unless the confidence interval is made larger or smaller in response.

The "value of information" approach to sample size calculation, in contrast, explicitly considers these other factors. This approach is more decision oriented than the classical approach and consequently more appropriate for some marketing research applications. Because the value of information approach is decision focused, it tends to work best with "problem-solving" research and is not very helpful for indicating how much data should be collected in a marketing information system used for market-monitoring purposes (Schlaifer, 1959).

Why Information Has Value

To understand the value of information approach to sample size, one must first understand why research has value. Every manager makes decisions, and marketing managers are no exception. These decisions are not always right. Because of uncertainty in the marketplace, even the most experienced and judicious of managers are sometimes wrong. The value of information is that it enables managers to be right more often and thus to increase their companies overall profits.

Suppose, for example, that a marketing manager makes 100 new-product introduction decisions. Given the manager's experience and judgment, let's say that he or she can make the right decision 65 percent of the time without conducting marketing research. Let's also say that marketing research would allow him or her to make the right decision 75 percent of the time (research information is never perfect, and competitors may react in unexpected ways).

What, then, is the value of information? Assume for simplicity that the profit from a correct decision is $1 million for a specified time period and the loss from a wrong decision is a negative $1 million. Simple arithmetic suggests that being right 65 times makes the firm $65 million and being wrong 35 times loses $35 million. The net profit is thus, $30 million. With marketing research and a 75 percent rate of correct decisions, the net profit is ($75,000,000 – $25,000,000) or $50 million. The difference between the firm's profits *with* and *without* research is $20 million; this, then, is the value of the research.

Note that we haven't said that the company actually makes $200,000 from each of the 100 research projects. On average this is true, but the value of any given research project can vary. Also, the value of any given project cannot be known for certain in advance. Information has value in a specific project only if it causes a change from an incorrect to a correct decision, and one cannot know in advance when this will happen. One can, however, note that information pays off only when decision makers change their minds. If research is designed to "play it safe" and reinforce rather than challenge management assumptions, it will not pay off.

Critical Thinking Skills

Given this information, what would the value of research be if the manager never changed his or her mind and had the same 65 percent hit rate with or without information? What if the research improved the hit rate to 85 percent? What if the potential gain from each decision was $2 million and the potential loss was $3 million? What if the potential gain from each decision was $20,000 and the potential loss was $30,000?

Factors Related to the Value of Information

The following factors relate to the value of information:

1. *Uncertainty about the proper course of action.* How much would you pay for information on the direction where the sun will rise tomorrow morning? Presumably nothing, because you already know the answer.

   Some managers are sure that they know what is happening in the market and will ignore research that contradicts their preconceptions. Research has no value for these managers and should not be done.

2. *Gains or losses available from the decision.* Who will pay more for a research project: General Motors in studying reactions to a new electric car or a hardware store owner in studying customers' perceptions about service at the store? The answer is "General Motors," and the reason is that GM has far more money at stake than the local hardware store owner does. Tooling up for and marketing a new car model can cost hundreds of millions of dollars.

   Note, by the way, that the value of information does not depend on ability to pay. It is not that GM has more money to spend; it is that it has more to gain from a good decision or lose from a bad one.

3. *Nearness to breakeven.* This indicates the likelihood that research will affect a decision. Suppose, for example, that a company is considering the introduction of a new home appliance and the break-even sales volume for this product is 100,000 units. Research is more valuable if the company's best preresearch estimate of the likely sales volume is 200,000 units than if the company's estimate is 1 million units.

   When the estimate is near the break-even point, whether below or above, new information has a high likelihood of affecting the decision. On the other hand, when the estimate is far above or below the break-even point, it is unlikely that the decision will be affected. New information might change the specific estimate of profits resulting from a product introduction, but the decision *whether* to introduce the product is less and less likely to change as we go farther from breakeven.

In Chapter 1, it was pointed out that the value of marketing research depends on (1) the level of uncertainty, (2) gains and losses associated with the decision, and (3) whether the research provides a clear direction for a decision. The discussion here is basically the same, although nearness to breakeven has been substituted for the more general discussion of whether the research provides clear direction.

CASE STUDY 14.2

I s a big sample size needed for marketing research to be effective? Not necessarily.

We recently consulted on a string of three projects for a major oil company. All three projects concerned new services that the company might introduce.

The first service involved oil well drilling on a contract basis for smaller oil companies. We interviewed ten potential customers in connection with this project. After talking with these ten people, it was obvious that the service did not appeal to the market. We discontinued interviewing, and the company dropped the idea.

The second service involved energy management services for certain kinds of factories. We interviewed fifteen potential customers in connection with this project. We found some interest in the service, but it appeared that potential revenues were unlikely to exceed $2 million per year. This revenue potential was nowhere near enough to fit the company's requirements for a new business, so we discontinued interviewing and the company dropped the idea.

The third service involved an environmental cleanup service. Early interviews indicated that this service might have a very high revenue potential. As a result, we planned a study that allowed us to make a fairly close estimate of that potential. This study involved more than 100 personal interviews—which is a large number in an industrial study—and cost more than $100,000.

Together, the three studies illustrate a point from the confidence interval approach to setting sample size. If rough information about the market is adequate for the purposes at hand, small sample sizes are adequate. If more precise information is needed, a larger sample is necessary.

The studies also illustrate some points about the value of information. If early information shows that a potential product or service will produce revenues that are far below those needed for introduction, further research is not needed except to evaluate possible product revisions. If the situation is not so clear-cut and there is a large amount of money to be gained or lost from a good or bad decision, expensive research may be justified.

The Value of Information and Sample Size

Information has value, but it also costs money to obtain. As with all economic goods, it is desirable to maximize the net gain from information after accounting for costs. This gain is maximized as follows: Each new unit of information—for example, each survey interview—provides some marginal improvement in our knowledge about the market and hence some marginal value. This marginal value decreases from unit to unit, because the more we know, the less value we get from an additional unit of information. Each unit of information also carries some marginal cost. This marginal cost tends to remain constant from unit to unit. The optimum sample size occurs when the marginal gain from one unit of new information is just equal to the cost of that unit of information.

Under certain assumptions, it is possible to compute the optimum sample size using the value of information approach. We describe this procedure in Appendix 14.2. Even firms that do not explicitly use the methods described in Appendix 14.2 use the concepts of value and cost of information in determining sample size. The nonstatistical methods described in the next section are often implicitly based on the value of information.

Nonstatistical Approaches to Sample Size

So far, two statistical approaches for setting sample size in a marketing research project have been discussed. Several nonstatistical approaches also are used. These include:

- Setting the sample size according to previous practice
- Setting the sample size according to typical practice
- Using a "magic number" to set sample size
- Setting the sample size to produce desired cell sizes in planned subgroup analyses
- Setting the sample size according to resource limitations
- Asking an expert to suggest a sample size

Let's discuss each of these methods in more detail.

Using Previous Sample Sizes

It is common for companies that do repetitive research to set sample sizes according to what has worked in previous projects. For example, we know of one pharmaceutical company that usually uses a sample size of 50 to measure doctors' opinions about its new drugs. If a new drug is deemed especially important, the company uses 100 doctors. The company's marketing staff is accustomed to these numbers and feels comfortable with them.

The simple approach of repeating sample sizes works well if situations are similar and the previous sample size was optimum. It is important to recognize, however, that different situations may require different sample sizes. Simply doing the same thing each time can lead to spending too much or too little on information relative to what it is worth.

Using Typical Sample Sizes

A related approach to setting sample size is to "follow the crowd" and use sample sizes similar to those that other companies have used. Marketing Research Tools 14.1 gives some typical sample sizes that can be used in this regard. Copying sample sizes has the same logic as repeating your own sample sizes—"if it worked before, it should work again"—and the same pitfalls. Different situations may require different sample sizes.

Using a Magic Number

Another nonstatistical approach to sample size determination is using what is called a "magic number." By this is meant a number that seems appropriate to managers who will be asked to support decisions based on the research.

Marketing research is most useful when it challenges conventional thinking and suggests new ways of doing things. After all, you don't need research to tell you to keep doing things the same way. However, research that suggests new ways of doing things almost always faces some resistance. The doubters and opponents of a

MARKETING RESEARCH TOOLS

14.1

TYPICAL SAMPLE SIZES USED IN MARKET RESEARCH

Number of Subgroup Analyses	Consumer Research		Business Research*	
	National Population	Special Population	National Population	Special Population
None/few	200–500	100–500	20–100	20–50
Average	500–1,000	200–1,000	50–200	50–100
Many	1,000+	500+	200+	100+

*Assumes that the total population size is large relative to these sample sizes.

research conclusion will seek ways of denying or invalidating that conclusion, and one of the most common ways is to say that the research is based on "only" X number of observations.

To maximize the acceptance of research conclusions and hence make them more valuable, it is important that the researcher measure managers' beliefs about appropriate sample sizes at the start of a research project. Be blunt—tell them, "You know, sometimes research studies produce unexpected findings," and ask, "If this study produces unexpected findings, what kind of sample size would make you feel comfortable that these findings are legitimate and not a fluke?" Probe until you get answers from the key managers who will receive and implement project findings. Then make sure that the sample size exceeds these expectations. This precaution will not forestall all criticism of the sample size, but it will minimize it, and it is an important part of producing research that satisfies managers' intuitive concerns.

In an organization that does a lot of research, the "magic number" is likely to be the same as previous sample sizes. In the pharmaceutical company that measures physician response to new drugs with standard sample sizes of 50 and 100, these sample sizes now go unnoticed—nobody thinks to question them, and research findings based on them are well accepted. If the research department were to do a study with some other sample size, such as 40 or 72, all attention would be on the unusual sample size rather than the results of the study. The research would face resistance because it would violate organizational standards that people have accepted.

Critical Thinking Skills

Pick an issue that is controversial in your area. Ask some people how big a sample they think would be needed to get a representative picture of public opinion on this issue. After hearing their answers, how big a sample do you think is needed for credibility?

Anticipating Subgroup Analyses

Our fourth nonstatistical method for setting sample size is anticipating subgroup analyses and planning minimum sample sizes in the smallest subgroups. Suppose, for example, that a hospital plans to measure customer satisfaction among inpatients. It plans to report separate analyses for various wards—orthopedic, maternity, and so on—and it wants all reports to be based on a minimum of fifty patients. Also suppose that the neurological ward is the smallest distinct ward, accounting for only 4 percent of inpatients. Under these circumstances, the hospital's customer satisfaction study must do one of the following: (1) use a total sample size of at least 1,250 ($50 \div .04 = 1,250$) so that the sample produces at least fifty neurological patients, (2) oversample neurological patients so that the subgroup minimum can be met despite a total sample of less than 1,250, or (3) plan not to issue a report for the neurological ward.

Using Resource Limitations

A fifth nonstatistical method is setting the sample size according to financial resource limitations. This is usually done as follows. Ask a decision maker how much she or he expects to pay for a particular research project. Subtract the fixed costs of the project from this number. Divide the remaining budget by the expected cost per observation to obtain a resource-based sample size.

Say, for example, that a hospital administrator is willing to spend no more than $20,000 for a patient satisfaction survey to be conducted by telephone. A research company might budget a certain number of hours to write the questionnaire and have it approved by the client, a certain number of hours for data analysis, a certain number of hours for report preparation, and a certain number for report presentation. These hours can be budgeted at appropriate pay rates, including overhead charges and profit. The research company will also budget interviewers' time for a pretest, supervisors' time to plan and supervise the pretest, professionals' time to conduct training for the pretest and the main study, professionals' time to prepare training materials, and so on. These are the fixed costs of the project.

Let's say, for example, that these fixed costs sum to $6,000. This leaves $14,000 for variable costs. Now the research company must estimate the variable cost per interview, which will depend on the length of the questionnaire, the number of long-distance calls needed, the screening rate, the costs of editing and coding (which depend on the number of open-ended questions), the costs of data entry, and other variables. Say these come to $15 per completed interview for the hospital satisfaction study. A $14,000 budget for variable costs will thus allow a sample size of 933 interviews ($14,000 ÷ $15).

A budget-based approach is, in our experience, the most common method used to set sample sizes in marketing research, particularly in smaller companies whose budgets and statistical knowledge are limited. The approach has intuitive appeal because it allows managers to talk about research in dollars and cents, a language they understand. The approach is also grounded in financial realities. In contrast to other approaches, which essentially budget a study and then ask whether managers are willing to pay that much, the budget-based approach fits the research effort to the funds available.

The weakness of the budget-based approach is that it does not explicitly consider information objectives. For example, 933 interviews may be more than a hospital needs to profile overall patient satisfaction, or it may be nowhere near enough to develop separate satisfaction profiles for various service areas. Just as statistical calculations must be checked against a budget to see whether the sample is affordable, it is desirable to check a budget-based sample size against information needs to see whether the sample will be satisfactory and efficient.

Critical Thinking Skills

A marketing research instructor is planning a class project that involves a telephone survey. The instructor has forty students in the class and wants each student to do a reasonable number of interviews for the project within a two-week period. What would be a reasonable number of interviews for each student to do? What will the resulting sample size be?

Ask an Expert

A final nonstatistical approach for setting sample size is to ask an expert. For example, you could call the nearest major university and ask for a professor who is expert in marketing research methods. Briefly describe your research project to this person and ask for suggestions regarding an appropriate sample size. The professor should be able to make suggestions or refer you to someone else. Of course, an expert will consider several of the approaches we have discussed in determining a sample size to recommend.

Marketing Research Tools 14.2 summarizes the possible methods of setting sample size.

MARKETING RESEARCH TOOLS

14.2

METHODS OF SETTING SAMPLE SIZE

1. The confidence interval approach
2. The value of information approach
3. Use of previous sample sizes
4. Use of typical sample sizes
5. Use of a "magic number"
6. Anticipation of subgroup analyses
7. Use of resource limitations
8. Use of expert guidance

Using Stratified Sampling to Improve Cost-Effectiveness

So far, the discussion of sample size has presumed that a simple random sample will be drawn. There are also situations in which the cost-effectiveness of a research project can be improved by using *stratified sampling* to reduce sampling errors or *cluster sampling* to reduce costs.

As mentioned in Chapter 13, stratified sampling separates the population into subgroups called "strata," then selects random samples from each subgroup (see Exhibit 14.3 on page 380 for a graphic depiction). Dividing the sampling effort in this fashion creates some extra work and extra cost. However, under some conditions, the estimates drawn from stratified samples have much lower sampling errors than estimates from simple random samples. This allows sampling error goals to be met with smaller sample sizes than are needed in simple random sampling and consequently lowers the total cost of research.

When Should Stratified Samples Be Used?

There are five conditions under which stratified sampling is cost effective: (1) when the primary research objective is to compare population subgroups, (2) when there are separate confidence interval goals for various population subgroups, (3) when population subgroups have different variances for some variable being studied, (4) when costs of data collection differ across population subgroups, and (5) when prior information about some variable of interest differs across population subgroups. These conditions are listed in Marketing Research Tools 14.3 (see page 381) and discussed in the following sections.

EXHIBIT 14.3

How Stratified Sampling Works

Assume companíes in a particular industry are to be sampled. The companies are of small, medium, or large size. If different-sized companies are to be compared on some dimension, or if there is more variation among the larger companies, *stratified sampling* might be used.

First, the companies are stratified into small, medium, or large **strata.**

Large companies

Medium companies

Small companies

A random sample is then drawn from each stratum. It is not necessary to sample the same number of companies from each stratum.

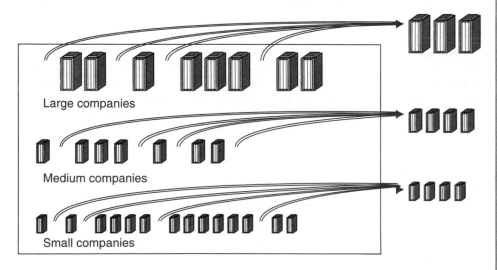

Large companies

Medium companies

Small companies

MARKETING RESEARCH TOOLS

14.3

REASONS FOR SAMPLE STRATIFICATION

1. The primary research objective is to compare groups.
2. There are separate confidence interval objectives by strata.
3. Variances differ by strata.
4. Costs differ by strata.
5. Prior information differs by strata.

When the Objective Is to Compare Subgroups

The first condition under which stratified sampling is cost effective is when the primary research objective is to compare population subgroups. For example, people who buy a certain brand and people who buy other brands might be compared to see whether the two groups differ significantly on any other variables.

The key significance tests in such research will be tests of differences between means (e.g., the mean for buyers versus the mean for nonbuyers). Sampling errors for differences between means are minimized when the sample size is equal in the groups being compared (assuming equal variances in the groups). If these groups differ in size in the population, they must be sampled at different rates to get equal sample sizes. This, of course, implies stratified sampling.

When There Are Separate Confidence Interval Goals

The second condition under which stratified sampling is cost effective is when there are separate confidence interval goals for various population subgroups. For example, separate estimates of mean income of people who buy a certain brand and people who buy other brands might be desired, with each estimate having a 95 percent confidence interval of ±$2,000. Assuming equal variances in the two groups, the sample sizes needed to reach your confidence interval goals are the same for each group. If the groups differ in size in the population, they must be sampled at different rates to get equal sample sizes.

Confidence interval goals need not be identical across groups to motivate stratified sampling. The existence of specific goals for each group implies specific needed sample sizes, whether or not the goals are identical, and these sample sizes may require different sampling rates in the different groups. Case Study 14.3 illustrates this point.

When Variances Differ Across Strata

The third condition under which stratified sampling is cost effective is when population subgroups have different variances for some variable being studied. This occurs because the squared sampling error, or **sampling variance,** for a total sample can be expressed as a weighted combination of sampling variance in various strata, as follows:

$$s_{\bar{x}}^2 = \Sigma \left(\frac{N_h^2}{N^2} \right) s_{\bar{x}_h}^2 .$$ **Equation 14.3**

where $s_{\bar{x}}^2$ is the sampling variance, N_h is the population size for stratum h, N is the total population size, and $s_{\bar{x}_h}^2$ is the sampling variance in the h stratum, computed as s_h^2/n_h.

CASE STUDY 14.3

The manager of market research for a hospital chain says that stratified sampling was used to solve a problem in the company's outpatient satisfaction surveys. She says:

At each hospital in our system, we conduct 2,400 telephone interviews per year with people who received outpatient services. We ask these people to rate our performance on various dimensions, and the results are used to evaluate the performance of each hospital as well as specific care units.

Until recently, we used a random sample of outpatients for these surveys. However, in the course of a year, we might treat 10,000 patients in the radiology [X-ray] unit of a hospital and only twenty patients in the occupational therapy unit. Therefore, in drawing a random sample of 2,400 patients, we might get 1,000 from radiology and two from occupational therapy. This gave us very narrow confidence intervals for radiology and very wide confidence intervals for occupational therapy. If the occupational therapy unit got poor results, the manager of that unit would scream bloody murder about the tiny sample size.

We've now switched to a stratified system which sets the sample size for each unit separately. This new system goes through the patient records for each hospital and counts the number of patients treated in each unit. It then calculates an initial sample size for each unit that will provide a .05 confidence interval around estimates of the percentage of patients who were "very satisfied" with each performance dimension. These sample size calculations use the "finite population correction," so smaller units get smaller sample sizes. The total initial sample size across all units adds to something less than 2,400, and the remaining available sample size is allocated to units in proportion to their initial sample size.

This system eliminates situations where we only have two or three observations for a unit, and it allows me to tell each unit manager that the results have a confidence interval of less than 5 percent. This has created much better acceptance of the results among the managers.

Since the overall sampling variance is a weighted composite of the strata sampling variances, it is possible to get a smaller overall sampling variance by giving a relatively larger sample to strata in which the variance is higher.

In a classic paper on stratified sampling, Jerzy Neyman (1934) showed that the minimum overall sampling error is obtained if sample allocations for each stratum are proportionate to the size of the stratum *and* to the standard deviation in that stratum for the variable being studied. Thus, the optimum sample size for a stratum is given as

$$n_b^* = \left[\frac{\pi_b s_b}{\Sigma(\pi_b s_b)} \right] n. \qquad \textbf{Equation 14.4}$$

where n_b^* is the optimum sample size in the bth stratum, π_b is the proportion of the population which is in the bth stratum, s_b is the standard deviation in the bth stratum for the variable being measured, and n is the total sample size to be allocated across strata.

If variances—and therefore standard deviations—are equal across the various strata, Equation 14.4 can be simplified to show that the allocation for each stratum should be proportional to its size in the population. However, when variances differ across strata, disproportionate sampling is optimal, with more sampling being done in the higher variance strata.

When do such situations arise? For most marketing variables, differences in variances across consumer groups are small, even if there are substantial differences in means. The big differences occur in research dealing with organizations. As a general rule, large organizations exhibit much more variation than small organizations do. Therefore, establishments should be stratified by size, and higher sampling rates should be used for the bigger organizations.

If variances among organizations are unknown before the research is conducted, measures of organizational size can be used to approximate them, because research has shown that size measures are highly correlated with variances. Size measures may be based on total annual sales, number of employees, value of assets, or other factors. If more than one size measure is available, the one most closely related to the critical variables in the study should be used. The formula for optimum sample selection using measures of size is given as

$$n_h^* = \left[\frac{MOS_h}{\Sigma MOS_h} \right] - n. \qquad \text{Equation 14.5}$$

where n_h^* is the optimum sample size in the hth stratum, MOS_h is the measure of size for the hth stratum, and n is the total sample size.

For example, suppose you want to study the market for uniforms for hospital employees. You plan to survey 1,000 hospitals in this study, and you want your sample to have the smallest possible sampling error for estimates of expenditure on uniforms. You expect expenditures on uniforms to correlate very highly with the number of employees.

Information on hospitals can be found in the annual "Guide" issue of *Hospitals* magazine, published by the American Hospital Association. Exhibit 14.4 divides the hospitals into six strata based on size and shows (1) the number of hospitals in each stratum, (2) the number of employees in each stratum, and (3) the standard deviation in the number of employees for hospitals in each stratum.

EXHIBIT 14.4

Characteristics of U.S. Hospitals

Number of Beds	Number of Hospitals	Number of Employees (in thousands)	s_h for Number of Employees
Fewer than 50	1,614	429	25
50–99	1,566	601	51
100–199	1,419	2,106	95
200–299	683	2,124	152
300–499	679	3,910	384
500 and over	609	6,677	826
Total	6,570	15,847	

Exhibit 14.5 uses this information to allocate a total sample of 1,000 across the various strata. The first column of Exhibit 14.5 shows proportional allocations based on the number of hospitals in each group; for example, hospitals with fewer than fifty employees account for 24.6 percent of the total number of hospitals (1,614/6,570), so they are assigned 24.6 percent of the sample, or 246. The second column of Exhibit 14.5 shows optimal allocations based on Equation 14.4 (see page 382), using number of employees as a measure of size. The bottom row of Exhibit 14.5 shows sampling variances for the two samples, based on using the standard deviation in number of employees (from Exhibit 14.4) as a proxy for the standard deviation in expenditures on uniforms.

Note that the optimal allocation produces a sampling variance that is only one-fourth as large as the sampling variance for the proportional sample. To put it another way, an optimum stratified sample of 1,000 hospitals produces the same sampling variance as a proportional sample of 4,000 hospitals.

In many business populations, the number of very large organizations is small but the variance in this stratum is huge. In these situations, optimum allocations using a size measure may yield a sample size for the stratum of largest businesses that is larger than the number of firms in that stratum. The solution is to take *all* the elements in this stratum, which is then called a "certainty" stratum because all of its members are included in the sample.

Case Study 14.4 provides an example of a stratified sample in which all key businesses are selected, along with a sampling of other businesses. Other well-known examples of such sampling are the monthly economic surveys conducted by the Census Bureau to measure sales and manufacturing activity. In these surveys, the largest 2,500 establishments fall into each month's sample with certainty and the rest of the sample is selected by probability procedures, asked for information for only a limited time, and then replaced.

Critical Thinking Skills

Use Equation 14.4 (see page 382), along with the information in Exhibit 14.4, to verify that the optimal allocation shown in Exhibit 14.5 is correct. Use Equation 14.3 (see page 381), along with the standard deviations given in Exhibit 14.4, to verify that the sampling variances are correct.

EXHIBIT 14.5

U.S. Hospitals: Sample Size Allocations, Given a Total Sample of 1,000

Number of Beds	Proportional Allocation	Optimal Allocation by Number of Employees
Fewer than 50	246	27
50–99	238	38
100–199	216	133
200–299	104	134
300–499	103	247
500 and over	93	421
Total sample	1,000	1,000
Overall sampling variance for mean number of employees	71.0	17.8

CASE STUDY 14.4

The vice president of marketing for an industrial tank–coating business also uses stratified sampling in customer satisfaction research. He says:

Our company sells industrial products and services. As is common for industrial companies, we have key customers who account for a large share of our business. Our top fifty customers represent 76 percent of our sales. The remaining 24 percent of sales is distributed across roughly 950 customers.

When we do customer satisfaction surveys, it makes no sense for us to treat all 1,000 customers equally. We could draw a random sample of customers and weight the results by the amount of business that each respondent does with us. However, the easiest approach for us is to separate the fifty key accounts from our other customers, survey all of the key accounts, and survey a sample of the other customers. We then keep results from the two groups separate so that our managers never lose sight of the key accounts.

When Costs Differ Across Strata

Neyman's (1934) famous paper also showed that optimum sample allocations across strata depend on the costs of gathering information in the various strata. Specifically, optimum allocations are *inversely* proportional to the square roots of per unit data collection costs in the different strata. Combining this result with Equation 14.4 (see page 382), the more general optimum is given as

$$n_h^* = \left[\frac{\pi_h s_h / \sqrt{C_h}}{\Sigma(\pi_h s_h / \sqrt{C_h})} \right] n. \qquad \textbf{Equation 14.6}$$

where C_h is the variable cost per observation in the hth stratum and all other terms are as defined in Equation 14.4.

If costs but not variances differ by strata—which sometimes happens in consumer research—then Equation 14.6 reduces to Equation 14.7. If neither costs nor variances differ by strata, the equation reduces to proportional allocation:

$$n_h^* = \left[\frac{\pi_h / \sqrt{C_h}}{\Sigma(\pi_h / \sqrt{C_h})} \right] n. \qquad \textbf{Equation 14.7}$$

There are two main situations in which costs differ by strata. The first is when combined data collection methods, such as mail surveys with telephone follow-ups, are used to improve the cost-effectiveness of research. Case Study 14.5 gives an example of this situation.

The second situation in which costs differ by strata is when a special consumer population of interest, such as Hispanic or African-American consumers, is geographically clustered so that there will be large differences in screening costs depending on location. For example, assume that Hispanics in a given region are to be sampled. To simplify the example, assume that some Hispanics in this region live in

CASE STUDY 14.5

Some years ago, the U.S. Public Health Service conducted a survey to determine physicians' smoking behavior and attitudes toward smoking. The results were intended for wide public dissemination, and a careful sample was required. A budget of $50,000 was allocated for data collection.

A mail survey was used for initial data collection to save money, since at the time mailing costs were only about $1 per completed questionnaire. It was recognized that only about 40 percent of physicians would respond to the mail survey, even after two follow-ups. The other 60 percent would require a long-distance telephone interview at a cost of about $25 per completed interview. Based on Equation 14.7, the optimum sample design was to take one-fifth of those who did not cooperate by mail since $\sqrt{(\$1/\$25)} = \frac{1}{5}$. For the given budget, this yielded a sample of 5,905 mail responders and 1,764 telephone responders, a total sample size of 7,669.

The reason why this is the best allocation can be seen by comparing it to other procedures:

- If the entire study had been done on the telephone, a sample size of only 2,000 could have been obtained ($50,000 data collection budget ÷ $25 per interview = 2,000 interviews) and the sampling error would have been more than 50 percent larger than in the optimum design.

- If the sample had been proportionate, instead of sampling from the telephone stratum at a lower rate, a sample of only 1,299 mail responders and 1,948 telephone responders could have been selected for the same total cost. In this case the sampling error is more than 15 percent larger than for the optimum design.

- Finally, the exclusive use of mail would yield the highest sample size but would create serious sample biases because, as we learned in this study, the physicians who did not respond by mail were much more likely to be smokers.

areas that are 100 percent Hispanic, and others live in areas that are only 5 percent Hispanic. Assume that the cost of each interview is $25, and that screening households to determine if they are Hispanic costs $10 per screen. Therefore, the total cost per completed case is $25 in the areas that are 100 percent Hispanic, since no screening is required, and $225 in the areas that are only 5 percent Hispanic, since there will be twenty screening calls at $10 per case for each completed interview. Since $\sqrt{(\$25/\$225)}$ is $\frac{1}{3}$, the sampling rate in those areas where Hispanics are rare should be one-third of that in the areas that are entirely Hispanic.

When Prior Information Differs Across Strata

Earlier in the chapter, it was shown that the value of information depends on how much is already known. If a great deal is already known about a given market, further information has less value than if very little is known.

Sometimes much more information is available for some strata than for others. In this case, the sampling rate will be lower in strata where more is already known, and in some cases there may be no sampling at all from these strata. An example is given here to illustrate this situation.

A manufacturer developed a new motor that was superior to existing motors but also was more expensive to produce. Market research was planned to determine customer acceptance of the new motor. The market for this product was stratified into a few large buyers, which accounted for about half the total sales of existing motors, and hundreds of other buyers, which each bought smaller quantities. In designing a sample for the market research, we recommended that the manufacturer omit all the large users and survey only the smaller ones.

The reason we made this recommendation is that the manufacturer was in steady communication with the largest customers and had already conducted detailed discussions with each of them about the new motor. Thus, additional research was not needed. Contact with the smaller customers was much less frequent and their views were not known, so research on this group was valuable.

Other Comments on Stratified Sampling

Inappropriate Uses of Stratification

Five situations in which stratified sampling is appropriate have been described. This procedure is also sometimes used in situations in which it is inappropriate. These are as follows.

First, people who do not trust probability sometimes ask that a sample be stratified so that variables such as age, race, gender, or income agree exactly with census estimates. The cost of doing this is prohibitive, because it requires extensive screening efforts as well as additional sampling costs, and the benefits are nonexistent. Stratification should not be used to ensure that a sample is exactly representative. Given a large enough sample size, uncontrolled chance does a very good job of generating a representative sample.

Another inappropriate use of stratification is to correct for major problems in survey cooperation rates. In poorly designed mail surveys with only one mailing, as little as 5 or 10 percent of the sample may participate. Researchers faced with such a disaster sometimes try to demonstrate that the sample is adequate by comparing its demographic characteristics with those of the total population. Usually, there will be noticeable biases for some variables. In an effort to salvage something from the wreck, the data are weighted on these variables to correct for sample biases. This weighting corrects the distributions for the weighted variables but is unlikely to eliminate the biases in the key variables of interest.

The use of weights to correct for sample biases due to noncooperation is called "poststratification" because it is done after the sampling. It is a legitimate procedure to correct for minor differences between the sample and population. For example, poststratification is sometimes used to adjust for lower cooperation in central cities than in rural areas and for the fact that younger respondents are less likely to be available for interviewing than are retired persons. Poststratification cannot, however, transform a low-quality sample into a jewel.

Stratification in Studies with Multiple Objectives

Market research studies often have multiple purposes, such as making estimates about the total population and also making comparisons among subgroups. In this case, no one sample design is optimum for both requirements simultaneously. The usual response to multiple objectives is to make some compromise: for example, in consumer research it is common to use proportional sampling constrained by minimum sample sizes for each stratum. The compromise that is made should reflect the relative importance of specific research objectives.

Using Cluster Sampling to Improve Cost-Effectiveness

Cluster sampling, like stratified sampling, can improve the cost-effectiveness of research under certain conditions. In cluster sampling, the population is divided into subgroups called "clusters," and a sample of clusters is drawn. Further sampling of population members may be done within clusters, and multistage cluster sampling (i.e., sampling clusters within clusters) is possible. Marketing Research Tools 14.4 gives examples of the kinds of clusters sometimes used in marketing research, and Exhibit 14.6 (see page 390) provides a graphic depiction of cluster sampling.

Cluster sampling differs from stratified sampling in that cluster sampling uses a *sample of clusters*, whereas stratified sampling draws a sample *within every stratum*. Cluster sampling also differs from stratified sampling in that stratified sampling is focused on reducing sampling errors, and cluster sampling is focused on reducing costs. Cluster samples actually have higher sampling errors than simple random samples of equal size, but, under the right conditions, cluster samples allow a large enough increase in sample size to more than offset their inefficiency, so that overall sampling error is reduced for any given budget.

The logic of cluster sampling can be seen in the context of a national survey of households. Assume that a nationwide sample of 500 households is desired and that interviews will be done in respondents' homes where product samples can be shown. A simple random sample of 500 households from the nation's more than 90 million households will produce something like the following: one household selected in Cedar Rapids, Iowa; one household in Fort Myers, Florida; one household in Helena, Montana; and so on. The travel and/or training costs for interviewing this sample will be staggering. Interviewers will travel from city to city for each interview, so the cost of each interview will reflect at least one intercity trip (more, if callbacks are needed).

Costs will be greatly reduced if the 500 households are selected in clusters rather than individually. For example, twenty-five counties nationwide might be drawn, four places per selected county, one census tract per selected place, one block per selected tract, and five households per selected block. The result will still be 500 households, but interviews will be concentrated in twenty-five counties with twenty interviews per county, and interviewers will go to only four places in each county. This approach will cost much less than a simple random sample. Or, if the same budget is used, this approach will allow far more than 500 interviews.

MARKETING RESEARCH TOOLS 14.4

EXAMPLES OF CLUSTERS

Population	Possible Clusters
Consumers	Standard metropolitan areas
	Counties
	Shopping malls
	Telephone exchanges
	Census tracts
	Blocks
	Households
College students	Colleges
	Dormitories
	Classes
Elementary or high school students	School districts
	Schools
	Grade levels
	Classes
Businesses	Counties
	Localities
	Plant sites
Hospital patients	Hospitals
	Wards

When Should Cluster Samples Be Used?

Cluster sampling is beneficial under three general conditions:

- *When travel costs can be reduced as a result.* This occurs in in-home or in-office interviews that are spread over broad geographic areas. It does *not* occur in mail or telephone surveys (long-distance charges do not vary enough to motivate clustered interviewing from localized facilities).

    In-home interviews for consumer populations have become rare in marketing research. However, many industrial studies are conducted with in-office interviews, and these studies benefit from clustering unless the target population is geographically compact.

- *When there are substantial fixed costs associated with each data collection location.* For example, if a research company is hired to interview people at a mall, there is usually a basic charge of at least $1,000 per mall, regardless of how many

EXHIBIT 14.6

How Cluster
Sampling
Works

Assume companies in a particular industry are to be sampled. The companies are located in several different cities. If it is necessary to travel to each company to conduct the research and it is desirable to minimize the number of cities to which researchers need to travel, *cluster sampling* will be cost effective.

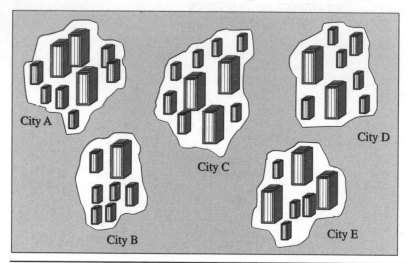

First, the population of companies is divided into clusters (in this case, cities) and a sample of clusters (cities) is drawn. Here, clusters B and D are selected.

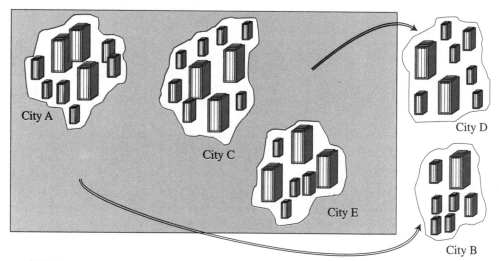

Then a sample would be drawn within each cluster to make up the sample.

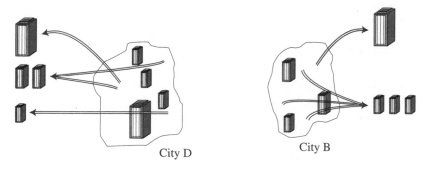

interviews are conducted. Gathering several interviews at each mall allows these fixed costs to be spread over the interviews.

■ *When there is a list of clusters but not of individual population members.* For example, if the preferences of local business managers regarding economic development activities for the area are to be studied, a researcher might start with a list of local businesses, select businesses from that list, then select managers from within those companies.

Optimal Clustering

If cost were the only concern in designing cluster samples, the logical approach would be to gather all data in a single cluster. After all, if you can save money by breaking 500 interviews into twenty-five counties with twenty interviews in each county, why not do all 500 interviews in one county and save even more?

The answer, obviously, is concern about the representativeness of the sample. Households within a single county may have product preferences or product usage patterns that are specific to the region. Consequently, research results from a single county may not provide a good picture of the nation as a whole.

In statistical terms, clustering increases sampling error because of correlations among cluster members. Two households in Cedar Rapids, Iowa, are likely to be more highly correlated in their behaviors and attitudes than a household in Cedar Rapids and a household in Fort Myers, Florida. The higher correlation means that a second household from Cedar Rapids adds less new information to the sample than a household from Fort Myers. In fact, if the households in Cedar Rapids were perfectly homogeneous, a second household from Cedar Rapids would add no new information and thus would have no research value. As a general rule, homogeneities are higher for smaller clusters, because people and companies next door to one another tend to be more similar than people and companies across town. Homogeneities in consumer populations also tend to be higher for variables that are economically related, because people who live near one another are usually economically similar.

Homogeneity (or similarity) within clusters is measured by a statistic called the "intracluster coefficient of homogeneity," expressed as ρ (rho). ρ functions like a correlation coefficient—a ρ of 0 indicates that the elements in a cluster are completely uncorrelated, and a ρ of 1.00 indicates that the elements in a cluster are perfectly homogeneous (correlation coefficients are discussed in Chapter 17). In most marketing studies, ρ falls in the range of 0 to .10 for most variables studied, and a value of .05 can be assumed for planning purposes.

Morris Hansen, William Hurwitz, and William Madow (1954) have shown that optimum cluster sizes can be determined by Equation 14.8, which uses (1) ρ, (2) the variable cost of each observation, and (3) the fixed costs associated with each cluster.

$$n_{opt} = \sqrt{\frac{C_1}{c_2}\left(\frac{1-\rho}{\rho}\right)}.$$ **Equation 14.8**

where n_{opt} is the optimum size of the clusters (the first-stage clusters if multi-stage sampling is used), C_1 is the fixed cost per cluster, and c_2 is the variable cost per observation.

This formula often produces optimum cluster sizes of 20 to 25 in marketing research projects for which clustering is appropriate. So, for example, a sample of 500 will usually be allocated to twenty data collection sites at twenty-five observations per site, or twenty-five collection sites at twenty observations per site.

Drawing Cluster Samples

Clusters tend to vary greatly by size. However, it can be shown that sampling errors arc minimized when the same sample size is taken from each cluster. The trick in drawing cluster samples, therefore, is to draw an equal sample size in each cluster, yet preserve equal probabilities of selection for population members within big and little clusters.

The problem can be illustrated with an example. Assume that we would like to draw a cluster sample of 2,000 American college students. We would like to draw 40 schools, then 50 students within each selected school, and we would like all students to have the same overall chance of selection.

If we draw schools with equal probabilities, a small school such as Milliken University will have the same chance of selection as a big school such as the University of Minnesota. Then, if we draw 50 students within each school, the Minnesota students will have a lower chance of selection. This is not what we want.

To achieve equal probabilities of selection for individual population members but equal sample sizes within clusters, the clusters—in our case, colleges—must be selected with different probabilities of selection. Specifically, clusters must be selected with probabilities that are proportional to their size (this is called "PPS sampling"). PPS sampling is done as follows:

1. The clusters are listed.

2. A cumulating measure of population size is recorded next to each cluster. If the first cluster is a university with 30,000 students, the cumulation to this point is 30,000, and that number is recorded next to the cluster. If the next cluster is a university with 27,000 students, the cumulation to this point is 57,000, and that number is recorded next to the cluster. This continues until all clusters have been cumulated and the entire population is accounted for.

4. A sampling interval is calculated by dividing the population size by the desired number of clusters. In the college example, there are about 8,000,000 American college students, so the interval would be $8,000,000 \div 40 = 200,000$.

5. A random start between 1 and i (the sampling interval) is chosen. Using the random number table in Appendix A at the back of this book, start from the top left of the table and read six-digit numbers downward, looking for a random start between 1 and 200,000. We therefore get 114,962 for our random start.

6. A systematic sample is drawn using the random start and the calculated interval. In our example, the selected numbers are 114,962 (s); 314,962 ($s + i$); 514,962 ($s + 2i$); 714,962 ($s + 3i$), and so on. A cluster is selected if a selected number falls into its sequence of numbers, that is, if a selected number is greater than the cumulative sum of all previous clusters but less than or equal to the cumulative sum including this cluster.

Any clusters that are larger than the sampling interval will fall into the sample with certainty, and some of them may be selected more than once. If a cluster is selected more than once, the sample size within that cluster is increased correspondingly. In our example, one selection for a college will mean that 50 students are selected, two selections will mean that 100 students are selected, and so on.

It can easily be seen that PPS sampling always gives each student an equal probability of selection since the probability of a college being selected is directly proportional to its size and the probability of a student being selected within that college is inversely proportional to the size of the college. Thus, college size cancels out and students at all colleges have equal probabilities of selection.

Computing Sampling Errors

If clustering or stratification is used to make a sampling more efficient, the procedures that are used to compute sampling errors for simple random samples no longer apply. Instead, new methods are used that depend heavily on the basic meaning of sampling variance and the power of computers.

Remember that the definition of sampling error involves the notion of repeated samples that exhibit chance variation. The sampling variance is defined as the variance across values of some statistic observed for these separate samples, and the square root of this variance is the sampling error.

In any given research project, there is only one sample. However, this sample can be split into subsamples, and the variation among these subsamples can be used to estimate sampling error. There are several computer programs that use this principle for calculating sampling errors for complex samples. The methods go by names such as "bootstrapping," "jackknifing," and "balanced random replication." All give satisfactory results. If you want to use one of them to estimate sampling errors for a complex sample, contact a statistical consultant at your university computing center (or, better yet, a social sciences computing center) for assistance.

Summary

This chapter discussed methods of determining sample size and increasing sample efficiency. The following points were covered:

1. What is sampling error?
The term "sampling error" refers to chance variation across repeated samples from a population. Specifically, for any given sample characteristic, such as the mean value of a measure, the sampling error of that characteristic is its standard deviation across all possible samples of the same size.

2. How can the sample size needed to produce a desired confidence interval be determined?
To set a sample size according to statistical objectives, start with a desired confidence interval, then calculate the sampling error needed to produce that interval. This

sampling error, in turn, implies a needed sample size. Use the tables in Appendix 14.1 or the SAMPLER software for help.

3. How can an optimum sample size be determined by using the value and cost of information?
Unlike the confidence interval approach, the value of information approach to sample size automatically considers the financial importance of the issue being studied and the level of uncertainty about what to do. This approach is illustrated in Appendix 14.2.

4. How can the sample size be set by using other guidelines?
Nonstatistical bases for setting the sample size include (1) using a sample size similar to what you have done before, (2) using a sample size similar to what others have done, (3) using a "magic number" that seems adequate to managers who will use the research, (4) anticipating subgroup analyses and planning minimum sample sizes in the small cells, (5) setting the sample size according to the available budget, and (6) asking an expert.

5. How is stratified sampling used to reduce sampling errors?
Stratified sampling separates the population into subgroups called "strata," then selects random samples from each stratum. Stratified sampling reduces sampling errors when (1) the major objective of the research is to compare population subgroups, (2) there are separate confidence interval goals for various strata, (3) variances differ across strata, (4) the costs of research differ across strata, or (5) more prior information is available about some strata than about others. Stratified sampling is almost always appropriate in studies of businesses.

6. How is cluster sampling used to increase the cost-effectiveness of research?
Cluster sampling divides the population into subgroups called "clusters" from which a sample is selected. Cluster sampling is cost effective when (1) travel costs are high, (2) there are substantial fixed costs associated with data collection at each location, and (3) there is a list of clusters but not of individual population members. Cluster sampling is usually appropriate for personal interviewing studies.

Suggested Additional Readings

The same books discussed in Chapter 13 should be consulted for most topics covered in this chapter. For a detailed discussion of the Bayesian approach to the value of information, see Robert Schlaifer, *Probability and Statistics for Business Decisions* (New York: McGraw-Hill, 1959).

Discussion Questions

1. Why should the "value of information" approach to sample size be used by marketing researchers? How does this approach differ from the classical approach?

2. What are the three things that a manager needs to know if he/she wishes to use the value of information approach to determine sample size?

3. What is a stratified sampling? When should it be used? What uses of stratified sampling are inappropriate?

4. What is cluster sampling? When should it be used?
5. How does cluster sampling differ from stratified sampling?
6. What is meant by sampling variance? What is meant by sampling error?

Marketing Research Challenge

You have been given the assignment of comparing current undergraduate student usage and needs for computer facilities by major academic units at your school. Assume the questionnaire will be self-administered by mail and you will attempt to obtain a sample of about 1,000 students. (If your school is small, take a sample of half the students.) Using a current student directory, describe how you would select a sample of students stratified by major academic units so that each of the major academic units is adequately sampled.

If no current mail list is available, or if mail is not feasible for some other reason, indicate how you might sample classes using a current semester class schedule. For either method, what problems might you face? How might you reduce these problems?

Internet Exercise

The Internet Exercise for Chapter 13 asked how you would obtain respondents for an Internet survey of Houston Astros fans. If your recommended procedures were used, what sample size would you expect to obtain? Can the sample size for an Internet survey be controlled? If the Astros wanted to stratify the sample into business season ticket buyers, personal season ticket buyers, and single-game ticket buyers, could this be done on the Web?

References

Hansen, Morris, William Hurwitz, and William Madow (1954). *Sample Survey Methods and Theory* (2 vols.) New York: Wiley.

Neyman, Jerzy (1934). "On the Two Different Aspects of the Representative Method: The Method of Stratified Sampling and the Method of Purposive Selection." *Journal of the Royal Statistical Society* 97, pp. 558–606.

Schlaifer, Robert (© 1959). *Probability and Statistics for Business Decisions*, pp. 706–707, 712. Reproduced with permission of The McGraw-Hill Companies.

Sudman, Seymour (1976). *Applied Sampling*. (New York: Academic Press).

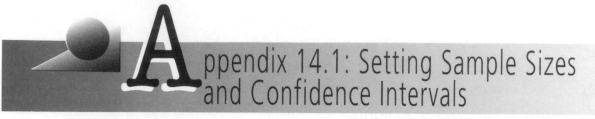

Appendix 14.1: Setting Sample Sizes and Confidence Intervals

Contents

Help Sheet 14.1A

Guide to Determining Sample Sizes

To Get . . .	Use
Sample size needed to achieve a desired 95% confidence interval around an estimated *proportion*	Table 14.1A
Sample size needed to achieve a desired 95% confidence interval around an estimated *mean*	Table 14.1B
Sample size needed to achieve a desired 95% confidence interval around an estimated *group size* (e.g., "How many *Time* subscribers took European vacations last year?")	Table 14.1A plus Adjustment 14.1A
Sample size needed to achieve a desired 95% confidence interval around an estimated *total amount* (e.g., "How much did *Time* subscribers spend on airline tickets to Europe last year?")	Table 14.1B plus Adjustment 14.1A
Sample size needed to achieve a desired 95% confidence interval around a *difference between two proportions*	Table 14.1A plus Adjustment 14.1B
Sample size needed to achieve a desired 95% confidence interval around a *difference between two means*	Table 14.1B plus Adjustment 14.1B

Help Sheet 14.1B

Guide to Determining Confidence Intervals

Given a Planned Sample Size, to Get . . .	Use
A 95% confidence interval around an estimated *proportion*	Table 14.1C
A 95% confidence interval around an estimated *mean*	Table 14.1D
A 95% confidence interval around an estimated *group size* (e.g., "How many *Time* subscribers took European vacations last year?")	Table 14.1C plus Adjustment 14.1A
A 95% confidence interval around an estimated *total amount* (e.g., "How much did *Time* subscribers spend on airline tickets to Europe last year?")	Table 14.1D plus Adjustment 14.1A
A 95% confidence interval around a *difference between two proportions*	Table 14.1C plus Adjustment 14.1B
A 95% confidence interval around a *difference between two means*	Table 14.1D plus Adjustment 14.1B

Table 14.1A

Sample Sizes Needed to Achieve Desired 95% Confidence Intervals Around Estimates of *Proportions*

Prestudy Estimate of the Proportion (*p*)	Sample size (*n*) Needed to Be 95% Confident the After-Study Estimate Is Within ±*l* of the True Proportion					
	l = .1%	.5%	1%	3%	5%	10%
1% or 99%	38,032	1,522	381	43	16	4
2% or 98%	75,296	3,012	753	84	31	8
5% or 95%	182,476	7,300	1,825	203	73	19
10% or 90%	345,744	13,830	3,458	385	139	35
20% or 80%	—	24,587	6,147	683	246	62
30% or 70%	—	32,270	8,068	897	323	81
40% or 60%	—	36,880	9,220	1,025	369	93
50%	—	38,416	9,604	1,068	385	97

Results that are not on this page can be determined by applying the following formula:

$$n = \left(\frac{1.96}{l}\right)^2 p(1-p),$$

where *l* is the desired confidence interval.

Table 14.1B

Sample Sizes Needed to Achieve Desired 95% Confidence Intervals Around Estimates of *Means*

Prestudy Estimate of the Standard Deviation (*s*)	Sample Size (*n*) Needed to Be 95% Confident the After-Study Estimate Is Within ±*l* of the True Mean					
	l = 1	5	10	50	100	500
2	16	—	—	—	—	—
5	97	4	—	—	—	—
10	385	16	4	—	—	—
30	3,458	139	35	—	—	—
50	9,604	385	97	4	—	—
100	38,416	1,537	385	16	4	—
500	—	38,416	9,604	385	97	4
1,000	—	153,664	38,416	1,537	385	16
5,000	—	—	—	38,416	9,604	385
10,000	—	—	—	153,664	38,416	1,537

Results that are not on this page can be determined by applying the following formula:

$$n = \left(\frac{1.96}{l}\right)^2 s^2,$$

where *l* is the desired confidence interval.

Table 14.1C

95% Confidence Intervals Obtained Around Estimates of *Proportions*, Given Various Sample Sizes

Prestudy Estimate of the Proportion (p)	Given Sample Size (n) Needed to be 95% Confident the After-Study Estimate Is Within ±*l* of the True Proportion						
	n = 50	100	200	300	500	1,000	5,000
1% or 99%	2.8%	2.0%	1.4%	1.1%	.9%	.7%	.3%
2% or 98%	3.9	2.8	2.0	1.6	1.3	.9	.4
5% or 95%	6.1	4.3	3.0	2.5	2.0	1.5	.6
10% or 90%	8.4	5.9	4.2	3.4	2.7	1.9	.9
20% or 80%	11.1	7.9	5.6	4.6	3.5	2.5	1.1
30% or 70%	12.7	9.0	6.4	5.2	4.0	2.9	1.3
40% or 60%	13.6	9.6	6.8	5.6	4.3	3.1	1.4
50%	13.9	9.8	7.0	5.7	4.4	3.1	1.4

Results that are not on this page can be determined by applying the following formula:

$$l = \frac{1.96\sqrt{p(1-p)}}{\sqrt{n}}$$

Table 14.1D

95% Confidence Intervals Obtained Around Estimates of *Means*, Given Various Sample Sizes

Prestudy Estimate of the Standard Deviation (s)	Given Sample Size (n) Needed to Be 95% Confident the After-Study Estimate Is Within ±*l* of the True Mean						
	n = 50	100	200	300	500	1,000	5,000
2	.56	.40	.28	.23	.18	.13	.06
5	1.39	.98	.70	.57	.44	.31	.14
10	2.8	2.0	1.4	1.2	.9	.7	.3
30	8.4	5.9	4.2	3.4	2.7	1.9	.9
50	13.9	9.8	7.0	5.7	4.4	3.1	1.4
100	28	20	14	12	9	7	3
500	139	98	70	57	44	31	14
1,000	278	196	139	114	88	62	28
5,000	1,386	980	693	566	439	310	139
10,000	2,772	1,960	1,386	1,132	877	620	278

Results that are not on this page can be determined by applying the following formula:

$$l = \frac{1.96\,s}{\sqrt{n}}$$

Adjustment 14.1A

Sample Sizes and Confidence Intervals for Estimates of *Group Sizes* and/or *Total Amounts*

Typical goal:	The number of Houstonians who visited San Antonio last year is to be estimated. The total amount of money they spent in San Antonio is also to be estimated.
Comments	Group sizes, such as the number of Houstonians who visited San Antonio, are obtained via estimates of proportions. A sample of Houstonians is taken, the proportion who visited San Antonio is estimated, then this proportion is multiplied by the population size (of Houstonians) to obtain an estimate of the total number.
	Total amounts, such as total dollars spent by Houstonians in San Antonio, are obtained via estimates of means. A sample of Houstonians is taken, their mean expenditure in San Antonio (including people who spent zero) is estimated, then this mean is multiplied by the population size to obtain an estimate of the total amount.

To find needed sample sizes for estimates of group size:

Step 1: Set the desired confidence level and confidence interval. For example, let's say you want to be 95 percent confident that your estimate of the number of Houstonians who visited San Antonio is within ±15,000 of the true number.

Step 2: Divide the confidence interval by N, the population size. In this example, 15,000 ÷ 3,000,000 (the approximate Houston population) = .005 (.5%). This is the adjusted confidence interval.

Step 3: Use Table 14.1A to find the needed sample size. The confidence interval, I, will be the adjusted result from Step 2, and the p will be the initial estimate of the proportion of Houstonians who visited San Antonio. For example, if we estimate $p = 20\%$, and we want I to be .005 (.5%), then we need $n = 24,587$.

To find needed sample sizes for estimates of total amounts:

Step 1: Set the desired confidence level and confidence interval. For example, let's say you want to be 95 percent confident that your estimate of total dollars spent by Houstonians in San Antonio is within ±$1.5 million of the true amount.

Step 2: Divide the interval by N, the population size. In this example, $1,500,000 ÷ 3,000,000 = $.50. This is the adjusted confidence interval.

Step 3: Use Table 14.1B to find the needed sample size. Proceed as if you were estimating a mean; in this example, it would be mean expenditure per Houstonian. For s, estimate the standard deviation of dollars spent in San Antonio across Houstonians.

To estimate confidence intervals for group sizes or total amounts:

Step 1: Given the planned sample size and the initial estimate of p or s, use Table 14.1C or 14.1D to find an expected confidence interval around the relevant proportion or mean.

Step 2:   Multiply the confidence interval (from the table) by *N*, the population size. The result is the confidence interval expected around the estimate of the total group size or total amount.

Adjustment 14.1B

Sample Sizes and Confidence Intervals for *Between-Group Comparisons* of Means or Proportions

To find needed sample sizes:

Step 1:   Set the desired confidence level and confidence interval for the comparison. Do you want to be 95 percent confident that your measured difference between two proportions is within ±1% of the true difference? 95 percent confident that your measured difference between two means is within ±10 of the true difference?

Step 2:   Use Table 14.1A or 14.1B (Table 14.1A for a 95% interval around a difference in proportions, Table 14.1B for a 95% interval around a difference in means) to find the needed sample size given the confidence level and confidence interval. If you expect *p* or *s* to differ between groups, use the *p* or *s* that gives a larger sample size.

Step 3:   Double the sample size obtained from the table. This doubled amount is the sample size needed *for each group*.

To find expected confidence intervals:

Step 1:   Estimate the sample size you expect from your *smaller* group.
Step 2:   Divide this sample size by two.
Step 3:   Given this divided result, use Table 14.1C or 14.1D to find the expected confidence interval for the measured difference.

Help Sheet 14.1C

How to Estimate *s* or *p*

To use Table 14.1A or 14.1C, you will need an initial estimate of *p* (the proportion of interest to you). Where will you get this estimate? Possibilities include:

1. Use 50% for your estimate, because 50% produces the largest (most conservative) sample size requirements. This works pretty well if *p* is likely to fall anywhere in the range of 30 to 70 percent.

2. Use your own good sense about the likely proportion. This works pretty well if *p* will fall in the 20-to-80 percent range.

3. Estimate *p* based on results obtained from other, similar studies.

4. Do a pilot study to estimate *p*. This can be combined with questionnaire pretesting.

To use Table 14.1B or 14.1D, you will need an initial estimate of s (the standard deviation). Possible ways of estimating s include:

1. Make an initial estimate of the mean you are interested in. (Say, for example, that you are interested in estimating mean dollars spent by Houstonians in San Antonio last year. What is your initial guess about this number, including people who spent zero? Is it $10? $20? $50?) Multiply your estimate by 1.5 for a "guesstimate" of s.

2. Instead of estimating the mean, estimate a high number that 99 percent of the observations will fall below. (What might be a high number for a Houstonian to have spent last year in San Antonio? $1,000? $1,500?) Also estimate a low number that 99 percent of the observations will be above. (For our example, this will be $0.) Calculate the range from high to low. (In our example, $1,500 minus $0 is a range of $1,500.) Divide this range by 6 for a "guesstimate" of s. (In our example, $1,500 ÷ 6 equals $250.)

    If you try methods 1 and 2 and get different results, use the higher number.

3. Estimate s based on results obtained from similar studies.

4. Do a pilot study to estimate s. This can be combined with questionnaire pretesting.

Appendix 14.2: Value of Information Calculations

For decisions such as whether or not to market a new product, it is possible to quantify prior uncertainty, gain or loss potential, and nearness to breakeven, and to compute a dollar value for information.

Let's start with a simple profit function for marketing a new product:

$$R = (kX - K),$$ **Equation 14.2A**

where R is the total profit or return on investment realized within some time period, K is the fixed cost necessary to market the product, k is the contribution to profit of each item sold (the difference between the selling price and variable costs), and X is the actual number sold in the specified time period. Given this profit function, the breakeven sales volume, X_b, is

$$X_b = K/k.$$ **Equation 14.2B**

For research planning purposes, the fixed cost, K, should not include "sunk costs." It should include expenditures for new plants and new equipment, if needed, and for introductory marketing costs, but it should not include costs of existing plants or research costs spent in developing the product. These costs have already been incurred regardless of whether the product is marketed and thus should play no role in the decision whether to market.

Estimating Prior Uncertainty

The first step in estimating the value of information for new product research is to get the decision maker to provide explicit estimates regarding (1) the number of units of the new product that can be sold and (2) a measure of uncertainty regarding this estimate.

Sales estimates are usually easy to get from managers. A manager is likely to have some idea of market size, competitive environment, and competitors' sales volumes in the product category (this information comes from the company's marketing information system). Knowing the advantages of the new product and its proposed selling price, the manager can make a preliminary estimate of sales. We label this estimate X_{prior}.

It is more difficult to get decision makers to quantify their uncertainty, but this also is possible. One can start by asking a question about the shape of the distribution around the best estimate, for example, "Is it equally likely that sales will be higher or lower than your best estimate?" Usually, this will be the case, and this implies that the decision maker's prior distribution is symmetric. The most widely known and easiest distribution to use is the normal distribution. It is not necessary that the decision maker's distribution be normal or even symmetric, but since it greatly simplifies discussion and computation of the value of information we shall assume normality.

The normal distribution is fully described by two parameters, the mean and the standard deviation. A natural measure of the decision maker's uncertainty is the standard deviation. The larger the standard deviation, the greater the uncertainty.

Decision makers often lack the statistical knowledge to answer a question such as "What standard deviation would you associate with the distribution of decision outcomes?," but it is not necessary to ask the question in this form. Any statement about the probability of some point other than X_{prior} on the prior distribution is sufficient to determine σ_{prior}, the standard deviation of the decision maker's estimate. For example, if the decision maker says that chances are about two out of three that estimated sales will be within $X_{prior} \pm a$, then $\sigma_{prior} = a$. If the decision maker says that the chances are 95 out of 100 that sales will be within $X_{prior} \pm b$, then $\sigma_{prior} = \frac{b}{2}$.

Gains and Losses

In calculating sample size under the value of information approach, potential gains and losses are simply expressed by k, the per unit contribution to profit. An incorrect decision not to market a product will result in an opportunity loss, that is, a lost potential contribution to profits.

Distance from Breakeven

Given managers' sales and uncertainty estimates, distance from breakeven is defined as

$$D = |X_{prior} - X_b| \div \sigma_{prior}.$$ **Equation 14.2C**

That is, D is not simply expressed as the absolute distance between the prior estimate and the breakeven point, it is expressed relative to uncertainty. If breakeven is 250,000 units and the chances are 95 out of 100 that sales will be between 150,000 and 200,000, the company is far from breakeven and is unlikely to seek new information or market the new product; on the other hand, if the company believes that chances are two out of three that sales will be between 100,000 and 300,000, it is closer to breakeven.

The Value of Perfect Information

The situation we have described is essentially a two-action problem (market/don't market) with linear costs and gains. For this case, Schlaifer (1959) has defined the value of information as

$$V = [k] \times [\sigma_{prior}] \times [G(D)],$$ **Equation 14.2D**

where V is the value of perfect information, k is the per unit profit contribution, σ_{prior} is the standard deviation of the sales estimate, D is the distance from breakeven, and $G(D)$ is the unit normal loss integral, a function first defined and used by Schlaifer. A table of the unit normal loss integral is found as Table 14.2A.

Note, in Table 14.2A, that $G(D)$ becomes smaller as D gets bigger. Therefore, the value of information declines as the distance from breakeven increases. However, the value of information increases as k (the gain or loss associated with the decision) and σ_{prior} (the prior uncertainty) increase. Thus, V simply quantifies our earlier discussion concerning the value of information.

TABLE 14.2A

Values of the Unit Normal Loss Integral G(D)

D	00	01	02	03	04	05	06	07	08	09
.0	.3989	.3940	.3890	.3841	.3793	.3744	.3697	.3649	.3602	.3556
.1	.3509	.3464	.3418	.3373	.3328	.3284	.3240	.3197	.3154	.3111
.2	.3069	.3027	.2986	.2944	.2904	.2863	.2824	.2884	.2745	.2706
.3	.2668	.2630	.2592	.2555	.2518	.2481	.2445	.2409	.2374	.2339
.4	.2304	.2270	.2236	.2203	.2169	.2137	.2104	.2072	.2040	.2009
.5	.1978	.1947	.1917	.1887	.1857	.1828	.1799	.1771	.1742	.1714
.6	.1687	.1659	.1633	.1606	.1580	.1554	.1528	.1503	.1478	.1453
.7	.1429	.1405	.1381	.1358	.1334	.1312	.1289	.1267	.1245	.1223
.8	.1202	.1181	.1160	.1140	.1120	.1100	.1080	.1061	.1042	.1023
.9	.1004	.09860	.09680	.09503	.09328	.09156	.08956	.08819	.08654	.08491
1.0	.08332	.08174	.08019	.07866	.07716	.07568	.07422	.07279	.07138	.06999
1.1	.06862	.06727	.06595	.06465	.06336	.06210	.06086	.05964	.05884	.05726
1.2	.05610	.05496	.05384	.05274	.05165	.05059	.04954	.04861	.04750	.04650
1.3	.04553	.04457	.04363	.04270	.04179	.04090	.04002	.03916	.03831	.03748
1.4	.03667	.03587	.03508	.03431	.03356	.03281	.03208	.03137	.03067	.02998
1.5	.02931	.02865	.02800	.02736	.02674	.02612	.02552	.02494	.02436	.02380
1.6	.02324	.02270	.02217	.02165	.02114	.02064	.02015	.01967	.01920	.01874
1.7	.01829	.01785	.01742	.01699	.01658	.01617	.01578	.01539	.01501	.01464
1.8	.01428	.01392	.01357	.01323	.01290	.01257	.01226	.01195	.01164	.01134
1.9	.01105	.01077	.01049	.01022	$.0^2 9957$	$.0^2 9698$	$.0^2 9445$	$.0^2 9198$	$.0^2 8957$	$.0^2 8721$
2.0	$.0^2 8491$	$.0^2 8266$	$.0^2 8046$	$.0^2 7832$	$.0^2 7623$	$.0^2 7418$	$.0^2 7219$	$.0^2 7024$	$.0^2 6836$	$.0^2 6649$
2.1	$.0^2 6468$	$.0^2 6292$	$.0^2 6120$	$.0^2 5952$	$.0^2 5788$	$.0^2 5628$	$.0^2 5472$	$.0^2 5320$	$.0^2 5172$	$.0^2 5028$
2.2	$.0^2 4887$	$.0^2 4750$	$.0^2 4616$	$.0^2 4486$	$.0^2 4358$	$.0^2 4235$	$.0^2 4114$	$.0^2 3996$	$.0^2 3882$	$.0^2 3770$
2.3	$.0^2 3682$	$.0^2 3558$	$.0^2 3453$	$.0^2 3352$	$.0^2 3255$	$.0^2 3159$	$.0^2 3067$	$.0^2 2977$	$.0^2 2889$	$.0^2 2804$
2.4	$.0^2 2720$	$.0^2 2640$	$.0^2 2561$	$.0^2 2484$	$.0^2 2410$	$.0^2 2337$	$.0^2 2267$	$.0^2 2199$	$.0^2 2132$	$.0^2 2067$
2.5	$.0^2 2004$	$.0^2 1943$	$.0^2 1883$	$.0^2 1826$	$.0^2 1769$	$.0^2 1715$	$.0^2 1682$	$.0^2 1610$	$.0^2 1580$	$.0^2 1511$
2.6	$.0^2 1464$	$.0^2 1418$	$.0^2 1373$	$.0^2 1330$	$.0^2 1288$	$.0^2 1247$	$.0^2 1207$	$.0^2 1169$	$.0^2 1132$	$.0^2 1096$
2.7	$.0^2 1060$	$.0^2 1026$	$.0^3 9928$	$.0^3 9607$	$.0^3 9295$	$.0^3 8992$	$.0^3 8699$	$.0^3 8414$	$.0^3 8138$	$.0^3 7870$
2.8	$.0^3 7611$	$.0^3 7359$	$.0^3 7115$	$.0^3 6879$	$.0^3 6660$	$.0^3 6428$	$.0^3 6213$	$.0^3 6004$	$.0^3 5802$	$.0^3 5606$
2.9	$.0^3 5417$	$.0^3 5233$	$.0^3 5055$	$.0^3 4883$	$.0^3 4716$	$.0^3 4555$	$.0^3 4398$	$.0^3 4247$	$.0^3 4101$	$.0^3 3959$

[1]From Schlaifer (71, pp. 706–707, Table IV). By permission of McGraw-Hill Book Co., Inc.

Read the top row as the second decimal place for D. For example, if $D = 1.25$, go to the 1.2 row and the 05 column to find $G(D) =$ .05059.

Read $.0^3 5417$ as .0005417.

To illustrate the calculation of V, suppose you are considering the introduction of a new home appliance. You plan to sell this appliance at about $40 with a unit profit of $k = \$10$. Your fixed costs K for production and marketing are estimated at $5,000,000. Thus your breakeven $X_b = 500,000$ units (K/k). Your prior distribution as to the number that can be sold is normal with an expected value (mean) of 450,000 and a standard deviation of 100,000. That is, $X_{prior} = 450,000$ and $\sigma_{prior} = 100,000$. What is the value of information?

First, compute $D = |500,000 - 450,000| \div 100,000 = .50$. Next, find $G(D)$ in Table 14.2A; in this case, $G(D) = .1978$. Finally, calculate $V = \$10 \times (100,000) \times (.1978) = \$197,800$.

As noted earlier, V does not really tell you how much money you will make or lose based on a specific decision. The value of information in a specific decision depends on actual sales and costs, which are estimated in this exercise but not known, and on whether the information changes your decision. V is a long-run estimate of how much more you would make per decision over many decisions of this type if you had *perfect* information (which, of course, you will never get).

What, then, is V good for? As shown in the next section, V can be used to measure the gain in information if new research is done. V can then be used to determine whether gathering new information is justified and, if so, how much new information should be gathered.

How Much Research Should Be Done?

If you think about Equation 14.2D (see page 404), you will see that the value of information declines as more of it is obtained. As more information is obtained, σ_{prior} becomes smaller and D becomes larger. As D gets larger, $G(D)$ becomes smaller. Therefore, since σ_{prior} and $G(D)$ become smaller, V, the value of perfect information, becomes smaller. This should come as no surprise if information is considered to be an economic good similar to, say, chocolate ice cream. We may love chocolate ice cream and be willing to pay a great deal for the first pint if we haven't had any for weeks, but we are not willing to pay as much for the tenth pint.

As you may remember from your basic economics courses, the solution to maximizing the net value of any good is purchasing the good until marginal gain equals marginal cost. This same principle holds for information. The marginal cost is simply the variable cost of information—in a survey, variable costs include interviewer time, telephone tolls, coding, and data processing. The marginal gain is more complex to compute. It requires that the value of information V' be recomputed after information is gathered, with the difference ($V - V'$) being the gain. There is no easy algebraic solution to this problem, but Schlaifer has produced a chart that provides the data needed to optimize n, the sample size. This chart is given as Table 14.2B. The next section describes how to compute an optimum sample size and then continues the example.

Computing an Optimum Sample Size

To compute an optimum sample size (n_{opt}), it is necessary to estimate the following terms:

- k, the unit contribution to profit
- σ_{prior}, the prior uncertainty

TABLE 14.2B

Values of *h* for given values of *Z* and *D*

Z \ D	.7	1	2	3	4	5	6	7	8	9	10	15	20	30	40	50	60
D																	
0	.01	.04	.16	.18	.18	.17	.16	.15	.14	.14	.13	1	.10	.08	.07	.06	.06
.1	-	.03	.16	.18	.18	.17	.16	.15	.14	.14	.13	.11	.10	.08	.07	.06	.06
.2	-	-	.15	.18	.18	.17	.16	.15	.14	.14	.13	.11	.10	.08	.07	.06	.06
.4	-	-	.10	.16	.17	.16	.15	.13	.13	.12	.12	.10	.08	.08	.07	.06	.06
.6	-	-	.10	.15	.15	.15	.14	.14	.13	.12	.12	.10	.08	.07	.06	.05	.05
.8	-	-	-	.10	.13	.13	.13	.12	.12	.11	.11	.09	.08	.07	.06	.05	.05
1.0	-	-	-	.10	.11	.11	.11	.11	.11	.10	.08	.07	.06	.05	.04	.04	.04
1.2	-	-	-	-	.07	.09	.10	.10	.10	.10	.09	.08	.07	.06	.05	.05	.04
1.4	-	-	-	-	-	.06	.07	.08	.08	.08	.07	.06	.06	.05	.04	.03	.03
1.6	-	-	-	-	-	-	.05	.06	.06	.06	.06	.05	.05	.04	.04	.03	.03
1.8	-	-	-	-	-	-	-	.04	.05	.05	.05	.05	.04	.04	.03	.03	.03
2.0	-	-	-	-	-	-	-	-	-	.03	.03	.03	.03	.03	.03	.02	.02
2.2	-	-	-	-	-	-	-	-	-	-	-	.02	.02	.02	.02	.02	.02
2.4	-	-	-	-	-	-	-	-	-	-	-	-	.02	.02	.02	.02	.02
2.6	-	-	-	-	-	-	-	-	-	-	-	-	.01	.01	.01	.01	.01
2.8	-	-	-	-	-	-	-	-	-	-	-	-	-	.01	.01	.01	.01

- Indicates no sampling justified

From Schlaifer (71, p. 712, Chart II). By permission of McGraw-Hill Book Co., Inc.

- σ, the population standard deviation (this would be estimated, as in Appendix 14.1)
- *D*, the distance from breakeven
- *c*, the variable cost (per observation) of research

The difference between σ and σ_{prior} is the same as that between the standard deviation of a population and the standard error of a mean. You will remember, from Equation 14.2 in this chapter (see page 367), that the standard error of the mean can be calculated as follows if the finite population correction is ignored:

$$\sigma_{\bar{x}} = \sigma \div \sqrt{n}. \qquad \textbf{Equation 14.2E}$$

From this equation, if we treat σ_{prior} as a form of $\sigma_{\bar{x}}$, we can solve for *n*, which in this case—since σ_{prior} represents our prior information about the market—represents not the sample size we need in our new research but rather the "sample size equivalent" of our prior knowledge. The solution for *n* is $n = (\sigma/\sigma_{prior})^2$.

If new information is obtained from an optimum sample of size n_{opt}, then n', the posterior sample size equivalent, will be the sum of this new sample size plus the *n* equivalent from our prior information. That is, $n' = n_{opt} + (\sigma/\sigma_{prior})^2$.

To compute the size of the optimum sample, n_{opt}, do the following:

1. Compute the value $Z = (\sigma_{prior}/\sigma)(k\sigma/c)^{1/3}$
2. Then compute the value *D* as defined in Equation 14.2C.
3. Using Table 14.2B, find the value of *h*.
4. The optimum sample size, $n_{opt} = (h) \times (k\sigma/c)^{2/3}$

These calculations can be illustrated via the previous example, in which you are considering the introduction of a new home appliance.

- Assume $\sigma = 1{,}000{,}000$.
- Assume $c = \$10.00$.
- Then $z = \frac{100{,}000}{1{,}000{,}000} \times (10 \times \frac{1{,}000{,}000}{10})^{1/3} = 10$.
- $D = .5$ (as before).
- $h = .12$ (from Table 14.2B—you should verify this).
- Therefore, $n_{opt} = .12 \times (100)^2 = 1{,}200$.

Is Research Justified?

In the preceding example, an optimum sample size has been computed, but it has not yet determined whether or not to do research at all. This decision will be based on the total costs of research, including fixed costs C that have not been considered up to now. The following steps must be performed to determine if research is justified:

1. Compute a new $V' = [k\sigma_{post}] \times [G(D')]$, where σ_{post} is calculated as $\sigma \div \sqrt{(n')}$ and D' is calculated as $D \div \sigma_{post}$.
2. Compute the gain in value of information, $V - V'$.
3. Compute total research cost $C + cn_{opt}$, where C is the fixed cost of research and c is the variable cost per observation.
4. Compute the net gain due to research, calculated as $(V - V') - (C + cn_{opt})$.

If the net gain is positive, research is justified; if not, research is not justified.
   Returning to our appliance introduction example:

- Suppose $C = \$10{,}000$.
- First, compute a new $\sigma_{post} = \sigma/(n')^{1/2}$
  Here $\sigma_{post} = 1{,}000{,}000/[1{,}200 + (10)^2]^{1/2}$
  $\qquad\qquad = 1{,}000{,}000/36.06 = 27{,}735$.
- Now compute $D' = 50{,}000/27{,}735 = 1.80$.
- Now compute $V' = 10 \times 27{,}735 \times G(1.80) = 277{,}350 \times .01428 = \$3{,}961$.
- Next, calculate the total research cost: $(C + cn_{opt}) = \$10{,}000 + \$10(1{,}200) = \$22{,}000$.
- Finally, calculate the net gain from research: $\$197{,}800 - \$3{,}961 - \$22{,}000 = \$171{,}839$.

The net gain is positive, so in this example research is justified with an optimum sample size of 1,200.
   You may wonder what the components of the fixed cost C are. These are of two kinds. The first are the fixed costs of marketing research, such as the costs of study design and interviewer training. The second are costs to the company developing the new product. Primarily, these are in the form of forgone profits if the new product is a success. The time required to conduct and analyze the study is time during which the product could be sold at a profit.

Analyzing Data

At this point in the book, you should have a pretty good idea of how to collect market research data. The next five chapters turn from data collection to data analysis. The discussion breaks analysis into the following steps:

1. Physically inspect the data.
2. Code the data.
3. Edit the data.
4. Enter data into a computer file.
5. Clean the data file.
6. Perform any desired data transformations.
7. Document the data set.
8. Analyze the data.

Chapter 15 covers the first seven steps, all of which involve preparing data for analysis. Chapters 16 to 19 then present various methods of data analysis. Chapter 16 covers univariate procedures; Chapter 17 describes bivariate procedures; and Chapters 18 and 19 describe multivariate procedures.

The chapters on data analysis are not intended to replace a course in statistics. Rather, they show how statistical analysis techniques are used for solving marketing problems. The most important thing to remember is that marketing research is done for *managerial* purposes. Data analysis is never a goal in itself: It is a means to an end. All decisions in data analysis should be motivated by an effort to improve marketing decisions. This means:

- If it is not known how an analysis will contribute to marketing decisions, do not do the analysis.
- The form of an analysis and the presentation of its results should be guided by a desire to be compelling as well as correct. An analysis can be mathematically correct but not useful if its results are not communicated effectively to management.

Sample Student Project

Data Analysis

After the computer use survey was completed, the data were entered on computer disks and collected into a single SPSS file using the procedures described in Chapter 15 of this book. The analysis was conducted by four teams of students. Each team had a copy of the SPSS file and used Chapters 16 and 17 to guide its use of univariate and bivariate analysis. Because of time constraints, there was very limited use of the multivariate procedures discussed in Chapters 18 and 19. The students then prepared a report based on their analysis. This is the part of the project that is always the most satisfying, since it provides the answers that are being sought. Almost always, there are important results that had not been anticipated.

The final student reports were longer than fifty pages including text, tables, and charts. Shown here are excerpts from the reports using both univariate and bivariate analysis and presenting the data in bar graphs and pie charts. Note that CCSO stands for Computing and Communications Services Office, but everyone on campus uses the abbreviation.

Computer Usage

Computer Program Applications Used by Respondents

Since 99 percent of the respondents claimed to use computers, it is pointless to illustrate graphically the percentage of users versus nonusers among both graduate students and undergraduate students. Instead, it is more meaningful to depict graphically the application usages for computers among the survey respondents. As the graph below illustrates, 96 percent of the respondents utilized the word processing applications, and 93 percent of the respondents utilized e-mail and Internet capabilities. One student responded, "I don't know much about [computers] because I do not use them for anything aside from typing papers and e-mail." These two applications greatly outdistanced the third most popular application, games.

Survey Respondents' Use of Computer Applications by Major

Depicting what students in a particular major use computers for enables a computer manufacturer to

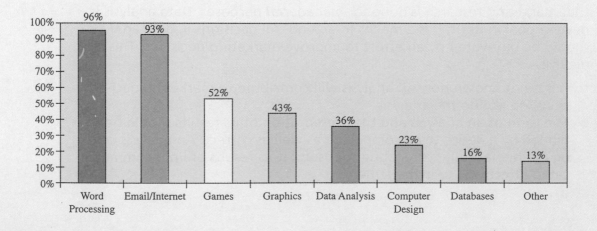

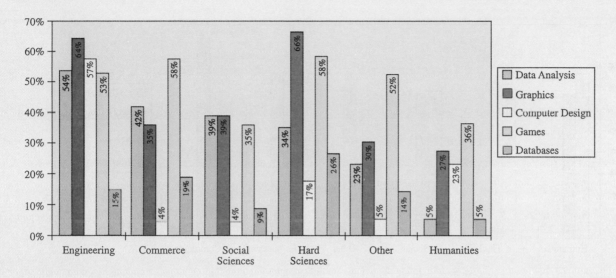

stress the features that the particular target market finds of value. The graph on the top of this page shows that engineers use computers for most of the applications asked on the questionnaire, with graphics as the primary use, followed by computer design, data analysis, and games. Other majors have a broader range of use depending on the application. Word processing and Internet uses are not depicted because of the high percentage of use across all majors.

Survey Respondents' Computer Usage at CCSO Sites

The graph below illustrates that 76% of survey respondents have used IBM-compatible computers

at a CCSO site, and 62% have used Apple computers. This fact could be due to the fact that there are more IBM-compatible computers at the sites or that survey respondents are more comfortable using IBM-compatible computers than Apple computers.

Survey Respondents' CCSO Site Usage by Major and Computer Type

Apple/Macintosh computers are used more at CCSO sites by majors in the humanities and social sciences, and IBM and IBM-compatible computers are used more at CCSO sites by commerce and engineering students. Among the humanities, hard sciences, and social sciences students, however,

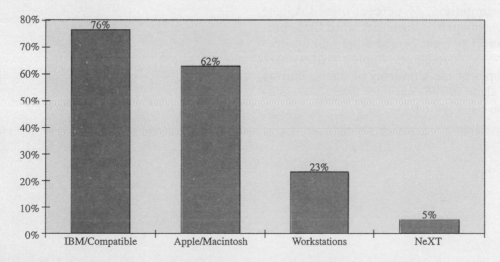

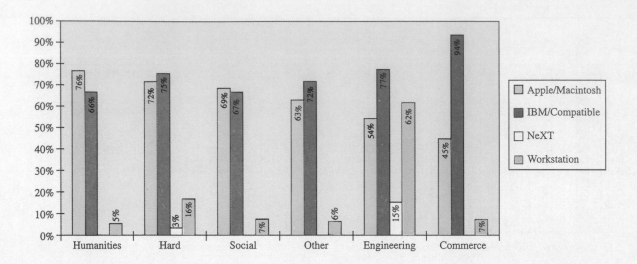

Apple and IBM-compatible users are relatively close in terms of percentages. See the graph on the top of this page.

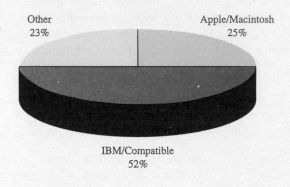

Computer Ownership/Purchasing

Computer Brand Ownership Percentages among Survey Respondents

The pie chart illustrates that of the 401 respondents who own computers, 25 percent owned Apple/Macintosh computers, 52 percent owned IBM-compatible, and 23 percent owned other brand-name, Intel chip–based computers. Apple's market share on the campus of the University of Illinois mirrors its market share in the consumer marketplace outside the university setting.

Note: In the pie chart, "other" refers to brand names that were not listed on the questionnaire but were filled in by the respondents. Assume that most are IBM-compatible brands.

15 Preparing Data for Analysis

OBJECTIVES

LEARNING

After reading this chapter, you should be able to answer the following questions:

❶ Why is it important to inspect data physically before analyzing them?

❷ What are the principles of data coding?

❸ How are data entered into a computer?

❹ How is a computerized data file cleaned of errors?

❺ When and how should data be transformed?

❻ How should a data file be documented?

❼ How does paper-based data entry differ from computer-based data entry?

Several steps are involved in preparing data for analysis. The data must be inspected, coded, edited, entered into the computer, cleaned, transformed if necessary, and documented. Marketing Research Tools 15.1 shows the steps involved in data preparation. In the following sections of this chapter, each of these steps is discussed in detail, under an assumption that the data have been recorded with some paper-and-pencil instrument such as a written questionnaire. At the end of the chapter, the differences in processing data that have been gathered directly by computer are discussed.

Physical Inspection of Paper Documents

The first step in preparing paper-based data for analysis is physical inspection of the data. No matter what type of data are concerned—accounting records, notes from secondary research, survey questionnaires, depth interview transcripts, whatever—data analysis should be started by *touching* the data.

Physical examination does three things. First, it gives a feeling for overall problems with the data, such as changes in accounting practices that cause irregularities in sales and expense records. Second, it reveals specific data points that may be a problem, such as survey questionnaires that have been completed only partially. Third, it gives ideas about how to analyze the data. This last point may not seem logical, but the concreteness of touching data seems to inspire ideas about their meaning—and this, in the end, is what data analysis is all about.

MARKETING RESEARCH TOOLS

15.1

STEPS IN PREPARING DATA FOR ANALYSIS

1. Physically inspect the documents.
2. Code the data in numeric form.
3. Prepare a codebook to document the codes.
4. Edit the data and correct any errors.
5. Enter the data into a computer file.
6. Clean the data file.
7. Make any desired data transformations.
8. Prepare documentation for the final data file.

If physical inspection of the data reveals records that are incomplete, there are three options:

- Using the observations as they are.
- Discarding the observations.
- Going back to get the missing information.

Data are usually used as is if only a small portion of a record is missing. However, substantially flawed records should not be used as is, because substantial defects call the quality of the entire record into question.

If incomplete records are not used as is, the least expensive alternative is to discard them. This course of action may have a biasing effect if the flawed records differ from the good ones in some systematic manner. For cost reasons, though, unacceptable records are generally discarded unless their number is large enough to cast doubt upon the quality of the entire data collection effort.

Going back to get the missing information is more expensive than simply discarding the record and generally is not done unless the value of individual observations is very high or if the number of unacceptable records is large enough to require a thorough data check (Roth, 1994).

Coding Data

Introduction to Coding

Once data have been inspected, they are coded into numeric form for analysis purposes. To understand the nature and purpose of coding, consider the following example.

Chapter 12 included a questionnaire that might be used by a chain of sporting goods stores to help decide whether to discontinue its credit card operation. A variation of this questionnaire is shown in Exhibit 15.1, along with the answers given by one respondent.

In Question 1, this particular respondent reports buying a basketball. Suppose that three other respondents answer, respectively:

- "A pair of running shoes."
- "A Prince tennis racket."
- "I recently bought a pair of tennis shoes."

In a focus group or depth interview study, these answers would be recorded and used verbatim. Each interview would be transcribed; then an analyst would read the transcript(s), make subjective decisions about the story to tell from the data, and "cut and paste" verbatim answers to illustrate this story.

In a survey, a more quantitative analysis of the data is generally desired. In this study, for example, different types of purchases might be classified, then the percentage

(*cont. on p.* 419)

EXHIBIT 15.1

A Sample
Questionnnaire

Hello, I'm _____ of _____, a marketing and opinion research firm. We are conducting a study with people who have purchased sporting goods, including athletic shoes or sportswear, during the past year.

A. Have you purchased any sporting goods, including athletic shoes or sportswear, during the past year?

B. IF NO: Has anyone else in your household purchased any sporting goods, including athletic shoes or sportswear, during the past year?

IF NO, TERMINATE.

CONTINUE INTERVIEW WITH A PERSON WHO HAS BOUGHT SPORTING GOODS

1. On your most recent purchase of sporting goods, athletic shoes, or sportswear, what did you buy?

(MERCHANDISE) *Basketball*

2. At what store did you make this purchase?

(STORE) *Kmart*

3. What was the most important reason you bought that merchandise at *(STORE IN Q1A)* rather than at some other store? (DO NOT READ CATEGORIES)

Price	①
Sale	2
Location/convenience	3
Merchandise quality	4
Merchandise selection	5
Salespeople	6
Availability of credit	7
(_____) ← Other (SPECIFY)	0

4. How much did you spend on that purchase? (TO NEAREST DOLLAR)

$ *20*

5. Did you pay cash, use a store charge account, or use another credit card such as a Visa, MasterCard, or American Express?

Paid cash (check)	①
Store charge	2
Other credit card	3

6. I have some specific factors that might influence where you would shop for sporting goods, including athletic shoes or sportswear. As I read each one, please tell me whether you generally consider that factor to be very important, somewhat important, or not important in choosing a store for this type of merchandise. How about . . .

	Very important	Somewhat important	Not important
The convenience of store locations?	3	②	1
The store's prices?	③	2	1
Special sales?	③	2	1
Whether the store takes credit cards such as Visa, MasterCard, and American Express?	3	②	1
Whether the store has its own charge accounts?	③	2	1
The quality of merchandise carried by the store?	③	2	1
The selection of merchandise?	③	2	1
The availability of your desired brand names?	③	2	1
How often the store is out of stock on the merchandise you want?	3	②	1
The helpfulness of the salespeople? .	③	2	1
The speed of service?	③	2	1

7. Now I'm going to read the same factors again and ask you to rate Smith's on each. Compared to other stores where you might buy this type of merchandise, would you consider Smith's to be well above average, above average, about the same, below average, or well below average. How about . . .

	Well Above Average	Above Average	About the Same	Below Average	Well Below Average
The convenience of store locations?	5	4	③	2	1
The store's prices?	⑤	4	3	2	1
Special sales?	⑤	4	3	2	1
Whether the store takes credit cards such as Visa, MasterCard, and American Express? . . .	⑤	4	3	2	1

Continued

EXHIBIT 15.1

A Sample
Questionnnaire
—Continued

	Well Above Average	Above Average	About the Same	Below Average	Well Below Average
Whether the store has its own charge accounts? .	⑤	4	3	2	1
The quality of merchandise carried by the store?	⑤	4	3	2	1
The selection of merchandise?	⑤	4	3	2	1
The availability of your desired brand names? .	⑤	4	3	2	1
How often the store is out of stock on the merchandise you want?	⑤	4	3	2	1
The helpfulness of the salespeople?	⑤	4	3	2	1
The speed of service? . . .	⑤	4	3	2	1

8. In total, about how much have you spent in the past twelve months on sporting goods including athletic shoes and sportswear?

(TO NEAREST DOLLAR) $ _100_

(IF RESPONDENT SPENT MORE THAN $0)

8A. About how much of that did you spend at Smith's Stores?

(TO NEAREST DOLLAR) $ _40_

9. Do you have a Smith's charge account?

Yes . . . . ① (ASK Q9A,B)
No . . . . 2 (GO TO Q10)

(IF YES)

9A. During the past twelve months, would you have spent more, about the same, or less at Smith's Stores if you did not have a Smith's charge account?

More . . . . 1 (ASK Q9A1)
Same . . . . ② (GO TO Q9B)
Less . . . . 3 (ASK Q9A1)

(IF MORE OR LESS)

9A1. How much do you think you would have spent at Smith's Stores?

(TO NEAREST DOLLAR) $ _40_

9B. A minute ago, you estimated that you spent _(GO TO Q8)_ at Smith's Stores in the past twelve months. About how much of that was charged to your Smith's account?

(TO NEAREST DOLLAR) $ _40_____

10. What is your age category? Is it . . .

Under 18?	1
18–24?	2
25–34?	3
35–49?	④
50–64?	5
65 and over?	6
Refused	7

11. Which of the following categories best describes your family income before taxes for 1996? Would it be . . .

Under $10,000?	1
$10,000–$14,999?	2
$15,000–$24,999?	3
$25,000–$49,999?	4
Over $50,000?	⑤
Refused	6

12. What is your home Zip Code?   (NUMBER) _77095_

13. (DON'T ASK) SEX   Male . . . . ①
                            Female 2

Those are all of our questions. Thanks for your help.

of respondents who mentioned credit availability as their most important reason for store choice might be measured to see whether it varies across purchase types.

Verbatim data are not well suited to quantitative analysis for two reasons. First, the analysis will almost certainly be done by computer, and it is not efficient to enter long verbatim answers into a computer data file. Second, and more important, verbatim data do not facilitate counting. A hundred different respondents might give a hundred different verbatim answers to a question. However, many of their answers might be similar enough to be grouped and counted together.

The purpose of coding is to accomplish this grouping. In the sporting goods example, codes might be established in which "1" refers to sporting goods, "2" refers to athletic shoes, and "3" refers to sportswear. Under these codes, respondents who reported buying a basketball or a tennis racket would be coded as "1," and respondents who reported buying running shoes or tennis shoes would be coded as "2."

Notice that the act of coding destroys some of the meaning of the data. The ability to recognize the similarity between "basketball" and "tennis racket" is accompanied by a loss of ability to recognize their differences once the coding is complete. It is possible to preserve the meaning of the data by using more elaborate codes—for example, 01 to 19 can refer to athletic equipment, with 04 being basketball equipment and 07 being tennis equipment, and codes 70 to 89 can refer to athletic shoes, with 72 being running shoes and 81 being tennis shoes—but some nuance of meaning is always lost.

Given this background on the nature and purpose of coding, let us turn to details regarding the development and application of codes. The discussion is organized into five topics:

- Who should develop codes
- When codes should be developed
- General coding principles
- Preparing a codebook
- Physically coding the data

Who Should Develop Codes

The first step in developing codes is deciding who should do the job. Three characteristics are needed to do this job well: (1) the code developer should know the technical coding principals discussed in the following sections, (2) the code developer should have some intuitive sense of what the raw data mean, and (3) the code developer should understand the managerial purposes of the research.

The value of these characteristics can be seen through the four respondents who were asked to describe their most recent sporting goods purchases. These people answered, respectively:

- "A basketball."
- "A pair of running shoes."
- "A Prince tennis racket."
- "I recently bought a pair of tennis shoes."

Technical knowledge will be sufficient to show that these answers should be given numerical codes and that code categories should be mutually exclusive and exhaustive. However, technical knowledge cannot determine whether tennis shoes should be grouped with running shoes or with tennis rackets. This requires a managerial judgment (for example, research done for Tennis Lady stores might group tennis shoes with tennis rackets, while research done for Foot Locker stores might group tennis shoes with running shoes). Also, technical knowledge cannot determine whether the answer "tennis shoes" actually refers to "shoes for tennis," since some people use the term "tennis shoes" as a generic term for all athletic shoes. A code designer who is sensitive to this fact will consider the possibility that "tennis shoes" means the same as "athletic shoes, unspecified."

For most studies, the person who designs the data collection form (e.g., the person who writes the questionnaire) is the person who is best suited to draft an initial coding system. This first draft can be checked by a manager and/or a data analysis specialist to correct any deficiencies.

When Codes Should Be Developed: Precoding Versus Free Coding

Codes can be developed either before or after data are collected. In Exhibit 15.1, (see page 416) question 3 uses **precoding;** that is, the codes are defined before the questionnaire is administered. When the respondent indicates price as his most important reason for shopping at Kmart, the interviewer simply circles the number corresponding to this answer. Questions 1 and 2, in contrast, are not precoded; the interviewer must record enough of the verbatim response to allow later coding. We use the term **free coding** to describe the coding of verbatim data.

Precoding is recommended wherever feasible. Precoding offers three advantages over free coding:

- It facilitates data collection by allowing data gatherers to circle numbers or check boxes rather than write verbatim observations. This improves the speed, cost, and uniformity of data collection.

- It helps data gatherers recognize codable information. For example, question 3 in Exhibit 15.1 has separate categories for "Price" and "Sale"; this will remind interviewers that "Price" responses must be probed to determine whether the respondent is referring to the store's everyday prices or to a special sale. This improves data quality.

- If there is any doubt about the proper classification of an observation, precoding forces the classification to be made at the point of data collection. This, in our opinion, is better than having the classification made by a coder who is operating secondhand.

Unfortunately, precoding is not always feasible. Precoding requires that (1) most of the different codes that might arise are known in advance and (2) the number of different codes is small enough to fit on the data collection form. These conditions are not always met.

Variables for which code possibilities cannot be known in advance tend to be subjective measures, such as questions about motives, likes, and dislikes. For example, it is very difficult to anticipate exactly what people will say when asked why they chose a particular store for sporting goods. In such a situation, there are two choices: either run a large pretest so that precoding categories can be derived from the pretest data (a large test is needed to ensure that some of the less common codes emerge), or gather verbatim data and free-code these data after data collection is finished.

Variables for which the code possibilities are too numerous to fit onto a data collection form tend to be variables such as questions 1 and 2 in Exhibit 15.1, which ask for specific types of merchandise purchased and specific purchase locations. Consider, for example, the location measure (question 2). In a large city, hundreds of stores

Critical Thinking Skills

Look at the questions in Exhibit 15.1 (see page 416). Which are precoded, and which need to be free-coded? Would you have coded any of the precoded questions differently?

might be cited. Unless these stores are grouped into categories for precoding purposes, the easiest thing to do is list the answers verbatim and free-code them later.

General Coding Principles

Whether defined via precoding or free coding, a coding system should reflect the following principles:

1. The records in a data set should be structured as a **matrix;** that is, a table of rows and columns. Each row should represent a particular data record (for example, a person who answered the questionnaire), and each column should represent a particular piece of information. The same information should appear in the same column for each data record. That is, if one respondent's answer to the question "At what store did you make this purchase?" is a three-digit code appearing in the ninth through eleventh columns of the data record, every respondent's answer to this question should be a three-digit code appearing in the ninth through eleventh columns. This structure is necessary for standard data analysis software packages.

   Matrix structure is easy to develop in any study for which information is gathered in a fixed sequence, such as a survey. Three rules should be followed:

   - If a particular item allows "all that apply" responses, these responses should be treated as separate variables. For example, if respondents to question 3 in Exhibit 15.1 (see page 416) were allowed to list *all* of their reasons instead of only their most important reason, the eight categories of reasons would be treated as eight separate variables even though they are measured by a single question. This ensures that every data record will have eight fields for this information regardless of how many reasons a particular respondent cites.

   - If a variable is not measured for a particular respondent because of a branching sequence, a "Not applicable" code should be used to hold place for the missing item. For example, if a respondent does not answer question 9A in Exhibit 15.1 because she does not have a Smith's credit card, this variable should be given a "Not applicable" code.

   - If a variable is missing for some other reason, a missing value code should again be used to hold place for the item. For example, if a respondent refuses to answer question 11 in Exhibit 15.1 (the income question), this variable should be coded as "Refused."

   Matrix structure is not so easy to obtain in studies for which information is obtained in an irregular sequence, such as focus groups and depth interviews. However, these types of data often are not computer-analyzed. In fact, they are often not coded at all and are simply used verbatim.

2. The second coding principle is that each record in a data set should carry an identifying code that is unique to that record. The purpose of this code is simply to identify the record within the data set; the code is not intended to provide any public identification of the record. It need not, and usually should not, be a meaningful identifier such as a telephone number.

3. Within any given variable, the codes should be exhaustive. Every observation should be codable, even if the code refers only to an "Other" category.

4. As part of being exhaustive, categories should be reserved for any forms of missing data that might occur. Common missing-data forms are "No answer," "Don't know," or "Not applicable" for questionnaire data and "Not able to observe" or "Not applicable" for observational data.

   Missing data should be coded according to fixed conventions; that is, with the same codes. "No answer," for example, should not be represented by 3 on one variable and 22 on another, because this is confusing and inefficient. Most statistical packages allow you to define "missing values" and exclude them from the analyses, and it is easier to make these definitions if all variables use the same codes.

   The simplest convention is coding all missing data with a "." (a period or dot). This convention is automatically recognized by standard statistical packages. A more elaborate convention is using different codes for different types of missing data, for example:

   - "Not applicable" may be coded as 0 (for a one-digit code), 00 (for a two-digit code), 000, 0000, and so on.
   - "No answer" or "Not observable" may be coded as 9, 99, 999, 9999, and so on.
   - "Don't know" may be coded as 8, 98, 998, 9998, and so on.

5. Code categories for any given variable should be mutually exclusive. If code categories overlap—for example, if one category of reasons for store choice is "merchandise selection" and another category is "availability of brand names"—the allocation of observations between these categories may be arbitrary and inconsistent.

6. If the categories being coded have some quantitative order (e.g., "Very satisfied" is higher than "Moderately satisfied" is higher than "Not satisfied"), the numbers assigned to those categories should reflect that order (e.g., "Very satisfied" = 3, "Moderately satisfied" = 2, "Not satisfied" = 1).

7. Related categories should be given related code numbers (e.g., codes 01 to 19 refer to athletic shoes, codes 70 to 89 refer to other athletic equipment). Keeping related categories near one another in the code list helps both coders and data gatherers locate the codes for related answers and thus improves coding accuracy. It also facilitates viewing the data at two levels—that is, how many observations were in the 01 to 19 range as well as how many were specifically at 1, 2, 3, and so on.

   Although simple groupings of related categories are a good idea, multidimensional relationship structures are usually not desirable. Consider, for example, a coding system for stores in which the first digit signifies whether the store is a sporting goods specialist (1 = sporting goods specialty store, 2 = other specialty store, 3 = non–specialty store), the second digit signifies whether the store is a discount store (1 = discount pricing, 2 = regular pricing), and the third through fifth digits signify the particular store. Under this system, Kmart might be coded as 31002 (3 for non–specialty store, 1 for discount store, 002 for

Author Tips

Separate codes for different types of missing data are needed only if you want to distinguish among them; for example, if you want to know how many people said "Don't know" as opposed to "No answer." This information is not needed in most projects, and a "." convention works fine. Some research organizations always use separate codes for different types of missing data because they want the information in some studies, and they want to use the same conventions for all studies.

Critical Thinking Skills

hat problems would you face if each of these six principles of coding is not followed?

Kmart). A system like this is misguided. Coding will be easier and data analysis more flexible if specialty versus other, discount versus regular, and specific store are simply treated as three separate variables, each with its own codes.

Incidentally, this example illustrates that a single piece of information can be coded in more than one variable. The fact that somebody shopped at Kmart simultaneously tells us that he or she bought at a non–specialty store, a discount store, and (specifically) at Kmart.

Preparing a Codebook

Once codes have been developed, a **codebook** should be prepared. The purpose of the codebook is to document the data set and to serve as a reference source for coders in free coding. A codebook should contain:

1. *Identifying information concerning the data set.* This includes the study number if applicable, a computer file name and file location if applicable, a brief verbal description of the study, identification of the research sponsor, identification of the organization that gathered the data, and identification of a person who can be contacted for information about the research.

2. *A list all of the variables, including the identification code, in the order in which they are found on each data record.* This list is the "table of contents" of the codebook. Each variable should be named and described, its location in the original data should be given, and its location in the coded data (that is, the data fields it occupies) should be given. For example:

   Variable name: V2
   Variable description: Type of merchandise last purchased
   Location on questionnaire: Q1
   Data fields: Columns 7, 8

3. *Coding information for each variable.* The variables should be taken in the same order as the variables list, that is, the same order in which they are found in the data records. After each variable is named, all of the codes for that variable should be listed and labeled, including the missing-value codes. For example:

   Variable: V2
   Variable description: Type of merchandise last purchased
   Codes: 01 = Shoes, unspecified
            02 = Cross-training shoes
            03 = Walking shoes
            04 = Running shoes
            05 = Aerobics shoes
            06 = Basketball shoes
            . . .
            99 = No answer

The codebook should become a permanent part of data set documentation, and one copy of the codebook should be retained in the research files.

For illustrative purposes, Appendix 15.1 at the end of this chapter provides the codebook developed for the questionnaire shown in Exhibit 15.1 (see page 416).

Physically Coding the Data

Once codes have been developed and a codebook has been written, it is time to code the data for entry into the computer. The biggest challenge at this stage is, of course, free coding. Coders will work from the list of codes contained in the codebook but must still decide which category to apply to each free-coded observation.

The key to good free coding is coder training. Coders should be given a training session that includes both lecture and practice components. First, a supervisor should go through the codebook and discuss the coding for every variable, including pre-coded items. Free-coded items should be illustrated through examples, and coders should be allowed to ask questions about the coding procedures. Then, after the codes have been discussed, coders should be asked to code a limited number of records (say, ten to twenty). These records should include some that are ambiguous on free-coded items. Still within the training session, the codes assigned to these records by different coders should be compared with one another, or with codes assigned by a coding supervisor, to identify coding discrepancies. The discrepancies should be discussed by the coders and coding supervisor, and a consensus should be reached concerning how to resolve them. Then, if the number of discrepancies was undesirably high, the process should be repeated with a new set of records. This testing process should be repeated until the **intercoder reliability** (the percentage of codes on which coders agree) reaches some acceptable level (usually at least 90 percent). At this point, coders with satisfactory levels of performance are considered qualified to work on their own.

Once qualified, a coder can begin to code data. The coder should go through each record from start to finish, examining precoded as well as free-coded items and marking the appropriate code for each item. Codes should be marked in the right-hand column of data collection forms so that data entry people can find them easily. The original data should have been recorded in pencil (so that data gatherers can correct their mistakes), and coders should work with a different-colored pencil so that their marks are distinguishable from data collectors' marks; for example, data gatherers could use regular black pencils and coders red pencils.

Strictly speaking, a coder need not mark precoded items unless they are missing data, in which case he or she should enter the proper missing-data code. However, coders should circle the proper code for precoded items to verify that these items have been reviewed.

In the process of going through data collection forms, coders may encounter data that are affected by problems such as illegibility, two or more precodes circled together, or uncodable ambiguity. These data must be *edited*; that is, they must be corrected or marked as missing. If a coder encounters data that require editing, he or she should mark the relevant portion of the data collection form—for example, by drawing a big circle around it—and continue coding.

Critical Thinking Skills

The question is "What was the most important reason you bought that merchandise at Smith's rather than at some other store?" Four possible answers are: "It was a good buy," "They were having a sale," "I like their stuff," and "It's a good store." What problems, if any, would you face in coding these answers?

Editing Data

After finishing with the form, the coder should place it into a separate collection area for forms that require **editing.** These forms should be gathered for supervisory review.

A data editor has the same options for dealing with flawed records that were noted earlier in this chapter: (1) using a record as is, which means entering missing-data codes for the uninterpretable portion of the record, (2) discarding the entire data record as being fatally flawed, or (3) replacing the missing information. The last course of action can involve returning to the original data source for additional information or using other information in the record to resolve ambiguity.

If only a few items are uninterpretable, an editor will probably use a record as is. If the missing items are crucial to the study and the value of each observation is high, then the editor probably will return the record to data collection people for further information. If a large portion of the record is unusable, the editor will probably discard the record.

Any marks made on a data collection form by an editor should be made in a color different from the colors used in data collection and coding; for example, black pencil can be used for original data collection, red pencil for coding, and blue or green pencil for editing.

Entering Data into a Computer File

Data Entry Options

Coded and edited data are ready for computer entry. It is possible to analyze a very small data set by hand if only a couple of key variables are to be counted, but any analysis beyond this level should be done by computer. Data entry is done directly from the coded, edited original data collection forms.

Data can be entered in any one of three ways:

1. A specialized data entry package that presents a series of screens onto which the data are copied can be used. The package will automatically create the data file.

2. A word processing package or spreadsheet package can be used to create an unlabeled ASCII file. **ASCII files** are in a standard format that can be read by any software, including any statistical package.

3. A data entry module in the statistical package may be used to create a labeled data file that is "customized" for that package.

In general, it is best to use a word processing package or spreadsheet to create ASCII files, unless good data entry software are available. These files are relatively quick to create and do not limit the researcher to any particular statistical package.

To illustrate how data are entered in this fashion, we will describe (1) how to create an ASCII data file with a word processing program and (2) how to read these data into a statistical package. SPSS for Windows will be used as an illustrative statistical package both here and in subsequent chapters.

Entering Data

To enter data using a word processing package, simply treat each data record as a line to be typed. Begin with the identification code and proceed to type the different variables in sequence. Blank spaces should be left at preset points in the record so it is easy to see whether the data have been entered without missing or excess characters.

In some data sets, the records are long enough to require more than one line per record. This does not create any problems in reading the data, but such data tend to be most easily transportable across software packages when each line is limited to no more than eighty spaces, including blanks.

When a record has been entered, advance to the next row (line) and enter the next record. Do not skip lines between records. When all the records have been entered, save the file in ASCII format. It can then be used as an input file for any analysis package.

An Example

Let us illustrate data entry by looking at the questionnaire in Exhibit 15.1. Assume that:

- Each record is given a three-digit identification number, with this observation being 001.

- The merchandise variable (Q1) is coded as a one-digit number, with 1 representing sporting goods.

- The store variable (Q2) is coded as a two-digit number, with 06 representing Kmart.

- The dollar expenditure questions—Q4, Q8, Q8A, Q9A1, Q9B—are coded as four-digit numbers to allow for a maximum expenditure of $9,997 on every item.

- The zip code (Q12) is coded as a five-digit number.

- "Not applicable" is coded as 0, 00, 000, an so on, depending on the length of the field.

- A blank space is placed after the identification number, Q5, Q6, Q7, and Q9.

Given these assumptions, the questionnaire in Exhibit 15.1 will generate a data record that looks as follows:

001 106100201 23323333233 35555555555 010000401200400040 45770951

The first block of numbers indicates the record identification number (001). The second block of numbers indicates the type of merchandise purchased (1), the store where the purchase was made (06), the most important reason for choosing that store (1), the amount spent on the purchase (0020), and the method of payment (1). The third block of numbers indicates the responses to the eleven attribute importance measures in question 6. The fourth block of numbers indicates the rating of Smith's on the eleven attributes in question 7. The fifth block of numbers indicates the total amount spent on sporting goods during the past twelve months (0100), the amount spent at Smith's (0040), whether the respondent has a Smith's credit card (1), how

Author Tips

In the process of entering so many numbers, mistakes are bound to occur. Most commercial data entry operations validate their work at a 100 percent rate in an effort to minimize errors in the finished data set. Every data record is entered by two different people, and the two records are checked against each other. If any inconsistencies appear, the record is entered a third time. This third record should match one of the first two, and the two matching records are assumed to be correct. One of the correct records is then retained for the final data file.

not having the card would have affected the respondent's spending (2), how much the respondent would have spent without the card (0040), and how much was charged to the card (0040). The final block of numbers indicates the respondent's age (4), income (5), zip code (77095), and gender (1).

A thousand questionnaires like the one shown in Exhibit 15.1 (see page 416) would generate a data set with 1,000 rows, each looking like our sample row (except, of course, that the specific numbers would change) and each with blanks in the same locations.

Reading ASCII Data into a Statistical Package

For data to be analyzed effectively, the unlabeled ASCII file must be converted into a labeled file for the statistical package to be used. For example, to analyze data with SPSS for Windows, the ASCII file must be converted to an SPSS file. This is done as follows.

Open SPSS for Windows and choose "Read ASCII Data" from the "File" menu. Access the appropriate disk drive, highlight the file, and click "Define." Enter the name of the first variable in the data set, the number of the column in which the variable starts, and the number of the column in which it ends (counting blank spaces). If the variable is not numeric, click on "Data Type" to define the variable's type. If missing values were coded as a number (e.g., 998), indicate the number in the space labeled "Value" under "Value Assigned to Blanks for Numeric Variables." Note that at this stage, only one number can be defined as a missing value. If more than one number was used to indicate missing values, such as a 9 to indicate "No answer" and a 0 to indicate "Not applicable," the SPSS file must be created first, "Define Variable" called up from the "Data" menu, and the additional values for missing variables indicated.

Once information about the variable has been entered, click "Add" to enter this variable into the list of defined variables. If you make a mistake or change your mind about the name of a variable, highlight the variable in the "Defined Variables" box, make the necessary changes, and click the "Change" button.

When all the variables in the data set have been entered, click the "OK" button. Save the file with a SAV extension (e.g., SPORT.SAV) to create a data set that can be opened directly by using the "Open" command from the "File" menu. Then, the next time you want to use SPSS for Windows to analyze the data, you won't have to define the variables again.

Critical Thinking Skills

The disk accompanying your textbook contains an ASCII data file called "SPORTS" and an SPSS for Windows file called "SPORTDAT.SAV" with the variables already defined. Practice entering data into SPSS for Windows with the SPORTS data and the codebook. Are you able reproduce the SPORTDAT.SAV file correctly?

Cleaning the Data File

Despite efforts to the contrary, the finished data file usually contains some coding and/or data entry errors. These errors should be **cleaned** from the data if possible.

The first step in cleaning a data set involves checking for *"out-of-range"* values on every variable. For example, the gender variable (V37) in the SPORTS data set allows only three legitimate codes: 1 (male), 2 (female), and 9 (no answer). Any other code in these data fields will indicate an error in coding or data entry.

Out-of-range observations are easy to locate. Just print the frequency distribution for each variable—that is, the code values that occur for this variable and the number of observations for each code value—and check for out-of-range codes. If any out-of-range values are observed, list the offending records. Once the offending records are identified, it is usually necessary to inspect the original data collection forms to determine what code values should have been entered. This inspection may show that the variable was coded incorrectly; if so, a correct code can be entered.

The second step in cleaning a data set involves checking for *logical inconsistencies.* For example, the questionnaire in Exhibit 15.1 imposes certain relationships among variables. If a respondent does not have a Smith's credit card (question 9 = 2), the fields for question 9A, question 9A1, and question 9B should be recorded as "Not applicable." The answer to question 9A1 should be greater than the answer to question 8A if the respondent answers "More" to question 9A and less than the answer to question 8A if the respondent answers "Less" to question 9A. The answer to question 8A should not exceed the answer to question 8, and the answer to question 9B should not exceed the answer to question 8A. Any violations of these relationships will indicate errors in coding or data entry. Logical inconsistencies are identified in the same way as out-of-range values.

The third and final step in cleaning a data set is checking for *unlikely observations.* For example, if a respondent to the questionnaire in Exhibit 15.1 reports that his most recent sporting goods purchase was a basketball and that the amount paid was $200, these answers make an unlikely combination.

Unlikely observations are difficult to locate, because there are no specific rules for finding them. Also, it is difficult to know how to clean these observations unless you return to the original data source to check the information. For these reasons, it is common not to do any formal checking for unlikely observations and to address them only if they create noticeable problems in the course of data analysis.

Of course, coding and/or data entry errors can occur in a data set without producing out-of-range values, logical inconsistencies, or even unlikely observations. A male can be coded as a female, a $30 purchase can be coded as a $40 purchase, and so on. These errors will never be discovered in data cleaning. They must be minimized through good training and good quality controls in the coding and data entry operations, including validation procedures in data entry.

Author Tips

To print out frequency distributions in SPSS for Windows, choose "Summarize" and then "Frequencies" from the "Statistics" menu. Highlight the variables you want distributions for (this will be all the variables if you are checking for out-of-range values). Click the arrow key, then click "OK."

To identify problem records, choose "Select Cases" from the "Data" menu. Click the "If" button and use the keyboard or on-screen calculator to indicate the problem (e.g., V37 = 3 if this is the out-of-range value). Click "Continue" and then "OK." SPSS will draw a diagonal line across the line number for all records that *do not* match the criteria selected (all records for which V37 does not equal 3). Any record that is not crossed out is a problem record.

Critical Thinking Skills

Run frequency distributions for all the variables in the SPORTS data set. Are all the variables within appropriate ranges?

Transforming the Data

After cleaning is completed, the data set is ready for analysis. Before documenting this data set and proceeding to analysis, you should consider whether you wish to transform the data in any way. The existing form of the data may not be the most desirable form for analysis purposes.

Let us illustrate this point through a simple example. When the questionnaire shown in Exhibit 15.1 (see page 416) was first shown in Chapter 12, the answers in question 6 were coded as 1 = "Very important," 2 = "Somewhat important," and 3 = "Not important." Left unchanged, these codes would have produced data in which higher importance is indicated by a lower number. A variable with an average importance score of 2.20 would have been *less* important than a variable with an average importance score of 1.91. To avoid this confusing situation, the coding was reversed so that 3 = "Very important," 2 = "Somewhat important," and 1 = "Not important."

Even if the codes had not been reversed before the data were collected, it would be possible to change the category definitions through **recoding**. Statistical software packages have recode commands that will change the coding with a single command. An instruction with the logic to RECODE these variables should be used so that (1 = 3), (2 = 2), (3 = 1). This instruction would produce a data transformation.

Many transformations may be applied to data. In general, transformations fall into three broad categories:

- Recoding a variable
- Rescaling a variable
- Combining variables

Recoding a Variable

As the name implies, recoding involves changing the code values assigned to some or all categories of a variable. Common reasons for recoding are:

- *To reverse the scoring on a variable that has been coded "backward."* Such an example has just been described.

- *To consolidate small categories into broader categories that contain more observations.* For example, say question 2 in Exhibit 15.1 is used to identify the stores where respondents bought sporting goods. When these data are to be analyzed, it may turn out that many stores have been named by only one or two people. To form bigger groups, a recode command can be used to gather them into broader categories (e.g., "Other").

- *To group similar codes together.* For example, in question 3 (reasons for store choice) in Exhibit 15.1, 2 might be recoded to 1 (2 = 1) to group all of the price buyers together and 5 to 4 (5 = 4) to group all of the merchandise buyers together. Case Study 15.1 shows how this type of recoding can change the implications of the data.

CASE STUDY 15.1

A survey of undergraduates at the University of Houston included this question: "If you could change any two things about the University of Houston, what two things would you change?" The answers were initially coded as follows:

Category	Students Who Named This as an Area to Change (%)
More parking	40%
Better teachers/fewer teaching assistants	18
More section offerings	14
Smaller classes	13
Fewer course prerequisites	9
Better on-campus housing	9
Easier registration	7
More spirit activities	6
Better food service	5
Less red tape	5
Other	36

The data then were recoded as follows (this recode includes classification of the "Other" responses):

Category	Students Who Named This as an Area to Change (%)
Education	74%
Parking	40
Social life	19
Registration	10
Housing	9
Food service	5
Red tape	5

Which coding is better? It's a judgment call. If you want to highlight educational issues, the second approach is better. If you want to highlight parking, the first approach is better. This example shows that data coding and data analysis often require judgments about how the data should be interpreted and used.

Author Tips

To recode a variable using SPSS for Windows, bring up the "Transform" menu and highlight "Recode." To create a new variable (rather than changing the existing one) choose "Into Different Variables." On the new screen, insert the name of the old variable in the "Input Variable →Output Variable:" box (by highlighting it from the list of variables and clicking the arrow key), and insert the new variable into the "Name:" box under "Output Variable." Click "Change." Next, define the specific transformation (e.g., old values of 18 through 24 are recoded to the new value of 1) by clicking the "Old and New Values" button. Click "Continue" and then "OK."

- *To convert a continuous variable into a categorical variable.* For example, a continuous age measure may be converted into the groups 18 to 24, 25 to 34, 35 to 49, 50 to 64, and 65 and over.

- *To distinguish between missing data and valid observations.* Look, for example, at question 9B in Exhibit 15.1 (see page 416). If a respondent has a Smith's credit card but did not use it during the previous twelve months, the answer to this question will be $0, coded as 0000. However, if the respondent does not have a Smith's credit card, so that this question does not apply, this variable will also be coded 0000. It may be desirable to recode this variable so that "$0" and "Not applicable" use different codes.

When recoding is done for the first and last purposes (reversing scoring or distinguishing between missing values and legitimate data), it is usually not desirable to use or retain the variable in its original form. Consequently, the transformation can be applied to the original variable and saved in the data file.

When recoding is done for purposes of consolidating small categories, grouping similar categories, or categorizing a continuous variable, it may be desirable to use the original data as well as the recoded data in different analyses. In such situations, it is better to create a new variable equal to the original variable, then to recode the new variable and leave the original variable unchanged. This approach allows for saving the new variable permanently, if desired, and leaves both the recoded variable and the original variable available for analysis.

When creating a new variable, one should not forget that the missing values for the original variable will carry into the new variable. The new variable will thus need the same missing-values declaration as the original variable.

Rescaling a Variable

In rescaling, the code numbers used for a variable are kept in sequence but converted to a different scale. For example, suppose that a group of customers has been asked to indicate their satisfaction with a product on the following scale:

Very dissatisfied			Neutral			Very satisfied
1	2	3	4	5	6	7

It might make more sense to score these data on a scale where dissatisfaction is represented by negative numbers and neutral feelings are represented by a zero, as follows:

Very dissatisfied			Neutral			Very satisfied
−3	−2	−1	0	1	2	3

However, this second scale would be more difficult to enter into the data, because additional fields and strokes would be needed for the negative signs. The best way of achieving this scale is not to code it directly but rather to code and enter the data via the first scale and then rescale the data by subtracting 4 from all respondents' answers.

Among the most common types of rescaling transformations are:

- *Transformations that change the average of the scale but otherwise leave it unaltered, as in the example just given.* For example, you might convert the measure "In what year were you born?" into a measure of age by subtracting the year the respondent was born from the current year.

- *Transformations that raise variables to powers.* Power transformations are used to analyze nonlinear relationships among variables, as discussed in later chapters.

- *Transformations that take logarithms of variables.* Like power transformations, logarithms can be used to express nonlinear relationships among variables. They also can be used to convert multiplicative functions into additive functions that can be analyzed more easily. This procedure takes advantage of the fact that

$$LOG(A \times B) = LOG(A) + LOG(B).$$

Therefore, if you start with a model such as

$$SALESPERSON\ PERFORMANCE = f(EFFORT \times EFFICIENCY)$$

and take logarithms of both sides, the model becomes

$$LOG(PERFORMANCE) = f[LOG(EFFORT) + LOG(EFFICIENCY)].$$

This additive model can be analyzed with multiple regression analysis, which is discussed in Chapter 18.

- *Transformations that normalize data in multi-item scales.* **Normalization** standardizes a series of related items so that they are more comparable with one another. For example, to normalize the eleven importance ratings obtained in question 6 in Exhibit 15.1, one would (1) calculate the mean score and standard deviation for the ratings given by a particular respondent, then (2) standardize each rating by subtracting the mean score and dividing by the standard deviation. This process would be repeated for every respondent. The purpose of this transformation is to remove differences in how respondents used the measurement scale.

In general, rescaling transformations are used less frequently than recoding or variable combinations. In certain types of analyses, though, they are fairly common.

When rescaling variables, do not forget to make specific provision for the missing values. Otherwise, the rescaling will change these values. For example, if a "No answer" to YEARBORN is coded as 9999 and this variable is rescaled as AGE = THISYEAR − YEARBORN without holding out the missing values, you will suddenly find the record full of respondents who are coded as being approximately −8,000 years old.

Author Tips

To rescale variables in SPSS for Windows, choose the "Compute" option under the "Transform" menu. Type the name of the new variable in the "Target Variable" box (if you type a new name, a new variable will be created; if you type the name of an existing variable, that variable will be changed). Highlight the variables you wish to change from the list and click the arrow key. Use the keyboard or the calculator displayed on the screen to create the desired transformation (e.g., AGE = 1998 − YEARBORN) in the "Numeric Expression" box. When you are finished, click "OK."

Combining Variables

Data can also be transformed by creating new variables from combinations of existing variables. This can be done by:

- *Adding variables.* For example, cost measures might be added to create a measure of total cost, satisfaction measures might be added to create an index of total satisfaction, and so on.

- *Subtracting variables.* For example, a variable called PROFIT might be created by subtracting COSTS from REVENUES.

- *Multiplying variables.* For example, a measure of purchase frequency might be multiplied by a measure of purchase amount to get a measure of total expenditure.

- *Dividing variables.* Profits might be divided by sales to create a measure of profit margin, store sales by store size to create a measure of sales per square foot, and so on.

- *Using conditional combinations of variables.* For example, to measure the potential market size for a new type of industrial valve, factory managers might be asked about the maximum stresses experienced by valves in their factory, their interest in the new valve, and their valve purchasing process. Then a series of conditions might be set on these variables to test whether the respondent is likely to buy the new valve: IF maximum stress is within some range AND interest is at some level AND the valve-purchasing process takes some particular form, THEN the respondent is likely to buy; otherwise the respondent is not likely to buy.

Again, don't forget to make provisions for missing values. For example, if MARGIN = PROFIT/REVENUES is computed and a particular data record has revenues coded as 00000 because the revenue measure does not apply to this record, the analysis program will crash (because the computer can't divide by zero) unless the missing values are held out of the analysis.

Critical Thinking Skills

Recode V3 in the SPORTS data (main reason for store choice). Consolidate some of the categories by combining "regular prices" with "sale prices" and "selection" with "merchandise quality." Run frequency distributions of both the original and new variables. Does the recoding change the interpretation of the main reason for choosing the store?

Documenting the Data Set

The final step in preparing data for analysis is documenting the data set. Documentation allows you to remember next week what you did today. It also allows other people to interpret the data set if they use it for secondary analysis.

Documentation for a data set should exist in two forms. One form is electronic, contained within the data file. The other form is a hard copy kept separate from the data file.

Electronic documentation is easy to develop in standard statistical packages. All of these packages have procedures for data definition, as well as statistical analysis. These procedures allow the following to be defined:

- *Variable names* that denote the variables. For example, the name "V1" might be used to denote the variable that corresponds to question 1 in the Smith's questionnaire.

- *Variable labels* that describe the variables. For example, V1 might be labeled "Type of merchandise last bought."

- *Value labels* for the different values that each variable might assume. For example, value labels for V1 might be 1 = "Sporting goods"; 2 = "Athletic shoes"; and 3 = "Sportswear."

- *Missing-value declarations* that tell the statistical package which values to ignore.

All of this definitional information is saved with the data file and is read every time the data are analyzed. The availability of this information within the data file allows analyses to be designed without consultation of the codebook. It also allows the statistical package to print appropriate labels on all outputs, which is a major convenience in interpreting results.

The other form of documentation that should be defined for a data set is the codebook, which we described earlier in this chapter. The codebook provides hardcopy documentation that is physically separate from the data file. It describes where that file is located, how it is identified, what variables it contains, and how those variables are coded. In most studies, the codebook will describe only the original variables in the data set. However, permanent recodes and transformations can also be described in the codebook, if desired.

Data Preparation for Computer-based Data

In some marketing research studies, data are gathered directly on the computer, rather than on paper. Computer-assisted telephone interview (CATI) systems are the major source of computer-based data.

The data processing procedures used for these studies have many similarities to the data processing procedures used for paper-based data. For example, the principles of coding are the same for all data, as are the procedures for cleaning and documentating a data set. However, there are some points of difference, as follows:

- *Definition of the data file.* CATI data are entered directly into a computerized data file. As a result, the nature of this file must be defined in advance of the study. One should not gather the data, then decide how the variables are to be defined.

- *The use of precoded categories.* All telephone interviews have a preference for questions with precoded categories, but this preference is particularly strong in CATI interviews, because direct data entry requires precoded categories.

- *The use of online editing.* The answers to precoded questions in CATI interviews are edited on line, as they are entered. If an out-of-range answer is entered, the interviewer receives an error message and is asked to reenter the answer. The computer can also be programmed to check for logic inconsistencies between questions. If an inconsistency occurs, the interviewer is instructed to check the current question to see if the correct answer has been entered. If the current answer has been entered correctly, the interviewer is asked to check the earlier question. Too many logic checks slow the interview, so they are usually limited to important questions where mistakes are likely to occur.

- *The capture method for open-ended responses.* CATI interviewers record the answers to open questions by typing them on the keyboard rather than writing them down. In the process, they seem to record open answers more completely, which makes these answers easier to code.

  Some CATI operations have experimented with using voice chips to capture open-ended responses. This technology has exciting potential, because it allows managers to hear customers in their own words.

Author Tips

By entering open-ended answers into the computer in raw text form, it is possible to use programs that search for specific words or phrases to help code the answers.

Summary

This chapter discussed how to prepare data for analysis. The following points were covered:

1. Why is it important to inspect data physically before analyzing them?

Physically inspecting the data gives a feeling for overall problems and irregularities with the data, reveals specific data points that may be a problem, and gives ideas about how to analyze the data.

2. What are the principles of data coding?

A data set should have a matrix structure in which the same information appears in the same location for each record. Each record in a data set should carry a unique identifying code. In coding specific variables, (1) the codes should be exhaustive, so that every observation is codable, (2) missing data should be coded according to fixed conventions, (3) categories should be mutually exclusive, (4) the numbers assigned to ordered categories should reflect the natural order of those categories, and (5) related categories should receive related code numbers.

3. How are data entered into a computer?

Data can be entered into an ASCII file, using a wide variety of software packages, or directly into a statistical package. We recommend creating an ASCII file, then reading this file into the statistical package of choice.

4. How is a computerized data file cleaned of errors?

Cleaning a data file involves three steps. First, check for "out-of-range" values on every variable. Second, check for logical inconsistencies in the relationships among variables. Third, check for unlikely observations.

5. When and how should data be transformed?

Data can be transformed through recoding, rescaling, or combining variables. *Recoding* involves giving a new value to some or all categories of a variable. This might be done to reverse the scoring, to consolidate small categories, to group similar codes together, to divide a continuous variable into categories, or to distinguish between missing data and valid observations. *Rescaling* involves converting the code numbers to a different scale while keeping them in sequence. This might be done to shift the average of a scale, to create nonlinear transformations such as powers and logarithms, or to normalize (standardize) data. *Combining* variables involves using some logical or arithmetic operation on two or more variables to create a useful new variable, for example, multiplying unit price and sales volume to calculate revenue.

6. How should a data file be documented?

Data should be documented electronically in a system file that contains all data definitions and transformation commands. In addition, hard-copy documentation should be kept in a location that is physically separate from the data file; this documentation should describe where the file is located, how it is identified, what variables it contains, and how those variables are coded.

7. How does paper-based data entry differ from computer-based data entry?

The major differences between paper-based and computer-based interviews are: (1) in computer-based interviews, the data file must be defined in advance; (2) because of this, questions are more likely to be precoded; (3) precoded questions are edited on line; and (4) open-ended responses are typed into the computer, which seems to have some advantages.

Discussion Questions

1. Who should develop the coding system for a questionnaire? Why do you think this person is best?

2. What is the difference between free coding and precoding? When would you use each?

3. What does it mean to "recode" data? For recodes that group categories together, why not just collect data under the broader categories to begin with?

4. How would you recode the following categories if you wanted to combine them into two? three? four? What would you name the categories?

A&W Rootbeer	Coke	Crush	Dr. Pepper	Pepsi
Mountain Dew	7-Up	RC Cola	Sprite	Squirt

5. A survey of adults asked respondents for the number of years of education completed. The data from this question range from six years to twenty-two years. How might you recode this data?

Marketing Research Challenge

Prepare codes for the new-product questionnaire you designed in Chapter 11. If you did not design a questionnaire, prepare codes for one of the questionnaires used as examples in Chapter 12.

Internet Exercise

How would you build the data file for an Internet-based survey? Would each response immediately enter a pre-specified data file, or would the data somehow be stored and entered in batches?

References

Roth, P. L. (1994). "Missing Data: A Conceptual Review for Applied Psychologists." *Personnel Psychology* 47 (Fall), pp. 537–560.

Appendix 15.1: Codebook for the SPORTS Data File

FILE NAME AND LOCATION: The data are coded in ASCII format and are found on the disk that came with your textbook. The file name is SPORTS. The disk also has an SPSS file called SPORTDAT.SAV that includes these codes.

LIST OF VARIABLES

Variable name: ID
Variable description: Identification number of record
Location on questionnaire: Written in upper right-hand corner on page 1
Data fields: Columns 1–3
Codes: 1–181; 183–218; 502–575

Variable name: V1
Variable description: Type of merchandise last bought
Location on questionnaire: Q1
Data fields: Column 5
Codes: 1 = Shoes   4 = Exercise equipment
            2 = Sportswear   5 = Other
            3 = Field and stream

Variable name: V2
Variable description: Store where last purchase was made
Location on questionnaire: Q2
Data fields: Columns 6–7
Codes: 00 = Other   06 = Kmart
            01 = Sears   07 = Wal-Mart
            02 = Academy   08 = Nevada Bob's
            03 = Target   09 = Smith's
            04 = Foley's   98 = No answer
            05 = Foot Locker

Variable name: V3
Variable description: Main reason for choosing store
Location on questionnaire: Q3
Data fields: Column 8
Codes: 0 = Other   5 = Merchandise selection
            1 = Price   6 = Salespeople
            2 = Sale   7 = Availability of credit
            3 = Location/convenience   8 = Don't know
            4 = Merchandise quality

Variable name: V4
Variable description: Amount of last purchase
Location on questionnaire: Q4
Data fields: Columns 9–12
Codes: $ amount
          9998 = Missing
          9999 = No answer

Variable name: V5
Variable description: How paid for last purchase
Location on questionnaire: Q5
Data fields: Column 13
Codes: 1 = Cash or check   3 = Other credit card
          2 = Store card   8 = Don't know

Variable name: V6
Variable description: Importance of location
Location on questionnaire: Q6
Data fields: Column 15
Codes: 1 = Not important   3 = Very important
          2 = Somewhat important   0 = No answer

Variable name: V7
Variable description: Importance of everyday price
Location on questionnaire: Q6
Data fields: Column 16
Codes: 1 = Not important   3 = Very important
          2 = Somewhat important   0 = No answer

Variable name: V8
Variable description: Importance of sales
Location on questionnaire: Q6
Data fields: Column 17
Codes: 1 = Not important   3 = Very important
          2 = Somewhat important   0 = No answer

Variable name: V9
Variable description: Importance of taking credit cards
Location on questionnaire: Q6
Data fields: Column 18
Codes: 1 = Not important   3 = Very important
          2 = Somewhat important   0 = No answer

Variable name: V10
Variable description: Importance of having store card
Location on questionnaire: Q6
Data fields: Column 19
Codes: 1 = Not important   3 = Very important
          2 = Somewhat important   0 = No answer

Variable name: V11
Variable description: Importance of merchandise quality
Location on questionnaire: Q6
Data fields: Column 20
Codes: 1 = Not important   3 = Very important
            2 = Somewhat important   0 = No answer

Variable name: V12
Variable description: Importance of merchandise selection
Location on questionnaire: Q6
Data fields: Column 21
Codes: 1 = Not important   3 = Very important
            2 = Somewhat important   0 = No answer

Variable name: V13
Variable description: Importance of brand names
Location on questionnaire: Q6
Data fields: Column 22
Codes: 1 = Not important   3 = Very important
            2 = Somewhat important   0 = No answer

Variable name: V14
Variable description: Importance of being out of stock
Location on questionnaire: Q6
Data fields: Column 23
Codes: 1 = Not important   3 = Very important
            2 = Somewhat important   0 = No answer

Variable name: V15
Variable description: Importance of helpfulness
Location on questionnaire: Q6
Data fields: Column 24
Codes: 1 = Not important   3 = Very important
            2 = Somewhat important   0 = No answer

Variable name: V16
Variable description: Importance of speed of service
Location on questionnaire: Q6
Data fields: Column 25
Codes: 1 = Not important   3 = Very important
            2 = Somewhat important   0 = No answer

Variable name: V17
Variable description: Smith's rating on location
Location on questionnaire: Q7
Data fields: Column 26
Codes: 1 = Well below average   5 = Well above average
            2 = Below average   8 = Don't know
            3 = About the same   9 = No answer
            4 = Above average

Variable name: V18
Variable description: Smith's rating on everyday price
Location on questionnaire: Q7
Data fields: Column 27
Codes: 1 = Well below average   5 = Well above average
          2 = Below average   8 = Don't know
          3 = About the same   9 = No answer
          4 = Above average

Variable name: V19
Variable description: Smith's rating on sales
Location on questionnaire: Q7
Data fields: Column 28
Codes: 1 = Well below average   5 = Well above average
          2 = Below average   8 = Don't know
          3 = About the same   9 = No answer
          4 = Above average

Variable name: V20
Variable description: Smith's rating on taking credit cards
Location on questionnaire: Q7
Data fields: Column 29
Codes: 1 = Well below average   5 = Well above average
          2 = Below average   8 = Don't know
          3 = About the same   9 = No answer
          4 = Above average

Variable name: V21
Variable description: Smith's rating on having own card
Location on questionnaire: Q7
Data fields: Column 30
Codes: 1 = Well below average   5 = Well above average
          2 = Below average   8 = Don't know
          3 = About the same   9 = No answer
          4 = Above average

Variable name: V22
Variable description: Smith's rating on merchandise quality
Location on questionnaire: Q7
Data fields: Column 31
Codes: 1 = Well below average   5 = Well above average
          2 = Below average   8 = Don't know
          3 = About the same   9 = No answer
          4 = Above average

Variable name: V23
Variable description: Smith's rating on merchandise selection
Location on questionnaire: Q7
Data fields: Column 32

Codes:	1 = Well below average	5 = Well above average
	2 = Below average	8 = Don't know
	3 = About the same	9 = No answer
	4 = Above average	

Variable name: V24
Variable description: Smith's rating on brand names
Location on questionnaire: Q7
Data fields: Column 33

Codes:	1 = Well below average	5 = Well above average
	2 = Below average	8 = Don't know
	3 = About the same	9 = No answer
	4 = Above average	

Variable name: V25
Variable description: Smith's rating on out-of-stock merchandise
Location on questionnaire: Q7
Data fields: Column 34

Codes:	1 = Well below average	5 = Well above average
	2 = Below average	8 = Don't know
	3 = About the same	9 = No answer
	4 = Above average	

Variable name: V26
Variable description: Smith's rating on helpfulness
Location on questionnaire: Q7
Data fields: Column 35

Codes:	1 = Well below average	5 = Well above average
	2 = Below average	8 = Don't know
	3 = About the same	9 = No answer
	4 = Above average	

Variable name: V27
Variable description: Smith's rating on speed of service
Location on questionnaire: Q7
Data fields: Column 36

Codes:	1 = Well below average	5 = Well above average
	2 = Below average	8 = Don't know
	3 = About the same	9 = No answer
	4 = Above average	

Variable name: V28
Variable description: Amount spent on sporting goods in past 12 months
Location on questionnaire: Q8
Data fields: Columns 37–40
Codes: $ amount
            9998 = Don't know
            9999 = Missing

Variable name: V29
Variable description: Amount spent at Smith's in past 12 months
Location on questionnaire: Q8A
Data fields: Columns 41–44
Codes: $ amount
            9998 = Don't know
            9999 = Missing

Variable name: V30
Variable description: Have a Smith's card
Location on questionnaire: Q9
Data fields: Column 45
Codes: 0 = Not applicable   2 = No
            1 = Yes   8 = Don't know

Variable name: V31
Variable description: How not having a card would affect spending
Location on questionnaire: Q9A
Data fields: Column 46
Codes: 0 = Not applicable   3 = Spend less
            1 = Spend more   8 = Don't know
            2 = Spend the same

Variable name: V32
Variable description: Amount would have spent on sporting goods without a card
Location on questionnaire: Q9A1
Data fields: Columns 46–49
Codes: $ amount
            9998 = Don't know
            9999 = Missing

Variable name: V33
Variable description: Amount charged on Smith's card in past 12 months
Location on questionnaire: Q9B
Data fields: Columns 50–53
Codes: $ amount
            9998 = Don't know
            9999 = Missing

Variable name: V34
Variable description: Age
Location on questionnaire: Q10
Data fields: Column 54
Codes: 1 = Under 18   5 = 50–64
            2 = 18–24   6 = 65 and over
            3 = 25–34   7 = Refused
            4 = 35–49

Variable name: V35
Variable description: Annual family income
Location on questionnaire: Q11
Data fields: Column 55
Codes: 1 = Under 10,000   4 = $25,000–$49,999
            2 = $10,000–$14,999   5 = Over $50,000
            3 = $15,000–$24,999   6 = Refused

Variable name: V36
Variable description: Zip Code
Location on questionnaire: Q12
Data fields: Columns 56–60
Codes: Zip code
            99999 = Missing

Variable name: V37
Variable description: Sex
Location on questionnaire: Q13
Data fields: Column 61
Codes: 1 = Male
            2 = Female
            8 = No answer

16 Univariate Data Analysis

 OBJECTIVES

After reading this chapter, you should be able to answer the following questions:

❶ What are the four kinds of scaling that might apply to univariate data?

❷ How are tabulations used to describe univariate data?

❸ How should missing values in data analyses be handled?

❹ How are summary measures of central tendency and dispersion used to describe univariate data?

❺ What are inferential statistics?

This chapter begins a discussion of data analysis in marketing research with coverage of univariate analysis procedures. **Univariate procedures,** as the name implies, involve only one variable.

The chapter starts by distinguishing among different types of variables according to their mathematical properties. *Descriptive* univariate analyses, that is, analyses that are used to describe the distribution of a variable, are then discussed. These procedures include tabulations, summary measures of central tendency (the mean, median, and mode), and summary measures of dispersion (the range, variance, standard deviation, and interquartile range). Which measures apply to which types of data are indicated, and the section ends with comments regarding the best descriptive procedures to use in different analysis situations.

After descriptive analyses for univariate data are discussed, *inferential data analyses* are described. These analyses—the calculation of confidence intervals and statistical significance tests—involve making inferences from the data at hand to some broader population. The inferential procedures used with various descriptive measures are described, and the general usefulness of inferential procedures in market research is discussed.

All of the procedures discussed in this chapter are illustrated using the SPORTS data described in Chapter 15. This data file appears on the computer disk that came with this book, along with the codebook containing descriptive labels for the data. SPSS for Windows was used to perform the analyses discussed in this chapter.

The material in this chapter is usually covered in a beginning course in statistics, which you may have already had. It is included in this book to show you how these basic statistical concepts can be used in marketing research.

Scale Types

Marketing research data are usually coded with numerical values whether or not the data are quantitative in nature. Consequently, the numerical values for a variable can represent:

- *Definite quantities,* such as the number of dollars spent on sporting goods during the past twelve months, where a code of 1 represents $1, 2 represents $2, and so on.

- *Indefinite quantities,* such as level of satisfaction with a purchase, where 1 represents "Not at all satisfied," 2 represents "Slightly satisfied," and so on.

- *Nonquantitative categories,* such as gender, where 1 represents "Male" and 2 represents "Female."

The numbers used to code these different types of variables all look the same, but they have different mathematical properties. Variables can be classified into four scale types according to these properties. The four scale types are ratio, interval, ordinal, and nominal.

Ratio scale variables have the properties of (1) order among scale points, (2) equal distances among all adjacent scale points, and (3) an absolute zero. An example is V4 in our SPORTS data, the amount spent on the most recent sporting goods purchase. This variable has order: $1 is less than $2, $2 is less than $3, and so on. It has equal distances among all adjacent points: the difference between $1 and $2 equals the difference between $2 and $3, $10 and $11, $400 and $401, and so on. Finally, it has an absolute zero: zero represents no expenditure at all.

The existence of equal distances among scale points makes addition and subtraction meaningful for ratio scale data: for example, $40 plus $20 equals $60. The existence of an absolute zero makes ratios between scale values meaningful: $40 is twice as much money as $20 (this existence of meaningful ratios gives ratio scales their name).

Interval scale variables have the properties of order among scale points and equal distances among scale points, but *not* the property of an absolute zero. The usual example of an interval scale variable is Centigrade or Fahrenheit temperature. On either scale, 41° is warmer than 40°, 21° is warmer than 20°, and the increase in heat needed to go from 40° to 41° equals the increase needed to go from 20° to 21°. However, the location of zero is arbitrary; zero does not represent an absolute absence of heat.

Interval data can be meaningfully added and subtracted: 40° plus 20° equals 60°. Because they can be added, they can also be averaged—the average of 40° and 20° is 30°. However, because the zero point is arbitrary, ratios are not meaningful: 40° is not twice as hot as 20°.

Ordinal scale variables have only the property of order among scale points. Product rankings are one example of the use of ordinal data: the highest-ranked product is better than the second-highest-ranked product, and the second-highest-ranked product is better than the third-highest-ranked product, but the distances among products are not necessarily equal. For example, if a person ranks Mercedes ahead of Buick ahead of Oldsmobile in preference, the distance from Mercedes to Buick may be different from the distance from Buick to Oldsmobile. These data are called "ordinal" because order is their highest property.

Since ordinal data do not have equal distances among scale points, addition and subtraction are not meaningful. For instance, $2 plus $1 equals $3, but a Buick plus an Oldsmobile doesn't necessarily equal a Mercedes. Also, ratios of ordinal data are not meaningful because of the absence of an absolute zero.

Nominal scale variables do not even have the property of order among scale points. The numbers are simply names for the categories, hence the term "nominal." An example of a nominal variable in our SPORTS data is V43 (gender). Another example is V3 (reason for store choice). These data can be counted (e.g., 138, or 47 percent, of the respondents were women and 153, or 53 percent, were men), but they cannot be ordered, added, subtracted, or put into meaningful ratios.

Nominal scale variables are also sometimes called **categorical variables** or **qualitative variables.** Ordinal, interval, and ratio scale variables are sometimes called **continuous variables** or **quantitative variables.** These distinctions are important because they determine what kinds of analyses are appropriate.

Descriptive Analyses of Univariate Data

As noted earlier in this chapter, univariate procedures analyze the distribution of a single variable. Let us begin by defining terms. A **variable** is some phenomenon that might assume at least two different values. Examples include gender (male, female), the type of sporting good last purchased (shoes, shorts, basketball, etc.), the amount spent on a sporting goods purchase ($0, $1, $2, etc.), and so on. The **distribution,** or **frequency distribution,** of a variable is a list of the different values that the variable can assume along with the number of times each value occurs.

Tabulations

A tabular presentation of a frequency distribution is called a **tabulation,** or **tab,** of that variable. Exhibit 16.1 (see page 451) shows tabs for three variables from our SPORTS data: V37 (gender), V3 (the most important reason for choosing the store at which respondents made their most recent sporting goods purchase), and V4 (the amount spent on that most recent purchase).

Author Tips

To generate tabs with SPSS for Windows, call up "Summarize" and then "Frequencies" from the "Statistics" menu. Highlight the variables you want to tabulate from the displayed list, and hit the arrow key.

Note that Exhibit 16.1 shows both the raw frequency and the percentage of observations in each category. This is a standard feature of computerized tabulation programs. The raw frequencies are translated into percentages because percentages are usually more meaningful. For example, in the tab for V37, learning that 47 percent of the respondents are female conveys the gender breakdown for this sample better than learning that 138 of the respondents are female.

Tabulations represent the most basic level of univariate data analysis, so basic, in fact, that people sometimes don't think of tabulation as a form of data analysis. However, if you think about Exhibit 16.1 in comparison with the underlying data, you can see that tabulations summarize and order data. A list of any one of these variables in the raw data would present 291 values occurring in no particular order. Exhibit 16.1, in contrast, shows the *different* values that occur for each variable, presents these values in order from low to high, and shows the number of observations at each value.

Even though tabulations organize data, a tab may be difficult to interpret if the variable assumes a large number of values. Exhibit 16.1 illustrates this point. The tab for V37, which has only two categories, is easy to interpret: the sample is almost evenly split between men and women with slightly more men (53%) than women (47%). However, the tab for V4, which has sixty categories, is difficult to interpret. It is apparent that expenditures ranged from $3 to $800, but other features of the distribution are difficult to grasp; the forest can't be seen for the trees.

When a tabulation has too many categories to allow quick interpretation of the results, interpretation is facilitated by recoding the data into fewer, broader categories. For example, Exhibit 16.2 (see page 453) recodes V4 into the following categories: "$20 or less," "$21 to $50," "$51 to $100," "$101 to $200," and "More

EXHIBIT 16.1

Tabulations of V37, V3, and V4 from the SPORTS Data

V37   Sex

Value Label	Value	Frequency	Percent	Valid Percent	Cum Percent
Male	1	153	52.6	52.6	52.6
Female	2	138	47.4	47.4	100.0
	Total	291	100.0	100.0	

Valid cases 291   Missing cases 0

- -

V3   Main Reason for Choosing Store

Value Label	Value	Frequency	Percent	Valid Percent	Cum Percent
Other	0	13	4.5	4.5	4.5
Regular prices	1	50	17.2	17.2	21.7
Sale	2	61	21.0	21.0	42.8
Location	3	64	22.0	22.1	64.8
Merch quality	4	30	10.3	10.3	75.2
Selection	5	54	18.6	18.6	93.8
Service	6	3	1.0	1.0	94.8
Credit	7	15	5.2	5.2	100.0
Don't know	8	1	.3	Missing	
	Total	291	100.0	100.0	

Valid cases 290   Missing cases 1

- -

V4   Amount of Last Purchase

Value Label	Value	Frequency	Percent	Valid Percent	Cum Percent
	3	3	1.0	1.2	1.2
	5	2	.7	.8	1.9
	8	1	.3	.4	2.3
	9	2	.7	.8	3.1
	10	6	2.1	2.3	5.4

Continued

EXHIBIT 16.1

Tabulation of V4 from the SPORTS Data—Continued

Value Label	Value	Frequency	Percent	Valid Percent	Cum Percent
	12	3	1.0	1.2	6.6
	14	1	.3	.4	7.0
	15	9	3.1	3.5	10.5
	18	1	.3	.4	10.9
	20	22	7.6	8.6	19.5
	22	2	.7	.8	20.2
	23	4	1.4	1.6	21.8
	24	2	.7	.8	22.6
	25	17	5.8	6.6	29.2
	28	3	1.0	1.2	30.4
	29	1	.3	.4	30.7
	30	19	6.5	7.4	38.1
	32	1	.3	.4	38.5
	35	9	3.1	3.5	42.0
	37	1	.3	.4	42.4
	39	2	.7	.8	43.2
	40	18	6.2	7.0	50.2
	45	9	3.1	3.5	53.7
	46	1	.3	.4	54.1
	49	2	.7	.8	54.9
	50	34	11.7	13.2	68.1
	52	1	.3	.4	68.5
	54	2	.7	.8	69.3
	55	3	1.0	1.2	70.4
	56	1	.3	.4	70.8
	60	7	2.4	2.7	73.5
	64	2	.7	.8	74.3
	70	4	1.4	1.6	75.9
	75	1	.3	.4	76.3
	80	6	2.1	2.3	78.6
	90	4	1.4	1.6	80.2
	95	1	.3	.4	80.5
	100	15	5.2	5.8	86.4
	112	1	.3	.4	86.8
	117	1	.3	.4	87.2
	120	3	1.0	1.2	88.3
	129	1	.3	.4	88.7
	130	2	.7	.8	89.5
	145	1	.3	.4	89.9
	150	6	2.1	2.3	92.2
	170	1	.3	.4	92.6
	175	1	.3	.4	93.0
	185	1	.3	.4	93.4

EXHIBIT 16.1

Tabulation of V4 from the SPORTS Data—Continued

Value Label	Value	Frequency	Percent	Valid Percent	Cum Percent
	200	1	.3	.4	93.8
	250	1	.3	.4	94.2
	300	4	1.4	1.6	95.7
	350	1	.3	.4	96.1
	400	3	1.0	1.2	97.3
	500	3	1.0	1.2	98.4
	560	1	.3	.4	98.8
	700	2	.7	.8	99.6
	800	1	.3	.4	100.0
	998	34	11.7	Missing	
		-------	-------	-------	
	Total	291	100.0	100.0	

Valid cases 257   Missing cases 34

EXHIBIT 16.2

Tabulation of V4 with Recoded Categories

V4 Amount of Last Purchase

Value Label	Value	Frequency	Percent	Valid Percent	Cumulative Percent
$20 or less	1	50	17.2	19.5	19.5
$21 to $50	2	125	43.0	48.6	68.1
$51 to $100	3	47	16.2	18.3	86.4
$101 to $200	4	19	6.5	7.4	93.8
More than $200	5	16	5.5	6.2	100.0
Don't know	998	34	11.7	Missing	
		-------	-------	-------	
	Total	291	100.0	100.0	

Valid cases: 257   Missing cases: 34

EXHIBIT 16.3

Tabulation of V4 with a Different Recode

```
V4 Amount of Last Purchase


                                                Valid      Cumulative
Value Label      Value   Frequency   Percent   Percent     Percent

Less than $20      1         28        9.6      10.9        10.9
$20 to $49         2        113       38.8      44.0        54.9
$50 to $99         3         66       22.7      25.7        80.5
$100 to $199       4         33       11.3      12.8        93.4
$200 to $499       5         10        3.4       3.9        97.3
$500 or more       6          7        2.4       2.7       100.0
Don't know       998         34       11.7     Missing
                            -------   -------   -------
                 Total      291      100.0     100.0

Valid cases:  257    Missing cases:   34
```

Author Tips

Since the interpretation of a tabulation depends on how the categories are drawn, you should study the original distribution, draw your own conclusions about the best way of interpreting that distribution for marketing purposes, and choose a categorization scheme that facilitates this interpretation. Numbers do not speak for themselves—you must give them a voice.

than $200." This reduces the tabulation from sixty categories to five categories and makes it much easier to interpret the data. A quick look at this table shows that virtually all respondents spent less than $200 on their most recent sporting goods purchase, most spent less than $50, and $21 to $50 was the most common range of expenditure.

Of course, there are other ways of recoding data, and different recodes may lead to different interpretations. Consider, for example, Exhibit 16.3. This tabulation makes small changes in the category boundaries used in Exhibit 16.2: it lowers the category boundaries by $1, and it splits the "More than $200" category into "$200 to $499" and "$500 or more." These are minor changes, but they affect the impression given by the tab. Compared with Exhibit 16.2, Exhibit 16.3 gives an impression of higher expenditures.

Recoding can also affect the interpretation of tabs with a smaller number of categories. Consider the tab for V3 that is shown in Exhibit 16.1. According to this tab, the reasons for store choice are pretty evenly split among location (22%), sales (21%), selection (19%), and everyday prices (17%), followed by merchandise quality (10%) and credit availability (5%). Reasons for store choice appear to be diffuse, with location narrowly on top. Now look at the tab for V3 that is shown in Exhibit 16.4. In this tab, everyday prices and sale prices have been combined into a single "Price" category, and merchandise selection and quality have been combined into a single "Merchandise" category. The result shows that reasons for store choice are concentrated in price (38%), merchandise (29%), and location (22%). This is a different story than the previous tab told.

EXHIBIT 16.4

Tabulation of V3 with Recoded Categories

V3 Main reason for choosing store

Value Label	Value	Frequency	Percent	Valid Percent	Cumulative Percent
Price	1	111	38.1	38.3	38.3
Merchandise	2	84	28.9	29.0	67.2
Location	3	64	22.0	22.1	89.3
Service	4	3	1.0	1.0	90.3
Credit	5	15	5.2	5.2	95.5
Other	6	13	4.5	4.5	100.0
Don't know	8	1	.3	Missing	
		-------	-------	-------	
Total		291	100.0	100.0	

Valid cases: 290   Missing cases: 1

How to Treat Missing Data

An issue that arises in data tabulation—as well as in subsequent data analyses—is how missing data should be handled. For example, the tabs for V3 and V4 in Exhibits 16.2 and 16.3 show that one person didn't answer the "reasons" questions and thirty-four didn't answer the "amount" question. In addition to these people, other people didn't respond to the survey at all. All of these lost observations constitute missing data.

The concern that arises in connection with missing data is that these data, if available, would lead to different research conclusions. The extent of this concern depends on the amount of missing data and the likelihood that these data would be different from the available results. For example, information on income is often missing in as many as 20 percent of cases. This can seriously distort analyses, since people who are unwilling to report incomes may generally have higher incomes than those who are willing to report. On the other hand, the interpretation of the tab for V2 would be unaffected by getting an answer from the one missing respondent, no matter how this person answered. Similarly, the interpretation of the V4 tabulation is unlikely to be affected by the disposition of the thirty-four missing respondents unless these people have really extreme expenditure levels.

If the volume of missing data is small enough that it is unlikely to affect the conclusions from an analysis, the best way of handling missing data is by simply excluding them from analyses. For example, in reading the tabulations for V2 and V3, the column labeled "Valid Percent," which excludes the missing data, should be used.

Critical Thinking Skills

What conclusions would you draw from Exhibit 16.4 about the importance of price in attracting customers to this store? How do these conclusions compare with the conclusions you would draw from Exhibit 16.1? Which table is better?

Author Tips

The worst mistake you can make with missing data is to fail to declare missing values in your software commands. For example, if you were to code "Don't know" answers for V4 as "998," a failure to declare missing values in the V4 tab would result in all "Don't know" observations being counted as expenditures of $998. This would clearly distort the results.

However, if the volume of missing data is large enough to affect the conclusions, the best way of handling missing data is by including them in the results. This can be done in two ways. The usual method is to retain missing values as a separate category and report this category in all results. For example:

Attitude Toward Brand	Percentage of All Respondents	Percentage of Aware Respondents
Favorable	36	60
Neutral	12	20
Negative	12	20
Don't know/not aware	40	

The less common method is to estimate values for the missing data from values of the nonmissing data. For example, if we could establish a relationship in the SPORTS data between V4 (amount of the most recent purchase) and V1 (type of merchandise bought), and if some of the people who didn't answer V4 *did* answer V1, the V1 answers might be used to estimate values for V4. This method, however, is normally not used in marketing research.

Summary Measures of Central Tendency

The data shown in a tabulation can be further summarized by measures that describe some characteristic of the distribution. These summary measures are grouped into **measures of central tendency** (i.e., measures that give some idea of a "typical" value) and **measures of dispersion**.

There are three principal measures of central tendency: the mean, median, and mode. The **mean** is the arithmetic average of a variable, computed as

$$\bar{x} = \frac{\Sigma x_i}{n},$$

where $\bar{x}$ represents the mean of some variable x, x_i represents the values of individual observations on that variable, and n represents the number of observations. The **median** is the value that has an equal number of observations above and below it, that is, the fiftieth percentile value. The **mode** is the value that is observed more frequently than any other value.

In SPSS for Windows, summary measures of central tendency can be obtained through a tabulation. Choose "Summarize" and "Frequencies" from the "Statistics" menu, click the "Statistics" button, and indicate which statistics you want.

The resulting output is shown in Exhibit 16.5. It repeats the tabulation shown in Exhibit 16.1 and adds various summary statistics at the bottom of the tabulation. As can be seen in Exhibit 16.5, the mean for V4 is $74.72, the median is $40, and the mode is $50.

EXHIBIT 16.5

Tabulation of V4 Along with Summary Statistics

V4 Amount of last purchase

Value Label	Value	Frequency	Percent	Valid Percent	Cumulative Percent
	3	3	1.0	1.2	1.2
	5	2	.7	.8	1.9
	8	1	.3	.4	2.3
	9	2	.7	.8	3.1
	10	6	2.1	2.3	5.4
	12	3	1.0	1.2	6.6
	14	1	.3	.4	7.0
	15	9	3.1	3.5	10.5
	18	1	.3	.4	10.9
	20	22	7.6	8.6	19.5
	22	2	.7	.8	20.2
	23	4	1.4	1.6	21.8
	24	2	.7	.8	22.6
	25	17	5.8	6.6	29.2
	28	3	1.0	1.2	30.4
	29	1	.3	.4	30.7
	30	19	6.5	7.4	38.1
	32	1	.3	.4	38.5
	35	9	3.1	3.5	42.0
	37	1	.3	.4	42.4
	39	2	.7	.8	43.2
	40	18	6.2	7.0	50.2
	45	9	3.1	3.5	53.7
	46	1	.3	.4	54.1
	49	2	.7	.8	54.9
	50	34	11.7	13.2	68.1
	52	1	.3	.4	68.5
	54	2	.7	.8	69.3
	55	3	1.0	1.2	70.4
	56	1	.3	.4	70.8
	60	7	2.4	2.7	73.5
	64	2	.7	.8	74.3
	70	4	1.4	1.6	75.9
	75	1	.3	.4	76.3
	80	6	2.1	2.3	78.6
	90	4	1.4	1.6	80.2
	95	1	.3	.4	80.5
	100	15	5.2	5.8	86.4
	112	1	.3	.4	86.8

Continued

EXHIBIT 16.5

Tabulation of V4 Along with Summary Statistics— Continued

Value Label	Value	Frequency	Percent	Valid Percent	Cumulative Percent
	117	1	.3	.4	87.2
	120	3	1.0	1.2	88.3
	129	1	.3	.4	88.7
	130	2	.7	.8	89.5
	145	1	.3	.4	89.9
	150	6	2.1	2.3	92.2
	170	1	.3	.4	92.6
	175	1	.3	.4	93.0
	185	1	.3	.4	93.4
	200	1	.3	.4	93.8
	250	1	.3	.4	94.2
	300	4	1.4	1.6	95.7
	350	1	.3	.4	96.1
	400	3	1.0	1.2	97.3
	500	3	1.0	1.2	98.4
	560	1	.3	.4	98.8
	700	2	.7	.8	99.6
	800	1	.3	.4	100.0
	998	34	11.7	Missing	
		-------	-------	-------	
	Total	291	100.0	100.0	

Mean	74.720	Std err	6.970	Median	40.000
Mode	50.000	Std dev	111.731	Variance	12483.710
Kurtosis	17.196	S E kurt	.303	Skewness	3.899
S E skew	.152	Range	797.000	Minimum	3.000
Maximum	800.000	Sum	19203.000		

Valid cases: 257   Missing cases: 34

Of the three measures of central tendency, the mean is the most influenced by extreme values in a distribution. V4, for example, has three unusually high observations at $700 and $800 that pull the mean upward. If these three observations—the top 1 percent—are removed from the data, the mean drops from $74.72 to $66.94, a change of about 10 percent. The median and mode, in contrast, remain unchanged at $40 and $50, respectively.

When the distribution of a variable is symmetric, such as in the well-known "normal" distribution, extreme values in each tail of the distribution will balance each other so that the mean falls in the middle of the distribution, near the median and mode. However, when the distribution is positively or negatively skewed (i.e., lopsided), extreme values in the long tail of the distribution will overbalance those in the short tail and pull the mean in their direction. This tends to make the mean a poor indicator of the distribution's "typical" value. In the V4 tab, for example, the mean of $72.74 is higher than 75 percent of the individual observations. When the mean is a poor indicator of the "typical" value, the median is usually used in its place.

Summary Measures of Dispersion

The dispersion, or variability, of a distribution can be measured in various ways. The most common measures are the range, variance, standard deviation, and interquartile range. The range, variance, and standard deviation can be found among the summary statistics at the bottom of Exhibit 16.5.

The **range** is simply the distance from the smallest to the largest value in a distribution. The data shown in Exhibit 16.5, for example, go from a low of $3 to a high of $800, for a range of $797. When presenting the range of a variable, it is usually desirable to present the actual extreme values; that is, rather than simply saying that the variable has a range of $797, say that values range from a low of $3 to a high of $800. This provides information about the location as well as the dispersion of the data.

The **variance** is the average squared distance between the values of individual observations on some variable and the mean of that variable, computed as

$$s^2 = \frac{\Sigma(x_i - \bar{x})^2}{n},$$

where s^2 represents the variance of some variable x, x_i represents the values of individual observations on that variable, $\bar{x}$ represents the mean of that variable, and n represents the number of observations. Since the variance indicates the average squared distance between the observations in a distribution and the mean of that distribution, a smaller variance indicates a tighter grouping of observations around the mean.

The **standard deviation**, symbolized as s, is the square root of the variance. As with the variance, a smaller standard deviation indicates a tighter grouping of observations around the mean of a distribution.

The **interquartile range** is the distance between the values that mark the first and third quartiles of a distribution. In Exhibit 16.5, the first quartile boundary—where the cumulative percentage of observations hits 25 percent—is $25. The second quartile boundary, or median, is $40. The third quartile boundary— where the cumulative percentage hits 75 percent—is $70. The interquartile range is $70 – $25 = $35.

Note that the interquartile range for these data, $35, is smaller than the standard deviation of $111.73. When data follow a "normal" distribution, the interquartile range is *larger* than the standard deviation. The fact that the standard deviation is larger than the interquartile range in these data indicates the presence of **outliers** (i.e., extreme values). Just as the mean is more sensitive to outliers than the median is, the standard deviation is more sensitive to outliers than the interquartile range is. Outliers inflate the variance and standard deviation without affecting the interquartile range much.

Summary Measures and Scale Types

Different measures of central tendency are appropriate for different scale types. The mean requires summing the observed values and dividing by the sample size; this is appropriate for ratio and interval scale data, which can be added meaningfully, but not for ordinal and nominal data. The median requires finding a point that has half the values above it and half the values below; this is appropriate for ratio, interval, and ordinal data, which have order in the data, but not for nominal data. The mode applies to any type of data: we can say that "1" is the most common value of V43 even if "1" is only a symbol for "male."

Measures of dispersion are even more restricted than measures of central tendency. The variance, standard deviation, range, and interquartile range all require addition or subtraction in their calculation and therefore apply only to interval and ratio scale data (for which addition and subtraction are meaningful). None of these measures applies to nominal or ordinal data.

Marketing Research Tools 16.1 summarizes the characteristics of various scale types and the applicability of various summary measures to different scale types.

Choosing Descriptive Analysis Procedures

Given the various procedures that *can* be used to describe univariate data, let us talk about the procedures that *should* be used in any given analysis situation. Two general situations will be considered: (1) the distribution of a single variable by itself is to be described and (2) the univariate distributions of two or more variables are to be compared.

MARKETING RESEARCH TOOLS

16.1

TYPES OF SCALES

Scale Type	Mathematical Properties	Applicable Summary Statistics
Nominal	None	Mode
Ordinal	Order	Mode, median
Interval	Order, equal intervals	All (mean, median, mode; variance, standard deviation, interquartile range)
Ratio	Order, equal intervals, absolute zero	All

Describing a Single Variable

Generally, tabulations are the best procedure to use when a variable is being analyzed with no comparisons to other variables. Tabs can be used for any type of data, no matter how the data are scaled, and a tab with properly chosen categories provides a better sense of the distribution than can be gotten from summary statistics.

For example, compare the tab of V4 shown in Exhibit 16.3 (see page 454) with the summary statistics shown in Exhibit 16.5. The tab gives a more vivid sense of the data. Tabs also facilitate graphic presentation of the results. They can be represented by pie charts or bar charts, while means, medians, and other summary statistics do not have any natural graphic representation.

This is not to say that summary statistics have no value. In presenting quantitative data such as expenditure results, it is a good idea to show both a tabulation *and* a summary measure of central tendency. For example, Exhibit 16.6 repeats Exhibit 16.3 but adds the median of the distribution. This approach provides the best of both worlds. The median was used rather than the mean because these data had a skewed distribution and the median seemed to fit the tabulation better.

Note that a summary measure of dispersion is not shown in Exhibit 16.6. The tab itself is sufficient to show the variation in the data, and some people find dispersion measures such as the variance or standard deviation too abstract to be meaningful.

Comparing Distributions for Two or More Variables

Sometimes it is appropriate to compare univariate distributions for two or more variables within a single table. In this situation, tabulations are usually too cumbersome to be effective, and some simplification or summarization of the data is necessary.

Consider Exhibit 16.7 (see page 462), which combines the tabs for V17 to V27 in the STORES data. These variables contain respondents' ratings of Smith's Stores along eleven dimensions. The eleven variables are combined into a single table for purposes of comparison, to show where Smith's Stores gets its highest and lowest ratings. However, it is difficult to make this comparison amid the confusion of Exhibit 16.7.

Exhibit 16.8 (see page 462) analyzes these data much more effectively. Instead of showing the full tabulation for each variable, Exhibit 16.8 shows only the percentage of respondents who rated Smith's "Much better than average" and reorders the

EXHIBIT 16.6

Amount Spent on Most Recent Sporting Goods Purchase

Category	Percent
$20 or less	19.5
$21 to $50	48.6
$51 to $100	18.3
$101 to $200	7.4
More than $200	6.2
Total	100.0

Median expenditure = $40

EXHIBIT 16.7

Ratings of Smith's Stores on Various Dimensions

	Percent of Respondents Who Rated Smith's . . .				
Dimension	Much Better Than Average	Better Than Average	About the Same	Worse Than Average	Much Worse Than Average
Location	61	18	17	3	1
Everyday prices	35	23	30	10	2
Sales	48	23	25	4	1
Taking credit cards	46	18	35	1	1
Having own card	54	18	26	1	1
Merchandise quality	59	20	17	3	1
Selection	56	16	19	9	1
Brand names	51	18	21	7	2
Having merchandise in stock	52	20	20	6	1
Helpful service	49	16	23	10	3
Speed of service	45	16	29	8	3

EXHIBIT 16.8

Ratings of Smith's Stores on Various Dimensions

Dimension	Percentage of Respondents Who Rated Smith's "Much Better Than Average"
Location	61
Merchandise quality	59
Selection	56
Having own credit card	54
Having merchandise in stock	52
Brand names	51
Helpful service	49
Sales	48
Taking credit cards	46
Speed of service	45
Everyday prices	35

eleven dimensions so they appear in high-to-low order. Simplification and organization of the results make the comparison among dimensions much easier to see. They also facilitate graphic presentation of the results. Exhibit 16.8 can easily be converted to a bar chart, as shown in Exhibit 16.9, while the full tabulations shown in Exhibit 16.7 (see page 462) would be difficult to graph.

The results could have been simplified by the use of measures other than the percentage of respondents who rated Smith's Stores "Much better than average." For example, the percentage of respondents who rated Smith's as *either* "Much better than average" or simply "Better than average" could have been used. Or the percentage who rated Smith's as better than average could have been calculated, the percentage who rated Smith's worse than average subtracted, and the difference used. Or the data could have been treated as if they had interval scaling and mean ratings used on each dimension. Any of these measures would have simplified the comparison across variables. The choice among measures depends on the scaling and distribution of the variables being studied and, more than anything else, on your opinion regarding which measure yields the most useful results.

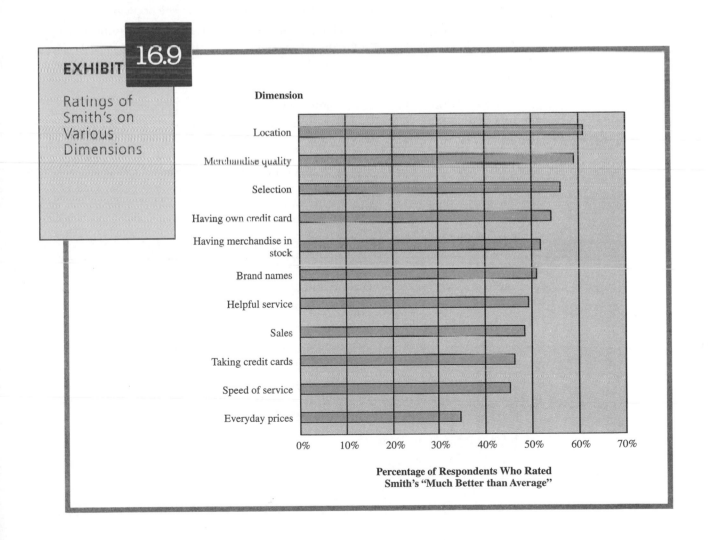

EXHIBIT 16.9

Ratings of Smith's on Various Dimensions

Inferential Data Analyses

What Are Inferential Data Analyses?

In most market research projects, the data available for analysis are a sample drawn from some broader population of possible observations. For example, the 291 people who provided the SPORTS data are a sample drawn from a larger population. Under these circumstances, **inferential data analyses** are used to measure the extent to which descriptive results from the sample represent or might differ from the population.

In the discussion of sampling error in Chapter 14, the following points were made:

- The value of a descriptive measure obtained from any given sample is usually not exactly equal to the value of that measure in the population; for example, the mean of a sample is usually not exactly equal to the mean of the population.

- Across repeated samples, the values obtained for the descriptive measure of interest will form a distribution around the population value of that measure.

- The variance of that distribution will be a function of the population variance for the variable being measured, the sample size, and the sample design.

Since descriptive measures will vary across samples from a population, one cannot be sure that the results obtained from any particular sample accurately reflect the population. It is, however, possible to estimate the distribution of possible sample results. This allows the calculation of **confidence intervals**, intervals within which a specified percentage, usually 90% or 95%, of the sample results should fall. It also allows the testing of the probability that any given population value would have led to the observed sample result. These are the two basic forms of inferential analysis.

Confidence Intervals

Based on the "normal" distribution, a 95% confidence interval around any descriptive measure—whether a mean, a percentage, a difference in means, a difference in percentages, or whatever—is calculated as

$\pm(1.96 \times$ Standard deviation of the measure).

In principle, the standard deviation of a measure would be obtained by (1) taking repeated samples from the population of interest, (2) calculating the measure for each sample, and (3) calculating the standard deviation across the sample measures. In practice, we usually have data from only one sample, and must estimate the standard deviation of the measure from information contained within that single sample.

Confidence Intervals for Means

The standard deviation of a mean is represented by the symbol $s_{\bar{x}}$ and is estimated as

$$s_{\bar{x}} = \frac{s}{\sqrt{n}},$$

where s is the standard deviation of the variable for which the mean has been calculated and n is the sample size.

At the bottom of Exhibit 16.5 (see page 458) is shown a "Standard error" among the summary statistics provided for tabulations in the SPSS software package. This statistic, which is not provided in all software packages, refers to $s_{\bar{x}}$ and saves the bother of calculating it. The standard error shown in Exhibit 16.5 is $6.97. Therefore, the 95% confidence interval for the mean of V4 is calculated as

$$\pm(1.96 \times \$6.97) = \pm\$13.66.$$

This confidence interval is interpreted as follows: if V4 has a standard deviation of $111.73 in this population, 95 percent of all random samples of size 291 drawn from this population will have a mean for V4 that falls within $\pm\$13.66$ of the population mean.

A 90% confidence interval is calculated in the same fashion as a 95% interval, except that 1.645 is used in place of 1.96. In our example, the 90% confidence interval for the mean of V4 is calculated as

$$\pm(1.645 \times \$6.97) = \pm\$11.47.$$

That is, if V4 has a standard deviation of $111.73 in this population, 90 percent of all random samples of size 291 drawn from this population will have means for V4 that fall within $\pm\$11.47$ of the population mean.

> ## Critical Thinking Skills
>
> For a frequency distribution with a mean of 102 and a standard error of 5, calculate the 90% and 95% confidence intervals for the mean.

Confidence Intervals for Proportions

Confidence intervals around proportions (percentages) are calculated the same way as confidence intervals around means. The only difference is that the standard deviation of a proportion is calculated as

$$s_p = \sqrt{\frac{p(1-p)}{n}},$$

where p is the sample percentage for the variable of interest and n is the sample size.

Say, for example, that one of the results to be derived from the SPORTS data is the percentage of respondents who spent more than $50 on their most recent sporting goods purchase, and the 95% confidence interval associated with this percentage is to be calculated. Exhibit 16.2 (see page 453) shows that this percentage equals 31.9 percent of the observations in the sample data (18.3% in the "$51 to $100" category plus 7.4% in the "$101 to $200" category plus 6.2% in the "More than $200" category). The standard deviation of this proportion is calculated as

$$\sqrt{\frac{.319(1-.319)}{257}} = .029$$

In this calculation, 257 was used as the sample size because 257 is the number of usable responses for V4. Given the result, the 95% confidence interval is calculated as

$$\pm(1.96 \times .029) = \pm.057 \text{ or } \pm 5.7\%.$$

This confidence interval is interpreted as follows: if the percentage of sporting goods buyers who spent more than $50 on their most recent purchase is 31.9 percent in this population, 95 percent of all random samples of size 291 drawn from this population will have a percentage of buyers who spent more than $50 that is within ±5.7% of the population figure.

The 90% confidence interval is calculated as

$$\pm(1.645 \times .029) = \pm.048 \text{ or } \pm4.8\%$$

Confidence Intervals for Differences Between Means or Proportions

Sometimes it is desirable to calculate confidence intervals associated with the difference between two means or two percentages. For example, 35.1 percent of respondents in the SPORTS data rated Smith's *everyday* prices as much better than average, and 48.4 percent rated Smith's *sale* prices as much better than average. The difference is 13.3 percent. It might be desirable to calculate a confidence interval associated with this difference.

The basic procedure for calculating confidence intervals around measures of difference is no different from the procedure for calculating intervals around means or percentages. The only difference lies in the computation of the standard deviation of the measure. The standard deviation of a difference between two means is calculated as

$$s_{(\bar{x}_1 - \bar{x}_2)} = \sqrt{\frac{(s_1)^2}{n_1} + \frac{(s_2)^2}{n_2}}$$

and the standard deviation of a difference between two proportions is calculated as

$$s_{(p_1 - p_2)} = \sqrt{\frac{p_1(1 - p_1)}{n_1} + \frac{p_2(1 - p_2)}{n_2}}.$$

To illustrate these calculations, the percentage of respondents in our SPORTS data who rated Smith's everyday prices "Much better than average" is 35.1 percent, with 288 usable observations. The percentage who gave this rating for Smith's sale prices is 48.4 percent, with 289 usable observations. The difference is 13.3 percent. The standard deviation of the difference is

$$\sqrt{\frac{.484(1 - .484)}{289} + \frac{.351(1 - .351)}{288}} = .041$$

and the 95% confidence interval around this difference is

$$\pm(1.96 \times .041) = \pm.080 \text{ or } \pm8.0\%.$$

This confidence interval does not take account of the fact that most of the people who rated Smith's everyday prices and Smith's sale prices are, in fact, the same people. A more appropriate procedure when comparing two measures that come from the same sample is to create a difference measure by subtracting one measure from the other. The mean and standard deviation of this difference

Author Tips

The formulas we have used to calculate the standard deviation of a measure apply to simple random samples. These formulas may not apply to data that were obtained with stratified and/or cluster sampling. If the data were obtained with a complex sampling design, the standard deviation of a measure can be estimated by means of a "pseudoreplication" technique such as jackknifing, bootstrapping, or balanced random replication, as noted in Chapter 14.

variable can be calculated directly, as can the standard deviation of the mean and a confidence interval. The result should be a smaller confidence interval than is obtained by treating the two measures as coming from separate samples.

Hypothesis and Significance Tests

Hypothesis tests, also known as **significance tests**, measure the probability that a hypothesized population value for the measure of interest could have led to the observed sample result. For example, the observed sample mean for V4 in our SPORTS data is $72.74. To test a hypothesis that the population mean for V4 is $100, the probability that a random sample of 291 people from this population would have exhibited a mean as extreme as $72.74 if the population mean is $100 is measured. If that probability is less than .05 (5%), we can say that a hypothesis that the population mean equals $100 is rejected at the .05 level. Alternately, we can say that the observed mean, $72.74, is "significantly different" from $100. If the probability is more than .05, we can say that the hypothesis cannot be rejected at the .05 level or that the observed mean is not significantly different from $100. The .05 level is conventional for hypothesis/significance testing, but the .10 level also receives some use, and researchers sometimes report significance at the .01 or .001 levels to indicate differences that are "highly significant."

Hypothesis tests concerning univariate means and proportions are usually done with *t* **tests.** A *t*-test is constructed as follows:

$$t = \frac{\text{Sample value} - \text{Hypothesized population value}}{\text{Standard deviation of the sample value}}.$$

The resulting *t*-value is compared with a table of values to determine whether it exceeds the "criterion values" that mark certain levels of probability. A *t*-table is provided as Appendix B at the back of this book. The criterion value for a .05 probability level, assuming a "two-tailed" test and a sample size over 100, is ±1.96. The criterion level for a .10 probability level is 1.645.

Let us illustrate this testing procedure with three examples that parallel our confidence interval calculations.

Example 1

First, let us test whether the mean for V4, the amount of the most recent sporting goods purchase, is significantly different from $100. In this example, the sample mean is $72.74 and the standard deviation of the mean is $6.97 (these numbers were used in the previous section). The hypothesized population value is $100. The calculation for this test is

$$t = \frac{72.74 - 100.00}{6.97} = -3.91.$$

The absolute value of *t* is higher than 1.96, which is the critical value for significance at the .05 level. In fact, it is also higher than 2.576, which is the critical value for significance at the .01 level, and 3.291, which is the critical value for significance at the .001 level. Given this result, we reject the hypothesis that the population mean is $100. To put it another way, we conclude that the sample mean is significantly different from $100.

Example 2

Next, let us test whether the percentage of respondents who spent more than $50 is significantly different from 30 percent. As shown in the confidence interval examples, the percentage of SPORTS respondents who spent more than $50 on their most recent sporting goods purchase is 31.9 percent. The standard deviation of this percentage is 2.9 percent. The calculation for this test is

$$t = \frac{.319 - .300}{.029} = .66.$$

The absolute value of t is less than 1.96, so the difference is not statistically significant at a .05 level. That is, we cannot reject, at the .05 level, the hypothesis that the population percentage is 30 percent. The absolute value of t is also less than 1.645, so the difference is not significant at the .10 level, either.

Example 3

Finally, let us test whether the percentage of respondents who rated Smith's "Much above average" on everyday prices is significantly different from the percentage who rated Smith's "Much above average" on sale prices. This can be restated as "Test whether the difference between these two percentages is zero."

As seen in the discussion of confidence intervals, the percentage of respondents who rated Smith's "Much above average" on everyday prices is 35.1 percent, the percentage for sale prices is 48.4 percent, and the difference is 13.3 percent. The standard deviation of this difference is 8.0 percent. The calculation for the test is

$$t = \frac{.133 - .000}{.080} = 1.66.$$

The absolute value of t is higher than 1.645 but lower than 1.96. Therefore, the hypothesis that these two percentages are the same in the population—that is, that the difference between them is zero—would be rejected at the .10 level but not at the .05 level.

The Role of Inferential Analyses in Market Research

Unlike descriptive analyses, inferential analyses do not provide information about the nature of the market. Instead, they serve a "checking" role, giving some idea of the confidence that can be placed in descriptive results. A researcher can use confidence intervals to convey the precision of results and can use significance tests to caution managers not to place too much importance on nonsignificant differences.

These uses of inferential analyses are generally legitimate and valuable. However, inferential analyses generally are less important in marketing research than descriptive analyses are. Descriptive results occupy the foreground of most market research reports, while inferential results are kept in the background or not reported at all. There are various reasons for this emphasis on description:

- *Inferential analyses simply do not apply in some marketing research situations.* Inference is not needed if the data represent the entire population, as sometimes occurs in business research or analyses of internal records. Also, if data are drawn

CASE STUDY 16.1

An entrepreneur planned to market a product called "Mr. SureStop." This was a funny-looking plastic head that people could hang in their garages as a stopping guide for automobiles ("When your windshield hits Mr. SureStop, it's time to stop!"). Since this entrepreneur had very little money for research, he conducted his own informal opinion poll with fifteen men and fifteen women. Most of the women said they would buy the product, but none of the men was interested. The entrepreneur used these results to decide that women were the better target market for his product.

The confidence interval related to these results would have been very large because the sample was small and might not even have been meaningful because the sample was haphazard. In the end, though, the entrepreneur had to make decisions based on the available data regardless of confidence intervals and significance tests. This is what we mean when we say that marketing decisions ultimately depend on descriptive results. Inferential results tell you how much confidence to place in descriptive results, but they cannot make decisions for you.

from a nonprobability sample (as in focus group studies) or from a sample of unknown characteristics (as in much secondary research), standard inferential procedures may be meaningless, because these procedures assume a random sample from the broader population.

- *Significance tests may be misleading.* Consider, for example, a marketer who wishes to compare men's and women's attitudes toward a new product. If the sample size is large, differences between men and women may be statistically significant but of no practical marketing importance. On the contrary, if the sample size is small, the differences may be of major marketing importance but not statistically significant.

- *Most importantly, the ultimate purpose of marketing research is to guide decisions.* Descriptive analyses guide decisions; and inferential analyses do not. Case Study 16.1 illustrates this point.

Summary

This chapter discussed univariate data analysis. The following points were covered:

1. What are the four kinds of scaling that might apply to univariate data?

A variable can have ratio, interval, ordinal, or nominal scale properties. *Ratio scale variables* have order among scale points, equal distances among adjacent scale points, and an absolute zero. *Interval scale variables* have order and equal distances among adjacent points but do not have an absolute zero. *Ordinal scale variables* have only the property of order among scale points, and *nominal scale variables* have none of these properties (the numbers simply identify categories).

2. How are tabulations used to describe univariate data?

A tabulation (or tab) is a tabular presentation that shows the frequency distribution for a variable (i.e., it shows the values assumed by that variable and the number of times each value is observed).

3. How should missing values in data analyses be handled?

Missing data should be excluded from analyses if the number of missing values is small. If there is a reasonable chance that the missing values might affect the conclusions, missing data should be shown as a separate category.

4. How are summary measures of central tendency and dispersion used to describe univariate data?

Measures of central tendency include the mean, median, and mode. They are used to give an indication of the "typical" value for a variable. Measures of dispersion include the range, variance, standard deviation, and interquartile range. They are used to show how much variability exists in the data.

5. What are inferential statistics?

Inferential analyses are used to measure the extent to which descriptive characteristics of the sample might differ from the population. Inferential analyses include confidence intervals and hypothesis/significance tests.

Suggested Additional Readings

There are a very large number of introductory statistics texts that cover the material in this chapter. You may wish to refer to the book you used in your statistics class for additional information. Two useful books that are widely used in business statistics courses are John Neter, William Wasserman, and Michael H. Kutner, *Applied Linear Statistical Models: Regression, Analysis of Variance, and Experimental Designs* (Homewood, Ill.: Irwin, 1990) and Paul Newbold, *Statistics for Business and Economics* (Englewood Cliffs, N.J.: Prentice Hall, 1991).

Discussion Questions

1. What are the four different scale types? Give examples of each.
2. Discuss the role of inferential analysis in marketing research.
3. Which is more important to the marketing manager, descriptive analysis or inferential analysis?
4. How should missing data be handled?
5. Discuss the difference between measures of central tendency and measures of dispersion. For each measure given, indicate whether that measure is a measure of central tendency or a measure of dispersion.

Mode	Variance
Range	Interquartile range
Mean	Median
Standard deviation	

6. What measures of central tendency could you calculate for each of the following scale types: Nominal? Ordinal? Interval? Ratio? What measures of dispersion could you calculate?

7. Discuss what is meant by hypothesis testing.

Marketing Research Challenge

Choose one or more of the variables on the SPORTS disk. Show the distribution of this variable both as a table and in some graphic form. If appropriate, give measures of central tendency and variance, and compute confidence intervals.

Internet Exercise

If you need a refresher course in basic statistics, visit SurfStat Australia, at:
http://frey.newcastle.edu.au/Stat/surfstat/surfstat.html.
This is an online statistics book by Keith Deer at the University of Newcastle.

17

Bivariate Data Analysis

 OBJECTIVES

LEARNING

After reading this chapter, you should be able to answer the following questions:

❶ How can cross-tabulation be used to analyze the relationship between two variables?

❷ How can comparison of means be used to analyze the relationship between two variables?

❸ How can correlation be used to analyze the relationship between two variables?

❹ How can bivariate linear regression be used to analyze the relationship between two variables?

This chapter discusses bivariate analyses, which measure the relationship of two variables. It considers four types of bivariate analyses that are used in marketing research: cross-tabulation, comparison of means, correlation, and bivariate regression analysis.

All of these procedures have the same goal, which is to measure the relationship between two variables. However, they are used for different types of data.

- *Cross-tabulation* is appropriate when both variables are categorical in nature (this includes quantitative variables that have been broken into categories).

- *Comparison of means* is appropriate when one variable is categorical and the other is quantitative.

- *Correlation* requires that both variables be quantitative.

- *Bivariate regression* is related to correlation analysis, and also requires that both variables be quantitative.

Marketing Research Tools 17.1 lists the four procedures, their data requirements, and examples of situations in which each procedure is appropriate.

MARKETING RESEARCH TOOLS

17.1

OVERVIEW OF BIVARIATE ANALYSES

Procedure	Data Requirements	Sample Research Question
Cross-tabulation	Both variables categorical	Is interest in our product (yes-no) related to gender (male-female)? That is, does the percentage who are interested in the product vary between men and women?
Comparisons of means	One variable categorical, one variable quantitative	Is level of expenditure on our product (continuous) related to gender (male-female)? That is, does the mean expenditure vary between men and women?
Correlation	Both variables quantitative	Is level of expenditure on our product (continuous) related to income (continuous)? That is, does the level of expenditure vary across levels of income?
Bivariate regression	Both variables quantitative	What is the linear equation that relates level of expenditure to income?

Cross-tabulation

Description of the Procedure

The simplest form of bivariate analysis is two-way **cross-tabulation** (also called **cross-classification**), which counts the number of observations in each cross-category of two variables. The basic descriptive result of a cross-tabulation is a frequency count for each cell in the analysis. For example, in cross-tabulating a two-category measure of gender (male-female) with a two-category measure of product interest (yes-no), the basic result is a cross-classification table showing the number of interested men, the number of noninterested men, the number of interested women, and the number of noninterested women.

As with simple tabulations, the results of a cross-tabulation are more meaningful if frequencies are expressed as percentages. This can be done in two ways. First, percentages can be calculated with respect to the total number of observations. For example, a cross-tab of product interest by gender can express the numbers of interested men, noninterested men, interested women, and noninterested women as percentages of the total. This analysis will show the relative size of the groups.

Second, percentages for one variable can be calculated within categories of the other. For example, a cross-tab of product interest by gender can calculate (1) the percentage who are interested and not interested within each gender category, or (2) the percentage of men and women within each interest category. Either analysis will show whether the variables are related, but from two points of view. The first calculation will show whether the probability of being interested is related to gender; the second calculation will show whether the probability of being male is related to interest.

Since the usual purpose of a cross-tabulation is to learn whether variables are related, category percentages are usually more useful than total percentages. The preferred basis for calculating category percentages depends on the nature of the relationship between the variables. If one of the variables can be viewed as dependent on the other, percentages for the **dependent variable** should be calculated within categories of the **independent variable**. For example, if product interest can be viewed as dependent on gender (gender is certainly not dependent on interest!), it is most useful to look at percentages of interest for each gender category. If the variables are simply related, with no dependence, either variable can be used as the basis for categorization.

An Example of Cross-tabulation

To illustrate cross-tabulation, Exhibit 17.1 (see page 476) shows the output from a cross-tab of V3 and V37 in the SPORTS data. The output has two sections: (1) a cross-tab table that contains the descriptive results, and (2) a statistics table that contains inferential information about the results.

EXHIBIT 17.1

Cross-tabulation of V3 and V37

V3 Main Reason for Choosing Store by V37 Sex

```
                      V37
             Count
             Row Pct   Male    Female
             Col Pct                        Row
             Tot Pct     1        2        TOTAL
V3           --------+--------+--------+
             0    |    6    |    7    |    13
Other             |   46.2  |   53.8  |    4.5
                  |    3.9  |    5.1  |
                  |    2.1  |    2.4  |
             +--------+--------+
             1    |   28    |   22    |    50
Regular prices    |   56.0  |   44.0  |   17.2
                  |   18.3  |   16.1  |
                  |    9.7  |    7.6  |
             +--------+--------+
             2    |   29    |   32    |    61
Sale              |   47.5  |   52.5  |   21.0
                  |   19.0  |   23.4  |
                  |   10.0  |   11.0  |
             +--------+--------+
             3    |   28    |   36    |    64
Location          |   43.8  |   56.3  |   22.1
                  |   18.3  |   26.3  |
                  |    9.7  |   12.4  |
             +--------+--------+
             4    |   14    |   16    |    30
Merchandise quality|  46.7  |   53.3  |   10.3
                  |    9.2  |   11.7  |
                  |    4.8  |    5.5  |
             +--------+--------+
             5    |   36    |   18    |    54
Selection         |   66.7  |   33.3  |   18.6
                  |   23.5  |   13.1  |
                  |   12.4  |    6.2  |
             +--------+--------+
             6    |    2    |    1    |     3
Service           |   66.7  |   33.3  |    1.0
                  |    1.3  |     .7  |
                  |     .7  |     .3  |
             +--------+--------+
             7    |   10    |    5    |    15
Credit            |   66.7  |   33.3  |    5.2
                  |    6.5  |    3.6  |
                  |    3.4  |    1.7  |
             +--------+--------+
         Column    153      137      290
          Total   52.8     47.2    100.0
```

Chi-square	Value	DF	Significance
Pearson	9.22311	7	.23703
Likelihood ratio	9.35434	7	.22821
Mantel-Haenszel test for linear association	2.87453	1	.08999

Minimum expected frequency: 1.417

Cells with expected frequency < 5: 2 OF 16 (12.5%)

Number of missing observations: 1

Each cell in the cross-tab table contains four numbers. The meaning of these numbers, indicated by a legend at the upper left-hand corner of the table, is as follows:

- The first number is a frequency count. For example, the count for the cell in which V3 = 1 and V37 = 1 is 28, which indicates that the data include 28 men who gave "regular price" as their most important reason for store choice.

- The second number expresses the cell count as a percentage of the row count. In the same cell, a row percentage of 56.0 indicates that of the 50 people who cited "regular price," 28, or 56.0 percent, are men.

- The third number expresses the cell count as a percentage of the column count. In the same cell, a column percentage of 18.3 indicates that of the 153 men, 18.3 percent cited "regular price" as their reason for store choice.

- The fourth number expresses the cell count as a percentage of the total number of observations in the table. In the same cell, a total percentage of 9.7 indicates that the 28 observations in this cell constitute 9.7 percent of 290 total observations with non-missing data on V3 and V37.

Overall, the cross-tab table is cluttered and should be simplified for purposes of presentation. The focus would be on row or column percentages, whichever are more useful in showing the relationship of interest.

Exhibit 17.2 shows the two alternatives. The upper half of Exhibit 17.2 contains a table drawn from the column percentages in Exhibit 17.1; this table shows reasons for store choice within each gender category (with reasons arranged in descending order of citation for men). The lower half of Exhibit 17.2 (see page 478) is a table drawn from the row percentages in Exhibit 17.1; this table shows the distribution of genders within each reason for store choice. The first analysis more clearly shows what we want to know and is the one we would use. This demonstrates the point that it is better to look at percentages for a dependent variable within categories of an independent variable.

Inferential Analyses for Cross-tabulations

The primary inferential question in a bivariate cross-tab is whether the overall relationship between the two variables significantly differs from zero. This issue is tested by means of a **chi-squared (χ^2) test,** which works in the following way:

- If two events are independent—i.e., not related to each other—the probability of their joint occurrence can be calculated by multiplying the probabilities of their individual occurrences. For example, the probability of drawing an ace of hearts from a deck of cards, which equals 1/52, can be calculated as the

EXHIBIT 17.2

Cross-tabulation Results Expressed as Percentages of Each Variable

Distribution of Reasons Within Genders

Main Reason for Store Choice	Men(%)	Women(%)
Merchandise selection	23.5%	13.1%
Sale	19.0	23.4
Everyday prices	18.3	16.1
Location	18.3	26.3
Merchandise quality	9.2	11.7
Credit availability	6.5	3.6
Service	1.3	.7
Other	3.9	5.1
Total	100.0%	100.0%

Comment: This table shows what we want to know—whether reasons for store choice differ by gender—and is the one we would use.

Distribution of Genders Within Reasons

Main Reason for Store Choice	Men(%)	Women(%)	Total
Merchandise selection	66.7%	33.3%	100%
Sale	47.5	52.5	100
Everyday prices	56.0	44.0	100
Location	43.8	56.3	100
Merchandise quality	46.7	53.3	100
Credit availability	66.7	33.3	100
Service	66.7	33.3	100
Other	46.2	53.8	100

Comment: This table does not show what we want to know and would not be used.

probability of drawing an ace (4/52, or 1/13) multiplied by the probability of drawing a heart (13/52, or 1/4).

- Following this logic, if two variables such as gender and store choice reason are independent, the probability of occurrence for men who chose on the basis of location should be equal to the probability of occurrence for men times the probability of occurrence for choosing on the basis of location. That is, P(Men, Location) should equal P(Men) × P(Location), which, in the cross-tab, equals .528 × .221, or .116. Similarly, P(Women, Location) should equal P(Women) × P(Location), P(Men, Everyday price) should equal P(Men) × P(Everyday price), and so on.

- If P(Men, Location) equals .116, a cross-tab with 290 observations should produce 33.77 observations in the Men, Location cell (.116 × 290 = 33.77). That is, we would expect this cell to have a frequency of 33.77 *if gender and reason for store choice were independent.* Expected frequencies for all other cells can be calculated in a similar fashion.

- The observed frequency in each cell can be compared with the frequency that would be expected if the variables were independent. For the Men, Location cell, the observed frequency is 28, versus an expected frequency of 33.76.

- Given observed and expected frequencies for each cell in the cross-tabulation, a chi-squared statistic is calculated as

$$\chi^2 = \Sigma \frac{(\text{Observed frequency} - \text{Expected frequency})^2}{\text{Expected frequency}},$$

where the sum is taken over all cells of the cross-tab.

- The resulting value can be compared with a table of critical χ^2 values to test whether the differences between observed and expected values are large enough to reject a hypothesis that the variables are independent. Appendix C at the back of this book contains such a table.

A chi-squared test was done on the cross-tab of V3 and V37, and the results appear in Exhibit 17.1 under the label "Chi-square." The first line of those results contains a standard χ^2 test. The first two numbers on this line show that the χ^2 value associated with this cross-tab is 9.22, with seven degrees of freedom (DF). The degrees of freedom associated with a cross-tab are calculated as $(R-1)(C-1)$, where R is the number of rows and C is the number of columns; in this case, $(8-1) \times (2-1) = 7$. The third number, labeled "Significance," shows that there is a .237 (23.7%) probability of getting a χ^2 value of 9.22 or larger in a cross-tab with seven degrees of freedom if the variables are independent. Since this probability is greater than .05, we cannot reject, at the .05 level, the hypothesis that V3 and V37 are independent. In common parlance, one would say that the relationship between V3 and V37 is not statistically significant. If the significance level had been below .05, we would have concluded that the relationship *was* significant.

Other information provided in the output goes beyond the basic χ^2 test. It provides alternatives to the basic test, as well as diagnostic information that can be used to determine whether there might be a problem in interpreting the results. This information can be useful, but we recommend that you not worry about it. Similarly, SPSS for Windows would have allowed us to request a variety of other statistics in connection with this analysis. All of these statistics can be useful, but we generally recommend that you stick with one basic procedure to minimize confusion. In a cross-tabulation, that basic procedure is a χ^2 test.

Note that a χ^2 test applies to the *overall* relationship between the variables. That is, it tests whether men and women differ in their overall distributions of reasons for choosing stores. It does not test for differences in one specific category, such as whether there is a significant difference between men and women in the percentage who cited location as their main reason for choosing a store. Hypotheses about differences in specific categories require further tests, which can be done in either of two ways:

Author Tips

When doing inferential testing, remember that statistical significance depends on sample size as well as the size of the relationship, so a large sample may produce significant results for a small relationship, and a small sample may fail to produce significance for a large relationship.

- If the analysis is to be done by computer, recode the dependent variable into the category of interest and all others, and cross-tabulate this abbreviated variable with the independent variable. For example, to test whether there is a significant difference between men and women in the percentage who cited location, recode reasons (V3) into "Location" and "Other." Then cross-tabulate the abbreviated V3 with V37. The χ^2 value for this cross-tab will test whether there is a significant difference between men and women in the probability of citing location.

- Alternately, the test can be performed by hand. To test whether there is a significant difference in the percentages of men and women who cited location, plug these percentages into the formula given in Chapter 16 for hypothesis tests involving differences in percentages. That formula was discussed in terms of comparing two variables, but the same procedure is used for comparing two groups.

Issues in Using Cross-tabulations

In Chapter 16, it was noted that tabulations can be difficult to interpret if the number of categories is large. This is doubly true for cross-tabulations and is the reason why cross-tabs should not be used for quantitative variables unless those variables are broken into categories.

Exhibit 17.3 shows the beginning of a cross-tabulation between V4 (amount of the most recent expenditure) and V3 (reason for store choice). This exhibit contains only the start of the table; V4 assumes 8 different values, and V3 assumes 60 different values, so the full cross-tab contains $8 \times 60 = 480$ cells and covers many pages of computer output. Since the data set has only 290 observations, many of the cells in this cross-tab are empty, and many others have only one observation in them. Overall, the size of the table and the sparseness of the data make it very difficult to get a sense of the relationship between these variables, which is the purpose of the analysis.

The problem of overly large cross-tabs has an easy solution, which is to recode the variables into broader categories. For example, Exhibit 17.4 (see page 482) takes this approach to the cross-tab between V4 and V3. The expenditure measure, V4, has been recoded into three categories, and the reason measure, V3, has been recoded into four categories. The result is a twelve-cell cross-tab that is much easier to interpret.

Of course, just as the selection of category boundaries can affect the interpretation of a tabulation, so can it affect the interpretation of a cross-tab. It is often useful to run several cross-tabs with different recodes in order to find the one that communicates best.

Critical Thinking Skills

Run the simplified cross-tab shown in Exhibit 17.4 (see page 482) to verify that you get the same results. Then run an analysis with V4 recoded into the following three categories: $0 to $19, $20 to $49, and $50 and over. Which recode do you think is better? Why?

EXHIBIT 17.3

Cross-tabulation of V4 and V3

V4 Amount of Last Purchase by V3 Main Reason for Choosing Store

V3   Page 1 of 16

Count Row Pct Col Pct Tot Pct	Other	Regular Prices	Sale	Location	Merchandise Quality	Row Total
V4	0	1	2	3	4	
3				2 66.7 3.6 .8		3 1.2
5	1 50.0 8.3 .4					2 .8
8	1 100.0 8.3 .4					1 .4

V4 Amount of Last Purchase by V3 Main Reason for Choosing Store

V3   Page 2 of 16

Count Row Pct Col Pct Tot Pct	Selection	Service	Credit	Row Total
V4	5	6	7	
3	1 33.3 2.0 .4			3 1.2
5	1 50.0 2.0 .4			2 .8
8				1 .4

(Table continues for a total of 480 cells.)

EXHIBIT 17.4

Simplified Cross-tabulation of V4 and V3

V4 Amount Spent on Last Purchase by V3 Main Reason for Choosing Store

	V3				Page 1 of 1
Count Row Pct Col Pct Tot Pct	Price 1.00	Merchandise 2.00	Location 3.00	Other 4.00	Row Total
V4					
1.00 Under $20	19 38.0 20.0 7.4	13 26.0 16.9 5.1	13 26.0 23.6 5.1	5 10.0 17.2 2.0	50 19.5
2.00 $21 to $50	48 38.7 50.5 18.8	30 24.2 39.0 11.7	30 24.2 54.5 11.7	16 12.9 55.2 6.3	124 48.4
3.00 More than $50	28 34.1 29.5 10.9	34 41.5 44.2 13.3	12 14.6 21.8 4.7	8 9.8 27.6 3.1	82 32.0
Column Total	95 37.1	77 30.1	55 21.5	29 11.3	256 100.0

Number of missing observations: 35

Comparison of Means

Description of the Procedure

The second type of descriptive bivariate analysis is **comparison of means**. This procedure calculates mean values for one variable within the categories of another variable and compares the means across categories. For example, in Exhibit 17.4, a cross-tabulation was used to determine whether the amount of the most recent expenditure (V4) was related to the reason for store choice (V3) in our SPORTS data. A comparison of means could also have been used to look at this relationship. This analysis would have involved calculating the mean expenditure within each reason category and comparing the results across categories to see whether some reasons were associated with higher average expenditures.

An Example of Comparison of Means

Exhibit 17.5 (see page 484) shows this analysis as obtained via the "Compare Means" command in SPSS for Windows. The output contains the mean amount spent by the respondents in each category of V3, as well as an analysis of variance table, which is used for significance testing. **Analysis of variance**, or **ANOVA,** is the inferential procedure used to test the significance of differences among group means.

Exhibit 17.6 (see page 485) uses the information in Exhibit 17.5 to create a table in which the various reasons for store choice are organized according to mean expenditure. Here it can easily be seen that people who cited merchandise quality as their main reason for choosing a store spent more than the other groups, people who cited location spent less than other groups, and most of the other groups spent similar amounts. Exhibit 17.6 also provides information about group sizes and the overall significance of the differences.

Inferential Analyses for Comparison of Means

Author Tips

To generate the SPSS for Windows output shown in Exhibit 17.5 (see page 484), choose "Compare Means" and then "Means" from the "Statistics" menu. Indicate that V4 is the dependent variable and V3 is the independent variable. Click the "Options" button, and indicate that you want the variable mean and count in the cells display and that you want an ANOVA table. Click "Continue" and then "OK."

Analysis of variance can be viewed as an extension of using t-tests to test the difference between two means, as discussed in Chapter 16. A t-test evaluates the difference between two means by making a ratio in which (1) the numerator contains the difference between the means that are being compared and (2) the denominator contains the pooled standard errors of those means. In essence, then, a t-test evaluates whether the observed difference between two means is larger than would be expected from their natural variation.

Analysis of variance extends this concept to more than two means. It establishes a ratio in which (1) the numerator contains the variance *between* the means being compared and (2) the denominator contains the pooled variance *within* the groups being compared. This ratio, which evaluates whether the observed differences among means are larger than would be expected given natural variation in the groups, forms an **F statistic**. It can be compared with a table of critical F values to determine whether the observed differences are statistically significant, that is, whether there is less than a .05 chance of getting such a large ratio if all groups have the same mean in the underlying population (see Exhibit 17.7, page 485) for a graphical depiction). Appendix D at the back of this book contains an F table.

The bottom part of Exhibit 17.5 contains analysis of variance results for the comparison of V4 means across categories of V3. This table is read as follows:

- The first column shows the sources of variation in V4. The "Between groups" line represents variation in mean expenditure across the various reason groups. The "Within groups" line represents pooled variation in expenditures within groups.

- The second column shows the sums of squares associated with each source of variation. The numbers in this column are analogous to the numerator of a variance calculation: $\Sigma(x_i - x)^2$.

(cont. on p. 486)

EXHIBIT 17.5

Comparison
of Mean
Expenditures
Across Reasons
for Store
Choice

```
                  - - Description of Subpopulations - -

Summaries of      V4          Amount of last purchase
By levels of      V3          Main reason for choosing store

Variable  Value  Label                    Mean      Std Dev    Cases

For entire population                    74.8164    111.9386     256

V3            0  Other                    71.0000     99.7943      12
V3            1  Regular prices           73.2857     99.8900      42
V3            2  Sale                     74.2642    113.2805      53
V3            3  Location                 51.4727     65.8809      55
V3            4  Merchandise quality     118.6923    192.9493      26
V3            5  Selection                79.1961    111.5991      51
V3            6  Service                  71.0000     57.9828       2
V3            7  Credit                   79.2667     98.7323      15


   Total cases = 291
Missing cases = 35 or 12.0 Pct


                  - - Analysis of Variance - -

Dependent variable  V4    Amount of last purchase
      By levels of  V3    Main reason for choosing store

Value Label                    Mean     Std Dev    Sum of Sq   Cases
    0 Other                  71.0000     99.7943   109548.000      12
    1 Regular prices         73.2857     99.8900   409098.571      42
    2 Sale                   74.2642    113.2805   667288.302      53
    3 Location               51.4727     65.8809   234375.709      55
    4 Merchandise quality   118.6923    192.9493   930735.538      26
    5 Selection              79.1961    111.5991   622718.039      51
    6 Service                71.0000     57.9828     3362.0000       2
    7 Credit                 79.2667     98.7323   136472.933      15
                            ---------------------------------------
Within-groups total          74.8164    112.0484  3113599.09      256
```

Source	Sum of Squares	d.f.	Mean Square	F	Sig.
Between groups	81617.2777	7	11659.6111	.9287	.4848
Within groups	3113599.0934	248	12554.8351		

Eta = .1598   Eta squared = .0255

EXHIBIT 17.6

Comparison of Mean Expenditures Across Reasons for Store Choice

Reason for Store Choice	Group Size	Average Amount of Purchase*
Merchandise quality	26	$118.69
Credit availability	15	79.27
Merchandise selection	51	79.20
Sale	53	74.26
Everyday prices	42	73.29
Other reasons	12	71.00
Service	2	71.00
Location	55	51.47
Overall	256	$74.72

*The overall differences among means are not statistically significant.

EXHIBIT 17.7

How Analysis of Variance Works

Comparison of the means of two groups is a test to see if the groups really are different in how they respond to the dependent variable or whether the difference we see in the mean scores might be due to sampling error. An analysis of variance (ANOVA) assesses whether the variability *between* the group means is greater than would be expected by chance based on the variability *within* the groups.

When the within-group variance is high relative to the between-groups variance, there is a lot of overlap between the two groups. In such a situation, we have little confidence that the group means are different in the population.

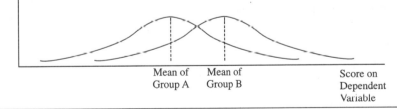

Number of Observations

Mean of Group A   Mean of Group B   Score on Dependent Variable

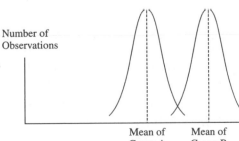

Number of Observations

Mean of Group A   Mean of Group B   Score on Dependent

When the within-group variance is low relative to the between-group variance, there is little overlap between the two groups. In such a situation, we can be reasonably sure that the group means are different in the population.

- The third column shows the degrees of freedom associated with each term. Degrees of freedom are related to sample size. V3 has eight groups, so there will be eight observations of group means, and $(k - 1) = (8 - 1) = 7$ degrees of freedom associated with the V3 effect. The total usable sample size is 256 observations, so the sample size for calculating overall variance is $(n - 1) = (256 - 1) = 255$ total degrees of freedom. The within-group degrees of freedom is calculated by subtracting the degrees of freedom for any effects being tested from the total degrees of freedom; in this example, $255 - 7 = 248$ residual degrees of freedom.

- The fourth column shows the mean squares associated with each source of variation. These are calculated by dividing the sum of squares by the degrees of freedom. They are analogous to variances: $\sum(x_i - x)^2/n$.

- The fifth column shows F statistics for the various effects. F values are computed by dividing the mean square for a particular effect by the residual mean square. In this analysis, the mean square associated with V3 is $11,659.611, and the mean square within groups is $12,554.835, so the F value for the V3 effect is $11,659.611 ÷ $12,554.835 = .929.

- The sixth column shows a significance level. This figure shows that, given seven degrees of freedom for the numerator and 255 degrees of freedom for the denominator, there is a .485 (48.5%) probability of obtaining an F of .929 or higher if there are no differences among group means in the population. Since this probability exceeds .05, the hypothesis that mean expenditures are equal across the various categories of V3 cannot be rejected. In more common terms, there are no significant differences in mean expenditure levels across the categories of V3. If the significance level were less than .05, one would conclude that there *were* significant differences.

Note that these are *overall* effects. The F test in this analysis does not test whether the mean expenditure for people who cited "Location" is different from the mean expenditure for people who cited "Credit availability" or whether the difference between the "Location" and "Merchandise quality" groups is significant. Rather, the F value provides a test of overall differences among groups.

If you want to test differences between specific groups, you have three choices:

- You can select only the data from groups of interest and run an analysis of variance among these data.

- You can compare group means by hand. The formula for testing the difference between the means of two groups is the same as the formula given in Chapter 16 for testing the difference between the means of two variables.

- Depending on your statistical software, you may be able to get "pairwise comparisons" among specific groups as

Author Tips

To get pairwise comparisons of means in SPSS for Windows, choose "Compare Means" and then "Independent Samples—t-tests" from the "Statistics" menu. The dependent variable (e.g., amount spent on sporting equipment) is the "test variable" and the independent variable (e.g., reason for choosing store) is the "grouping variable." Click "Define Groups" and indicate which two levels of the grouping variable you wish to compare. Click "Continue" and then "OK."

an option when using the ANOVA command (discussed in Chapter 18).

Issues in Using Comparison of Means

There are two issues to consider in using comparison of means. The first issue is that the calculation of a mean must be appropriate for the variable that is being averaged. For example, it is reasonable to calculate means for V4 within categories of V3—that is, it is reasonable to calculate average purchase size within reasons for store choice—but it would *not* be reasonable to calculate means for V3 within categories of V4. V3 is a categorical variable for which numbers simply represent different reasons, and it makes no sense to calculate an "average reason."

Strictly speaking, the calculation of means is appropriate only for variables that have interval or ratio scaling. However, as a practical matter, means calculated on ordinal opinion measures usually produce acceptable results. For example, we could compare men and women on the mean importance score given to location (V6 in the SPORTS data) and get reasonable results, even though the location importance measure is an ordinal variable scaled as 3 = "Very important," 2 = "Somewhat important," and 1 = "Not important."

In some situations, a variable that is appropriate for calculating means can be made inappropriate as the result of a recode. For example, in the SPORTS data, the original form of V4 (dollar amount of the most recent sporting goods purchase) is appropriate for calculating a mean. However, if this variable is recoded so that 1 = "$20 or less," 2 = "$21 to 50," and 3 = "More than $50," a mean calculated on the recoded data might be misleading.

The second issue that affects the usefulness of comparisons among means is the direction of dependence between the variables. In the discussion of cross-tabs, it was noted that percentages should be calculated for the dependent variable within categories of the independent variable if a dependence relationship exists. This same logic applies to comparisons of means: the dependent variable should be averaged within categories of the independent variable.

Consider Exhibit 17.6 (see page 485), which shows mean purchase sizes across various reasons for store choice. If the goal of the analysis is to measure how purchase size (V4) influences the basis for store choice (V3), Exhibit 17.6 is not what is wanted. The question is whether people who make large purchases are more likely to choose a store on the basis of credit availability, not whether people who choose a store on the basis of credit make smaller purchases on average. The two points are related, but they are not the same.

Given an analysis situation with a categorical dependent variable and a quantitative independent variable—as would be the case if store choice reason were viewed as a dependent variable and purchase size as an independent variable—a comparison of means is not the best analysis to use. In this situation, it is best to categorize the independent variable and run a cross-tab, as was done in Exhibit 17.4 (see page 482).

Critical Thinking Skills

Using the SPORTS data set, compare the mean importance scores given for the importance of having a store credit card (V10) by gender (V37). What do you conclude from this analysis? Cross-tabulate these same variables. Do you draw the same conclusion? Which analysis would you rather show a manager? Why?

Correlation

Description of the Procedure

The third type of descriptive bivariate analysis is **correlation**, which can be used to measure the relationship between two quantitative variables. The **correlation coefficient** is calculated by the following formula:

$$r = \frac{\Sigma(x_i - \bar{x})(y_i - \bar{y})}{s_x\, s_y},$$

where r is the correlation coefficient, x_i represents individual observations on one of the variables being correlated, $\bar{x}$ is the mean of that variable, s_x is the standard deviation of that variable, y_i represents individual observations on the second variable, $\bar{y}$ is the mean of that variable, and s_y is the standard deviation of that variable.

Correlation coefficients can range from +1.00 to –1.00. A correlation of +1.00 indicates a perfect positive relationship; for example, the correlation between heights measured in inches and meters would equal +1.00. A correlation of –1.00 indicates a perfect negative relationship. A correlation of 0.00 indicates no relationship (the variables are independent of each other).

The good thing about a correlation is that it is concise. A correlation coefficient summarizes the relationship between two variables in a single number. There is no cross-tab filling a page, no column of group means—just a single number.

The bad thing about a correlation is that it is abstract. For example, if annual expenditure on sporting goods correlates .22 with annual family income, this means that the two variables are related, but it does not indicate how much money people spend on sporting goods or the difference in expenditure between people with high and low incomes. Cross-tabs and comparisons of means provide information about the levels of the variables as well as their relationship; correlation measures only the relationship.

An Example of Correlation

The fact that correlation coefficients are concise makes them well suited to summarizing relationships among a series of variables. Exhibit 17.8 shows correlations among V17 to V27 in the SPORTS data, which contain eleven different ratings of Smith's Stores. It would take fifty-five cross-tab tables to show the relationships among all these variables, but fifty-five correlations can be shown in a single table.

Exhibit 17.8 shows that all of the rating dimensions are positively correlated. The most highly correlated dimensions are V26 and V27, with a correlation of .71, and V22 and V23, with a correlation of .68. Unfortunately, the correlation output does not print the variable labels, so the codebook must be checked to determine that V26 and V27 are ratings for helpfulness of service and speed of service, respectively, and V22 and V23 are ratings for merchandise quality and merchandise selection.

(*cont. on p. 491*)

EXHIBIT 17.8

Correlations Among Ratings of Smith's Stores

- - Correlation Coefficients - -

	V17	V18	V19	V20	V21	V22
V17	1.0000 (282) p= .	.4144 (281) p= .000	.3370 (280) p= .000	.2647 (271) p= .000	.2308 (275) p= .000	.3188 (281) p= .000
V18	.4144 (281) p= .000	1.0000 (288) p= .	.5343 (286) p= .000	.2508 (277) p= .000	.2172 (280) p= .000	.2534 (287) p= .000
V19	.3370 (280) p= .000	.5343 (286) p= .000	1.0000 (289) p= .	.3468 (277) p= .000	.2679 (281) p= .000	.3455 (288) p= .000
V20	.2647 (271) p= .000	.2508 (277) p= .000	.3468 (277) p= .000	1.0000 (278) p= .	.5725 (274) p= .000	.3624 (278) p= .000
V21	.2308 (275) p= .000	.2172 (280) p= .000	.2679 (281) p= .000	.5725 (274) p= .000	1.0000 (283) p= .	.3739 (282) p= .000
V22	.3188 (281) p= .000	.2534 (287) p= .000	.3455 (288) p= .000	.3624 (278) p= .000	.3739 (282) p= .000	1.0000 (290) p= .
V23	.3131 (279) p= .000	.3041 (284) p= .000	.2854 (285) p= .000	.2510 (274) p= .000	.3244 (280) p= .000	.6756 (286) p= .000
V24	.3626 (279) p= .000	.3107 (285) p= .000	.2899 (287) p= .000	.2616 (276) p= .000	.3020 (281) p= .000	.5753 (287) p= .000
V25	.3871 (280) p= .000	.2411 (286) p= .000	.2903 (287) p= .000	.2727 (276) p= .000	.2669 (281) p= .000	.4787 (288) p= .000
V26	.2818 (282) p= .000	.1832 (288) p= .002	.2892 (289) p= .000	.2330 (278) p= .000	.3103 (283) p= .000	.3770 (290) p= .000
V27	.3277 (282) p= .000	.2303 (288) p= .000	.2820 (289) p= .000	.1640 (278) p= .006	.2144 (283) p= .000	.3032 (290) p= .000

(Coefficient / (Cases) / 2-tailed significance)

" . " is printed if a coefficient cannot be computed.

Continued

EXHIBIT 17.8

Correlations
Among Ratings
of Smith's
Stores—
Continued

```
                  - - Correlation Coefficients - -

            V23        V24        V25        V26        V27

V17         .3131      .3626      .3871      .2818      .3277
          (  279)    (  279)    (  280)    (  282)    (  282)
          p= .000    p= .000    p= .000    p= .000    p= .000

V18         .3041      .3107      .2411      .1832      .2303
          (  284)    (  285)    (  286)    (  288)    (  288)
          p= .000    p= .000    p= .000    p= .002    p= .000

V19         .2854      .2899      .2903      .2892      .2820
          (  285)    (  287)    (  287)    (  289)    (  289)
          p= .000    p= .000    p= .000    p= .000    p= .000

V20         .2510      .2616      .2727      .2330      .1640
          (  274)    (  276)    (  276)    (  278)    (  278)
          p= .000    p= .000    p= .000    p= .000    p= .006

V21         .3244      .3020      .2669      .3103      .2144
          (  280)    (  281)    (  281)    (  283)    (  283)
          p= .000    p= .000    p= .000    p= .000    p= .000

V22         .6756      .5753      .4787      .3770      .3032
          (  286)    (  287)    (  288)    (  290)    (  290)
          p= .000    p= .000    p= .000    p= .000    p= .000

V23        1.0000      .6173      .5644      .4133      .3441
          (  287)    (  285)    (  286)    (  287)    (  287)
          p= .      p= .000    p= .000    p= .000    p= .000

V24         .6173     1.0000      .5650      .3906      .3761
          (  285)    (  288)    (  286)    (  288)    (  288)
          p= .000    p= .      p= .000    p= .000    p= .000

V25         .5644      .5650     1.0000      .4378      .4096
          (  286)    (  286)    (  289)    (  289)    (  289)
          p= .000    p= .000    p= .      p= .000    p= .000

V26         .4133      .3906      .4378     1.0000      .7085
          (  287)    (  288)    (  289)    (  291)    (  291)
          p= .000    p= .000    p= .000    p= .      p= .000

V27         .3441      .3761      .4096      .7085     1.0000
          (  287)    (  288)    (  289)    (  291)    (  291)
          p= .000    p= .000    p= .000    p= .000    p= .

(Coefficient / (Cases) / 2-tailed significance)

" . " is printed if a coefficient cannot be computed.
```

Inferential Analyses for Correlations

The most common inferential test involving correlations is to test whether a coefficient is significantly different from 0. This can be done with a t-test employing the following formula:

$$t = \frac{r\sqrt{(n-2)}}{\sqrt{1-r^2}},$$

where r is the correlation coefficient and n is the sample size. If this calculation produces a t-value with an absolute value larger than 1.96, there is less than a .05 probability that a correlation this large or larger would have been observed if the correlation in the broader population is 0. Given such a result, one would reject the hypothesis that the population correlation is zero; in other words, one would conclude that there is a statistically significant relationship between the variables that were correlated.

In our example, the p-values in Exhibit 17.8 allow us to test the significance of the various correlations without running t-tests by hand. A p-value lower than .05 indicates that the associated correlation is significantly different from 0 at the .05 testing level. For example, the correlation between V17 and V18 is .4144. The associated p-value is .000, indicating that there is less than a .001 probability that such an extreme correlation would have been observed in this sample if the correlation in the population is 0. Based on this result, we would conclude that the correlation between V17 and V18 is significantly different from 0.

Issues in Using Correlations

Since correlations have the benefit of being concise and the drawback of being abstract, they are best suited for summarizing the relationships among a series of variables. If it is desirable to measure and describe the relationship between just two variables, a cross-tab or a comparison of means is usually a better analysis, because these procedures provide more description and hence more vivid results.

Of course, correlation analysis is appropriate only if it is appropriate to calculate means for the variables involved. The correlation procedure requires the calculation of deviations from the mean, and this calculation is not meaningful if the mean is not meaningful. For example, it would be inappropriate to correlate V3 and V4 in the SPORTS data—reason for store choice and amount of purchase—because V3 is a nominal variable.

However, it should be noted that correlations can be usefully calculated for most ordinal measures; in fact, the correlations in Exhibit 17.8 derive from just such measures. Correlations can also be calculated for sets of rankings (which by definition are ordinal in nature). Consider, for example, the information in Exhibit 17.2 (see

Author Tips

To obtain the output shown in Exhibit 17.8 in SPSS for Windows, choose "Correlate" and then "Bivariate" from the "Statistics" menu. Highlight V17 to V27 on the variables list, and click the arrow key. The correlations shown in the output are "Pearson correlations."

Critical Thinking Skills

Using the SPORTS data set, compute correlations for V6 to V16 (the importance ratings of various store attributes). Are the correlations between those variables as strong as the correlations among V17 to V27 (the ratings of Smith's on the same attributes) shown in Exhibit 17.8? Why do you think that is?

Critical Thinking Skills

Given the three procedures discussed so far—cross-tabulations, comparisons of means, and correlation coefficients—which has the fewest restrictions on use? The most restrictions? Which would be easiest to present to a manager?

page 478), which shows the percentages of men and women who cited various reasons for store choice. These percentages could be converted into rankings for each gender group, that is, merchandise selection ranked first for men but fourth for women, sale prices ranked second for both groups, and so on. The rankings could then be correlated to arrive at a summary measure of the similarity between men and women. Most statistics books show a special formula for calculating correlations between sets of rankings—the procedure is called a **rank order correlation** or a **Spearman rank order correlation**—but a regular correlation calculation will produce similar results.

Bivariate Regression

Description of the Procedure

The fourth, and final, descriptive bivariate analysis procedure is bivariate regression. **Bivariate regression** is an extension of correlation analysis that, in addition to measuring the correlation between two variables, measures the *linear relationship* between them. The linear relationship is expressed by an equation of the form

$$y = B_0 + B_1x,$$

where y is the dependent variable and x is the independent variable (if the two variables do not have a causal relationship, the decision as to which variable should be x and which variable should be y is arbitrary). The B_0 term is the y-axis intercept, and the B_1 term is the slope coefficient that shows the number of units of change in the y variable associated with each unit of change in the x variable. In regression terminology, the B terms are called **beta coefficients** or **beta weights.** Exhibit 17.9 provides a graphical depiction of regression analysis.

An Example of Bivariate Regression

Exhibit 17.10 (see page 494) shows an example of a bivariate regression analysis. We constructed this analysis as follows:

- We started with V29 and V32 in our SPORTS data. V29 is an estimate of how much money the respondent spent at Smith's Store during the previous twelve months. V32 is an estimate of how much money the respondent would have spent at Smith's if the respondent had not had a Smith's credit card.

- In the original data, V32 was asked only if respondents said that their spending at Smith's would have changed without the card. If they said that their spending would have remained the same (V30 = 2), V32 was coded as "Not applicable." We now recoded V32 = V29 if V30 = 2; that is, we recoded spending without the card to be the same as actual spending if respondents said their spending would not have changed.

EXHIBIT 17.9

How Regression Analysis Works

Graph of independent X and dependent variable Y. Obs_1 is located at X_1, Y_1 because it has a value of X_1 on variable X and a value of Y_1 on variable Y.

Regression analysis looks for a linear relationship between the variables. Of the infinite number of lines that *could* be drawn through the points, regression analysis finds the *one* line that minimizes the total distance of the line from all the observations.

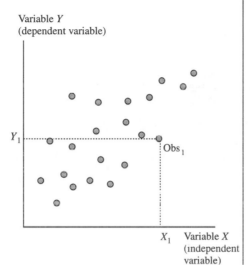

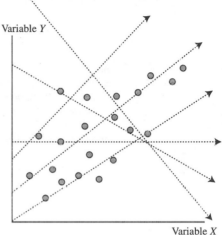

The distance between Obs_1 and the line shown below is $Y_1 - \hat{Y}_1$, (the value of the observation is X_1, Y_1 and the corresponding point on the line is X_1, $\hat{Y}_1$). The total variation of all the observations from the line is the sum of the squared distances, $\sum(Y_i - \hat{Y}_i)^2$.

The line that has the smallest sum of squared differences is taken as the regression line. The line has the equation $Y = B_0 + B_1\hat{x}$, where B_0 is the intercept and B_1 is the slope of the line. Holding all else constant, a change in X of one unit would lead to a change of B_1 units in Y.

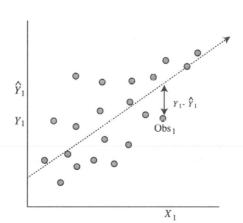

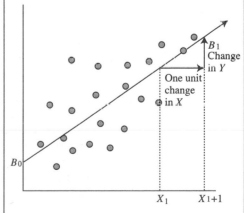

EXHIBIT 17.10

Regression
Analysis of
V101 on V10

```
      * * * *  M U L T I P L E   R E G R E S S I O N  * * * *

Listwise deletion of missing data

Equation number 1  Dependent variable . .  V101  Decline in spending

Block number 1.    Method: Enter V10

Variable(s) entered on step number
   1 . .  V10        Importance of having store card

Multiple R          .06779
R square            .00459
Adjusted R square   .00082
Standard error   108.76966

Analysis of Variance
                    DF      Sum of Squares      Mean Square
Regression           1        14417.76961      14417.76961
Residual           264      3123341.34693      11830.83844

F =       1.21866      Signif F =  .2706

----------------- Variables in the Equation ------------------

Variable            B         SE B        Beta         T    Sig T

V10           8.406863    7.615399     .067786      1.104   .2706
(Constant)    3.430635   16.626908                   .206   .8367

End block number   1   All requested variables entered.
```

- We calculated a new variable, V101, as the difference between V29 and V32. We also gave that new variable a label: DECLINE IN SPENDING IF NO CARD.

- We tabulated V101 to make sure it looked correct (that tab is not shown here). (You should always tabulate new variables to make sure they look right.)

- We then ran a regression analysis with V101 as the dependent variable and V10 as the independent variable. V10 is the importance given to store credit cards by the respondent in choosing where to shop (3 = "Very important," 2 = "Somewhat important," 1 = "Not important"). The purpose of the regression was to measure the relationship between the importance of store credit to respondents and the expected decline in patronage that would result from withdrawing the card.

Proceeding down the output shown in Exhibit 17.10, we see the following information.

- *The fact that the analysis used "listwise deletion" of missing values.* This means that observations were excluded from the analysis if they had missing values for any of the contributing variables.

- *"Multiple R," "R square," and "Adjusted R square."* These are measures of the overall relationship between the regression equation and the dependent variable. *Multiple R* represents the correlation between the *y* variable and all of the *x*'s taken together. In a bivariate regression, there is only one *x* variable, so the "multiple R" is simply the bivariate correlation between *x* and *y*. *R square* is, as the name implies, the "multiple R" value squared. This measure indicates the percentage of total variance in the dependent variable, which is "explained" by variation across the levels of the independent variable. In our example, R^2 is .00459, which indicates that the regression equation accounts for less than one-half of one percent of the variance in V101. *Adjusted R square* represents the R^2 value after an adjustment for the number of *x* variables in the equation.

- *An analysis of variance for the overall regression.* These analyses will be discussed later in this chapter.

- *Coefficients for the regression equation.*

The *B* terms shown in this section are called *raw beta weights*. They indicate that the raw linear relationship between V101 and V10 can be expressed as

$$V101 = 3.43064 + 8.40686 \ (V10).$$

The weight for V10 is interpreted as follows: for every one unit that V10 increases, V101 increases by 8.41 units. In this case, for every one scale point that V10 increases, V101 increases by \$8.41. The fact that the coefficient is positive means that the importance of store credit is positively associated with the expected spending decline if credit is withdrawn.

On the same line as the *B* weights, we find "Beta" terms. These are standardized beta coefficients, which represent the beta coefficients if the *x* and *y* variables were standardized. A variable is *standardized* by subtracting the mean from every observation and dividing by the standard deviation, which has the effect of giving the variable a mean of 0 and a standard deviation of 1.0. The standardized coefficient for V10 in this analysis, .067786, indicates that each increase of one standard deviation in V10 is associated with an increase of .068 standard deviation in V101. Note that the standardized beta coefficient in a bivariate regression is the same as the correlation between the variables. Also, the standardized intercept term is always 0.

Author Tips

The output in Exhibit 17.10 was generated in SPSS for Windows. To recode V32 = V29 when V30 = 2, choose "Compute" from the "Transform" menu. The "Target Variable" is V32 and the "Numeric Expression" is V29. Click the "If . . . " button and type "V30 = 2" in the "Include if case satisfies condition" box. Click "Continue" and then "OK." Then, to calculate V101, choose "Compute" from the "Transform" menu, type "V101" under "Target Variable" and "V29–V32" under "Numerical Expression." Remember to cancel the "If . . . " condition from the previous computation before you hit "OK."

To run the regression analysis, choose "Regression" and then "Linear" from the "Statistics" menu. Indicate that V101 is the dependent variable and V10 is the independent variable. The method is "Enter," meaning all the independent variables you specified (in this case, just V10) will be entered into the regression equation regardless of their level of significance in predicting the dependent variable.

Inferential Analyses in Bivariate Regression

Inferential tests in regression analyses are conducted at two levels: (1) a significance test for the entire regression equation and (2) significance tests for individual coefficients.

The significance test for the overall equation is found in the analysis of variance (ANOVA) table. This analysis breaks the variance in the dependent variable into two components: "regression" variance, which is explained by the regression line, and "residual" variance around the line. The ratio of these variances (or "mean squared deviations") forms an F statistic that tests whether the R^2 value is significantly different from zero. In this example, the probability associated with F is .27, which is larger than .05, so one would conclude that R^2 is not significantly different from zero.

The significance tests for individual coefficients are found in the same section of the output as the coefficients. Along with the B coefficients, we find:

- Standard errors for these coefficients (marked "SE B").
- A t-value for each coefficient (obtained by dividing the coefficient by its standard error).
- A significance figure for each t-value.

In this analysis, the .2706 significance figure for V10 indicates that if the value of this coefficient in the population is 0 and the standard error of the coefficients is 7.61, there is a 27 percent probability that this sample would exhibit a coefficient of 8.41 or larger. Since this probability is larger than .05, the hypothesis that the coefficient for V10 in the broader population is 0 cannot be rejected. In other words, the coefficient for V10 is not significantly different from 0.

Note that the significance level for the V10 coefficient is exactly the same as the significance level for the entire equation. This is because V10 is the only independent variable in the equation. In multiple regression, which is discussed in Chapter 18, there are two or more independent variables, and the significance levels for these variables would generally not be identical to the overall significance level.

Critical Thinking Skills

Create a new variable in the SPORTS data set representing the amount spent at competing stores by subtracting V29 (the amount spent at Smith's in the past twelve months) from V28 (the total amount spent on sporting goods in the past twelve months). Use a bivariate regression analysis to test the effect of Smith's rating on location (V17) on the new variable. What interpretation would you place on the results?

Issues in Using Regression

Two issues arise in using bivariate regression analysis. The first issue relates to scaling. A bivariate regression analysis requires that both variables be quantitative. If one or both of the variables are categorical, regression analysis is not appropriate.

The second issue relates to the general usefulness of the method. In many situations, regression analysis is less useful than cross-tabs, comparisons of means, or correlations.

If only the relationship between two variables is to be described, a cross-tabulation or a comparison of means often provides a more vivid picture of the

EXHIBIT 17.11

Comparison of Means for V101 Across Levels of V10

Importance of Having a Store Credit Card as a Factor in Choosing a Store for Sporting Goods	Percentage of Respondents	Average Amount by Which Annual Spending at Smith's Would Decline If No Smith's Card*
"Not important"	38%	$14.12
"Somewhat important"	23	12.74
"Very important"	38	30.93
Total	100%	$24.12

*Overall differences among groups are not statistically significant.

relationship than a regression. For example, compare the regression equation obtained from Exhibit 17.10 (see page 494) with the table in Exhibit 17.11, which shows a comparison of mean values of V101 across categories of V10. A comparison of means is easier for many people to understand. A comparison of means also makes nonlinear aspects of the relationship between V10 and V101 more obvious. It is interesting to see that the increase in V101 is concentrated among respondents who consider store credit to be "Very important."

If it is desirable to describe relationships among a series of variables, regression results are not as concise as correlation coefficients. Consider Exhibit 16.7 (see page 462), which summarizes the relationships among V17 to V27. A series of regression equations relating all of these variables would take far more space and be less handy to read. Correlation is the best type of analysis for this situation.

One situation in which regression analysis *is* useful is when the goal of the analysis is to predict values of the dependent variable. For example, a regression equation that predicts sales volume on the basis of time might be used. However, in such a situation, one is rarely limited to one independent variable. Instead, several variables that might help predict the dependent variable are used, and multiple regression analysis is thus appropriate.

Summary

This chapter discussed bivariate data analysis. The following points were covered:

1. How can cross-tabulation be used to analyze the relationship between two variables?

A cross-tabulation shows the joint tabulation of two variables. If moving from one category to another on one variable produces a change in the percentage distribution of the other variable, the two variables are related.

2. How can comparison of means be used to analyze the relationship between two variables?

A comparison of means shows mean values of one variable within each category of another variable. If moving from one category to another on the categorical variable produces a change in the mean value of the other variable, the two variables are related.

3. How can correlation be used to analyze the relationship between two variables?

A correlation shows the extent to which two quantitative variables are related. Correlations can range from +1 to –1, with a correlation of +1.00 indicating a perfect positive relationship between the variables, a correlation of 0.00 indicating no relationship, and a correlation of –1.00 indicating a perfect negative relationship.

4. How can bivariate linear regression be used to analyze the relationship between two variables?

A bivariate regression expresses the relationship between two variables in the form of a linear equation $y = B_0 + B_1x$. The B_1 coefficient indicates how many units the y variables change, on average, for each unit of change in the x variable.

 # Suggested Additional Readings

There are really no books that concentrate on bivariate analysis. See the previous chapter for recommendations on general statistics texts, or look at the recommended books at the end of the next chapter on multivariate methods.

 # Discussion Questions

1. What is the primary difference between simple bivariate regression and correlation analysis?

2. Suppose that a catalog manager has data on the number of catalogs sent to 481 customers. In particular, suppose that every customer was classified in two ways: (1) by whether they were sent one or more catalogs, and (2) by whether they bought from the catalog(s) or not. These two classifications cross to form the following two-way cross-tabulation. The catalog manager wants to test the hypothesis that the probability of a purchase for one-catalog customers equals the probability of a purchase for multiple-catalog customers. Based on the findings given, should the catalog manager accept or reject the hypothesis? Interpret the results for the catalog manager.

Number of Catalogs	Buyers	Nonbuyers	Total
One	80 (24%)	251 (76%)	331
Multiple	84 (56%)	66 (44%)	150
Total	164	317	481

$\chi^2 = 46.54$, df = 1, $p < .05$

3. The marketing manager of a tax preparation service administered a customer satisfaction survey to a random sample of the firm's customers. The manager then correlated the customer satisfaction scores with the customer's preparation fee. The correlation between customer satisfaction and the preparation fee paid by the customers turned out to be –.17. How should the marketing manager interpret this finding? Is there a strong or a weak relationship between these two variables?

4. The brand manager for a new brand of popcorn believed that household expenditures on snack food is a function of the total number of hours of TV watched within a household. Which of the data analysis procedures covered in this chapter is most appropriate for testing the brand manager's theory?

5. The marketing director of a monthly newsletter for pet owners wants to test three different direct mail promotion pieces to determine which mail piece "pulls" the best. That is, which mail piece brings in the most sales. Which of the data analysis procedures covered in this chapter is most appropriate for answering the marketing director's research question?

Marketing Research Challenge

We suggest that you first duplicate the analyses in this chapter using the SPORTS disk. For additional practice, select a new pair (or pairs) of variables from the disk and analyze the relationship between them using the SPSS for Windows procedures described in this chapter.

Internet Exercise

For an interactive primer on which analyses are appropriate for different types of variables, visit Bill Trochim's homepage, out of Cornell University. It is located at http://trochim.human.cornell.edu/selstat/ssstart.htm.

18 Multivariate Analysis with Dependent Variables

 OBJECTIVES

After reading this chapter, you should be able to answer the following questions:

1 What are the purposes and procedures of multivariate analysis with dependent variables?

2 How can complex cross-tabulations be used to analyze multivariate data?

3 How can comparisons of means be used to analyze multivariate data?

4 How can multiple regression be used to analyze multivariate data?

5 How can discriminant analysis be used to analyze multivariate data?

The next two chapters discuss **multivariate analysis** procedures, which involve three or more variables. These procedures are separated into two broad categories: (1) *analyses with dependent variables,* which measure the relationship between one or more dependent variables and two or more independent variables, and (2) *grouping procedures,* which use three or more variables without treating any of these variables as being dependent on the others. This chapter discusses multivariate analyses with dependent variables, and Chapter 19 discusses multivariate grouping procedures.

The Purposes of Multivariate Analysis with Dependent Variables

Multivariate analysis with dependent variables can be used for three broad purposes:

- It can be used *to explore or confirm the existence of relationships between the dependent and independent variables.* For example, if respondents' annual expenditures at Smith's Stores (V29 in the SPORTS data) might depend on their evaluations of Smith's along dimensions such as location, price, and merchandise selection (V17–V27), this relationship can be tested by running an analysis in which V29 is the dependent variable and V17 to V27 are the independent variables.

- It can be used *to measure the relative contribution of each independent variable to the overall relationship.* Such an analysis is used to identify key variables for marketing and/or segmentation efforts. For example, if evaluations of merchandise quality seem to be the key to spending, Smith's should focus on this marketing variable.

- It can be used *to establish a prediction equation that allows the dependent variable to be predicted as a function of the independent variables.* For example, if a company can establish an equation in which sales volume is the dependent variable and price, advertising, and other marketing inputs are the independent variables, this equation can be used for purposes of sales forecasting.

Procedures to Be Discussed in This Chapter

Multivariate analysis procedures are usually classified according to how the independent and dependent variables are scaled. Such a classification is followed in this chapter.

- The chapter begins with a discussion of **complex cross-tabulations,** which are cross-tabs involving three or more variables. Complex cross-tabs are appropriate when the independent and dependent variables all are categorical in nature.

- Next are discussed **comparisons of means,** which are appropriate when the dependent variable is quantitative but the independent variables are categorical.

- Next is discussed **multiple regression analysis.** This is appropriate when the dependent and independent variables are all quantitative.

- Next is discussed **discriminant analysis,** which is used when the dependent variable is categorical and the independent variables are quantitative.

Marketing Research Tools 18.1 lists these procedures, their data requirements, and examples of situations in which each procedure is appropriate.

Although these four procedures are the basic tools of multivariate dependence analysis, there are also some other procedures that are used in certain situations. They include *stepwise multiple regression, logistic regression, LOGIT analysis, log-linear regression, canonical correlation analysis,* and *structural equations modeling.* These procedures are discussed in Appendix 18.1 at the end of this chapter.

MARKETING RESEARCH TOOLS

18.1

OVERVIEW OF MULTIVARIATE ANALYSES WITH DEPENDENT VARIABLES

Procedure	Data Requirements	Sample Research Question
Complex cross-tabs	All variables categorical	Is interest in our product (yes-no) related to gender (male-female) and age group (18–24, 25–34, 35–49, 50–64, 65+)?
Comparisons of means	Dependent variable quantitative, independent variables categorical	Is level of expenditure on our product (continuous) related to gender and age group?
Multiple regression	All variables quantitative	Is level of expenditure on our product (continuous, ratio-scaled) related to various attitudes (ordinal or interval)?
Discriminant analysis	Dependent variable categorical, independent variables quantitative	Is choice of brand (categorical) related to attitudes toward various brands (ordinal or interval)?

Format of the Discussion

The general format for discussion of the procedures in this chapter is as follows:

- First is given a description of the procedure: its structure, the descriptive statistics associated with it, the inferential tests associated with it, and the types of data to which it applies.
- Second, marketing research applications for the procedure are described.
- Third, illustrative SPSS for Windows outputs for the procedures you are most likely to use are provided.
- Finally, issues that arise in using the procedure are discussed.

The discussion operates at an input-output level without getting into the mathematical details of each technique. The goal is not to make you an expert in the mathematics of these procedures but simply to make you aware that the procedures exist, how they might be used, and what their limits are.

If this is your first exposure to multivariate analysis, you may find the subject a bit overwhelming. The best thing to do is read about the procedures in this chapter, then practice them with the SPORTS data or another data set. This will give you some "hands-on" training in the techniques and provide you with a feeling for which analyses you have the confidence to do on your own and which will require expert guidance.

Complex Cross-tabulations

Description of the Procedure

Complex cross-tabulations, also known as **complex contingency tables,** are a direct extension of bivariate cross-tabs to three or more variables. This procedure can be applied to any type of data, as long as the variables have been categorized.

The basic *descriptive* measure that results from a complex cross-tabulation is a count of the number of observations in each cell of the cross-tab. These raw frequencies are not very useful by themselves, and results are generally expressed in percentage terms. If one of the variables in the analysis can be taken as a dependent variable (i.e., a variable that is assumed to be caused by the other variables), percentages are calculated with reference to the dependent variable. This point is illustrated in the following examples given.

The basic *inferential* procedure used for cross-tabs is the chi-squared (χ^2) test, which was described in Chapter 17. This test measures the extent to which observed cell frequencies differ from what would be expected if the variables in the cross-tab were unrelated. A significant χ^2 result is evidence of a statistically significant deviation from independence *somewhere* in the table, but it does not indicate where this relationship is located. The relationship might be specific to certain variables or to certain categories, but the χ^2 test does not reveal this fact. Specific testing can be done by collapsing categories or by using *t*-tests to compare the percentages in specific categories, as was discussed in Chapter 17.

Marketing Research Applications of Complex Cross-tabulations

In commercial marketing research, complex cross-tabs are primarily used for segmentation purposes, to learn whether the percentage of purchase or interest in some product varies across possible market segments. For example, a marketing manager for Valvoline motor oil might cross-tabulate oil buyers with respect to (1) brand of motor oil last purchased, (2) age of buyer, and (3) region of the country. The manager would look to see whether the percentage who bought Valvoline varies across age groups and/or geographic regions. The purpose of this analysis would be to identify age and/or geographic segments within which Valvoline is strong or weak.

An Illustrative Analysis

Exhibit 18.1 (see page 506) provides an illustration of a complex cross-tabulation, condensed to save space. It shows a three-variable cross-tab from the SPORTS data. We recoded V2 (store choice) so that it indicates whether or not respondents made their most recent sporting goods purchases at Smith's Stores. We then cross-tabulated V2 with V17, a rating of Smith's Stores on location, and V18, a rating on everyday prices. The purpose of the analysis is to see whether ratings of Smith's location and/or everyday prices influence the probability of choosing Smith's for a purchase.

Issues in Using Complex Cross-tabulations

The major issue that arises with complex cross-tabs is difficulty of interpretation. Complex cross-tabs usually do *not* yield intuitive, easy to understand results. For example, consider Exhibit 18.1. This table relates to an analysis that is relatively simple as complex cross-tabs go. Even so, the full cross-tab contains $2 \times 5 \times 5 = 50$ possible categories and is too complicated for easy reading. Most people cannot look at this table and form a quick conclusion as to whether ratings of location and everyday prices (V17 and V18) influence the probability of shopping at Smith's (V2).

Interpreting a complex cross-tab can be made easier by simplifying the table. For example, Exhibit 18.2 (see page 507) condenses the cross-tab shown in Exhibit 18.1 to facilitate

Author Tips

In the Valvoline example, the relationship between brand choice and age could be established with a bivariate cross-tab between those two variables. Similarly, the relationship between brand choice and region could be established with a bivariate cross-tab. The purpose of the complex cross-tab is to look at age and region simultaneously. This is appropriate if the Valvoline manager expects these segmenting variables to interact in some way. If the effects of age and region on brand choice are independent of each other, a multivariate analysis will not add to the bivariate results.

EXHIBIT 18.1

A Three-way
Cross-
tabulation
with V2, V17,
and V18

This output has been edited to show only levels 1 and 5 of V18. Had the output been shown in its entirety, there would also be tables for levels 2, 3, and 4 of V18.

```
V2 Store where made last purchase by V17 Smith's location
Controlling for..
V18 Smith's prices Value = 1 Well below average
```

Count Row Pct	V17 Below average 2	About the same 3	Above average 4	Well above average 5	Row Total
V2					
0 Other stores	1 20.0	2 40.0	1 20.0	1 20.0	5 83.3
1 Smith's		1 100.0			1 16.7
Column Total	1 16.7	3 50.0	1 16.7	1 16.7	6 100.0

Page 1 of 1

```
(V18 = 2, 3, 4 have been edited out)
V18 Smith's prices Value = 5 Well above average
```

Count Row Pct	V17 Below average 2	About the same 3	Above average 4	Well above average 5	Row Total
V2.1					
0 Other stores	1 3.4	1 3.4	4 13.8	23 79.3	29 29.0
1 Smith's		4 5.6	5 7.0	62 87.3	71 71.0
Column Total	1 1.0	5 5.0	9 9.0	85 85.0	100 100.0

```
Number of missing observations:  15
```

Author Tips

To generate the output shown in Exhibit 18.1 using SPSS for Windows, recode V2 into two categories using the "Recode" option under the "Transform" menu. Generate (cont. on p. 507)

interpretation. In Exhibit 18.2, separate categories for the dependent variable are no longer shown; instead, the percentage of respondents in each cell who made their most recent purchase at Smith's are shown. This reduces the three-way table to a two-dimensional presentation that is easier to read.

Although Exhibit 18.2 is easier to read than Exhibit 18.1, it still is not easy to interpret. Part of the problem relates to having too many categories for quick interpretation, and part of the problem relates to having small cell sizes. Many of the cells in Exhibit 18.2

EXHIBIT 18.2

A Condensed Version of the Three-way Cross-tabulation

For different ratings of Smith's Stores regarding location and everyday prices, the percentage of respondents who made their last sporting goods purchase at Smith's . . .

V17: SMITH RATING ON LOCATION	V18: SMITH'S RATING ON EVERYDAY PRICES (compared with other stores)				
	Much worse	Somewhat worse	About same	Somewhat better	Much better
Much worse	-- (n=0)	0% (1)	-- (0)	-- (0)	-- (0)
Somewhat worse	0% (1)	67% (3)	67% (3)	100% (1)	0% (1)
About same	33% (3)	63% (8)	54% (24)	63% (8)	80% (5)
Somewhat better	0% (1)	50% (4)	67% (18)	53% (19)	56% (9)
Much better	0% (1)	70% (10)	63% (38)	48% (33)	73% (85)

have fewer than ten people in them, which causes unstable results. The problem of small cell sizes is common in complex cross-tabulations, because the data are split across so many cells.

To reduce the number of categories and boost cell sizes, V17 and V18 were recoded into just two categories each. Both variables were split into respondents who rated Smith's Stores as "much better" than other stores versus respondents who gave any other rating. The variables were split at this point because it gave the most balanced cell sizes. From a "managerial appeal" point of view, one also could argue for splitting the ratings into "better than other stores" versus "same or worse."

Exhibit 18.3 (see page 508) shows the subsequent $2 \times 2 \times 2$ cross-tabulation of V2, V17, and V18, and Exhibit 18.4 (see page 509) shows this cross-tab condensed to show only the percentages of respondents who made their last purchase at Smith's Stores. Exhibit 18.4 is much easier to interpret than the original cross-tab. In it, it is immediately obvious that people who rate Smith's Stores as much better than other stores on *both* price and location are more likely to have made their last purchase at Smith's than everyone else. The same results are available in the earlier cross-tabs, but they are much harder to see.

The problem of interpreting complex cross-tabs is magnified as the analysis becomes more complex. For this reason, researchers usually do not use this procedure with more than three variables.

Author Tips—Continued

the cross-tab by choosing "Summarize" and "Crosstabs" from the "Statistics" menu. We specified V2 as the row variable, V17 as the column variable, and V18 as the "Layer 1 of 1" variable. Note that the second column variable goes into a different box than the first column variable; putting them into the same box will generate two one-way cross-tabs rather than a two-way cross-tab. A fourth variable would be added to the cross-tab by clicking the "Next" button to move to "Layer 2 of 2."

EXHIBIT 18.3

A Three-way
Cross-
tabulation
with Reduced
Categories

V2 Store by V17 Smith's rating on location
Controlling for..
V18 Smith's rating on everyday price Value = 1 Not "much better"

```
                          V17
                Count
                Row Pct  Not "much  Much
                Col Pct  better"    better    Row
                            0          1      Total
V2              --------+--------+--------+
        0               |    41  |     35 |    76
Other stores            |  53.9  |   46.1 |  43.2
                        |  43.6  |   42.7 |
                        +--------+--------+
        1               |    53  |     47 |   100
Smith's                 |  53.0  |   47.0 |  56.8
                        |  56.4  |   57.3 |
                        +--------+--------+
                Column       94         82     176
                Total      53.4       46.6   100.0
```

V2 Store where made last purchase by V17 Smith's rating on
location
Controlling for..
V18 Smith's rating on everyday price Value = 2 Much better

```
                          V17          Page 1 of 1
                Count
                Row Pct  Not "much  Much
                Col Pct  better"    better    Row
                            0          1      Total
V2              --------+--------+--------+
        0               |     6  |     23 |    29
Other stores            |  20.7  |   79.3 |  29.0
                        |  40.0  |   27.1 |
                        +--------+--------+
        1               |     9  |     62 |    71
Smith's                 |  12.7  |   87.3 |  71.0
                        |  60.0  |   72.9 |
                        +--------+--------+
                Column       15         85     100
                Total      15.0       85.0   100.0
```

Number of missing observations: 15

EXHIBIT 18.4

A Condensed Version of the Reduced Three-way Cross-tabulation

For different ratings of Smith's Stores regarding location and everyday prices, the percentage of respondents who made their last sporting goods purchase at Smith's . . .

V17: SMITH'S RATING ON LOCATION	V18: SMITH'S RATING ON EVERYDAY PRICES (compared with other stores)	
	Worse, same, or somewhat better	Much better
Worse, same, or somewhat better	56% (n=94)	60% (15)
Much better	57% (82)	73% (85)

Comparison of Means

Description of the Procedure

Just as complex cross-tabs are a direct extension of bivariate cross-tabs, multivariate comparisons of means are a direct extension of bivariate comparisons of means. In **multivariate comparison of means,** values for a dependent variable are compared across the categories of two or more independent variables. The dependent variable must be quantitative in nature so that a mean can meaningfully be calculated. The independent variables are used in categorical form.

The basic *descriptive* measure that results from a multivariate comparison of means is mean values for the dependent measure across various categories of the independent variables. The basic *inferential* procedure associated with comparisons of means is **analysis of variance (ANOVA),** which was discussed in Chapter 17.

Marketing Research Applications of Comparisons of Means

One use for multivariate comparisons of means is to test the results of marketing experiments. For example, Chapter 9 discussed an experiment in which a supermarket chain varied wall colors and lighting levels in produce departments. In analyzing the

Critical Thinking Skills

Using the SPORTS data, cross-tabulate V2 (store where last purchase was made), V27 (Smith's ratings on speed of service), and V35 (family income). Should these variables be recoded into two categories each? If so, where should the cutoff between categories be? What do you conclude from the analysis? Would your conclusions change if you recoded the variables in a different way?

results of that experiment, comparisons of means would be used to test whether average produce sales differed across the categories of wall color and lighting.

Comparisons of means can also be used for segmentation purposes, to see whether mean expenditures on a product vary across possible market segments. For example, a marketing manager for Revlon might use comparisons of means to learn how spending on hair care products varies across women with different hair types in different age categories.

 # An Illustrative Analysis

Author Tips

The output shown in Exhibit 18.5 was generated with the ANOVA command in SPSS for Windows. Many statistical packages use an ANOVA command, which refers to the inferential procedure used for testing differences among means, to access the means themselves.

To generate this output, choose "ANOVA Models" and "Simple Factorial" from the "Statistics" menu. Indicate that V29 is the dependent variable and V17 and V18 are the factors. After specifying each factor, click "Define Range" to indicate that both V17 and V18 have five levels (categories). Click the "Options" button and indicate that the "Method" is "Experimental" and that you want "Means and Counts." Click "Continue" and then "OK." Note that SPSS uses the language of experimentation in this analysis, but the data need not come from an experiment.

Exhibit 18.5 shows a comparison of means using V29 as a dependent variable and V17 and V18 as independent variables. V29 measures respondents' total expenditures at Smith's Stores during the past year, and V17 and V18 are ratings of Smith's location and everyday prices. The purpose of this analysis is to learn whether higher ratings of Smith's appear to result in higher expenditures at Smith's.

The first thing shown in Exhibit 18.5 is the overall mean for V29, the dependent variable. This is followed by the mean of V29 for each category of the independent variables taken one at a time, then the mean of V29 for each cross-category of the independent variables.

After showing all of the means, Exhibit 18.5 shows an analysis of variance table with inferential results. The right-most column of the ANOVA table indicates the following:

- The "main effect" for V17 is statistically significant, with a p-value of .000. The p-value is interpreted as follows: if there is no difference in mean values of V29 across categories of V17 in the broader population, and if V29 has the level of random variance indicated by the residual mean square (i.e., the within-group variance), there is a .000 probability that there would have been as much variation in the mean values of V29 across categories of V17 as was observed. Since this probability is less than .05, we reject the hypothesis that there is no difference among category means in the broader population. In other words, one can conclude that there are statistically significant differences in V29 across the categories of V17; that is, there is a significant effect of V17 on V29.

- The main effect for V18 has a p-value of .076. This effect is not significant at the .05 level but is significant at the more lenient .10 level ($p < .10$).

- Taken together, the combined "main effects" of V17 and V18 are statistically significant ($p = .000$).

- The interaction effect for V17 and V18 is not significant ($p = .999$). This means that the effect of V17 on V29 does not vary significantly across the categories of V18; likewise, the effect of

EXHIBIT 18.5

Comparison of Means for V29 over the Categories of V17 and V18

```
              * * * C E L L   M E A N S * * *

        V29        How much spent at Smith's in 12 months
     by V17        Smith's location
        V18        Smith's prices

Total population

    228.51
 (   261)

V17
       1          2          3          4          5

   1500.00     136.67     170.13     229.67     242.97
 (      1)  (      9)  (     47)  (     49)  (    155)


V18
       1          2          3          4          5

     84.17     273.89     179.42     198.10     286.55
 (      6)  (     27)  (     79)  (     58)  (     91)


       V18
              1          2          3          4          5
V17
       1        .00    1500.00        .00        .00        .00
             (   0)  (      1)  (      0)  (      0)  (      0)

       2     105.00     125.00     100.00     150.00     300.00
             (   1)  (      3)  (      3)  (      1)  (      1)

       3       6.67     206.25     186.13     113.13     228.00
             (   3)  (      8)  (     23)  (      8)  (      5)

       4     190.00     305.00     185.88     218.24     309.33
             (   2)  (      4)  (     17)  (     17)  (      9)

       5        .00     240.91     178.69     210.16     287.53
             (   0)  (     11)  (     36)  (     32)  (     76)
```

Continued

V18 on V29 does not vary significantly across the categories of V17. Essentially, this means that V17 and V18 affect V29 independently.

- Since there are only two independent variables in the analysis, and hence only one interaction term, the same p-value applies to the total of all interaction effects.

EXHIBIT 18.5

Comparison of Means for V29 over the Categories of V17 and V18—Continued

```
* * * A N A L Y S I S   O F   V A R I A N C E * * *

         V29      How much spent at Smith's in 12 months
   by V17         Smith's location
      V18         Smith's prices

         EXPERIMENTAL sums of squares
         Covariates entered FIRST
```

Source of Variation	Sum of Squares	DF	Mean Square	F	Sig of F
Main effects	2396878	8	299609.766	5.016	.000
V17	1665710	4	416427.377	6.972	.000
V18	511610	4	127902.434	2.141	.076
2-way interactions	111809	11	10164.448	.170	.999
V17 V18	111809	11	10164.448	.170	.999
Explained	2508687	19	132036.161	2.211	.003
Residual	14394564	241	59728.482		
Total	16903251	260	65012.505		

```
291 cases were processed.
30 cases (10.3 pct) were missing.
```

- The total "explained variance," which combines both main effects and interactions, is significant ($p < .05$). This means that V29 exhibits statistically significant variation across the combined categories of V17 and V18.

    As a general rule, the total explained variance will be significant if any of the main effects or interaction terms is significant. However, this need not be the case. Also, it is possible for total explained variance to be significant even though none of the individual effects are significant.

Issues in Using Comparisons of Means

Four principal issues arise in connection with multivariate comparisons of means. These are as follows:

- The dependent variable must be quantitative (suitable for the calculation of a mean), and the independent variables must be categorical. However, a quantitative independent variable can be broken into categories for purposes of this analysis. Also, the dependent variable can be a "dummy" variable.

    A **dummy variable** is a variable with two categories coded "0" and "1". The mean of such a variable is simply the percentage of observations that fall into the

"1" category. For example, if V2 (store where most recent purchase was made) had been recoded into a dummy variable for which 1 = Smith's Stores and 0 = Other, and a comparison of means with the recoded V2 as a dependent variable and V17 and V18 as independent variables had been run, the resulting mean values would have been the same as the numbers shown in Exhibit 18.2 (see page 507).

- As with cross-tabs, comparisons of means can be confusing when a large number of variables and/or categories are involved. For example, before Exhibit 18.5 (see page 511) is presented to a manager, categories could be combined to simplify the table.

- Interaction terms involving three or more independent variables are usually ignored, even if they are statistically significant, because they cannot be described in "manager-friendly" terms.

- The number of independent variables that can be accommodated in most ANOVA software routines is limited. For example, SPSS for Windows allows only five independent variables in ANOVA. This is not a serious limitation, because the difficulties in complex interaction effects discourage long lists of independent variables.

- As with any procedure involving means, a comparison of means is sensitive to the presence of extreme values (outliers). The presence of one or two outliers can make a cell mean deceivingly high or low, especially when cell sizes are small.

Other Techniques Involving Comparisons of Means

In addition to being used on their own, comparisons of means form the basis for two other procedures that are used in marketing research: multivariate analysis of variance (MANOVA) and Automatic Interaction Detector (AID) analysis.

Multivariate Analysis of Variance (MANOVA)

Multivariate analysis of variance (MANOVA) extends the logic of analysis of variance to two or more dependent variables. For example, Exhibit 18.5 showed how ANOVA can be used to measure the effects of V17 and V18 on V29. Suppose one is also interested in the effects of V17 and V18 on the probability of making a purchase at Smith's (obtained from V2). A separate ANOVA could be done for V2, or a MANOVA could be used to measure the effects of V17 and V18 on V29 and V2 taken together.

From a descriptive point of view, MANOVA adds nothing to ANOVA. Rather, MANOVA is used to get significance tests that simultaneously relate the independent variables to a series of dependent variables. Since descriptive results are of pri-

Critical Thinking Skills

Use the "Comparison of Means" command in SPSS to test the bivariate effect of V18 (Smith's rating on price) on the amount spent at Smith's (V29). Run the same analysis with the "ANOVA Models" command. Compare the two outputs. How are they similar? How are they different? Compare the bivariate ANOVA output to Exhibit 18.5. What happens to the effect of V18 on V29 when V17 (Smith's rating on location) is added to the model?

Critical Thinking Skills

Check the distribution of V29. Does it have any outliers? What is the effect of outliers, if any, on the analysis shown in Exhibit 18.5 (see page 511)?

Author Tips

To conduct a MANOVA analysis using SPSS for Windows, choose "ANOVA Models" and then "Multivariate" from the "Statistics" menu.

mary interest in commercial research, MANOVA gets little use in that environment. The technique is used mostly in academic marketing research to test hypotheses involving multiple measures of a dependent phenomenon.

Automatic Interaction Detector (AID) Analysis

Automatic Interaction Detector analysis, better known as **AID analysis,** is an exploratory procedure that uses comparisons of means for market segmentation purposes. It is called automatic because the segmentation is done by a computer program, not by an analyst. The procedure works as follows:

- It begins by creating all the possible ways in which every independent variable can be split into two groups.

- For all of these splits, on all of the independent variables, the AID procedure calculates the ratio of between-groups variance to within-group variance in the dependent variable, which is usually an expenditure measure.

- It locates the split with the highest ratio and defines that split as the first split or segmentation in the data.

- Then, within each group formed by the first split, the AID procedure again makes all possible splits and uses the ratio of between to within group variance to identify a second split. It continues to split groups until it reaches some minimum group size or a minimum ratio of between to within group variance.

For example, Exhibit 18.6 shows AID results reported by Douglas MacLachlan and John Johansson (1981) in a segmentation of telephone users. The dependent variable in this analysis is the size of the monthly telephone bill, which averaged $11.23 for the entire sample. The AID procedure first split this sample into those with annual incomes above $20,000 versus those with incomes of $20,000 and below. Mean phone bills were $13.88 for the higher-income group and $9.82 for the lower-income group. The lower-income group was subsequently split into those with one to two phones in their home versus those with three or more phones; the higher-income group was split into those who own their home and those who rent. The analysis continued until the "tree" shown in Exhibit 18.6 was completed.

Note that groups formed by AID can be split on different variables; for example, the high-income group was split on homeownership, and the low-income group was split on telephone ownership. These differences reflect interaction patterns among the independent variables and are the source of the name "Automatic Interaction Detector."

Issues that arise in using AID include the following. First, it is important to set minimum group sizes that are fairly large; otherwise, the procedure will split off tiny groups that have little value as market segments. Second, since the data are being split and resplit and it is desirable to have fairly large groups in the end, AID works best with a very large sample. Most applications of AID use data sets with at least 1,000 observations.

Critical Thinking Skills

What do you see as the advantages of using AID analysis rather than defining your own splits in the data and running comparisons of means? What do you see as the advantages of defining your own splits?

EXHIBIT 18.6

An Example of AID Analysis (Dependent Variable = Monthly Telephone Bill)

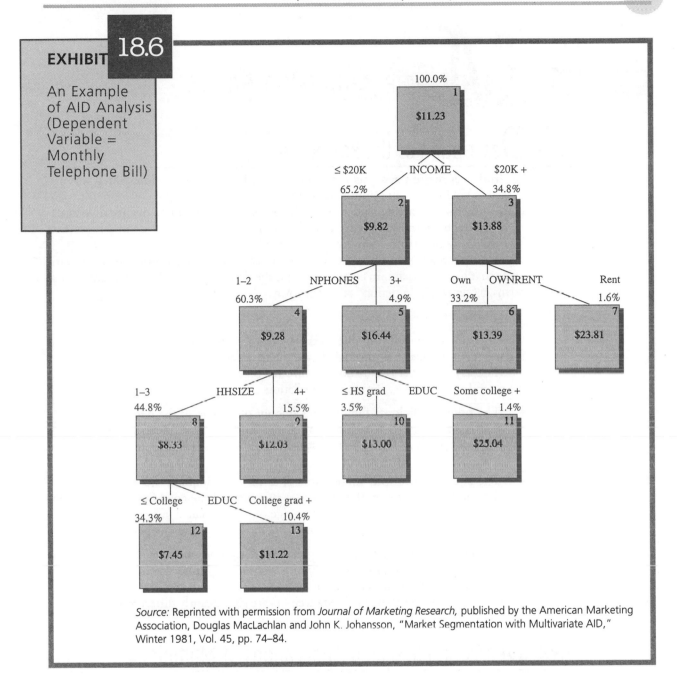

Source: Reprinted with permission from *Journal of Marketing Research,* published by the American Marketing Association, Douglas MacLachlan and John K. Johansson, "Market Segmentation with Multivariate AID," Winter 1981, Vol. 45, pp. 74–84.

Multiple Regression Analysis

Description of the Procedure

Multiple regression analysis is an extension of bivariate regression, which was discussed in Chapter 17. In multiple regression analysis, there are two or more independent variables and one dependent variable. All variables should be quantitative in nature, although, as will be discussed, categorical variables can be used in a regression by converting them into "dummy" (0–1) variables.

Multiple regression finds the weighted linear combination of independent variables that has the maximum correlation with the dependent variable. In mathematical terms, a "regression function" takes the form

$$y = B_0 + B_1x_1 + \ldots + B_kx_k$$

where y is the dependent variable, x_1 through x_k are the k independent variables, B_0 is the intercept term, and B_1 through B_k are the beta coefficients.

The key *descriptive* results obtained from a regression analysis are the beta coefficients and R^2, the squared multiple correlation:

- The **beta coefficients** indicate the amount of change in the dependent variable that is associated with each unit of change in the various independent variables. For example, if B_1 is 13.38, this means that each unit of change in x_1 is associated with 13.38 units of change in y.

- The **squared multiple correlation** is, as its name implies, the squared value of the correlation between the dependent variable and the combination of independent variables. It indicates the percentage of total variance in the dependent variable that is "explained" by variation across the levels of the independent variables.

Key *inferential* tests in multiple regression are significance tests. These tests measure (1) whether the multiple correlation is significantly different from 0, thus indicating a significant overall relationship between the dependent and independent variables, and (2) whether individual beta weights are significantly different from 0.

Marketing Research Applications of Multiple Regression

Multiple regression is used for a wide variety of purposes in marketing research. A regression might be run to test whether an overall relationship exists; for example, a regression might be run with V29 (amount spent at Smith's Stores during the past twelve months) as the dependent variable and V17 to V27 (ratings of Smith's on various dimensions) as the independent variables, to see whether expenditures are related to the ratings. This regression might also be run to measure the relative importance of the various rating dimensions, that is, to see which rating dimensions seem to have the biggest effects on expenditure.

Multiple regression is also used for predictive purposes, especially for sales forecasting. Companies develop regression models to express sales as a function of time, economic variables, and/or marketing inputs. They then plug values for the independent variables into the equation to generate predicted sales levels.

An Illustrative Analysis

Exhibit 18.7 (see page 518) shows the results of a multiple regression analysis with V29 as the dependent variable and V17 to V27 as the independent variables. The purpose of this analysis is to see whether the ratings of Smith's Stores on various dimensions (V17–V27) are related to annual expenditures at Smith's (V29).

The following information can be found in Exhibit 18.7:

■ First, there is some general descriptive information regarding the dependent and independent variables. Means and standard deviations are given for each variable, followed by bivariate correlations among all of the variables.

The column of correlations between V29 and the various independent variables provides information about the strength of bivariate relationships between the dependent and independent variables. This column shows that none of the correlations is larger than .20 and two are actually negative (the correlations involving the two "service" ratings, V26 and V27).

The correlation table also shows sizable correlations among the independent variables. Correlation among independent variables is called **multicollinearity** and can cause problems in interpreting the relative sizes of regression coefficients for the various independent variables. This point will be discussed when issues in multiple regression are considered.

■ Following the correlation table, Exhibit 18.7 shows that all eleven variables have been entered into the multiple regression analysis. Appendix 18.1 discusses the "stepwise" option in multiple regression, where variables may be entered in stages.

■ Next is information about the overall relationship between the dependent and independent variables. The multiple correlation between the dependent variable and the weighted combination of independent variables is .31, the squared multiple correlation (R^2) is .09, and the adjusted R^2, which adjusts for the number of variables in the equation, is .05. An R^2 value of .09 indicates that 9 percent of the variation in V29 is attributable to variation across the levels of the eleven rating variables. This is a fairly weak relationship, since the remaining 91 percent is "unexplained" variance. There is no rule as to what fraction of the variance needs to be explained to make the relationship strong, but many researchers would consider an R^2 of .3 or larger to be at least moderately strong.

■ Finally, Exhibit 18.7 shows the "raw" and standardized regression equations, along with significance tests for the individual variables.

Author Tips

To generate the output shown in Exhibit 18.7 (see page 518) in SPSS for Windows, choose "Regression" and then "Linear" from the "Statistics" menu. Indicate that V29 is the dependent variable and V17 to V27 are the independent variables. Click the "Statistics" button and indicate that you want "Estimates," "Descriptives," and "Model Fit." Click "Continue" and then "OK."

EXHIBIT **18.7**

A Multiple Regression with V29 Dependent and V17 to V27 Independent

```
* * * * M U L T I P L E   R E G R E S S I O N * * * *

Listwise deletion of missing data


              Mean      Std Dev    Label

V29        230.661      261.076    How much spent at Smith's in 12 months
V17          4.326         .914    Smith's location
V18          3.760        1.112    Smith's prices
V19          4.095         .957    Smith's sales
V20          4.045         .943    Smith's credit policy
V21          4.244         .912    Smith's own cards
V22          4.281         .996    Smith's merchandise quality
V23          4.153        1.099    Smith's selection
V24          4.045        1.098    Smith's brands
V25          4.128        1.049    Smith's stock
V26          3.917        1.206    Smith's helpfulness
V27          3.876        1.153    Smith's speed of service


Number of cases:  242


Correlation


       V29    V17    V18    V19    V20    V21    V22    V23    V24    V25    V26    V27

V29  1.000   .052   .141   .158   .058   .193   .098   .138   .014   .041  -.018  -.013
V17   .052  1.000   .404   .311   .243   .228   .327   .314   .345   .415   .300   .322
V18   .141   .404  1.000   .548   .236   .213   .245   .298   .318   .268   .214   .232
V19   .158   .311   .548  1.000   .312   .263   .320   .290   .308   .323   .309   .266
V20   .058   .243   .236   .312  1.000   .575   .353   .241   .250   .292   .251   .173
V21   .193   .228   .213   .263   .575  1.000   .372   .339   .295   .266   .309   .238
V22   .098   .327   .245   .320   .353   .372  1.000   .688   .607   .498   .379   .291
V23   .138   .314   .298   .290   .241   .339   .688  1.000   .623   .570   .435   .323
V24   .014   .345   .318   .308   .250   .295   .607   .623  1.000   .568   .382   .362
V25   .041   .415   .268   .323   .292   .266   .498   .570   .568  1.000   .438   .387
V26  -.018   .300   .214   .309   .251   .309   .379   .435   .382   .438  1.000   .730
V27  -.013   .322   .232   .266   .173   .238   .291   .323   .362   .387   .730  1.000
```

Continued

The "raw" or *unstandardized*, beta coefficients are given in the column labeled *B*. The regression equation indicated by this column is

$$V29 = -50.78 - 1.05 \times V27 - 28.23 \times V20 + 17.19 \times V18 + 40.98 \times V23$$
$$- 2.09 \times V17 + 34.68 \times V19 + 64.85 \times V21 - 3.01 \times V25 - 35.60$$
$$\times V24 + 6.04 \times V22 - 28.78 \times V26.$$

These coefficients can be read as follows: For every scale point that V27 increases, holding other independent variables constant, V29 decreases by 1.05 units (in this case by $1.05). For every scale point that V20 increases, V29 decreases by 28.23 units. And so on.

This equation can be used for predictive purposes if desired. For example, if a person rates Smith's Stores as a "4" (somewhat better) on all eleven dimensions

```
* * * * M U L T I P L E   R E G R E S S I O N * * * *

Equation number 1  Dependent variable . .  V29 How much spent at Smith's in 12 months

Variable(s) entered on step number
     1. .   V27      Smith's speed of service
     2. .   V20      Smith's credit policy
     3. .   V18      Smith's prices
     4. .   V23      Smith's selection
     5. .   V17      Smith's location
     6. .   V19      Smith's sales
     7. .   V21      Smith's own cards
     8. .   V25      Smith's stock
     9. .   V24      Smith's brands
    10. .   V22      Smith's merchandise quality
    11. .   V26      Smith's helpfulness


Multiple R           .30602
R square             .09365
Adjusted R square    .05030
Standard error    254.42588

Analysis of Variance
                    DF     Sum of Squares      Mean Square
Regression          11        1538297.25008    139845.20455
Residual           230       14888480.96479     64732.52593

F =        2.16035      Signif F =  .0174


---------          Variables in the Equation ------------------


Variable            B          SE B          Beta         T    Sig T

V17            -2.093806    21.342196     -.007328     -.098   .9219
V18            17.185038    18.768174      .073207      .916   .3608
V19            34.683755    21.663502      .127164     1.601   .1107
V20           -28.230588    22.249117     -.102013    -1.269   .2058
V21            64.852500    22.974043      .226638     2.823   .0052
V22             6.041296    24.902359      .023039      .243   .8085
V23            40.983096    23.458061      .172596     1.747   .0820
V24           -35.603620    21.431490     -.149724    -1.661   .0980
V25            -3.006355    21.489840     -.012076     -.140   .8889
V26           -28.775917    21.374053     -.132893    -1.346   .1795
V27            -1.047885    21.363899      .004627     -.049   .9609
(Constant)    -50.779164   110.918760                  -.458   .6475
```

(V17–V27), it could be predicted that this person's annual expenditure at Smith's (V29) is equal to

$$V29 = -50.78 - 1.05(4) - \ldots - 28.78(4) = \$160.85.$$

The *standardized* regression equation is given in the column labeled "Beta." These coefficients are read as follows: For every one standard deviation that V17 increases, holding other independent variables constant, V29 decreases by .007 standard deviations. And so on.

Significance tests for the beta coefficients are given in the column labeled "Sig T." This column shows that only the coefficient for V21 is significant at $p < .05$ ($p = .0052$). In addition, V23 and V24 are significant at $p < .10$.

Chapter 17 noted that the standardized beta coefficient given to the independent variable in a bivariate regression is the same as the correlation between the independent and dependent variables. In a multiple regression, the standardized regression coefficients are generally smaller than the corresponding correlations. This occurs because the standardized regression coefficient is a measure of correlation between an independent variable and the dependent variable when other independent variables are taken into account. The usual effect of taking other variables into account is to share effects with them, which makes the standardized beta smaller than the correlation coefficient. In a bivariate regression, there are no other variables to share with, so the correlation and the standardized beta are the same.

Sharing effects among independent variables may cause a variable that has a significant bivariate relationship with the dependent variable to be pushed below significance in a multivariate context. In fact, it is possible to have a multiple regression with a significant overall equation but no significant coefficients, either because the overall effect is a "team effort" or because shared correlation leaves no single variable with a large enough effect to be significant.

Correlation among the independent variables can lead to other odd features in a multiple regression. In our example, V17, V20, V24, and V25 all have positive bivariate correlations with V29. However, all of these variables receive *negative* beta coefficients in the regression, which indicates that they are negatively related to V29 when the other independent variables are taken into account.

Such sign reversals can be both legitimate and meaningful. A famous example from the field of education is the relationship between participation in Head Start programs and subsequent school performance; the bivariate relationship between Head Start participation and school performance is negative, but this is because Head Start participants are disproportionately poor. When family income is taken into account, the relationship between Head Start participation and school performance turns positive.

No such logic applies to the sign reversals in Exhibit 18.7 (see page 518). The negative coefficients in this regression do not appear to be meaningful. Rather, they appear to reflect the fact that correlation among independent variables makes the assignment of effects arbitrary and consequently causes the regression coefficients to be unreliable. Solutions to this problem are discussed later in this chapter.

Critical Thinking Skills

Practice multiple regression analysis using the SPORTS data set. Use V29 (amount spent at Smith's in the past twelve months) as the dependent variable and Smith's ratings on various dimensions as the independent variables. Before running the analysis, create new variables by combining attributes. Add V18 (everyday prices) and V19 (sales) to form a single price variable, add V20 (credit) and V21 (store cards) to form a credit variable, add V22 (merchandise), V23 (selection), V24 (brands), and V25 (stock outs) to form a merchandise variable, and add V26 (helpfulness) and V27 (speed) to form a service variable. Use V17 (location) and the new variables as the independent variables. Compare the result with Exhibit 18.7 (see page 518). What do you conclude?

Issues in Using Multiple Regression

The Linearity Assumption

New users of multiple regression are sometimes dazzled by the power of the procedure. It seems almost magical that many independent variables can be considered simultaneously, while, in comparison, the number of variables in cross-tabs or ANOVA is limited by sample sizes, interpretive difficulties, and/or software limitations. Regression also summarizes the effect of each independent variable with a single coefficient.

The power of multiple regression comes from a crucial assumption of the procedure: that the relationship between the dependent variable and the independent variables is *linear*. Cross-tabs and comparisons of means will reveal *any* pattern of variation in the dependent variable across levels of the independent variables, but a regression analysis will reveal only relationships that follow a linear trend.

Consider, for example, the relationship between age and income. In the U.S. population, average income rises across age groups until the age of sixty-five, when many people retire. From that point on, average income declines across age groups. A comparison of means across age groups will reveal this pattern, but a regression analysis will not. A regression will simply do the best it can at fitting a linear trend line to this nonlinear relationship.

Nonlinear relationships can be accommodated in a multiple regression by means of data transformations. To do this, nonlinearities must first be identified. This can be done in two ways:

- Nonlinear relationships can be identified on theoretical grounds prior to running the regression. For example, we could anticipate a nonlinear relationship between age and income.

- Nonlinear relationships also can be discovered *after* running a regression, by examining plots of the **residuals.** These are differences between (1) the actual value on the dependent variable for each observation in the data set and (2) the value that the regression equation would predict for that observation based on its independent variable scores. Most regression packages have an output option that plots the values of the residuals against values of the independent variables. If the residuals show any systematic pattern—such as a U, or inverted U pattern—this systematic pattern is evidence of nonlinearity.

If nonlinear effects are hypothesized or discovered, data transformations can be used to incorporate these effects into the regression. For example, one can introduce polynomial terms ($income^2$, $income^3$, etc.) to pick up bends in the relationship. It also is possible to take logarithms, convert variables to trigonometric functions, or apply other transformations. A problem with transformations is that they make the results more difficult for most managers to comprehend.

Author Tips

To plot residuals in SPSS for Windows, click the "Plots" button on the linear regression screen and click "Produce all partial plots."

Other General Issues in Using Multiple Regression

In addition to the question of linearity, other issues arise in connection with multiple regression analysis. General issues to consider regardless of the purpose of the analysis are as follows:

- All of the variables used in a regression analysis should be quantitative in nature. However, categorical variables can be used in the form of dummy (0–1) variables.

  A categorical variable that has more than two categories can be converted into a series of dummy variables. For example, a four-category measure of "region" (1 = East, 2 = North, 3 = South, 4 = West) can be converted into three dummy variables: "East" (1 = East, 0 = Other), "North" (1 = North, 0 = Other), and "South" (1 = South, 0 = Other). The number of dummy variables is always one less than the number of categories, because the final category is simply indicated by a series of zeros on the dummy variables that represent the other categories.

  A four-category region measure could also be dummied as 1 = East and 0 = Other, 1 = East/North and 0 = West/South, or something else. For example, in the earlier use of V2 (store where last purchase was made), V2 was dummied into 1 = Smith's and 0 = Other.

- Multiple regression is sensitive to the presence of outliers. Outliers will show up as extreme values on a plot of residuals. If outliers are discovered, consider whether the regression results provide a fair picture of the data. If not, the analysis should be run with outliers excluded.

- Multiple regression is usually applied as a "main effects only" analysis. The equation in Exhibit 18.7 (see page 518) shows that it does not include interaction terms. If some of the independent variables are expected to interact in their effects on the dependent variable, an interaction variable can be computed by multiplying the appropriate independent variables (e.g., compute V118, price interaction, as V18 × V19), and that interaction variable can be used as an independent variable in the regression analysis.

Author Tips

Interaction terms often correlate highly with the contributing variables; for example, V18 × V19 would be likely to correlate with V18 and V19. Using all of these variables in the same analysis can cause problems with multicollinearity, as discussed in the section "Issues in Using Regression to Measure the Importance of Variables."

Issues in Using Regression to Measure the Importance of Variables

When regression results are used to measure the relative importance of various independent variables, some additional issues arise, as follows:

Source: Fugitive from the Cubicle Police, 1996. DILBERT, Scott Adams. Reprinted by permission of United Feature Syndicate, Inc.

- Conclusions about the importance of different variables should be based on standardized beta weights, not on unstandardized (raw) weights, because unstandardized weights are affected by the scale magnitude of a variable. Say, for example, that a regression is run with income in thousands of dollars as an independent variable and a raw coefficient of 34.2 for income is obtained. If the analysis is rerun using income in dollars rather than income in thousands, the raw income coefficient will change to .0342. That is, if a change of $1,000 affects the dependent variable by 34.2 units, a change of $1 will affect the dependent variable by .0342 unit. However, the standardized coefficient would remain unchanged because standardization removes the effects of scale.

- If the independent variables are correlated among themselves, this creates a situation in which their relationships with the dependent variable will overlap. This situation is called *multicollinearity*.

    When multicollinearity exists, the regression analysis apportions overlapping relationships to the contributing independent variables, but the apportionment tends to be unstable over repeated samples. Consequently, a variable that seems important in one sample can seem *un*important in another sample. Also, if the analysis contains a different number of measures for different independent variables—for example, if there are two measures of price but only one measure of location—the independent variables with more "redundancy" tend to be shortchanged because they must share more of their effects. For these reasons, conclusions about the relative importance of variables should be made very cautiously in the presence of multicollinearity (Mason and Perreault, 1991).

    One way of evaluating the extent of multicollinearity in a multiple regression is by looking at the correlations among independent variables. Individual correlations above .30 indicate possible interpretation problems for the related variables.

    If multicollinearity becomes a concern, there are several ways of reducing its effects. The simplest approach is to exclude redundant variables from the regression equation. Thus, in a regression equation where education and income are both used to predict purchases, one might drop education because it is highly correlated with income, and income is a better predictor of purchasing behavior.

    Another approach is to combine the correlated variables into a single scale. For example, income, education, and occupation are often combined into a scale that is labeled "Socioeconomic status."

    Combined scales also can be obtained by means of a procedure called *factor analysis*. This is discussed in the next chapter.

- Related to the issue of multicollinearity is the issue of **specification effects.** The "specification" of a regression equation refers to the independent variables that are used in that equation. Since the coefficient that is calculated for an independent variable can depend on that variable's correlations with other independent variables, it follows that the coefficient can depend on which independent variables are specified in the analysis. Adding an independent variable to a regression equation can change the apparent importance of other variables in the equation.

    To minimize the possibility of misleading results from specification error, it is best to include all possible independent variables, to minimize the risk of excluding a key variable. However, this is rarely possible.

- An independent variable that has shown no variation will get no weight in a regression analysis, even though it might be an important variable to consider. For example, if regression is used to relate a company's sales to various marketing in-

Critical Thinking Skills

Which of these issues, if any, apply to the multiple regression shown in Exhibit 18.7? How might these issues be addressed?

puts and sales force compensation policies have been constant throughout the data-gathering period, compensation will have no ability to explain variation in sales and will get a weight of 0. However, if sales force compensation policies are changed, this change might have a strong impact on sales.

- Similarly, a **restricted range** of variation might limit the weight attached to an independent variable. An example is the relationship between SAT scores and college grades; SAT scores correlate about .70 with college grades, but the correlation would be even higher if people with low SAT scores were allowed into college.

- An independent variable may require some transformation before its importance can be measured properly. For example, in a regression that relates sales to marketing inputs, the relative price of a brand (i.e., its price divided by the price of another brand) may work better than absolute price as an independent variable.

Issues in Using Regression for Prediction

Using regression results for prediction purposes brings another set of issues, as follows:

- A regression done for prediction purposes should use independent variables that will be readily available when needed. For example, in developing a regression for sales-forecasting purposes, it is better to use historical sales figures, which are readily available at the time of the forecast, than to use unemployment statistics, which may not be available until after the forecast period.

- The predictive equation obtained from a regression might not apply outside the range of independent variable values over which the regression was developed. For example, if a regression is developed to relate height to age for children aged three to twelve, and the obtained formula is used to predict the height of a twenty-five year old, the prediction will probably not be accurate.

    Many sales-forecasting methods project sales as a function of time. In a sense, these methods always predict outside the observed range, because they predict into future time periods for which no observations are available.

- The predictive equation might not apply if the environment changes. For example, if new competitors enter a market after a forecasting equation is developed, then forecasts are likely to be inaccurate.

- If the data are heteroskedastic, the accuracy of prediction will vary over the range of the independent variables. **Heteroskedasticity** is a condition in which the variance of the dependent variable is not constant across levels of the independent variables. For example, if a regression uses expenditures on some industrial product as the dependent variable and company size as an independent variable, the variance in expenditures among big companies is usually much larger than among small companies. When this occurs, prediction accuracy will be better than expected in the low-variance portion of the range and worse than expected in the high-variance portion of the range.

- The squared multiple correlation, R^2, provides information about the accuracy of prediction. A high R^2 indicates that observed values for the dependent variable fall close to the values predicted by the regression equation. It should be noted that R^2 overstates the real accuracy of prediction because it represents the ability of the regression equation to fit the same data on which it was generated. To get a better idea of prediction accuracy, the regression equation should be tested on a "holdout" sample that is set aside for testing purposes. This is done as follows: (1) enter the regression equation by hand to calculate a new variable in the holdout sample, (2) correlate that new variable with the dependent variable, and (3) compute the squared correlation.

General Comments

Marketing Research Tools 18.2 summarizes the various issues associated with multiple regression. Despite these many issues, multiple regression is very popular among

MARKETING RESEARCH TOOLS

18.2

ISSUES IN USING MULTIPLE REGRESSION

General issues:

- Are all variable quantitative (or dummies)?
- Are the relationships linear?
- Are the results distorted by outliers?
- Should interactions among independent variables be considered?

Issues in Judging the importance of variables:

- Standardized coefficients should be used for this purpose.
- Are some of the coefficients misleading because of multicollinearity?
- Has the regression model been properly specified?
- Are coefficients for some of the independent variables dampened because the variables have a restricted range?
- Should some variables be transformed to get a better measure of their effects?

Issues in using regression for predictive purposes:

- Will the independent variables be available at the time of prediction?
- Has the environment changed since the equation was developed?
- Is the equation valid outside the range of values for which it was developed?
- Will prediction accuracy vary across levels of the independent variables because of heteroskedasticity?
- Has predictive accuracy been tested on a holdout sample? (R^2 overstates prediction accuracy.)

analysts who work with multivariate data. It is viewed as a flexible technique that can be used for a wide variety of data, given its limitations.

Because multiple regression is so popular, variations on the procedure have been developed to fit analysis situations and data conditions other than those discussed. We discuss some of these variations on multiple regression in Appendix 18.1.

Discriminant Analysis

Description of the Procedure

Discriminant analysis is similar to multiple regression analysis in form, except that discriminant analysis uses a categorical dependent variable. **Discriminant analysis** relates one dependent variable and two or more independent variables and develops a linear function of the form

$$z = B_0 + B_1 x_1 + \ldots + B_k x_k.$$

The weighted combination of independent variables—which is called the **discriminant function**—is calculated to be the formula of the line that best discriminates among categories of the dependent variable (hence the name "discriminant analysis"). Specifically, the discriminant function is calculated so as to maximize the ratio of between-groups variation to within-group variation in z-scores across different categories of the dependent variable (see Exhibit 18.8 for a graphical depiction).

If the dependent variable has two groups, discriminant analysis produces one discriminant function that best separates those two groups. If the dependent variable has *three* groups, discriminant analysis produces *two* discriminant functions. The first function defines the single line that best separates the three groups. The second function makes the maximum incremental separation of the groups, subject to the constraint that it is independent of the first function (z-scores obtained from the second function are uncorrelated with z-scores obtained from the first function). In general, if the dependent variable has k groups, discriminant analysis generates $k - 1$ discriminant functions, each making the maximum separation among groups, subject to the constraint that it is uncorrelated with the preceding functions.

Marketing Research Applications of Discriminant Analysis

One use of discriminant analysis in marketing research is development of credit-scoring equations. Companies separate their credit customers into "good payers" and "bad payers," then run a discriminant analysis with good pay/bad pay as the dependent variable. The result is used to define an equation to screen applicants for credit approval. Here, discriminant analysis is being used for predictive purposes—the goal is to predict whether a particular applicant is a good credit risk.

EXHIBIT **18.8**

How
Discriminant
Analysis Works

Figure A: Graph of the relationship between three variables. Variable x_1 and x_2 are independent variables. The dependent variable is membership in Group A or Group B.

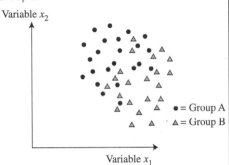

Figure B: The group means, called centroids, are calculated.

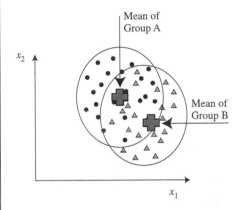

Figure C: Along the x_1 axis, the groups have high overlap (a low ratio of between-groups variance to within-group variance), and there is not much discrimination between the groups.

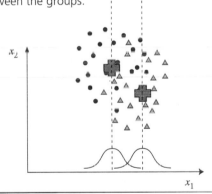

Figure D: Similarly, along the x_2 axis, the groups have high overlap, and there is not much discrimination between them.

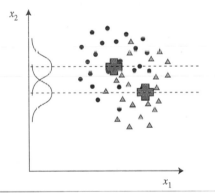

Figure E: Discriminant analysis finds the new axis, the discriminant axis, on which overlap is minimized.

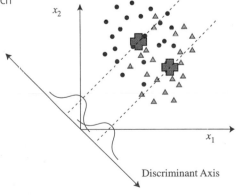

Another marketing research use of discriminant analysis is identification of variables that discriminate between buyers and nonbuyers of a product, or among buyers of different brands. Here, discriminant analysis is used in an exploratory manner to identify variables that are worth considering in segmenting the market or identifying good sales prospects.

A third use of discriminant analysis is development of *product space maps*. A product space map is a picture that shows the relative positions of brands within a market. This use of discriminant analysis is discussed after an example of discriminant analysis.

 # An Illustrative Analysis

Author Tips

To generate the output shown in Exhibit 18.9 in SPSS for Windows, choose "Classify" and then "Discriminant" from the "Statistics" menu. Indicate that V5 is the "Grouping Variable" and that it ranges from 1 to 3. Indicate that V4, V9, V10, V34, V35, and V37 are the independent variables. Click the "Classify" button and indicate that probabilities should be computed from group size, you want a separate-groups plot, the covariance matrix should be within-group, and a summary table should be displayed. Click "Continue" and then "OK."

Exhibit 18.9 shows an example of discriminant analysis drawn from the SPORTS data set. The dependent variable is V5 (method of payment used for the most recent purchase of sporting goods). This variable has three categories: cash or check, store credit card, or another credit card. The independent variables are V4 (dollar amount of purchase), V10 (importance of store credit cards in choosing where to buy sporting goods), V9 (importance of other credit cards), V34 (respondent's age), V35 (respondent's family income), and V37 (respondent's gender). The purpose of this analysis is to see how well method of payment relates to these independent variables and to see which independent variables seem to be most important.

Exhibit 18.9 contains the following information:

- First, it shows the number of observations available from each category of the dependent variable. Of 200 respondents who provided answers to all of these questions, 93 paid for their most recent purchase with cash or check, 73 paid with a store credit card, and 34 paid with another credit card.

- Next, it shows "prior probability" figures for each group. These are estimates of each group's size in the underlying population. The analysis package was directed to set each group's "prior probability" according to the group's size within the observed sample. For example, the first group, people who paid with cash or checks, is assumed to be 46.5 percent of the population because it accounts for $93/200 = 46.5$ percent of the sample on which this analysis is based. The prior probability has no effect on the calculation of discriminant functions, but it does affect how those functions are used to predict category membership.

- Next, it shows standardized coefficients for each independent variable on each discriminant function (since the independent variable has three categories, there are two discriminant functions). According to these coefficients, the first discriminant function (standardized) is

$$z = -.31632 \times V4 - .07964 \times V9 + .44720 \times V10 + .74982 \times V34 - .57674 \times V35 + .05302 \times V37.$$

EXHIBIT 18.9

Discriminant
Analysis of
Payment Type

```
- - - - - - - - D I S C R I M I N A N T   A N A L Y S I S - - - - - - - -

On groups defined by V5      How paid for last purchase

        291 (Unweighted) cases were processed.
         91 of these were excluded from the analysis.
        200 (Unweighted) cases will be used in the analysis.

Number of cases by group

                    Number of cases
       V5        Unweighted      Weighted   Label
          1          93            93.0     Cash or check
          2          73            73.0     Store charge
          3          34            34.0     Other credit card

       Total        200           200.0

Direct method: all variables passing the tolerance test are entered.
       Minimum tolerance level    .00100

Canonical discriminant functions

       Maximum number of functions                     2
       Minimum cumulative percent of variance   100.00
       Maximum significance of Wilks' Lambda    1.0000

Prior probabilities

       Group      Prior    Label
          1        .46500   Cash or check
          2        .36500   Store charge
          3        .17000   Other credit card

       Total    1.00000

                    Canonical Discriminant Functions

                Pct of   Cum  Canonical  After   Wilks'
   Fcn Eigenvalue Variance Pct  Corr      Fcn   Lambda   Chi-square   df   Sig

                                            :   0  .875264   25.913     12  .0110
    1*    .0862    62.47   62.47   .2818  :   1  .950742    9.825      5  .0804
    2*    .0518    37.53  100.00   .2219  :

   * Marks the 2 canonical discriminant functions remaining in the analysis.
```

Continued

Since the function is standardized, these coefficients can be used to make judgments about the relative importance of each variable. V34 makes the largest contribution to the first discriminant function, followed by V35 and V10. These judgments are subject to the same issues discussed in connection with using multiple regression coefficients to judge the importance of independent variables.

- Next, under the heading "Structure matrix," it gives the correlations between each independent variable and the two discriminant functions. These

EXHIBIT 18.9

Discriminant
Analysis of
Payment
Type—
Continued

Standardized canonical discriminant function coefficients

	Func 1	Func 2
V4	−.31632	.05084
V9	−.07964	.92194
V10	.44720	−.23955
V34	.74982	.20516
V35	−.57674	.40394
V37	.05302	−.25257

Structure matrix:
Pooled within-group correlations between discriminating variables
                                  and canonical discriminant
                                  functions
(Variables ordered by size of correlation within function)

	Func 1	Func 2
V34	.59656*	.30882
V10	.48412*	.12129
V35	−.43003*	.34310
V4	−.32668*	.02387
V9	.20581	.81662*
V37	.02314	−.28910*

* Denotes largest absolute correlation between each variable and
any discriminant function.

Canonical discriminant functions evaluated at group means (group
centroids)

Group	Func 1	Func 2
1	−.26265	−.13141
2	.37576	−.06288
3	−.08835	.49444

Classification results

Actual Group	No. of Cases	Predicted Group Membership 1	2	3
Group 1	93	75	18	0
Cash or check		80.6%	19.4%	.0%
Group 2	73	41	32	0
Store charge		56.2%	43.8%	.0%
Group 3	34	20	13	1
Other credit card		58.8%	38.2%	2.9%

Percent of "grouped" cases correctly classified: 54.00%

correlations provide a second way of looking at the relative importance of the independent variables, because a high correlation indicates that a variable is closely associated with the discriminant function.

- Next, it shows "group centroids." These are the mean z-scores for each category of the dependent variable on each discriminant function. Note that the first discriminant function primarily separates the first and second categories of V5— these are the two groups with the widest separation in means—and the second discriminant function primarily separates the third category of V5 from the first two categories. In other words, the first discriminant function primarily separates people who paid with cash or check from people who used store credit. The second discriminant function primarily separates people who used "third-party" credit such as Visa from people who paid in some other way.

- Finally, Exhibit 18.9 (see page 529) shows "Classification results." These results are obtained as follows: (1) the discriminant functions are applied to every observation in the data set, and each observation gets a z-score on each function; (2) given these z-scores, each observation is assigned to the category with the nearest centroid; (3) these predictions are compared with the actual category membership for each observation.

    The classification indicates that the V5 categories are not well separated by the discriminant functions. Overall, only 54 percent (108/200) of the observations were correctly classified: 81 percent of the observations in Category 1 were correctly classified, 44 percent in Category 2, and only 3 percent in Category 3.

Critical Thinking Skills

In what ways is discriminant analysis similar to multiple regression? In what ways does it differ?

Using Discriminant Analysis to Map Product Spaces

Exhibit 18.10 (see page 532) shows an example of a **product space map.** This map was developed by Johnson (1971) to show the beer market in Chicago, Illinois, as it existed in 1968.

Product space maps can be developed with discriminant analysis in the following way:

- First, the products or brands to be mapped are evaluated on various attributes. In this example, beer drinkers scored Budweiser, Schlitz, and other beers on each of the attributes shown in the space—pale golden color, a good beer to drink when drinking alone, and so on.

- Next, the data are arranged so that each participant's scores for each product are treated as a single data record. For example, if Larry and Stan are participants, the first data record might be Larry's ratings of Budweiser, and the second record might be his ratings of Schlitz. After all of Larry's beer ratings are accounted for, with a separate data record for each brand, we begin with Stan's ratings, then the next participant's ratings, and so on. If 100 participants each score eight products, the resulting data set will have 800 records.

- One variable in the resulting data set represents the identities of the products being scored: 1 = Budweiser, 2 = Schlitz, and so on. The other variables represent the various attributes, for example, pale golden color. So if 100 participants

EXHIBIT 18.10

A Product Space Map from Discriminant Analysis

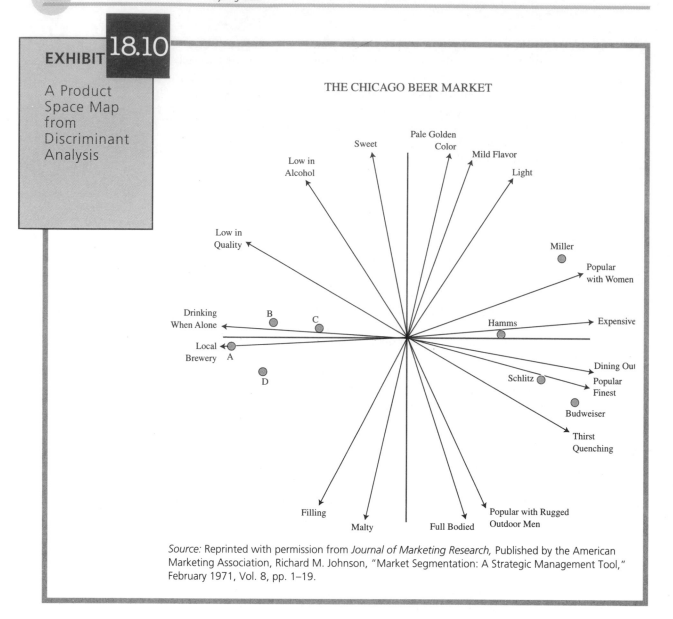

THE CHICAGO BEER MARKET

Source: Reprinted with permission from *Journal of Marketing Research,* Published by the American Marketing Association, Richard M. Johnson, "Market Segmentation: A Strategic Management Tool," February 1971, Vol. 8, pp. 1–19.

score eight products on six attributes, the resulting data set will have 800 rows and seven columns (one column to identify the product and six columns to give its ratings).

- Now a discriminant analysis is done with the product identities as the dependent (grouping) variable and the various attributes as the independent variables. This produces $k - 1$ discriminant functions, where k is the number of products used in the analysis.

- The observations can then be mapped against the first two discriminant functions. To make a cleaner picture in product space maps, it is customary to show only the group centroids.

This is how the beer brands have been mapped into Exhibit 18.10. The axes of the product space map represent the first two discriminant functions obtained from the analysis. The location of each brand represents the centroid (the mean) of z-scores for that brand on each discriminant function.

- If desired, the attributes on which the products were scored can be mapped into the space, as they have been in Exhibit 18.10. When data are mapped in this fashion, it can be mathematically demonstrated that the cosine of the angle between two variables equals the correlation between those variables. Thus, if a particular attribute is correlated .58 with the first discriminant function and −.41 with the second discriminant function, a line representing the attribute is drawn at an angle of 54° with the first axis (.58 is the cosine of 54°) and an angle of 114° with the second axis (−.41 is the cosine of 114°). If the line cannot be perfectly set in the indicated position—which is common—it is set as close as possible.

We should note that product space maps are usually based on buyers' perceptions. In physical content, Miller beer is quite similar to Budweiser beer, but in 1968 these two brands held different positions in beer drinkers' minds. At that time, Miller was positioned as a light beer; subsequently, Miller Lite has been introduced and Miller has been "repositioned" to be closer to Budweiser. Since product space maps are usually based on buyers' perceptions, they are also called **product perception maps.**

Author Tips

Product space maps are useful because they show product positionings in a pictorial form that is easy to interpret. Managers can see which products are seen as similar or dissimilar, which attributes define similarities and differences among products, and whether there are open spaces that might represent opportunities for new products.

Issues in Using Discriminant Analysis

Most of the issues that arise in connection with discriminant analysis parallel issues involved with multiple regression, as follows:

- The independent variables should be quantitative, though dummy variables can be used. If you check the scaling for the independent variables used in Exhibit 18.9 (see page 530), you will see that we pushed this assumption pretty hard in that analysis.

- Discriminant analysis is fundamentally linear. If an independent variable has nonlinear effects—for example, Group 1 membership is associated with low and high levels of the independent variable and Group 2 membership is associated with a medium level—some transformation will be needed to see these effects.

- Discriminant results can be affected by outliers.

- Discriminant analysis is usually implemented as a "main effects only" analysis. However, interaction terms can be created and used if desired.

- Judgments about the relative importance of independent variables should be based on standardized discriminant coefficients.

- Multicollinearity and model specification can influence the apparent importance of an independent variable.

- If an independent variable is observed over a restricted range, this will dampen its apparent importance.

- If the discriminant analysis will be used for predictive purposes, independent variables should be used that will be readily available at the time of prediction.

- If the environment changes, the predictive value of a discriminant analysis may be lost or diminished.

- The classification results obtained from a discriminant analysis will overstate the true predictive power of the discriminant functions, because these results show how well the functions can classify the same data that were used to generate them. To get a better idea of prediction accuracy, the discriminant functions should be tested on a "holdout" sample that is set aside for testing purposes.

In addition to these issues, one other issue arises in connection with predictive uses of discriminant analysis. This is the issue of unequal costs of misclassification across groups. Assume, for example, that discriminant analysis is being used to sort credit applicants and that historical records show that a good credit customer will be worth $10,000 in profits over the life of his or her buying relationship while a bad credit customer will cause $2,000 in losses before credit is revoked. In these circumstances, misclassifying a good customer as bad (and denying the application) costs $10,000, and misclassifying a bad customer costs $2,000. Therefore, it is better to err on the side of approval, up to the point where five bad applications are erroneously included for every good application rejected. The *percentage* of misclassifications is not as relevant as the *cost* of misclassifications.

Under such circumstances, the declaration of prior probabilities can be used to overstate the size of "high-cost" groups and hence shift the classification boundaries in favor of these groups.

Summary

This chapter discussed multivariate procedures with dependent variables. The following points were covered:

1. What are the purposes and procedures of multivariate analysis with dependent variables?

Multivariate analysis with dependent variables is data analysis that uses at least one dependent variable and two or more independent variables. It can be used (1) to explore or confirm the existence of a relationship between the dependent and independent variables, (2) to measure the relative contribution of each independent variable to that relationship, and/or (3) to establish a prediction equation that allows the dependent variable to be predicted as a function of the independent variables. Analyses with dependent variables include complex cross-tabs, comparison of means, multiple regression, and discriminant analysis.

2. How can complex cross-tabulations be used to analyze multivariate data?

A complex cross-tab is the joint tabulation of three or more variables. Relationships between variables are measured by the extent to which the distribution of one variable changes across the categories of another.

The primary issue in using complex cross-tabs is that results must often be simplified before they can be interpreted.

3. How can comparisons of means be used to analyze multivariate data?

A multivariate comparison of means involves the calculation of mean values for a dependent variable across the categories of two or more independent variables. If the mean value of the dependent variable changes across categories of the independent variables, then the variables are related.

Issues in using comparisons of means include the following: (1) the dependent variable must be quantitative, (2) the technique is sensitive to outliers, (3) the results can be confusing when a large number of categories are involved, (4) interactions of the independent variables can be detected but may be difficult to describe, and (5) the number of independent variables that can be included is limited in many statistical software packages.

4. How can multiple regression be used to analyze multivariate data?

A multiple regression expresses the relationship between a dependent variable and two or more independent variables in the form of a linear equation ($y = \beta_0 + \beta_1 x_1 + \ldots + \beta_k x_k$). The coefficients indicate how many units the y variables change, on average, for each unit of change in each x variable. A multiple regression also produces an R^2 measure, which indicates the percentage of total variance in the dependent variable that is "explained" by the independent variables.

Issues that arise in using multiple regression include the following: (1) all variables should be quantitative, (2) the procedure is sensitive to outliers, (3) the procedure is usually applied as a "main effects only" analysis, (4) conclusions about the importance of different variables should be based on standardized beta weights and should be made cautiously when the independent variables are correlated, (5) a restricted range of variation will limit the weight given to an independent variable, (6) an independent variable may require transformation before its importance can be measured properly, (7) a regression done for prediction purposes might not apply outside the range of values over which the equation was developed, and (8) R^2 overstates the real accuracy of prediction because it represents the ability of a regression equation to fit the same data on which it was generated. Also, a multiple regression expresses only linear relationships (though nonlinearities can be captured by raising independent variables to powers or making other transformations).

Despite the many issues that arise in using multiple regression, the technique is very useful and receives wide application in marketing research.

5. How can discriminant analysis be used to analyze multivariate data?

Discriminant analysis relates a categorical dependent variable to two or more quantitative independent variables. It uses the independent variables to form linear equations that maximally discriminate among the categories of the dependent variable. The coefficients in these equations indicate the extent to which each independent variable contributes to the discrimination and hence is related to the dependent variable. The equations can be used to predict an observation's category on the dependent variable, for example, to predict whether a credit applicant is a good risk.

Issues that arise in using discriminant analysis basically parallel the issues in regression analysis.

Suggested Additional Readings

Multivariate analysis is a complicated topic, but there are several good books to consult. Unfortunately, many require a fairly high level of mathematical sophistication. Two of the easier ones to use are by Joseph F. Hair Jr., Ralph E. Anderson, and Ronald L. Tatham, *Multivariate Data Analysis: With Readings* (New York: Macmillan, 1987), and Richard Harris, *A Primer of Multivariate Statistics* (Orlando, Fla.: Academic, 1985). Paul Green and J. Douglas Carroll, *Mathematical Tools for Applied Multivariate Data Analysis* (Orlando, Fla.: Academic, 1976), provides the basic mathematics needed to be aware of what is really happening in multivariate analysis.

Some of the more advanced books that may be useful are William W. Cooley and Paul R. Lohnes, *Multivariate Data Analysis* (Malabar, Fla.: Krieger, 1985); Brian S. Everitt and Graham Dunn, *Applied Multivariate Data Analysis* (New York: Oxford University Press, 1992); Daniel H. Freeman, *Applied Categorical Data Analysis* (New York: Dekker, 1987); Johannes P. van de Geer, *Introduction to Multivariate Analysis for the Social Sciences* (San Francisco: Freeman, 1971) and *Multivariate Analysis of Categorical Data* (Newbury Park, Calif.: Sage, 1983); Paul Green and J. Douglas Carroll, *Analyzing Multivariate Data* (Hinsdale, Ill.: Dryden, 1978); and James Stevens, *Applied Multivariate Statistics for the Social Sciences* (Hillsdale, N.J.: Erlbaum, 1992).

 # Discussion Questions

1. What are three general uses for multivariate analysis with dependent variables?

2. What multivariate statistical techniques would you use to address each of the following marketing problems?
    a. Talbots wants to know if there is a difference in the number of returns made by catalog buyers and retail buyers.
    b. Philip Morris wants to know if there is an association between gender, race, and brand of beer consumed.
    c. An advertising agency wants to predict the market share for a particular brand based on an ad's (1) reach, (2) frequency, and (3) recall.
    d. An industrial manufacturer wants to understand the causal relationships between conflict, communication, and trust on distributor satisfaction with the manufacturer.
    e. The circulation manager of *Business Week* wants to predict subscription renewal based on the number of times the subscriber has renewed in the past, the original subscription price paid by the subscriber, the subscriber's income, and the subscriber's age.
    f. The brand manager of a new brand of snack food wants to create a product space map of the leading brands of snack food.

3. What is stepwise regression (see Appendix 18.1)? Why do some market researchers use this type of analysis? What are some of the problems with this statistical tool? What are the two basic forms of stepwise regression and how do they differ?

4. What is multicollinearity? Why can multicollinearity cause problems in regression? How can you get around the problems?

 # Marketing Research Challenge

We suggest that you first use the variables that we have used in the examples given in this chapter to see if you can duplicate the results. If you can understand these, you may then want to choose other variables from the SPORTS disk and repeat the analyses with them.

Internet Exercise

To learn more about structural equation modeling, visit Ed Rigdon's homepage, out of Georgia State University. It's located at http://www.gsu.edu/~mkteer/sem.html.

References

Johnson, (1971). "Market Segmentation: A Strategic Management Tool." *Journal of Marketing Research* 8, pp. 1–19.

MacLachlan and Johansson (1981). "Market Segmentation with Multivariate AID." *Journal of Marketing Research* 45, pp. 74–84.

Mason, Charlotte H., and William O. Perreault (1991). "Collinearity, Power and Interpretation of Multiple Regression Analysis." *Journal of Marketing Research* 28, p. 268.

Appendix 18.1: Variations on Multiple Regression

This appendix discusses some analysis techniques that extend the logic of multiple regression to additional contexts.

Stepwise Multiple Regression

Stepwise multiple regression is an exploratory analysis technique that builds regression equations in a series of steps. It works as follows:

- In the first step of an uncontrolled "forward" stepwise regression, the analysis routine forms a regression equation between the dependent variable and the one independent variable that correlates most highly with it.

- In the second step, the routine evaluates the remaining independent variables to see which variable makes the largest incremental contribution to the variable already in the equation and adds that second variable if the contribution is statistically significant.

- Step by step, the procedure continues to add variables to the equation until none of the remaining variables makes a significant incremental contribution.

Exhibit 18.1A shows an example of a forward stepwise multiple regression. The dependent variable is V34, amount spent at Smith's, and the independent variables are V17 to V27. These are the same variables used in the nonstepwise regression shown in Exhibit 18.7.

The analysis in Exhibit 18.1A never goes past the first step. In the first step, V21, Smith's having its own credit card, enters the equation. This variable receives a raw beta weight of 55.19 and a standardized weight of .19. Once V21 is in the regression, none of the remaining independent variables are significant at a .05 level, so the analysis stops at that point.

Stepwise multiple regression can also be implemented in "backward" form. An uncontrolled backward stepwise multiple regression starts with a regression equation that contains all of the independent variables. On the second step, it eliminates the variable with the smallest incremental contribution if that contribution is not statistically significant. The procedure continues until all remaining variables make a statistically significant incremental contribution.

The purpose of uncontrolled stepwise multiple regression, whether forward or backward, is to let the data build the regression equation. The goal is a parsimonious yet powerful regression equation. However, a potential problem with stepwise multiple regression is that stepwise results may be unstable across repeated samples if there is substantial correlation among the independent variables. It is especially important with stepwise multiple regression procedures to have a holdout sample to confirm the results of an exploration (Steckel and Vanhonacker, 1993).

EXHIBIT ## 18.1A

Stepwise
Regression
with V29 as
the Dependent
Variable and
V17–V27
as the
Independent
Variables

```
                 * * * * M U L T I P L E   R E G R E S S I O N  * * * *

Listwise deletion of missing data

Equation number 1 Dependent variable . . V29 How much spent at Smith's in 12 months
Block number  1.  Method: Stepwise        Criteria   PIN  .0500    POUT   .1000
    V17        V18        V19        V20        V21       V22       V23       V24
    V25        V26        V27

Variable(s) entered on step number
   1. .   V21         Smith's own cards


Multiple R              .19287
R square                .03720
Adjusted R square       .03319
Standard error       256.70764


Analysis of Variance
                        DF       Sum of Squares      Mean Square
Regression               1          611063.83736    611063.83736
Residual               240        15815714.37752     65898.80991


F =         9.27276        Signif F =   .0026

------------------ Variables in the Equation ------------------
Variable                 B         SE B        Beta         T   Sig T

V21              55.190055   18.124095     .192871     3.045   .0026
(Constant)       -3.554491   78.665342                 -.045   .9640

--------------- Variables Not in the Equation --------------

Variable            Beta In   Partial   Min Toler        T   Sig T

V17                 .008849   .008782    .948171      .136   .8921
V18                 .104463   .104014    .954541     1.617   .1072
V19                 .115113   .113180    .930735     1.761   .0795
V20                -.078962  -.065829    .669158    -1.020   .3088
V22                 .030204   .028574    .861672      .442   .6589
V23                 .081504   .078142    .885015     1.212   .2268
V24                -.047269  -.046023    .912725     -.712   .4770
V25                -.011330  -.011129    .928997     -.172   .8635
V26                -.085543  -.082918    .904622    -1.286   .1996
V27                -.062722  -.062086    .943384     -.962   .3372

End block number 1  PIN = .050  Limits reached.
```

Some statistical software packages allow you to control the order of entry of independent variables into a stepwise regression and to enter variables in sequential groups. If used in this fashion, the technique is not really exploratory. Rather, it allows for confirmation of the existence of a relationship between the dependent variable and a parsimonious set of independent variables.

Logistic Regression

Logistic regression is a variation on multiple regression analysis that is designed for dummy (0-1) dependent variables. It draws its name from the fact that it uses a logistic function in the process of estimating the regression equation, but this point is not important except for those who wish to become expert in the mathematics of the procedure.

Logistic regression is an appropriate procedure to use when data are being analyzed for purposes of building a prediction equation. The logistic procedure, with its classification-based outcomes, allows a 0-1 dependent variable to be predicted in the form it actually takes. However, if the purpose of doing an analysis is simply to determine whether the dependent variable relates to the independent variables, or if the purpose is to compare the relative contributions of various independent variables, logistic regression is not needed. A conventional multiple regression will provide satisfactory results in these circumstances.

LOGIT Analysis

LOGIT analysis is appropriate when the dependent variable is a proportion bounded by 0 and 1. To get around the constraint of having a dependent variable bounded by 0 and 1, LOGIT forms a regression equation with the dependent variable transformed as follows:

$$ln\left[\frac{p}{1-p}\right] = b_0 + b_i x_i$$

where p is the proportion represented by the dependent variable and ln indicates the natural logarithm. This transformed dependent variable can range from minus infinity (if $p = .00$) to positive infinity (if $p = 1.00$).

As with logistic regression, LOGIT analysis is not really needed unless the regression analysis is being done for prediction purposes. Its value is that it allows predictions that fit the constrained form of the dependent variable. If the analysis is being done for purposes other than prediction, conventional regression analysis will yield satisfactory results.

Log-Linear Models

Log-linear models allow you to analyze complex cross-tabs in a regression format. The dependent variable in a log-linear regression is the logarithm of the number of observations in each cell of the cross-tabulation. The independent variables are a series of dummy variables representing the various categories of the variables involved in the cross-tab. By analyzing the data in this fashion, log-linear models can measure not just whether there is an overall relationship among the variables in the analysis, but also where this relationship is located. In contrast, a complex cross-tab with a χ^2 test can identify the existence of an overall relationship but cannot locate the specific variables or categories involved in that relationship.

The use of log-linear models is growing, and they may become common in marketing research in the future. At the present time, though, it is best to stick to cross-tabs to analyze multivariate relationships in categorical data. Complex cross-tabs can be difficult to interpret, but they are easier to comprehend than log-linear regressions.

Canonical Correlation Analysis

Earlier in the chapter, multivariate analysis of variance was described, and the fact that it extends analysis of variance to situations in which there is more than one dependent variable was noted. In like fashion, **canonical correlation analysis** extends multiple regression analysis—or something like it—to these situations.

Canonical correlation takes the form

$$C_1y_1 + \ldots + C_my_m = B_1x_1 + \ldots + B_kx_k,$$

where the x's are independent variables, the y's are dependent variables, and the B's and C's are weights applied to these variables. The analysis procedure calculates the B and C weights so as to maximize the correlation between the weighted combination of independent variables and the weighted combination of dependent variables.

The B weights in a canonical correlation are interpreted in a manner similar to regression analysis. If $B_1 = .23$, this means that a change of one unit in x_1 is associated with a change of .23 units in the weighted combination of dependent (y) variables. However, it does not mean that any particular dependent variable changes by .23 units, or even that any particular dependent variable changes at all.

Since changes in the independent variables cannot be connected with specific amounts of change in specific dependent variables, canonical correlation is not really useful for prediction. If a series of dependent variables is to be used in a predictive exercise, it is best to run separate multiple regressions for each dependent variable or to create a simple unweighted additive scale from the dependent variables (i.e., $y_{scale} = y_1 + \ldots + y_k$). Canonical correlation is also not particularly well suited for exploratory work—if x and y variables that are related to each other are to be identified, results that are more precise and easier to interpret will be derived from a series of bivariate correlations. Like MANOVA, canonical correlation is most valuable for its ability to provide a single inferential test that summarizes the relationship between a series of independent and dependent variables. This procedure gets relatively little use in marketing research.

Structural Equations Modeling

Structural equations modeling is used to analyze relationships among variables that are connected in some type of multistage causal system. This type of analysis is also known as **causal modeling, structural relations modeling,** and **LISREL analysis. LISREL,** which stands for Linear Structural Relations, is the name of the software package that is usually used to perform this procedure (Bagozzi and Yi, 1989).

To illustrate multistage systems, assume that annual expenditure on books is influenced by a person's income and education and that income depends partly on education. The relationships among these variables can be depicted as in the following figure:

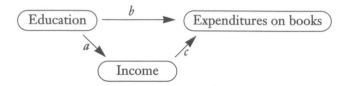

In this diagram, the connecting lines indicate relationships between variables, and the arrows indicate the direction of causality for those relationships (noncausal relationships are drawn with arrows pointing in both directions). The *a*, *b*, and *c* terms are standardized regression coefficients that indicate the magnitude of each relationship.

This system of relationships can be represented in mathematical form by the following equations:

Income = *a*(Education) + Prediction error
Books   = *b*(Education) + *c*(Income) + Prediction error.

These equations are called "structural equations" because they define the structure of the system.

There are two ways of measuring multistage relationships like those shown in our example:

- *Through a sequence of regressions.* A regression could be run with income as the dependent variable and education as the independent variable, to get a coefficient for the connection between education and income. Then a regression could be run with expenditure on books as the dependent variable and education and income as the independent variables, to derive coefficients for those connections.

- *Through structural equations modeling.* Structural equations software simultaneously calculates all of the coefficients in a system of relationships, so as to maximize the likelihood of the values observed in the data.

In a simple situation such as the education–income–book-spending example, a series of regressions would be used to estimate the desired coefficients, because these analyses would be easy to run and would not require any specialized software. However, structural equations modeling becomes more attractive as the model becomes more complex and/or when latent variables enter the model.

An **observed variable** is one that is subject to direct measurement; for example, if salespeople are asked to rate how hard they intend to work during the next six months, their answers would constitute an observed variable. A **latent variable** is one that is measured *indirectly* through a series of observed *indicators*. For example, if salespeople are asked to rate how hard they intend to work during the next six months, how careful they will be in their work, and how willing they are to help their manager, these ratings might be taken as indicators of an underlying "motivation" variable.

There are three different ways of obtaining a latent variable from its indicators. One approach is to construct a simple, unweighted additive scale of the indicators. A second approach is to use a technique called **factor analysis** to identify the weighted combination of indicators that maximizes the squared multiple correlation between the weighted combination and the indicators themselves (factor analysis is discussed in Chapter 19). A third approach is to estimate weights for the indicators at the same time as other portions of the system of relationships are estimated, and to derive these weights to optimize the entire system. This is the approach used by LISREL, which simultaneously fits (1) the measurement model that connects latent variables with their indicators and (2) the structural model that defines the structural relationships among variables.

Exhibit 18.1B illustrates an analysis situation that features latent variables and multistage causality. The topic of the research is realignments of sales force territories. The researcher has (1) three measures of actions that might have been taken by sales managers in connection with sales territory realignments, (2) five measures of the extent to which salespeople perceive that the realignment was fair, (3) two measures of salespeople's expected levels of sales and income after the realignment, and (4) five measures of salespeople's motivation. The researcher believes that:

- The five fairness perceptions can be treated as indicators of a latent "perceived fairness" variable.

- The two expectancy measures can be treated as indicators of a latent "expected income" measure.

- The five motivation measures can be treated as indicators of a latent "motivation" variable.

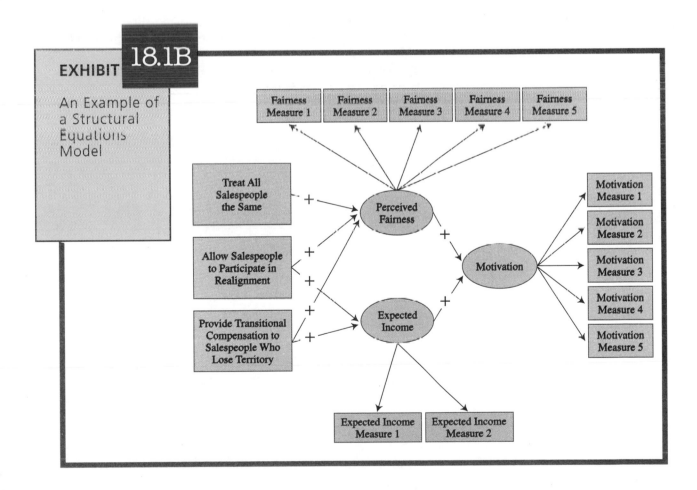

EXHIBIT 18.1B

An Example of a Structural Equations Model

- The action of treating all salespeople the same will positively affect perceived fairness.
- The action of allowing salespeople to participate in the realignment process will positively affect both perceived fairness and expected income.
- The action of providing a transitional compensation for salespeople who lose territory will positively affect perceived fairness and expected income.
- Perceived fairness and expected income will positively affect motivation.

All of these relationships are shown in Exhibit 18.1B (see page 543). The observed variables are shown as boxes, the latent variables are shown as ovals, and the relationships among variables are shown as arrows. This type of model, with multistage relationships and latent variables, represents a perfect context for LISREL analysis.

Structural equations modeling is not appropriate for exploratory analysis in marketing research, because it requires defining a theoretical system before the analysis is run. However, if a complex, multistage theory about a market is to be tested, structural equations modeling allows for this to be done and for latent variables to be incorporated into the analysis.

References

Bagozzi, Richard P., and Youjae Yi (1989). "On the Use of Structural Equation Models in Experimental Designs." *Journal of Marketing Research* 26 (August), pp. 271–284.

Steckel, J. H., and W. R. Vanhonacker (1993). "Cross-Validating Regression Models in Marketing Research." *Marketing Science* 12, pp. 415–427.

19 Multivariate Grouping Procedures

◨ OBJECTIVES

After reading this chapter, you should be able to answer the following questions:

❶ What are the purposes of multivariate grouping procedures?

❷ How can factor analysis be used to analyze data?

❸ How can cluster analysis be used to analyze data?

❹ How is multidimensional scaling used in marketing research?

This chapter, which finishes the coverage of data analysis methods, discusses **multivariate grouping procedures.** Multivariate grouping procedures involve three or more variables, with none of the variables being treated as dependent on the others. The goal of these analyses is not to predict values of some dependent variable or to describe causal relationships but simply to form groups of some type.

The Purposes of Multivariate Grouping Procedures

Multivariate grouping procedures are used for three general purposes in market research:

- One purpose is to group *variables* into broader, underlying factors. For example, in our SPORTS data, V6 to V16 measure the importance of eleven store characteristics in deciding where to buy sporting goods. These characteristics are:

  V6   Importance of store location
  V7   Importance of everyday prices
  V8   Importance of sale prices
  V9   Importance of taking third-party credit cards
  V10   Importance of having a store credit card
  V11   Importance of merchandise quality
  V12   Importance of merchandise selection
  V13   Importance of having desired brand names
  V14   Importance of having merchandise in stock
  V15   Importance of helpfulness of employees
  V16   Importance of speed of service

  A grouping analysis applied to these variables might show that V7 and V8 can be grouped into a broader "price" factor, V9 and V10 can be grouped into a "credit" factor, V11 to V14 can be grouped into a "merchandise" factor, V15 and V16 can be grouped into a "service" factor, and V6 ("location") stands alone.

- A second purpose is to group *customers* into market segments based on their similarities across several variables (Mitchell, 1995; Riche, 1990). For example, respondents in the SPORTS data might be grouped according to similarities in their answers to V6 to V16.

- A third purpose is to group *products or services* to show patterns of competition among them. For example, Chapter 18 described how discriminant analysis can be used to generate product space maps that show how products or services are positioned in relation to each other. Product space maps can also be generated by means of grouping analyses.

We discuss three types of grouping procedures in this chapter: *factor analysis*, *cluster analysis*, and *multidimensional scaling (MDS)*. Factor analysis is most commonly used to group variables, cluster analysis is most commonly used to group customers, and MDS is most commonly used to group products. However, each procedure can be used for other purposes as well. The procedures are differentiated not so much by their purposes as by the methods and/or data used to accomplish these purposes.

Format of the Discussion

The general format for discussing these procedures is the same as in Chapter 18:

- First, a description of each procedure is given: its structure, the descriptive statistics associated with it, the inferential tests associated with it, and the types of data to which it applies are described.
- Second, marketing research applications for the procedure are described.
- Third, illustrative outputs are provided.
- Finally, there is a discussion of issues that arise when the procedure is used.

The discussion operates at an input/output level without getting into the mathematical specifics of each technique. Again, our goal is not to make you expert in the mathematics of these procedures but simply to make you aware that the procedures exist, how they might be used, and issues that should be considered.

Factor Analysis

Description of the Procedure

Factor analysis is a procedure that groups items—usually variables—on the basis of correlations. A factor analysis will form groups of variables that have strong correlations (either positive or negative) with one another. Because the technique relies upon correlations, all variables should be quantitative in nature, though dummy (0-1) variables can be used.

More specifically, a factor analysis calculates a series of **factors**, each of which is a weighted combination of the variables being analyzed. These combinations take the form:

$$F = w_1 x_1 + w_2 x_2 + \ldots + w_k x_k$$

where F is the factor, x_1 through x_k are the variables being analyzed, and w_1 through w_k are weights applied to these variables. The weights for each factor are determined so as to maximize the sum of squared correlations between this factor and the various contributing variables, subject to a constraint that each factor be uncorrelated with all preceding factors.

Descriptive Results

The key descriptive results obtained from a factor analysis are *factor loadings*, *eigenvalues*, and possibly *factor scores*, as follows:

- **Factor loadings** are the correlations between a factor and the individual variables being analyzed. For example, if a factor analysis shows that V6 has a loading of –.12 on Factor 2, this means that the correlation between V6 and the second factor is –.12.

  Each factor will have loadings for all of the variables being analyzed. Variables that have loadings with absolute values larger than .50 are said to "load highly" on the factor and are considered to be members of a group of variables identified by the factor. Variables that have loadings with absolute values of less than .50 are usually ignored in interpreting the factor.

  For example, in the SPORTS data, if V7 (importance of everyday prices) and V8 (importance of sale prices) are the only two variables to load higher than .50 on a particular factor, this factor identifies a group formed by V7 and V8. Since both of the variables relate to price, this factor would be referred to as a "price" factor. Note that the names of the factors do not come directly from the data but depend on the researcher's interpretation.

- The **eigenvalue** for a factor equals the sum of the squared loadings for all variables on that factor—in other words, the sum of the squared correlations between that factor and all of the variables in the analysis. Since the first factor is chosen so as to maximize the sum of the squared correlations without any constraints, the first factor naturally has the largest eigenvalue. The second factor has the second largest eigenvalue, the third factor has the third largest eigenvalue, and so on.

  The eigenvalues provide a measure of the percentage of variance in the contributing variables that is "explained" by the factor. The sum of the eigenvalues represents the total amount of variance to be explained in the analysis, and the ratio of each individual eigenvalue to that sum indicates the percentage of variance explained by the relevant factor. For example, if the sum of the eigenvalues in a factor analysis is 11.00 and the eigenvalue for the first factor is 2.17, the first factor accounts for 2.17/11.00 = .197, or 19.7 percent, of the total variance.

- The third descriptive measure available from a factor analysis is **factor scores.** When a factor analysis is used to group variables, the resulting factors can be treated as new variables that represent combinations of the original variables. Appropriate values for each observation on these new variables (the factors) can be calculated. These values are called **"factor scores."** As a general rule, statistical software packages that have factor analysis routines will calculate and save factor scores if desired.

Inferential Results

Three types of inferential analyses are appropriate in a factor analysis:

- Testing whether the overall analysis is "significant" in the sense of effectively accomplishing its grouping objectives

- Testing whether a particular factor makes a significant contribution to the overall analysis, and consequently should be retained for purposes of interpretation and/or further analysis

- Testing whether a particular variable is significantly associated with a particular factor and consequently should be considered part of the group of variables defined by that factor

In factor analysis, these inferential goals are primarily achieved by using "rules of thumb" rather than formal statistical tests (Acito, Anderson, and Engledow, 1980). These rules include the following:

- The overall factor analysis generally can be considered effective if the total percentage of variance explained by the retained factors exceeds 70 percent. If the retained factors account for less than 70 percent of the variance, this fact should be noted in reports.

    This is not to say there is anything wrong with the retained factors when the explained variance is less than 70 percent. It simply means that the original variables contained a substantial amount of information that the factors were not able to capture, so the factors should not be viewed as a good summary of the original variables.

    An alternative, nonquantitative criterion for determining the effectiveness of a factor analysis is simply to judge whether the factors can be meaningfully interpreted and are useful for some purpose. If the results are meaningful and useful, the analysis should be deemed a success.

- The number of "significant" or meaningful factors can be determined in various ways. The most common approach is to retain all factors with eigenvalues larger than 1.0. In most applications of factor analysis, an eigenvalue of 1.0 is regarded as the amount of variance attributable to a single variable. Therefore, factors with eigenvalues of less than 1.0 are viewed as "explaining" less than one variable's worth of variance. Since the purpose of the analysis is to form groups with two or more variables, these factors are considered to be nonsignificant and are dropped from further consideration.

    A second approach is to use a **scree test,** a procedure that uses decreases in eigenvalues to determine the factors to be retained. A scree test can be done either graphically or numerically; the eigenvalues are arranged in descending order and a dramatic drop between two eigenvalues is looked for. If a dramatic drop is seen, it might be best to retain only the factors whose eigenvalues come before that drop. For example, if the first eigenvalue is 5.44, the second eigenvalue is 4.32, and the third eigenvalue is 1.40, only the first two factors might be considered significant. If a dramatic drop is not seen, it is time to fall back on the rule of thumb that significant factors must have eigenvalues greater than 1.0.

    A third approach is to retain factors according to theoretical and/or interpretive judgments. For example, a factor analysis of V6 to V16 in the SPORTS data might produce four factors with eigenvalues larger than 1.0, and V6 (location) might not load highly on any of these factors because this variable is unique. Rather than proceed with an analysis that ignores location as a store choice factor, one can simply assert a fifth factor consisting of V6 by itself.

- In measuring the contribution of individual variables, each variable is usually assigned to the factor for which it has the highest loading (measured in terms of

Critical Thinking Skills

Is factor analysis an objective technique, a subjective technique, or a combination of both? Explain your answer.

absolute value). If this loading is larger than .50, the variable is considered to be part of the group of variables defined by the factor. Variables with loadings of less than .50 usually are ignored in interpreting factors.

In some situations, this quantitative rule will be overridden by judgmental considerations. For example, a variable with a loading in the .35 to .50 range might be assigned to a particular factor if the variable has a theoretical relationship with other variables that load highly on that factor, especially if the variable does not load highly on any other factor. Similarly, a variable that loads highly on a factor but bears no explainable relationship to the other high-loading variables might be ignored in interpreting the factor.

Marketing Research Applications of Factor Analysis

It has already been noted that factor analysis is primarily used for purposes of grouping variables. The procedure has three possible purposes in this regard:

- One purpose is to show the structure underlying a large number of variables. This provides insight into the data. For example, a factor analysis of V6 to V16 in the SPORTS data will show whether there are eleven different dimensions of store choice or a smaller number of underlying dimensions. It will also illuminate the nature of individual variables by showing how they fit into the bigger picture.

- A second purpose is to simplify discussion of the data. For example, instead of talking to managers about eleven different store choice variables, it might be better to focus on four broad factors.

- A third purpose is to create new, combined variables for use in other analysis procedures. For example, it was noted in Chapter 18 that multicollinearity (correlation among the independent variables) can cause problems in analysis procedures such as multiple regression and discriminant analysis. One way of reducing multicollinearity is to (1) run a factor analysis to identify sets of related variables, (2) combine these related variables into broader scales, and (3) use the broader scales in subsequent analyses.

There are two ways of combining related variables into broader scales. One method is to save factor scores from the factor analysis, then use the factors as variables in subsequent analyses. Another method is simply to add together the variables that are found to be related (i.e., SCALE = V1 + V2 + . . . + Vk). This latter approach often produces more reliable results because factor scores may be unstable.

In addition to being used to group variables, factor analysis can be used to group respondents who share similar response patterns across some set of variables. A factor analysis used for this purpose is called a **Q-type factor analysis.** The usual goal of Q-type factor analysis is the identification of market segments.

Q-type factor analysis does not differ from regular factor analysis in its basic method or interpretation. However, since Q-type factor analysis requires that the data be analyzed across rows of the data set (the observations) instead of across columns (the variables), it constitutes a special option that is not available in all software packages.

An Illustrative Analysis

Exhibit 19.1 (see page 552) shows the results of a factor analysis applied to V6 to V16 in the SPORTS data. As with the analyses shown in previous chapters, this output was generated with SPSS for Windows.

Exhibit 19.1 contains the following information:

- First, the results are obtained from a principal components analysis, which is the most common type of factor analysis. In **principal components analysis (PCA),** the goal is to develop factors that explain the maximum amount out of the *total* variance in the variables being analyzed. This method can be contrasted to **common factor analysis (CFA),** in which the goal is to explain the maximum amount out of the variance shared in common by the variables in the analysis (excluding the unique variance associated with each variable).

- Next come the initial **communalities** associated with each variable in the analysis. The communalities indicate the percentage of variance in each variable that is being used in the analysis. Since a principal components analysis is being performed, the initial communalities shown in Exhibit 19.1 are all 1.00, indicating that the full variance of each variable is being used.

- Next comes a listing of factors, eigenvalues for each factor, and variance explained. There are eleven factors because there were eleven variables in the analysis, and a factor analysis will generate as many factors as variables (or as many factors as the number of observations, if that is smaller than the number of variables). The eigenvalue associated with the first factor is 2.16949, the eigenvalue associated with the second factor is 1.52651, and so on.

  The sum of the eigenvalues, which is not shown in the output but can easily be calculated, is 11.00 (the sum of the initial communalities). This represents the total amount of variance to be explained in the eleven variables used in the analysis. The first factor accounts for $2.16949 \div 11.00 = .197$ or 19.7 percent of that total variance. The second factor accounts for $1.52651 \div 11.00 = 13.9$ percent of the variance. Together, the first two factors account for a cumulative $19.7\% + 13.9\% = 33.6\%$ of the variance.

  Four factors have eigenvalues larger than 1.0. According to a default decision rule built into the software package, only these four factors are retained for further analysis and display. This default could have been overridden if desired.

  Collectively, the four retained factors account for only 55.1 percent of the total variance in the eleven variables. This figure is lower than desired. It indicates that the variables contain substantial information that is not captured by the four factors.

- Next comes the factor matrix, which is the matrix of loadings for the eleven variables on the four retained factors. These loadings show that all of the variables load moderately well on the first factor, with loadings ranging from .29 for V13 to .58 for V7. The second factor has strong negative loadings for V9 and V10 (importance of taking third-party credit cards and having a store credit card) and strong positive loadings for V11 and V12 (importance of merchandise quality

Author Tips

To generate the output shown in Exhibit 19.1 (see page 552) using SPSS for Windows, choose "Data Reduction" and then "Factor" from the "Statistics" menu. Indicate that you want the analysis to include V6 to V16. Click the "Rotation" button and indicate that the method is "Varimax." Click "Continue" and then "OK."

```
- - - - - - - - -  F A C T O R    A N A L Y S I S  - - - - - - - -

Analysis number 1   Listwise deletion of cases with missing values

Extraction   1 for analysis    1, Principal components analysis (PCA)

Initial Statistics

Variable      Communality  *  Factor  Eigenvalue  Pct of Var  Cum Pct
                           *
V6            1.00000      *    1      2.16949       19.7        19.7
V7            1.00000      *    2      1.52651       13.9        33.6
V8            1.00000      *    3      1.21401       11.0        44.6
V9            1.00000      *    4      1.15647       10.5        55.1
V10           1.00000      *    5       .96236        8.7        63.9
V11           1.00000      *    6       .87942        8.0        71.9
V12           1.00000      *    7       .85297        7.8        79.6
V13           1.00000      *    8       .66626        6.1        85.7
V14           1.00000      *    9       .53738        4.9        90.6
V15           1.00000      *   10       .52335        4.8        95.3
V16           1.00000      *   11       .51179        4.7       100.0

PCA    extracted   4 factors.

Factor Matrix

              Factor  1     Factor 2     Factor 3     Factor 4

V6            .48560       -.12155      -.07395      -.06825
V7            .58666        .09163      -.02889      -.55312
V8            .54770       -.02185       .04303      -.57749
V9            .39640       -.60705       .38974       .17432
V10           .35969       -.54833       .44081       .30950
V11           .38471        .54709       .23438       .23660
V12           .41746        .62452       .21684       .24121
V13           .29287        .34152       .23684       .25259
V14           .32883       -.01266       .12861      -.18292
V15           .51387       -.14700      -.56898       .25883
V16           .47201       -.07712      -.60109       .32830
```

and merchandise selection). The third factor has strong negative loadings for
V15 and V16 (importance of helpful people and speedy service), and the fourth
factor has strong negative loadings for V7 and V8 (importance of everyday prices
and sale prices).

Overall, the results shown in this initial factor matrix are not easily interpretable. The first factor is undifferentiated, indicating that all of these variables

```
Final Statistics

Variable      Communality  *   Factor  Eigenvalue  Pct of Var   Cum Pct
                           *
V6                .26071   *      1      2.16949       19.7        19.7
V7                .65934   *      2      1.52651       13.9        33.6
V8                .63580   *      3      1.21401       11.0        44.6
V9                .70793   *      4      1.15647       10.5        55.1
V10               .72015   *
V11               .55822   *
V12               .66950   *
V13               .32230   *
V14               .15829   *
V15               .67640   *
V16               .69783   *


VARIMAX   rotation   1 for extraction   1 in analysis   1 - Kaiser
Normalization.  VARIMAX converged in 5 iterations.

Rotated Factor Matrix

                 Factor 1     Factor 2     Factor 3     Factor 4

V6                .36546       .06511       .18934       .29505
V7                .79984       .07763      -.06487       .09675
V8                .79629      -.00448       .02915       .02918
V9                .15127      -.05338       .82375       .06026
V10               .02942       .04742       .84551       .04631
V11               .09471       .73985      -.02890       .03338
V12               .11222       .80498      -.07804       .05309
V13               .02100       .56048       .08585       .01874
V14               .36187       .10251       .12972       .00240
V15               .10702       .01431       .06299       .81288
V16               .02578       .06364       .00754       .83250

Factor Transformation Matrix

                 Factor 1     Factor 2     Factor 3     Factor 4

Factor 1          .65867       .42707       .35056       .51076
Factor 2          .00673       .71817      -.68128      -.14157
Factor 3          .06402       .36272       .54023      -.75663
Factor 4          .74968       .41264       .34802       .38287
```

move together to some extent. The second factor is a mixture of disparate elements. The third and fourth factors are cleaner, though negative. This type of result—somewhat messy and not easy to interpret—is often obtained from the first stage of a factor analysis.

■ The next section of Exhibit 19.1 shows the final communalities for the eleven variables. These communalities indicate the percentage of variance in each

EXHIBIT 19.2

A Scree Plot
for the Factor
Analysis of V6
to V16

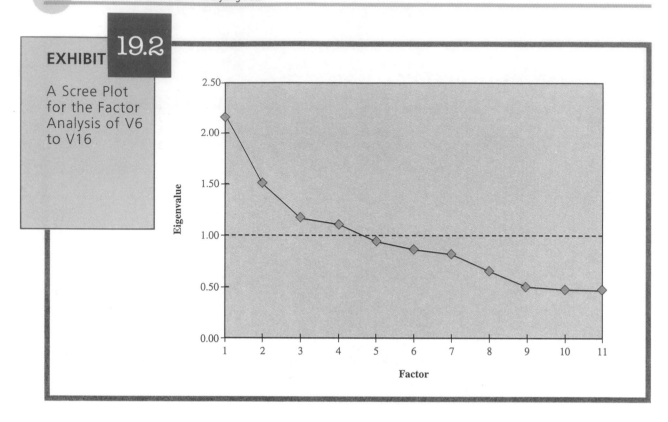

Critical Thinking Skills

Exhibit 19.2 shows a scree plot for the eigenvalues in this analysis. Considering this plot, the eigenvalues themselves, and your interpretation of the factors, how many factors would you retain in this analysis? Why?

variable that is explained by the four retained factors. They are calculated as the sums of the squared loadings for each variable across the four factors.

The communality for V6 (importance of location) is .26071, which indicates that the four retained factors account for only 26 percent of the variance in this variable. The communality for V14 (importance of having merchandise in stock) is even lower, at .15829. The low communalities mean that these variables are not well captured by the four retained factors. If we wish to retain these variables for purposes of interpretation or analysis, then we will need to retain them as individual variables in addition to the factors obtained from the factor analysis.

■   The next section of the exhibit shows a "rotated" factor matrix. The concept of factor rotation is explained in Marketing Research Tools 19.1 and illustrated in Exhibit 19.3 (see page 556).

The rotated factors shown in Exhibit 19.3 are easier to interpret than the initial factors. The first factor is clearly a price factor, with very high loadings for V7 and V8 (importance of everyday prices and sale prices) and low loadings for all other variables. The second factor is clearly a merchandise factor, with high loadings for V11, V12, and V13 (importance of merchandise quality, merchandise selection, and brand names). The third factor is clearly a credit factor, with high loadings for V9 and V10 (importance of taking credit cards and having a

MARKETING RESEARCH TOOLS

19.1

HOW FACTOR ROTATION WORKS

The purpose of factor rotation is to improve the interpretability of the factors.

In graphic terms, the variables in a factor analysis can be represented as lines running through a space defined by the factors, as shown in Exhibit 19.3A (See page 556). The distance of the line which represents a variable from the axis, which represents a factor is determined by the variable's loading on that factor. A high loading means a high correlation between the variable and the factor, so the lines are close to each other. A low loading means a low correlation, so the lines are far away from each other.

A factor rotation program literally rotates the factors so they become closer to some variables and farther from others. The goal is to sharpen the definition of the factors.

For example, in Exhibit 19.3B, the factors have been rotated so that Factor 1 is closer to Variables 1 and 2 and farther from Variable 3, and Factor 2 is closer to Variable 3 and farther from Variable 1. Now, instead of having medium-sized loadings for all of the variables on all of the factors, Factor 1 will be clearly defined by Variables 1 and 2, and Factor 2 will be clearly defined by Variable 3. This exhibit shows **orthogonal rotation,** in which the repositioning of the factors is subject to a constraint that they remain at right angles (orthogonal) to each other; that is, the factors must remain uncorrelated.

Exhibit 19.3C shows a different factor rotation. The principle is the same; Factor 1 has been moved closer to Variables 1 and 2, and Factor 2 has moved *very* close to Variable 3. This exhibit shows **oblique rotation,** in which the factors are not constrained to remain at right angles; i.e., the factors can become correlated.

Rotation creates sharp loading patterns, with some variables loading very highly on a factor and the other variables loading as close to zero as possible. The interpretation of the factors may completely change in the process.

---

store card). The fourth factor is a service factor, with high loadings for V15 and V16 (importance of helpful people and speedy service). The names given to these factors are a judgment call by the analyst.

Given this rotated factor matrix, the eleven original variables can be grouped as follows:

Store Choice Factors	Corresponding Variables
Price	V7, V8
Merchandise	V11, V12, V13
Credit availability	V9, V10
Service	V15, V16
Location	V6
Having goods in stock	V14

Keep in mind that this list does *not* reflect the importance of these factors in determining store choice for any given store. The list simply represents a grouping of the original eleven variables.

EXHIBIT **19.3**

How Factor
Rotation
Works

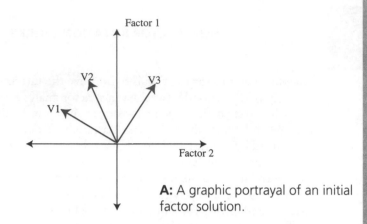

A: A graphic portrayal of an initial factor solution.

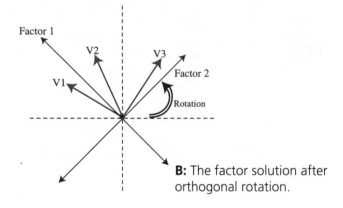

B: The factor solution after orthogonal rotation.

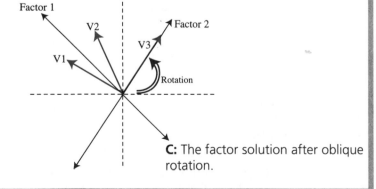

C: The factor solution after oblique rotation.

- The final section of Exhibit 19.1 (see page 553) shows the factor transformation matrix associated with the factor rotation. The numbers in this matrix are the correlations between the original four factors and the rotated factors. These correlations have no particular application or interpretation in market research.

Issues in Using Factor Analysis

Issues that arise in doing or interpreting factor analyses include the following:

- All of the variables in a factor analysis should be quantitative in nature, so that correlations are meaningful. Strictly speaking, this means that the variables should have interval or ratio scaling. However, as a practical matter, ordinal variables (such as V6 to V16) and dummy (0-1) variables also produce satisfactory results.

- Factor analysis relies on *linear* relationships among variables. If some variables are expected to have nonlinear relationships, and you want the analysis to reflect these relationships, then some type of data transformation may be appropriate. In practice, this is seldom done.

- A factor analysis can be either a principal components analysis or a common factor analysis, as discussed earlier in this chapter. A principal components analysis will explain a lower percentage of the available variance because it has been asked to explain unique as well as common variance, but the two methods usually produce similar interpretation patterns in other regards. It is best not to worry about the distinction between these methods. It is best just to run principal components analysis when doing factor analysis; this is the method used in most market research applications of factor analysis.

- Since there is no formal significance test to indicate whether the overall results of a factor analysis are meaningful, it is necessary to make a judgment in this regard. One way of making this judgment is by using a rule of thumb that a meaningful factor analysis should account for at least 70 percent of the total variance in participating variables. However, this is not a hard-and-fast rule. For example, the factor analysis of V6 to V16 seems meaningful even though the four "significant" factors explain only 55 percent of the variance.

- Judgment is also necessary to determine the number of factors that should be retained and/or interpreted. A good rule of thumb is to retain only as many factors as have eigenvalues larger than 1.0. However, this approach may fail to account for meaningful items. For example, in the interpretation of the V6 to V16 results, two single-variable factors (for V6 and V14) were added to account for variables not captured in the four "significant" multivariate factors.

Author Tips

It is almost always useful to rotate the initial results obtained from a factor analysis. The decision between orthogonal and oblique rotations depends on the objectives of the analysis. If the purpose of a factor analysis is to remove multicollinearity from a set of variables and produce uncorrelated factors that can be used in subsequent analyses, orthogonal rotations are the way to go. If the purpose of a factor analysis is to get the sharpest possible definition of factors, oblique rotations are appropriate (though orthogonal rotations may also produce satisfactory results). In SPSS for Windows, the "Varimax" option will produce an orthogonal rotation and the "Direct oblimin" option produces an oblique rotation).

- Judgment is also needed to label or interpret factors. As stated earlier, the usual rule of thumb is to ignore variables with loadings less than .50 (in absolute value) and to name the factor based on the variables with high loadings. However, this rule is open to judgment.

- If the purpose of the factor analysis is to simplify the data by reducing the number of variables, there are various ways of using the results. Two options were discussed earlier in this chapter. One option is to use the factors themselves as the new variables. Another option is to use the factor analysis simply to identify variables that should be combined and to combine them with simple summated scales. A third option is to choose one representative variable from each group and simply ignore other variables. In general, summated scales tend to work the best.

- Our final issue concerns the difference between **exploratory factor analysis** and **confirmatory factor analysis.** The focus in this discussion has been on "exploratory" analysis, in which the analyst makes no prior specification of groups and the computer forms the groups according to purely mathematical criteria. In the alternative, "confirmatory" approach, the analyst specifies variable groupings and tests whether this grouping scheme seems to provide adequate fit to the data. Confirmatory factor analysis can be done as a subset of structural equations modeling, which was briefly discussed in Appendix 18.1.

   In general, confirmatory factor analysis is more appropriate when the purpose of the analysis is to test a theory of multivariate relationships. If the purpose of the analysis is simply to describe or simplify the data, exploratory analysis is appropriate.

Critical Thinking Skills

Using the SPORTS data set, run a factor analysis on V17 to V27 (Smith's ratings on the various dimensions). How many factors should be retained? Which variables load on these factors? How much of the variance is explained? How does this amount compare to the amount of variance explained in Exhibit 19.1 (see page 552)?

Cluster Analysis

Description of the Procedure

As noted in the previous section, factor analysis groups items on the basis of their correlational patterns. It can group either variables or observations but is usually used to group variables. **Cluster analysis,** in contrast, is usually used to group observations. It is commonly used to identify market segments.

Cluster analysis also differs from factor analysis in that it does not group observations on the basis of correlational patterns but rather on the basis of absolute differences (distances) across a series of variables. To see the difference between grouping by correlations and grouping by distances, imagine four observations that take the following values for four variables:

	VAR1	VAR2	VAR3	VAR4
Observation 1	1	2	2	1
Observation 2	6	7	7	6
Observation 3	2	1	2	1
Observation 4	7	6	7	6

In grouping these observations, a correlational procedure will group Obs1 with Obs2 and Obs3 with Obs4, because these observations rise and fall together. A grouping procedure based on distances, such as cluster analysis, will group Obs1 with Obs3 and Obs2 with Obs4, because they have similar values across the four variables.

The groups obtained from a cluster analysis are called, not surprisingly, **clusters.** Given a data set with n usable observations, a full-scale cluster analysis routine produces a "one-cluster solution," in which all of the observations are lumped into a single cluster, a "two-cluster solution," in which the observations are grouped into two clusters, a "three-cluster solution," in which the observations are grouped into three clusters, all the way to an "n-cluster solution," in which each observation constitutes a cluster all by itself. Exhibit 19.4 (see page 560) provides a visual representation of clustering using Observations 1, 2, and 3 in the preceding example.

The various levels of cluster solutions can be obtained either through aggregation or disaggregation. If aggregation is used, the cluster analysis starts with the "n-cluster solution" in which each observation is distinct (such as is shown in Exhibit 19.4B). The analysis then merges observations, step by step, until it reaches the completely aggregated "one-cluster solution" (Exhibit 19.4D). At each step, distances are calculated among all of the observations and/or clusters defined on the previous step, and the two observations or clusters that are nearest each other are merged.

Disaggregation works in the reverse fashion. It starts with the "one-cluster solution" (Exhibit 19.4D) and separates the most distant observations or clusters from one another, step by step, until it reaches the completely disaggregated "n-cluster solution" (Exhibit 19.4B).

Distances can be measured in various ways. The two most common methods are called *Euclidean distance* and *city block distance*. The **Euclidean distance** between two observations, Obs$_i$ and Obs$_j$, is measured as

$$D_{ij} = \Sigma(x_{ik} - x_{jk})^2,$$

where D_{ij} is the distance between observations i and j, x_{ik} is the value of observation i for variable x_k, x_{jk} is the value of observation j for variable x_k, and the squared differences are calculated and summed across all variables being used in the analysis. The **city block distance** between the same two observations is measured as the sum of the absolute differences:

$$D_{ij} = \Sigma|x_{ik} - x_{jk}|.$$

For example, let us go back to the hypothetical observations given and calculate the distances among the first three observations:

	VAR1	VAR2	VAR3	VAR4
Observation 1	1	2	2	1
Observation 2	6	7	7	6
Observation 3	2	1	2	1

EXHIBIT 19.4

How Cluster
Analysis Works

A: Representation of the distances between observations 1, 2, and 3.

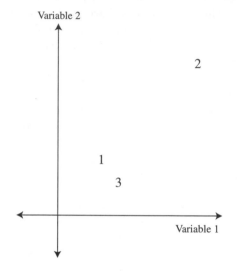

B: A three-cluster solution would have each observation in a separate cluster.

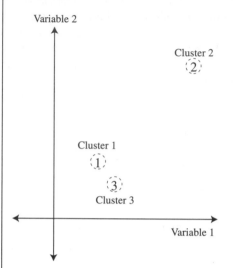

C: A two-cluster solution would have observations 1 and 3 in one cluster and observation 2 in another cluster.

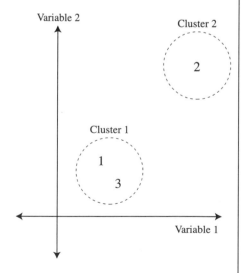

D: A one-cluster solution would have all the observations in the same cluster.

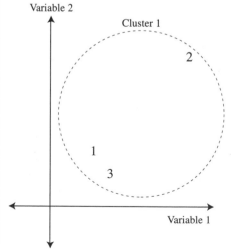

The Euclidean distances among these observations, measured across the four variables, are

$$D_{12} = (1-6)^2 + (2-7)^2 + (2-7)^2 + (1-6)^2 = 100$$
$$D_{13} = (1-2)^2 + (2-1)^2 + (2-2)^2 + (1-1)^2 = 2$$
$$D_{23} = (6-2)^2 + (7-1)^2 + (7-2)^2 + (6-1)^2 = 102.$$

The city block distances are

$$D_{12} = |1-6| + |2-7| + |2-7| + |1-6| = 20$$
$$D_{13} = |1-2| + |2-1| + |2-2| + |1-1| = 2$$
$$D_{23} = |6-2| + |7-1| + |7-2| + |6-1| = 20.$$

No matter which distance measure is used, an aggregating cluster analysis applied to these observations will start with the three observations in separate clusters and will, on the next step, combine Obs1 and Obs3 because the distance between these observations is smallest. A disaggregating procedure will start with all three observations in a single cluster and will, on the next step, split Obs2 into a cluster by itself because its distance from the other two observations is largest. In this example, the two different distance measures and the two different clustering approaches (aggregating versus disaggregating) produce the same clusters, however, this does not always happen.

Once observations are placed into clusters, a question arises as to how the distances between clusters should be measured. Two approaches are used:

- One is to use the distances between the "nearest neighbors" from each cluster. For example, given Euclidean distances for the three observations, the distance from Obs2 to the Obs1-Obs3 cluster would be measured as the distance from Obs2 to Obs1 (i.e., 100), because Obs1 is Obs2's nearest neighbor in the cluster. This approach is similar to measuring the distance from New York City to New Jersey by comparing their closest points and ignoring the fact that parts of New York and New Jersey are much farther apart.

- Another is to use the distance between the cluster centroids, or averages. Given the observations, the Euclidean distance between Obs2 and the Obs1-Obs3 cluster centroid is

$$(6-1.5)^2 + (7-1.5)^2 + (7-2)^2 + (6-1)^2 = 100.5.$$

This approach is similar to measuring the distance between New York City and New Jersey by taking the distance between the geographic center of New York City and the geographic center of New Jersey.

Descriptive Results

Three descriptive results are obtained at each stage of a cluster analysis:

- *The cluster centroids.* These centroids help us describe each cluster by showing the variables on which it has high or low average values.

- *The number of observations belonging to each cluster.* If cluster analysis is used to identify market segments—which is the usual purpose of using this procedure—the size of the cluster indicates the size of the market segment.

Critical Thinking Skills

Pat gives Smith's a rating of 5 (the maximum) on everyday prices, and 1 (the minimum) on merchandise quality. John rates Smith's 3 on both dimensions. Jane rates Smith's 5 on both dimensions. If Euclidean distance is used, who is closer to Jane? If city block distance is used, who is closer to Jane? Which measure do you think is more appropriate in this situation? Why?

- *The determination of cluster membership for specific observations.* This result may be desired in subsequent analyses; for example, we might use a cluster analysis to define market segments, then use a discriminant analysis with segment membership as the dependent variable to identify variables that predict segment membership.

Inferential Results

Two types of inferential analysis are appropriate in a cluster analysis:

- Testing whether the overall analysis is "significant" in the sense of effectively accomplishing its grouping objectives
- Testing the number of clusters that should be retained; in other words, which cluster solution should be used

As with factor analysis, the inferential results in a cluster analysis are achieved through rules of thumb rather than formal statistical tests:

- The overall significance of the analysis is decided purely by judgment. If the results are meaningful and useful, the analysis is a success. Otherwise, it is not.
- There are three ways of determining the number of clusters to keep. One approach is to use a **scree test** to look for jumps in the distances used at each stage of the analysis. Consider, for example, the three observations for which distances have already been calculated. Possible cluster solutions for these observations are as follows:

Number of Clusters	Clusters	Euclidean Distance Traveled to Join Nearest Neighbors
3	Obs1, Obs2, Obs3	0
2	Obs1-Obs3, Obs2	2
1	Obs1-Obs3-Obs2	100

In the three-cluster solution, all of the observations lie in their own clusters, and there is no distance between members of the same cluster. To form the two-cluster solution, Obs1 is grouped with Obs3, and the distance traveled to make this grouping is 2 (the distance between Obs1 and Obs3). To form the one-cluster solution, Obs2 is joined with the Obs1-Obs3 cluster, and the distance traveled to make this grouping is 100 (the distance between Obs2 and its nearest neighbor in the Obs1-Obs3 cluster).

In this example, the distances traveled to form clusters show a big jump between the two-cluster solution and the one-cluster solution. This suggests that the clustering procedure has grouped dissimilar observations to get the one-cluster solution. As a result, the two-cluster solution should probably be used.

A second approach to choosing a cluster solution is to rely on the interpretability of the cluster centroids. If a three-cluster solution produces clusters that correspond to managers' understanding of market segments and a four-cluster solution produces segments that seem odd, the three-cluster solution would be preferable.

A third approach to deciding the number of clusters is simply to specify the number of clusters in advance of the analysis. For example, when 1,000 buyers are cluster-analyzed for purposes of defining market segments, an 800- or 900-cluster solution is not useful, because each cluster will be too small to be meaningful. In this case, it would probably be better to use three to ten market segments. Rather than run all possible solutions, it makes sense to restrict the analysis to a plausible range of outcomes and then to use distance measures or judgment to select a solution from within that range.

Marketing Research Applications of Cluster Analysis

Cluster analysis is mostly used in marketing research to form groups of customers for market segmentation purposes. This is done at two levels. Within specific industries, customers can be grouped according to behaviors and preferences for the particular product category. For example, Case Study 19.1 describes how Mobil Oil has segmented gasoline buyers according to the ways in which they use gasoline stations and the things they care about.

At a broader level, consumers can be grouped according to "values, attitudes, and lifestyles," to give companies a broader view of the kinds of people who buy their products. For example, Case Study 19.2 describes how Claritas Corporation has created "geodemographic" segments to help companies identify the geographic areas they should target for marketing purposes.

Cluster analysis also can be used for other purposes. For example, products can be clustered according to their scores across some set of variables. Variables can also be clustered by (1) calculating correlations among all of the variables to be clustered, (2) subtracting the absolute value of each correlation from 1.0, (3) using the resulting values as measures of distance between the variables, and (4) clustering on the basis of these distances. These applications of cluster sampling are much less common than segmentation applications.

An Illustrative Analysis

Exhibit 19.5 (see page 566) shows an example of cluster analysis. In this example, the 291 respondents in the SPORTS data set are clustered according to their answers to V6 to V16 (these variables measure the importance of eleven store characteristics in choosing a place to buy sporting goods). The purpose of this analysis is to learn whether we can identify groups who care about different things in choosing a store.

The clustering has been done in SPSS for Windows using the "K-means cluster" command; this is an efficient clustering routine that requires the analyst to specify in advance the number of clusters that will be obtained. Three clusters have been specified for this analysis in the hope that all of the clusters will be reasonably large.

Exhibit 19.5 starts with, in succession, "Initial Cluster Centers," "Change in Cluster Centers," and "Final Cluster Centers." Of these, we are interested in only the final cluster centers, which represent the group centroids for the three final clusters. The initial cluster centers and change in cluster centers are intermediate results that are generated by the software as it goes about its work.

Author Tips

To generate the output shown in Exhibit 19.5 (see page 566) in SPSS for Windows, choose "Classify" and then "K-means cluster" from the "Statistics" menu. Specify that you want the analysis to include V6 through V16 and that you want three clusters. Click "OK."

CASE STUDY 19.1

With cappuccino in the convenience store, a concierge to assist customers, and what may be the cleanest gas station bathrooms ever, Mobil is going upscale at the pump. The new amenities are part of a major overhaul in the company's marketing strategy. Until recently, Mobil tried to lure gasoline buyers with low prices—and found profitability to be elusive. Now, a segmentation study with more than 2,000 motorists has shown the company an alternative.

Mobil's study revealed five groups of gasoline buyers, which have been labeled as follows:

- *Road warriors* are heavy users who care about credit cards, convenience stores, and car washes. They account for 16 percent of gas buyers.

- *True blues* are loyal to a brand and sometimes to a particular station. They account for 16 percent of gas buyers.

- *Generation F3* wants food and fuel, fast. These younger people account for 27 percent of gas buyers.

- *Homebodies* drive kids around and use whatever gas station is convenient and comfortable. They account for 21 percent of buyers.

- *Price shoppers* are not loyal to a brand or a station; they just look for the lowest price. They account for 20 percent of buyers.

Since only 20 percent of motorists fall into the "price shopper" group, Mobil's new approach is to "blow the customer away with product quality and service," according to Borden Walker, a Mobil executive. The company expects prices to remain reasonably competitive but is no longer interested in getting into price wars. Mobil believes that buyers will forsake lower prices in favor of "a quality buying experience."

Of course, cluster analysis was used to perform the segmentation on which Mobil's new strategy is based. If the analysis and the strategy are correct, the payoff for Mobil will be substantial. An extra 2¢ per gallon would translate into $118 million a year for the company: an extra 30¢ per share in earnings.

Source: Taken from Allanna Sullivan, "Mobil Bets Drivers Pick Cappuccino Over Low Prices," *The Wall Street Journal,* Jan. 30, 1995, p. B1. Reprinted by permission of *The Wall Street Journal,* © 1995 Dow Jones & Company, Inc. All Rights Reserved Worldwide.

The final cluster centers show each cluster's average value on V6 to V16, the eleven variables that form the basis of the clustering. An examination of these averages reveals that Cluster 2 is relatively high on V9 and V10, which measure the importance of credit availability. This cluster might be called the "credit-oriented" segment of respondents. Clusters 1 and 3 have no clear identifying features. Cluster 1 seems to contain people who gave relatively low ratings across the board, and Cluster 3 is similar to Cluster 2 except for V9 and V10.

After showing the cluster centroids, Exhibit 19.5 gives the cluster sizes. Both weighted and unweighted results are shown; the weighted results allow the analyst to

CASE STUDY 19.2

One tool marketers use in targeting consumer groups is PRIZM (Potential Rating Index by Zip Market), a "geodemographic" segmentation system developed by Virginia-based Claritas Inc. PRIZM has used information on demographic characteristics, lifestyles, and buying habits to group zip codes into sixty-two clusters that have been given descriptive names such as "Furs and Station Wagons," "Pools and Patios," and "Hispanic Mix."

Restaurants, banks, and stores use PRIZM to pinpoint the areas that have the highest potential for new outlets. Other marketers use it to target mailings and advertising. Often, they find surprises; for example, the blue-collar households of "Rural Industria" are a good market for pagers, and "Golden Ponds" seniors love theme parks.

The U.S. Army found that its top clusters for recruiting high school graduates were zip codes labeled "Shotguns and Pickups," "Mines and Mills," and "Blue Collar Nursery." The worst clusters for the army were "Bohemian Mix," "Blue Blood Estates," "Money and Brains," and "Urban Gold Coast." The army found that *Field & Stream* and *Mechanix Illustrated* were good media for reaching its top clusters.

A PRIZM report costs as little as $99, but marketers that use PRIZM heavily can pay more than $100,000 in annual licensing fees.

Source: Michael J. Weiss, *The Clustering of America* (New York: Harper & Row, 1988); Christina Del Valle and Jon Berry, "They Know Where You Live—and How You Buy," *Business Week,* Feb. 7, 1994, p. 89.

---

weight certain variables more heavily in the classification exercise. In this example, no weights have been used, so the weighted and unweighted results are the same. These results show that Clusters 2 and 3 are of similar size, with 113 and 115 members, respectively (40 percent and 41 percent of the sample). Cluster 1 is smaller, with 53 members (19 percent).

These results can be interpreted in either of two ways. One interpretation is that the general failure to find sharp differences among segments on specific variables indicates that these variables do not provide a basis for meaningful market segmentation. Another possible interpretation is that the results show a meaningful, "credit-oriented" segment that represents 40 percent of the sample.

To decide which interpretation is better, it helps to look at another solution. Accordingly, the analysis shown in Exhibit 19.6 (see page 568) was run. This is a K-means cluster analysis for which *five* clusters have been specified.

Start with the last section of Exhibit 19.6, which shows cluster sizes. The five-cluster solution produced three small clusters (Clusters 2, 3, and 4) and two larger clusters (Clusters 1 and 5).

The final cluster centroids show that Clusters 1 and 5 are similar. Both clusters are relatively high on V11 to V13 (importance of merchandise quality, merchandise selection, and brand names). Overall, it seems appropriate to regard these two clusters as two slightly different versions of the same thing—a "merchandise-oriented"

EXHIBIT 19.5

An Illustration of Cluster Analysis

```
* * * * * * * * Q U I C K   C L U S T E R * * * * * * * * *
Initial Cluster Centers

Cluster       V6            V7            V8            V9

   1        3.0000        3.0000        2.0000        1.0000
   2        1.0000        1.0000        1.0000        3.0000
   3        1.0000        3.0000        3.0000        1.0000

Cluster       V10           V11           V12           V13

   1        1.0000        1.0000        1.0000        1.0000
   2        3.0000        3.0000        3.0000        1.0000
   3        1.0000        3.0000        3.0000        3.0000

Cluster       V14           V15           V16

   1        3.0000        2.0000        2.0000
   2        1.0000        3.0000        3.0000
   3        1.0000        2.0000        1.0000

Convergence achieved due to no or small distance change. The
maximum distance by which any center has changed is .0625.
Current iteration is 7.
Minimum distance between initial centers is 4.6904.

Iteration        Change in Cluster Centers.
                    1          2          3
   1            2.93E+00   3.51E+00   3.03E+00
   2            4.55E-01   3.73E-01   2.67E-01
   3            2.86E-01   1.29E-01   1.66E-01
   4            3.73E-01   5.87E-02   1.60E-01
   5            2.39E-01   2.20E-02   9.87E-02
   6            1.53E-01    .0000     7.06E-02
   7            1.22E-01    .0000     5.26E-02
```

segment of respondents. If we regard the two clusters in this way and merge them into a single "supercluster," this single cluster accounts for 170 of the 281 usable observations (60 percent).

The second, third, and fourth clusters are ambiguous as well as small. Cluster 2 has relatively high scores on V9 and V10 (credit availability) and might be interpreted as a small, "credit-oriented" segment accounting for 11 percent of the sample. Clusters 3 and 4 have no particular distinguishing features.

Overall, there is quite a bit of interpretive difference between the five-cluster solution and the three-cluster solution. The failure to find convergence suggests that there is no natural, robust segment structure in the data. One might continue to play around with other cluster solutions to gain further insight, but at this point the best interpretation may be that respondents in the SPORTS data cannot be meaningfully segmented on the basis of their answers to V6 to V16.

```
Final Cluster Centers

Cluster        V6              V7              V8              V9

    1        2.2830          2.2075          1.8679          1.4528
    2        2.8053          2.8407          2.6903          2.8230
    3        2.6783          2.9217          2.8087          1.6783

Cluster        V10             V11             V12             V13

    1        1.6415          2.7547          2.7170          2.1887
    2        2.7965          2.8673          2.8496          2.6637
    3        1.3913          2.9478          2.9217          2.7826

Cluster        V14             V15             V16

    1        2.4151          2.2264          2.2642
    2        2.7345          2.7965          2.7434
    3        2.7217          2.7826          2.8087


Number of Cases in Each Cluster.

Cluster   Unweighted Cases   Weighted Cases

    1              53.0              53.0
    2             113.0             113.0
    3             115.0             115.0

Missing cases:          10
Valid cases:         281.0             281.0
```

Issues in Using Cluster Analysis

Issues that arise in doing or interpreting cluster analyses include the following:

- All of the variables that are used in a cluster analysis should be quantitative (though ordinal variables and dummy variables generally produce satisfactory results). The procedure relies upon calculation of distances among items, and distances are meaningful only for variables with interval or ratio scaling.

- In conducting a cluster analysis, it must be decided (1) whether to aggregate or disaggregate at successive stages of the analysis, (2) which distance measure to use, and (3) how to measure distances among clusters. All three of these issues were discussed earlier in this chapter.

EXHIBIT 19.6

Another Illustration of Cluster Analysis

```
* * * * * * * * * Q U I C K   C L U S T E R * * * * * * * * * *

Initial Cluster Centers

Cluster        V6              V7              V8              V9

    1        1.0000          3.0000          3.0000          1.0000
    2        3.0000          3.0000          3.0000          3.0000
    3        3.0000          1.0000          1.0000          3.0000
    4        3.0000          3.0000          2.0000          1.0000
    5        1.0000          3.0000          1.0000          3.0000

Cluster        V10             V11             V12             V13

    1        1.0000          3.0000          3.0000          3.0000
    2        3.0000          3.0000          1.0000          1.0000
    3        1.0000          3.0000          3.0000          3.0000
    4        1.0000          1.0000          1.0000          1.0000
    5        3.0000          2.0000          3.0000          3.0000

Cluster        V14             V15             V16

    1        1.0000          2.0000          1.0000
    2        1.0000          3.0000          3.0000
    3        1.0000          3.0000          3.0000
    4        3.0000          2.0000          2.0000
    5        3.0000          3.0000          2.0000

Convergence achieved due to no or small distance change.
The maximum distance by which any center has changed is
.0607.
   Current iteration is 6.
Minimum distance between initial centers is 4.2426.

Iteration      Change in Cluster Centers
                  1          2          3          4          5
        1      2.57E+00   2.41E+00   2.52E+00   2.61E+00   2.65E+00
        2      1.65E-01   2.96E-01   2.38E-01   2.24E-01   2.28E-01
        3      2.00E-01   3.06E-01   2.90E-01   1.95E-01   1.09E-01
        4      1.28E-01   2.30E-01   2.45E-01   1.14E-01   5.04E-02
        5      1.38E-01   1.27E-01   2.47E-01   1.33E-01   1.33E-02
        6      8.61E-02      .0000   1.23E-01   8.00E-02   3.32E-02
```

Most cluster analysis situations will produce similar results no matter which decisions are made in response to these questions. However, this is not always true. To determine whether results are sensitive to these issues, the analysis must be run using different approaches. If different approaches produce different results, the results that are most meaningful and useful should be used. There is no "correct" approach.

■ Since cluster analysis groups observations on the basis of absolute distances, it is sensitive to the scale magnitude of the variables. For example, consider the following three people:

```
* * * * * * * * * Q U I C K   C L U S T E R * * * * * * * * *

Final Cluster Centers

Cluster        V6              V7              V8              V9

     1        2.4861          2.6250          2.5417          1.0694
     2        2.5625          2.7813          2.7188          2.7813
     3        2.6383          2.8723          2.7660          2.4894
     4        2.5625          2.5625          1.9688          1.4063
     5        2.8469          2.8469          2.6837          2.6633

Cluster       V10             V11             V12             V13

     1        1.5278          2.9583          2.9028          2.9028
     2        2.7188          2.8438          2.6563          1.5313
     3        1.1277          2.9362          2.8511          2.8298
     4        1.4375          2.6250          2.6563          1.6250
     5        2.7245          2.8878          2.9490          3.0000

Cluster       V14             V15             V16

     1        2.6111          2.5833          2.6111
     2        2.5313          2.7188          2.6875
     3        2.5532          2.6170          2.7660
     4        2.5313          2.5000          2.4688
     5        2.8571          2.8367          2.7551

Number of Cases in Each Cluster

Cluster       Unweighted Cases      Weighted Cases

     1              72.0                 72.0
     2              32.0                 32.0
     3              47.0                 47.0
     4              32.0                 32.0
     5              98.0                 98.0

Missing cases:            10
Valid cases:            281.0                281.0
```

	Gender	Years of Education	Annual Income
Ann	2	18	$37,000
Betty	2	18	$35,000
Carl	1	10	$34,500

Intuitively, it might seem that Ann and Betty are most similar among these three people. Ann and Betty have the same gender, the same level of education (master's degree), and almost the same income. Carl has a different gender and a much different level of education, though almost the same income.

However, a cluster analysis will start by grouping Carl and Betty, because the scale of the income variable will dominate the analysis. The fact that Betty is only $500 away from Carl, compared with $2,000 away from Ann, will overwhelm the fact that she matches Ann and differs from Carl on gender and education.

In order to avoid a situation in which variables with high magnitudes completely dominate the cluster analysis, it is appropriate to *standardize* all of the variables before running the analysis, that is, to express observations in terms of units of standard deviation for each variable. However, if all of the variables are measured on a similar scale, scale magnitude is usually not a problem. For example, the data were not standardized when the SPORTS data were clustered on the basis of V6 to V16 because all eleven of those variables were measured on the same four-point scale.

- A related matter is the issue of overlapping or redundant variables. Consider, for example, V6 to V16 in the SPORTS data. These variables include one variable to measure the importance of store location (V6) and three or four variables to measure the importance of merchandise (V11, V12, V13, and possibly V14). This means that the overall distance measure between two observations will reflect three scores for the merchandise dimension, compared with only one for the location dimension. As a result, the merchandise dimension will tend to have more influence in the analysis.

  This problem can be addressed in a couple of ways. One approach is to combine the overlapping variables into a single summated scale, then standardize this scale to eliminate the extra magnitude introduced by the summation. Another approach is to factor-analyze the variables, then use the factors as a basis for cluster analysis. Either approach works well.

Critical Thinking Skills

Cluster respondents in the SPORTS data set on the basis of the ratings of Smith's Stores. Calculate a three-group solution and a five-group solution. What conclusions do you draw?

Multidimensional Scaling (MDS)

Description of the Technique

In the previous chapter, we described how discriminant analysis can be used to generate product space maps that illustrate similarities and dissimilarities among products. **Multidimensional scaling (MDS)** is an alternative procedure for accomplishing the same purpose. MDS can be used for other purposes as well, but in marketing research it is used almost exclusively for product space mapping.

In product space maps generated with MDS, the products need not be rated on any specific variables. Instead, respondents are simply asked to indicate the overall similarities of the products to be mapped. These similarities can be obtained through paired comparisons (e.g., the similarity between Coke and Pepsi is greater than the similarity between Coke and Sprite) or through numerical ratings of similarity (e.g., on a ten-point scale where "0" represents that the items are identical and "10" represents complete dissimilarity, the similarity between Coke and Pepsi is 1 and the similarity between Coke and Sprite is 7).

Given similarity data, an MDS program (there are several) constructs a network of distances in which the most similar products are closest to each other and the least similar products are farthest from each other. The program then tries to reproduce these distances in a one-dimensional mapping of the data, a two-dimensional mapping, a three-dimensional mapping, and so on.

Consider the following example. A consumer is asked to rate the similarities of four beverages: Coke, milk, coffee, and orange juice. The consumer is asked to rate these similarities on a ten-point scale where "0" means "completely similar" and "10" means "completely dissimilar." The consumer gives the following ratings:

Products	Similarity Rating
Coke, milk	8
Coke, coffee	3
Coke, orange juice	4
Milk, coffee	6
Milk, orange juice	5
Coffee, orange juice	4

Since the higher numbers represent *dissimilarity* in these ratings, we will use the ratings as direct measures of distance. Therefore, in mapping these data, the distance should be 8 between Coke and milk, 3 between Coke and coffee, 4 between Coke and orange juice, and so on.

Now let us try to reproduce these distances in a one-dimensional space—that is, on a line. We will start by locating Coke on a line (it does not matter which product we start with, and it does not matter where we locate it—only the distances are meaningful). We will locate milk, coffee, and orange juice on the same line at distances of 8, 3, and 4 from Coke. The result is as follows:

Coke			Coffee	Orange Juice				Milk	
0	1	2	3	4	5	6	7	8	9

So far, so good. However, problems emerge when we check the distances of milk, coffee, and orange juice from each other. According to the data, these distances should be 6 between milk and coffee, 5 between milk and orange juice, and 4 between coffee and orange juice. However, in this mapping, the distances are 5, 4, and 1, respectively. We can express the differences between the target distances and the observed distances as follows:

Products	Target Distance	Observed Distance	Squared Discrepancy
Coke, milk	8	8	0
Coke, coffee	3	3	0
Coke, orange juice	4	4	0
Milk, coffee	6	5	1
Milk, orange juice	5	4	1
Coffee, orange juice	4	1	9
Total			11

Different mappings will produce different results. For example, if milk is moved one space to the right in our mapping, so its distance from Coke becomes 9, the results are as follows:

Products	Target Distance	Observed Distance	Squared Discrepancy
Coke, milk	8	9	1
Coke, coffee	3	3	0
Coke, orange juice	4	4	0
Milk, coffee	6	6	0
Milk, orange juice	5	5	0
Coffee, orange juice	4	1	9
Total			10

We would like to find the mapping of these data that minimizes the sum of the squared discrepancies between the target distances and the observed distances. A multidimensional scaling program will find that mapping. Similarly, an MDS program will find the optimal two-dimensional mapping, the optimal three-dimensional mapping, and so on. (In this particular example, there will be no more than three dimensions, because k objects can define no more than $k - 1$ dimensions.)

Issues in Using Multidimensional Scaling

The following issues arise in using MDS:

- There are several MDS packages, each of which uses a particular type of input data. It is necessary to check on software availability *before* data are gathered and to make sure that the data are gathered in a form that is compatible with the MDS software available.

- It should also be considered how respondents will react to the data collection burden imposed by MDS. For example, if a space containing 10 different products is to be mapped and respondents are to provide similarity data on all possible pairs of products, each respondent must be asked to rate 45 pairs (k items form $k(k - 1)/2$ pairs). Eleven products generate 55 pairs, 15 products generate 105 pairs, 20 products generate 190 pairs, and so on.

- Results can vary according to the specific products used in an MDS. For example, if people are asked to rate the similarity of Coke, Pepsi, and Sprite, most will rate Sprite as being *dissimilar* to Coke. However, if they are asked to rate the similarity of Coke, Sprite, and milk, they will rate Sprite as being *similar* to Coke.

- An MDS analysis will produce a one-dimensional solution, a two-dimensional solution, and so on. Which of these solutions is the best?

There are two ways of making this decision. One approach is to compare the sums of squared discrepancies for the one-dimensional solution,

Author Tips

In our experience, people start getting restless when the number of comparisons gets near 20. Consequently, MDS analyses using more than 6 to 7 products (15 to 21 pairs) may require that you obtain only partial ratings from any one respondent.

two-dimensional solution, three-dimensional solution, and so on, and look for a jump in the sum of squared discrepancies. For example, consider these results:

Number of Dimensions	Sum of Squared Discrepancies
4	9
3	22
2	681
1	904

These results suggest the use of a three-dimensional mapping. The sum of squared discrepancies for this mapping is almost as good as that of the four-dimensional mapping and much better than that of the two-dimensional mapping. This suggests that whatever is being mapped fits pretty well into three dimensions but not into two dimensions.

Another approach is to rely on judgments about the usefulness of results. Despite the jump in squared discrepancies shown in this example, it might still be best to use the two-dimensional mapping if it seems easier to comprehend than the three-dimensional mapping and it produces similar insights into the structure of the market.

- In interpreting MDS results, remember that the specific location of products is arbitrary. The distances among products are the only thing that is meaningful. The map can be rotated, reversed, and turned upside down without changing the distances among products. Such movement may be needed to get a better perspective on the map and make the results more interpretable.

- As the previous point might suggest, MDS outputs are unlabeled. The axes are arbitrary and have no natural meaning. This absence of labeling can make MDS results difficult to interpret.

    The advantage of generating product space maps through a method that uses attribute ratings, such as discriminant analysis, is that the product attributes can be mapped into the results along with the products. This makes the maps easier to interpret. On the other hand, rating products on a series of attributes can be a tedious task for respondents, and it requires the analyst to know the relevant dimensions in advance. The advantage of MDS is that it allows customers to impose their own structure on the market.

As discussed in Chapter 18, product space maps are very useful tools for determining your position relative to your competitors, and both discriminant analysis and multidimensional scaling are widely used.

Summary

This chapter discussed multivariate grouping procedures. The following points were covered:

1. What are the purposes of multivariate grouping procedures?

Multivariate grouping procedures are used for three general purposes: (1) to group variables into broader, underlying factors, (2) to group customers into market segments based on their similarities across several variables, and (3) to group products or services so as to show patterns of competition among them.

2. How can factor analysis be used to analyze data?

The usual purpose of factor analysis is to see whether a large number of variables can be represented by a smaller number of underlying factors. The analysis calculates a series of linear combinations of the variables being analyzed. Each combination is called a factor, and the variables with high weights on that factor are associated with it.

Issues that arise in using factor analysis include the following: (1) all of the variables should be quantitative, (2) the analysis relies on linear relationships, (3) decisions about whether factors are meaningful are ultimately based on judgment, and (4) it is usually useful to rotate the initial results obtained from a factor analysis.

3. How can cluster analysis be used to analyze data?

Cluster analysis is used to group observations; in particular, to group customers into market segments that have similar behaviors and/or attitudes. The observations are measured on a series of variables, then are grouped according to their differences on these variables. At each step of the analysis, either the two closest observations are joined (this is an aggregating approach) or the two farthest elements are separated (this is a disaggregating approach).

Issues that arise in cluster analyses are as follows: (1) all of the variables in a cluster analysis should be quantitative, (2) it must be decided whether to aggregate or disaggregate, (3) how to measure distances must be decided, (4) cluster analysis is sensitive to the scale of the variables, (5) correlated or redundant variables will contribute disproportionately to the grouping, and (6) the interpretation of a cluster analysis is ultimately based on judgment.

4. How is multidimensional scaling used in marketing research?

In MDS, respondents indicate overall similarities among some objects, usually products. The analysis procedure then constructs product space maps in which the most similar objects are closest to each other, the least similar objects are farthest apart, and the relative distances among objects reflect their relative similarity.

Issues that arise in using MDS include the following: (1) different MDS routines use different inputs, and it is necessary to gather data in a form that is compatible with the software available, (2) MDS can impose a substantial data collection burden on respondents, (3) the results may vary according to the specific products used in the analysis, (4) only the distances among products are meaningful, (5) the axes are arbitrary and have no natural meaning, and (6) it may be helpful to rotate the results for better interpretation.

Suggested Additional Readings

The books suggested at the end of Chapter 18 are also useful if you wish to learn more about multivariate grouping procedures.

Discussion Questions

1. What are three general purposes for using multivariate grouping procedures?
2. Listed are three multivariate grouping procedures used in marketing research. How are each of these procedures commonly used in marketing research?

Factor analysis
Cluster analysis
Multidimensional scaling

3. Listed are six questions taken from a survey of heavy equipment dealers that was conducted by a manufacturer. The market researcher ran a factor analysis on these six items. Two factors were extracted. The rotated factor matrix is presented alongside the six questions. Interpret the findings. Which questions load on which factors? How would you name each of the factors?

	Factor 1	Factor 2
Q1. Overall, we are very satisfied with this manufacturer.	.703	.286
Q2. We feel good about the working relationship we have with this manufacturer.	.642	.309
Q3. We look forward to continuing our business relationship with this manufacturer.	.743	.251
Q4. This manufacturer always performs ahead of its peers.	.243	.714
Q5. This manufacturer is a market leader.	.356	.639
Q6. This manufacturer is achieving its sales potential.	.332	.624

4. Give three reasons why a market researcher might want to use factor analysis to group variables.

5. What information does the cluster centroid provide the analyst when using cluster analysis? Why might the number of observations within a cluster be important?

6. What are produce space maps? Why would they be important to a marketer? What analysis procedures could an analyst use to create a product space map?

Marketing Research Challenges

1. Look through business magazines as well as professional journals such as the *Journal of Marketing* or *Journal of Marketing Research* for one or more examples of the use of multivariate grouping procedures or of situations where such procedures might have been used. For each example you find, summarize briefly why and how a procedure was used or could have been used.

2. Using the SPORTS disk, replicate the results shown in the examples of this chapter with the same or different variables.

Internet Exercise

The Stanford Research Institute's VALS and VALS2 typologies are psychographic segmentation systems similar to the PRIZM system discussed in Case Study 19.2 (VALS stands for Values And Lifestyles). Visit the VALS homepage at http://future.sri.com/vals/valshome.html to learn more about these typologies, which were developed through cluster analysis. While you are at the site, fill out a questionnaire, and the system will classify *you*.

References

Acito, Franklin, Ronald D. Anderson, and Jack L. Engledow (1980). "A Simulation Study of Methods for Hypothesis Testing in Factor Analysis." *Journal of Marketing Research* 7 (September), pp. 141–150.

Mitchell, Susan (1995). "Birds of a Feather." *American Demographics* 17 (February), pp. 40–42.

Riche, Martha Farnsworth (1990). "New Frontiers for Geodemographics." *American Demographics* 12 (June), p. 20.

Issues in Research Management

The last four chapters of this book focus on some vital issues in marketing research management: presenting research reports, managing international research, research ethics and current issues in marketing research. These chapters are not at the end of the book because they are less important than earlier chapters: in fact, they are four of the most important chapters. They are placed here because we believe the background of the earlier chapters is necessary to appreciate fully the issues discussed.

Chapter 20 is about effectively communicating research results in both written and oral reports. Effective communication is crucial to your future success and that of the people you work with, and we believe it is possible for everyone to be an effective communicator. Effective communication, however, depends on having something valuable to communicate. The successful researcher has both good technical skills and good communication skills. Neither is a substitute for the other.

Chapter 21 discusses some of the special issues that arise when marketing research moves from one country to an international level. In addition to all the issues discussed in earlier chapters, researchers face additional issues when working in an international environment.

Chapter 22 considers ethical issues in marketing research. This chapter shows the ethical standards that have been recommended by various professional organizations and discusses both how researchers should treat research participants and how research clients and suppliers should treat each other.

Finally, Chapter 23 describes some issues that will face market researchers in the twenty-first century—the use of the Internet for research and the use of research for relationship marketing, database marketing, new-product development, total quality management, and measuring customer satisfaction.

Sample Student Project: Presenting Results to Management

Each of the class teams made two presentations to Apple management about students' use of and attitudes toward computers, using the recommendations in Chapter 20 of this book. The first presentation dealt with the results of the secondary analysis and focus groups, the second with the analysis of the survey results. The presentations used PowerPoint, transmitting computer images directly onto the screen. The presentations were kept deliberately short so that Apple management could ask questions and comment on the findings. Final written reports were also prepared by each team. A summary of the report presented by one of the teams is given here.

At the end of the semester, the Apple representative and Apple management expressed satisfaction with the information that had been obtained and initiated changes in their marketing activities. As one example, Apple staff had initially been concerned about how students rated the Micro Computer Order Center (MCOC), which was the primary source of Apple computers at the university. They learned through the survey that a large majority of students had no contact with the Micro Computer Order Center and bought their computers off campus. As a result of this, Apple decided to expand their distribution efforts with these noncampus outlets.

Students generally reported high satisfaction with the project and what they had learned while doing it. Several of the students used copies of the final report (with permission) on job interviews to illustrate their writing and analysis skills, and at least one student was hired, not by Apple but by an Apple competitor.

Brief Summary of Findings

Nearly all students on campus (99.2 percent) have had some exposure to computers. As one might expect, there is a trend that indicates an increase in computer use with year in school, which may be driven by students moving out of campus locations (where computers are easy to access) into apartments or other living arrangements (where computers are not as easy to access). The average student tends to visit the university CCSO sites 3.4 times per week, with engineers and business students tending to visit more often than other majors. Almost all students used computers for e-mail and Internet and to sign up for classes. Graphics, data analysis, and computer-aided design/programming languages were the major uses of computers related to specific majors.

Graduate students are the greatest percentage of computer owners, and of all Apple Macintosh computers, they own 45 percent of the Apple computers on campus. Freshmen are least likely to own Apple Mac computers. Unfortunately, the market for computers on campus is shrinking because an increasing percentage of students entering the university each year come with their personal computer. Still, there is a high percentage of noncomputer owners who live in apartments who are forced to use the university labs (CCSO sites). For those who own computers, the largest influence is personal friends. The important attributes of a computer (for computer owners) were reliability, ease of use, memory, price, and speed, but the characteristics the owners were looking for varied.

Buyer loyalty was also examined. Apple brand-loyals were approximately 7 percent of the computer owners. The expectation that students have about using computers after school is the largest determinant of brand loyalty. The results showed that owners of Apple computers had a higher percentage of brand switchers than those who owned IBM-compatibles, indicating a "softness" in the Apple installed base. Key target audiences for Apple were found to be the routinized brand switchers and the nonusers—their attitudes about Apple were closest to favorable, indicating they are ready targets for brand attitude improvements leading to trial. Communication objectives for Apple should be to improve the perceptions of Apple brand computers in the areas of available software, speed, reliability, and price. Word of mouth is the most effective medium for all buyer loyalty categories. Apple brand-loyals tend not to purchase through mail orders but use computer retailers. The largest percentage of Apple brand-loyals was found in the humanities, which has the largest percentage of Apple Macintosh owners.

A little over half of the students surveyed were aware of the MCOC, which is driven by computer ownership and possibly purchase intention. A majority of the students who own computers had heard of the MCOC, whereas fewer than half of the nonowners are aware of the MCOC. The indication is that awareness of the MCOC is at least in part driven by the search process when potential buyers look to buy a computer. Only half of the students who were aware of the MCOC actually visited the facility, but 20 percent who did visit the MCOC bought their computer there. Of the computers bought at the MCOC, Apple Macintosh computers dominated.

When comparing Apple Macintosh and IBM-compatible ownership, one can see different items of importance to each owner. One can also see different perceptions when evaluating the opposing computer. Apple Macintosh owners rated IBM-compatible machines as equal or better in the attributes of speed and price. A very important attribute to Apple Macintosh owners is ease of use. Finally, the Apple Macintosh owners seemed to be "pickier" than other computer owners, in that the ratings of each attribute varied considerably for IBM-compatible and Apple Macintosh when expressed by Apple owners. The ratings of both competing brands expressed by IBM-compatible owners were more even across the board.

The remainder of the document will, in more detail, discuss the findings and explain the results we determined to be relevant and important. Each section opens with a summary of findings for that section to assist the reader in locating the important points of that section.

Conclusions/Recommendations

There is a high percentage of computer ownership among freshmen and graduate students, suggesting that these two groups are a good target group. One concern is that these groups already meet or exceed the average computer ownership of 57 percentage. This may spell trouble if the market does not grow any larger than it is, especially with respect to freshmen. On the other hand, we saw from the data that freshmen and graduate students visit the MCOC at much higher rates compared with other classes, so this may imply a growing market. What is of concern is that only about 4 percent of freshmen bought their computers at the MCOC. This means that the ratio of purchasers to visitors is very low among freshmen. It may be prudent to direct promotions toward freshmen and their families. This may be done by sending brochures to their homes before they begin school so that they delay their purchase until after they have arrived at U. of I. Promotions directed toward freshmen on Quad Day may also be helpful.

We have noted the importance of positive word of mouth and how much consumers rely on advice from others when purchasing a computer. Additionally, Apple owners found brochures an important source for information, but IBM-compatible owners referred to magazines. Magazine ads are more a concern for the Apple Corporation and not the MCOC. The aspects of friends, brochures, and salespeople are sources of information the MCOC can and should concentrate on.

All of these can probably be taken care of by achieving higher awareness of the MCOC (only 57 percent of students are aware of its existence). The brochures and salespeople are useless unless people actually come in to the MCOC, so getting them in there is the first stage of the battle.

The second problem is that only about 20 percent of the MCOC visitors actually purchase a computer there. This is probably where the highest gains can be made. Just bringing this number up to 40 percent would double the MCOC sales. This directly relates to the MCOC operations. The ratings of the MCOC are fairly low; the ratings on convenience are the highest ratings amongst purchasers and nonpurchasers. This makes sense considering the location of the MCOC. Price, salesperson knowledge, before-sales service, and selection are lower in each aspect, and these are areas where there can be more improvement. Price does seem to be the greatest concern from these ratings, but it is unclear whether this refers to Dell, Apple, or both. We mentioned earlier that first-time purchasers had a high priority on ease of use; one of the tactics a salesperson should use is to assess whether this is a first purchase for the prospective buyer so as to know how to approach the customer.

Although IBM-compatibles are the popular choice, Apple still has an opportunity to gain market share with approximately 35 percent of the students who do not have a strong preference for either an IBM-compatible or Apple computer. This is where a strong salesperson would help tilt these people toward Apples.

Besides freshmen, the other two demographics identified in the paper as potential targets were humanities and the Greeks. Humanities have a slightly higher preference of Apples over IBM-compatibles, but they have a lower action response rate, so getting them to visit the MCOC would be a place to start. Additionally, we saw that nobody from Greek housing has purchased a computer (thus they have a low awareness, low action response, and no response action). This may also be an avenue for increased sales. Also, since word of mouth is one of the biggest factors in computer purchases, this should really apply to fraternity/sorority houses.

The rest of these concerns do not apply as much to the MCOC but more to Apple as a whole. Ease of use seems to be the main competitive advantage that Apple has (ease of use is the most important feature to Apple owners). Compatible owners ranked reliability as the most important feature, followed by price, memory size, etc. We did notice that Apple may begin to lose market share since fewer than half of their owners (49 percent) are considered brand-loyals and the same amount (49 percent) are considered brand switchers. As mentioned earlier, although this is a very high priority for all computer users, IBM-compatibles have a higher loyalty compared to Apples, which implies that ease of use becomes secondary as a computer user matures. Also, this gap may eventually close as Windows 95 catches on in the market.

Price, speed, and software availability have become higher priorities since our society is much more price-sensitive and the expectations of computer users have risen. This only makes sense. Although we did not explore prices of Apples and IBM-compatibles, the gap in price may be explained by a comment that was made in our focus group, where it was felt that Apple has a monopoly and therefore its prices will always be high.

Apple owners are not very aware of their computers' speed—since IBM-compatibles are sold and priced on the basis of their processor and speed, their owners are well aware of the computers' capabilities. On the other hand, if Apple Mac owners are not aware of their computers' speed, they may be benchmarking their computers' speed based on a compatible with a faster speed. This may be where the problem of perception comes in. Intel has gone to great lengths to let the public know how great the 80486 chip is. Motorola has not done this at all when it comes to the 86040 chip. Thus, whether or not a 75-MHz Motorola chip is superior to Intel's, the public is unaware of this.

20 Communicating Research Results

 OBJECTIVES

After reading this chapter, you should be able to answer the following questions:

❶ What information should be included in a research report?

❷ How can numerical tables be presented so they are easy to understand?

❸ How can charts and graphs be presented in an effective manner?

❹ How can multivariate results be communicated?

❺ How can effective oral presentations be made?

It hardly seems necessary to stress the importance of communication, both written and oral, in the business world. Over and over, we have heard about people who were hard workers but did not succeed because they could not communicate well with others. This principle applies to marketing research as well. The ultimate value of a research project depends on how well its results are communicated.

This chapter provides guidelines for preparing effective written research reports and effective oral presentations. Topics discussed in the chapter are (1) proper contents and organization of a research report, (2) how to make numerical tables that effectively communicate results, (3) how to make effective charts and graphs, (4) how to communicate multivariate results, and (5) how to make effective oral presentations. Other people may prefer somewhat different formats from those described here, but the general concepts will be applicable everywhere.

The Contents of a Research Report

In preparing a marketing research report, the key thing to remember is that a decision maker's scarcest resource is time. A report should present information in a way that minimizes the time needed to absorb the meaning of the results and allows readers to skip results that are less important to them (Mohn and Land, 1989; Payne, 1989).

A research report is more like a newspaper story than a mystery novel. The reader should be able to get the key information at the beginning of the report without having to read to the final page to discover "whodunit." Also, knowing when to omit unnecessary details is as important as knowing what to include. Inexperienced people sometimes provide excruciating detail about every step they went through in designing and analyzing the research. This is a mistake.

The outline of a typical research report is presented in Marketing Research Tools 20.1. The following text sections describe some guidelines for preparing each of these parts of the report.

Title Page

The title page gives the title of the report and indicates the source of information. In some cases, this will be the names of the individual authors; in other cases, the name of the vendor or the research department. It is also useful to give an address and a phone number that readers can call for additional information. The date of the report should also be provided for future reference. Finally, if the report has been revised, this should be noted.

Table of Contents

The table of contents gives the titles and page locations of major sections in the report. Additional mention may be made of important subsections, although a table of

MARKETING RESEARCH TOOLS

20.1

AN OUTLINE FOR MARKETING RESEARCH REPORTS

  I. Title page
 II. Table of contents
III. Executive summary
 IV. Brief description of research methods
  V. Detailed results
    A. Topic 1
      1. Topic heading
      2. Introduction and conclusions concerning this topic
      3. Detailed (text) discussion of results
      4. Supporting exhibits
        a. Numerical tables, if any
        b. Graphic displays, if any
    B. Topic 2
      1. Topic heading
      2. Introduction and conclusions concerning this topic
      3. Detailed (text) discussion of results
      4. Supporting exhibits
        a. Numerical tables, if any
        b. Graphic displays, if any
 VI. Appendices
    A. Detailed description of methods, if desired
    B. Data collection instruments
    C. Raw data and/or miscellaneous analyses

contents with too much detail is self-defeating because it takes too much time to use. If there are a large number of tables or figures, it is useful to list them separately.

Executive Summary

Special attention must be given to the executive summary, because this is the only part of the research report that is certain to be read. The executive summary starts with a brief statement of the problem the study addresses, followed by the key findings and the recommendations (if any). Normally, this should be condensed to one or at most two pages. There is usually no discussion of research methods in the executive summary except possibly an indication of when the study was done, who did the study, and what the sample size was.

The inclusion of recommendations depends on whether or not the decision maker wants them. Some decision makers don't want recommendations in research reports because they believe that printed recommendations narrow their flexibility; if so, do not give them recommendations. Also, do not invent recommendations. Some research projects—particularly "problem identification" research—do not lend themselves to action recommendations. It is inappropriate to offer recommendations unless they are firmly based on study results. This is not the place for a researcher to demonstrate creativity.

Description of Research Methods

After the executive summary, the report should begin with a *brief* description of the research methods. This description should take no more than one page of text. Its purpose is not to provide full detail on the methods employed but simply to give readers some background to help them interpret the results.

Typical elements included in this section of the report are:

- The research methods that were used (focus groups, survey, analysis of internal records, etc.)
- The locations where data were collected
- The key measures that were used
- The number of observations
- Possibly an exhibit showing general characteristics of the research participants

Any additional details about the sampling and data analysis procedures should be presented in an appendix at the back of the report, where interested readers can find them. Similarly, copies of the data collection instruments or transcribed interviews should be presented in appendices.

Detailed Results

The largest part of the research report will be the detailed discussion of findings. This part of the report may range from a few pages to several hundred pages, depending on the complexity of the study. As suggested by our outline, the detailed findings are most easily communicated if split into topic sections, each of which concentrates on a main theme. Thus, in a study reporting consumer attitudes toward a new product, there might be separate sections on buying intentions, features of the new product that are liked and disliked, how people would use the new product, characteristics of likely buyers, and so on.

Topic sections can be ordered according to either of two principles. One possibility is to order them by importance, with the most important sections first. Another is to order sections according to some logical progression, for example, who buys, what they buy, why they buy. Either way, the order of sections in the research report need not correspond to the order of topics in a questionnaire or to the chronological order of data collection.

Each section of findings should have a heading that describes the section topic. Sections are sometimes numbered as well, but this is not universal. The topic heading, which is listed in the table of contents, should be sufficiently explicit to enable readers to determine whether or not they wish to read that section.

After the topic heading, a section of results should open with an introduction and conclusions regarding the topic. This material, which should usually be no more than two paragraphs long, should introduce readers to the purpose and major conclusions of the section. These major conclusions are repeated in the executive summary.

The text should then proceed to a detailed discussion of the results. This discussion should refer to the exhibits that present the results of analyses, give a brief description of each exhibit, and interpret the meaning of each exhibit. All exhibits *must* be discussed in the text. The text may contain comments that are unrelated to exhibits, but in general it is best if the findings are described through a combination of text, tables, and displays, as multiple presentation modes make it easier for readers to understand the results. We discuss how to present readable tables and displays later in this chapter.

Appendices

Appendices to the research report include copies of all measurement instruments, along with copies of materials such as interviewer instructions and coding and processing specifications.

Appendices may also include data tabulations or other results that are not crucial to the report but may be of interest to some readers.

An Example

To illustrate the presentation of marketing research reports, a real report is shown in Appendix 20.1 (see page 602), with some graphics omitted to save space. Note that the data analyses shown in Appendix 20.1 are quite simple. As a general rule, the main sections of research reports should present simple, easily visualized data unless the researcher knows that the audience is limited to people who already have a good knowledge of sophisticated data analysis methods. The researcher may do sophisticated analyses for his or her own benefit or may provide sophisticated analyses in subsidiary tables, but the central purpose of marketing research is to give decision makers results that are comprehensible, nonintimidating, and intuitively appealing. For most decision makers, this means results that are analytically simple, even though they may be conceptually rich.

Designing Effective Numerical Tables

Tables of numerical data are one of the major ways in which information is conveyed in marketing research reports. We have all seen tables in newspapers, such as daily stock prices or batting averages. It is important to recognize the difference between these types of tables and those in a marketing research report.

Author Tips

An old Alka-Seltzer commercial featured a man standing at a medicine cabinet. From the other room, his newlywed wife asks him how he liked dinner. "Great," he says morosely. "I never saw such a big meatball." His wife says, "I thought of making a lot of little ones, but I wanted to impress you." Without comment, he takes his Alka-Seltzer, obviously feeling the effects of this indigestible meatball.

Novice researchers often make the "giant meatball" mistake in tables. They add information until a table looks sufficiently impressive and in so doing make it harder to read and interpret. This is a mistake. Simpler is better.

The tables in a newspaper are designed to provide general information to a large number of users. These tables are often long and complex, and users must pick out the information they need. In contrast, a table in a marketing research report should have a clearly defined single purpose and be easily understood by a reader with limited time.

Table Format

Principles of table format include the following:

- Each table should be numbered, so it can be referred to in the text.
- Each table must have a title that describes its major purpose.
- Each row and column of a table should have a descriptive heading so that readers know what the numbers represent.
- The sample size(s) on which statistics are based should be shown somewhere in the table. This information can be given in a footnote or wherever works best.
- Rows or columns may be ordered in one of two ways. Some variables, such as age or expenditure, have a natural numerical order, and the data should be arranged accordingly. Exhibit 20.1 shows an example, using V4 from the SPORTS data (amount of most recent expenditure on sportswear, athletic shoes, or sporting goods). Other variables, such as preferred brand or reason for buying, do not have a natural order. Here, the rows or columns should be arranged in descending order of magnitude. Exhibit 20.2 shows an example, using V3 (reason for store choice).

EXHIBIT 20.1

Amount Spent on Most Recent Purchase (V4 in SPORTS Data)

Amount	Percentage of Respondents ($n = 257$)
Less than $20	11%
$20–$49	44
$50–$99	26
$100–$199	13
$200–$499	4
$500 or more	3
Total	100%

Categories that have a natural order, such as spending levels, should be presented in that order.

- If a table has multiple columns, the proper ordering of categories may vary across columns. In this situation, the ordering of categories should be based on a "total" column if the table has one. If not, the ordering should be based on the first numerical column in the table. Exhibit 20.3 shows an example in which the proper ordering of "main reason for store choice" varies between men and women.

EXHIBIT 20.2

Main Reason for Store Choice (V3 in SPORTS Data)

Reason	Percentage of Respondents (n = 290)
Location	22%
Sale prices	21
Merchandise selection	19
Regular prices	17
Merchandise quality	10
Credit	5
Service	1
Other	5
Total	100%

Categories that do not have a natural order, such as reasons for choice, should be presented in declining order of magnitude.

EXHIBIT 20.3

Main Reason for Store Choice (V3), for Men and Women (V37 in SPORTS Data)

Main Reason for Store Choice	Men	Women
Merchandise selection	23.5%	13.1%
Sale prices	19.0	23.4
Regular prices	18.3	16.1
Location	18.3	26.3
Merchandise quality	9.2	11.7
Credit	6.5	3.6
Service	1.3	.7
Other	3.9	5.1
Total	100.0%	100.0%

If categories have a different ordering sequence across columns, present them in order for the "total" column. If there is no "total" column, present the categories in order for the first column.

Critical Thinking Skills

Ⓘn a research report, every table should be interpreted in the text. Write brief interpretations of Exhibits 20.1 to 20.3.

■ Every row and column in a table adds to the complexity of reading that table. Therefore, rows or columns that represent small groups may be combined into broader categories. If this group cannot be well described, it may be labeled "Other." Exhibits 20.2 and 20.3 (see page 587) both use an "other" category.

Effective Charts and Graphs

Charts and graphs improve the interest and readability of a research report. They do not replace the use of text and tables but are used in addition to them.

Following are some comments regarding the preparation of charts and graphs. The discussion is limited to the three major types: (1) pie charts, (2) bar charts, and (3) line graphs. First, each type of chart and when it should be used is described. Then, some general principles of effective graphic design are discussed.

Appropriate Uses for Different Types of Charts

Pie charts use segments of circles to represent percentages. They are good for showing the breakdown of some variable within the total population. For example, Exhibit 20.4 uses a single pie chart to show an overall breakdown for V3 in the SPORTS data set (main reason for choosing a store). This chart provides a clear, visual sense of the overall breakdown.

Pie charts are not so good for showing comparisons across groups. For example, Exhibit 20.5 uses a double pie chart to compare the breakdown of V3 between men and women. In this exhibit, we can see that women are higher on location and sales and lower on merchandise selection, but our inability to see comparisons on a direct, side-by-side basis makes it difficult to evaluate the magnitude of differences.

Bar charts use bars to show the breakdown of a variable, or the value of a variable across groups. The big advantage of bar charts, compared with pie charts, is that the figures in bar charts need not represent the breakdown of some total. However, if the purpose of the chart is to show a breakdown, bar charts are not as effective as pie charts. For example, Exhibit 20.6 (see page 590) shows the breakdown of V3 in bar chart form. This chart shows the relative sizes of the various categories but is less vivid than the pie chart shown in Exhibit 20.4.

Bar charts are very good for comparing groups. For example, Exhibit 20.7 (see page 590) shows a double bar chart that compares the breakdown of V3 between men and women. This chart reveals the magnitude of differences more clearly than the double pie chart in Exhibit 20.5.

Line graphs use lines to show the movement of one variable relative to another. They are appropriate if the purpose of the chart is to show how the variable on the

(cont. on p. 591)

EXHIBIT 20.4

Pie Chart of Main Reason for Store Choice (V3)

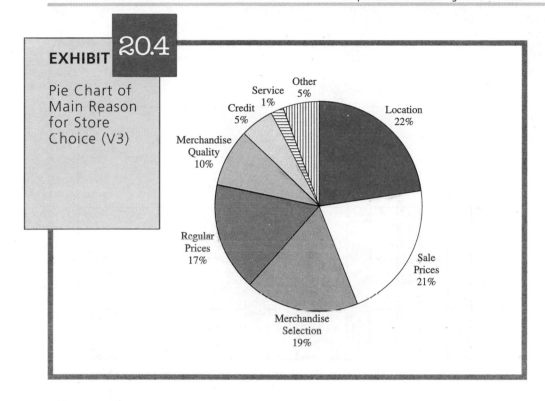

EXHIBIT 20.5

Pie Charts of V3, Main Reason for Store Choice (V3) for Men and Women (V37)

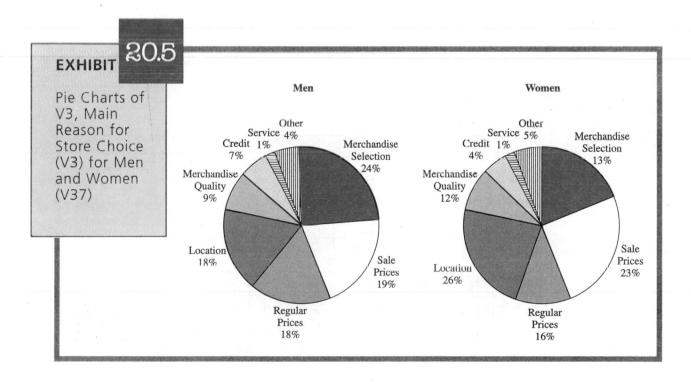

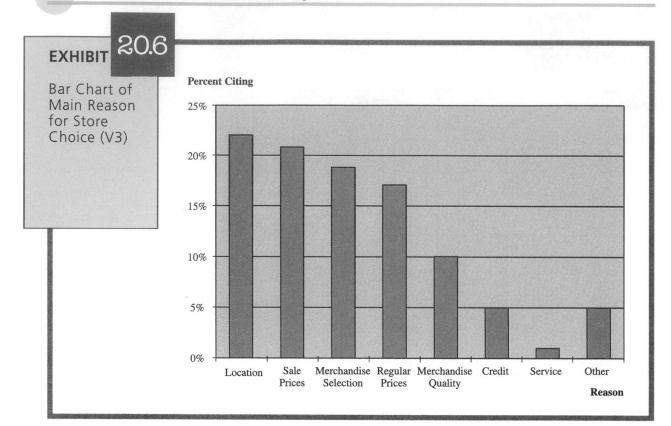

EXHIBIT 20.6

Bar Chart of Main Reason for Store Choice (V3)

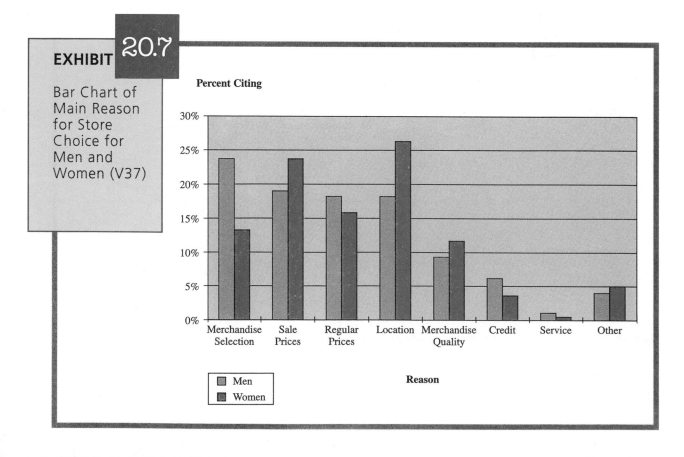

EXHIBIT 20.7

Bar Chart of Main Reason for Store Choice for Men and Women (V37)

y-axis trends with respect to the variable on the *x*-axis. For example, Exhibit 20.8 shows how V29 in the SPORTS data, annual expenditures at Smith's Stores, trends across V22, ratings of Smith's on merchandise quality. This chart shows that expenditures tend to rise as the ratings increase, though the relationship is not perfect.

If the variable on the *x*-axis is categorical, a line graph is not appropriate. For example, Exhibit 20.9 (see page 592) shows how V29 varies across categories of V3, reasons for store choice. This chart creates an impression of trend that is not appropriate given the categorical nature of V3. A bar chart would be a better way of showing this relationship.

Regardless of which type of chart is most appropriate for a particular application, the guidelines for preparing effective charts are similar to those for preparing effective tables:

- Each chart should be numbered and given a title.
- Charts should be kept simple.
- Data should be scaled appropriately.
- Every element of a chart should be labeled.

Critical Thinking Skills

What form of visual presentation would you use to:

1. Show the expenses of the U.S. federal budget by agency?
2. Show trends in the sales of CD players over the past seven years?
3. Compare the amount of money spent on sporting goods by low-, middle-, and high-income households for 1990, 1993, and 1996?

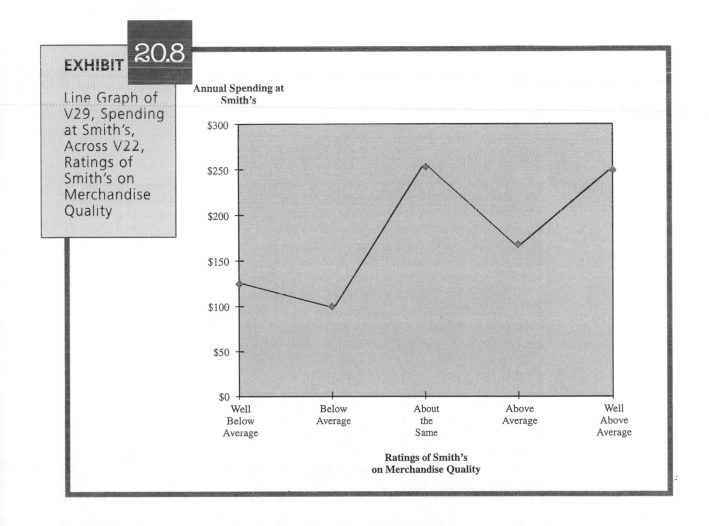

EXHIBIT 20.8

Line Graph of V29, Spending at Smith's, Across V22, Ratings of Smith's on Merchandise Quality

Annual Spending at Smith's

Ratings of Smith's on Merchandise Quality

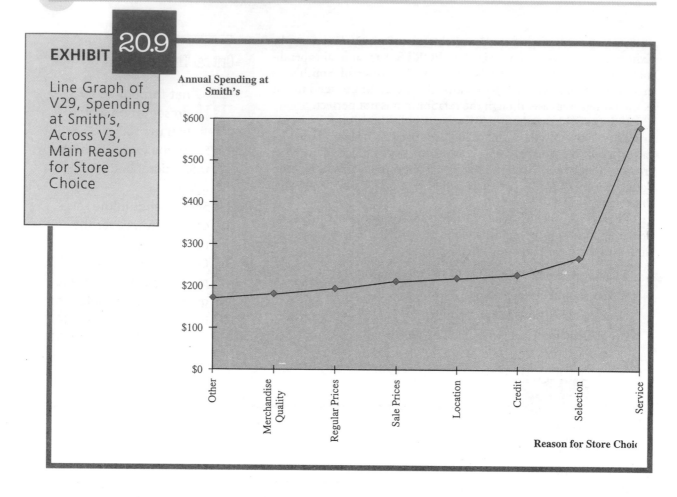

EXHIBIT **20.9**

Line Graph of V29, Spending at Smith's, Across V3, Main Reason for Store Choice

Keeping Charts and Graphs Simple

An important principle of creating effective charts and graphs is to keep them simple. Problems occur when too much information is presented at one time. For example, consider Exhibit 20.10, which shows how V29, expenditures at Smith's, relates to ratings of Smith's on eleven dimensions. When the relationship between V29 and one rating variable was graphed in Exhibit 20.8 (see page 591), the result was easy to read and useful. When eleven different lines are shown, as in Exhibit 20.10, the result is a mess.

The solution is to use a line graph but to edit the graph to eliminate all but the two or three lines of most interest. The use of different colors for different lines is another way of making a graph easier to read.

Scaling Line and Bar Charts

Line and bar charts can be scaled so as to make large differences appear small or small differences appear large. Differences will appear smaller if the scale is expanded on the vertical axis, that is, by counting in tens rather than ones, hundreds rather than tens, and so on. Differences will appear larger if (1) the scale of the vertical axis is shrunk or (2) the scale of the vertical axis is begun at a number higher than zero.

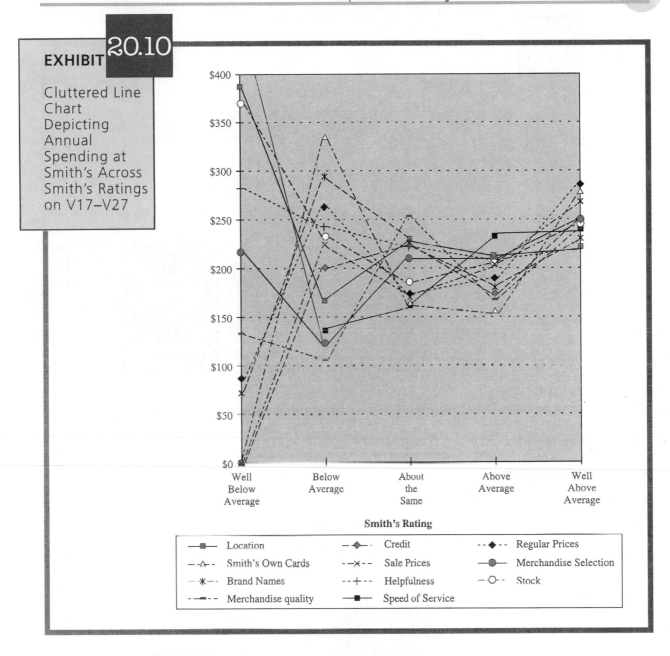

EXHIBIT 20.10

Cluttered Line Chart Depicting Annual Spending at Smith's Across Smith's Ratings on V17–V27

Exhibits 20.11 and 20.12 (see page 594) demonstrate this last point. Exhibit 20.11 shows annual expenditures at Smith's for men and women. Men are seen to spend about 10 percent more than women. Exhibit 20.12 shows the same comparison, but on a scale that starts at $150 rather than $0. Here, it looks as if men spend twice as much as women, which is deceptive.

In preparing a research report, you may feel some urge to exaggerate the importance of small results to make a graph more interesting. However, a research presentation should not mislead or even appear to mislead. Charts should be scaled so that differences that are important for decision-making purposes are clearly noticeable and differences without decision-making significance are minimized.

EXHIBIT 20.11

Bar Chart of V29, Annual Spending at Smith's by Men and Women (V37)

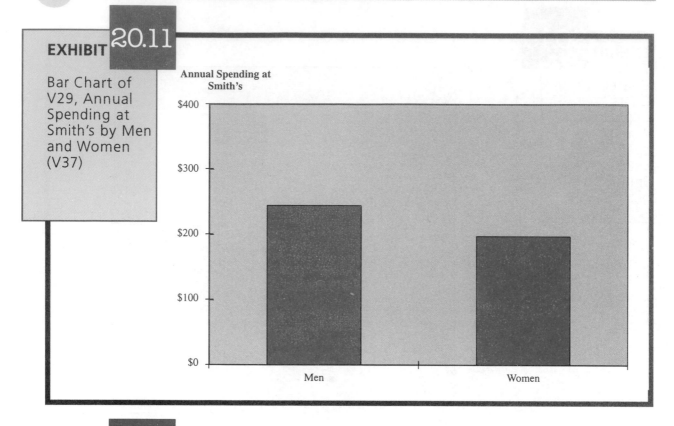

EXHIBIT 20.12

Rescaled Bar Chart of V29, Annual Spending at Smith's by Men and Women (V37)

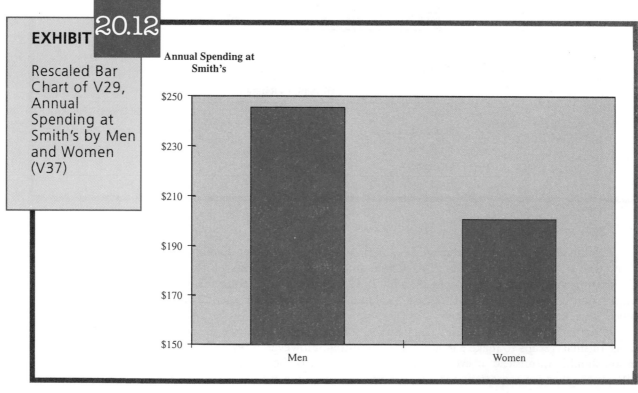

Using Titles and Labels

One similarity between charts and numerical tables is the need to provide self-explanatory titles and to label each element for easy comprehension. This should be done even if the presenter will be giving an oral explanation of the chart, since the chart may get additional use when this information will not be available.

Communicating Multivariate Results

Chapters 18 and 19 described a range of multivariate analysis methods with application to marketing research problems. Multivariate procedures raise special problems of communicating research findings to managers who may not be statistically sophisticated. For example, tables of beta weights are mysteries to most managers. How, then, should these results be presented?

The results of multivariate procedures should be translated into simple text, tables, and graphics. Say, for example, that a multiple regression analysis shows that the probability of using disposable diapers on an infant is related to the parents' age, economic status, and concern for environmental issues. These results do not have to be presented as a multiple regression equation; one can create (1) a simple graph or table that shows the relationship of disposable diaper use to the parent's age, (2) a simple graph or table that shows the relationship to the parent's economic status, and (3) a simple graph or table that shows the relationship to environmental concern. These graphs or tables should be shown in order of importance, with the strongest relationship shown first.

The multiple regression procedures can either be described in an appendix or omitted entirely, depending on readers' preferences and your desire to impress them with the fancy techniques that were used in the study. Some sophisticated readers may want to know the details. Most, however, will not be interested in the analytic details of the research—only in its implications for decision making. Once again, it is important to know what to leave out of a report.

Oral Presentations

Most of the foregoing comments about written reports also apply to oral presentations. There are, however, some special features of oral presentations, which are discussed here.

Organizing a Presentation

In making an oral presentation, it is a cliché, but true, that you should tell the audience what you are going to tell them, then tell them, then tell them what you told them. This means that a presentation should start with an overview of the subsequent material: in effect, a table of contents. This portion of the presentation should take only a few seconds.

The overview of the presentation should use an outline format. This helps audience members to grasp quickly the structure of the presentation. Subsequently, in the main body of the presentation, the outline structure should be shown on the visuals again. Members of the audience may lose attention at some point, and reshowing the structure of the presentation will help them get reoriented.

After the overview, the main body of the presentation should follow the same sequence as a written report:

- A *brief* presentation of the problem, the key results, and the recommendations (if any) should be given.
- A *brief* description of the methods used should be given.
- Key results should be shown in more detail.
- Less important results should be shown as time allows.
- Finally, the presentation should be briefly reviewed.

Staying on Time

There is no such thing as a good presentation that runs overtime. Listeners have other tasks scheduled and will start getting antsy. They will lose track of what you are saying, because all they can think is "When will this end?"

The surest way of staying on time is to rehearse your presentation before you give it in a meeting. Almost always, you will find the first time you try it that it runs too long. You will need to think about what the highest-priority issues to be covered in the oral presentation are and what can be left to a written report.

Be aware that presenting a talk to yourself takes less time than making the same talk at a meeting, where you will need time to present visuals and give the participants a chance to absorb them. To avoid running long, plan to use only two-thirds of the time allocated to you (this assumes that your live presentation will take 50 percent longer than your rehearsal). If you finish early, you can be sure that no one will mind.

During your rehearsal, you may want to include time breaks for the various sections of your presentation. Then, during the presentation, if you see that you have gone more slowly than you expected, you will know that you need to start skipping material. Notice that we say "skipping material," not "moving faster." It is a mistake to rush a presentation. Listeners will have trouble following you, they will tune out, and the whole presentation will be a failure. Give any material you discuss enough time to be comprehended, and stay on schedule by editing rather than rushing.

A key piece of advice is not to be too ambitious. Most novice presenters try to cram too much material into too little time. It is easier to edit in advance than in the middle of the presentation.

Relating to the Participants

The effectiveness of an oral presentation depends heavily on the extent to which you relate to the participants. If you simply read your notes without looking up or turn your back on the participants to look at your visual aids, they will find the presentation less interesting, and you will lose an opportunity to learn how well it is being accepted.

Notice that we have used the word "participants," rather than "audience," to suggest that the listeners may participate in the presentation by asking questions. Take questions in a way that fits you best. A presentation is most effective if clarifying questions can be asked and answered as they arise, but some inexperienced presenters have trouble staying on time if they take questions and do best if they hold questions until the end. Of course, if a question comes up that will be answered later in the presentation, you can simply tell the questioner that this will be covered a bit later.

Your ability to relate to participants will be much greater if your presentation style is interesting, rather than a mere presentation of facts. Practice voice modulation, and use different tones and speed at different points in your presentation to keep your listeners' interest. Enthusiasm is contagious, and you should make it clear that you find the data interesting and important. If not, why present at all?

Author Tips

Jokes are not needed in a research presentation. There is nothing wrong with jokes if (1) you have jokes that relate to the topic, (2) your jokes are not offensive, (3) your jokes are funny, and (4) you can tell a joke effectively. If you cannot meet these requirements, leave the jokes to a comedian. Audience members want a professional presentation to be professional, and humor is optional.

Using Effective Visuals

In any oral presentation, the use of visual aids greatly improves the ability of the audience to absorb and understand the results. Here are some guidelines for using effective visuals:

- The entire presentation, from start to finish, should be supported by visual aids.

- Don't put too much onto each visual.

- Use a separate visual for each topic. This helps keep visuals clean and helps the audience group material into sections.

- Show your outline structure on the visuals from time to time. This helps the audience keep track of the presentation.

- Show headings, not content. Your audience is there to hear a presentation, not read a report. The purpose of visual aids is to show structure and guide the audience, not to make the presentation for you.

- Use charts and graphs to enhance the impact of the presentation. Pictures can help audience members grasp a point.

- Keep visuals up long enough for the audience to absorb them. As a general rule, a visual should be up for at least ninety seconds. It may be helpful to talk the audience through the visual and use a pointer to show where you are.

- Do not play with your pointer. Point, then either put the pointer down or hold it steady while you discuss the topic. Do not wave it.

- Text and graphics on visual aids must be large enough for the audience to read. Visual aids are not much use if the audience cannot read them.

- Fit the medium to the room. Charts or flip charts may be the best devices in a small room where there is not enough space to project a big image, but they are too small for big rooms. Overhead projectors fit most medium-sized and large rooms. Slide projectors usually require a large room to get a big enough image.

- Check the room's audiovisual capacities before preparing a presentation, and make arrangements for proper equipment to be available. Also, arrive early enough to test the equipment and make sure you know how to use it.

Marketing Research Tools 20.2 summarizes these tips for giving effective oral presentations.

MARKETING RESEARCH TOOLS

20.2

TIPS FOR MAKING EFFECTIVE ORAL PRESENTATIONS

Organize the presentation.

- Tell them what you are going to tell them, then tell them, then tell them what you told them.
- Use an outline format and show it on your visuals.
- Follow the same sequence as you would in a written report.

Stay on time.

- Rehearse.
- Plan to use only two-thirds of the allotted time.
- In your notes, record time breaks by section so you can see if you are behind.
- If you fall behind, edit material rather than rushing.
- Do not be too ambitious.

Relate to your listeners.

- Face the participants and try to look at them.
- Take questions in the way that fits you best.
- Do not worry about making jokes.

Use effective visuals.

- The entire presentation, start to finish, should be supported by visual aids.
- Do not put too much onto each visual.
- Use a separate visual for each topic.
- Show your outline structure on the visuals.
- Show headings, not content.
- Use charts and graphs.
- Keep visuals up long enough for the audience to absorb them.
- Do not play with your pointer.
- Text and graphics must be large enough to read.
- Fit the medium to the room.
- Check the room's audiovisual capacities in advance.
- Test the audiovisual equipment in advance of the presentation.

Summary

This chapter discussed how to communicate research results. The following points were covered:

1. What information should be included in a research report?

A research report should contain a title page, a table of contents, an executive summary, a research methods section, a results section split into topic sections, and appendices that contain copies of all measurement instruments, interviewer instructions, and coding and processing specifications.

2. How can numerical tables be presented so they are easy to understand?

Each table should be numbered and given a title. Within the table, each row and column should be given a descriptive heading, so readers know what the numbers mean. The total sample size(s) on which any percentages or statistics are based should be shown. Data should be arranged according to their natural order if they have one, or according to descending order of frequencies or average scores if they do not. Rows or columns that represent small groups should be combined into broader categories, and tables should be kept two-dimensional if at all possible.

3. How can charts and graphs be presented in an effective manner?

Visuals should be clean and simple. In general, simple bar charts and line charts work best. Charts should be scaled so that differences with decision-making significance are clearly noticeable and differences without decision-making significance are minimized. Each chart should be given a self-explanatory title, and all elements should be labeled for easy comprehension.

4. How can multivariate results be communicated?

Unless an audience is very sophisticated, multivariate results should be expressed through simpler bivariate comparisons. The multivariate results can be described in an appendix or omitted entirely.

5. How can effective oral presentations be made?

The first step is to *organize the presentation*. Start with an overview in outline format, follow the format of a written report, and finish with a brief review.

Second, *stay on time*. Rehearse your presentation before you give it, and plan to use only two-thirds of the time allocated to you. If you find yourself falling behind, edit the material rather than speeding up the presentation.

Third, *relate to the listeners*. Do not turn your back on the audience, and, if possible, take questions as they arise. Be enthusiastic about your presentation, and do not use humor unless it is relevant and you are good at it.

Fourth, *use effective visuals*. Support the entire presentation with visual aids. Do not put too much onto each visual, use a separate visual for each topic, and show your outline structure on the visuals. Show topic headings, not detailed content, and use charts and graphs to enhance the impact of the presentation. Keep each visual up at least ninety seconds, do not wave your pointer, make text and graphics large enough for the audience to read, fit the audiovisual medium to the room, and check the room's audiovisual capacities before making a presentation.

Suggested Additional Readings

You may have had a course in business writing at your school. If so, you may want to look back at your text for that course for additional pointers on communication. Some of these texts are: Shirley Kuiper and Philip Wolf Morris, *Effective Communication in Business* (Cincinnati: South-Western, 1994); Roy W. Poe and Rosemary T. Fruehling, *Business Communication: A Case Method Approach* (St. Paul, Minn.: Paradigm, 1995); Claudia Rawlins, *Business Communications* (New York: Harper Perennial, 1993); Tim J. Saben, *Practical Business Communications* (Burr Ridge, Ill.: Irwin/Mirror Press, 1994).

In addition, reading business newspapers and magazines will give you models that may be useful. One book on data presentation that has become a classic is Hans Zeisel, *Say It with Figures* (New York: Harper and Row, 1985).

Discussion Questions

1. What is the purpose of the marketing research report?
2. What are some common pitfalls of the marketing research report?
3. What should the researcher keep in mind as he/she prepares the marketing research report?
4. How should the research report be formatted?
5. Discuss the six basic components of the research report. What information is included in each section? What criteria would you use to evaluate a research report?
6. What information should be included in an executive summary? What information should not be included in an executive summary?
7. Should the researcher include action recommendations in the executive summary?
8. What can you do to ensure the success of an oral presentation?

Marketing Research Challenge

Look in the business press and find good and poor examples of a table and good and poor examples of a graphic presentation. Discuss how the poor examples might be improved.

Internet Exercise

For tips on how to present research results in a nonmisleading manner, check "Pitfalls of Data Analysis (or How to Avoid Lies and Damned Lies)," by Clay Helberg of SPSS, Inc. The site is located at http://maddog.fammed.wisc.edu/pitfalls/.

References

Mohn, N. Carroll, and Thomas H. Land (1989). "A Guide to Quality Marketing Research Proposals and Reports." *Business* 39 (January–March), pp. 38–40.

Payne, Melanie S. (1989). "Good Writing Skills Perk Up Dull Reports." *Marketing News* 23 (June 19), p. 10.

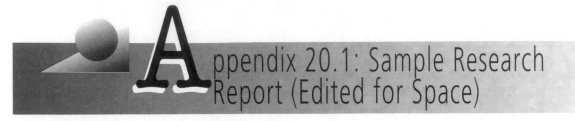

Appendix 20.1: Sample Research Report (Edited for Space)

DOWNTOWN RETAIL SURVEY:

Final Report

for the

Downtown Houston Association

July 1988

CONTENTS

I. EXECUTIVE SUMMARY

This report describes the results of a self-administered survey applied to the Downtown Houston work force. Our broad objectives in conducting this survey (the Downtown Retail Survey) were as follows:

1. To describe Downtown workers in terms of demographic characteristics, mobility to Downtown, and mobility within Downtown.

2. To determine how Downtown workers use Downtown retail. Where do they shop Downtown, when do they shop, what do they buy, how much do they spend?

3. To examine shopping differences across subgroups of workers.

4. To measure workers' perceptions of Downtown retail service.

5. To evaluate possible changes that might increase retail sales Downtown.

Our key findings were as follows:

1. Most Downtown workers shop Downtown at least occasionally and have the income to be excellent retail customers. However, shopping is focused upon the lunch hour, and many workers use transportation arrangements (to and from Downtown) that inhibit carrying merchandise. Because of time and transport constraints, shopping by Downtown workers tends to be directed toward small, personal items. It is not clear that any significant increase in shopping can be expected given the existing constraints facing Downtown workers.

2. There is some evidence that Downtown has become a set of retail "islands." Workers patronize Foley's, the Tunnel, and The Park, but little else in between.

3. Downtown workers rate Downtown lower than their usual shopping malls in every dimension considered in this study. Not surprisingly, Downtown scores lowest in store selection, parking, and other transportation factors. "Convenience" is the dimension along which Downtown shopping is most competitive with the shopping malls.

4. The changes most likely to increase Downtown shopping by Downtown workers relate to store selection, parking, and the "ecology" of the area (cleanliness, security). Indeed, free parking was the first choice among respondents asked to cite specific changes that would encourage more Downtown shopping.

5. However, Downtown workers seem to account for a relatively small portion of the recent decline in Downtown retail sales. Most of the decline is centered elsewhere; presumably in people who used to come Downtown to shop and no longer do so. Common sense suggests that parking, store selection, wayfinding systems, and possibly ecological factors will be key elements in bringing these people back Downtown, although their perceptions were not directly measured in this survey.

II. DESCRIPTION OF THE RESEARCH

Results shown in this report are drawn from the Downtown Retail Survey conducted in February, 1988. This self-administered survey was distributed to 1,119 office workers at 21 participating companies scattered throughout Downtown Houston. Questions asked of each respondent can be seen in the copy of the questionnaire that is appended. The overall response rate of the survey was 74 percent.

Some of the results shown in this report might have been different if we had a different mix of respondents. For example, the exact percentage of respondents who said they shop "often" at The Park would have changed if we had more or fewer respondents from office buildings near The Park. Our key findings, however, are not likely to be sensitive to sample composition. The findings that Downtown workers shop primarily during their lunch breaks, that they don't travel far to shop, that most of the decline in Downtown retail trade is *not* attributable to the Downtown work force; these findings should be steady. Overall, we believe the results of this survey to be accurate and stable.

The economic context suggesting the need for this survey is graphically illustrated in the following chart that shows the trend in retail sales in Houston's Central Business District from 1978 to 1986.

Retail Sales—Central Business District
Zip Codes 77001, 77002, 77010
(Real Dollars 1982 = 100)

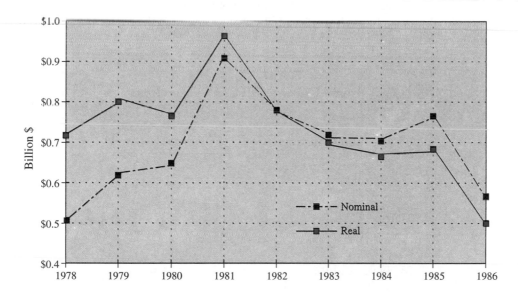

III. GENERAL DESCRIPTION OF THE RESPONDENTS

Our first objective in the Downtown Retail Survey was simply to describe the Downtown work force. How old are they? How much money do they make? How do they get Downtown, and how long does it take them? What about mobility within Downtown?

Tables 3.1, 3.2 and 3.3 provide answers to these questions. Table 3.1 shows that the Downtown work force—at least as represented by our respondents—contains people who should be attractive to retail merchants. The respondents mostly are in their 30s or 40s. Half (51 percent) of them report family incomes over $50,000 (Houston's average household income estimated from the 1980 census is $31,837) and almost three-fourths say that they are the principal shopper in their household. One has to be careful in interpreting these numbers—many of the higher-income respondents are men, and many of them are not the principal shopper in their households—but the Downtown work force clearly has the income to be a good source of retail trade.

Whether this income can be captured is another question. Table 3.2 shows that only 8 percent of the Downtown work force live within ten minutes of Downtown and only one-third (32 percent) live within twenty minutes. Longer commutes, which are likely to discourage evening and weekend shopping, are the norm. Also, only 57 percent of our respondents said they drive their own cars. The others have transportation arrangements that tend to require strict schedules and make transportation of goods somewhat inconvenient. These people can't just throw a bag into their back seat.

Table 3.3 offers some data regarding mobility within Downtown. About one-third of the respondents (34 percent) believe their office to be within a five-minute walk from Foley's; almost four-fifths (79 percent) consider themselves to be within

TABLE 3.1
Background Characteristics of Respondents

Background Characteristic	Percentage of Respondents
Male	42%
Female	58%
Married	66%
Not married	34%
Under 35 years old	39%
35–49 years old	45%
More than 49 years old	16%
Income of $25,000 or less:	16%
$25,001 to $50,000	33%
$50,001 to $100,000	37%
More than $100,000	14%
Principal shopper in household	72%
Not principal shopper	28%

TABLE 3.2
Mobility to Downtown

Driving Time from Residence to Downtown	Percentage of Respondents[1]
1–10 minutes	8%
11–20 minutes	24%
21–30 minutes	24%
31–45 minutes	30%
46–90 minutes	14%

Usual Mode of Transportation	
Drive own car	57%
Metro Park and Ride	27%
Car or van pool	14%
Other	1%

[1]Percentages may not sum to 100 due to rounding.

TABLE 3.3
Mobility Within Downtown

Perceived Walking Time	Percentage of Respondents
Workplace to Foley's:	
5 minutes or less	34%
10 minutes or less	79%
Workplace to The Park:	
5 minutes or less	23%
10 minutes or less	54%
Workplace to Jones Hall:	
5 minutes or less	42%
10 minutes or less	67%
Have used The Park Trolley	46%
Have used Metro Downtown circulators	45%

ten minutes. The 79 percent figure reflects Foley's central location, and it is noticeably higher than the figure for The Park. (Just over half the respondents consider themselves within ten minutes of The Park.) In general, the figures in Table 3.3 remind us that peripheral Downtown locations such as The Park, Market Square, and the Albert Thomas Center will depend upon motorized transport services to make themselves adequately accessible to Downtown workers. Respondents appear willing to use such services; 46 percent of respondents said that they have used The Park Trolley, and an equal number reported having used the Metro Downtown circulators.

IV. DOWNTOWN SHOPPING PATTERNS

Our second objective in the Downtown Retail Survey was to profile workers' shopping patterns. Where do these workers shop Downtown? When do they shop? What do they buy? How much do they spend?

Table 4.1 starts to answer these questions by showing how often Downtown workers patronize various shopping attractions. As befits its convenient location, Foley's has the highest levels of patronage. Almost 90 percent of respondents claim to shop Foley's at least occasionally, and almost one-third say they shop there often. The Park fares well for occasional shopping but has only half as many frequent shoppers (compared with Foley's). The Park's lower ratio of "often" to "occasional" shoppers presumably reflects its distance from many Downtown workers.

Perhaps the most eye-catching number in Table 4.1 is the 7 percent who shop often at "other Downtown stores." This number is quite discouraging. It suggests that Downtown retail has evolved, even for people who work Downtown, into a set of islands; an area where specific destinations are well patronized but the general area is not.

Table 4.2 shows that lunch is by far the primary shopping time for Downtown workers.

Table 4.3 shows that people are more likely to purchase personal items such as clothing, books, and candy Downtown compared with other types of merchandise. The emphasis is on portable items requiring limited shopping effort. This corresponds with time and transport constraints on Downtown workers, such as having to shop during lunch, having to transport merchandise by foot and/or public transportation, and possibly having to store merchandise for a period of time at one's place of work before taking it home.

Tables 4.4 and 4.5 relate to levels of expenditures. The average respondent reported spending $221 Downtown over the ninety days preceding the survey (Table 4.4). This amount does not include parking and restaurant expenditures, and it does cover the Christmas shopping period. Ten percent of the respondents spent nothing at all, whereas 53 percent spent more than $100.

TABLE 4.1
Frequency of Shopping at Selected Locations

Location	Respondents Who Shop Here at Least "Occasionally"	Respondents Who Shop Here "Often"
Foley's	89%	31%
The Park	77%	16%
Other Downtown stores	72%	7%
The Tunnel	63%	19%

TABLE 4.2
When Shopping Occurs

Time	Respondents Who Shop at This Time at Least "Occasionally"	Respondents Who Shop at This Time "Often"
Lunch	94%	51%
After work	50%	5%
Weekend	30%	4%
Afternoon break	26%	2%
Time off work	24%	3%
Morning break	19%	1%
Before starting work	12%	0%

TABLE 4.3
Probability of Buying Various Types of Merchandise Downtown

Merchandise	Percentage of Respondents Who Buy This Merchandise	Of Those Who Buy, Percentage Who Made Last Purchase Downtown
Candy	90%	54%
Office supplies	75%	51%
Books	94%	48%
Shoes	100%	41%
Clothing	100%	40%
Cosmetics/toiletries	96%	34%
Baked goods	95%	33%
Jewelry	94%	33%
Hosiery	79%	33%
Tobacco	28%	32%
Flowers	88%	31%
Eyeglasses	79%	29%
Drugs/medicines	98%	19%
Kitchenware	93%	16%
Records/tapes	92%	16%
Sporting goods	85%	14%
Computers/software	33%	12%
Household appliances	94%	9%
Radio/TV/electronics	94%	9%
Beer/wine/liquor	82%	9%
Hardware	87%	3%
Furniture	92%	2%
Auto parts	81%	2%

TABLE 4.4
Total Dollars Spent Downtown
on Merchandise During Past 90 Days

Range of Expenditure	Respondents Spending in This Range[1]
$0 (zero)	10%
$1–$100	38%
$101–$250	24%
$251–$500	21%
More than $500	7%
Average expenditure	$221

[1]Percentages may not sum to 100 due to rounding.

TABLE 4.5
Dollars Spent Downtown Today Versus Five Years Ago
(taken as a percentage of total spending)

Spending Level	Percentage of All Respondents	Percentage of Respondents Who Worked Five Years Ago[1]
Spend higher % today	21%	28%
Spend about the same %	29%	38%
Spend lower % today	26%	34%
Didn't work Downtown then	25%	

[1]Percentages may not sum to 100 due to rounding.

Table 4.5 indicates there has been a slight decline in Downtown spending among people who have worked Downtown at least five years. Twenty-eight percent of our respondents who have been Downtown at least five years said that Downtown accounts for a larger percentage of their total spending today than five years ago, but 34 percent said they spend less Downtown now. The impact of this decline on overall Downtown sales will be discussed later.

V. SPENDING LEVELS ACROSS RESPONDENT SUBGROUPS

The previous section gives a clear picture of how Downtown workers use Downtown retail services. Shopping is done primarily during the lunch hour, is focused on small personal and convenience items, and occurs primarily at a few retail "islands" within Downtown.

Table 5.1 addresses another aspect of Downtown shopping; specifically, whether there are differences in spending levels across subgroups of Downtown workers. The findings are as follows:

1. Workers who have been Downtown longer average a higher amount of spending.

2. Workers who live closer to Downtown spend more; the dividing point is roughly a ten-mile radius.

TABLE 5.1
Downtown Spending by Respondent Groups

Respondent Characteristic	Percentage of Respondents[1]	Average Dollars Spent per Respondent in Past 90 Days
Worked Downtown 5 years or more	75%	$244
Worked Downtown less than 5 years	25%	$151
10 zip codes closest to Downtown	12%	$238
Outside 10 closest zip codes but within 10 miles of Downtown	27%	$233
10 to 20 miles from Downtown	45%	$214
More than 20 miles from Downtown	17%	$214
Male	42%	$219
Female	58%	$221
Married	66%	$233
Not married	34%	$195
Under 35 years old	39%	$184
35–49 years old	45%	$241
More than 49 years old	16%	$252
Family income $25,000 or less	16%	$124
$25,001 to $50,000	33%	$200
$50,001 to $100,000	37%	$244
More than $100,000	14%	$312

[1]Percentages may not sum to 100 due to rounding.

3. Men and women spend about the same amounts.
4. Married people spend more.
5. Older workers spend more
6. Spending rises with income.

The most interesting of these results are the findings that older workers and longer-time workers spend more. These findings partly correlate with income—the older, more senior workers have higher incomes and more money to spend—but also reflect a tendency for younger workers not to shop Downtown at all. It seems that some of the younger workers have never acquired the habit of Downtown shopping.

VI. PERCEPTIONS OF DOWNTOWN

Table 6.1 examines workers' perceptions of Downtown shopping compared with their usual malls. It is not surprising, though certainly not encouraging, to see that Downtown scored worse than the malls in every area. Particularly unfavorable ratings center on access (cost and ease of parking, store hours, and ease of getting around), merchandise variety, and the availability of desired stores.

Our purpose in measuring workers' perceptions of Downtown was not to identify areas of weakness but rather to identify areas of strength that might be exploited. In this regard, "convenience" clearly is Downtown's best dimension. A sizable group of Downtown workers consider Downtown more convenient than their usual malls, and convenience is the best predictor of Downtown spending level among the perceptions considered here (this result is not shown in a table).

It seems that promotional efforts directed at Downtown workers should stress the convenience of Downtown shopping and draw attention to mobility aids such as The Park Trolley.

TABLE 6.1
Perceptions of Downtown

Dimensions of Evaluation	Respondents Who Rate Downtown Better	Respondents Who Rate Mall Better	"Balance"
Helpfulness of salespeople	8%	17%	−9
Convenience	36%	50%	−14
Quality of merchandise	6%	31%	25
Prices	8%	34%	−26
Value for your money	5%	31%	−26
Personal safety	6%	52%	−46
Cleanliness	8%	56%	−48
Variety of merchandise	6%	73%	−67
Ease of getting around	8%	76%	−68
Getting merchandise home	3%	72%	−69
Having the stores you want	4%	81%	−77
Ease of parking	6%	85%	−79
Store hours	1%	81%	−80
Cost of parking	2%	94%	−92

VII. POSSIBLE CHANGES FOR DOWNTOWN

Our final—and most important—objective in the Downtown Retail Survey was to identify changes in Downtown that might have a positive effect on retail sales.

Table 7.1 shows workers' evaluations of the extent to which possible changes might increase their Downtown shopping, and Figure 7.1 provides a bar chart of these results. Parking draws the most votes, with improved merchandise selection and ecological factors coming next.

Table 7.2 splits these evaluations by respondents who shop Downtown more than they did five years ago and respondents whose Downtown shopping has declined. In general, both groups have similar profiles; free parking scores highest, valet parking scores lowest, etc. It is interesting to note that respondents who shop less appear slightly more sensitive to ecological factors, whereas respondents who shop more are slightly more sensitive to access issues.

Tables 7.3 and 7.4 show respondents' reactions to various stores that might be opened Downtown. Department stores and discount stores score highest among types of stores, with Macy's and Target tops among specific stores. Macy's, of course, is probably the hottest department store in the U.S. right now.

Overall, Tables 7.1 through 7.4 suggest that parking improvements, better store selection (especially the addition of another department store), and general ecological upgrading are the keys to increased shopping from Downtown workers. We consider all of these to be plausible changes, with store selection probably the single most important issue.

A more fundamental issue is the extent to which increased shopping by the Downtown work force will restore overall Downtown sales. Table 7.5 (with Table 7.6 supporting) provides a handle on this issue by estimating the decline in retail sales attributable to each of various sources.

TABLE 7.1
**Rankings of Possible Changes for Downtown Considered
Most Likely to Increase Shopping (limited to four choices)**

Possible Changes	Percentage of Respondents
Free parking	70%
Add higher-quality stores	54%
Clean up streets and sidewalks	49%
Expand and unify store hours	47%
Increase police officers/security	44%
Add less expensive stores	32%
Expand The Park Trolley service	28%
Provide delivery service	20%
Extend public transit schedules to allow after-work shopping	19%
Valet parking	5%

Possible Changes

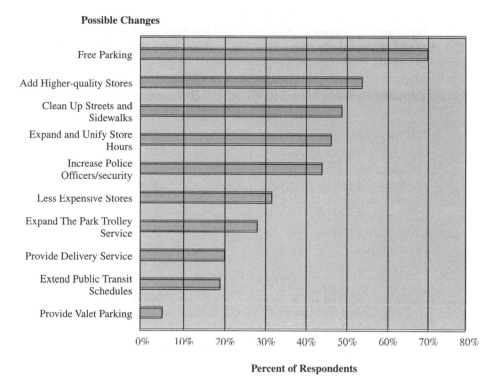

Percent of Respondents

Figure 7.1 Rankings of Possible Changes for Downtown Considered Most Likely to Increase Shopping (limited to four choices)

TABLE 7.2
**Rankings of Possible Changes for Downtown Considered
Most Likely to Increase Shopping by Respondent Group
(limited to four choices)**

Possible Changes	Percentage of Respondents Who:	
	Shop Downtown More Than 5 Years Ago	Shop Downtown Less Than 5 Years Ago
Free parking	70%	70%
Add higher-quality stores	54%	57%
Clean up streets and sidewalks	47%	57%
Expand and unify store hours	49%	44%
Increase police officers/security	45%	50%
Add less expensive stores	34%	30%
Expand The Park Trolley service	34%	25%
Provide delivery service	19%	21%
Extend public transit schedules to allow after-work shopping	20%	16%
Valet parking	5%	6%

TABLE 7.3
Rankings of Types of New Stores That Respondents Would Most Likely Patronize (limited to three choices)

Types of Possible New Stores	Percentage of Respondents
New department store	72%
Discount/off-price store	62%
Car care center	28%
Hardware store	26%
Grocery store	25%
Children's store	21%
Child care center	7%
None of these	9%

TABLE 7.4
Rankings of Specific New Stores That Respondents Would Most Likely Patronize (limited to three choices)

Possible New Stores	Percentage of Respondents
Macy's	68%
Target	60%
Dillard's	39%
Bloomingdale's	37%
J.C. Penney	29%
Mervyn's	24%
Loehman's	14%
None of these	4%

This table, while rough, gives clear indication that Downtown office workers account for a relatively small portion of the total decline in Downtown sales. Specifically, we estimate that 15 percent of Downtown's sales loss was caused by office workers—mostly because of decreased employment—whereas 85 percent came from other sources. The most likely "other source" is destination shoppers; people who used to go Downtown to shop and no longer do so.

Clearly, a revival of Downtown retail trade will depend more heavily on bringing shoppers back to Downtown than on encouraging extra sales to Downtown workers. Another way to view this point is as follows. We estimate that Downtown workers account for about $130,000,000 in merchandise sales per annum. Even if this number is increased by 50 percent—which is highly unlikely given the current local economy and given the time and transport constraints that Downtown workers face in shopping—it would represent a $65 million solution to a $250 million problem.

The Downtown Retail Survey was focused on office workers, so we do not have data on the changes that might attract destination shoppers to Downtown. Common sense suggests that free parking, improved wayfinding systems, improved store selection, and possibly ecological improvements will be crucial factors, but any firm conclusions must await appropriate data.

TABLE 7.5
Estimated Components of the Decline
in Downtown Retail Spending, 1980–1986 (in 1982 $)

Source	Amount of Decline	Percentage of Decline
1. Total decline in Downtown sales[1]	$250,000,000	100%
2. Decline caused by reduced employment Downtown	$24,476,128	10%
3. Decline caused by newer workers spending less than older workers	$13,586,184	5%
4. Decline caused by reduced spending among older workers	$2,780	0%
5. Decline caused by other sources (particularly patronage from destination shoppers)	$221,134,908	85%

[1]Decline in CBD retail sales estimated from Texas Comptroller of Public Accounts.

TABLE 7.6
Supporting Calculations for Table 7.5

Source	Amount	Percent
1. Total decline in Downtown sales[1]	$250,000,000	100%

Approx. 1980 sales	$750,000,000
– Approx. 1986 sales	500,000,000
Total decline	$250,000,000

Source	Amount	Percent
2. Decline caused by reduced employment Downtown	$24,476,128	10%

Average amount spent in past 90 days by respondents who spend same % now as then: $244

Assume annual expenditure is $4 \times \$244 = \$976$

Estimated 1980 work force	173,543
– Estimated 1986 work force	148,465
Decline in work force	25,078

25,078-person decline in work force × $976 expenditure per person = $24,476,128 decline in spending caused by reduced employment

[1]Decline in CBD retail sales estimated from Texas Comptroller of Public Accounts.

TABLE 7.6
Suppporting Calculations for Table 7.5 (in 1982 $)—Continued

Source	Amount	Percent
3. Decline caused by newer workers spending less than older workers	$13,586,184	5%

Average amount spent in 90 days by workers
who spend same % as before: $244
– Average amount spent in 90 days
$\underline{\text{by newer workers:}\hspace{2em}\$151}$
Difference per worker $ 93

Assume annual difference is $4 \times \$93 = \$372$

Number of newer workers:
$24.6\% \times 148,465$ total workers = 36,522

$372 decline per newer worker ×
36,522 newer workers = $13,586,184 decline in
spending caused by newer workers spending less

| **4. Decline caused by reduced spending among older workers** | $2,780 | 0% |

A. Average amount spent in 90 days
by workers who spend *more* than
5 years ago: $339
– Average amount spent in 90 days
by workers who spend same
$\underline{\text{\% as before:}\hspace{4em}\$244}$
Difference per worker $ 95

Assume annual difference is $4 \times \$95 = \$380$

Number of workers who spend more:
$20.6\% \times 148.465$ total workers = 30,584

Amount of gain:
$380 \times 30,584$ total workers = $11,621,920

B. Average amount spent in 90 days
by workers who spend same
% as before: $244

– Average amount spent in 90 days
by workers who spend *less* than
$\underline{\text{5 years ago:}\hspace{4em}\$169}$
Difference per worker $ 75

Assume annual difference is $4 \times \$75 = \$300$

Number of workers who spend less:
$26.1\% \times 148,465$ total workers = 38,749

Amount of decline:
$300 \times 38,749$ total workers = $11,624,700

C. Net decline:
$11,624,700 – $11,621,920 = $2,780

Continued

Source	Amount	Percent
5. Decline caused by other sources	$221,134,908	85%

Total decline $250,000,000
– Decline from work force
     decline   24,476,128
– Decline from lower spending
     among newer workers   13,586,184
- Decline from reduced spending
     among older workers   2,780
Decline from other
sources $221,134,908

Appendix 20.2: Questionnaire Used in the Survey

Location   Code

DOWNTOWN RETAIL SURVEY

1. How often do you shop at the following Downtown locations? (CIRCLE ONE ANSWER FOR EACH PLACE)

	Often	Occasionally	Never
Foley's	1	2	3
The Park shopping center	1	2	3
The tunnel	1	2	3
Other Downtown stores	1	2	3

2. When do you shop Downtown? (CIRCLE ONE ANSWER FOR EACH TIME)

	Often	Occasionally	Never
Before starting work	1	2	3
Morning break	1	2	3
During lunch	1	2	3
Afternoon break	1	2	3
After work	1	2	3
Time off from work	1	2	3
Weekend	1	2	3

3. Where did you last buy each of the following types of merchandise? (CIRCLE DOWNTOWN, ELSEWHERE, OR NEVER BUY)

	Downtown	Elsewhere	Never Buy
Auto parts	1	2	3
Baked goods	1	2	3
Beer, wine, or liquor	1	2	3
Books	1	2	3
Candy	1	2	3
Clothing	1	2	3
Computers or software	1	2	3
Cosmetics/toiletries	1	2	3
Eyeglasses	1	2	3
Flowers	1	2	3

Furniture	1	2	3
Hardware	1	2	3
Hosiery	1	2	3
Household appliances	1	2	3
Jewelry	1	2	3
Kitchenware	1	2	3
Office supplies	1	2	3
Prescription or nonprescription drugs	1	2	3
Radio, television, or other electronics	1	2	3
Records or tapes	1	2	3
Shoes	1	2	3
Sporting goods	1	2	3
Tobacco	1	2	3

4. Counting merchandise only—not meals, parking, etc.—about how much did you spend Downtown during the past ninety days?

$ _____

5. Taken as a percentage of your total spending, how does your Downtown spending these days compare with five years ago? (CIRCLE ONE ANSWER)

1 You spend *a higher percentage* Downtown now

2 You spend *about the same percentage* now as then

3 You spend *a lower percentage* Downtown now

4 You didn't work Downtown then

6. How do you think Downtown compares with your usual mall in the following areas? (CIRCLE ONE RATING FOR EACH AREA)

	Downtown Much Better	Downtown Somewhat Better	About Same	Mall Somewhat Better	Mall Much Better
Having the stores you want	5	4	3	2	1
Variety of merchandise	5	4	3	2	1
Quality of merchandise	5	4	3	2	1
Prices	5	4	3	2	1
Value for your money	5	4	3	2	1
Convenience	5	4	3	2	1
Cleanliness	5	4	3	2	1
Ease of parking	5	4	3	2	1
Cost of parking	5	4	3	2	1
Ease of getting around	5	4	3	2	1
Getting merchandise home	5	4	3	2	1
Personal safety	5	4	3	2	1
Store hours	5	4	3	2	1
Helpfulness of salespeople	5	4	3	2	1

7. Of the following, what four changes in Downtown would be most likely to increase your Downtown shopping? (CIRCLE FOUR ITEMS)

1 Add higher-quality stores
2 Add less expensive stores
3 Clean up streets and sidewalks
4 Free parking
5 Valet parking

6 Expand Park Shopping Center Trolley service
7 Provide delivery service
8 Increase police officers/security
9 Expand and unify store hours
10 Extend public transit schedules to allow after-work shopping

8. Which three of the following would you most likely patronize if they opened Downtown? (CIRCLE THREE)

1 Grocery store
2 New department store
3 Children's store
4 Hardware store

5 Car care center
6 Discount/off-price store
7 Child care center
8 NONE OF THESE

9. Which three of the following stores would you most likely patronize if they opened Downtown? (CIRCLE THREE)

1 Bloomingdale's
2 Macy's
3 Dillard's
4 J. C. Penney

5 Mervyn's
6 Loehman's
7 Target
8 NONE OF THESE

10. About how many minutes would it take you to walk from where you work: to Foley's? _____   The Park? _____   Jones Hall? _____

11. Have you ever used (CIRCLE EACH THAT APPLIES)

1   The Park Trolley   2   Metro's downtown circulators

12. What is your home zip code?   77 _____

21 International Marketing Research

OBJECTIVES

LEARNING

After reading this chapter, you should be able to answer the following questions:

❶ How do expenditures on marketing research vary across different parts of the world?

❷ What are some good sources of primary, secondary, and syndicated data for international markets?

❸ How do data collection methods differ across countries?

❹ How do questionnaire design, sampling, and interviewer supervision procedures differ across countries?

❺ What are important managerial issues in international marketing research?

Marketing is increasingly an international activity. Much of what we buy comes from other countries, and much of what we sell is bought in foreign markets. Similarly, marketing research has become an international activity practiced in virtually all countries. International marketing research is any form of marketing research conducted in one or more countries anywhere in the world.

This chapter discusses the ways in which international marketing research differs from research in an American context. The principles of good research remain the same everywhere, but international research may involve (1) different research suppliers, (2) different sources of secondary or syndicated data, (3) different methods of gathering primary data, and/or (4) different questionnaire design or sampling procedures.

The following sections of this chapter discuss differences between countries. After discussing these differences, we discuss the management of international marketing research. We give special attention to procedures for designing cross-national studies that are done in multiple countries for the same product at about the same time.

International Marketing Research Expenditures

According to a study by ESOMAR (the European Society for Market Research), international spending on marketing research was more than $5.4 billion in 1988. Approximately 40 percent of that spending was done in the United States, 40 percent in western Europe, 10 percent in Japan, and 10 percent in the rest of the world. Three points can be seen in these numbers:

- The United States is the largest single country for marketing research.

- However, more than half of the world's marketing research business is done outside the United States.

- The marketing research business is concentrated in industrialized nations, where people have high levels of discretionary income.

Since the publication of that study, the fastest growth in world research spending has been in countries in Asia (Katori, 1990; Miller, 1991, 1994) and Latin America. (Namakforoosh, 1994). In western Europe, the greatest increase in research has been in business-to-business research (Milmo, 1990). It is likely that the United States and western Europe still provide more than 70 percent of world expenditures on market research, but developing nations are increasingly important as a place to do marketing and, consequently, as a place to do marketing research.

As one might expect with a service business such as marketing research, the companies that provide international research are not necessarily the same as in the United States. Marketing Research Tools 21.1 shows the top ten research companies

TOP RESEARCH COMPANIES (BY U.S. AND NON-U.S. REVENUES)

Top Ten Marketing Research Companies According to U.S. Revenues

Company	1993 U.S. Revenues (in millions of dollars)
Nielsen/IMS International	$710
Information Resources Inc.	284
Arbitron Co.	172
VNU Business Information Services	160
Westat	113
Abt Associates	85
Gallup Organization	76
Maritz Marketing Research	74
Walsh International/PMSI	72
NFO Research	57

Top Ten Marketing Research Companies According to Non-U.S. Revenues

Company	1993 Non-U.S. Revenues (in millions of dollars)
Nielsen/IMS International	$1,158
Video Research, Ltd.	132
Research International Group	124
MRB Group	69
Walsh International/PMSI	54
Global Market Research	51
Information Resources Inc.	50
Milward Brown	47
Gallup Organization	28
Louis Harris & Associates	19

Source: Reprinted with permission from the November 28, 1994 issue of *Advertising Age*, pp. 28, 30. Copyright, Crain Communications Inc. 1994.

according to U.S. revenues (in 1993) and the top ten research companies according to non-U.S. revenues. Four companies appear on both lists (Nielsen/IMS International, Information Resources Inc., the Gallup Organization, and Walsh International/PMSI), but the other names differ. A couple of points can be inferred from these lists:

- The fact that top non-U.S. companies show lower revenues than top U.S. companies, despite the fact that total research spending is higher outside the United States, reflects the fact that the international research business is more diffuse, involving more companies in more countries with less total revenue per company than in the United States.
- The fact that different companies appear on the two lists shows that multinational companies are likely to deal with different research suppliers in different

CASE STUDY 21.1

There are 350 million neophyte consumers in places such as Poland, Hungary, and the former Soviet republics. Inquiring American marketers want to know all about them. In eastern Europe, borders are moving, politics are new, currencies are evolving, and uncertainties are multiplying. But some western businesses say it is not too soon to begin figuring out how Ivan shaves or what Olga uses to wash her hair.

"The alternative is to say, 'Gee, we'll wait until things settle down,'" which might allow rivals to get ahead in the new marketplace, says Ken White, marketing research director for Gillette, which has agreed to a joint venture in Saint Petersburg, Russia, to make razor blades and razors.

Gillette is among several companies that are eagerly attempting to map eastern Europe's consumer landscape despite a population unfamiliar with market concepts and a primitive communication system that means pollsters must rely on shoe leather and face-to-face interviews.

When Olivia Scheffler, eastern Europe research manager for Eastman Kodak's professional products business began seeking information in 1989, all she could dig up were general trade flow and production statistics. There were no industry associations to tap and certainly no consumer data.

For marketing research companies actually supervising surveys, the problems can loom large, thwarting even the most ingenious ploys. Special attention must be paid to training local interviewers and reviewing their work. Heads of local polling concerns are knowledgeable, but those below the top level are not. A woman being trained to be a focus group moderator in Moscow was like a drill sergeant: "I asked you a question, and you have to respond," she said.

Despite the obstacles, a fledgling marketing research industry has emerged over the past three years in Budapest, Prague, Warsaw, and Moscow, fed by marketing research companies from western Europe. Meanwhile, dozens of local companies headed by sociologists from government ministries and academic institutions have sprung up to do the legwork for western researchers.

Pollsters are pleasantly surprised to find that, unlike blasé Western consumers, people in eastern Europe are more than willing to answer questions. Gallup's Mr. Manchin recounts how an elderly lady in Hungary thanked an interviewer at the end of an hour-long session. "It was such a wonderful experience to have a chance to talk to you for so long," she said. "How much do I pay you?"

Source: Taken from Lourdes Lee Valeriano, "Western Firms Poll Eastern Europeans to . . .," *The Wall Street Journal,* Apr. 27, 1992, p. B1. Reprinted by permission of *The Wall Street Journal* © 1992 Dow Jones & Company, Inc. All Rights Reserved Worldwide.

countries. A listing of companies involved in international marketing research is given in the annual *Greenbook* prepared by the New York chapter of the American Marketing Association.

■ Three of the companies that appear on both lists—Nielsen/IMS International, IRI, and Walsh International/PMSI—provide syndicated tracking data for the packaged goods and pharmaceutical industries. Companies in these industries can get international data from the same suppliers, but companies in other industries are likely to get syndicated data that are not standardized across countries, if they can get syndicated data in international markets at all.

International Marketing Research Sources

The most striking difference in marketing research across various countries is the varying availability of secondary and syndicated data. Many data sources that we take for granted in the United States do not exist in less developed countries. Nevertheless, even limited data may be highly useful.

Some common sources of secondary and syndicated information about international markets are described in the following sections. The secondary sources are available in most U.S. university libraries. In fact, odd as it may seem, the United States may be the best place to do secondary research on a foreign market. It is often easier to find data in the United States than in the country in question, because many U.S. libraries feature powerful access systems and interlibrary loans (MacFarlane, 1991; Rabin, 1994). In some other countries, information is kept only in specific libraries or government offices, and computer-based access is rudimentary.

Secondary Sources

There are three major sources of information about world markets that every market researcher should know about: the United Nations, the World Bank, and the U.S. Department of Commerce. The *United Nations* publishes a wide range of general economic statistics in its *Statistical and Demographic Yearbooks*. Similar information is published by the World Bank. The U.S. Department of Commerce publishes global market surveys and *Overseas Business Reports*. Summaries of this information, as well as other data, are provided by the Worldcasts division of Predicasts, whose U.S. services were discussed in Chapter 6.

Potential sources of more specific information include the following:

■ For statistics on a particular industry, try the *Yearbook of Industrial Statistics*, Euromonitor's *International Marketing Data and Statistics*, and/or the *World Market Share Reporter*.

- For nonstatistical information on an industry, use *Predicasts F & S International Index*. This is an extension of the *F & S Index* mentioned in Chapter 6. Another useful source of information about industry events is the *International Trade Fairs and Conferences Directory*.

- For information about a specific company, use the *Predicasts F & S International Index*. To learn whether the company you are studying is owned by another, try *Who Owns Whom* or *International Companies and Their Brands*. Market share data in various countries are reported in the *World Share Reporter* (Reddy and Lazich, 1995). Annotated guides to sources are available (Weekly and Cary, 1986) but rapidly become dated.

These sources are just the tip of the iceberg in international research. Many countries have ministries that compile statistical data on economic activity, and there are an increasing number of online databases that provide information on international trade. Ask your librarian for help, and check the Internet.

Syndicated Sources

The availability of syndicated data for international markets is growing rapidly. Nielsen/IMS International, the world's largest research company, is now authorized to operate in more than ninety countries. This is an extreme example, but a major trend in the research business is for companies with syndicated services to expand their international operations so they are able to serve global marketers as shown in Case Study 21.2.

Despite this trend toward expansion, three general principles govern the availability of syndicated data:

- Companies in the packaged goods and pharmaceutical industries can buy similar data in a wide variety of countries.

CASE STUDY 21.2

A.C. Nielsen Marketing Research and Information Resources Inc. have been battling for several years to dominate the scanner data syndicated service market. In 1994, Nielsen had several major victories, luring back Bristol-Myers Squibb and signing General Mills. The major reason for these triumphs was that these new clients sell their products around the world and need global marketing data.

"That's Nielsen's big advantage," said James Goss, an analyst for Duff and Phelps. "Three-fourths of their business is overseas, and companies like Johnson and Johnson are actively engaged in those markets. When Nielsen markets itself, the first word out of its mouth is 'global.'" IRI has not been sitting idly by. Last month it announced that it signed an agreement to acquire Survey Research Group of Hong Kong, Asia's largest marketing research firm. IRI executives say the company is headed for major international expansion.

Source: Taken from Ronald E. Yates, "Johnson & Johnson Chooses Nielsen," *Chicago Tribune,* Mar. 9, 1994, p. D1.

- Other companies face spotty availability of syndicated data across countries. If data are available, they are likely to be provided by different suppliers with some amount of inconsistency in measures and formats.
- Syndicated data are difficult to find in less developed countries.

In short, it is difficult for large multinational companies to get the consistent data that they would like to have across international markets.

International Differences in Data Collection Methods

There are various differences in data collection methods across countries. Rates of literacy, levels of technology, culture, and tradition all affect data collection methods. The following discussion of these differences is organized according to data collection method.

Focus Groups

In principle, focus groups can be used anywhere. In practice, they receive little use outside the United States. They are uncommon in most of western Europe and are virtually unknown in less developed countries.

Focus groups are uncommon outside the United States because personal interviewing is more feasible. In the United States, focus groups serve as a way of getting unstructured, face-to-face information from customers. Personal interviews with a broader group of respondents would be preferred in many situations, but this type of interviewing is deemed too expensive. This is less true in other countries. In European nations, short distances and high population density make personal interviewing more cost effective than in the United States. In less developed countries, low interviewer pay rates reduce the relative cost of personal interviews.

Personal Surveys

In all countries, personal interviewing is the method of choice for business-to-business research. For consumer research, personal interviewing is rare in the United States but is far more common in other countries, for the reasons already given.

Telephone Surveys

The use of telephone interviewing varies widely across countries. In Sweden and Switzerland, as in the United States, telephone interviewing is the most common

CASE STUDY 21.3

The environment for market research can vary widely across countries, especially between industrialized and less developed nations.

We once bid on a contract to do a large survey in Afghanistan. To help prepare for this project, we contacted other researchers who had worked in Afghanistan to learn about their experiences. They told us that:

- Telephone interviewing would be impossible because of low phone ownership and cultural expectations; all interviewing would have to be done in person.
- The interviewers would have to be men, because it was not considered appropriate for women to do this sort of work.
- The interviewers would have to interview female respondents in the company of their husbands or fathers.
- Strong, healthy men should be hired as interviewers because in some places the interviewer might be required to show his worth by wrestling the village wrestling champion or riding a horse bareback.

The project was canceled because of a revolution, so we never got a chance to experience these things firsthand. However, the preparation for the project was enough to convince us that research in Afghanistan is different from research in America. In America, our interviewers never had to wrestle anyone or ride a horse bareback to get an interview!

method of conducting market research surveys. In Italy and Spain, telephone interviewing is hardly ever used, and telephone surveys are virtually unknown in less developed countries. Researchers in countries such as France, England, and the Netherlands do some phone interviewing, but not as much as in the United States.

The variation in telephone interviewing across European countries may be related to cultural attitudes about the polite way of approaching people. Mediterranean countries such as Italy and Spain are considered to have more "personal" cultures, and we have heard researchers say, "If you want information, you must appear in person to show respect and deference." However, the differences in telephone interviewing may also be attributable to industry custom.

In less developed countries, the absence of telephone interviewing is attributable to low levels of telephone ownership. Marketing Research Tools 21.2 shows that telephone coverage is much lower in less developed countries than in industrialized nations.

A low level of telephone availability has two deleterious effects on telephone surveys. First, it limits the extent to which a telephone survey can cover the population. This is less of a problem than it might appear, because middle- and upper-class people are more likely to have telephones, and most market research in developing nations is directed at these people. However, a low level of telephone availability also tends to be associated with a low level of telephone usage, and people who have telephones do not expect to have them used for research purposes.

MARKETING
RESEARCH
TOOLS

21.2

**TELEPHONE AVAILABILITY
IN VARIOUS COUNTRIES**

Country	Number of People per Telephone
Canada	1.3
United States	1.3
Germany	1.6
France	1.6
Italy	1.5
Spain	4.1
United Kingdom	3.7
Japan	1.8
Czech Republic	2.6
Poland	8.5
Russia	10.3
El Salvador	38.1
Guatemala	62.0
Mexico	10.4
Argentina	9.7
Brazil	11.3
Colombia	13.0
Ecuador	27.4
India	191.0
Pakistan	164.0
Malaysia	11.7
Singapore	2.2
South Korea	5.4
Taiwan	3.2
Thailand	52.6
Australia	1.8
New Zealand	1.5
Egypt	35.6
Iran	26.5
Iraq	18.6
Israel	2.6
Nigeria	366.7
South Africa	6.9

Source: From *The Economist Book of Vital World Statistics,* by The Economist Books Limited. Copyright 1990 by The Economist Books Limited. Reprinted by permission of Times Books, a division of Random House, Inc.

Mail Surveys

The use of mail surveys obviously depends on literacy levels and mail systems within a country. Countries with high literacy levels and good mail systems are reasonable places to do mail surveys. Countries with low literacy levels and/or bad mail systems are not well suited to mail surveys (though even in these countries, the population of interest for marketing research purposes is likely to be literate). Marketing Research Tools 21.3 shows literacy rates in various countries.

Apart from the issue of literacy, there may be country differences that local researchers will know about. In the Netherlands and the Scandinavian countries, there have recently been strong protests about government censuses and surveys as invasions of privacy. This has led to reduced cooperation for all surveys, especially by mail.

Critical Thinking Skills

What differences, if any, would you expect between the United States and Mexico in methods of administration for consumer research studies? How about the United States and Canada?

Mall Surveys

The number of malls is higher in the United States than elsewhere in the world. In many other countries, few malls exist. For this reason, mall studies are far less common outside the United States. However, other forms of intercept surveys may be used. "Street-corner" intercepts, for example, are common in some European countries.

# International Marketing Research Design Issues

Questionnaire Design

Although wordings and meanings differ in each country, the principles of questionnaire design are stable across cultures. That is, the discussion in Chapters 10 to 12 would apply anywhere.

One difference that does occur between countries is in the degree of deference given the interviewer. In some countries, there is a strong culture of politeness and a greater tendency on the part of respondents to try to figure out what answer would please the interviewer and to give that answer. This is to some extent, but not completely, a function of level of development. It is also more characteristic of eastern than western countries.

MARKETING
RESEARCH
TOOLS

21.3

LITERACY RATES ACROSS COUNTRIES

Country	Estimated Percentage of Population Who Can Read and Write	Country	Estimated Percentage of Population Who Can Read and Write
North America		**Middle East**	
Canada	97	Egypt	46
Mexico	88	Iran	72
United States	99	Iraq	89
Central America		Israel	95
El Salvador	70	**Africa**	
Guatemala	55	Ethiopia	24
South America		Nigeria	51
Argentina	96	South Africa	78
Brazil	80	**Europe**	
Colombia	88	France	99
Asia		Germany	99
China	78	Italy	97
India	52	Poland	98
Pakistan	26	Portugal	85
South Korea	88	Russia	98
Taiwan	88	United Kingdom	99
Thailand	93		
Australasia			
Australia	99		
New Zealand	99		

Source: International Marketing Data and Statistics 1997, London: Euromonitor, 1977, p. 438, and *European Marketing Data and Statistics 1997*, London: Euromonitor, 1977, p. 380.

Sample Quality and Sample Design

High-quality samples can be selected from almost every country in the world, although there may be logistical problems in executing the sample. In many European countries, sampling of consumer populations is far easier than in the United States because registers exist. **Registers** list all persons or all adults in a country. Legitimate

Author Tips

There is some tendency for respondents to try to please the interviewer in every country, including the United States. The questionnaire designer must be aware of this tendency and keep from asking leading questions. Also, interviewers in all countries must be trained to ask questions in a neutral way.

marketing research firms are generally permitted to sample from these registers for modest fees. In some cases, such as in Great Britain, the register is a public document available at no cost except that of copying from it.

Where telephones are common, telephone directories usually form an excellent sampling frame, since, at least up to now, there were only a few unlisted numbers in countries other than the United States. In several European countries, one must pay a fairly substantial fee to remain unlisted.

In countries where lists are unavailable and data are gathered through personal interviews, researchers often use **quota sampling** procedures. These specify an area that an interviewer must cover and sometimes a travel pattern. The interviewer is also given quotas by gender and sometimes other variables but is not required to call back if no one is home. This procedure saves significant amounts of money and time. It was once common in the United States but has now become rare since little face-to-face interviewing is done in U.S. marketing research.

Quota sampling has been fairly successful in Europe. This is because European behaviors and attitudes based on social class have been more rigid than in the United States. Generally, in Europe, social class is more closely related to where people live and what they buy than it is in the United States.

In many developing countries, marketing research is still mainly done in the large cities and the areas immediately surrounding them. Sending interviewers long distances into inaccessible areas makes no sense since it is very expensive and there is unlikely to be much of a distribution system for the product of interest outside the cities.

Interviewer Selection, Training, and Supervision

The quality of the available interviewing force varies from country to country, depending on alternative job opportunities and the education of the labor force. In general, the quality of interviewers as measured by education and intelligence is higher in many developing countries than in the United States and other developed countries. This is because job opportunities are fewer in developing countries, so interviewing jobs are more highly regarded.

Critical Thinking Skills

What differences, if any, would you expect between the United States and Mexico in interviewer selection and training procedures? How about the United States and Canada?

Interviewer training and supervision procedures are similar across most countries. The one exception is that where telephones are more common, supervision is usually by telephone; where telephones are rare, supervision is face to face regardless of the data collection method.

Validation procedures also vary according to telephone ownership rates. If a country has high telephone coverage, verification of research interviews is by phone; otherwise, verification is by

CASE STUDY 21.4

International beer companies have a hot new market in a surprising place: Saudi Arabia. The country bans alcoholic beverages, but nonalcoholic beers have become popular. As a result, companies such as Heineken, Bass, and Stroh have jumped into the market.

Although the beer companies know that nonalcoholic beer is selling, they are not sure who is buying it. Saudi Arabia is a tough place to do market research. Focus groups are a problem because the government officially bans most gatherings of four or more people, with the exceptions of family and religious meetings. There are no published electoral rolls or Western-style phone books to use in contacting consumers for a random survey. And it is technically illegal to stop strangers on the street or knock on the door of someone's house. "Pretty much you obtain a group of respondents through word of mouth," says Ajay Shrikhande, chairman of Dubai ad agency Lintas Gulf. "You spread the word and say, `Let's get together.' It's not ideal for getting a random sample."

Getting to know your audience is even harder if your product appeals to women, brewers say. Sales of Bass's Barbican with Lemon malt beverage are booming in Saudi Arabia, and company officials "suspect it's women who like it best," says Huw Williams, sales director for Bass Beers Worldwide. "But in a country where the women are covered head to toe, and they can't drive, and they can't speak to you on the street, we can't be sure."

Source: Adapted from Tara Parker-Pope, "Nonalcoholic Beer Hits the Spot in Mideast," *The Wall Street Journal,* Dec. 6, 1995, p. B1. Reprinted by permission of *The Wall Street Journal,* © 1995 Dow Jones & Company, Inc. All Rights Reserved Worldwide.

mail. In some countries, validation is not routinely done; however, we think that this is a mistake and that research clients should always insist on validation.

Research Interpretation

Regardless of how data are collected, the crucial issue in marketing research is the implications of research results for marketing programs. Data do not speak for themselves; the interpretation of research is an active process in which data are studied, interpreted, and then presented to best effect.

International marketing research does not present any special challenges in interpreting objective data such as sales results, market populations, and so on. These data may not speak for themselves, but whatever meaning they hold is literal, with no culture-bound shadings. Self-report data, in contrast, are very much influenced by cultural context. Literal interpretations of questions or answers can easily distort their meaning. For this reason, questionnaire design and data interpretation are usually more satisfactory if done by someone who shares the respondents' culture (Samiee, 1994).

Managing International Marketing Research

General Management and Staffing Issues

The need to understand cultural context in marketing research presents a simple implication for marketing research management: research is best performed by native researchers within a country. This implication applies to data collection, of course, but also to research design. A company that sells abroad should use local market researchers who have the same "gut feel" for their markets that we have for ours.

Within this context, the research management principles discussed in Chapter 3 apply to international as well as domestic marketing. Typically, the marketing research staff for any given country will be small and data will be obtained from local suppliers. Contracting procedures should be similar to those used in domestic research, though suppliers are more likely to demand advance payment through a letter of credit and views about the importance of a contract may differ from one country to the next.

Some companies prefer to centralize research operations. **Centralized marketing research** is done by using a single research group everywhere in the world or a single group for major regions of the world. Even if research is not centralized, some countries may be too small to warrant the cost of a separate marketing research staff, so a company might have a single research group for several geographically contiguous

CASE STUDY 21.5

Procter & Gamble has improved its marketing success in developing countries by changing the way it researches and develops products. P&G's traditional approach is to study how people use a product, learn how it might be improved, do lab research to make the improvements, then market the improved product at a premium price. This approach has been extremely successful in America and Europe. In developing nations, though, it too often results in products that consumers cannot afford.

P&G's new research approach in developing nations is to start with an income analysis to determine how much customers can afford. The company then tries to develop products that can be sold within those limits. This approach has produced successful products such as Pampers Uni in Brazil, a less expensive diaper that allows Brazilians to start on the Pampers line until their incomes rise enough to buy regular Pampers.

Source: Taken from Bill Saporito, "Behind the Tumult at P&G," *Fortune,* Mar. 7, 1994, pp. 74–82. © 1994 Time Inc. All rights reserved.

countries despite language and cultural differences among those countries. When research is centralized, either globally or regionally, it is helpful if someone on the staff is a native of or an expert on each country and has a good knowledge of the secondary sources available, as well as a good ability to work with local research suppliers.

Local adaptation is essential; the opposite side of the coin is maintenance of research quality. In many developed countries, the training and experience of market researchers is similar to that obtained in the United States, and there is no need for any special training. In some developing countries, though, employees may have had limited training in relevant skills. In such cases it is useful for the international firm to give additional training to foreign nationals. This training might consist of both academic and on-the-job training in the United States or another developed country and might take several years. The trained researchers then return to their home countries.

Because of varying standards in educational or training systems, there is some temptation for corporate-level marketing researchers in international companies to try to control quality by micromanaging research activities in individual countries. This is a bad idea, because corporate-level researchers generally do not have detailed knowledge about a specific country. Corporate-level researchers have an important role to play in coordinating research activities across countries but should not try to replace locals in research operations.

Our emphasis on the use of native researchers may be disappointing to some of you who have envisioned yourselves as going to live in a country and working in marketing research. However, this is the way things are. Some jobs do still exist, especially in developing countries, for foreign researchers who have western training and have lived in the host country long enough to develop a full command of the language and a feeling for the culture. Even these opportunities will diminish as the availability of well-trained natives increases.

Interestingly, familiarity with foreign languages improves career opportunities for Americans who are willing to work for foreign companies that market in the United States. These companies face exactly the same problems as do U.S. companies selling abroad. They want native marketing researchers, but it is very helpful if these researchers can communicate with corporate management in the managers' native language.

Managing Cross-National Projects

There is a trend in international marketing toward "globalized" programs that offer the same products under the same brand names, same benefit positionings, and same advertising themes in a variety of countries. Globalization is a response to increasingly homogeneous consumer markets in the developed nations, as well as distribution systems and advertising media that increasingly cross borders.

Globalized (or even regionalized) marketing programs often require **cross-national research,** which studies the same topics concerning the same product in several countries at the same time. Given the differences that exist among countries, it is obvious that careful planning and coordination are necessary for such projects to be successful. This coordination is accomplished through the corporate research group.

In planning multicountry marketing research programs, there may be a planning and design committee that has representatives from each of the countries involved in the research plus representatives from corporate research. This committee is responsible for designing research that has maximum similarity across countries yet accommodates the differences among them. The planning committee may hold one or two face-to-face meetings, but much of its work will be done via conference calls, voice mail, and fax. After the planning committee has reached reasonable consensus on the general research design, each individual country can make adaptations to fit its special needs.

In attempting to maximize similarities across countries, special attention is paid to sample design and to questionnaires. Sample design issues are fairly straightforward. The first major decision by the planning committee should be *who or what* the universe for the study is. The same universe definition should be used across countries. There should also be some decision on the approximate cooperation rate needed in each country and the level of effort required to achieve that cooperation. It would generally make no sense to use a single mailing in one country and get a very low cooperation rate while interviewers in another country conduct expensive door-to-door interviews with callbacks.

On the other hand, it is not necessary that identical data collection methods be used in every country. Some countries might use telephone sampling, some face-to-face quota samples, and some mail if the type of questionnaire makes this possible. As noted in Chapter 7, these different modes of data collection generally yield similar data quality, so it is reasonable to use whichever method best fits a country. It is also not necessary for the sampling procedure to be identical from one country to the next. Each country staff will use its own standard lists and methods.

Every country should use the questionnaire adopted by the planning committee as a starting point. If this draft is prepared in English or any other language, it will have to be translated into the various languages used in each country. After this is done, the standard practice is to have another translator retranslate the questionnaire back into English. This process is called **backtranslation.** Backtranslation is done to ensure that the translation does not distort the original meaning of the questions. If the backtranslation produces a question with a different meaning than the original question, the question designers and translators must iron out the differences.

There may be some questions in the initial questionnaire draft that are inappropriate, meaningless, or confusing in one or more of the countries. Normally, it is the responsibility of that country's representatives to point this out during the design of the first draft. It is sometimes possible to design a more general question that works in all countries. In some cases, however, a question asked in some countries is simply omitted in others. Conversely, a question might be added for some countries but not for others.

Once each country has a draft in the proper language, a simultaneous pretest should be held in each country. Any difficulties with question wording uncovered in the pretest can be handled by either the planning committee or the country staff. To be safe, the revised questionnaires should again be backtranslated to make sure that the concepts have not been distorted.

It is evident that the process of developing a study and questionnaire to be used in several countries is slower and more cumbersome than simply doing the same thing in a single country. However, cross-national research can be a powerful and efficient alternative to uncoordinated research studies in separate countries.

CASE STUDY 21.6

International markets are becoming increasingly homogeneous, but important differences remain among nations. These differences make it important to do multinational research and not assume that knowledge from one country will transfer to another.

Take refrigerators as an example. Northern Europeans want large refrigerators because they tend to shop once a week in supermarkets; southern Europeans want smaller refrigerators because they shop more frequently. Northerners like their freezers on the top, whereas southerners like their freezers on the bottom. The British, who eat lots of frozen food, like refrigerators with 60 percent freezer space. Americans want even larger refrigerators than northern Europeans do, and Asians want even smaller refrigerators than southern Europeans. White is the preferred color in most countries, but bright colors are preferred in developing Asian nations, where refrigerators are often placed in the living room.

These differences limit the international transferability of research. For example, using American market research to develop a refrigerator for the Spanish market would be a big mistake.

Source: Based on William Echikson, "The Trick to Selling in Europe," *Fortune,* Sept. 20, 1993, p. 82, and Rahul Jacob, "The Big Rise: Middle Classes Explode Around the Globe, Bringing New Markets and New Prosperity," *Fortune,* May 30, 1994, pp. 74–90.

If one is analyzing data from multiple countries, a decision must always be made whether to do a single analysis when country (or segment within country) is one of the explanatory variables, or to do a country-by-country analysis. The issue is the same as when an analysis is done across different market segments in the United States.

It is easier to do a single analysis, but this will be misleading if there are significant differences among countries. For example, Spam canned meat is seen in some countries as a superior good purchased by the rich and in others as an inferior good purchased by the poor. In such a case, combining data from several countries would make the data impossible to interpret. Analyses should always be done at the country (or segment) level first before similar segments and countries are combined.

Summary

This chapter discussed international marketing research. The following points were covered:

1. How do expenditures on marketing research vary in different parts of the world?

The United States is the largest country for marketing research spending but accounts for less than half of worldwide expenditures. Together, the United States and western Europe account for about 80 percent of worldwide expenditures, but the fastest-growing areas are the developing nations.

2. What are some good sources of secondary and syndicated data for international markets?

Major sources of secondary information on international markets include U.N. publications, World Bank publications, U.S. Department of Commerce publications, *Predicasts Worldcasts*, and *Predicasts F & S International Index*. The availability of syndicated data for international markets is growing rapidly. However, it is still difficult to find syndicated data for less developed countries, and data across countries are likely to be provided by different suppliers with some amount of inconsistency in measures and formats.

3. How do data collection methods differ across countries?

Differences between the United States and other countries in data collection methods include (1) personal interviews for consumer research are used more often in other countries than in the United States, (2) focus groups are used less often in other countries, (3) telephone interviews are generally less common in other countries and are inappropriate in some nations because of low telephone ownership, (4) the use of mail surveys varies depending on literacy rates and the quality of mail service, and (5) mall surveys are uncommon outside the United States because malls are uncommon, though "street-corner" surveys are common in some countries.

4. How do questionnaire design, sampling, and interviewer supervision procedures differ across countries?

The general principles of questionnaire design are the same across countries. Sampling principles are also the same, but in some countries marketing research firms can sample consumers from government registers of the population, and telephone books are more useful because there are few unlisted numbers. In countries where lists of consumers are unavailable for sampling purposes, researchers often use quota sampling procedures to obtain personal interviews within selected geographic areas.

Interviewer training and supervision procedures are similar across countries. Verification of research interviews is done by phone in countries with high telephone coverage and by mail elsewhere. The quality of the interviewing force in a particular country depends on alternative job opportunities and the education of the labor force.

5. What are important managerial issues in international marketing research?

Better results are obtained if research is designed and analyzed in the country where it is done. This implies local research staff, although some companies prefer to centralize. Also, marketing research for any given country should typically be bought from local suppliers.

Suggested Additional Readings

Ley Groves, *Principles of International Marketing Research* (Cambridge, Mass.: Blackwall Business, 1994) and Susan P. Douglas and C. Samuel Craig, *International Marketing Research* (Englewood Cliffs, N.J.: Prentice Hall, 1983) provide a full-scale discussion of issues raised in this chapter.

Discussion Questions

1. Discuss some of the unique problems a researcher faces in conducting international survey research.

2. What are some major sources of information about world markets?

3. How might use of the following data collection methods and procedures differ when conducting marketing research in a foreign country? What should the researcher keep in mind before using each of these methods?
   a. Face-to-face interviews
   b. Telephone interviews
   c. Mail surveys

4. What is meant by cross-national research? When is cross-national research generally beneficial?

5. What is the major objective of cross-national research? How can the researcher minimize country differences in a coordinated study?

6. After the U.S., what countries would you think would be big users of marketing research?

Marketing Research Challenge

Imagine you are working for one of the major fast-food chains such as McDonald's or Burger King. How would you organize your international marketing research operation? Look in the business press for discussions of what these companies actually do to compare with your proposed organizational structure.

Internet Exercise

Pick two countries: one for which you think syndicated data will be easy to obtain and one for which you think syndicated data will be difficult to obtain. Access the A. C. Nielsen site at http://acnielsen.com/home/countries/world.htm and see what industries Nielsen tracks in your chosen countries. Were you correct in your assumptions about your chosen countries?

References

Katori, Kazuaki (1990). "Recent Developments and Future Trends in Marketing Research in Japan Using New Electronic Media." *Journal of Advertising Research* 30 (April–May), pp. 53–57.

MacFarlane, Ian (1991). "Do-It-Yourself Marketing Research." *Management Review* 80 (May), pp. 34–37.

Miller, Cyndee (1991). "European In-Store Marketing Research Grows." *Marketing News* 25 (July 2), p. 1.

Miller, Cyndee (1994). "China Emerges as Latest Battleground for Marketing Researchers." *Marketing News* 28 (Feb. 14), pp. 1–2.

Milmo, Sean (1990). "Business-to-Business Research Booms in Western Europe." *Business Marketing* 75 (April), p. 26.

Namakforoosh, Naghi (1994). "Data Collection Methods Hold Key to Research in Mexico." *Marketing News* 28 (Aug. 29), p. 28.

Rabin, Steve A. (1994). "How to Sell Across Cultures." *American Demographics* 16 (March), pp. 56–57.

Reddy, Marlita A., and Robert S. Lazich (1995). *World Market Share Reporter: A Compilation of Reported World Market Share Data and Rankings on Companies, Products, and Services, 1995–96* (Detroit: Gale Research).

Samiee, Saeed (1994). "Customer Evaluation of Products in a Global Market." *Journal of International Business Studies* 25, pp. 579–604.

Weekly, James K., and Mary K. Cary (1986). *Information for International Marketing: An Annotated Guide to Sources* (New York: Greenwood Press).

22 Ethical Issues in Marketing Research

OBJECTIVES

After reading this chapter, you should be able to answer the following questions:

❶ What ethical obligations do researchers have to research participants?

❷ What ethical obligations do researchers have to clients?

❸ What ethical obligations do clients have to research suppliers?

❹ When research findings are made public, what ethical issues are involved?

E thical questions arise in marketing research, as in all other aspects of life. Consider the following scenarios:

- A hospital employee calls competing hospitals in the area, pretending to be a university student who is doing a class project on hospital marketing. Under this guise, she gathers data on competitors' marketing plans. Is this ethical?

- A researcher conducts a marketing survey and makes no promises of anonymity or confidentiality. The names of respondents who express interest in a new product are given to the company's sales department for follow-up. Is this ethical?

- A research company does a customer satisfaction study for a client. Later, the research company learns that the client is misrepresenting the results in sales presentations. The research company asks the client to stop doing this, but the client refuses. Does the research company have the *right* to make a public statement contradicting the client's representation of the findings? Does the research company have an ethical *obligation* to do so?

Ethical questions such as these permeate marketing research. They require you to have some knowledge of ethical standards, not only so that you can feel comfortable with your own actions but also so that you can act in a way that other people find ethical. Ethical behavior is good for business, at least over the long run, because most people respect ethical behavior and most businesspeople have learned that unethical people make poor associates.

This chapter summarizes the most common ethical issues seen in marketing research and provides guidelines for dealing with them. These issues are separated into four broad areas: (1) researchers' obligations to participants, (2) research suppliers' obligations to clients, (3) clients' obligations to suppliers, and (4) disclosure requirements when publicly reporting research results.

The following discussion draws from codes of ethics established by various professional organizations. Three such codes, those of the American Marketing Association, the American Association for Public Opinion Research, and the American Psychological Association are shown as Appendices 22.1, 22.2, and 22.3 at the end of this chapter. We encourage you to read these codes of ethics because they can alert you to what are and are not appropriate practices. You may someday find yourself asked to do something unethical, and codes of ethics come in handy at such times. Most requests for unethical behavior come from managers who simply do not know the ethical issues involved in research. If you make them aware that their requests violate written ethical standards, they almost always drop the requests.

All ethical decisions are ultimately personal (Akaah, 1989, 1990; Akaah and Riordan, 1989; Castleberry, French, and Carlin, 1993; Kelley, Ferrell, and Skinner, 1990). If you find yourself confronted by an ethical question that is not specifically addressed in this chapter, just follow three simple maxims:

- Do unto others as you would have them do unto you.

- Do not do anything that you would not be willing to have published in the newspaper.

- If your instincts tell you that something is wrong, follow them.

Researchers' Obligations to Research Participants

Researchers have some general obligations to the people who provide data in marketing research studies. These include:

- Participants should not be harmed.
- Participants should not be deceived.
- Participation should be willing and informed.
- Data should be held in confidence.

Few people would dispute these obligations in principle. However, what do they mean in practice?

Participants Should Not Be Harmed

The first obligation of researchers to participants is not to harm them in any way. At a physical level, this means that participants should not be burned, shocked, prodded, nauseated, or generally subjected to discomfort. For example, a food company should inquire about allergies before having people participate in a taste test. At an emotional level, the obligation not to harm participants means that they should not be embarrassed, ridiculed, belittled, or generally subjected to mental distress.

Taken to the extreme, the obligation not to hurt participants might seem to make research impossible. Any marketing research survey, for example, will encounter people who do not really want to participate but are not forceful enough to refuse. One can argue that these people are harmed by being "pressured" into participation—even though the researcher is unaware of the respondent's feelings. Similarly, many surveys will produce moments in which some respondents are embarrassed that they have not bought some product, their income is not higher, or whatever. If the dictum that research should not harm participants is taken to mean that not even one participant should experience the slightest bit of discomfort, it would be impossible to find research that satisfies this test.

The approach taken by most researchers who have pondered this issue is to apply two standards. First, researchers should *minimize* the potential discomfort of a research project and *maximize* respondents' convenience. This entails practices such as:

- Avoiding embarrassing or prying questions if possible; for example, do not ask about income unless you absolutely need it.
- Reminding research participants that they need not answer any question they prefer not to answer.
- Scheduling interviewing so as to minimize disruptions in respondents' lives; for example, calls to consumers should generally not be placed before 9:00 A.M. or after 9:00 P.M.

Second, once the potential harm of a research project has been minimized, its risks should be compared to risks that people face in everyday life. Nothing is absolutely risk-free—we take a risk of being run over every time we cross the street. If the risks posed by the research are no greater than those posed by everyday life, the research is not viewed as posing serious ethical issues.

Ethical issues do arise when a person who is asked to participate in research does not instantly agree. Is it ethical to try to persuade someone to participate and, if so, how much effort is permissible before it becomes harassment? There is a story told about a U.S. Census Bureau interviewer who never got a refusal. When asked how he did it, he said, "I tell them that there are thirty other interviewers in my group, and if they turn me down they will have to face each of them, one by one." This approach worked for him, but was it ethical?

The approach that many researchers have adopted is to distinguish between hard and soft refusals. A soft refusal is when a person says, "I'm too busy right now" or "This isn't a good time." A hard refusal is one when a person says, "No, I'm not interested." Hard refusals are not followed up, but soft refusals may be. Even for soft refusals, there will almost never be more than one follow-up effort.

For mail surveys, respondents who send back the questionnaire indicating that they do not wish to participate are not followed up, but those who do not mail it back receive subsequent reminder mailings.

Participants Should Not Be Deceived

There are many ways in which researchers might deceive respondents. For example, a researcher might misrepresent herself as a student doing a class project, as cited earlier in this chapter. A research company might advise an interviewer to identify herself to respondents as "Joan Alden," so that her real identity is protected from people who might become obsessed with her. A research company might not disclose the name of the research sponsor to participants. An interviewer might tell respondents that a ten-minute interview will "take only a few minutes." A researcher might promise anonymity in a study where respondents can be identified or might use what respondents thought were confidential answers to research questions as the basis for qualifying sales prospects.

Is it ever ethically permissible to deceive participants in marketing research? We feel that several situations can be distinguished.

Sales Prospecting and Fund-raising Under the Guise of Surveys

Because so many people are willing to participate in marketing research studies, some unscrupulous marketers and fund-raisers pretend to do research, especially surveys, when they actually have no interest in obtaining information. This is a clear violation of all ethical codes that deal with marketing research (Advertising Research Foundation, 1986). If something is represented to participants as marketing research, it should be legitimate marketing research and the results should not be used for other purposes without the express consent of participants.

As an example of phony research, a major car company conducted a large telephone survey some time ago, indicating to respondents that the purpose of the survey was to measure their attitudes about cars and their buying intentions for marketing research purposes. This information was then turned over to local dealers, who made sales calls to likely buyers. This study was done on behalf of the marketing group of this car company without the knowledge of the marketing research group. When the researchers heard about this phony survey, they persuaded management never to do it again. Not only is such behavior an unethical deception of respondents, but such phony surveys ultimately lead to reduced cooperation on legitimate surveys, killing the goose that lays the golden eggs.

One of the most common uses of phony marketing research is to raise money. Fund-raisers have discovered that people are more likely to contribute money if they have a chance to express their views on issues related to the fund-raising. Thus, a brief survey, usually of four or five questions, is included with a request for a contribution. The survey results are typically thrown away after the checks are cashed and no attention is given to them. This technique is practiced by major political parties as well as by many other nonprofit groups. Despite the worthy goals of many of these organizations, it is our view, and the view of all professional organizations involved in marketing research, that fund-raising under the guise of doing research is deceptive and unethical.

Misidentification of the Researcher or Research Sponsor

One of our examples of deception involved misidentification of the researcher or the research sponsor. In our opinion, such misidentification is acceptable if it serves a legitimate purpose of interviewer security or data integrity *and* it does not encourage participation from people who otherwise would not participate.

Consider, for example, a telephone interviewer using a name that is not her own. We do not see this as an ethical problem. The security concern is not a large one, but it is legitimate, and it is doubtful that participants care whether the interviewer is "Joan Alden" or "Hannah Schnitzer."

Similarly, consider a survey about car attitudes done on behalf of the Ford Motor Company. If respondents are told that Ford is the research sponsor, they may shade their answers to be more favorable toward Ford cars. This gives a legitimate reason not to disclose the research sponsor. At the same time, it seems unlikely that people who are willing to participate in a survey about automobiles would suddenly withdraw that participation if they knew that Ford was the sponsor. Therefore, we do not see an ethical problem with failing to disclose the sponsor's identity at the start of the survey.

Participants who ask the identity of the sponsor can be handled in at least two different ways. One approach is to tell them that the sponsor's name is confidential and let them decide whether or not they will participate under these circumstances. Another approach is to promise to identify the sponsor at the end of the interview and give participants an opportunity to withdraw their responses at that time.

If there is reason to believe that the sponsor's identity will affect people's willingness to participate in the research, the sponsor should be identified. Our example of the hospital employee who poses as a student describes clearly unethical behavior, whether or not the employee actually is a student. The key factor is not whether the person is a student but whether other hospitals would participate if they knew the research was benefiting one of their competitors. Along these lines, we always insist that students who do projects under our supervision clearly identify if the project is being done for some company.

Critical Thinking Skills

A hospital employee calls competing hospitals and gathers information on their marketing plans by telling them she is a university student doing a project on hospital marketing. If the employee actually *is* a student and uses the data for a term paper as well as for her employer's benefit, is this ethical? Why or why not?

Deception in Experiments

As discussed in Chapter 9, one of the threats to internal validity in an experiment is **treatment effects,** in which subjects respond to the fact that they are in an experiment and try to behave in ways that will please the researcher. Of course, this is not what researchers want. They want honest responses.

To reduce or eliminate treatment effects, researchers often disguise the real purpose of an experiment while it is in progress. There are different ways of doing this, based on what subjects are told or not told.

One common approach is actively to misdirect the subject about the purpose of the experiment. **Misdirection** is deliberately falsifying the purpose of the study to get more useful responses from respondents. Chapter 9 gave the example of "theater test" procedures for testing television ads. Subjects see ads embedded in a real program, as they would while watching TV at home. They are told that their task is to evaluate the program, and they are given questions about program content as well as questions intended to measure the effectiveness of advertising. The purpose of the deception is to keep people from paying *too much* attention to the ads, which would detract from the study's external validity. This procedure obviously constitutes deception, even though it is not a large deception.

The standard method of dealing with active misdirection is to debrief subjects at the end of the experiment. **Debriefing** involves telling the subjects the real purpose of the experiment and why the deception was necessary. We believe that this procedure satisfies the experimenter's ethical obligations to the subject. Our reason is that, in our experience, virtually all subjects are satisfied with the debriefing and understand why concealing the real aim of the experiment was necessary.

Another way of disguising the purpose of a survey or experiment is by including a series of distractors so the respondent or subject does not know exactly what the researcher is looking for. In testing ads, for example, the test ad is usually grouped with five or six other ads so that no single ad is given undue attention.

Like active misdirection, this type of camouflage can be covered by debriefing at the end of an experiment. However, it is our belief that debriefing is not usually required in this situation, since no active deception has been practiced and the design has primarily been used to make the experiment more real world.

Deceiving Participants about the Length of the Task

Imagine a researcher who wants to do an interview that will take ninety minutes. The researcher does not mention how long the interview will last during the introduction because of concern that many respondents will refuse to cooperate if they know its length. In this case, we believe this is deception by omission and is unethical.

In general, we believe that the length of an interview should be specified when seeking cooperation if it is possible to do so. For interviews where the length varies depending on the answers, it is often possible to specify a range. One might argue that it really is not ethically necessary to give the time needed for a short interview, but it still is useful to do so because it may increase cooperation.

Participation Should Be Willing and Informed

The ethical issue of how much information to give research participants so they can make informed decisions on whether to participate is a difficult one. Respondents should be given adequate information, but one obviously does not want to take twenty minutes to explain a ten-minute questionnaire. Such a detailed explanation increases the total time required from respondents and provides no clear benefits.

The general principle that guides informed consent is that the amount of information should be related to the risk facing the participant in the study. Most marketing research involves only small risks, if any, for the participants (in comparison, say, with medical research), and therefore only minimal information need be given at the beginning. For example, a typical survey introduction in marketing research would need only three kinds of information:

- Who is doing the study?
- What is the study about?
- How long will it take?

An example might be "Hello, I'm [NAME] from the Danbury Research Organization. We are doing a study concerning people's feelings about ready-to-eat cereal. It should last about fifteen minutes."

You might also want to add (after obtaining permission to proceed): "Your participation in this study is, of course, completely voluntary. Feel free to refuse to answer any questions you feel are too personal." Such a phrase makes respondents' rights more explicit and has been found to reassure people and make them *more* likely to participate.

Earlier in this chapter, we gave our opinion that the research sponsor need not be given in most studies. However, the interviewer and the research organization should be identified so that participants can confirm that the study is legitimate and complain if they are unhappy with the process.

We consider it unethical to falsify the name of the research firm or the client. If the research is done in house by a company, that company should be willing to be identified. Some companies have established in-house marketing research operations and given them different names to conceal the parent company's identity. We consider this to be borderline ethical behavior.

Observational studies pose special questions regarding the issue of informed consent. For example, if a department store wants to measure how people move through the store and gathers this information by observing customers without notifying them, is this ethical? In this situation, one can argue that consent procedures are not needed because the participants are in a public place. On the other hand, cameras in dressing rooms would be an invasion of privacy, as would observation without consent in any private place.

Data Should Be Held in Confidence

The final researcher obligation to participants is the obligation to hold data in confidence. In many studies, participants are told something such as "All answers to this study will be confidential." Whether or not this promise is made, research participants have a right to confidentiality unless they specifically waive this right.

This means that data-gathering organizations should routinely separate information that can identify a specific respondent from the information the respondent gives. This cannot usually be done at the time of a survey interview because it is necessary to have identifying information for purposes of verifying that the interview was conducted. It may also be necessary to call respondents back if interviews are incomplete or crucial answers are unclear. However, once verification and data editing are complete, identifying information should be separated from the answers and never supplied to the client or anyone else. In fact, the identifying information should be destroyed unless there are plans to conduct follow-up research in which the same respondents are reinterviewed. In that situation, the identifying information should be retained in a file separate from the data, and respondents should not be promised anonymity (though it is possible to promise confidentiality).

Some researchers believe that confidentiality should not be violated under any circumstances, but we believe that research participants may waive this right if they wish. In some research projects, participants are asked if they would be willing to be identified so that someone from the sponsoring company can talk with them to follow up their comments. Since such follow-ups are done with the permission of participants, we do not see any violation of ethical principles.

A rare but troublesome problem in marketing research is to have data subpoenaed for court cases. When data are subpoenaed, there are only limited legal safeguards for respondent confidentiality. If identifying information has already been routinely removed, of course, respondent confidentiality can be maintained, but this information cannot be destroyed *after* being requested by a court.

Critical Thinking Skills

A researcher tells survey participants that their answers will remain anonymous. Strictly speaking, it is possible to use sampling records from the study to identify individual respondents. These records are retained in case they are wanted for follow-up research, but the researcher keeps them separate from the questionnaires and makes no other use of them. Is this ethical? Why or why not?

Marketing Research Suppliers' Obligations to Clients

A marketing research supplier is a professional who is ethically obligated to meet professional standards. These standards can be categorized into four main areas:

- Proper procedures should be used.
- Benefits of the research should not be overestimated.
- Clients' information should be kept confidential.
- Results should not be distorted.

Proper Procedures Should Be Used

The Code of Professional Ethics and Practices of the American Association for Public Opinion Research, shown as Appendix 22.2 at the end of this chapter, starts with the following statement:

> We shall exercise due care in developing research designs and survey instruments, and in collecting, processing and analyzing data, taking all reasonable steps to assure the reliability and validity of results.
>
> We shall recommend and employ only those tools and methods of analysis which, in our professional judgment, are well suited to the research problem at hand.
>
> We shall not select research tools and methods of analysis because of their capacity to yield misleading results.

It is sometimes difficult to separate poor competence from poor ethics, but researchers are ethically bound to do the best they can for clients and to advise clients against inappropriate courses of action.

Problems most often arise when a client proposes procedures that the researcher believes to be inappropriate. Sometimes this is because the client really believes that the proposed method is better than the one recommended by the researcher. Other times, though, the client may be proposing a procedure that will yield a desired result. For example, we once did a study in which the marketing research manager of an industrial products company insisted on naming the people to be interviewed, because this manager was fighting with his company's service department and wanted to pick people who would criticize the service department.

Many marketing research companies, faced with the possibility of losing the revenue from a project, will simply do whatever the client wants. However, an ethical researcher will attempt to persuade the client to change the design, and, if this is not possible, will refuse to do the study rather than be associated with an inappropriate project. Of course, the client might also persuade the researcher that the client's approach is better or at least as good.

Do real-world researchers ever turn down business? Believe it or not, they do. Many ethical firms refuse to do work that they consider unprofessional. In the long run, both they and their clients benefit from this behavior (Moorman, Deshpandi, and Zaltman, 1990).

Benefits Should Not Be Over-Promised

In order to win projects, research companies sometimes promise results at a level of accuracy greater than is possible with currently available research techniques. We believe that this is unethical behavior (Axelrod, 1992). The AAPOR Code puts it this way:

> We shall be mindful of the limitations of our techniques and capabilities and shall accept only those research assignments which we can reasonably expect to accomplish within these limitations.

In a widely publicized case a few years ago, a marketing research firm claimed to have developed a method for predicting the success of new products with a high level of accuracy. It was sued by a large client when the actual sales of a new product fell significantly below what had been predicted (Jarvis, 1993). Although the case was settled out of court, it sent a strong message to research suppliers that it is good legal practice as well as good ethical practice to make the limitations of research clear to clients.

Clients' Information Should Be Kept Confidential

Clients often need to reveal proprietary information about their marketing plans and product development to research suppliers in connection with projects. Such information could, of course, be valuable to competitors, and researchers have an ethical responsibility to keep it confidential.

It is unlikely that any supplier would be foolish enough to reveal proprietary information while still working with a client, since this would cause an instant dissolution of the relationship. Researchers are ethically bound, however, to keep former clients' data confidential even if they are now working for a competitor. Again, this is simply good business. If a researcher reveals information about a previous client to a current one, the new client will be unwilling to trust the researcher with any proprietary information.

Results Should Not Be Distorted

Again we quote from the AAPOR code:

> We shall not knowingly make interpretations of research results, nor shall we tacitly permit interpretations that are inconsistent with the data available.
>
> We shall not knowingly imply that interpretations should be accorded greater confidence than the data actually warrant.

Note that this code not only requires researchers to avoid making false claims about their work but also requires them to speak out when their client or someone else makes incorrect *public* statements about the data. This is not easy to do, and not all firms do it, but ethical research firms do. Note that the researcher has no ethical obligation regarding use of a study within the client's own organization and usually has no way of knowing if data are misrepresented within the client firm.

Typical public situations in which clients distort research findings occur when findings are used in advertising or in public sales presentations at meetings or conventions. Then, if the researcher is unable to persuade the client to withdraw the distorted findings, the researcher's ethical obligation is to set the record straight. Note that this is not a violation of the confidentiality requirement, because the client has made the data public.

Realistically, a situation in which client and researcher find themselves in an adversarial relationship is uncomfortable for both sides. Sometimes the client backs off. Sometimes the researcher does. Researchers who allow distorted data to be made public must recognize, however, that their reputations will also be damaged if the data are challenged.

Ethical issue: Is it in the client's best interests to sugar-coat negative results?

Source: Build a Better Life by Stealing Office Supplies: Dogbert's Big Book of Business, 1991. DILBERT, Scott Adams. Reprinted by permission of United Feature Syndicate, Inc.

Clients' Obligations to Research Suppliers

The main ethical obligation of the client is not to ask suppliers to do unethical research. In addition:

- A client should not request research proposals from suppliers if it has no intention of using those suppliers for the work.

CASE STUDY 22.1

In recent years, research studies have become one of America's most powerful and popular tools of persuasion. Once confined to a small circle of polling and research companies and a few universities, the business of studying public opinion and consumer habits has exploded in the past two decades. Today, studies have become vehicles for polishing corporate images, influencing juries, shaping debate on public policy, selling shoe polish, and satisfying the media's—and the public's—voracious appetite for information.

Yet although studies promise a quest for truth, many are little more than vehicles for pitching a product or opinion. An examination of hundreds of recent studies indicates that the business of research has become pervaded by bias and distortion. The result is a corruption of information used every day by America's voters, consumers, and leaders.

While described as "independent," a growing number of studies are actually sponsored by companies or groups with a real—usually financial—interest in the outcome. And often the study question is posed in such a way that the response is predictable:

- When Levi Strauss & Co. asked students which clothes would be most popular this year, 90 percent said Levi's 501 jeans. They were the only jeans on the list.

- A survey for Black Flag said, "A roach disk . . . poisons a roach slowly. The dying roach returns to the nest and after it dies is eaten by other roaches. In turn these roaches become poisoned and die. How effective do you think this type of product would be in killing roaches?" Not surprisingly, 79 percent said "Effective."

- A Gallup Poll sponsored by the disposable diaper industry asked, "It is estimated that disposable diapers account for less than 2 percent of the trash in landfills. In contrast, beverage containers, third-class mail, and yard waste are estimated to account for 21 percent of the trash in landfills. Given this, in your opinion, would it be fair to ban disposable diapers?" Eighty-four percent said no.

"There's been a slow sliding in ethics" says Eric Miller, who, as editor of the newsletter *Research Alert,* reviews some 2,000 studies a year. "The scary part is, people make decisions based on this stuff. It may be an invisible crime, but it's not a victimless one."

"You can't have an industry study done by that industry be 100 percent objective," says Carl Lehrburger, who has studied the environmental impact of cloth versus disposable diapers for the cloth-diaper industry. "There are too many judgment calls, too many meetings between the sponsor and the organization doing the study. We're dealing with degrees of objectivity and degrees of truth." He adds, though, that it is the researcher's responsibility to get as close to the truth as possible.

Source: Taken from Cynthia Crossen, "Margin of Error," *The Wall Street Journal,* Nov. 14, 1991, p. 1. Reprinted by permission of *The Wall Street Journal,* © 1991 Dow Jones & Company, Inc. All Rights Reserved Worldwide.

- A client should not show one supplier's proposal to another supplier for a competitive bid.
- A client should not misrepresent research findings.

The first two guidelines about proposals are based on the fact that marketing research companies are usually not paid for proposals. Proposals serve as "free estimates" that advise clients how research should be done as well as how much it will cost. They can require substantial effort and expertise to prepare and are done as a business proposition with some reasonable expectation of getting the work. Under these circumstances, it is obviously not fair to give an expert researcher's proposal to a cheaper researcher for execution. It is also not fair to ask a researcher to prepare a proposal simply to see what ideas she or he might have.

The situation is, of course, different if a client pays for the proposal. If suppliers understand that their time will be fairly compensated and their proposals may be given to other companies for execution, there is no problem. Similarly, it is ethical for a client to hire a supplier to evaluate another supplier's proposal as long as the evaluating supplier does not bid to do the same work.

Critical Thinking Skills

What are the practical business reasons why research suppliers and clients would want to behave ethically toward each other?

Disclosure Requirements When Results Are Publicized

Earlier in this chapter, it was noted that marketing research data should be handled in such a way as to protect the confidentiality of clients and participants. This naturally limits the disclosure of methods and results. For example, a research company should not describe research that it has done for clients, or even disclose the existence of research, unless the clients have given their permission.

However, if research results are publicized by the client in an effort to persuade other people to take some action, the client and the researcher have an ethical obligation to provide those people with enough information to evaluate the research. The confidentiality of individual participants should be sacrosanct, but the researcher or client should make available:

- A copy of the questionnaire
- A description of the sample design and execution
- A description of where, when, and how the data were collected
- Data analyses relevant to the conclusions of the report

Sometimes organizations commission research for persuasive purposes but find results that are the opposite of what they want. For example, a company might do a customer satisfaction survey to show how happy its customers are, only to find that they give the company poor marks on some dimensions. The usual reaction in this situation is to suppress the study. We do not believe such behavior is itself unethical, because we do not believe that ethical behavior requires making public everything you know.

The issue changes, however, if unfavorable results are suppressed and favorable results are publicized. In our opinion, this is a form of misrepresenting the research findings. Researchers have an ethical obligation to protest and, if necessary, to set the record straight.

Conclusion

These guidelines cover many of the ethical questions that arise in marketing research, but not all. If you encounter situations that fall outside these guidelines, you will be all right if you follow simple moral maxims and trust your own judgment. Behaving ethically is a difficult task that may not always be fully achieved. We think it is useful, however, to remember the famous quotation by Leo Burnett that is the motto of the ad agency he started:

> Reach for the stars. You may not get there, but you won't grab a fistful of mud either.

Summary

This chapter discussed marketing research ethics. The following points were covered:

1. What ethical obligations do researchers have to research participants?
The first obligation of researchers is to do no physical or emotional harm to research participants. The second is not to deceive participants. The third is to ensure that the participant is willing and informed. The fourth is to hold data in confidence.

2. What ethical obligations do researchers have to clients?
Researchers' ethical obligations to their clients are as follows. Researchers are ethically bound to do the best they can for clients and to advise clients against inappropriate courses of action. Benefits should not be over-promised. Clients' information should be kept confidential, now and forever. Results should not be distorted. Researchers are required not only to avoid making false claims about their work but also to speak out when a client makes incorrect public statements about the data.

3. What ethical obligations do clients have to research suppliers?
Clients should not ask suppliers to do unethical research. Clients should not request research proposals from suppliers if they have no intention of using those suppliers for the work. Clients should not show one supplier's proposal to another supplier for a competitive bid. Clients should not misrepresent research findings.

4. When research findings are made public, what ethical issues are involved?
A research company should not describe research that it has done for clients, or even disclose the existence of research, unless the clients have given their permission. If

research results are publicized by the client in an effort to persuade other people to take some action, the client and the researcher have an obligation to provide those people with enough information to evaluate the research. If the results of a study commissioned for persuasive purposes do not turn out as expected, there is no ethical obligation to publicize them; however, it is unethical to suppress unfavorable parts of the results while publicizing favorable parts.

Suggested Additional Readings

As a start, you should read and think about the ethical codes presented in the Appendices to this chapter. For additional reading, see Eugene R. Laczniak and Patrick E. Murphy, *Ethical Marketing Decisions: The Higher Road* (Boston: Allyn and Bacon, 1993). Also, Sisella Bok's *Lying* (New York: Vintage, 1989) is thought-provoking.

Discussion Questions

1. Discuss researchers' obligations to participants.

2. If the researcher pays the participants $100 for their participation in a study, do the researcher's obligations to the participants change?

3. What are some unethical practices being used by some marketing researchers today? Why do you consider them to be unethical?

4. Discuss the difference between anonymity and confidentiality.

5. Discuss suppliers' obligations to clients.

6. The following nine scenarios describe ethical dilemmas. Discuss whether you approve or disapprove of the research director's actions in each scenario. [*Source:* Merle C. Crawford, "Attitudes of Marketing Executives Toward Ethics in Marketing Research," *Journal of Marketing Research*, April 1970, pp. 46–52.

Selected Research Techniques

1. *Ultraviolet Ink*
"A project director recently came in to request permission to use ultraviolet ink in pre-coding questionnaires on a mail survey. He pointed out that the letter referred to an anonymous survey, but he said he needed respondent identification to permit adequate cross-tabulations of the data. The marketing research director gave his approval."

2. *Hidden Tape Recorders*
"In a study intended to probe rather deeply into the buying motivations of a group of wholesale customers by use of a semi-structured personal interview form, the marketing research director authorized the use of the department's special attache cases equipped with hidden tape recorders."

3. *One-Way Mirrors*
"One product of the X Company is brassieres, and the firm has recently been having difficulty making some decisions on a new line. Information was critically needed concerning the manner in which women put on their brassieres. So the marketing research director designed a study in which two local stores cooperated in putting one-way mirrors in their foundations dressing rooms. Observers behind these mirrors successfully gathered the necessary information."

4. *Fake Long Distance Calls*
"Some of X Company's customers are busy executives, hard to reach by normal interviewing methods. Accordingly, the market research department recently conducted a study in which interviewers called 'long distance' from near-

by cities. They were successful in getting through to busy executives in almost every instance."

5. *Fake Research Firm*

"In another study, this one concerning magazine reading habits, the marketing research director decided to contact a sample of consumers under the name of Media Research Institute. This fictitious company name successfully camouflaged the identity of the sponsor of the study."

6. *Exchange of Price Data*

"X Company belongs to a trade association that includes an active marketing research subgroup. At the meetings of this subgroup, the marketing research director regularly exchanges confidential price information. In turn, he gives the competitive information to the X Company sales department, but he is careful not to let the marketing vice-president know about it. Profits are substantially enhanced, and top management is protected from charges of collusion."

The Role of the Marketing Research Director

7. *Advertising and Product Misuse*

"Some recent research showed that many customers of X Company are misusing Product B. There's no danger; they are simply wasting their money by using too much of it at a time. But yesterday, the marketing research director saw final comps on Product B's new ad campaign, and the ads not only ignore the problem of misuse, but they actually seem to encourage it. He quietly referred the advertising manager to the research results, well known to all people on B's advertising staff, and let it go at that."

8. *Distortions by Marketing Vice-President*

"In the trial run of a major presentation to the board of directors, the marketing vice-president deliberately distorted some recent research findings. After some thought, the marketing research director decided to ignore the matter, since the marketing head obviously knew what he was doing."

9. *Possible Conflict of Interest*

"A market testing firm, to which X Company gives most of its business, recently went public. The marketing research director had been looking for a good investment and proceeded to buy some $20,000 of its stock. The firm continues as X Company's leading supplier for testing."

 ## Marketing Research Challenge

Have you yourself or any of your friends ever been treated unethically in a research setting? If you think so, describe the situation and what the researcher should have done. If you have no personal experience, look for an example of unethical behavior in the business press or professional journals.

 ## Internet Exercise

In various places in this book, we recommend posting questions to online newsgroups to get advice or opinions. Are there circumstances where this practice could cross the boundaries of ethical behavior or good "netiquette"? What if a researcher working for a company initiated a discussion of the company's products without identifying himself or herself as working for the company? What if a researcher posted an irrelevant or inappropriate message to a site? (This is called *spamming*, which is described in more detail at the DejaNews site: http://www.dejanews.com/help/dnglossary_help.html.)

References

Advertising Research Foundation (1986). *Phony or Misleading Polls* (New York: Advertising Research Foundation).

Akaah, Ishmael P. (1989). "Differences in Research Ethics Judgments Between Male and Female Marketing Professionals." *Journal of Business Ethics* 8 (May), pp. 375–381.

Akaah, Ishmael P. (1990). "Attitudes of Marketing Professionals Toward Ethics in Marketing Research: A Cross-National Comparison." *Journal of Business Ethics* 9 (January), pp. 45–53.

Akaah, Ishmael P., and Edward A. Riordan (1989). "Judgments of Marketing Professionals About Ethical Issues in Marketing Research: A Replication and Extension." *Journal of Marketing Research* 26 (February), pp. 112–120.

Axelrod, Joel N. (1992). "Observations: Politics and Poker: Deception and Self-Deception in Marketing Research." *Journal of Advertising Research* 32 (November–December), pp. 79–82.

Castleberry, Stephen B., Warren French, and Barbara A. Carlin (1993). "The Ethical Framework of Advertising and Marketing Research Practitioners: A Moral Development Perspective." *Journal of Advertising* 22 (June), pp. 39–46.

Exter, Thomas (1989). "What's a Researcher to Do?" *American Demographics* 11 (February), p. 8.

Jarvis, Susan S. (1993). "Potential Malpractice Lawsuits: New Impetus for the Marketing Profession to Adopt Research Standards?" *Journal of Business & Industrial Marketing* 8, pp. 13–16.

Kelley, S. W., O. C. Ferrell, and S. J. Skinner (1990). "Ethical Behavior Among Marketing Researchers: An Assessment of Selected Demographic Characteristics." *Journal of Business Ethics* 9 (August), pp. 681–688.

Moorman, Christine, Rohit Deshpandi, and Gerald Zaltman (1990). "Factors Affecting Trust in Market Research Relationships." *Journal of Marketing* 57, p. 81.

O'Boyle, Edward J., and Lyndon E. Dawson Jr. (1992). "The American Marketing Association Code of Ethics: Instructions for Marketers." *Journal of Business Ethics* 11 (December), pp. 921–932.

Excerpt from the American Marketing Association's
Code of Ethics (as it Pertains to Research)

Responsibilities of the Marketer

Marketers must accept responsibility for the consequences of the activities and make every effort to ensure that their decisions, recommendations, and actions function to identify, serve, and satisfy all relevant publics; customers, organizations and society.

Marketers' professional conduct must be guided by:

1. The basic rule of professional ethics: not knowingly to do harm;
2. The adherence to all applicable laws and regulations;
3. The accurate representation of their education, training, and experience, and;
4. The active support, practice, and promotion of this Code of Ethics.

Honesty and Fairness

Marketers shall uphold and advance the integrity, honor, and dignity of the marketing profession by:

1. Being honest in serving consumers, clients, employees, suppliers, distributors, and the public;
2. Not knowingly participating in conflict of interest without prior notice to all parties involved; and
3. Establishing equitable fee schedules including the payment or receipt of usual, customary and/or legal compensation for marketing exchanges.

Rights and Duties of Parties in the Marketing Exchange Process

Participants in the marketing exchange process should be able to expect that:

1. Products and services offered are safe and fit for their intended uses;
2. Communications about offered products and services are not deceptive;
3. All parties intend to discharge their obligations, financial and otherwise, in good faith; and
4. Appropriate internal methods exist for equitable adjustment and/or redress of grievances concerning purchases.

It is understood that the above would include, but is not limited to, the following responsibilities of the marketer in the area of marketing research:

1. Prohibiting selling or fundraising under the guise of conducting research;
2. Maintaining research integrity by avoiding misrepresentation and omission of pertinent research data; and
3. Treating outside clients and suppliers fairly.

Source: Reprinted with permission from the American Marketing Association.

The American Association for Public Opinion Research's
Code of Ethics and Practices

I. Principles of Professional Practice in the Conduct of Our Work

A. We shall exercise due care in developing research designs and survey instruments, and in collecting, processing, and analyzing data, taking all reasonable steps to assure the reliability and validity of results.

　1. We shall recommend and employ only those tools and methods of analysis which, in our professional judgment, are well suited to the research problem at hand.

　2. We shall not select research tools and methods of analysis because of their capacity to yield misleading conclusions.

　3. We shall not knowingly make interpretations of research results, nor shall we tacitly permit interpretations that are inconsistent with the data available.

　4. We shall not knowingly imply that interpretations should be accorded greater confidence than the data actually warrant.

B. We shall describe our methods and findings accurately and in appropriate detail in all research reports, adhering to the standards for minimal disclosure specified in Section III.

C. If any of our work becomes the subject of a formal investigation of an alleged violation of this Code, undertaken with the approval of the AAPOR Executive Council, we shall provide additional information on the survey in such detail that a fellow survey practitioner would be able to conduct a professional evaluation of the survey.

II. Principles of Professional Responsibility in Our Dealings with People

A. The Public:

　1. If we become aware of the appearance in public of serious distortions of our research, we shall publicly disclose what is required to correct these distortions, including, as appropriate, a statement to the public media, legislative body, regulatory agency, or other appropriate group, in or before which the distorted findings were presented.

B. Clients or Sponsors:

　1. When undertaking work for a private client, we shall hold confidential all proprietary information obtained about the client and about the conduct and findings of the research undertaken for the client, except when the dissemination of the information is expressly authorized by the client, or when disclosure becomes necessary under terms of Section 1-C or II-A of this Code.

continued

2. We shall be mindful of the limitations of our techniques and capabilities and shall accept only those research assignments which we can reasonably expect to accomplish within these limitations.

C. The Profession:

1. We recognize our responsibility to contribute to the science of public opinion research and to disseminate as freely as possible the ideas and findings which emerge from our research.

2. We shall not cite our membership in the Association as evidence of professional competence, since the Association does not so certify any persons or organizations.

D. The Respondent:

1. We shall strive to avoid the use of practices or methods that may harm, humiliate, or seriously mislead survey respondents.

2. Unless the respondent waives confidentiality for specified uses, we shall hold as privileged and confidential all information that might identify a respondent with his or her responses. We shall also not disclose or use the names of respondents for nonresearch purposes unless the respondents grant us permission to do so.

III. Standard for Minimal Disclosure

Good professional practice imposes the obligation upon all public opinion researchers to include, in any report of research results, or to make available when that report is released, certain essential information about how the research was conducted. At a minimum, the following items should be disclosed:

1. Who sponsored the survey, and who conducted it.

2. The exact wording of questions asked, including the text of any preceding instruction or explanation to the interviewer or respondents that might reasonably be expected to affect the response.

3. A definition of the population under study, and a description of the sampling frame used to identify this population.

4. A description of the sample selection procedure, giving a clear indication of the method by which the respondents were selected by the researcher, or whether the respondents were entirely self-selected.

5. Size of samples and, if applicable, completion rates and information on eligibility criteria and screening procedures.

6. A discussion of the precision of the findings, including, if appropriate, estimates of sampling error, and a description of any weighting or estimating procedures used.

7. Which results are based on parts of the sample, rather than on the total sample.

8. Method, location, and dates of data collection.

Source: Reprinted with permission from the American Marketing Association.

Appendix 22.3

Excerpt from the American Psychological Association's *Ethical Principles of Psychologists and Code of Conduct* (as it Pertains to Research)

6.06 Planning Research

(a) Psychologists design, conduct, and report research in accordance with recognized standards of scientific competence and ethical research.

(b) Psychologists plan their research so as to minimize the possibility that results will be misleading.

(c) In planning research, psychologists consider its ethical acceptability under the Ethics Code. If an ethical issue is unclear, psychologists seek to resolve the issue through consultation with institutional review boards, animal care and use committees, peer consultations, or other proper mechanisms.

(d) Psychologists take reasonable steps to implement appropriate protections for the rights and welfare of human participants, other persons affected by the research, and the welfare of animal subjects.

6.07 Responsibility

(a) Psychologists conduct research competently and with due concern for the dignity and welfare of the participants.

(b) Psychologists are responsible for the ethical conduct of research conducted by them and by others under their supervision and control.

(c) Researchers and assistants are permitted to perform only those tasks for which they are appropriately trained and prepared.

(d) As part of the process of development and implementation of research projects, psychologists consult those with expertise concerning any special population under investigation or most likely to be affected.

6.08 Compliance with Law and Standards

Psychologists plan and conduct research in a manner consistent with federal and state law and regulations, as well as professional standards governing the conduct of research, and particularly those standards governing research with human participants and animal subjects.

6.09 Institutional Approval

Psychologists obtain from host institutions or organizations appropriate approval prior to conducting research, and they provide accurate information about their research proposals. They conduct the research in accordance with the approved research protocol.

6.10 Research Responsibilities

Prior to conducting research (except research involving only anonymous surveys, naturalistic observations, or similar research), psychologists enter into an agreement with participants that clarifies the nature of this research and the responsibilities of each party.

6.11 Informed Consent to Research

(a) Psychologists use language that is reasonably understandable to research participants in obtaining their appropriate informed consent (except as provided in Standard 6.12). Such informed consent is appropriately documented.

(b) Using language that is reasonably understandable to participants, psychologists inform participants of the nature of the research; they inform participants that they are free to participate or to decline to participate or to withdraw from the research; they explain the foreseeable consequences of declining or withdrawing; they inform participants of significant factors that might be expected to influence their willingness to participate (such as risks, discomfort, adverse effects, or limitations on confidentiality, except as provided by Standard 6.15); and they explain other aspects about which the prospective participants inquire.

(c) When psychologists conduct research with individuals such as students or subordinates, psychologists take special care to protect the prospective participants from adverse consequences of declining or withdrawing from the research.

(d) When research participation is a course requirement or opportunity for extra credit, the prospective participant is given the choice of equitable alternative activities.

(e) For persons who are legally incapable of giving informed consent, psychologists nevertheless (1) provide an appropriate explanation, (2) obtain the participant's assent, (3) obtain appropriate permission from a legally authorized person, if such substitute consent is permitted by law.

6.12 Dispensing with Informed Consent

Before determining that planned research (such as research involving only anonymous questionnaires, naturalistic observations, or certain kinds of archival research) does not require the informed consent of research participants, psychologists consider applicable regulations and institutional review board requirements, and they consult with colleagues as appropriate.

6.13 Informed Consent in Research Filming or Recording

Psychologists obtain informed consent from research participants prior to filming or recording them in any form, unless the research involves simply naturalistic observations in public places and it is not anticipated that the recording will be used in a manner that could cause personal identification or harm.

6.14 Offering Inducements for Research Participation

(a) In offering professional services as an inducement to obtain research participants, psychologists make clear the nature of the services, as well as the risks, obligations, and limitations.

(b) Psychologists do not offer excessive or inappropriate financial or other inducements to obtain research participants, particularly when it might coerce participation.

6.15 Deception in Research

(a) Psychologists do not conduct a study involving deception unless they have determined that the use of deceptive techniques is justified by the study's prospective scientific, educational, or applied value and that equally effective alternative procedures that do not use deception are not feasible.

(b) Psychologists never deceive research participants about significant aspects that would affect their willingness to participate, such as physical risks, discomfort, or unpleasant emotional experiences.

(c) Any other deception that is an integral feature of the design and conduct of an experiment must be explained to participants as early as is feasible, preferably at the conclusion of their participation, but no later than at the conclusion of the research.

6.16 Sharing and Utilizing Data

Psychologists inform research participants of their anticipated sharing or further use of personally identifiable research data and of the possibility of unanticipated future uses.

6.17 Minimizing Invasiveness

In conducting research, psychologists interfere with the participants or milieu from which data are collected only in a manner that is warranted by an appropriate research design and that is consistent with psychologists' roles as scientific investigators.

6.18 Providing Participants with Information About the Study

(a) Psychologists provide a prompt opportunity for participants to obtain appropriate information about the nature, results, and conclusions of the research, and psychologists attempt to correct any misconceptions that participants might have.

(b) If scientific or humane values justify delaying or withholding this information, psychologists take reasonable measures to reduce the risk of harm.

6.19 Honoring Commitments

Psychologists take reasonable measures to honor all commitments they have made to research participants.

6.20 Care and Use of Animals in Research

(Not excerpted for this appendix)

6.21 Reporting of Results

(a) Psychologists do not fabricate data or falsify results in their publications.

(b) If psychologists discover significant errors in their published data, they take reasonable steps to correct such errors in a correction, retraction, erratum, or other appropriate publication means.

6.22 Plagiarism

Psychologists do not present substantial portions or elements of another's work or data as their own, even if the other work or data source is cited occasionally.

6.23 Publication Credit

(a) Psychologists take responsibility and credit, including authorship credit, only for work they have actually performed or to which they have contributed.

(b) Principal authorship and other publication credits accurately reflect the relative scientific or professional contributions of the individuals involved, regardless of their relative status. Mere possession of an institutional position, such as Department Chair, does not justify authorship credit. Minor contributions to the research or to the writing for publications are appropriately acknowledged, such as in footnotes or in an introductory statement.

(c) A student is usually listed as principal author on any multiple-authored article that is substantially based on the student's dissertation or thesis.

6.24 Duplicate Publication of Data

Psychologists do not publish, as original data, data that have been previously published. This does not preclude republishing data when they are accompanied by proper acknowledgement.

6.25 Sharing Data

After research results are published, psychologists do not withhold the data on which their conclusions are based from other competent professionals who seek to verify the substantive claims through reanalysis and who intend to use such data only for that purpose, provided that the confidentiality of the participants can be protected and unless legal rights concerning proprietary data preclude their release.

Source: Copyright by the American Psychological Association. Reprinted with permission.

23 Current Issues in Marketing Research

OBJECTIVES

After reading this chapter, you should be able to answer the following questions:

❶ How can the Internet be used in marketing research?

❷ How can marketing research be used in relationship marketing?

❸ How can marketing research be used in database marketing?

❹ How can marketing research be used in new-product development?

❺ How can marketing research be used in total quality management (TQM)?

❻ What issues arise in conducting and using customer satisfaction research?

The previous chapters have provided a general foundation in marketing research. They have discussed the steps involved in a research project, what to do at each step, and how to manage the research function in an organization. This final chapter considers some special topics that are of current interest in marketing research.

Six topics are addressed. First is a discussion of the latest place to do marketing research: the Internet. Various Internet issues have been discussed throughout the book, and that discussion is pulled into one section here. Four areas of application for marketing research are then discussed: relationship marketing, database marketing, new-product development, and Total Quality Management (TQM). Why each topic is of interest to marketers is discussed, as are the marketing research issues related to each. Finally, customer satisfaction research, which has seen rapid growth in recent years, is considered, and the issues involved in doing and using this type of research are discussed.

The Internet

Among other things, the **Internet** is a place to do marketing research. The Internet can be used to seek out secondary data, gather observational data on website visitors, administer surveys to website visitors, and post questions to newsgroups or listservs to get advice about research techniques and sources. Following is a discussion of each of these topics.

Using the Internet as a Source of Secondary Data

One of the best uses of the Internet in marketing research is as a source of secondary data. The Internet provides access to a wide variety of information, some free, some at a charge.

For information on a specific company, the first place to look is the company's **homepage,** if it has one. Internet addresses for these sites are easy to guess; for example, Nike's homepage is at http://www.nike.com, and Microsoft is at http://www.microsoft.com. Homepages usually have background information on the company and information about the company's products.

For financial data on companies and industries, the best sources are sites that provide information for investors. Three such sites are Wall Street Research Net (http://www.wsrn.com), CompanyLink (http://www.companylink.com), and Deloitte & Touche PeerScape (http://www.peerscape.com). These sites provide industry performance profiles, stock prices, and financial data for individual companies, as well as general information such as news clippings and press releases.

For other types of information, there are many Internet sites of potential interest. For example, the U.S. Census homepage (http://www.census.gov) provides access to a wide variety of industry and demographic statistics, including the *County and*

City Data Book and the *Statistical Abstract of the United States*. The American Marketing Association homepage (http://www.ama.org) provides links to various AMA publications. Marketing Research Tools 23.1 lists these sites, along with others that might be of interest in marketing research projects.

Of course, it is also possible to find information on the Internet without knowing specific sites. Just access an Internet **search engine** such as Infoseek or Alta Vista, enter keywords for the search, and follow the links that come up. For example, if you want market size information for vacuum cleaners, try keywords such as "vacuum cleaners" + "sales statistics", and follow the resulting trail.

MARKETING RESEARCH TOOLS

23.1

SOME INTERNET SITES RELATED TO MARKETING RESEARCH

Name of Site	Web Address	Description
Newsgroups and Listservs:		
Deja News	http://www.dejanews.com	Newsgroup searching and archival service
Mousetracks	http://www.nsns.com/MouseTracks/tloml/general.html	List of marketing-related listservs
Investment Advice:		
Deloitte & Touche Peerscape	http://www.peerscape.com	Includes industry benchmarks, financial information, and industry and company reports
CompanyLink	http://www.companylink.com	Includes recent news articles, press releases, stock prices, and SEC filings
Wall Street Company Research Profiles	http://www.wsrn.com/home/companyResearch.html	Includes stock prices, financial statistics, industry comparisons, and market guide reports
Product Information:		
U.S. Patent Office	http://patents.cnidr.org/access/access.html	Searches for patent numbers or companies that have applied for patents
Product Development and Management Association	http://www.pdma.org	Describes the activities of the PDMA

Continued

SOME INTERNET SITES RELATED TO MARKETING RESEARCH—Continued

Name of Site	Web Address	Description
Links to Marketing Research Resources:		
Business Resources on the Web	http://www.idbsu.edu/carol/ busnessl.htm#Marketing (note the spelling of "busness")	Links the user to sites containing demographic information, business news, industry information, and much more
Marketing Research Index	http://www.cba.uh.edu/ ~reinartz/resl.html	Links the user to marketing research companies and data sources
Targeting & Segmentation Links	http://advertising.utexas.edu/ world/Target.html#Top	Links the user to sites with cultural and lifestyle information
Statistical Data:		
U.S. Census Page	http://www.census.gov	Allows access to a wide variety of industry and demographic statistics
Survey Research Center at Princeton University	http://www.princeton.edu/ ~abelson/index.html	Allows access to a wide variety of demographic and public opinion data sets
Academic Marketing Research:		
Publications of the American Marketing Association	http://www.ama.org/pubs.htm	Provides information about publications available through the AMA
Marketing Science Institute	http://cism.bus.utexas.edu/ ravi/marketing_science.html	Provides information about the MSI
Current Research in Marketing	http://www.cba.uh.edu/crim	Provides information about doctoral dissertations in progress, research activities of selected scholars, and current research topics

At the present time, the biggest problem in using the Internet for general searches is that search engines are not efficient enough to cope with the huge amount of available information. This leads to two problems. The first is too much volume. It is as if you sent someone to a huge library to get information on vacuum cleaners sales, and that person brought back every single document that had the words "clean" or "sales" anywhere in them. The second problem is not enough prioritization. A search for vacuum cleaner sales may elicit a document that provides exactly what you want, but this document may be buried amid thousands of useless documents. This inefficiency can make general Internet searches frustrating.

By the time you read this chapter, the efficiency of Internet research may have been substantially enhanced by new generations of search engines. Even if problems remain, use of the Internet is a must for any thorough secondary research project. One of the basic goals in a secondary research project is to obtain all available information, and there is an excellent chance that the Internet will contain information that cannot be found in a local library. The Internet is especially useful in identifying commercial and international data sources that are not available in most libraries.

Critical Thinking Skills

Pick a country. Using the Internet, try to find sources that provide information for that country on (1) general social statistics, such as population, income, and housing; (2) sales of durable goods, such as automobiles and washing machines; (3) sales of nondurable goods, such as laundry detergents and fruit juices; and (4) sales of industrial goods, such as industrial ball valves.

Using the Internet for Observational Data

Observational data can be gathered on the Internet in various ways. The simplest form of observation is to count the "hits" on various parts of a website or the number of "downloads" for various material. These measures can provide useful information. For example, when Cadillac runs a promotional campaign for its Catera model, it can use the number of hits on its Catera web page (shown in Exhibit 23.1, page 672) as an indicator of the extent to which the campaign has sparked interest in the car. This measure is similar, in spirit, to traditional measures such as counting the number of entrants in a promotional contest. Hits also can be used as measures of advertising effectiveness. For example, many web advertisers such as Procter & Gamble pay for web "banner" ads only if viewers of those ads use the link to hit the advertiser's homepage.

Technology companies such as Sun Microsystems and BMC Software have another way of using hit counts. These companies place a lot of technical support information on their websites. Making information available in this way allows companies to save money by reducing the number of calls to support centers. It also provides research feedback by allowing the companies to use hit counts on various pages to measure the number of users with questions about various aspects of the equipment or software.

In addition to simply counting hits, companies can monitor the points of origin for visitors to their websites and can ask visitors to register at the site. These measures provide the company with background information on the visitors to their websites. Point-of-origin data are also used by advertising companies to target messages. For example, when Internet users go to a new site, an advertising service called DoubleClick can observe the type of site they came from, and can use this information to choose advertising that might be of interest to them.

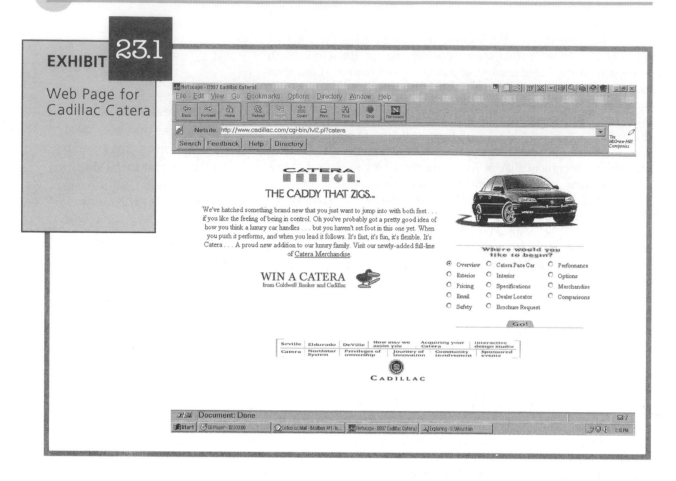

The McGraw-Hill Companies

EXHIBIT 23.1

Web Page for Cadillac Catera

Two issues arise in using observational information such as point-of-origin data on the Internet. The first issue is practical; the value of this information is limited by the fact that many users access the Internet from public sites, such as university modem banks, and cannot be specifically identified. The second issue is ethical and involves concerns about privacy and informed consent. Because of ethical issues, the general trend in Internet tracking is toward systems that (1) notify users when they are being observed and (2) use information about the user's characteristics without recording the user's specific identity.

Using the Internet for Surveys

At the time this chapter was written, Internet-based surveys were not a significant form of marketing research. However, they have the potential for explosive growth.

So far, marketing surveys on the Internet have primarily been done by companies that ask visitors to their websites to answer questions about product usage and product preferences. Surveys of this type have been used by Domino's Pizza, Qantas Airlines, Jelly Belly candies, and others. These surveys provide "quick-and-dirty" information to the companies that use them. However, they suffer from three severe sampling limitations:

- First, the population using the Internet is not representative of the broader population. At the time this chapter was written, there were an estimated 40 million Internet users out of a total U.S. population of 250 million. Exhibit 23.2 compares the characteristics of these users with the general U.S. population. It shows that Internet users are younger, better educated, more technologically adept, and more likely to be male. Many consumers goods are bought by women, and many industrial goods are bought by senior managers, but both groups are underrepresented on the Internet.

- Second, if a questionnaire is posted on a company's website, the sample is limited to people who have an active interest in the company. This sample might be ideal for some purposes, but it certainly does not represent the market at large.

- Third, response rates for Internet surveys are *very* low. Most people who hit a site will not bother to complete a questionnaire, and respondents to an Internet survey should be viewed as people who volunteered for the research.

Because of these limitations, the Internet is not acceptable as a *sole* method of administering most marketing surveys. However, the Internet is perfectly acceptable as a *secondary* method of administering surveys, and this is the context in which there is tremendous growth potential. Research companies that run large survey programs—such as the companies that run consumer panels

Author Tips

Surveys have shown that many Internet users do not object to having their activity tracked if the information is used for their benefit. For example, most users approve of using such information to guide them to web content that is likely to fit their interests. These attitudes are similar to people's attitudes about "junk mail": most people don't object to junk mail that they find useful, such as sale announcements from their favorite stores.

EXHIBIT 23.2

Demographic Differences Between Internet Users and the Total U.S. Population

Characteristic	World Wide Web Users (%)	Total U.S. Population (%)
Age under 35	52%	39%
Male	65	48
College graduate	64	28
Professional/technical	49	24
Household income over $50,000	49	34

Source: A. C. Nielsen Co., "Internet Demographics and Statistics," http://www.otn.com/aboutinternet/Demographics-Nielsen.html.

Critical Thinking Skills

Do you have a website or know someone who does? Post a brief questionnaire on the site, and see who responds. Do these respondents represent the population of interest?

with tens of thousands of households—can save large sums in mailing and processing costs by allowing respondents to participate via the Internet. We expect this type of activity to explode in the future.

Using the Internet as a Source of Advice

If you want general information from the Internet, such as advice on how to use some research procedure or where to find some data, you can post your question to a newsgroup or listserv and hope for a reply from someone who knows the answer. **Newsgroups** are electronic bulletin boards where messages can be read by anyone who accesses the site. **Listservs** are electronic mailing lists that automatically send messages to all list subscribers.

The Internet has thousands of newsgroups and listservs, so, whatever your question, there is likely to be an appropriate place for you to ask it. You can locate and access newsgroups by using an Internet browser, such as Netscape Navigator, and a newsgroup-searching service, such as Deja News (http://www.dejanews.com). You can find a list of marketing-related listservs at Mousetracks (http://nsns.com/Mouse-Tracks).

Relationship Marketing

Relationship marketing is a growing area of application for marketing research. Here relationship marketing is described, and the associated marketing research issues are discussed.

What Is Relationship Marketing?

Relationship marketing is a marketing perspective that emphasizes relationships rather than transactions, and individual customers rather than market segments. The goal is to build strong, lasting relationships with customers. Relationship marketing is focused not on today's sale but rather on the long-term value of a customer. The key concepts in relationship marketing are "lifetime revenue" and "share of customer."

Lifetime Revenue

Lifetime revenue is the amount of revenue a company gains from a customer over the entire life of the customer's relationship with the company. It can be calculated as follows:

$$\text{Lifetime revenue} = \text{Revenue per transaction} \times \text{Transactions per year} \times \text{Years in the relationship}$$

For example, a customer who spends an average of $10 when she or he buys Texaco gasoline, buys gasoline an average of fifty-two times per year, and spends five years in his or her relationship with a Texaco station represents a lifetime revenue of $2,600 to that station. Or, as Exhibit 23.3 shows, a pair of college roommates who spend $10 per pizza, and order 100 pizzas per year for four years, represent a lifetime revenue of $4,000 to a campus pizzeria. Along these lines, Pizza Hut estimates that a loyal Pizza Hut customer represents a lifetime revenue of $8,000 to the company. Cadillac estimates $300,000.

The lifetime revenue concept is important for two reasons. First, it helps companies calculate the amount they can reasonably spend to recruit and retain a customer. Second, it emphasizes the value of customer service. For example, in working with Texaco employees, we ask if they would exert themselves to grab $1,000 if they saw it blowing down the street. Of course they say, "Yes." We then point out that customer service deserves the same level of exertion, because a loyal customer will generate $1,000 in revenue to a gas station in less than two years.

Share of Customer

Share of customer, the other important concept in relationship marketing, is a company's share of the total amount spent by a particular customer in a product or service category. For example, if a person spent $800 on gasoline last year and $400 of that went to Texaco, Texaco's share of customer is 50 percent. As with all market share measures, share of customer is sensitive to the way in which the category is defined. For example, Pizza Hut may have 80 percent of a pair of roommates' pizza spending but only 20 percent of their total fast-food spending.

The share of customer concept is important because it measures the strength of a company's relationship with a customer. In effect, it is a behavioral measure of brand loyalty.

Elements of Relationship Marketing

Relationship marketing programs can have a wide variety of operational elements, but all these elements are centered around the concepts of lifetime revenue and share of customer. On the lifetime revenue side, possible elements of a relationship marketing program include:

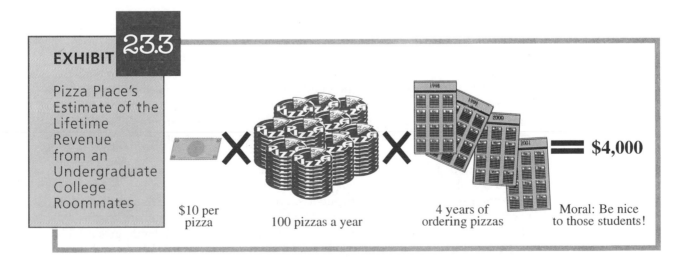

EXHIBIT 23.3

Pizza Place's Estimate of the Lifetime Revenue from an Undergraduate College Roommates

$10 per pizza × 100 pizzas a year × 4 years of ordering pizzas = $4,000

Moral: Be nice to those students!

- Running a "star" customer program in which key customers get special services to enhance their loyalty
- Maintaining order histories so repeat orders are quickly and easily filled
- Maintaining personal dossiers on industrial customers so relationships can be personalized
- Using multifunctional selling teams for industrial customers so relationships can survive the loss of an individual salesperson or an individual buyer
- Compensating salespeople on the basis of salary rather than commissions to remove disincentives for time spent in customer service
- Monitoring customer satisfaction

All these elements have the purpose of increasing lifetime revenue by strengthening relationships and extending their life.

With regard to share of customer, possible elements of a relationship marketing program include:

- Working closely with industrial customers (through programs such as data interchange or joint product development) to serve them better and encourage them to use only one vendor in a category
- Using "loyalty programs," such as frequent flyer programs, to enhance customer loyalty as well as to increase the life of customer relationships

Marketing Research Issues in Relationship Marketing

Marketing research is used for four broad purposes in relationship marketing programs. These purposes are (1) to measure the lifetime revenue associated with various customer groups, (2) to measure share of customer for various customer groups, (3) to evaluate whether relationship marketing efforts are effective in building lifetime revenues and/or loyalty, and (4) to measure customer satisfaction.

Measuring Lifetime Revenue

For businesses that sell directly to their customers, such as catalog companies and many industrial firms, the best way of calculating lifetime revenue is usually from **customer information files (CIFs).** At a minimum, a CIF contains identifying information for each customer, such as address and telephone number, and a record of the customer's purchases. This information allows the company to calculate the average purchase amount (for each customer and in total), the average purchase frequency (for each customer and in total), and the average length of relationship. The CIF also may contain other information such as customer demographics, which allows the company to compare the value of different customer groups. This information is usually obtained from credit applications (and, in fact, credit card companies have the best CIFs available).

For companies that do not sell directly, the best way of estimating lifetime revenue is usually by using survey data. A random sample of customers is asked about their purchase frequency, average purchase amount, and length of relationship, as well as other questions such as demographics. The results are used to estimate lifetime revenue for the average customer and for the average customer in different groups. The results are not as accurate as those obtained from purchase records, but are still useful.

In some cases, companies that sell directly to their customers do not maintain customer information files; for example, if you think about retail stores you patronize, you will realize that many of them do not track you as an individual customer. In these cases, lifetime revenue information would be drawn from a survey. On the other hand, some companies that do *not* sell directly are able to use membership programs to build information files on individual customers. For example, Marlboro smokers can join a program that allows them to receive information and win awards—and allows Philip Morris to keep track of them. Similarly, frequent flyer programs allow airlines to keep track of customers who buy their tickets through travel agents.

Measuring Share of Customer

Regardless of whether or not a company has direct contact with its customers, share of customer estimates must be drawn from a survey. A customer information file will show only a customer's purchases from your company and will not capture purchases from competitors. A survey can be used to measure cross-purchasing behavior and, if desired, the specific competitors that customers patronize.

Measuring the Effectiveness of Relationship Marketing Programs

The same sources that are used to measure lifetime revenue and share of customer are used in measuring the effectiveness of relationship marketing programs. For example, if a company wants to know whether a membership program has the effect of increasing its share of customer among members, it would most likely use a survey to measure share of customer, then would measure program effectiveness by either (1) comparing the average share of customer between members and nonmembers or (2) comparing the average share of customer for members before and after enrollment in the program.

Cross-sectional comparisons (i.e., comparisons between groups) are the more common approach for evaluating the effectiveness of relationship marketing programs, but they often raise questions about causality. For example, every company in the gasoline industry has found that "share of customer" is higher for people who use the company's credit card than for people who do not. Because of this finding, most gasoline retailers encourage customers to use the company's credit card, even though it might be cheaper to process other forms of payment. However, it is not clear whether using the card makes customers more loyal or customers who are more loyal are simply more likely to use the card. Cross-time comparisons can be more difficult to make than cross-sectional comparisons but raise fewer questions about causality.

Measuring Customer Satisfaction

The final use for marketing research in relationship marketing is in measurement of customer satisfaction. Satisfaction data are used to indicate whether the company's relationship with its customers is healthy or there are problems in the relationship.

Customer satisfaction is usually measured by surveys. Various issues involved in conducting these surveys and using their results are discussed later in this chapter.

Critical Thinking Skills

An automobile dealer has historically paid his salespeople on a commission basis. As a result, they are very aggressive about closing sales, and many customers find the buying experience to be unpleasant. The dealer is thinking about switching to salary-based compensation for his salespeople, in order to provide better customer service and enhanced customer relationships. In your opinion, what benefits and losses might the dealer experience if this switch is made? What marketing research would you recommend to help the dealer evaluate the switch *before* it is made? What marketing research would you suggest to evaluate the switch *after* it is made?

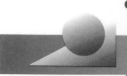

Database Marketing

Another growing area of application for marketing research is **database marketing.** Here, database marketing is described, and the associated marketing research issues are discussed.

What Is Database Marketing?

The term "database marketing" refers to any marketing program that is based on analysis of a company's customer database. These programs are directed at either or both of two goals: (1) enhancing customer retention and/or (2) enhancing the efficiency of marketing expenditures. In the first regard (enhanced customer retention), there is an overlap between database marketing and relationship marketing.

Possible applications of database marketing include:

- Modeling interpurchase times to know when to call on customers or send them a buying reminder

- Modeling interpurchase times to know when a customer is late and a special offer is justified (for example, Exhibit 23.4 shows a catalog with a special offer for a customer who has not ordered in a while)

- Modeling interpurchase times to know when to drop a customer from the active customer database and cut promotional activities

- Calculating the profitability of individual customers so that price incentives and/or promotional expenditures can be matched to the profitability of each customer

- Using records of item purchases to cross-sell other items (e.g., using records of appliance purchases to sell warranty extensions when the warranties expire)

- Using purchase records along with demographic information to model the demographic characteristics of high-value customers, so these groups can be targeted for new marketing efforts

Marketing Research Issues in Database Marketing

The basic data source for database marketing programs is customer information files. In many applications of database marketing, the only information needed is the customer's purchasing history. In some applications, the purchasing history must be augmented with other information such as demographic data, which can be obtained from sources such as credit applications or loyalty program enrollment forms, as shown in Exhibit 23.5 (see page 680).

The biggest research-related issue in database marketing is how to build the database. Much of the interest in database marketing comes from consumer goods manufacturers, who do not have direct relationships with consumers and therefore

(cont. on p. 681)

EXHIBIT 23.4

The Paragon Catalog

WILL THIS BE YOUR LAST PARAGON CATALOG?

Dear Friend,

We don't want to remove your name from our mailing list, but we haven't heard from you in a long time! We must assume that you may no longer wish to receive our catalogs.

However, just place an order from this catalog and you'll be moved back onto our active list to continue receiving future catalogs.

We hope to hear from you soon.

Sincerely,

John McCormick

The Paragon
HOLIDAY PREVIEW 1996

"Will this be your last Paragon Catalog?" Paragon's database marketing system has noticed that this customer hasn't bought in a while.

EXHIBIT 23.5

Continental
One Pass
Application

Frequent flyer programs allow airlines to track their relationships with their best customers. The applications also provide identifying information that allows airlines to link up with other databases.

do not have a natural way of building customer information files. To build files, these companies have to assemble a mixture of customer contact information, such as contest entries, along with secondary data, such as magazine subscription lists, home ownership lists, and automobile registration lists.

If a company sells directly to its customers—such as a catalog company, a retailer, or an industrial company with direct sales—the raw materials for customer information files are more readily available, but the files still do not build themselves. The company must decide what information it wants to capture, have a way of matching purchases with customers, have a structure for maintaining the data records, have enough data storage capacity to handle the files, and have a plan for analyzing and using the data. All these needs can be viewed as an extension of designing and using a marketing information system.

Once customer information files are available, the challenge is to analyze those files in useful ways. Some of the desired analyses are simple; for example, it is quite easy to calculate the revenues and profits obtained from a customer. Some of the desired analyses are mathematically simple but statistically complex; for example, it is quite easy to calculate the mean and variance of a customer's interpurchase times, but a solid knowledge of statistics is needed to convert that information into judgments that the customer is late or gone. Some of the analyses require advanced analytic skills; for example, the procedures used to distinguish high-value from low-value customers can include discriminant analysis (see Chapter 18), AID analysis (see Chapter 18), and neural network analysis (which can be viewed as an extension of AID analysis). In most companies, the people who are best able to do these analyses are found in the marketing research department.

Critical Thinking Skills

If you were asked to develop a database marketing program for the largest supermarket chain in your area, what information would you put into the customer information files? How would you obtain this information? Physically, what would a CIF look like? How would you analyze the data? How would you use the results?

New-Product Development

New-product development is a hot topic in the business world. Businesspeople believe that the world is changing faster and faster and new products are needed to meet this change. This attitude is especially strong in technology-related businesses such as computing, software, telecommunications, home electronics, medical diagnostics, and chemicals.

In an effort to make new-product development more systematic, the development process has been broken down into a series of steps. Marketing research plays a role in three of these steps: (1) concept generation, (2) concept screening, and (3) product optimization.

Using Marketing Research in Concept Generation

The first step in the new-product development process is **concept generation,** or generation of product ideas. Analyses of innovation leaders such as Hewlett-Packard and 3M have shown that new-product development is a numbers game. To get good product ideas, you need *lots* of product ideas; and to get lots of product ideas, you have to seek them out, rather than waiting for them to come to you.

New-product ideas can be found either inside or outside a company. Internal sources include (1) technical research and development, (2) employee suggestion programs, (3) brainstorming, and (4) periodic review of ideas filed in an "idea bank" for later consideration. External sources of ideas include (1) new-product announcements in the trade press, (2) reviews of patent applications, (3) customer request forms filled out by salespeople, (4) ideas suggested by customers in focus groups, (5) a "champions of innovation" program, (6) "concept engineering," (7) product space mapping, and (8) conjoint analysis. Several of these techniques can be viewed as forms of marketing research.

Brainstorming sessions, for example, can be viewed as a type of focus group. One form of brainstorming is the **idea conference.** Employees are invited to participate in the conference on a voluntary basis, and a list of topics is set (these topics can be solicited from participants, if desired). Once the conference begins, attendees are formed into groups of four to eight people drawn from different parts of the company. Each group is assigned a topic, and the groups are given twenty to thirty minutes to generate as many product ideas on their topics as they can. Each group or subgroup records its ideas on a flip pad. The conference then moves to a presentation phase in which each group presents its ideas and other attendees are allowed to comment, elaborate, and make additional suggestions. The groups can then be given additional time to elaborate on their best ideas, if desired. All flip pads are retained, and the ideas are transcribed into an "idea bank" for future reference.

The **"champions of innovation" program** is a six-step system for turning literature searches into new-product ventures. It is oriented toward alliances and joint ventures for technical companies. In the first step, a team is drawn from different parts of the organization and is given a mandate and a budget to generate new-product concepts in specific areas of interest. In the second step, the team scans six months of technical and trade journals in the targeted areas of interest, looking for embryonic ideas rather than finished products. Any organization that is identified as the source of more than one idea is labeled a "champion of innovation." On average, a scan of 20,000 articles will yield 500 innovations and 40 "champions of innovation." In the third step, the team makes site visits to "champions of innovation" to discuss the identified innovations, other innovations, and potential partnering opportunities. In the fourth step, the team translates these discussions into product ideas and picks the best six to twelve ideas. In the fifth step, the best ideas are screened for market size and customer interest, using inexpensive marketing research. In the sixth and final step, the best one or two ideas are developed for presentation to senior management, using additional marketing research.

Critical Thinking Skills

Get a few of your friends together and run your own idea conference to generate ideas about new products or services that might be successful at a campus bookstore. What further research, if any, would you recommend before the bookstore introduces any of these ideas?

Concept engineering is a five-step system for turning customer visits into product ideas. It is oriented toward product improvements, especially for industrial products. In the first step, a cross-functional team is formed, and team members visit selected customers to observe how they use the company's products and to hear their opinions. In the second step, the team uses this information to set customers' most important requirements for the product and interrelationships among those requirements. In the third step, the team defines measures that will identify whether a new-product concept meets customer requirements. In the fourth step, the team generates ideas about how to meet better customers' requirements and turns these ideas into product/service concepts. In the fifth step, the team selects the most promising concepts, possibly with the help of additional marketing research.

A **product space map** is a pictorial device that shows how customers perceive the relative positioning of existing products. Product space maps were discussed in Chapters 18 and 19. To use product space maps for new-product development, customers are asked to rate existing products on various attributes or to rate the similarity of existing products. Customers are also asked to rate their ideal products on the same attributes or to rate the similarity of their ideal products to existing products. Discriminant analysis or multidimensional scaling is used to make a space map of the existing products, and the ideal products descriptions are overlaid on this map. The goal is to identify market segments whose ideal products are different from the existing products. Reputedly, Pebbles cereal was the first product ever developed through this procedure.

Conjoint analysis and choice modeling were discussed in Chapter 9. These techniques allow companies to estimate the value that different customers place on specific product attributes. Given this information, it is possible to (1) estimate how the market share and/or profitability of an existing product can be improved by changing its features and/or price, (2) identify optimal features and/or pricing for a new product, (3) identify the extent to which a new product will draw business from existing products, and (4) identify optimal responses to competitors' new products.

In general, the new-product concepts that result from various idea generation techniques can be sorted into two broad categories: (1) repositionings or improvements of an existing product and (2) really new products. Repositionings and product improvements are cheaper and less risky to develop than really new products but will not create exciting new markets. Really new products may create exciting new markets and get you out "in front of the wave" but are costly and risky to develop. As a general rule, the idea generation techniques that are based in market research will produce ideas for repositionings and improvements but will usually not produce ideas for really new products. The reason is that customers can tell you how to improve products, but they usually cannot tell you how to make totally new products.

Using Marketing Research in Concept Screening

Once new-product concepts are identified, they are put through a series of evaluation screens. Marketing research has an obvious role to play in this process.

The first step in screening a product concept is to evaluate whether it is a *strategic fit*. Marketing research is not required at this stage. The concept is simply evaluated for consistency with the organization's mission statement and business strategy.

The second step in screening a concept is to evaluate it for *risk/reward ratio*. Questions to be asked in this regard include the current market size, market growth prospects, buyer characteristics, identities of leading competitors, current price points, how the product would be distributed, how the product would be promoted and sold, trends in the business environment, and the capital and human resources needed to get into the business. As a general rule, these questions would be answered on the basis of information found in secondary sources. A standard list of questions should be applied to all concepts evaluated by a company, and the concepts should be scored on a common basis.

The third step in screening a concept is to evaluate it for *customer acceptance*. This is usually done through focus groups, as described in Chapter 8. The data collection procedure should be matched with the ultimate marketing environment. If a company plans to market the product through personal selling and will thus have a chance to explain the product to potential customers in detail, it is appropriate to explain the product to focus group participants before measuring their response. If the product will be marketed through advertising, a "first-impression" reaction may be more appropriate. Regardless of how the product is presented, the goal is to classify response into three broad categories: customers love the concept, hate the concept, or are somewhere in between. Remember that customers must understand the concept to provide valid responses. Customer response is not reliable for really new products.

The fourth step in screening a concept is to refine the estimate of *sales potential*. This is usually done through a survey. Ask questions that allow you to estimate the number of potential customers who would benefit from the product, can afford it, and have some interest in trying a new product. Do not worry about the number who say they will buy the product. The goal is to estimate the number of qualified sales prospects, not to estimate sales. Actual sales will depend on marketing execution and competitors' reactions.

As with focus groups, customers must understand the product before they can provide valid responses in surveys. Also, the results will be more realistic if customers are given a product price as well as a product description. In addition, if one of the research goals is to identify market segments that show the best response to the product, the sample must be large enough to allow subgroup analysis with acceptable confidence intervals.

Using Marketing Research in Product Optimization

Once a company makes a decision to go forward with a new-product concept, it typically faces a series of decisions about optimal product design. For example, once Motorola decides to go forward with a new cellular telephone, it must decide on the phone's height, width, thickness, color, features, and price.

Customer preferences play an important role in these decisions. Conjoint analysis or choice modeling can be used to measure the value that customers place on specific product attributes. In turn, these results can be combined with cost information to choose the product design that is likely to yield the highest profits.

Total Quality Management

Marketing Research Issues in Total Quality Management

The word "quality," when applied to products and services, refers to their level and consistency of performance. In the context of "quality control," quality particularly refers to consistency of performance. The idea is that a product or service should have specified performance characteristics and that quality can be measured as the level of conformance with these specifications. By this definition of quality, Mazda automobiles can have higher quality than Jaguars if Mazdas fit their specifications more consistently than Jaguars and perform more reliably.

Almost all businesses have increased their emphasis on quality control in recent years, and many have installed **total quality management (TQM)** programs. They have had two reasons for doing so. The original motive for TQM programs was to cut costs by reducing scrap, rework, and unnecessary activities. Quality experts claim that companies without quality management programs typically lose 25 percent of their costs to waste, and that the costs of a quality management program are more than offset by reductions in this figure (this is the "quality is free" idea). More recently, the dominant motive for quality management programs has been to achieve marketing objectives. Managers talk about "market-driven quality" aimed at providing "total customer satisfaction," with the presumption that higher satisfaction will lead to more customers, higher loyalty, and less price sensitivity among customers.

Defining "total customer satisfaction" as the ultimate goal of a TQM program has two implications that involve marketing research. First, it implies that the specifications against which quality is measured should be set according to customers' preferences. Marketing research is needed to determine those preferences. Second, a goal of "total customer satisfaction" implies that customer satisfaction should be used as the ultimate test of quality. This requires marketing research to measure customer satisfaction.

This section of the chapter discusses how marketing research can be used to set quality standards. Customer satisfaction research is discussed later in the chapter.

Using Market Research to Set Quality Standards

In setting quality standards, companies must decide (1) which product/service characteristics will be subjected to goal setting and performance monitoring, (2) what levels of performance will be expected on those dimensions, and (3) what trade-offs will be made when goals for different characteristics come into conflict. A "market-driven" system will base these decisions on market research. The characteristics that are monitored will be those that influence outcomes important to customers, and the performance standards applied to these characteristics will reflect customers' utilities for different levels of performance as well as the trade-offs that customers are willing to make when different performance goals come into conflict.

For example, if market research shows that customers of an appliance repair service consider response time to be important, response time should be monitored; otherwise, it should not. If research shows that customers' satisfaction with response time is roughly equal for any same-day response but drops significantly for response the next day, the performance goal should be same-day response, and performance on this dimension should be measured by the percentage of service requests that are answered the same day they are made (other measures such as average response time would be less useful). If research shows that customers would rather have a repair job start tomorrow than start today and finish tomorrow, the goal of same-day response should be made subordinate to the goal of same-day completion.

Choosing Characteristics to Be Monitored

The first step in developing customer-based performance standards is choosing the product or service characteristics that will be subjected to performance goals. This is done as follows:

- First, depth interviews or focus groups should be used to identify dimensions that customers consider relevant to quality. The goal at this stage is not to quantify the importance of dimensions but simply to identify possible dimensions.

  This interviewing can be done in many ways. For example, participants might be asked to name high- and low-quality products or services of the type in question, then asked to discuss the differences between them. Or participants might be asked whether they ever bought the product or service in question; if so, they might be asked which brand they chose and how they knew that brand was better than the others. Projective techniques can also be used. For example, customers can be asked to draw a picture of a good appliance repair person and a picture of a bad appliance repair person. Exhibit 23.5 (see page 680) shows such a picture, which reveals that hair grooming and neatness of attire lead to inferences about competence.

  It is important to ask about low quality as well as high quality because people may take some dimensions for granted in discussing high-quality products. For example, many people who are asked to describe a high-quality appliance repair service will not mention the quality of repair; acceptable repair is taken for granted. When asked to describe a *low*-quality repair service, though, most people will begin by saying "A low-quality service does not fix the appliance properly."

- Once possible quality dimensions are identified, a survey should be done to measure the importance of various dimensions. These measures usually take the form of direct questions about attribute importance ("How important is . . . ?").

- Finally, the most important dimensions should be chosen.

Many companies skip the first step in this process and simply use judgment to develop a list of possible quality dimensions. The danger of this approach is that important dimensions may be overlooked. Dimensions that lead to inferences about product or service quality—for example, whether an appliance repair person looks

EXHIBIT 23.6

A Consumer's Drawings of High- and Low-Quality Repair Persons

High Quality

Low Quality

neat—are particularly likely to be missed, because these dimensions bear no obvious relationship to quality except in the customer's mind.

Setting Performance Standards

Once important quality dimensions have been identified, the next step is to set appropriate performance standards on these dimensions. The goal is to measure customers' utility functions for dimensions to be controlled—that is, the value customers attach to different levels of performance on these dimensions—so that standards can be set at or near optimum levels.

One approach is to measure customer satisfaction over some period of time, then plot satisfaction scores against performance levels on the dimension being studied. This method will show levels of performance where satisfaction peaks, plus any "elbow points" where satisfaction begins to decline rapidly. For example, Exhibit 23.7 shows the percentage of customers at a midpriced restaurant chain who said they were "very satisfied" with how quickly their food came, plotted against the length of time actually taken. The plot shows that satisfaction starts to decline at the five-minute mark and plummets after ten minutes. This graph suggests that the restaurant should set a goal of serving customers within five minutes and should set ten minutes as an absolute deadline.

Another way of measuring customers' utility functions is by using conjoint analysis, which was discussed in Chapter 9. People can be given descriptions of vari-

EXHIBIT 23.7

Relationship Between Service Time and Customer Satisfaction at a Midpriced Restaurant Chain

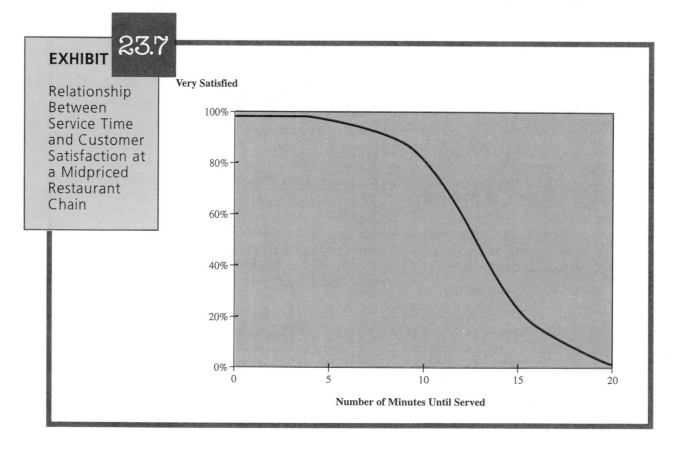

ous performance scenarios and asked to rank these scenarios according to acceptability. For this approach to be useful, people must be able to give meaningful reactions to *descriptions* of various performance levels (as opposed to actual performance).

A third way of identifying performance standards is by asking customers direct questions about their performance expectations. For example, a restaurant can ask customers how long they would be willing to wait while their food cooks. Different

CASE STUDY 23.1

In designing total quality management (TQM) programs, many companies do not take the time to measure customers' specific preferences and trade-offs. Instead, they set general improvement goals based on customer satisfaction surveys. The result can be a TQM system that is not fully efficient.

For example, a retail stockbrokerage tried to reduce the length of time taken by its brokers to return telephone calls. This issue was targeted because customer surveys showed low satisfaction with callback time. The company exhorted its brokers to return calls more quickly and began to track average callback time on a monthly basis. The company president set a goal of reducing the average callback time to less than thirty minutes, based purely on his own opinion regarding appropriate performance.

Further research showed this system to be misguided, because average callback time was not really the issue. Customers were found to call the brokers for two general reasons: (1) to discuss investment portfolios and strategies and (2) to execute trades. Calls made for the first purpose were not time-sensitive—the utility function for callback time did not show any significant decline until more than a day had passed. In contrast, calls made for trading purposes *were* time-sensitive—customers wanted their trades executed as soon as possible, and the utility function for callback time declined sharply from the very start. These were the calls that were prompting customer complaints about callback time.

The findings suggested a split system in which callers were given the option of ringing through to their brokers or ringing through to a trading desk. For calls placed to the brokers, response time was not worth measuring because very few of the callbacks fell outside a tolerance zone. For calls that went to the trading desk, crucial performance measures were the percentage of calls that got busy signals and the length of time callers had to hold the line. A system of measuring and improving callback times was not needed for either type of call, although it *seemed* to respond to customers' concerns.

This example shows that quality improvement efforts based on satisfaction data alone, without specific measures of customers' utility functions, can be suboptimal. It also illustrates a point familiar to any marketing research person: that customers' utility functions may vary across market segments and usage contexts. For this reason, a performance monitoring system that applies the same goals and measures to all service events, or that borrows goals and measures from other companies or organizational units, is likely to be less than optimal.

people will give different answers, but a performance standard can be chosen that falls within the range of acceptability for some desired percentage of customers. Like conjoint analysis, this approach requires participants to consider descriptions of performance rather than respond to actual performance.

A fourth way of setting performance standards is through **benchmarking,** which uses a combination of buyer opinions and competitor analysis. Buyers are asked to identify the company that has the best performance on some dimension (this company need not be in the same industry). That company's performance is measured, and a goal of meeting or beating that benchmark is established as the performance standard.

Identifying Internal Quality Dimensions

Most businesses have important performance dimensions that are invisible to customers and consequently do not emerge in interviews with buyers. For example, the dispatching operations in an appliance repair service are not seen by customers, but they do influence whether service people arrive in a timely manner. We will call these dimensions *internal* quality dimensions. It is necessary to identify important internal quality dimensions and set performance standards for them.

One way of identifying important internal dimensions is by conducting focus groups with employees. In these discussions, a session moderator presents customer-based performance goals to employees and asks them to name internal operations that affect the organization's ability to meet these goals. Once possible dimensions are recognized, group discussions can be combined with analyses of operations to select dimensions for performance monitoring and set performance standards on these dimensions.

In some companies, group discussions involving employees are conducted by the human resources department because this department has responsibility for all research involving employees. In other companies, the research is done by marketing research staff or suppliers because the procedures that are used are familiar to marketing researchers.

Critical Thinking Skills

In your opinion, what does it mean for a university to have high quality? What research would you recommend to a university that was interested in implementing a quality management program?

Customer Satisfaction Research

The rising popularity of relationship marketing and quality management programs in recent years has led to a tremendous increase in the use of customer satisfaction data. This information is almost always gathered by means of a customer survey.

The general discussion of surveys, questionnaires, and samples (in Chapter 7 and Chapters 10–14) is relevant to the design and use of customer satisfaction research. In addition, the following specific issues arise in doing and using customer satisfaction surveys.

Sampling Issues in Satisfaction Surveys

Several sampling issues arise in doing customer satisfaction research. These issues cover the full range of the sampling process, from population definition to sample design to sample execution to sample size. They are as follows:

1. *Satisfaction research is limited to customers.* The first issue in customer satisfaction research is that it is limited to a company's own customers. This is not a problem if the company simply wants to know how satisfied its customers are. However, if it intends to use satisfaction data to change a product or service with the ultimate objective of attracting new customers, it must remember that people who *do* buy the product or service cannot tell you why people *don't* buy it. For example, a Chrysler minivan buyer can tell how the minivan could be improved for people like her, but she cannot recommend how to attract sports car buyers.

2. *Transactions versus relationships.* A basic question in satisfaction research is whether the proper unit of observation is transactions or relationships. The two are not identical; for example, a customer may be dissatisfied with the speed of service on a specific trip to McDonald's but may be satisfied with McDonald's usual speed of service. The choice of a population unit is likely to depend on the purpose of the research. A quality management program is likely to focus on whether individual transactions meet performance specifications, whereas a relationship marketing program is likely to focus on the overall relationship.

3. *People versus companies versus dollars.* Should the measuring system give one vote per person, one vote per company, one vote per dollar, or what? To put this another way, is one customer's satisfaction more important than another customer's satisfaction? In consumer markets, the answer is usually "no," and it is appropriate to weigh responses equally. In business markets, the answer usually

CASE STUDY 23.2

What is the proper population unit for customer satisfaction research? Is it the transaction or the relationship? Is it the person, the company, or the sales dollar?

A salesperson for Link Industrial Services, which provides temporary workers for light industrial jobs, recently told us, "My company can afford occasional goof-ups. We just can't afford too many, and we can't afford to goof up the first time we do business with somebody." This comment suggests that satisfaction with the buying relationship is more relevant for Link than satisfaction with the transaction is.

The same salesperson said, "Right now, the good news is that I only have one dissatisfied customer. The bad news is that it's my largest customer, and I could lose about 20 percent of my billings." This comment suggests that a "key customers" reporting system is more appropriate for Link than a system that counts a large customer as just one more questionnaire in the data set.

is "yes," and it is desirable to distinguish between large and small customers. The easiest way of doing so is simply to show separate satisfaction results for key accounts.

4. *Who speaks for the customer?* An issue related to population units is the question of who speaks for the customer, especially in industrial contexts. For example, a construction company working on a large project deals with engineers, site managers, purchasing agents, financial managers, and other people within client organizations. Each of these people has a different perspective on the project and can speak about different aspects of the construction company's performance. Data obtained from any one person are incomplete, but data obtained from multiple respondents can be difficult to assemble into a coherent response.

   Such a situation raises various questions for data collection and data handling. For example, should different respondents within a client organization be asked different questions—the field managers asked about field issues, the purchasing managers asked about price and paperwork, and so on? If so, should the answers be entered into separate data files or stuck together into long, multirespondent observations? How should differing levels of satisfaction be handled? Should a client organization be counted as satisfied only if everyone in it is satisfied (which has the effect of treating unhappy people as vetoes within their organizations)? Should some respondents but not others be given veto power? If a client organization counts only as satisfied when everyone in it is satisfied, how should data from clients in which some people do not respond to the satisfaction questionnaire be handled? These questions usually cannot be answered in a completely satisfying manner, but they must be considered.

5. *How often will people respond?* Another issue for customer satisfaction research in business markets is the question of how often people will respond. In consumer markets, where companies have thousands of customers, it is easy to do repeated satisfaction surveys with different respondents each time. However, in business markets, it may be necessary to measure key accounts over and over. Since the usual rule of thumb is not to question people more than once every six months, this means that satisfaction cannot be monitored more than twice a year or, if more frequent results are desired, that key accounts must be split across administrations.

6. *Sample stratification.* An important sample design issue in customer satisfaction research is whether to use stratified sampling. Obviously, satisfaction research should use random samples of customers, to avoid bias in the selection process. Also, as our previous discussion suggests, stratification is usually appropriate when measuring satisfaction levels among business customers.

7. *Nonresponse.* Quality problems can be hidden by nonresponse if alienated customers fail to participate in data collection efforts. This is particularly a problem when data are gathered via mailed surveys or customer comment cards. Some disgruntled customers make a special point of venting their dissatisfaction, but many simply decide to cut their losses and ignore the company. These customers will express their opinions if called or visited but will not bother to complete self-administered questionnaires.

   This is not to say that self-administered questionnaires are inappropriate for customer satisfaction research. However, self-administered measures should be supplemented with periodic efforts to check whether nonrespondents differ from respondents.

8. *Sample size.* Our final sampling issue regarding customer satisfaction research relates to sample size. Sample size is rarely a problem in onetime satisfaction studies but may become a problem if a company uses repeated studies to track changes in satisfaction.

For example, we recently encountered a hospital that measured patient satisfaction on a quarterly basis, with sample sizes of 500 per quarter (2,000 per year). In a typical report, 90 percent of patients surveyed would indicate that they were "very satisfied" with the hospital. Given an annual sample size of 2,000, the 95 percent confidence interval around these estimates was approximately ±.013 (±1.3%). At this onetime level of analysis—reporting that 90 percent of patients were very satisfied, with a confidence interval of ±1.3%—the confidence interval is impressive. However, in testing the difference in satisfaction levels from quarter to quarter, the confidence interval is 3.7 percent (try these calculations yourself), and at this level of analysis—reporting that satisfaction changed by 1 percent or so last quarter, with a confidence interval of ±3.7 percent—the confidence interval seems unsatisfactory.

Such a situation is the rule, not the exception. Very few companies spend enough on customer satisfaction research to establish tight confidence intervals around quarter-to-quarter comparisons. The situation is perfectly acceptable, as long as the results are interpreted accordingly. A problem arises when small changes in satisfaction are made into a big managerial issue without taking the wide confidence intervals into account. In this example, the hospital had established an employee bonus program in which quarterly satisfaction changes of more than 1 percent would trigger changes in everybody's bonus. This program was an employee relations disaster waiting to happen.

Critical Thinking Skills

If you were asked to design a customer satisfaction research program for McDonald's, how would you define the population of interest? Would you measure transactions, relationships, or both? What sampling frame would you use? Would you stratify the sample? How often would you report results, and what sample sizes would you use?

Measurement Issues in Satisfaction Research

Customer satisfaction research also presents a series of measurement issues. These include the following:

1. *Whether to measure satisfaction.* The most basic measurement issue in any research project is whether the right questions have been asked. Ask yourself: Do you want satisfaction or repurchase intention? Satisfaction or what a customer would tell a friend? Satisfaction or suggestions for improvement? Satisfaction or perceived quality? Satisfaction is often the first thing that people think of measuring, because satisfaction research is popular, but satisfaction is not always the best thing to measure.

2. *When to measure satisfaction.* Should customer satisfaction be measured at the time of purchase? A week later? Three months later? A year later? The answer depends on the nature of the product and the focus of the research. For example, J. D. Power and Associates measures the satisfaction of new-car buyers several

months after the purchase, but satisfaction with individual fast-food transactions must be captured almost immediately.

One of the complications of customer satisfaction research is that the best time to measure one dimension may be different from the best time to measure another. For example, satisfaction with speed of service is best measured right after a purchase, but satisfaction with product reliability is best measured after a fairly lengthy usage period.

3. *Unipolar versus bipolar response categories.* Response categories for satisfaction measures can be unipolar (e.g., completely satisfied to not satisfied) or bipolar (completely satisfied to completely dissatisfied). We prefer bipolar categories, because we think some people are actively dissatisfied and we like to give them a chance to say so.

4. *Number of response categories.* Chapter 10 contained a discussion of how many response categories to use. A smaller number of categories is easier to label and administer, although a larger number of categories allows more discrimination. Most satisfaction measures use three to seven categories.

5. *Labeled versus unlabeled categories.* The issue of labeled versus unlabeled categories is related to the number of categories. Short scales, with only three or four categories, are easy to label, and the labeling gives the data vividness (for example, "55 percent of respondents said they were completely satisfied" is more vivid than "55 percent of respondents rated their satisfaction as 'four' on a four-point scale."). However, labels become increasingly difficult to develop and administer as scale length increases.

6. *Allowing room for improvement.* When satisfaction data are used on a onetime basis, almost any response scale can be used. Whether unipolar or bipolar, short or long, labeled or unlabeled, the scale will show that satisfaction in some areas of performance, and in some groups of respondents, is higher than in others. The specific numbers are not that important. However, when satisfaction data are used on an ongoing basis, it is desirable to have a scale that allows room for improvement.

For example, we recently encountered a company that measured satisfaction on a scale of "very satisfied, somewhat satisfied, or not satisfied." Given this scale, 95 percent of respondents said they were "very satisfied" with the company's service. The company's managers were happy with this result, but when they tried to improve service—because they knew the company was not perfect—they found that the high scores gave them nowhere to go. They could not use the results to convince employees that improvements were necessary, and they could not use improvements in the results to motivate employees.

We like to measure customer satisfaction with the following scale: "completely satisfied, mostly satisfied, somewhat satisfied, or dissatisfied." This scale is unbalanced, but we find that it works well. Labeling the top category "completely satisfied" and providing a category that says "mostly satisfied" cuts down the number of respondents who pick the top category and consequently provides room for improvement. Also, the "dissatisfied" category identifies respondents who are actively unhappy.

7. *Questionnaire length.* Companies sometimes use long questionnaires that measure every little aspect of their performance. In our opinion, this is a mistake, because

it is boring for respondents and costly for the company. A better approach is to use a limited number of questions—usually no more than ten—to measure satisfaction with broad aspects of the company's performance. Then, if a respondent expresses dissatisfaction in some area, a follow-up question can be asked for more detail.

8. *Reactive measurement conditions.* Some customer satisfaction programs are affected by reactive measurement conditions. For example, if an industrial company does a satisfaction survey and the company's sales force hears about it, salespeople are likely to ask their customers to give favorable comments when they get the survey. The same thing happens in customer satisfaction studies done by companies such as Ford to evaluate their dealers. Hopefully, the effects of these conditions will be constant across time, so that changes in satisfaction will be meaningful even if the baseline score is inflated.

Critical Thinking Skills

If you were asked to design a customer satisfaction research program for McDonald's, what topics would you cover? What response scales would you use? How many questions would you ask? When would you administer the questionnaire? What measurement problems, if any, would you encounter?

Issues in Using Satisfaction Data

Even if customer satisfaction surveys are well done, frustrations and inefficiencies can arise when the data are used without recognizing their limitations. Specific issues include the following:

1. *High areas are not beyond improvement.* Satisfaction data are always relative to the current market context. Consider, for example, American cars in the 1960s. These cars ruled the road, and at the time some of them would have scored very high on fuel economy, reliability, and "fit-and-finish" quality. Yet if these same cars were rated today, they would be unacceptable in these areas. While American manufacturers slept, Japanese manufacturers redefined what it meant to have satisfactory fuel economy, reliability, and fit-and-finish quality. Satisfaction measures reflect evaluations based on *what is*, not *what can be*.

    This point has some profound implications, including the possibility that the most fruitful area for improvement may be one in which a company currently scores high. High ratings do not mean that an area is beyond improvement.

2. *Satisfiers versus dissatisfiers.* The natural reaction of any company that does a satisfaction study is to target the areas with relatively low scores for improvement. However, just as the areas with high scores are not beyond improvement, the areas with low scores may not be the best priorities for improvement. These low-scoring areas may be "dissatisfiers" that cause complaints but do not attract customers.

    For example, at the University of Houston, where most students commute to campus, the aspect of the school that draws the lowest satisfaction ratings is the parking, but it is hard to argue that parking should be the school's top priority for improvement. In fact, the campus has excellent parking facilities—the low ratings stem from the fact that people do not think about parking when it goes well but are dissatisfied when it goes poorly. Also, parking is not the reason why people come to the university. If the university's goal is to draw more students or enhance student retention, improved parking will not do the job, unless the parking is so bad that it is driving people away.

3. *Satisfaction data have random error.* Any company that tracks customer satisfaction over time will experience random fluctuations that cannot be explained. These fluctuations are an inevitable consequence of sampling variation and measurement error, but can be very disturbing to people who are evaluated on the basis of customer satisfaction. It is necessary to take movements in the data with a grain of salt and not to overreact to every momentary shift in the data.

4. *Appropriate standards may vary.* Different satisfaction standards may be appropriate for evaluating different business units and/or different performance dimensions. In hospitals, for example, satisfaction ratings for service in the maternity ward are usually higher than ratings for the cancer ward, because the maternity ward is the "happy ward." Satisfaction with the hospital's doctors is usually higher than satisfaction with its business office. Satisfaction with hospitals in smaller cities is usually higher than satisfaction with hospitals in larger cities. These differences make comparisons across business units tenuous.

   Despite the tenuousness of cross-unit comparisons, many companies make them. These comparisons can lead managers from lower-rated units to become defensive about their results and disparage the whole measurement process. To minimize this problem, it is necessary to emphasize that each unit has its own scale and that comparisons across units or performance dimensions should be made with extreme caution.

5. *Haloing affects multi-item measures.* Multi-item satisfaction measures can be heavily influenced by "haloing," in which ratings of specific performance dimensions are influenced by overall satisfaction with the product or service. Happy customers tend to rate everything high, and unhappy customers tend to rate everything low. The result can be mistaken conclusions about ways to enhance satisfaction.

   For example, at some universities, the questionnaire that is used for course evaluations includes an item about the instructor's punctuality. This item usually correlates highly with the overall course evaluations. At face value, this correlation suggests that low evaluations can be improved by improving the instructor's punctuality, but this is usually not true. The punctuality ratings are caused by overall satisfaction, not vice versa.

6. *Diagnosing is not the same as curing.* In general, knowing that customers are less than fully satisfied does not tell managers how to improve the situation. Customers must be asked not only how satisfied they are but also how the situation can be improved. Even this may fail to provide adequate direction; customers are better at saying things are wrong than at knowing how to fix them.

   The overall effect of these issues is that managers and employees often find themselves in an unappealing position when they are evaluated on the basis of customer satisfaction. Their satisfaction scores vary for reasons they cannot explain, the system seems to give some people better scores than others, and they are not sure what to do with the results. This causes defensiveness and disparagement of the research process.

   To minimize these problems, managers must be given realistic expectations concerning the limitations of satisfaction data and must be asked to accept the idea that customer satisfaction data are valuable despite these limitations. Also, the focus must be on opportunity, not evaluation—that is, what *we* can do better, not what *you* did wrong. It is helpful to develop an operational plan intended to improve targeted aspects of customer satisfaction, then reward employees and managers for implementing that plan, whether or not satisfaction actually changes.

Marketing Research Tools 23.2 summarizes the various issues involved in conducting and using customer satisfaction research.

MARKETING RESEARCH TOOLS

23.2

ISSUES IN CUSTOMER SATISFACTION RESEARCH

Sampling issues:

- Satisfaction research is limited to customers.
- Do you want to measure transactions or relationships?
- Are you interested in people or companies or dollars?
- Who speaks for the customer?
- How often will people respond?
- Should the sample be stratified?
- Is nonresponse bias a problem?
- Is the sample size large enough to support the desired analyses?

Measurement issues:

- Is satisfaction the right thing to measure?
- When should satisfaction be measured?
- Should unipolar or bipolar response categories be used?
- How many response categories are appropriate?
- Should response categories be labeled or unlabeled?
- Will the scale allow room for improvement?
- Is the questionnaire too long?
- Is there a problem with reactive measurement conditions?

Application issues:

- High areas can still be improved.
- Low areas may not be the best priorities for improvement.
- Random error can cause meaningless shifts in the data.
- Appropriate standards may vary across business units.
- Specific items may be influenced by haloing.
- Knowing that customers are dissatisfied does not tell people how to improve.

Summary

This chapter discussed current issues in marketing research. The following points were covered:

1.   How can the Internet be used in marketing research?

The Internet can be used as a source of secondary data, to gather observational data, to collect survey information, and/or to get advice about research techniques and sources. Secondary data may be obtained from a company's homepage, websites that provide investment advice, and government and academic pages. Observational data may be obtained by counting the "hits" on a website, monitoring the points of origin for website visitors, and/or asking visitors to register. Surveys can be administered via the Internet but are best used as a supplementary method because of sampling concerns. The Internet can also be used as a source of advice by posting a question to a newsgroup or listserv.

2.   How can marketing research be used in relationship marketing?

Marketing research is used in relationship marketing to measure the lifetime revenue obtained from customers, to measure share of customer, to measure the effectiveness of relationship marketing programs, and to measure customer satisfaction. Lifetime revenue is measured by means of customer information files containing purchase information, or by means of survey data. Share of customer is measured using survey data. The effectiveness of relationship marketing programs is assessed by estimating the effect of a program on lifetime revenue and/or share of customer. Customer satisfaction is measured with surveys.

3.   How can marketing research be used in database marketing?

Marketing research techniques are used to build and analyze customer databases. Companies that do not sell directly to their customers can use customer contact records and secondary information to build customer information files, whereas companies that sell directly can use a marketing information system to gather and store customer information. Regardless of how the database is built, it is analyzed with the same procedures used in marketing research.

4.   How can marketing research be used in new-product development?

Marketing research plays a role in the concept generation, concept screening, and product optimization stages of new-product development. New-product concepts can be generated through idea conferences, "champions of innovation" programs, concept engineering, product space maps, and conjoint analysis, all of which use marketing research procedures. The steps taken when screening new-product concepts include determining risk/reward ratios with secondary data, evaluating customer acceptance with focus groups, and estimating sales potential with survey data. Conjoint analysis and choice modeling techniques can be used to find optimal new-product designs.

5.   How can marketing research be used in total quality management (TQM)?

Qualitative marketing research can be used to determine which dimensions of quality might be subjected to performance goals, and surveys and/or conjoint analysis can be used to assess the relative importance of these dimensions. Employee focus groups can be used to determine internal quality dimensions. Once a quality program is in place, surveys can be used to measure customer satisfaction.

6. What issues arise in conducting and using customer satisfaction research?

Sampling issues, measurement issues, and application issues arise in customer satisfaction research. Sampling issues include the fact that satisfaction research is limited to customers, whether the proper unit of analysis is transactions or relationships, whether responses from large customers should be weighted differently than those from small customers, who should speak for the customer, how often people will respond, whether the sample should be stratified, how to handle nonresponse error, and whether the sample size is large enough for tracking purposes. Measurement issues include whether to measure satisfaction, when to measure it, whether to use unipolar or bipolar measurement scales, what the appropriate number of response categories is, whether to use labeled or unlabeled categories, how to allow room for improvement, how long a questionnaire should be, and problems due to reactive measurement conditions. Issues in using satisfaction data include the facts that areas scoring high on satisfaction are not necessarily beyond improvement, areas that score low do not necessarily need to be improved, shifts in tracking data can be produced by random error, appropriate standards may vary across business units or performance dimensions, multi-item measures are affected by haloing, and diagnosing problems does not necessarily tell how to cure them.

Suggested Additional Readings

More information about the Internet is contained in Paul Gilster, *The New Internet Navigator* (New York: John Wiley and Sons, 1995). More information about relationship marketing is contained in Terry G. Vavra, *After-Marketing: How to Keep Customers for Life* (Chicago: Irwin, 1995). More information about database marketing is contained in Arthur M. Hughes, *The Complete Database Marketer: Second-Generation Strategies and Techniques for Tapping the Power of Your Customer Database* (Chicago: Irwin, 1996). More information about new-product development is contained in Glen L. Urban and John R. Hauser, *Design and Marketing of New Products* (Englewood Cliffs, N.J.: Prentice Hall, 1993). More information about customer satisfaction is contained in Alan Dutka, *AMA Handbook for Customer Satisfaction: A Complete Guide to Research, Planning and Implementation* (Chicago: NTC Business Books, 1994).

Discussion Questions

1. The most common way to measure online marketing success is by monitoring the number of hits on a web page. Do you think that this is the best way to measure the effectiveness of a firm's web page? Why or why not? How might this information be misleading?

2. According to a 1996 Lou Harris survey conducted by Equifax, 64 percent of the respondents do not agree that providers of online services should be able to track the places they go online to send users targeted offers. As a marketer, how do you feel about this finding? How is this different from a database marketer tracking purchases? Or a direct salesperson recording his/her customer's sales and service in a sales log? Or a car dealership tracking inquiries?

3. Do you think that tracking customers online is a violation of their privacy? Why? How does tracking this information benefit customers? How might it hurt them?

4. Why aren't Internet surveys always effective? What are some of the sampling limitations? When might you want to use an Internet survey?

5. The key concepts in relationship marketing are "lifetime revenue" and "share of customer." What is meant by each of these concepts? Why is measuring each of these concepts important to marketers?

6. What is meant by database marketing? What firms, do you think, maintain the largest databases? How do databases help marketers pursue a relationship marketing strategy? What type of customer information do you think the airline companies keep in their frequent-flyer customer databases?

7. When developing new products, how might marketing research be used in concept screening? Would you use primary or secondary data? What questions would you want to answer?

8. How can marketing research be used to set performance standards to be used as part of a total quality management program?

9. If you were asked to conduct a customer satisfaction survey for your local cable television company, how would you define the population of interest? Who would you have participate in the survey? What sampling frame would you use? What mode of administration would you use? What aspects of the service would you want to measure? How could you ensure a high cooperation rate?

Marketing Research Challenge

Design a survey to measure customer satisfaction with the academic advising process at a college. What questions should you ask? How long should the questionnaire be? Who should you sample? When should the survey be conducted? How should it be administered? How would you use the information once it was collected?

Internet Exercise

Marketing Tools 23.1 lists some Internet sites related to marketing research. Visit these sites. Which sites do you find most useful? What additional useful sites can you find, either by using our links or by exploring on your own? Make a list of the most useful sites and exchange them with other students in the class.

Appendix A

Table of Random Numbers

```
51007 80734   07258 74728   99882 41207   73851 00696   73571 21824
50993 20854   71363 91172   45289 30176   08979 75432   73320 09776
56399 22815   50260 05461   32433 21577   94273 36728   08620 11493
93213 13826   01331 34446   56094 79667   06823 74797   45438 12185
45930 66561   71732 62923   01098 81822   60191 85889   58466 19515

54387 42768   58715 29596   04916 94472   47999 69096   67057 69908
97224 27900   63750 37092   36637 18427   68522 49900   37713 36681
26625 56816   45580 64476   17499 52251   55575 14035   73024 51186
73443 84351   35589 81476   40628 29830   81595 16840   96129 71333
37590 97538   06142 94434   04253 15066   85501 57084   54335 13447

73413 36988   70451 47926   83971 32328   44695 12958   84357 53115
11496 92757   69239 06336   56596 57099   84186 36638   53632 39081
84601 77979   29868 11119   23337 83205   89136 46279   94089 79207
96000 08615   79589 73578   20322 88887   27932 67282   71110 64262
96898 60366   74335 69336   53283 06635   59679 80169   53603 62523

36283 61872   58475 91199   41151 33525   43496 33827   94191 88271
04016 25914   44877 77888   06064 83757   52800 24354   23595 78220
00260 06705   16874 61853   82761 58275   80492 76863   78702 28043
26375 70420   68631 83407   39930 75611   02479 49160   34292 90021
44291 46530   44695 72479   46924 92533   10036 69208   20560 00622

03447 83134   77495 65529   25125 83219   31940 25236   28539 53797
39087 55841   98208 12529   89823 66316   34302 45910   91984 08691
48683 12906   65254 61193   14843 37996   21800 39377   06590 22774
67797 33853   61219 24273   68652 26159   30289 44134   98760 95552
86282 18362   91092 41298   73865 85621   67829 99314   03338 80335

08571 42691   55695 27066   11443 99032   29044 38474   01338 70552
55132 23711   94498 02134   86292 96651   84019 96174   68786 46927
39184 32262   23881 38557   65778 11881   60933 00586   99386 93969
39250 72763   34345 82088   85364 16247   56831 41457   25702 44809
85560 41695   80906 27909   24905 94396   52442 00531   76631 19166

37134 84055   27525 13246   47265 66181   94140 90776   81863 46221
67596 33170   74500 55559   80249 15742   84873 82617   12615 45465
88195 65393   65690 00406   64209 98213   95491 40198   95499 11390
99911 04206   20407 92252   17539 57188   23540 42010   44950 14134
91848 03861   19547 02282   10792 82859   55555 89775   75764 57950

15694 35494   20103 07733   50761 57061   88933 04867   36939 08699
00363 71866   56135 64728   57154 19187   61176 18315   73154 30079
24894 44634   56288 15351   71522 43506   80301 21557   50969 92512
08475 30747   15721 40900   27475 07698   75083 28732   99301 38014
67100 21538   60366 11193   19765 63697   49377 21208   07615 37404

83457 52575   20958 31316   05254 82913   77345 91811   94181 10983
49341 09170   19642 99719   66177 39455   07641 78710   35507 57972
58754 68118   05067 79790   41945 08960   96439 97149   87407 76860
10995 58595   78474 70308   46882 28003   27757 26473   05673 54121
08319 88047   25951 68555   03797 74696   57201 00979   71156 65324

19616 32344   87887 12113   81295 35587   96460 61219   06050 91332
09886 57505   42123 06869   13106 40182   95865 57049   70378 35347
49574 81649   56499 52154   08046 21674   75762 65810   56955 63162
22505 76575   42051 51254   69305 73428   80645 09081   18932 31770
00985 86126   73348 94049   98078 16043   78746 70679   21992 06519
```

85550	09773	96718	78300	16879	45651	78924	68516	22811	02383
05039	11210	65432	16227	61988	04945	47279	13355	41710	33305
76332	20189	62253	06318	53712	66292	43800	96681	96177	18152
97882	87090	55361	63357	06614	04806	81959	93138	17600	01994
55227	87106	08229	21994	48540	94485	69871	64934	74144	81199
43262	44994	61596	76831	66443	55574	35467	89068	99010	50993
67123	18956	62755	37646	88771	32557	99289	26409	18248	26925
96985	93706	81756	50806	76684	31084	45005	42704	86278	28894
05100	80566	94459	92567	70878	58651	97155	93686	88706	44583
81811	11745	20247	25758	02885	30050	64078	78665	42711	68913
74622	93907	23648	78526	33335	54990	17604	51242	32043	48557
84981	47445	00278	92681	08803	32292	73080	34996	78659	91251
39804	26443	83687	21295	10925	14773	60507	09327	65182	41169
00338	80335	34561	60070	59111	73027	41810	12022	14515	92590
94824	92098	21954	10017	07011	89783	30868	25498	96732	90235
89906	04541	53678	73179	51918	77367	80808	30621	14821	93318
70226	37307	18392	52601	08109	84853	83356	72818	78173	32213
83519	48021	76798	59099	82159	81365	17659	48472	84340	90038
89340	86194	51216	03518	73005	12149	31682	13536	57288	62154
19055	18598	53389	05535	30459	83054	55821	89090	72664	78421
86703	47341	45470	70886	21031	11416	89086	53958	21538	08803
30870	79601	74279	23404	29780	25500	19547	57510	78677	87306
24654	57804	67962	25649	40873	75393	74019	56185	67982	94603
62894	66197	70701	03054	47281	47594	26608	52374	49690	84189
19835	13990	10071	84196	24492	48904	27184	51410	95938	83364
36436	58815	82296	67042	51288	31920	25697	95897	37703	39188
67048	63204	02638	24169	96786	32632	92137	18014	29947	72033
09972	85398	06647	13198	95739	01025	89847	29697	64375	99501
66846	02821	57298	64159	87738	92265	30367	71150	46899	43270
58759	11497	10101	59242	73742	77325	29741	20781	08297	86827
72055	37088	03929	36036	05892	65736	48583	06118	14889	59139
72275	63361	95768	68627	88030	34100	29930	45213	91344	44535
12780	08581	54121	22555	74271	64451	36984	97234	77198	87192
40420	14645	68505	47064	49595	19072	82043	77926	18856	24898
16408	40091	02929	56945	08410	88874	89275	58164	72505	08310
93192	17078	71240	53772	40839	11421	16495	27052	38116	00879
49896	79132	53541	84508	43701	83442	57412	58975	56095	82946
94360	35708	57395	88700	73459	06525	21190	52703	99350	67362
42062	86952	89744	17452	47192	18458	85195	18527	64558	73618
00377	37232	42034	12137	50611	02137	28155	42822	07952	32871
35425	69501	69720	73942	74797	10607	59301	58887	35231	62848
96667	71233	99819	54640	54458	89224	09569	66444	13273	48482
51858	91274	29278	92460	57802	36684	10500	04138	10060	64776
37075	25686	12992	11296	49002	10918	38606	80474	30351	80792
80184	89258	07569	26971	61626	75150	01553	32386	00042	85503
30084	67339	30094	37093	76724	88353	93056	60325	11232	10537
13910	81798	05258	51264	87575	90079	87679	86835	98797	42367
90987	00733	03827	78990	78154	98215	80577	46118	39109	67793
05051	04864	38995	59575	64832	20866	84637	98593	14618	71905
48512	54401	95545	81420	26322	73539	15399	90779	38461	73045

Source: The Rand Corporation. *A Million Random Digits with 100,000 Normal Deviates.* New York: The Free Press (1955), pp. 350–351.

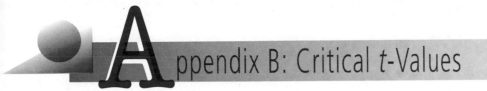

ppendix B: Critical *t*-Values

This table shows critical *t*-values to be used in hypothesis testing. See Chapter 16, p. 467, for a description of how *t*-values are used in hypothesis tests.

Use this table as follows:

1. Perform your *t* calculation.

2. Calculate your degrees of freedom, *df*. This is calculated as (n − 1), where n is the sample size used in your *t* calculation. If you are testing the difference between two samples, $df = (n_1 − 1) + (n_2 − 1)$.

3. Choose a significance level, *p*. This table shows three levels that are commonly used: .10, .05, and .01. They apply to "two-tailed" tests where *t* could be positive or negative, which is the usual situation. If only one direction of results is possible, cut the listed *p* level by half; in other words, *p* = .10 in this table should be treated as *p* = .05 if the test is one-tailed.

4. Use this table to find the critical *t*-value which corresponds to your degrees of freedom and desired significance level. For example, if you have a sample size of 30 and want to do a significance test at the .05 level, the critical *t*-value is 2.045 (*df* = 24, *p* = .05). If you have a sample size of 200 and want to do a significance test at the .05 level, the critical *t*-value is 1.960.

5. Compare your calculated *t*-value with the critical value from the table. If your calculated value is larger, then the difference being tested is significant at the indicated *p* level. For example, if your calculated *t*-value for the difference between two sample means is 4.72, and the sample size in each group is 200, then the difference between the two means is significant at the *p* = .05 level, because your calculated *t*-value of 4.72 is larger than the table's critical value of 1.96.

Critical *t*-values

df	p (two-tailed)		
	.10	.05	.01
1	6.314	12.706	63.657
2	2.920	4.303	9.925
3	2.353	3.182	5.841
4	2.132	2.776	4.604
5	2.015	2.571	4.032
6	1.943	2.447	3.707
7	1.895	2.365	3.499
8	1.860	2.306	3.355
9	1.833	2.262	3.250
10	1.812	2.228	3.169
11	1.796	2.201	3.106
12	1.782	2.179	3.055
13	1.771	2.160	3.012
14	1.761	2.145	2.977
15	1.753	2.131	2.947
16	1.746	2.120	2.921
17	1.740	2.110	2.898
18	1.734	2.101	2.878
19	1.729	2.093	2.861
20	1.725	2.086	2.845
21	1.721	2.080	2.831
22	1.717	2.074	2.819
23	1.714	2.069	2.807
24	1.711	2.064	2.797
25	1.708	2.060	2.787
26	1.706	2.056	2.779
27	1.703	2.052	2.771
28	1.701	2.048	2.763
29	1.699	2.045	2.756
30	1.697	2.042	2.750
40	1.684	2.021	2.704
60	1.671	2.000	2.660
120	1.658	1.980	2.617
∞	1.645	1.960	2.576

df = degrees of freedom.
Source: Taken from Sheldon M. Ross, *Introductory Statistics,* McGraw-Hill, 1996.

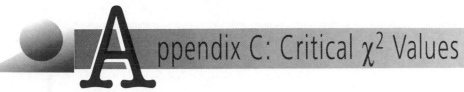

Appendix C: Critical χ^2 Values

This table shows critical χ^2 values to be used in hypothesis testing. See Chapter 17, p. 479, for a description of how χ^2 values are used in hypothesis tests.

Use this table as follows:

1. Perform your χ^2 calculation.

2. Calculate your degrees of freedom, *df*. In cross-tabs, *df* is calculated as $(r - 1) \times (c - 1)$, where r is the number of rows and c is the number of columns in the cross-tab.

3. Choose a significance level, *p*. This table shows three levels that are commonly used: .10, .05, and .01.

4. Use this table to find the critical χ^2 value which corresponds to your degrees of freedom and desired significance level. For example, if you are testing a cross-tab with five rows and three columns ($df = 4 \times 2 = 8$), and you want to do a significance test at the .05 level, the critical value of χ^2 is 15.51. For a 2×2 cross-tab ($df = 1 \times 1 = 1$), the critical value of χ^2 at a .05 significance level is 3.84.

5. Compare your calculated χ^2 value with the critical value from the table. If your calculated value is larger, then the relationship being tested is significant at the indicated *p* level. For example, if your calculated χ^2 value for a 2×2 cross-tab is 7.12, then the relationship between the variables is significant at the $p = .05$ level, because the calculated χ^2 value of 7.12 is larger than the table's critical value of 3.84.

Critical χ² values

df	.10	.05	.01
1	2.71	3.84	6.63
2	4.61	5.99	9.21
3	6.25	7.81	11.34
4	7.78	9.49	13.28
5	9.24	11.07	15.09
6	10.65	12.59	16.81
7	12.02	14.07	18.48
8	13.36	15.51	20.09
9	14.68	16.92	21.67
10	15.99	18.31	23.21
11	17.28	19.68	24.72
12	18.55	21.03	26.22
13	19.81	22.36	27.69
14	21.06	23.68	29.14
15	22.31	25.00	30.58
16	23.54	26.30	32.00
17	24.77	27.59	33.41
18	25.99	28.87	34.81
19	27.20	30.14	36.19
20	28.41	31.41	37.57
21	29.62	32.67	38.93
22	30.18	33.92	40.29
23	32.01	35.17	41.64
24	33.20	36.42	42.98
25	34.28	37.65	44.31
26	35.56	38.89	45.64
27	36.74	40.11	46.96
28	37.92	41.34	48.28
29	39.09	42.56	49.59
30	40.26	43.77	50.89
40	51.81	55.76	63.69
50	63.17	67.50	76.15
60	74.40	79.08	88.38
70	85.53	90.53	100.42
80	96.58	101.88	112.33
90	107.57	113.14	124.12
100	118.50	124.34	135.81

df = degrees of freedom.
Source: Taken from Sheldon M. Ross, Introductory Statistics, McGraw-Hill, 1996.

Appendix D: Critical F Values

The following tables show critical F values to be used in hypothesis testing. See Chapter 17, p. 483, for a description of how F values are used in hypothesis tests.

Use these tables as follows:

1. Perform your F calculation.
2. Calculate the associated degrees of freedom, *df*, for the numerator and denominator of your F ratio. If your F relates to the "main effect" of an independent variable, then *df* for the numerator is calculated as $(k - 1)$, where k is the number of levels for the independent variable. If your F relates to an "interaction effect" involving two independent variables, then *df* for the numerator is calculated as $(k_1 - 1) \times (k_2 - 1)$. The *df* for the denominator usually is the "residual *df*," calculated as the "total *df*" minus the sum of the *df* for all effects tested. The total *df* is calculated as $(n - 1)$, where n is the total sample size.
3. Choose a significance level, *p*. These tables show three levels that are commonly used: .10, .05, and .01.
4. Use the table which corresponds to your desired *p* level, and find the critical F value that corresponds to your degrees of freedom for the numerator and denominator. For example, if your *df* for the numerator and denominator are (4, 225), and you want to do a significance test at the .05 level, the critical value of F is 2.37.
5. Compare your calculated F value with the critical value from the table. If your calculated value is larger, then the relationship being tested is significant at the indicated *p* level. For example, if your calculated F value is 4.51, with *df* = (4, 225), then the differences among groups are significant at the $p - .05$ level, because the calculated F value of 4.51 is larger than the table's critical value of 2.37.

Critical F values

$p = .10$ (See following pages for $p = .05$ and $p = .01$)

Degrees of freedom for the numerator (df_1)

df_2	1	2	3	4	5	6	7	8	9	10	12	15	20	24	30	40	60	120	∞
1	39.86	49.50	53.59	55.83	57.24	58.20	58.91	59.44	59.86	59.86	60.19	60.71	61.22	61.74	62.00	62.26	62.53	62.79	63.06	63.33
2	8.53	9.00	9.16	9.24	9.29	9.33	9.35	9.37	9.38	9.39	9.41	9.42	9.44	9.45	9.46	9.47	9.47	9.48	9.49
3	5.54	5.46	5.39	5.34	5.31	5.28	5.27	5.25	5.24	5.23	5.22	5.20	5.18	5.18	5.17	5.16	5.15	5.14	5.13
4	4.54	4.32	4.19	4.11	4.05	4.01	3.98	3.95	3.94	3.92	3.90	3.87	3.84	3.83	3.82	3.80	3.79	3.78	3.76
5	4.06	3.78	3.62	3.52	3.45	3.40	3.37	3.34	3.32	3.30	3.27	3.24	3.21	3.19	3.17	3.16	3.14	3.12	3.10
6	3.78	3.46	3.29	3.18	3.11	3.05	3.01	2.98	2.96	2.94	2.90	2.87	2.84	2.82	2.80	2.78	2.76	2.74	2.72
7	3.59	3.26	3.07	2.96	2.88	2.83	2.78	2.75	2.72	2.70	2.67	2.63	2.59	2.58	2.56	2.54	2.51	2.49	2.47
8	3.46	3.11	2.92	2.81	2.73	2.67	2.62	2.59	2.56	2.54	2.50	2.46	2.42	2.40	2.38	2.36	2.34	2.32	2.29
9	3.36	3.01	2.81	2.69	2.61	2.55	2.51	2.47	2.44	2.42	2.38	2.34	2.30	2.28	2.25	2.23	2.21	2.18	2.16
10	3.29	2.92	2.73	2.61	2.52	2.46	2.41	2.38	2.35	2.32	2.28	2.24	2.20	2.18	2.16	2.13	2.11	2.08	2.06
11	3.23	2.86	2.66	2.54	2.45	2.39	2.34	2.30	2.27	2.25	2.21	2.17	2.12	2.10	2.08	2.05	2.03	2.00	1.97
12	3.18	2.81	2.61	2.48	2.39	2.33	2.28	2.24	2.21	2.19	2.15	2.10	2.06	2.04	2.01	1.99	1.96	1.93	1.90
13	3.14	2.76	2.56	2.43	2.35	2.28	2.23	2.20	2.16	2.14	2.10	2.05	2.01	1.98	1.96	1.93	1.90	1.88	1.85
14	3.10	2.73	2.52	2.39	2.31	2.24	2.19	2.15	2.12	2.10	2.05	2.01	1.96	1.94	1.91	1.89	1.86	1.83	1.80
15	3.07	2.70	2.49	2.36	2.27	2.21	2.16	2.12	2.09	2.06	2.02	1.97	1.92	1.90	1.87	1.85	1.82	1.79	1.76
16	3.05	2.67	2.46	2.33	2.24	2.18	2.13	2.09	2.06	2.03	1.99	1.94	1.89	1.87	1.84	1.81	1.78	1.75	1.72
17	3.03	2.64	2.44	2.31	2.22	2.15	2.10	2.06	2.03	2.00	1.96	1.91	1.86	1.84	1.81	1.78	1.75	1.72	1.69

Degrees of freedom for the denominator (df_2)

18	3.01	2.62	2.42	2.29	2.20	2.13	2.08	2.04	2.00	1.98	1.93	1.89	1.84	1.81	1.78	1.75	1.72	1.69	1.66
19	2.99	2.61	2.40	2.27	2.18	2.11	2.06	2.02	1.98	1.96	1.91	1.86	1.81	1.79	1.76	1.73	1.70	1.67	1.63
20	2.97	2.59	2.38	2.25	2.16	2.09	2.04	2.00	1.96	1.94	1.89	1.84	1.79	1.77	1.74	1.71	1.68	1.64	1.61
21	2.96	2.57	2.36	2.23	2.14	2.08	2.02	1.98	1.95	1.92	1.87	1.83	1.78	1.75	1.72	1.69	1.66	1.62	1.59
22	2.95	2.56	2.34	2.22	2.13	2.06	2.01	1.97	1.93	1.90	1.86	1.81	1.76	1.73	1.70	1.67	1.64	1.60	1.57
23	2.94	2.55	2.35	2.21	2.11	2.05	1.99	1.95	1.92	1.89	1.84	1.80	1.74	1.72	1.69	1.66	1.62	1.59	1.55
24	2.93	2.54	2.33	2.19	2.10	2.04	1.98	1.94	1.91	1.88	1.83	1.78	1.73	1.70	1.67	1.64	1.61	1.57	1.53
25	2.92	2.53	2.32	2.18	2.09	2.02	1.97	1.93	1.89	1.87	1.82	1.77	1.72	1.69	1.66	1.63	1.59	1.56	1.52
26	2.91	2.52	2.31	2.17	2.08	2.01	1.96	1.92	1.88	1.86	1.81	1.76	1.71	1.68	1.65	1.61	1.58	1.54	1.50
27	2.90	2.51	2.30	2.17	2.07	2.00	1.95	1.91	1.87	1.85	1.80	1.75	1.70	1.67	1.64	1.60	1.57	1.53	1.49
28	2.89	2.50	2.29	2.16	2.06	2.00	1.94	1.90	1.87	1.84	1.79	1.74	1.69	1.66	1.63	1.59	1.56	1.52	1.48
29	2.89	2.50	2.28	2.15	2.06	1.99	1.93	1.89	1.86	1.83	1.78	1.73	1.68	1.65	1.62	1.58	1.55	1.51	1.47
30	2.88	2.49	2.28	2.14	2.03	1.98	1.93	1.88	1.85	1.82	1.77	1.72	1.67	1.64	1.61	1.57	1.54	1.50	1.46
40	2.84	2.44	2.23	2.09	2.00	1.93	1.87	1.83	1.79	1.76	1.71	1.66	1.61	1.57	1.54	1.51	1.47	1.42	1.38
60	2.79	2.39	2.18	2.04	1.95	1.87	1.82	1.77	1.74	1.71	1.66	1.60	1.54	1.51	1.48	1.44	1.40	1.35	1.29
120	2.75	2.35	2.13	1.99	1.90	1.82	1.77	1.72	1.68	1.65	1.60	1.55	1.48	1.45	1.41	1.37	1.32	1.26	1.19
∞	2.71	2.30	2.08	1.94	1.85	1.77	1.72	1.67	1.63	1.60	1.55	1.49	1.42	1.38	1.34	1.30	1.24	1.17	1.00

Source: Taken from Sheldon M. Ross, *Introductory Statistics*, McGraw-Hill, 1996.

Critical F values

$p = .05$

	Degrees of freedom for the numerator (df_1)																		
df_2	1	2	3	4	5	6	7	8	9	10	12	15	20	24	30	40	60	120	∞
1	161.4	199.5	215.7	224.6	230.2	234.0	236.8	238.9	240.5	241.9	243.9	245.9	248.0	249.1	250.1	251.1	252.2	253.3	254.3
2	18.51	19.00	19.16	19.25	19.30	19.33	19.35	19.37	19.38	19.40	19.41	19.43	19.45	19.45	19.46	19.47	19.48	19.49	19.50
3	10.13	9.55	9.28	9.12	9.01	8.94	8.89	8.85	8.81	8.79	8.74	8.70	8.66	8.64	8.62	8.59	8.57	8.55	8.53
4	7.71	6.94	6.59	6.39	6.26	6.16	6.09	6.04	6.00	5.96	5.91	5.86	5.80	5.77	5.75	5.72	5.69	5.66	5.63
5	6.61	5.79	5.41	5.19	5.05	4.95	4.88	4.82	4.77	4.74	4.68	4.62	4.56	4.53	4.50	4.46	4.43	4.40	4.36
6	5.99	5.14	4.76	4.53	4.39	4.28	4.21	4.15	4.10	4.06	4.00	3.94	3.87	3.84	3.81	3.77	3.74	3.70	3.67
7	5.59	4.74	4.35	4.12	3.97	3.87	3.79	3.73	3.68	3.64	3.57	3.51	3.44	3.41	3.38	3.34	3.30	3.27	3.23
8	5.32	4.46	4.07	3.84	3.69	3.58	3.50	3.44	3.39	3.35	3.28	3.22	3.15	3.12	3.08	3.04	3.01	2.97	2.93
9	5.12	4.26	3.86	3.63	3.48	3.37	3.29	3.23	3.18	3.14	3.07	3.01	2.94	2.90	2.86	2.83	2.79	2.75	2.71
10	4.96	4.10	3.71	3.48	3.33	3.22	3.14	3.07	3.02	2.98	2.91	2.85	2.77	2.74	2.70	2.66	2.62	2.58	2.54
11	4.84	3.98	3.59	3.36	3.20	3.09	3.01	2.95	2.90	2.85	2.79	2.72	2.65	2.61	2.57	2.53	2.49	2.45	2.40
12	4.75	3.89	3.49	3.26	3.11	3.00	2.91	2.85	2.80	2.75	2.69	2.62	2.54	2.51	2.47	2.43	2.38	2.34	2.30
13	4.67	3.81	3.41	3.18	3.03	2.92	2.83	2.77	2.71	2.67	2.60	2.53	2.46	2.42	2.38	2.34	2.30	2.25	2.21
14	4.60	3.74	3.34	3.11	2.96	2.85	2.76	2.70	2.65	2.60	2.53	2.46	2.39	2.35	2.31	2.27	2.22	2.18	2.13
15	4.54	3.68	3.29	3.06	2.90	2.79	2.71	2.64	2.59	2.54	2.48	2.40	2.33	2.29	2.25	2.20	2.16	2.11	2.07
16	4.49	3.63	3.24	3.01	2.85	2.74	2.66	2.59	2.54	2.49	2.42	2.35	2.28	2.24	2.19	2.15	2.11	2.06	2.01
17	4.45	3.59	3.20	2.96	2.81	2.70	2.61	2.55	2.49	2.45	2.38	2.31	2.23	2.19	2.15	2.10	2.06	2.01	1.96

Degrees of freedom for the denominator (df_2)

18	4.41	3.55	3.16	2.93	2.77	2.66	2.58	2.51	2.46	2.41	2.34	2.27	2.19	2.15	2.11	2.06	2.02	1.97	1.92
19	4.38	3.52	3.13	2.90	2.74	2.63	2.54	2.48	2.42	2.38	2.31	2.23	2.16	2.11	2.07	2.03	1.98	1.93	1.88
20	4.35	3.49	3.10	2.87	2.71	2.60	2.51	2.45	2.39	2.35	2.28	2.20	2.12	2.08	2.04	1.99	1.95	1.90	1.84
21	4.32	3.47	3.07	2.84	2.68	2.57	2.49	2.42	2.37	2.32	2.25	2.18	2.10	2.05	2.01	1.96	1.92	1.87	1.81
22	4.30	3.44	3.05	2.82	2.66	2.55	2.46	2.40	2.34	2.30	2.23	2.15	2.07	2.03	1.98	1.94	1.89	1.84	1.78
23	4.28	3.42	3.03	2.80	2.64	2.53	2.44	2.37	2.32	2.27	2.20	2.13	2.05	2.01	1.96	1.91	1.86	1.81	1.76
24	4.26	3.40	3.01	2.78	2.62	2.51	2.42	2.36	2.30	2.25	2.18	2.11	2.03	1.98	1.93	1.89	1.83	1.79	1.73
25	4.24	3.39	2.99	2.76	2.60	2.49	2.40	2.34	2.28	2.24	2.16	2.09	2.01	1.96	1.92	1.87	1.82	1.77	1.71
26	4.23	3.37	2.98	2.74	2.59	2.47	2.39	2.32	2.27	2.22	2.15	2.07	1.99	1.95	1.90	1.85	1.80	1.75	1.69
27	4.21	3.35	2.96	2.73	2.57	2.46	2.37	2.31	2.25	2.20	2.13	2.06	1.97	1.93	1.88	1.84	1.79	1.73	1.67
28	4.20	3.34	2.95	2.71	2.56	2.45	2.36	2.29	2.24	2.19	2.12	2.04	1.96	1.91	1.87	1.82	1.77	1.71	1.65
29	4.18	3.33	2.93	2.70	2.55	2.43	2.35	2.28	2.22	2.18	2.10	2.03	1.94	1.90	1.85	1.81	1.74	1.70	1.64
30	4.17	3.32	2.92	2.69	2.53	2.42	2.33	2.27	2.21	2.16	2.09	2.01	1.93	1.89	1.84	1.79	1.74	1.68	1.62
40	4.08	3.23	2.84	2.61	2.45	2.34	2.25	2.18	2.12	2.08	2.00	1.92	1.84	1.79	1.74	1.69	1.64	1.58	1.51
60	4.00	3.15	2.76	2.53	2.37	2.25	2.17	2.10	2.04	1.99	1.92	1.84	1.75	1.70	1.65	1.59	1.53	1.47	1.39
120	3.92	3.07	2.68	2.45	2.29	2.17	2.09	2.02	1.96	1.91	1.83	1.75	1.66	1.61	1.55	1.50	1.43	1.35	1.25
∞	3.84	3.00	2.60	2.37	2.21	2.10	2.01	1.94	1.88	1.83	1.75	1.67	1.57	1.52	1.46	1.39	1.32	1.22	1.00

p = .01

Degrees of freedom for the numerator (df_1)

	1	2	3	4	5	6	7	8	9	10	12	15	20	24	30	40	60	120	∞
1	4052	4999.5	5403	5625	5764	5859	5928	5982	6022	6056	6106	6157	6209	6235	6261	6287	6313	6339	6366
2	98.50	99.00	99.17	99.25	99.30	99.33	99.36	99.37	99.39	99.40	99.42	99.43	99.45	99.46	99.47	99.47	99.48	99.49	99.50
3	34.12	30.82	29.46	28.71	28.24	27.91	27.67	27.49	27.35	27.23	27.05	26.87	26.69	26.60	26.50	26.41	26.32	26.22	26.13
4	21.20	18.00	16.69	15.98	15.52	15.21	14.98	14.80	14.66	14.55	14.37	14.20	14.02	13.93	13.84	13.75	13.65	13.56	13.46
5	16.26	13.27	12.06	11.39	10.97	10.67	10.46	10.29	10.16	10.05	9.89	9.72	9.55	9.47	9.38	9.29	9.20	9.11	9.02
6	13.75	20.92	9.78	9.15	8.75	8.47	8.26	8.10	7.98	7.87	7.72	7.56	7.40	7.31	7.23	7.14	7.06	6.97	6.88
7	12.25	9.55	8.45	7.85	7.46	7.19	6.99	6.84	6.72	6.62	6.47	6.31	6.16	6.07	5.99	5.91	5.82	5.74	5.65
8	11.26	8.65	7.59	7.01	6.63	6.37	6.18	6.03	5.91	5.81	5.67	5.52	5.36	5.28	5.20	5.12	5.03	4.95	4.46
9	10.56	8.02	6.99	6.42	6.06	5.80	5.61	5.47	5.35	5.26	5.11	4.96	4.81	4.73	4.65	4.57	4.48	4.40	4.31
10	10.04	7.56	6.55	5.99	5.64	5.39	5.20	5.06	4.94	4.85	4.71	4.56	4.41	4.33	4.25	4.17	4.08	4.00	3.91
11	9.65	7.21	6.22	5.67	5.32	5.07	4.89	4.74	4.63	4.54	4.40	4.25	4.10	4.02	3.94	3.86	3.78	3.69	3.60
12	9.33	6.93	5.95	5.41	5.06	4.82	4.64	4.50	4.39	4.30	4.16	4.01	3.86	3.78	3.70	3.62	3.54	3.45	3.36
13	9.07	6.70	5.74	5.21	4.86	4.62	4.44	4.30	4.19	4.10	3.96	3.82	3.66	3.59	3.51	3.43	3.34	3.25	3.17
14	8.86	6.51	5.56	5.04	4.69	4.46	4.28	4.14	4.03	3.94	3.80	3.66	3.51	3.43	3.35	3.27	3.18	3.09	3.00
15	8.68	6.36	5.42	4.89	4.36	4.32	4.14	4.00	3.89	3.80	3.67	3.52	3.37	3.29	3.21	3.13	3.05	2.96	2.87
16	8.53	6.23	5.29	4.77	4.44	4.20	4.03	3.89	3.78	3.69	3.55	3.41	3.26	3.18	3.10	3.02	2.93	2.84	2.75
17	8.40	6.11	5.18	4.67	4.34	4.10	3.93	3.79	3.68	3.59	3.46	3.31	3.16	3.08	3.00	2.92	2.83	2.75	2.65

Degrees of freedom for the denominator (df_2)

18	8.29	6.01	5.09	4.58	4.25	4.01	3.84	3.71	3.60	3.51	3.37	3.23	3.08	3.00	2.92	2.84	2.75	2.66	2.57
19	8.18	5.93	5.01	4.50	4.17	3.94	3.77	3.63	3.52	3.43	3.30	3.15	3.00	2.92	2.84	2.76	2.67	2.58	2.59
20	8.10	5.85	4.94	4.43	4.10	3.87	3.70	3.56	3.46	3.37	3.23	3.09	2.94	2.86	2.78	2.69	2.61	2.52	2.42
21	8.02	5.78	4.87	4.37	4.04	3.81	3.64	3.51	3.40	3.31	3.17	3.03	2.88	2.80	2.72	2.64	2.55	2.46	2.36
22	7.95	5.72	4.82	4.31	3.99	3.76	3.59	3.45	3.35	3.26	3.12	2.98	2.83	2.75	2.67	2.58	2.50	2.40	2.31
23	7.88	5.66	4.76	4.26	3.94	3.71	3.54	3.41	3.30	3.21	3.07	2.93	2.78	2.70	2.62	2.54	2.45	2.35	2.26
24	7.82	5.61	4.72	4.22	3.90	3.67	3.50	3.36	3.26	3.17	3.03	2.89	2.74	2.66	2.58	2.49	2.40	2.31	2.21
25	7.77	5.57	4.68	4.18	3.85	3.63	3.46	3.32	3.22	3.13	2.99	2.85	2.70	2.62	2.54	2.45	2.36	2.27	2.17
26	7.72	5.53	4.64	4.14	3.82	3.59	3.42	3.29	3.18	3.09	2.96	2.81	2.66	2.58	2.50	2.42	2.33	2.23	2.13
27	7.68	5.49	4.60	4.11	3.78	3.56	3.39	3.26	3.15	3.06	2.93	2.78	2.63	2.55	2.47	2.38	2.29	2.20	2.10
28	7.64	5.45	4.57	4.07	3.75	3.53	3.36	3.23	3.12	3.03	2.90	2.75	2.60	2.52	2.44	2.35	2.26	2.17	2.06
29	7.60	5.42	4.54	4.04	3.73	3.50	3.33	3.20	3.09	3.00	2.87	2.73	2.57	2.49	2.41	2.33	2.23	2.14	2.03
30	7.56	5.39	4.51	4.02	3.70	3.47	3.30	3.17	3.07	2.98	2.84	2.70	2.55	2.47	2.39	2.30	2.21	2.11	2.01
40	7.31	5.18	4.31	3.83	3.51	3.29	3.12	2.99	2.89	2.80	2.66	2.52	2.37	2.29	2.20	2.11	2.02	1.92	1.80
60	7.08	4.98	4.13	3.65	3.34	3.12	2.95	2.82	2.72	2.63	2.50	2.35	2.20	2.12	2.03	1.94	1.84	1.73	1.60
120	6.85	4.79	3.95	3.48	3.17	2.96	2.79	2.66	2.56	2.47	2.34	2.19	2.03	1.95	1.86	1.76	1.66	1.53	1.38
∞	6.63	4.61	3.78	3.32	3.02	2.80	2.64	2.51	2.41	2.32	2.18	2.04	1.88	1.79	1.70	1.59	1.47	1.32	1.00

activity report: report of a salesperson's activities over some time period; how many calls were made, to whom, and on what dates

adoption rate: the percentage of potential buyers who buy (adopt) a product within some time period, or the percentage who will ultimately buy the product

aggregate cluster solution: a cluster analysis solution that is found by starting with distinct observations and merging those observations that are nearest to one another

AID analysis: abbreviation for **Automatic Interaction Detector analysis**

American Statistics Index (ASI): a guide to statistical sources published by the U.S. government

analysis of variance (ANOVA): inferential procedure used for testing the significance of differences among group means

ANOVA: abbreviation for **analysis of variance**

ASCII file: a file written in a standard computer language that can be read by any software

ASI: abbreviation for **American Statistics Index**

Automatic Interaction Detector (AID) analysis: an exploratory procedure that uses comparisons of means for market segmentation purposes

backtranslation: retranslation of a questionnaire into the original language after it has been translated into another language

backward stepwise regression: a stepwise linear regression procedure that begins with all independent variables in the equation, and, in a series of steps, removes from the equation the independent variables that do not explain a significant amount of variance in the dependent variable

benchmarking: a method for setting performance standards by comparing customers' opinions about a company with their opinions about its best-performing competitor

beta coefficients: terms in a bivariate or multiple regression that indicate the direction and amount of change in the dependent variable which is associated with each unit of change in the independent variable(s); also called **beta weights**

beta test site: a survey method in which a few customers are recruited to use a new product and give feedback about it

beta weights: see **beta coefficients**

bipolar measure: a question with a response scale that has positive and negative responses (e.g., satisfied–dissatisfied)

bivariate regression: an extension of correlation analysis that, in addition to measuring the correlation between two variables, expresses the linear relationship between them

blocking: designing one or more nonmanipulated variables into an experiment to ensure that the treatment groups are equalized on those variables

bounded recall: a procedure in which respondents are interviewed at the start of a time period to set a baseline, then interviewed at the end of the period to identify changes

branching: asking or not asking certain questions depending on whether a qualifying answer has been given to a previous question; also called **skipping**

brand loyalty: the extent to which a consumer repurchases the same brand instead of alternative brands of the same product

browser: a program such as Netscape Navigator that is used to navigate the World Wide Web

Business Periodicals Index: an index to articles in general business magazines

buyer awareness: a measure of how well a product or service is known

call report: a salesperson report that shows the time and date of sales calls, the company and person visited, the issues discussed, and the outcome of the visit

canonical correlation analysis: a multivariate procedure for determining the relationship between two groups of variables

categorical variables: see **nominal scale variables**

causal modeling: see **structural equations modeling**

Census of Agriculture: a government report containing statistical information about the agricultural industry, published every five years

Census of Construction Industries: a government report containing statistical information about construction firms, published every five years

Census of Governments: a government report containing statistical information about government agencies, published every five years

Census of Manufactures: a government report containing statistical information about manufacturing firms, published every five years

Census of Population and Housing: a government report containing demographic information about U.S. households, published every ten years

Census of Retail Trade: a government report containing statistical information about retail trading firms, published every five years

Census of Service Industries: a government report containing statistical information about service firms, published every five years

Census of Wholesale Trade: a government report containing statistical information about wholesale trading firms, published every five years

census tract: a smaller area within a metropolitan area for which census information is reported

CFA: abbreviation for **common factor analysis**

"champions of innovation" program: a six-step program in which trade publications are used to identify highly innovative companies

checklist question: a question that asks about a series of items with a common response format

chi-squared (χ^2) test: an inferential test used to assess whether variables in a cross-tabulation are related

CIF: abbreviation for **customer information file**

city block distance: the distance between two observations across two or more variables, measured by calculating the difference on each variable and summing the absolute value of those differences

cleaning data: correcting errors in a computer data file

closed question: a question with response categories

cluster analysis: a data analysis technique used to group observations on the basis of their absolute differences (distances) across a series of variables

clustering (in sampling frames): a frame problem in which a single element in the frame corresponds to two or more population members

cluster sampling: drawing a probability sample by grouping population members into clusters and drawing a sample of clusters

codebook: a document that defines the variables in a data set and serves as a reference source for coders

cognitive interview: a questionnaire testing method in which people from the target population come to a central location and go through the interview, thinking out loud while they do so

common factor analysis (CFA): an analysis that groups variables solely on the basis of their common variance, without accounting for the unique variance associated with each variable

communality: the percentage of a variable's variance that is accounted for by the retained factors in a factor analysis

Compact Disclosure **system:** a computerized source of data taken from the annual reports of publicly traded companies

comparison of means: an analysis in which mean values for a dependent variable are compared across the categories of an independent variable

complex contingency table: the result of a complex cross-tabulation

complex cross-tabulation: an analysis that classifies observations into the intersecting categories of three or more variables

concept engineering: a five-step program that identifies new-product ideas from the ways customers use a company's products

concept generation: an early stage of marketing research in which ideas for new products and services are developed

concept test: an evaluation of whether buyers like a new-product concept, usually done with a focus group

confidence interval: the distance from a population value within which 95% (or 90%) of possible sample results will fall for a sample of a given size

confirmatory factor analysis: a factor analysis in which the analyst prespecifies variable groupings and tests whether this grouping scheme seems to provide adequate fit to the data

conjoint analysis: a "what-if" experiment in which buyers are presented with different combinations of product attributes and are asked to evaluate these combinations in some way, usually by ranking them in order of preference

continuous variables: numeric variables that are not broken into categories

control group: an experimental group that does not experience any manipulations of the experimental variables and therefore provides a baseline comparison for the results from other groups

controlled experiment: an experiment that uses some control procedure, such as a laboratory environment or a control group, to minimize the chance that extraneous variables influence the relationship between the manipulated and dependent variables

convenience sample: a nonprobability sample obtained by using whatever population members are easily available

Corporate and Industry Research Reports: a source of information on industries and companies, prepared by stockbrokerage companies to guide investment decisions

correlation coefficient: a number ranging from −1 to +1 that shows the level of relationship between two variables

County and City Data Book: a source of population data and business activity data for U.S. counties and cities

County Business Patterns: a source of business data at the county level by Standard Industrial Classification code

criterion variable: see **dependent variable**

cross-classification: an analysis that classifies observations into the intersecting categories of two (or more) variables; also called **cross-tabulation**

cross-tabulation: see **cross-classification**

cue: any type of spoken or printed reminder that is given to a respondent to improve memory

curbstoning: fabricating interview results

customer information file (CIF): a file on a particular customer that contains identifying information (such as an address and/or telephone number), purchasing data, and possibly demographic data

database marketing: any marketing program based on the analysis of a company's customer database

debriefing: describing the actual purpose of a research project to participants who have been misdirected regarding that purpose

Delphi method: a method of gathering executive judgments in which each executive makes an independent judgment, then is given information about other people's judgments and an opportunity to change his or her mind

demand effect: a type of treatment effect that occurs when study participants act the way they think they should

demographic characteristics: customer background characteristics such as age and gender

dependent variable: a variable of interest that depends on one or more independent variables; for example, sales volume depends on advertising; also called **criterion variable**

depth interview: an unstructured, probing interview with an individual respondent

Directory of Corporate Affiliations or Who Owns Whom: a publication that shows whether a company is a subsidiary of another company

disaggregation (in cluster analysis): an approach to cluster analysis in which all observations are initially placed in one big cluster and smaller clusters are formed by disaggregation

discriminant analysis: an analysis procedure that relates a categorical dependent variable to two or more independent variables

discriminant function: in a discriminant analysis, the weighted combination of independent variables that best discriminates among categories of the dependent variable

distribution: the distribution or frequency distribution of a variable is a list of the different values which the variable can assume along with the number of times each value occurs

dummy variable: a variable with two categories

Dun & Bradstreet's Industry Norms and Key Business Ratios: a source of financial ratios

Dun & Bradstreet's Market Profile Analysis: a source of population data at the level of census tracts

Dun & Bradstreet's Million Dollar Directory: a publication that indicates whether a company is public or private

duplication (in sampling frames): a problem that occurs when population members are duplicated in the sampling frame

editing: correcting miscoded or missing data

eigenvalue: in factor analysis, the sum of the squared correlations between a factor and all of the variables in the analysis

Encyclopedia of Associations: a source that provides names and addresses for all kinds of associations

Euclidean distance: the distance between two observations across two or more variables, measured by calculating the difference on each variable, summing the squared differences, and taking the square root of the sum

evaluation apprehension: in experiments, a type of treatment effect that occurs when subjects change their behavior because they view the experiment as a test

executive judgments: opinions and insights from key executives in a company

expense ratio: the ratio of some expense category to sales; for example, the ratio of advertising to sales

experiment: a study in which a researcher actively manipulates one or more causal variables, then measures the effects of this manipulation on one or more dependent variables of interest

experimental factors: see **experimental variables**

experimental group: a group that is exposed to a particular level of an experimental manipulation

experimental variables: causal variables that are manipulated in an experiment to see if they have an impact on some variable of interest; also called **experimental factors**

exploratory factor analysis: a factor analysis in which the analyst does not prespecify variable groupings and groups are formed according to purely mathematical criteria

extended internal information: information from companies that supply goods or services to a company

external validity: the extent to which the effects that occur in the experiment approximate those in the actual market situation; also called **generalizability**

factor (in experiments): a manipulated variable

factor (in factor analysis): a weighted combination of items—usually variables—in which the items with high positive or negative weights are considered to form a group

factor analysis: an analysis technique that groups items—usually variables—on the basis of correlations

factor loading: the weight assigned to a particular variable on a factor; it is the correlation between the variable and the factor

factor score: the value of an observation on a factor

F & S Index: see *Predicasts F & S Index*

field experiment: an experiment that measures the phenomena of interest in a natural setting

financial leverage: the ratio of liabilities to net worth

financial ratios: figures used to evaluate the financial health and performance of a business, such as net profit margin, return on assets, and financial leverage

Financial Studies of the Small Business: a source of financial ratios for small businesses

focus group: a moderated group discussion in which the moderator follows a topic guide but does not use a fixed questionnaire

focus group moderator: a person who moderates a focus group

forward stepwise regression: a stepwise linear regression procedure that begins with no independent variables in the equation, and, in a series of steps, adds to the equation the independent variables that explain a significant amount of variance in the dependent variable

fractional design: a multifactor experiment that omits some combinations of manipulation levels; also called a **fractional factorial design**

frame: a list or system that identifies every member of a population so that a sample can be drawn without physically contacting every member of the population

free coding: assigning open-ended responses to categories

frequency distribution: a list of the different values a variable can assume and the number of times each value occurs

F statistic: an inferential test used to measure whether the mean value of a dependent variable differs across the levels of one or more independent variables

full factorial design: a multifactor experiment in which all possible combinations of manipulation levels are used

funnel sequence: a series of questions ordered from general to specific

generalizability: see **external validity**

Hawthorne effect: a type of treatment effect that occurs when experimental groups react to being in the experimental spotlight

heteroskedasticity: a condition in which the variance of a dependent variable changes across the levels of one or more independent variables

history effect: a threat to internal validity that occurs when an outside event affects the dependent variable during an experiment

home page: the entryway into a Web site

hypothesis test: an inferential analysis that measures the probability that a hypothesized population value for the measure of interest could have led to an observed sample result; also called **significance test**

idea conference: a type of brainstorming session in which employees generate new product ideas

independent variable: a variable that influences a dependent variable of interest; for example, advertising influences sales volume; also called **predictor variable**

ineligibility: a problem that occurs when a sampling frame contains elements that are not members of the population of interest

inferential data analyses: analyses that measure the probability that a hypothesized population value for the measure of interest could have led to an observed sample result

intercept survey: a survey administered by intercepting visitors to some public place such as a shopping mall or a city street

intercoder reliability: the percentage of code assignments on which two coders agree

internal validity: the extent to which an experiment controls the effects of all extraneous variables so that differences among experimental groups on the dependent variable can be regarded as valid effects of the manipulations

Internet: a worldwide matrix of connecting computers; the term internet (with a lowercase *i*) refers to a network that is separate from the worldwide Internet.

interquartile range: the distance between the values that mark the first and third quartiles of a distribution

interval scale variables: variables that have the properties of order among scale points and equal distances among scale points, but not the property of an absolute zero

interviewer report form (IRF): a record of efforts to contact and interview a survey respondent

intracluster coefficient of homogeneity: in cluster sampling, a coefficient, symbolized by the Greek letter rho (ρ), that indicates the homogeneity among elements in a cluster and can range from 0 to 1

inventory turnover: the ratio of sales to inventory

inverted funnel: a series of questions ordered from specific to general

IRF: abbreviation for **interviewer report form**

judgment sampling: nonprobability sampling in which judgment is used to produce a representative sample

labeled scale: a response scale for which the categories are labeled

laboratory experiment: an experiment that measures the phenomena of interest in a controlled environment, outside their natural setting

latent variable: a variable that is not measured directly but rather through a series of indicators; can be contrasted to an **observed variable**

Leo Troy's Almanac of Business and Industrial Financial Ratios: a source of financial ratios

lifetime revenue: the amount of revenue a company can expect to gain from a customer over the entire life of the customer's relationship with the company

LISREL: abbreviation for *Li*near *S*tructural *Rel*ations; a popular software package for structural equations modeling

listserv: an electronic mailing list that distributes information on some topic of interest to subscribers

loaded question: a question that encourages a certain response

logistic multiple regression: a variation of multiple regression used for 0–1 dependent variables

logit analysis: a variation of multiple regression used when the dependent variable is a proportion

log-linear regression: a variation of multiple regression used with categorical independent and dependent variables

lost sales report: a salesperson report that provides information on a lost sales opportunity

mail survey: a self-administered survey conducted via mail

Major U.S. Private Companies: a source that provides information about privately held companies

MANOVA: abbreviation for multivariate analysis of variance

marketing information system (MKIS): a system of gathering and transmitting repetitive marketing research information

marketing research: all activities that provide information to guide marketing decisions

market segmentation: grouping buyers by certain characteristics or behaviors such that different marketing tactics are optimal for different segments

market size: total dollar sales for a product category

matching: sorting experimental subjects into sets that are matched on some variable and randomly assigning an equal number of subjects from each set into each experimental treatment group to ensure that the treatment groups are equal on that variable

matrix: a table of rows and columns

maturation effect: a threat to internal validity that occurs when some change that is unrelated to the manipulations, but affects the dependent variable, occurs within subjects during an experiment

MDS: abbreviation for **multidimensional scaling**

mean: the average value of a variable, calculated as the sum of all observations divided by the number of observations

measures of central tendency: measures that indicate the "typical" value of a variable; these measures include the **mean, median,** and **mode**

measures of dispersion: measures that indicate the dispersion of values for a variable; these measures include the **range, variance, standard deviation,** and **interquartile range**

median: the value of a variable that has an equal number of observations above and below it

misdirection: leading research participants to think the purpose of a project is different from the actual purpose, so as to obtain more valid data

MKIS: abbreviation for **marketing information system**

mode: the value of a variable that is observed more frequently than any other value

mortality effect: a threat to internal validity that occurs when some subjects fail to complete an experiment

multicollinearity: the correlation among independent variables in a multivariate analysis

multidimensional scaling (MDS): a data analysis technique used to impute multivariate distances among some set of objects (such as products), based on overall measures of similarity or order among the objects

multiple regression analysis: an analysis procedure that finds the weighted linear combination of independent variables that has the maximum correlation with a dependent variable

multivariate analysis of variance: an analysis of variance with two or more dependent variables

multivariate analysis: a data analysis procedure that involves three or more variables

multivariate comparison of means: an analysis in which mean values for a dependent variable are compared across the categories of two or more independent variables

multivariate grouping procedure: an analysis procedure involving three or more variables in which none of the variables is treated as dependent on the others

net profit margin: the ratio of net profit to total sales

newsgroup: an electronic bulletin board, usually related to a certain topic, on which public messages can be posted

nominal scale variables: variables for which numbers simply identify categories and do not have mathematical properties such as order; also called **categorical variables** or **qualitative variables**

nonprobability sample: a nonrandom sample selected by judgment or convenience

nonsampling error: an error in an estimate that is unrelated to the sampling of respondents, including error that occurs because people give incorrect answers, error that occurs because of failures or fluctuations in physical measurement instruments, and error that occurs in coding or data entry

normalization: standardization of individual respondents' answers to a series of questions with common response categories, so that each respondent has the same mean and variance across these questions

objective quantitative phenomena: phenomena that are objective and numerical in nature, such as age or income

oblique rotation: a rotation of factors that allows the factors to become correlated

observational data: data gathered through direct observation as opposed to self-reports

observed variable: a variable that is measured directly (though not necessarily by means of observation); can be contrasted to a **latent variable**

obtrusive measurement: a measurement in which people being measured are aware of the measurement

omission: a problem that occurs when a sampling frame omits population elements

open question: a question without response categories

operating ratios: figures used to evaluate a business's operating performance, such as inventory turnover and expense ratios

order effect: a problem that occurs when the answer to a particular question is influenced by previous questions

ordinal scale variables: variables that have only the property of order among scale points

orthogonal rotation: a rotation of factors that keeps them uncorrelated

outlier: an extreme value of a variable

panel: a group of research participants that provides information over time

PCA: abbreviation for **principal components analysis**

periodicals: magazines, newspapers, and other publications that are issued periodically; also called **serials**

periodicity: a recurring sequence or pattern that exists in a sampling frame; for example, male-female-male-female

personal interview: a form of survey research conducted face to face, usually at a respondent's home or workplace

physical sampling: drawing a sample from physical sources such as printed directories or file drawers

pilot test: administration of a questionnaire under field conditions to a small sample in order to time it and/or uncover problems; also called **pretest**

population: the set of elements of interest in a research project; also called **universe**

population boundaries: the conditions that separate those who are of interest in a research project from those who are not

potential market: the total number of potential customers for a product, or the sales a product would have if all potential customers bought it

precoding: defining how the possible responses to a question will be coded before the questionnaire is administered

Predicasts Basebook: a source of historical statistics on industries

Predicasts F & S Index: a source of nonstatistical information on industries and companies

Predicasts Forecasts: a source of future projections for industry statistics

predictor variable: see **independent variable**

pretesting: see **pilot test**

pretest-versus-posttest comparisons: controlling for initial differences among the subjects in an experiment by measuring the dependent variable before and after manipulations and using the difference as the dependent variable

primary information: information that is freshly gathered for a particular research question (as opposed to **secondary information**)

principal components analysis (PCA): a factor analysis that accounts for all variance in the variables being analyzed, including the unique variance associated with each variable

probability sample: a sample in which every population element has a known, nonzero chance of selection and chance is used to obtain representativeness; also called **random sample**

problem identification research: research done to help managers identify problems and opportunities in marketing programs

problem-solving research: research done to help managers decide between clearly defined courses of action

product perception map: see **product space map**

product space map: a graphic representation of similarities and dissimilarities among products; also called **product perception map**

professional respondent: a respondent who has participated in many previous studies

projective measure: a measure that encourages respondents to project their ideas onto some indefinite stimulus; for example, to learn how people view the usage context for Tostitos chips, they might be asked to draw a picture of people eating Tostitos

proxy respondent: a respondent who provides information about another member of his or her household or organization

psychographic (lifestyle) characteristics: psychological characteristics such as attitudes, tastes, and preferences

Psychological Abstracts: an index of articles from academic journals that cover psychological issues

Q-type factor analysis: a factor analysis used to group respondents who share similar response patterns across some set of variables

qualitative phenomena: question topics that have categories, rather than numbers, as possible answers

qualitative variables: see **nominal scale variables**

quantitative variables: variables for which numerical codes have mathematical properties such as order and equal distances among scale points

quota sampling: drawing a nonprobability sample by giving data gatherers quotas for the number of observations to be gathered in various population groups

random digit dialing (RDD): dialing random numbers in working telephone exchanges so that unlisted people can be included in a survey

randomization: random assignment of experimental subjects to treatment groups

random sample: see **probability sample**

range: the distance from the smallest to the largest value in a distribution

rank order correlation: a special formula for calculating correlations between sets of rankings; also called **Spearman rank order correlation**

ratio scale variables: variables that have the properties of order among scale points, equal distances among all adjacent scale points, and an absolute zero

RDD: abbreviation for **random digit dialing**

reactive measurement: measurement in which the object being measured reacts by changing in some way

Reader's Guide to Periodical Literature: an index of general-interest magazines

recoding: changing the coding of a variable after the data have been entered in the computer

register: a list of all persons or all adults in a country

relationship marketing: a marketing perspective that emphasizes relationships rather than transactions and individual customers rather than market segments

repeated measures design: an experiment in which subjects experience different treatment conditions at different points in time and the dependent variable is measured each time for each subject

research professional: a project manager who works with line managers in planning special projects

research technician: an employee who performs structured, relatively noncreative tasks such as data collection and data analysis

residual: the difference between the actual value on a dependent variable for each observation in a data set and the value that a regression equation would predict for that observation

restricted range: a lack of variation in an independent variable (which might limit the weight attached to that variable)

return on assets: the ratio of net profit to assets

rho (ρ): symbol for the intracluster coefficient of homogeneity

Robert Morris Associates' Annual Statement Studies: a source of financial ratios for various industries

sample: a subset of a larger population

sample bias: systematic differences between a sample and the population it is intended to represent

sampling error: an error in an estimate that is due to random variation in the sample; also called **sampling variance**

sampling variance: see **sampling error**

scree test: a "rule of thumb" procedure in which sharp changes in eigenvalues are used to decide how many factors to retain in a factor analysis or sharp changes in distance measures are used to decide how many clusters to retain in a cluster analysis

search engine: a program that provides links to Web sites and will search for sites related to a particular topic

secondary information: information that has already been collected for some other purpose

selection bias: a threat to internal validity that occurs when differences between treatment groups in an experiment are caused by differences in the subjects rather than by the manipulations

self-report data: information gathered by asking people to report their own opinions and/or activities

serials: see **periodicals**

service shoppers: people who are paid to visit a store or restaurant, make a purchase, and evaluate the service

share of customer: a company's share of the total amount spent by a particular customer in a product or service category

SIC Manual: a listing of the products covered by each Standard Industrial Classification code number

significance test: see **hypothesis test**

simple random sampling (SRS): a sampling procedure in which population elements are numbered and a sample is selected by drawing a series of random numbers

skipping: see **branching**

sleeper: a fictitious brand included in a brand-awareness survey in order to measure the extent to which knowledge is being overclaimed

social desirability bias: a threat to the validity of self-report data that occurs when respondents change their answers to comply with perceived social norms about which answers are desirable

Spearman rank order correlation: see **rank order correlation**

specification effects: potentially misleading results that occur in a multiple regression analysis (or other multivariate dependence techniques) because the weight assigned to a particular independent variable depends on which other variables are specified (used) in the equation

squared multiple correlation: the squared correlation between a dependent variable and a weighted combination of independent variables; also called R^2.

SRI: abbreviation for *Statistical Research Index*

srs: abbreviation for **simple random sampling**

Standard & Poor's Industrial Surveys: a source of reports on business conditions in various industries as well as statistical data on leading competitors

standard deviation: the square root of the variance

Standard Periodical Directory: a list of periodicals

Standard Rate and Data Service (**SRDS**) **publications:** a source of information regarding costs and audiences for various advertising media

State and Metropolitan Area Data Book: a source of population and business activity data for U.S. states and metropolitan areas

Statistical Abstract of the United States: a source of a wide variety of statistical information

Statistical Research Index (**SRI**): a guide to private statistical sources

stepwise linear regression: an exploratory multivariate analysis technique that builds a regression equation in a series of backward or forward steps; see backward stepwise regression and forward stepwise regression

stepwise multiple regression: an iterative search procedure for determining which of a group of independent variables explain the largest amount of the variance of the dependent variable

stratified sampling: a sampling procedure in which population elements are separated into subgroups called "strata" and samples are drawn within each stratum

"street news": gossip about customers' or competitors' activities

structural equations modeling: analysis of the relationships among variables that are connected in a multistage causal system; also known as **causal modeling, structural relations modeling,** or **LISREL analysis**

structural relations modeling: see **structural equations modeling**

subjective quantitative phenomena: phenomena that are subjective and quantitative in nature, such as levels of satisfaction

survey: a research method in which self-report data are collected by means of a fixed questionnaire

Survey of Buying Power: a source of population, income, and expenditure data for counties and cities

syndicated data: data sold to multiple users

syndicated research services: providers of syndicated data

systematic sampling: a sampling procedure in which the population size is divided by the desired sample size to set an interval i, then every ith member of a population is selected after a random start between 1 and i

tab: see **tabulation**

tabulation: a tabular presentation of a frequency distribution; also called **tab**

telephone survey: a survey in which data are gathered through interviews conducted over the telephone

test marketing: introducing new or revamped products into selected markets to test their market performance

testing effect: a threat to internal validity that occurs when the process of measuring a dependent variable influences the way that subjects respond to experimental manipulations and/or to later measures of the dependent variable

Thomas Register of American Manufacturers: a directory of manufacturers

Total Quality Management (TQM): a management philosophy of continuous monitoring and improvement of customer satisfaction with a firm's products and services

TQM: abbreviation for **total quality management**

trade associations: associations to which companies in an industry belong

treatment effects: a threat to internal validity that occurs when differences between study groups are caused by the very act of conducting the study rather than by the manipulations

t-test: an inferential analysis used to test whether a sample statistic is significantly different from some hypothesized value (for example, whether a sample mean is significantly different from 0) or whether two sample statistics are significantly different from each other

U.S. Industrial Outlook: a source of statistical data for the current year plus economic projections for the next five years for about 350 industries

Ulrich's International Periodical Directory: a list of periodicals

unipolar scale: a question with a response scale that contains only one valence, positive or negative (e.g., not at all happy to very happy)

univariate procedure: a data analysis procedure that involves only one variable

universe: see **population**

variable: a quantity that can assume at least two different values

variance: the average squared distance between the values of individual observations on some variable and the mean of that variable

volunteer sample: a sample composed of people who happen to be present at a certain location and agree to participate in a study

The Wall Street Journal Index: abstracts of articles published in *The Wall Street Journal*

wsorld wide web: the place on the Internet where individuals and organizations provide information about the products and services they provide

Index